An Autobiography

VOLUME 2

1911–1969

By The Same Author

An Autobiography, Volume 1: 1880–1911

History and Politics

International Government

Empire and Commerce in Africa

Co-operation and the Future of Industry

Socialism and Co-operation

Fear and Politics

Imperialism and Civilization

After the Deluge (*two volumes*)

Quack, Quack!

Principia Politica

Barbarians at the Gate

The War for Peace

Criticism

Hunting the Highbrow

Essays on Literature, History and Politics

Fiction

The Village in the Jungle

Stories of the East

The Wise Virgins

Drama

The Hotel

A Calendar of Consolation: A Comforting Thought for Every Day in the Year

AN AUTOBIOGRAPHY

LEONARD WOOLF

VOLUME 2

1911–1969

Oxford New York Toronto Melbourne

OXFORD UNIVERSITY PRESS

1980

Oxford University Press, Walton Street, Oxford OX2 6DP

OXFORD LONDON GLASGOW
NEW YORK TORONTO MELBOURNE WELLINGTON
KUALA LUMPUR SINGAPORE JAKARTA HONG KONG TOKYO
DELHI BOMBAY CALCUTTA MADRAS KARACHI
NAIROBI DAR ES SALAAM CAPE TOWN

First published in three volumes as Beginning Again, Downhill all the Way, *and* The Journey not the Arrival Matters *by The Hogarth Press Limited 1964, 1967, 1969*
First published as an Oxford University Press paperback 1980 at the suggestion of Kate Bath

British Library Cataloguing in Publication Data

Woolf, Leonard
An autobiography.
Vol. 2: 1911—1969
1. Woolf, Leonard
2. Publishers and publishing—Great Britain—Biography
I. Woolf, Leonard. Beginning again
II. Woolf, Leonard. Downhill all the way
III. Woolf, Leonard. The journey not the arrival matters
070.5'092'4 Z325.W/ 80-40480
ISBN 0-19-281290-4

Note: References to what was the present at the time of writing have not been updated in the paperback edition

Typeset by Blackmore Press, Shaftesbury and printed in Great Britain by Cox & Wyman Ltd, Reading

Contents

Illustrations

Beginning Again

1911–1918

To Trekkie

Sein Blick ist vom Vorübergehen der Stäbe
so müd geworden, daß er nichts mehr hält.
Ihm ist, als ob es tausend Stäbe gäbe,
und hinter tausend Stäben keine Welt.

His gaze from going through the bars has
grown so weary that it can take in nothing more.
For him it is as though there were a thousand
bars and behind the thousand bars no world.

Rilke: *Der Panther*

FOREWORD

In writing this third volume[1] of my autobiography I have often been haunted by the lines from Rilke's superb poem 'Der Panther' which I have had printed at the beginning of this book. This volume is the record of my life during the first great war and all through the war one felt that one was behind bars, and now recalling those years it seems to me that one was looking at the world and one's own life through bars. But then another thought, a terrible doubt, came to me. There are other bars, permanent bars of the cage of one's life, through which one has always and will always gaze at the world. The bars of one's birth and family and ancestors, of one's school and college, of one's own secret and sinuous psychology. Has not my mind, my soul, if I have a soul, for the last eighty-two years been pacing up and down like the panther, backwards and forwards, behind these bars and gazing through them until, so weary, I have seen, not the world or life, but only the bars—a thousand bars and behind the thousand bars no world?

I have to thank the Public Trustee and The Society of Authors for allowing me to quote Bernard Shaw's letter.

[1] Leonard Woolf's autobiography was originally published in five volumes, of which *Beginning Again* was the third.

1

London and Marriage 1911 and 1912

On Wednesday 24 May 1911, I left Ceylon on leave after my six and a half years there as a civil servant. My leave was for one year. I sailed in the *Staffordshire* with my sister Bella, who had married R. H. Lock, the Assistant Director of the Peradeniya Botanical Gardens. Seventeen days later, on Saturday June 10, we arrived in Marseille. It was a dull and rather dreary voyage. I like all voyages out, for you sail into the future, the unknown, into a widening horizon. And so all return journeys are somewhat depressing, even if you are on a year's leave and terribly eager to arrive and be once more home. You are going back to what you know—the horizon narrows. I feel that somehow my youth ended on Wednesday 24 May 1911—though I was already thirty-one, I was a young man when I left Colombo, but slightly middle-aged when I reached Marseille.

It was, of course, very strange and exciting to walk up the Marseille street. What astonished and entranced us most in our first view of Europe was the shops full of every kind of chocolate creams; we ate them steadily on the long train journey to Paris. I remember nothing of the France and Europe of my journey home except the chocolate creams. When we got off the boat at Folkestone, my brothers, Herbert and Edgar, were there to meet us—they had become strangers to me in six and a half years. And when we got into a taxi at Charing Cross and drove into Trafalgar Square, I felt at once, in the rhythm of the streets, that I had come back to a new world. The world of the four-wheeler and the hansom cab, which I had left in 1904, no longer existed. I felt for the moment like a relic from a slower age, for the life into which I was plunging out of Charing Cross railway station had a tempo clearly faster and noisier than what I was accustomed to. I faced it with caution and reserve and some depression.

We drove out to Putney in a London summer afternoon of perfect sunshine—1911 was one of those rare years, an unending summer of the snakeless meadow—in 1911 a summer which began in early spring and gently died away only in late autumn. In 1904 when I landed in Colombo and walked round to the Secretariat, to report my arrival, through the sun and sights and sounds and smells of Asia, I felt, as I wrote in *Growing*, as if my whole past life in London and Cambridge had suddenly vanished, fading away into unreality. And yet Colombo and myself walking in its dusty streets were not entirely real; then and all through my years in Ceylon I felt a certain unreality, theatricality, as if out of the corner of my eye I observed myself acting a part. The curious thing about my return to England was that, driving out from Charing Cross to Putney through the mechanised, bricked up sunshine of this London summer, I felt almost exactly what I had felt seven years ago in Colombo. My life in Ceylon, in Jaffna, Kandy, and Hambantota, suddenly vanished into unreality; but London and myself driving through its ugly streets did not acquire any reassuring reality. Out of the corner of my eye I seemed to observe myself once more acting a part in the same complicated play in front of a new backcloth and with different actors and a different audience.

I was born an introspective intellectual, and the man or woman who is by nature addicted to introspection gets into the habit, after the age of fifteen or sixteen, of feeling himself, often intensely, as 'I' and yet at the same time of seeing himself out of the corner of his eye as a 'not I', a stranger acting a part upon a stage. I always feel, from moment to moment, that my life and the life around me is immediately and extraordinarily real, concrete, and yet at the same time there is something absurdly unreal about it, because, knowing too well what I am really like inside, I cannot avoid continually watching myself playing a part upon a stage. This is the result of observing oneself objectively. It has a curious psychological effect; it helps one, I think, to bear with some equanimity both the ills one has and the ills one knows not of. If you begin to regard yourself objectively, you begin to find out what matters so violently to you subjectively hardly matters at all to the objective you.

Thus it was that driving out to Putney on Sunday 11 June 1911, about 4 p.m. in the Fulham Road I suddenly once more became aware of a kind of split in my personality, of the I, the real I, sitting in the taxi talking to my sister Bella and my brothers, Herbert and Edgar, and of that other I who had already begun to play a new part in Scene I, Act 1, of a quite new play. Today fifty-one years later, in June 1962, I am still playing my part in that play.

When we reached our destination, the house in Colinette Road, Putney, the mixture of reality and unreality, of familiarity and strangeness, was bewildering. This was the same house to which my mother with her nine children had migrated nearly twenty years before, when owing to my father's death we became overnight comparatively poor. It was the house from which, seven years before, I had set out for Ceylon. On the surface very little had changed in the house, the garden, and its inhabitants—except age. The furniture in the house, the pear tree in the garden, my mother, my brothers and sisters, and I myself were all twenty years older. There we all were, the ten of us, all together round the same dinner table as we had been seven years ago and seventeen years ago. Only the cat and the dog were missing, dead, and Agnes the parlourmaid who after twenty-five years 'service' had retired. I felt a slight feeling of claustrophobia. After the unending jungle, the great lagoons, the enormous sea pounding on the shore below my bungalow, the large open windowless rooms in Hambantota, I felt the walls of the Putney dining-room pressing in upon me, the low ceiling pressing down on me, the past and twenty years closing in on me. I went to bed somewhat depressed.

During the next few days slight depression continued, for the return is nearly always an anticlimax. But I decided, with some misgiving—for I did not know what I should find there—to plunge straight back into the life of Cambridge which I had left seven years ago. Three days after my arrival in Putney I took the train to Cambridge to stay with Lytton Strachey, who was living there in rooms in King's Parade. It was a formidable plunge. I dined at the high table in Trinity, and went to see McTaggart and Bertrand Russell, and played bowls on the Fellows Bowling Green with G. H. Hardy, who was a remarkable mathematician, became Professor at Oxford, and was one of the strangest and most charming of men. I saw my brother Cecil, who was at Trinity and later become a Fellow, and Walter Lamb, who became Secretary of the Royal Academy, and Francis Birrell. On Saturday evening I dined with Lytton and Rupert Brooke and we went on to a meeting of the Society. I had heard from Lytton a good deal about Rupert when he came up to King's from Rugby and was elected to the Society. He was twenty-three when I first met him on that June evening in 1911, the year in which his book of poems was published. In the narrow circle of Cambridge he had already a considerable reputation—for beauty, character, intellect, and poetry. His looks were stunning—it is the only appropriate adjective. When I first saw him, I thought to myself: 'That is exactly what Adonis must have looked like in the eyes of Aphrodite.' The well-known photograph of him by Schell in 1913, which is the frontispiece of his posthumous book, *1914 and Other Poems,* neither flatters not libels him. It is almost incredible, but he really did look like that. The photograph, of course, does not show his colouring—the red-gold of his hair and the brilliant complexion. It was the sexual dream face not only for every goddess, but for every sea-girl wreathed with seaweed red and brown and, alas, for all the damp souls of housemaids sprouting despondently at area gates.

Rupert had immense charm when he wanted to be charming, and he was inclined to exploit his charm so that he seemed to be sometimes too much the professional charmer. He had a very pronounced streak of hardness, even cruelty, in his character, and his attitude to all other males within a short radius of any attractive female was ridiculously jealous—the attitude of the farmyard cock among the hens. I never knew him at all well, though I used to see him fairly often when he was in England between 1911 and 1914. Before his quarrel with Lytton he was friendly both to me and to Virginia. He had a considerable respect for her, I think. He once stayed with her in Firle over a weekend and on Sunday morning they went and sat in Firle Park. He began to write a poem, his method being to put the last word of each line of rhyming quatrains down the sheet of paper and then complete the lines and so the poem. At one moment he said: 'Virginia, what is the brightest thing you can think of?' 'A leaf with the light on it,' was Virginia's instant reply, and it completed the poem.

In the short time between my meeting him and his death, Rupert quarrelled violently with Lytton and nearly all his Cambridge friends, and though we were uninvolved in and, indeed, ignorant of the quarrel, he included Virginia and me to some extent in his hostility. In 1915, just before he went out to the Dardanelles and died in the Aegean, walking down Holborn one morning we met him by chance. We stopped to talk and for the first moment there was hostility and even anger in his look and voice. But almost immediately they seemed to evaporate, and he was suddenly friendly and charming and we went into a near-by restaurant and had lunch. He was gay and affectionate, just as he had been that first evening at dinner in Cambridge.

Lytton and Rupert, Bertie Russell and Hardy, Sheppard[1] and

[1] Later Sir John Sheppard, Provost of King's College, Cambridge.

Goldie[1] at the Society on Saturday evening—all this was a wonderful plunge direct from the three years in Hambantota. In the train back to London, I came to the surface once more a little out of breath and slightly dizzy. At the same time I felt the warmth of a kind of reassurance. I had enjoyed my week-end. There was Cambridge and Lytton and Bertie Russell and Goldie, the Society and the Great Court of Trinity, and Hardy and bowls—all the eternal truths and values of my youth—going on just as I had left them seven years ago. Though I was fresh from the sands of Jaffna and Hambantota and from the Kiplingesque, Anglo-Indian society of Ceylon, I found that I was still a native of Trinity and King's, a Cambridge intellectual. My seven years in Ceylon had added a touch to my reserve and aloofness, but I had no difficulty in taking up the thread of friendship or conversation with Lytton and the others where I had left them in 1904.

When I got back from Cambridge, I pursued energetically the pleasures of London life and old friendships. I went to see Leopold Campbell,[2] who was now a clergyman, and Harry Gray,[3] who was now a successful surgeon, and Saxon,[4] who was now a civil servant in the Treasury. I went to see the Russian dancers, Shaw's *Fanny's First Play*, *Traviata*, and Adeline Genee dance at the Coliseum. I went to the Corona Club dinner where I met many Ceylon civil servants, including J. P. Lewis.[5] The next night I went to the Society dinner where I sat between Lytton and Maynard Keynes, and met once more Moore[6] and Desmond MacCarthy.[7] All this in a fortnight. Then on Monday 3 July, only three weeks after I had arrived in England, I went and dined with Vanessa and Clive Bell in Gordon Square. I was alone with them at dinner, but afterwards Virginia, Duncan Grant, and Walter Lamb came in. This was, I suppose, so far as I was concerned, the beginning of what came to be called Bloomsbury.

'What came to be called Bloomsbury' by the outside world never existed in the form given to it by the outside world. For 'Blooms-

[1] G. Lowes Dickinson.
[2] See Volume 1, pp. 113-15.
[3] See Volume 1, pp. 111-12.
[4] Saxon Sydney-Turner; see Volume 1, pp. 65-9 and 72-5.
[5] See Volume 1, pp. 155-6.
[6] See Volume 1, pp. 83-95 and 98-100.
[7] See Volume 1, pp. 90-1, 110-11 and 126-8.

bury' was and is currently used as a term—usually of abuse—applied to a largely imaginary group of persons with largely imaginary objects and characteristics. I was a member of this group and I was also one of a small number of persons who did in fact eventually form a kind of group of friends living in or around that district of London legitimately called Bloomsbury. The term Bloomsbury can legitimately be applied to this group and will be so applied in these pages. Bloomsbury, in this sense, did not exist in 1911 when I returned from Ceylon; it came into existence in the three years 1912 to 1914. We did ourselves use the term of ourselves before it was used by the outside world, for in the 1920s and 1930s, when our own younger generation were growing up and marrying and some of our generation were already dying, we used to talk of 'Old Bloomsbury', meaning the original members of our group of friends who between 1911 and 1914 came to live in or around Bloomsbury.

Old Bloomsbury consisted of the following people: The three Stephens: Vanessa, married to Clive Bell, Virginia, who married Leonard Woolf, and Adrian, who married Karin Costello; Lytton Strachey; Clive Bell; Leonard Woolf; Maynard Keynes; Duncan Grant; E. M. Forster (who will be referred to in this book as Morgan Forster or Morgan); Saxon Sydney-Turner; Roger Fry. Desmond McCarthy and his wife Molly, though they actually lived in Chelsea, were always regarded by us as members of Old Bloomsbury. In the 1920s and 1930s, when Old Bloomsbury narrowed and widened into a newer Bloomsbury, it lost through death Lytton and Roger and added to its numbers Julian, Quentin, and Angelica Bell, and David (Bunny) Garnett, who married Angelica.[1]

That Monday night of 3 July 1911, when I dined with Vanessa and Clive in Gordon Square, as I said, Bloomsbury had not yet actually come into existence. The reasons were geographical. At that moment only Vanessa and Clive and Saxon lived in Bloomsbury. Virginia and Adrian lived in Fitzroy Square and Duncan in rooms nearby. Roger lived in a house outside Guildford; Lytton in Cambridge and Hampstead; Morgan Forster in Weybridge; Maynard Keynes, as a Fellow of King's College, in Cambridge. I was a visitor

[1] There is proof of this chronological classification. We had what we called a Memoir Club, i.e. we met from time to time and we each in turn read a chapter, as it were, of autobiography. The original thirteen members of the Memoir Club were the thirteen members of Old Bloomsbury given above. Twenty years later the four younger persons were members.

from Ceylon. Ten years later, when Old Bloomsbury had come into existence, Vanessa, Clive, Duncan, Maynard, Adrian, and Lytton all lived in Gordon Square; Virginia and I were in Tavistock Square; Morgan in Brunswick Square; Saxon in Great Ormond Street; Roger in Bernard Street. Thus we all lived geographically in Bloomsbury within a few minutes walk of one another.

I am not, in this book, writing a history of Bloomsbury in any of its forms or manifestations, real or imaginary, and I shall have, after these first pages, very little to say about it. I am trying to write my autobiography, a true account of my life in relation to the times and the society in which I have lived, to the work I have done, and to people, whether intimates, acquaintances, or public persons. The twelve included by me in the previous paragraph as members of Old Bloomsbury had a great influence upon my life. The account of what happened to me during the ten or twelve years after my return from Ceylon will necessarily show how we came to congregate in those nostalgic London squares and the real nature of our congregation. Here there are one or two facts about us which I want to insist upon before going on with my narrative. We were and always remained primarily and fundamentally a group of friends. Our roots and the roots of our friendship were in the University of Cambridge. Of the thirteen persons mentioned above three are women and ten men; of the ten men nine had been at Cambridge, and all of us, except Roger, had been more or less contemporaries at Trinity and King's and were intimate friends before I went to Ceylon.

There is another point. In the first volume of my autobiography, in dealing with my years at Cambridge, I said that it was 'necessary here to say something about the Society—The Apostles—because of the immense importance it had for us, its influence upon our minds, our friendships, our lives'.[1] Of the ten men of Old Bloomsbury only Clive, Adrian and Duncan were not Apostles. Of the other seven of us, Desmond, Morgan, Lytton, Saxon, Maynard, and I, all overlapped more or less at Cambridge and had already grown into a peculiar intimacy there as active members of the Society. I tried in *Sowing* to give some idea of the character of G. E. Moore and of his tremendous intellectual (and also emotional) influence upon us and upon the Society of those days. The main things which Moore in-

[1] See Volume 1, particularly pp. 81-3 and 95-6.

stilled deep into our minds and characters were his peculiar passion for truth, for clarity and common sense, and a passionate belief in certain values. I have said that Moore's influence upon us was lifelong. How profound it was is shown by what Maynard Keynes wrote in his book *Two Memoirs*. What Moore and his *Principia Ethica* gave to us as young men and what we sixty years ago embraced with the violence and optimism of youth Maynard calls a religion and he is affectionately critical of its and our adolescent one-sidedness and absurdities. But as a final summing up he writes.

> It seems to me looking back that this religion of ours was a very good one to grow up under. It remains nearer the truth than any other that I know, with less irrelevant extraneous matter and nothing to be ashamed of; though it is a comfort today to be able to discard with a good conscience the calculus and the mensuration and the duty to know *exactly* what one means and feels. It was a purer, sweeter air by far than Freud cum Marx. It is still my religion under the surface.

That is the point: under the surface all six of us, Desmond, Lytton, Saxon, Morgan, Maynard, and I, had been permanently inoculated with Moore and Moorism; and even Roger, who was seven years older than Moore and highly critical of his philosophy, continually proved by his criticism of Moorism that he was 'under the surface' a Moorist. Through us and through *Principia Ethica* the four others, Vanessa and Virginia, Clive and Duncan, were deeply affected by the astringent influence of Moore and the purification of that divinely cathartic question which echoed through the Cambridge Courts of my youth as it had 2,300 years before echoed through the streets of Socratic Athens: 'What do you mean by that?' Artistically the purification can, I think, be traced in the clarity, light, absence of humbug in Virginia's literary style and perhaps in Vanessa's painting. They have the quality noted by Maynard in Moorism, the getting rid of 'irrelevant extraneous matter'.

There have often been groups of people, writers and artists, who were not only friends, but were consciously united by a common doctrine and object, or purpose artistic or social. The utilitarians, the Lake poets, the French impressionists, the English Pre-Raphaelites were groups of this kind. Our group was quite different. Its basis was friendship, which in some cases developed into love and marriage. The colour of our minds and thought had been given to us by the climate of Cambridge and Moore's philosophy, much as the climate of England gives one colour to the face of an Englishman while the climate of India gives a quite different colour to the face of a Tamil. But we had no common theory, system, or principles which we wanted to convert the world to; we were not proselytisers, missionaries, crusaders, or even propagandists. It is true that Maynard produced the system or theory of Keynsian economics which has had a great effect upon the theory and practice of economics, finance, and politics; and that Roger, Vanessa, Duncan, and Clive played important parts, as painters or critics, in what came to be known as the Post-Impressionist Movement. But Maynard's crusade for Keynsian economics against the orthodoxy of the Banks and academic economists, and Roger's crusade for post-impressionism and 'significant form' against the orthodoxy of academic 'representational' painters and aestheticians were just as purely individual as Virginia's writing of *The Waves*—they had nothing to do with any group. For there was no more a communal connection between Roger's 'Critical and Speculative Essays on Art', Maynard's *The General Theory of Employment, Interest and Money*, and Virginia's *Orlando* than there was between Bentham's *Theory of Legislation*, Hazlitt's *Principal Picture Galleries in England*, and Byron's *Don Juan*.

I can now return to Monday night 3 July 1911. In Cambridge during my week-end there, as I have said, I had had the reassuring pleasure of finding men and things, truths and values, to whom or to which I had given the love or loyalty of youth, unchanged and unchanging. In Gordon Square I re-entered a society which had completely changed since I left it seven years before, but in which I found myself immediately and completely at home. Nothing is more silly than the principle, which too often fatally influences practice, that you ought to be consistent in your feelings and your likes and dislikes. Where taste is concerned there is no law of contradiction. It is absurd to think, as many people do, that the love of cats or claret is a reason or excuse for not loving dogs or burgundy. So I get as much pleasure from the comfort of finding that nothing has changed as from the excitement of finding that everything is new.

There had certainly been a profound revolution in Gordon Square. I had dined in 46 Gordon Square with Thoby and his two sisters, the Misses Stephen, in 1904 only a few days before I left England for Ceylon. Now seven years later in the same rooms meeting again for the first time Vanessa, Virginia, Clive, Duncan, and Walter Lamb I found that almost the only things which had not changed were the furniture and the extraordinary beauty of the two Miss Stephens. Vanessa was, I think, usually more beautiful than Virginia. The form of her features was more perfect, her eyes bigger and better, her complexion more glowing. If Rupert was a goddess's Adonis, Vanessa in her thirties had something of the physical splendour which Adonis must have seen when the goddess suddenly stood before him. To many people she appeared frightening and formidable, for she was blended of three goddesses with slightly more of Athene and Artemis in her and her face than of Aphrodite. I myself never found her formidable, partly because she had the most beautiful speaking voice that I have ever heard, and partly because of her tranquillity and quietude. (The tranquillity was to some extent superficial; it did not extend deep down in her mind, for there in the depths there was also an extreme sensitivity, a nervous tension which had some resemblance to the mental instability of Virginia.) There was something monumental, monolithic, granitic in most of the Stephens in the two generations which descended from the Sir James Stephen who ruled the Colonial Office in the middle of the nineteenth century. His son, Sir James Fitzjames Stephen, the judge, was an outsize monolithic Stephen; Leslie, his brother and two sisters whom I knew personally—Miss Stephen the Quaker and Miss Stephen, Principal of Newnham—all had the quality, but less exaggeratedly. There was a magnificent and monumental simplicity in Thoby[1] which earned him his nickname The Goth. Vanessa had the same quality expressed in feminine terms. Like him she had a monolithic character and monolithic common sense and, as with him and her uncle, the judge, there was often something adamantine in the content and language of her judgments. It was the strange combination of great beauty and feminine charm with a kind of lapidification of character and her caustic humour which made her such a fascinating person.

Virginia was a very different kind of person beneath the strong family resemblances in the two sisters. She was, as I said, normally less beautiful than Vanessa. When she was well, unworried, happy, amused, and excited, her face lit up with an intense almost ethereal beauty. She was also extremely beautiful when, unexcited and unworried, she sat reading or thinking. But the expression, even the

[1] See Volume 1, pp. 75, 78-81.

shape of her face changed with extraordinary rapidity as the winds of mental strain, illness, or worry passed over its surface. It was still beautiful, but her anxiety and pain made the beauty itself painful.

Virginia is the only person whom I have known intimately who had the quality which one had to call genius. One has to call it genius because the mental process seems to be fundamentally different from those of ordinary or normal people and indeed from the normal mental processes of these abnormal persons. Virginia had a great enjoyment of ordinary things, of eating, walking, desultory talking, shopping, playing bowls, reading. She liked and got on well with all kinds of everyday people, as soon as they got to know her well and she them. (She had a curious shyness with strangers which often made them uncomfortably shy.) In this day to day, everyday life and intercourse with other people she talked and thought and acted, to a great extent, no doubt, as other ordinary people, though it is a curious fact that there was about her something, some intangible aura, which made her very often seem strange to the 'ordinary' person.

During our life together there was one fantastic recurring example of this fact which again and again I noted with astonishment. If you walk in the streets of London or any other large European city, you will see every now and then persons, particularly women, who in the eyes of God must appear indescribably ridiculous. There will be fat or lean middle aged or elderly, women dressed up in some exaggeration of the exaggerated contemporary fashion which could in fact only—and that doubtfully—be carried off by some rare and lovely young thing. They are ludicrous and laughable caricatures of female charm. Virginia, on the other hand, by any standard of taste was a very beautiful woman and many people would have applied to her the rather dubious description 'distinguished looking'; she had, too, I think, a flair for beautiful, if individual, dresses. Yet to the crowd in the street there was something in her appearance which struck them as strange and laughable. I am one of those people who merge in a crowd anywhere. Even in a foreign town, though I am not dressed exactly like the native inhabitants, no one notices and I pass—in appearance—for a Spaniard in Barcelona or a Swede in Stockholm. But in Barcelona and in Stockholm nine out of ten people would stare or stop and stare at Virginia. And not only in foreign towns; they would stop and stare and nudge one another—'look at her'—even in England, in Piccadilly or Lewes

High Street, where almost anyone is allowed to pass unnoticed. They did not merely stop and stare and nudge one another; there was something in Virginia which they found ridiculous. Some monstrous female caricature, who was accepted as ordinary by the crowd, would go into fits of laughter at the sight of Virginia. I always found it difficult to understand exactly what the cause of this laughter was. It was only partly that her dress was never quite the same as other people's. It was partly, I think, because there was something strange and disquieting, and therefore to many people ridiculous, in her appearance, in the way she walked—she seemed so often to be 'thinking of something else', to be moving with a slightly shuffling movement along the streets in the shadows of a dream. The hags and harridans and bright young things could not restrain their laughter or their giggles.

This laughter of the street distressed her; she had an almost morbid horror of being looked at and still more of being photographed—which is the reason why there are very few photographs of her in which she looks her natural self, the real everyday self which one saw in her face in ordinary life from hour to hour. A curious example of this nervous misery which she suffered from being looked at occurred when Stephen Tomlin (Tommy, as he was always called) sculpted the bust of her now in the National Portrait Gallery. With the greatest reluctance she was eventually induced by him to sit for him. The object of each sitting was naturally to look at her, which Tommy did with prolonged intensity. It was a kind of Chinese torture to her. He was a slow worker and worked away for an hour or so quite unconscious of what was going on in the mind of his tortured sitter. The sittings ended only just in time; if they had gone on much longer, they would have made Virginia seriously ill. A shadow of her misery has, I think, been caught by Tommy and frozen into the clay of the portrait.

I was saying that in her day to day, everyday life she thought and talked and acted, to a great extent, as other people do, though there was always this element or aura in her which was strange and disquieting to ordinary people so that in self-defence, in order to reassure themselves, they giggled or roared with laughter. I think this element was closely connected with the streak in her which I call genius. For in conversation she might, at any moment, leave the ground, as I used to call it. She was an unusually amusing talker in the usual way of talk and talkers, her mind being very quick and intelligent, witty and humorous, appropriately serious or frivolous as the occasion or subject demanded. But at any moment, in a general conversation with five or six people or when we were alone together, she might suddenly 'leave the ground' and give some fantastic, entrancing, amusing, dreamlike, almost lyrical description of an event, a place, or a person. It always made me think of the breaking and gushing out of the springs in autumn after the first rains. The ordinary mental processes stopped, and in their place the waters of creativeness and imagination welled up and, almost undirected, carried her and her listeners into another world. Unlike most good or brilliant talkers, she was never boring, for these displays—and displays is a bad word to describe them for they were so spontaneous—were always short.

When she soared away into one of these fantasias, one felt it to be a kind of inspiration. The thoughts and images fountained up spontaneously, not directed and consciously controlled as they were ordinarily by her in conversation and are always by most people. In the description in her diary of how she wrote the last pages of *The Waves* I recognise the same mental process:

> *Saturday, February 7th*
>
> Here in the few minutes that remain, I must record, heaven be praised, the end of *the Waves*. I wrote the words O Death fifteen minutes ago, having reeled across the last ten pages with some moments of such intensity and intoxication that I seemed only to stumble after my own voice, or almost after some sort of speaker (as when I was mad) I was almost afraid, remembering the voices that used to fly ahead.[1]

'Stumble after my own voice' and 'the voices that fly ahead'—here surely is an exact description of the inspiration of genius and madness, showing how terrifyingly thin is the fabric of thought often separating the one from the other, a fact recognised at least 2,000 years ago and often recognised since. 'Nullum magnum ingenium sine mixtura dementiae fuit'—there has never been great genius without a mixture of madness in it—says Seneca, which Dryden echoed in the hackneyed tag:

> Great wits are sure to madness near allied,
> And thin partitions do their bounds divide

This breaking away of the mind from the ordinary modes of

[1] *A Writer's Diary*, p. 169.

thought which I have described in Virginia is, I think, a kind of inspiration or genius. It produces more often than other modes of thought what Sir Thomas Browne called 'a glimpse of incomprehensibles and thought of things which thoughts do but tenderly touch'. There is evidence that the greatest of great geniuses experience it. Beethoven, every now and again, used to have what his faithful disciple called 'a raptus', a kind of volcanic creative outburst. In one sense however, there is nothing mysterious about this. The raptus or inspiration is clearly only a rare and wonderful form of a well-known everyday mental process. Graham Wallas in *The Art of Thought* rightly insisted upon the importance of bouts of idleness and of not thinking for creative thought. Nearly everyone must have had the experience of grinding away unsuccessfully at some intellectual or even emotional problem and then suddenly, when one has given it up in desperation and is thinking of something entirely different, the solution comes with a flash—'like an inspiration'—into the mind. Or you may even go to bed with an unsolved problem and wake next morning to find you have solved it in your sleep. The most famous example of this phenomenon is the triumphant 'Eureka!' of Archimedes when he leapt from his bath, having seen in a sudden flash the scientific principle which had so long eluded him in his study. The writer's 'inspiration' and Beethoven's raptus are of the same nature. One proof of this is that the inspiration is only the end process of a prolonged period of persistent conscious thought, often of trial and error. In Beethoven's case this is proved by his Notebooks. It was also true of Virginia. I have never known any writer who thought, ruminated so continually and so consciously over what she was writing, turning her problems over in her mind persistently while sitting in a chair in front of the winter fire or going for her daily walk along the bank of the Sussex Ouse. She was able to reel across the last ten pages of *The Waves* stumbling after her own voice and the voices that flew ahead only because of the hours of intense, conscious thought she had given to the book for weeks and months before the words were actually put upon paper—just as Archimedes would never have been able to shout his 'I have found it!' if he had not already consciously and laboriously worked for hours upon the problem.

After this second digression—though it is a highly relevant digression—I can return once more to the evening of Monday 3 July 1911. There were two things which immediately made me feel that I had entered a society wonderfully different from that which I had left in Gordon Square in 1904, not to speak of the Kiplingesque society in which I had lived from 1904 to 1911 in Ceylon. The first was an immediate sense of intimacy which was both emotional and intellectual. It carried back, and carried me back, to the Cambridge of my youth. What was so exhilarating in Cambridge and particularly in the Society in those years from 1900 to 1904 was the sense of profound intimacy with a number of people whom one liked and who were passionately interested in the same things and pursued the same ends—and who were always ready to laugh at themselves and at the universe, even the serious things in the universe that they took very seriously. But that was a state of things which applied only to Cambridge and the Society, to a small number of people who were Apostles. It did not in 1904 apply to Gordon Square and above all, it excluded all women. What was so new and so exhilarating to me in the Gordon Square of July 1911 was the sense of intimacy and complete freedom of thought and speech, much wider than in the Cambridge of seven years ago, and above all including women.

People who were born too late to experience in boyhood and adolescence the intellectual and moral pressure of Victorianism have no idea of the feeling of fog and fetters which weighed one down. In the first part of my autobiography, *Sowing*, I described the excitement with which we found ourselves, as young men in Cambridge, taking part 'in the springtime of a conscious revolt against the social, political, religious, moral, intellectual, and artistic institutions, beliefs, and standards of our fathers and grandfathers.'[1] Some reviewers lectured me severely for exaggerating or inventing this revolt and the part which my generation played in it. One can only congratulate the lecturers on their good fortune in never having suffered the burden of Victorianism and in having benefited so much from our revolt against it—clearly that revolt which Shaw and his generation began and my generation helped to extend was so effective that our successors are not even aware how and why, while we were born in chains, they are comparatively free.

In 1904 we had reached complete freedom of thought and speech among a few intimate friends, but the circle of friends was entirely male and extremely narrow and it is extraordinary to look back from today and remember how formal society was in those

[1] See Volume 1, pp. 96-8 and 102-7.

days. When I went to Ceylon—indeed even when I returned—I still called Lytton Strachey Strachey and Maynard Keynes Keynes, and to them I was still Woolf. When I stayed for a week with the Stracheys in the country in 1904 or dined in Gordon Square with the Stephens, it would have been inconceivable that I should have called Lytton's or Thoby's sisters by their Christian names. The social significance of using Christian instead of surnames and of kissing instead of shaking hands is curious. Their effect is greater, I think, than those who have never lived in a more formal society imagine. They produce a sense—often unconscious—of intimacy and freedom and so break down barriers to thought and feeling. It was this feeling of greater intimacy and freedom, of the sweeping away of formalities and barriers, which I found so new and so exhilarating in 1911. To have discussed some subjects or to have called a (sexual) spade a spade in the presence of Miss Strachey or Miss Stephen would seven years before have been unimaginable; here for the first time I found a much more intimate (and wider) circle in which complete freedom of thought and speech was now extended to Vanessa and Virginia, Pippa and Marjorie.

In the last six months of 1911 I lived a life of pleasure, just unmitigated, pure, often acute pleasure, such as I had never had before and have never had again. To have a full six months of unalloyed pleasure and even happiness is a very rare thing and a salutary thing, temporarily smoothing the lines and wrinkles which time and life grave upon the face, the mind, and the soul. There was first the weather. I do not remember any year as sunny as 1911. The sun was always blazing in a cloudless sky. In Ceylon I had lived for years in a very hot district and had never suffered from the heat, but at Stockholm in the first week of August it was so hot that, for the first and only time in my life, it was almost too much for me. It seemed absurd to have to come from the equator to latitude 60° north in order to feel too hot.

The climate and the weather, the sun and the rain, and the wind on the heath, have an immense effect upon our happiness, as Jasper Petulengro so rightly and so poetically explained to George Borrow. So too has the climate of opinion. In the decade before the 1914 war there was a political and social movement in the world, and particularly in Europe and Britain, which seemed at the time wonderfully hopeful and exciting. It seemed as though human beings might really be on the brink of becoming civilised. It was partly the feeling of relief and release as we broke out of the fog of Victorianism. The forces of reaction and barbarism were still there, but they were in retreat. They had suffered a tremendous defeat in the Dreyfus case. In the Zabern incident and the Denshawi incident a new note began to be heard in what may be called world opinion. It seemed at last to be generally agreed that for a German officer to beat a German cobbler was 'an outrage against law and order and decency and civilisation'. When at Denshawi a British court passed savage sentences upon Egyptian villagers for killing a British officer who insisted upon killing the villagers' pigeons, a cry went up, not against the villagers, but against the insolence of the officers and the vindictiveness and savagery of the judges. For the first time in the history of the world the rights of Jews, cobblers, and coloured men not to be beaten, hanged, or judicially murdered by officers, Junkers, or white men were publicly admitted; it looked for a moment as if militarism, imperialism, and antisemitism were on the run.

We were, of course, mistaken in thinking that the world really might become civilised, but the fact that it didn't does not prove that our optimism was foolish or credulous. It is so easy and foolish to be historically wise after the event. It was, I still believe, touch and go whether the movement towards liberty and equality—political and social—and towards civilisation, which was strong in the first decade of the twentieth century, would become so strong as to carry everything before it. Its enemies saw the risk and the result was the war of 1914; they postponed the danger of our becoming civilised for at least a hundred years. But the future could not alter the fact that it was exciting to be alive in London in 1911 and that there was reason for exhilaration. Profound changes were taking place in every direction, not merely politically and socially. The revolution of the motor car and the aeroplane had begun; Freud and Rutherford and Einstein were at work beginning to revolutionise our knowledge of our own minds and of the universe. Equally exciting things were happening in the arts. On the stage the shattering impact of Ibsen was still belatedly powerful and we felt that Ibsen had a worthy successor in Shaw as a revolutionary. In literature one seemed to feel the ominous lull before the storm which was to produce in a few years *A la Recherche du Temps Perdu, Ulysses, Prufrock* and *The Waste Land, Jacob's Room* and *Mrs Dalloway*. In painting we were in the middle of the profound revolution of Cézanne,

Matisse, and Picasso which miraculously followed so closely upon the no less profound revolution of Renoir, Monet, Degas, and Manet. And to crown all, night after night we flocked to Covent Garden, entranced by a new art, a revelation to us benighted British, the Russian Ballet in the greatest days of Diaghilev and Nijinsky.

For six months or more I lived in a kaleidoscopic dream and it is only by giving some details that I can give any idea of what life was like to the Ceylon civil servant on leave in Europe before the 1914 war. Two days after my dinner in Gordon Square Harry Gray took me, disguised as a surgeon, to West Ham Hospital to see him perform a terrific operation on an elderly man. I lived in those days on the principle that I wanted to know everything and experience everything and I therefore jumped at the chance when Harry offered to let me see a formidable operation. The spectacle was surprising and rather disconcerting. The operation was to take a growth out of the man's inside; it lasted an unconscionable time and what astonished me was that, after the first use of the knife, it was hardly used again, for Harry after a long and tremendous struggle and the use of great force, working away with his bare hands in the man's inside, at last triumphantly, as it seemed to me, drew out the growth. The heat and smells of the operating theatre and the sympathetic tension of those straining hands in the man's belly all but made me disgrace myself and Harry by fainting. I only just managed to remain conscious and on my feet.

Two days later I went and stayed for four days with Leopold at Frome. Leopold, who, when I knew him at Cambridge, was Leopold Colin Henry Douglas Campbell, was now the Rev. Leopold Colin Henry Douglas Campbell-Douglas, married and vicar of Frome in Somerset. The change from Gordon Square and the Russian dancers to the Somerset vicarage was fascinating. Leopold, it is true, was not by any means an ordinary English country parson. He was in the direct succession to the Barony of Blythswood and eventually, owing to the deaths of uncles, father, and brothers, did become Lord Blythswood. He was indelibly marked with the hereditary stigmata of Eton, the Scots Guards, Manchester Square, wealth and aristocracy. He really did call hunting and fishing 'huntin and fishin'. By some Freudian twist of the unconscious he had become a clergyman of the Church of England instead of Colonel of the Scots Guards, a post which had been occupied by his uncle, father, and brother and which they themselves seemed to regard as a kind of family heirloom. Up to a point Leopold took his religion pretty seriously and was about as High, I suppose, as an Anglican parson can be this side Rome and popery. It was probably true, as I wrote in *Sowing*, that 'the Church was to him exactly what the Scots Guards were to his father, his uncle, and his brother'.

It was fascinating to watch him now shepherding his sheep in the somnolent, typically agricultural, profoundly English parish instead of (and as if) paternally commanding his 'men' in the platoon, the company, or the regiment. He loved the High Church paraphernalia and properties, the incense, banners, images, genuflexions, chasubles, just as his relations had loved the standards, the uniforms, the pomp and circumstance of the daily drill on the Guards parade ground of the barracks in Birdcage Walk. In 1911 Somerset was still rural and Frome a typical market town with fewer than 10,000 inhabitants. These Somerset parishes were unlikely to be astonished by the idiosyncrasies or antics of any incumbent presented to a living by a Lord of the Manor or still more remote owner of an advowson, since for 500 years or more they had experienced the strange, motley succession of rectors or vicars who had appeared in and disappeared from their village churches. There were things about the Rev. Leopold Campbell-Douglas which ecclesiastically some of his parishioners did not approve, but beneath the sometimes irritating and foolish surface he had a singularly simple, honest, and charming character which endeared him to most people. Owing to the incorrigible snobbery of all classes in rural England the fact that his father was Lord Blythswood and that he would almost certainly succeed one day to the title probably endeared him to even more people in Frome and more securely than the charm of his character.

Fifty years ago life in Somerset still moved exceedingly slow and the well oiled wheels of Leopold's life moved slowly in the rhythm of the life around him. It seemed almost incredibly archaic and remote and to have nothing to do with realities, the reality of life in Jaffna or Hambantota, the reality of the Dreyfus case or Zabern, the reality of the Russian dancers. I went to church with Leopold and heard him preach an absurd sermon which I do not think the rest of the congregation thought absurd; I went with him to visit some of his parishioners which seemed to me even more absurd; we sat through the long sunny summer afternoons in the garden heavy with leaves and flowers; we ate heavy meals of juicy joints, Somerset cream and butter, home-made bread, peas and beans and raspberries; we drove slowly to Bath which with its peeling buildings still slept peacefully in the eighteenth century. Except that the car was ousting the parson's gig and the railway had ousted the stage coach, the life which I dipped into for four days in the Frome rectory in 1911 was centuries old. I don't think the essence or rhythm of it had changed much from the days of the Rev. Laurence Sterne, Vicar of Sutton-in-the-Forest in Yorkshire, or the Rev. Gilbert White in Selborne, Hampshire. I am glad to have lived in it briefly, just as I am glad to have lived briefly in the antediluvian life of the Ceylon jungle village. Both of them have finally passed away, becoming as extinct as the pterodactyl and the mammoth, destroyed by the motor car and the motor omnibus and the aeroplane and high explosives and bombs—man's passion for speed and destruction. Being a modern man, I too have a passion for speed, always moving faster and faster from place to place. But I am old enough and sensible enough to remember the pleasure of travelling slow and living slow and to recognise the folly and emptiness of speed.

On 11 July the kaleidoscope flickered violently again, for I went straight from Leopold and Frome and stayed with Lytton and Moore at Beckey House, Manaton, on Dartmoor. Beckey belongs also to an almost extinct past, for I doubt whether anything quite like it is now obtainable in England. It was a largish house in a remote, narrow, rocky Dartmoor valley. Behind it was a waterfall, the Beckey Falls, and through the valley and the trees past the house rushed the Beckey stream. A working class man and his wife and children lived in the house and they let lodgings, a large sitting-room and a few bedrooms. It was incredibly remote and rather primitive, but the people were very nice. The week I spent with Moore and Lytton was intellectually pretty astringent; to pass straight from the conversation of Leopold's parishioners to that of the authors of *Principia Ethica* and *Eminent Victorians* was as though one were stepping straight out of the society of the Vicar of Wakefield into that of Voltaire and Diderot. Astringency exactly describes the flavour of life with Moore and Lytton. Moore was never easy to talk to, though I found him less difficult in 1911 than he had been in 1904. It was extremely difficult to live up to his extraordinary simplicity and integrity, which were combined with great intellectual power. Talking to him one lived under the shadow of the eternal, though silent, question: 'What exactly do you mean by that?' It is a menacing question, particularly when you know that muddle and not knowing 'exactly what you mean by *that*' will cause to Moore almost physical pain which he will show involuntarily in his eyes.

In the morning Lytton used to sit in one part of the garden, with a panama hat on his head, groaning from time to time over his literary constipation as he wrote *Landmarks in French Literature* for the Home University Library; in another part of the garden sat Moore, a panama hat on his head, his forehead wet with perspiration, sighing from time to time over his literary constipation as he wrote *Ethics* for the Home University Library. Lytton used to complain that he was mentally constipated because nothing at all came into his mind, which remained as blank as the paper on his knees. Moore on the contrary said that his mental constipation came from the fact that as soon as he had written down a sentence, he saw either that it was just false or that it required a sentence to qualify it which would require another sentence to qualify the qualification. This, as we pointed out to him, would go on ad infinitum, and the 60,000 words which he had bound himself to write on ethics for the Home University Library would, after he had written a first sentence which was not 'just false', consist of an infinite series of qualifications to it only cut short by the fact that the publishers would not print more than 60,000 words.

In the afternoons we went for long walks over Dartmoor. Moore had a passion for bathing, and, whenever we came upon one of those long, deep, black pools which you find in the rocks among the Dartmoor tors, he would strip off his clothes and jump in. Nothing would induce Lytton to get into water in the open air, and so I felt I must follow Moore's example. It nearly killed me. I do not think that I have ever felt any water colder than in those Dartmoor rock pools; after the delicious evening plunge into the warm waves of the Indian Ocean at Hambantota, this was real torture. In the evenings Moore sang Adelaide, Schubert songs, or the Dichterliebe, or he played Beethoven sonatas. It was good to see again the sweat pour down his face and hear his passion in the music as he played the Waldstein or the Hammerklavier sonata.

A week after I got back from Dartmoor, I set off with my brother Edgar for Göteborg in Sweden. One of my aunts, my mother's sister, had married a Dane and lived in Copenhagen. When we were children, we used sometimes in the holidays to go and stay with her in Denmark. She had a large family and Charlotte, one of her daughters, had married a Swede who lived in Göteborg; he was a lawyer and Member of Parliament. Edgar and I went and stayed with Charlotte and her family at the fishing village of Fiskebackshil in Bohuslan, on the coast north of Göteborg. From there we went by steamer through fiords and canals and reached Rattvik on Lake Siljan and thence to Stockholm. Finally we went to Denmark and stayed in a large country house with Aunt Flora not far from Copenhagen.

Even after fifty years I can recall those three weeks in Scandinavia with extraordinary vividness. It was just three years before the Serbian student Princip fired the shot in Sarajevo which killed the Archduke Francis Ferdinand of Austria and destroyed the civilisation of Europe. Civilisation is a way of life and the war of 1914 destroyed a new, and civilised or semi-civilised, way of life which had established itself or was establishing itself all over Europe. I doubt whether anyone born after 1900 has any idea of what life was like before 1914 in England, France, or Sweden. We live today, and have lived ever since the shot was fired at Sarajevo, with a background of battle, murder, and sudden death. When the B.B.C. voice announces: 'This is the Home Service with the programme of news and current affairs', we know that the news is always bad; it will be ninety-nine per cent political and will tell us of some new acts of organised communal barbarism and violence in Russia or Hungary, Spain or Portugal, South Africa or Algeria. The motives and motifs in these events are fear and hatred, and we feel, as we listen to the announcer's voice—such a well-bred voice of doom—that the doom is threatening, not only our country and its allies, but ourselves, helpless individuals, in our personal lives with every kind of disaster and horror. Human beings are, we know, like Habbakuk, 'capable of anything'; they will accustom themselves to live their lives clinging to the side of a volcano which, they are aware, may at any moment overwhelm them with hot ashes and burning lava—and so we too in the last fifty years have schooled ourselves to live more or less contentedly under the menace of news and current affairs.

But it was really not like that before 1914. Thanks to the doctrines of nationalism and patriotism, of fascists, nazis, and communists, happiness is now politically a dirty word. I think the main difference in the world before 1914 from the world after 1914 was in the sense of security and the growing belief that it was a supremely good thing for people to be communally and individually happy. Coming to Europe after seven years in the purely Asiatic civilisation and barbarism of Ceylon, I was peculiarly sensitive to the civilised and barbarous variations in European countries. Life in Scandinavia, and particularly in Sweden, had a quality, an atmosphere and flavour, of its own, markedly different from that of Britain or France, Italy or Germany. Bohuslan has a lovely northern rocky coastline. In Fiskebackshil we lived in a house outside the village on a narrow estuary. The sea was studded with tiny islands of bare rock often only a few inches above the water. We used to row out to them and spend all day swimming in the sea or lying on the little islands talking, reading, eating, and sleeping. The sky and sea were bright blue; the sun beat down upon us in this marvellous eternal summer; the Swedes—advanced in everything—bathed, men, women, and children, naked and unashamed, so that scattered round one saw tall, fair-haired, naked men and women on the little islands or plunging into the sea. In the evening we rowed back to the mainland and walked out to the headland overlooking the estuary and called altogether in a long-drawn, lilting unison across the water: 'Re-gi-na! Re-gi-na!' Then, from the tiny rocky bay across the estuary, came the ferry boat rowed by Regina, an elderly woman, statuesque, with a face of great beauty, touched slightly by sadness and nobility. And as Regina rowed us across the water, and the soft, lilting Swedish merged or mingled with the gentle lapping of the water against the prow, there descended upon us from the cloudless, darkening sky that delicious melancholy which steals over one when one is completely happy and at the end of a summer day twilight steals across one's happiness.

The Swedes were in those days, and still are, more civilised than most Europeans. Their civilisation was their own. It was a little too self-conscious, too antiseptic and sterilised and municipalised for my taste, but it was refreshingly alive and vigorous. The Scandinavians have a passion for knowledge and for asking questions, and we were always having to try to satisfy this thirst for information in our cousins and their children and friends, in naked strangers whom we met on the rocks of Bohusland or in fully clothed strangers whom we met in trains, steamers, trams, and buses. 'Do you belong to the Church of England?' 'Do you believe in God?' 'What is the constitution of the Stock Exchange?' Can you divorce your wife in England if she is insane?' This conscientious, relentless, somewhat humourless pursuit of knowledge occasionally filled me with despair—Virginia used to say that in similar circumstances a look would sometimes cross my face which made her fear that I would stand up and howl like a child of three, suddenly aware that the bottom has dropped out of its world. Up to the age of fifty, I did, I think, often feel like that, but one of the consolations of age is that, if one does not exactly learn to suffer bores gladly, one learns at least to disregard them with equanimity. These Swedish searchers for truth were, too, so sympathetic, so civilised, that it was impossible not to like them even when for the twentieth time one explained that one was not a member of the Church of England and was unfortunately ignorant of how the London Stock Exchange was governed.

Edgar and I saw a good deal of the life of Scandinavia in the short time that we were there. On Lake Siljan, in Gefvle, and Stockholm we saw it as tourists from the outside; in Göteborg, Fiskebackshil, and in Denmark we saw it from the inside, from the inside of an enormous Danish family. It was a bourgeois life and civilisation, nineteenth-century bourgeois civilisation developing to its apogee. Society in Britain, France, and Italy has never been of a purely middle class type; it has always been tainted or tempered by an aristocracy, a peasantry, or a working class. If you wanted to see a bourgeois society in its purest and most advanced form, you had to go to Amsterdam and The Hague; but Scandinavia in 1911 was not far behind Holland. In my aunt's large country house at Gentofte, in the comfortable houses and flats of her innumerable relations in Copenhagen, in the house, swarming with children, which one of my cousins owned at a seaside place on The Sound, we sat down, usually ten to twenty or even thirty people, to vast meals; we swam and sailed and rowed; we talked interminably. Here, as in Sweden, I felt a sense of civilised stability and security, a wide and widening prosperity and communal happiness, humane, progressive, and, though partly philistine, also intellectually and artistically alive and eager.

It was a patriarchal or matriarchal society such as exists no longer, I suppose, anywhere in Europe. When my brother Herbert and I once went and stayed with my aunt and uncle one summer in their country house near Copenhagen, we came in for the wedding of their daughter Mary. The wedding ceremony was performed in the house in the presence of about 150 guests. After the ceremony there was a wedding breakfast for about 120 people, all relations. It was a colossal feast and lasted from twelve to three-thirty or four. There were innumerable speeches, young women got up and recited poems, children in white dresses and pink sashes rose from their seats and sang what I imagined to be Danish epithalamiums. At four the bride and bridegroom drove away in a shower of confetti, white satin slippers, laughter, tears, and cheers. Then the guests began to drift away, although about thirty of them remained to dinner. The scale of family reunions was nearly always gigantic. The patriarch of patriarchs lived in Copenhagen, an incredibly ancient man in his nineties. We were taken ceremonially to have lunch with him and I felt that I was expected to realise that I was going to have lunch with a kind of tribal totem or a cross between Methuselah and Melchizedek or even Jehovah. There were some thirty relations at lunch and Methuselah gave us, as Englishmen, an enormous sirloin of beef with marmalade.

Edgar and I returned to England in the middle of August and the next five months were the most exciting months of my life. During them 'Bloomsbury' really came into existence and I fell in love with Virginia. I felt the foundations of my personal life becoming more and more unstable, crisis after crisis confronting me, so that I had at short notice to make decisions whether I should or should not turn my life upside down. There is nothing more exhilarating than having to make that kind of decision, with the (no doubt false) feeling that you are the captain of your soul, the master of your fate. The shadow in the background of my life was Ceylon. Here in London and Cambridge during the next few months I was plunged into a life which was in every way the exact opposite of what I had left in Hambantota and what I should go back to at the end of my leave. Even before I decide to ask Virginia to marry me, I knew that I should sooner or later have to decide whether I would go back to the Ceylon Civil Service or throw the whole thing up.

A few days after I returned from Denmark I began to write *The Village in the Jungle*. The jungle and the people who lived in the Sinhalese jungle villages fascinated, almost obsessed me in Ceylon. They continued to obsess me in London, in Putney or Bloomsbury, and in Cambridge. *The Village in the Jungle* was a novel in which I tried somehow or other vicariously to live their lives. It was also, in some curious way, the symbol of the anti-imperialism which had been growing upon me more and more in my last years in Ceylon.

The Sinhalese way of life, in those entrancing Kandyan hills or the rice fields and coconut plantations of the low country, and above all those strange jungle villages, was what engrossed me in Ceylon; the prospect of the sophisticated, Europeanised life of Colombo, the control of the wheels of the intricate machinery of central administration, with the dreary pomp and circumstance of imperial government, filled me with misgiving and disgust. And I knew that if I went back to Ceylon it was almost certain that I would be returning, not to the village in the jungle, but to the seats of power in Colombo. The more I wrote *The Village in the Jungle*, the more distasteful became the prospect of success in Colombo.

Virginia and Adrian Stephen at this time were living in a large house in Fitzroy Square and had an 'evening' once a week. Virginia also leased a red-brick villa house in Firle, near Lewes, and she asked me to come there for a long weekend in September. It was still the unending summer of that marvellous year, and it seemed as if the clouds would never again darken the sky as we sat reading in Firle Park or walked over the downs. This was the first time that I had seen the South Downs as it were from the inside and felt the beauty of the gentle white curves of the fields between the great green curves of their hollows; I have lived close to them ever since and have learnt that, in all seasons and circumstances, their physical loveliness and serenity can make one's happiness exquisite and assuage one's misery. After that I began to see a great deal of Virginia and the circle around her in Fitzroy Square, and around Vanessa and Clive Bell in Gordon Square. The Russian Ballet became for a time a curious centre for both fashionable and intellectual London. It was the great days of Diaghilev with Nijinsky at the height of his powers in the classical ballets. I have never seen anything more perfect, nor more exciting, on any stage than Scheherezade, Carnaval, Lac des Cygnes, and the other famous classics. There develops in nearly all arts, and indeed in games like cricket, at various periods after an archaic, vague, or inchoate beginning, a classical style which combines great power and freedom and beauty with a kind of self-imposed austerity and restraint. In the hands of a great master, like Sophocles, Thucydides, Virgil, Swift, La Fontaine, La Bruyere,[1] this combination of originality and freedom with formal purity and

[1] I saw the same classical qualities in the batting of W. G. Grace and A. C. Maclaren and in the bowling of J. T. Hearne, Richardson, and Rhodes.

restraint is tremendously moving and exciting, and it was this element of classicism in the ballets of 1911 which made them so entrancing. One's pleasure was increased because night after night one could go to Covent Garden and find all round one one's friends, the people whom one liked best in the world, moved and excited as one was oneself. In all my long life in London this is the only instance in which I can remember the intellectuals going night after night to a theatre, opera, concert, or other performance as, I suppose, they have and do in other countries and cities, for instance Bayreuth or Paris.

Bayreuth recalls another motif of the autumn of 1911. Among the frequenters of the Russian Ballet there was, strangely enough, a vogue for Wagner—strangely, because one can hardly imagine two products of the human mind and soul more essentially hostile. Virginia and Adrian with Saxon Sydney-Turner used to go, almost ritualistically, to the great Wagner festival at Bayreuth, as Hugh Walpole and many others did later. It was, I think, Saxon who in our circle was the initiator or leader of the Wagner cult; the operas appealed to him, partly because, as I explained in *Sowing*,[1] he collected them as if they were postage stamps, and partly because the intricate interweaving of the 'themes' gave scope to his extraordinary ingenuity in solving riddles; spotting the Wotan or Siegfried theme interweaving with the fire music theme gave him the same kind of pleasure as that from fitting the right piece into a picture puzzle or solving a crossword puzzle. In 1911 I knew nothing about Wagner, but I saw that it was time for me to set about him seriously. I therefore took a box in Covent Garden for the *Ring* in October, and Virginia came to *Das Rheingold*, *Siegfried*, and *Götterdämmerung*, with Adrian and Rupert Brooke to *Die Walküre*. It was a formidable experience: the operas started in the afternoon and ended after eleven, and we used to go back after them to supper in Fitzroy Square. I am glad that I sat through those four operas of the *Ring*, though I have never had the courage or desire to do it again. I see that in its way the *Ring* is a masterpiece, but I dislike it and dislike Wagner and his art. There are passages in *Das Rheingold*, *Walküre*, and *Götterdämmerung* of considerable beauty and it is occasionally moving and exciting, but I find it intolerably monotonous and boring. The Germans in the nineteenth century developed a

[1] See Volume 1, p. 66.

tradition, a philosophy of life and art, barbarous, grandiose, phoney. Wagner was both cause and effect of this repulsive process which ended in the apogee and apotheosis of human bestiality and degradation, Hitler and the Nazis. There are, as I said, moments of beauty and excitement in the *Ring*; there is still more, perhaps, to be said for the early Wagner, as in *Lohengrin*, and for the *Meistersinger*. But I did not enjoy the *Ring* in my box, with Virginia by my side, in 1911, and *Tristan* and *Parsifal* when I came to hear them repelled me and far outdid the *Ring* in tediousness and monotony.

In October Virginia and Adrian had to find a new house as the lease of their house in Fitzroy Square came to an end. They took a large four-storied house in Brunswick Square, which they proposed to run on—for those days—original lines. Adrian occupied the second floor and Virginia the third. Maynard Keynes and Duncan Grant shared the ground floor, and I was offered the fourth floor, or rather a bedroom and sitting room there. They had a wonderful old family cook inherited from the nineteenth century, Sophie,[1] and a

[1] The following letter from Sophie to Virginia, written in 1936, shows in an interesting way the curious psychology of these devoted female servants to the families for whom they worked—sometimes without exorbitant recognition—in the nineteenth century:

My dear Miss Genia,

You are much too good to me. I dont deserve such kindness. I am sure I dont.

Thank you very much your very generious cheque arrived this morning. It was sent from Dalingridge to 33 Chester Square ware Lady Margaret has a house until the end of August. then on to me.

Thank you also for your nice letter and all the bits of news. I do enjoy hearing all about Miss Nessa and her charming children there is nobody just like you all are to me. I shall look forward to seeing you all again one day. I keep all your letters and read them over and over I also have some snaps that Sir George sent me. he had taken them of you all when he went to Charlston with Mr Brony and her Ladyship. They are all Treasures of mine. I took them one day to show Mr & Mrs Gerald. I am including one that Miss Stella took of me at St Ives also one Mr Gerald took. At least it might have been a copy of them thay was found with some others after Sir George died he always thought he had taken them. One day your beloved Mother found me in the kitchen shelling peas. and said thats whot I like to see you doing wait until I fetch Miss Stella to take a snap of you. then come Mr Gerald oh said I like to see you stirring with a big spoon. So hear they are Lady Margaret gave them to me after Sir George died Will you Please dear Miss Genia return them. . . . Thanks again for all your kindness to me. May I send my love to Mr Woolf

parlourmaid of the same vintage. Breakfast was provided for all the occupants and every morning one notified in writing on a tablet in the hall whether one would be in for lunch and dinner. All meals were put on trays in the hall and one carried one's tray up to one's room and, having eaten, left it again in the hall. We shared all the expenses of the house and establishment. On 4 December I went into residence and from that moment began to see Virginia continually. We often lunched or dined together, we went together to Gordon Square to see Vanessa or have a meal there, we walked in the country, we went to the theatre or to the Russian Ballet.

By the end of 1911 I knew that I was in love with Virginia and that I should have to make up my mind rapidly what I was to do about it. Should I ask her to marry me? What was I to do about Ceylon? In a few months time my leave would end and I should have to return to Colombo. If she married me, I should, of course, resign, but what should I do if she refused me? As I explained at the end of *Growing*, if she did not marry me, I did not want to go back to Ceylon and succeed in the Civil Service and end as a Governor. I had a vague notion that I might return and immerse myself for ever in the administration of a remote, backward district like Hambantota, but at the back of my mind I must have known that this was a mere fantasy. For a few weeks in a kind of perpetual social motion I contrived to put off the moment of making a decision. I went to Cambridge and stayed in Trinity as Hardy's guest, and the following week I was there again as Moore's guest for the Commem. feast. I stayed with Bob Trevelyan in his bitterly cold house on the North Downs near Dorking. In the new year—on 8 January 1912—I went down to Frome in Somerset to stay for a week with Leopold.

The change from the incessant whirl of London to the quiet somnolence of a Somerset rectory was like passing straight from a tornado into a calm, or from a saturnalia into a monastery. At last I

and to you. I am quite well but feel old I am going to be 76 next May. its 50 years last Friday that I fust cooked your Christmas dinner. May I send my Love to Miss Nessa and remain yours obediently Sophia

Sir George was George Duckworth, half-brother of Vanessa and Virginia; Lady Margaret was his wife; Mr and Mrs Gerald were Gerald Duckworth and his wife; Miss Stella was George and Gerald Duckworth's sister. Miss Nessa was Vanessa Bell. Sophie's life, as the letter shows, had become entirely absorbed in the life of the Stephen family.

had time to think. It took me forty-eight hours to come to a decision and on Wednesday I wired to Virginia asking whether I could see her next day. Next day I went up to London and asked her to marry me. She said she did not know and must have time—indefinite time—to see more of me before she could make up her mind. This put me in a quandary with regard to my leave and I thought, so far as my decision was concerned, I had better postpone taking any irrevocable step until it was forced on me. So I wrote to the Secretary of State for the Colonies, as I recounted in the last chapter of *Growing*, and asked him to extend my leave. When he refused, I resigned from the Ceylon Civil Service. In *Growing* I gave verbatim the correspondence which I had with the Colonial Office about my leave and resignation, and I was a little surprised and amused by the reactions of some reviewers to this. One reviewer could not understand why I included these rather dull letters verbatim. I did so because I thought—and still think—them interesting as a period piece. They show, I think, the economy and restraint on both sides which fifty years ago was considered right and proper in official relations and communications. As an official, I was in those days a stickler for what was officially right and proper. The result seems to me slightly interesting and amusing. Another reviewer criticised me severely on the ground that the Colonial Office behaved so well to me and I gave no recognition of this. But one of the reasons why I gave the letters in full was just that: to show how decently the Secretary of State treated his subordinate, giving me every opportunity to withdraw my resignation. I saw no reason to say this, just as I saw no reason to say that the Secretary of State's treatment of me may have been in part due to the fact that he knew that I had been a highly competent civil servant.

My resignation from the Ceylon Civil Service came into effect on 20 May 1912. Until that date I drew my salary of twenty-two pounds a month, on which I found it possible to live comfortably in London before the war. Those were the days of economic paradise for the bourgeoisie, and my total bill for the most comfortable lodging and first-class cooking at Brunswick Square was between eleven pounds and twelve pounds a month. But I had to face the fact that after 20 May I should be without a job and means of subsistence. It is true that I had saved a sum of about £600. This was mainly the result of my winning £690 in a sweepstake in 1908. That £690 has given rise to one of those completely false legends the origin of which is inexplicable. I have often been told and I have seen it stated more than once in print that Virginia and I started the Hogarth Press on the money which I had won in the sweepstake. The statement is ludicrously untrue. We started the Hogarth Press in 1917 on a capital of £41 15s. 3d. This sum was made up of £38 8s. 3d., which we spent on a small printing machine and type, and £3 7s. 0d. which was the total cost of production of the first book which we printed and published. We made a profit of £6 7s. 0d. in the first year on the first publication and that 'went back into the business', so that at the end of 1917 the total capital which we had put into the Hogarth Press was £35. After that the business financed itself out of profits and we never had to 'find capital' for it.

However this is a digression and I must return to the economic problem which faced me at the beginning of 1912. The problem faced me, but in fact I did not face the problem. I simply ignored it or rather postponed any serious consideration of it. I could keep going in my present way of life on my £600 for about two years. After that I should have to find some means of earning a living. I had a vague idea of trying to earn a living by writing, but I decided that for the present I should make no attempt to find a job—I would go on writing *The Village in the Jungle*.

During the first six months of 1912 I lived an extremely social life. I went up to Cambridge more than once for week-ends, and even read a paper to the Society. I stayed with Roger Fry in Guildford, with Bob Trevelyan near Dorking. I got to know the Morrells—Philip, the Liberal M.P., and Lady Ottoline, his wife—and went to the kind of salon Ottoline presided over in Bedford Square, and later for week-ends in Garsington Manor near Oxford. I saw a good deal of Henry Lamb, the artist, who painted my portrait. I used to take him out riding on Wimbledon Common. We hired horses in Putney, lazy, somnolent old hacks, as that kind of horse practically always is, but Henry was a congenitally incompetent rider. The ancient hacks, of course, realised this as soon as he was on their backs, and often when we got to the middle of the Common his horse would take charge of him and canter back down Putney Hill to its stable near Putney Bridge. I found that it was no good my trying to stop this, for as soon as I pursued Henry's horse to turn it back, its canter would change to a gallop, and, though Henry could just stick on at a trot or canter, he was liable to fall off if his horse broke into a gallop. Sometimes Philip Morrell, Adrian

Stephen, and Ka Cox joined Henry and me on these rides over Wimbledon Common or in Richmond Park.

All this time I was seeing a great deal of Virginia, and an event took place which in future years greatly affected our lives for it brought us permanently into Sussex. When I was staying with her in her Firle villa, we walked over the downs one day from Firle to the Ouse valley, and in one of those lovely folds or hollows in the down we came upon an extraordinarily romantic looking house. It was upon the Lewes–Seaford Road, but a great field, full of sheep, lay between it and the road. It faced due west, and from its windows and terrace in front of the house you looked across the great field and the Ouse valley to the line of downs on the west of the river. Behind it was a steep down, on the south and north were lines of elm trees running down on each side of the field to the road. There were barns behind the house, but there were no other buildings anywhere visible from it, indeed the only building anywhere near it was the shepherd's cottage. Its name was Asham House, sometimes written Asheham or Ascham. The house was empty, though it was, I think, occasionally occupied by a worker on the farm—Itford Farm. Its history was curious. The large Itford Farm was bought about 1820 by a Lewes solicitor. It was worked by a bailiff who lived in the very ancient farm-house at Itford over a quarter of a mile from Asham. The solicitor built himself Asham House in the hollow of the down and used it as a summer residence. An L-shaped house, it had two large sitting-rooms on the ground floor, four bedrooms on the second, and a vast attic. Its front was flat, plain, serene, yellow washed, with large french windows opening on to a small terrace. Just below the terrace was a small piece of grass and from it the great field swept straight away, joining with the Ouse valley to meet the downs which lay two miles away as the crow flies across the river.

We made enquiries and found that Asham and the whole farm belonged to the solicitor's granddaughter who lived in Rugby. From her Virginia got a five-year lease of Asham, and she gave up her Firle villa. On 9 February there was a house warming, a week-end party consisting of Virginia, Vanessa, Clive, Adrian, Roger Fry, Duncan Grant, and myself. It was the first of many such week-ends. Asham was a strange house. The country people on the farm were convinced that it was haunted, that there was treasure buried in the cellar, and no one would stay the night in it. It is true that at night one often heard extraordinary noises both in the cellars and the attic. It sounded as if two people were walking from room to room, opening and shutting doors, sighing, whispering. It was, no doubt, the wind sighing in the chimneys, and, when there was no wind, probably rats in the cellar or the attic. I have never known a house which had such a strong character, personality of its own—romantic, gentle, melancholy, lovely. It was Asham and its ghostly footsteps and whisperings which gave Virginia the idea for *A Haunted House*, and I can immediately see, hear, and smell the house when I read the opening words:

> Whatever hour you woke there was a door shutting. From room to room they went, hand in hand, lifting here, opening there, making sure—a ghostly couple.

There was a small dishevelled walled garden on one side of the house. The great elms towered up above it on the south. The grass of the garden and field seemed almost to come up to the sitting rooms and into the windows facing west. One often had a feeling as if one were living under water in the depths of the sea behind the thick, rough glass of the room's long windows—a sea of green trees, green grass, green air. One day when Virginia was ill in London, after we were married, I had to go down myself to Asham to get something or make some arrangements. I arrived late in the evening of an early summer day and spent the night there, sleeping outside on a mattress. In the night there was not a sound. I might have been miles from any other human being. Suddenly in the early morning there burst out a tremendous chorus as if every thrush and blackbird in England has started to sing round the house and every wood pigeon in Sussex had started 'bubbling with content'—in Virginia's *Haunted House* 'from the deepest wells of silence the wood pigeon drew its bubble of sound'. When this ecstatic hosanna or alleluia woke me, I really felt, lying there on the ground, for a moment that I was submerged by the uncut grass towering above my head, the rose leaves above the grass, and the elms above the rose leaves. I wonder if it is age and its dullness of hearing, the spraying of crops, or insecticides which make it seem that there are now no such great convocations of birds in my garden, no such passionate bursts of song, no such 'fantastic summer's heat' as one knew forty years ago.

It was a lovely house and the rooms within it were lovely. There was a slight sadness always over it and in it—an almost comforting sadness. Behind it was one of the most perfect hollows running right back into the down, the hill rising perpendicular behind and on each side of it. In the late summer and autumn the hollow was full of mushrooms. It was so remote and undisturbed that once a vixen had her cubs in an earth half way up the down behind the house and one could go out and watch the fox cubs playing about on the grass, with the mother lying full length outside her earth keeping an eye on them. There was only one objection to Asham House, but it was, as we eventually found, a serious one. With the down behind it on the east and the elms high above it on the south, for a great part of the year it was in shadow the better part of the day. The sun shone upon it so little that it felt damp spring, autumn, and winter, even though in fact the floors, walls, and ceilings were quite dry. The consequence was that, if one stayed in it for more than a week or two, one began to feel slightly depressed or even vaguely unwell.

All through the spring and summer of 1912, usually twice a month, I went with Virginia for the week-end to Asham. As a rule, Adrian, Vanessa, and Roger Fry came too, sometimes Lytton or Marjorie Strachey. The shepherd's wife, Mrs Funnell, from the cottage across the road came up and 'did' for us, making the beds, cleaning the house, and washing up. She was a great character and a great talker. After washing up, she used to come into the sitting room and stand talking for a long time. She was pure Sussex and used ancient words which have now, after fifty years, completely dropped out of the Sussex villagers' vocabulary. They were words like 'dishabille' and 'terrify'. After a storm she would tell us that all the flowers in her garden were 'dishabille'. When we first went to Rodmell, I had a man who did my garden and talked the same language. Dedman would say to me: 'Them birds do so terrify the peas, I must put a net over them.'

Mrs Funnell was a woman of iron will, but, in so far as her hard life allowed it, of good will. She became fond of Virginia and, to a much lesser degree, of me. She brought up a family of sons and daughters, in spotless cleanliness and considerable fear of their mother, on the starvation wage of her husband. Within the limits of her profound ignorance of the world outside a four-mile radius from her cottage—there were no buses in those days and it was only rarely that she could leave her cottage and go the four miles to Lewes or Newhaven—she had sagacity, understanding, curiosity, intelligence. I think she had scarcely ever read a book, but one day one of our visitors left a copy of Ethel M. Dell's *The Way of an Eagle* in the kitchen and Mrs. Funnell became completely engrossed in it—it was my first experience of the mysterious, devastating power of the great born best seller, which acts like a force of nature, an earthquake or hurricane, upon the mind and heart of unsophisticated millions.

I only once saw Mrs Funnell in any way upset or put out. One evening about an hour after she had done the washing up and talking and had gone back into her cottage, there was a knock on the sitting room door and there stood Mrs Funnell again, obviously 'in a state', a dark, fierce, but worried look upon her broad, lined, handsome face. Without beating about the bush, she told us that her unmarried daughter was at the moment giving birth to a child and that it was quite impossible to get a doctor. So bare was the home of a Sussex shepherd fifty years ago that she had not the necessary towels, basins, cans, and she had come to borrow them from us. The child was safely delivered, the father being, it was said, the bailiff, but Mrs Funnell never mentioned the subject again.

In the fifty years since we had Asham House, the physical basis of life in the English countryside has been revolutionised. Conditions in Sussex in 1912 were pretty primitive, and our daily life was probably nearer that of Chaucer's than of the modern man with water from the main, electricity, gas, cars, motor buses, telephone, wireless. When we went down to Asham for a week-end we sometimes got a fly, which the dictionary tells us correctly was 'a one-horse hackney carriage', from Lewes; but more often than not, wet or dry, we walked the four miles along the river bank and across the fields with knapsacks on our backs. All the water we used in the house we had to pump from the well. Sanitation consisted of an earth closet. We cooked on an oil stove or a primus; at night we used candles and oil lamps. Even in 1919, when we bought Monks House and moved across the river to a house in the middle of a village, conditions were just the same—no buses, no water, no gas or electricity and the only 'sanitary convenience', as it was called, an earth closet discreetly, but ineffectively, hidden in a grove of cherry laurels in the middle of the garden.

In 1917 when we had to renew our lease of Asham in the middle of the war, Mr Hoper, the Rugby solicitor, told us that they found the farm too big and that after the war they would divide it into two. They would then require Asham House for a bailiff to live in, and so could give us only a yearly tenancy while the war lasted. In 1918, when the war at last ended, they gave us a year's notice, which meant that we should have to leave Asham in September 1919. Then began a desperate attempt to find a house to take the place of Asham. We could find nothing to suit us and our purse, and in despair in the middle of the year we bought for £300 a very strange little house up on the hill in the middle of Lewes near the castle. It was called The Round House and it was indeed completely round, for it had been converted into a house from the old mill.

No sooner had we bought The Round House than in the village of Rodmell two miles away from Asham across the river old Jacob Verrall died; and Monks House, in which he had lived for many years, was to be sold by auction on 1 July 1919. As soon as we saw Monks House, we decided that we must, if we possibly could, buy it. It was said to date from the fifteenth or sixteenth century, a weatherboarded house with eight or nine oak-beamed rooms. But the rooms were mostly small as four of them had in fact been formed by thin partitions from what originally were biggish rooms, and we removed the partitions and restored the house to what it originally must have been. It had about an acre of garden which adjoined the churchyard, and it was said to have got its name because it belonged in the fifteenth century to the monks of Lewes Priory who used it for their 'retreats'. I hope this story is true, but I never believe such legends about houses unless there is documentary evidence for them, for if you know an English village for fifty years, you see strange things happen. For instance, I have seen two cottages converted into a gentleman's residence to be sold twenty years later as a fifteenth century Sussex farmhouse. Our monks, I am afraid, are probably equally mythological.

Chronologically I have got too far ahead, for Monks House and all this belongs to life after I married and after the 1914 war, and should therefore come later in this volume. And in my experience what cuts the deepest channels in our lives are the different houses in which we live—deeper even than 'marriage and death and division', so that perhaps the chapters of one's autobiography should be determined by the different periods in which one has lived in different houses, and the man who had lived the whole of his life in one house would have no life to write about. On the other hand the purchase of and move across the river to Monks House follow logically on our seven years interlude with Asham House and Mrs Funnell, and I shall therefore ignore chronology for a moment and finish the story of our acquisition of Monks House.

We had often noticed the house and garden before 1919, for walking up or down the lane between Rodmell church and the village street you could look over the wall into the orchard and garden and catch a glimpse of the back of the house. The orchard was lovely and the garden was the kind I like, much subdivided into a kind of patchwork quilt of trees, shrubs, flowers, vegetables, fruit, roses and crocus tending to merge into cabbages and currant bushes. In the middle of the nineteenth century it had belonged to the miller whose windmill stood on Mill Hill, the down above the village, and the great millstones were brought to Monks House, when the mill was pulled down, and still pave the garden. Jacob Verrall, the last owner, was a great character. The first extant reference to him is in the Rodmell Vestry Minute Book of 1882. He was then the Surveyor of Highways, the Assessor and Collector of Taxes, and an Overseer of the Poor. As Surveyor he was paid a sum of £10 per annum. In the first minutes recorded in this book, for the Vestry Meeting on 25 March 1882, the Overseers were requested to provide a new Vestry Minute Book as 'the old one cannot be found'; it is clear therefore that Jacob Verrall held all these parish posts even before 1882. He continued to hold them and to attend every Vestry Meeting until 1910, and even in 1918 just before his death at the age of seventy-four he attended the Parish Meeting, which had taken the place of the old Vestry Meeting.

Old Verrall, as he was always called when I first knew Rodmell, lies now in his narrow cell beneath rugged elms and the yew-trees' shade in Rodmell churchyard. He was, I think, a typical rude forefather of the hamlet such as Gray described in his famous Elegy in 1751; this kind of men and the society to which they belonged still existed 250 years after Gray wrote when I first knew Rodmell. They have died out with the earth closets in the laurel shrubberies. I am glad that I knew them and for a short time lived in the village among them, just as I am glad to have lived for a time in the primeval and rapidly disappearing life of the Ceylon jungle village. There was a great deal to be said against both, and yet one can say without any sentimentality that there was an element of earthy strength and individuality which gave not only some aesthetic satisfaction to the outsider, but some compensation to the victims.

Verrall's wife Lydia was a descendant of the miller and I think it was she who brought him Monk's House. She died seven years before him and of course, like him, lies under the elms and the yews in the churchyard. After she died, he lived by himself, cultivating his garden, grafting (not entirely successfully) his fruit trees, and collecting riddles for which he had a passion. Every Monday morning Mrs. Dedman came in from the neighbouring cottage and cooked him a large joint which he ate hot the first day and cold for the remainder of the week. The rest of his diet consisted of the vegetables from his garden, which he always ate raw, and the produce of his fruit trees. In the last years of his life he spent most of his time lying in bed in the tiniest room in the house which overlooked the garden and an immense gaunt cherry tree which grew out of a flower border into which the cabbages had to some extent penetrated. In the cherry season Verrall lay on his bed with one end of a long cord attached to his big toe while the other end of the cord was attached to a large bell hanging from the topmost bough of the cherry tree. Whenever he saw any birds approaching the tree, he jerked his foot so that the bell rang and scared the birds away.

Most of my information about Verrall came from the Rodmell rector who belonged entirely to that same ancient English village way of life which in Sussex has completely disappeared. The first time I ever saw Mr Hawkesford, I mistook him for a farm hand. He came suddenly round a corner into the footpath along which I was walking, a tall grizzled man of about sixty with an untidy beard in dirty old clothes carrying a ladder on his shoulder. He looked at me with the rapid, sideways, cautious glance with which the countryman in those days habitually greeted a stranger. Later on I got to know him fairly well for he liked to come and sit with me in the garden and talk about flowers and vegetables, the village history, and the curious characters of men and women who now lay buried in the churchyard. I never heard him say a word about religion or his work as a clergyman. Sometimes on Sunday I have seen him come out of the church during the service and stand in the churchyard smoking a cigarette, while the congregation sang the hymn or the psalm. His wife, poor woman, suffered intensely, but not silently, from the boredom of village life. People today have no conception of the long drawn out torture of boredom and empty lives in villages which in those days devoured the minds and souls of large numbers of middle class women whose only interests and pleasures could be found in the bourgeois society of a London suburb. There were no 'gentry' in the neighbourhood with whom Mrs Hawkesford could consort. She hated Rodmell, for she had nothing to look forward to—so she one day told us—but the hot bath on Thursday night when Mary, the devoted maid, carried up the brass cans full of hot water to the hipbath in front of the fire in her bedroom. Mrs Hawkesford had once stayed for a few days with a friend or relation in a house in West Kensington which overlooked Queen's Club, where in those days the Oxford and Cambridge football matches and high class tennis tournaments were held. She more than once told us about this and how she had never enjoyed herself more than sitting at the window and watching these exciting events; her ambition in life, never to be attained, was to live in a house backing on Queen's Club.

When the rector died, Mrs Hawkesford went and lived in Brighton. And there she lived for years until indeed she became an old bedridden woman who had lost even her memory. Her maid, Mary, went with her and looked after her—served her, as they used to say, devotedly—until they were parted by death. The lives of modern, civilised human beings can be incredibly strange—and sad. For the greater part of a long life Mrs Hawkesford lived in a nice large house, in a charming village, in beautiful country, comfortably off and with no apparent troubles, but miserable, bored, discontented, longing for a house in West Kensington. And to this peevish—though probably quite nice—woman and to her family Mary devoted absolutely the whole of *her* life. Not only her life but her universe seemed to be the Hawkesford family, her youth, her middle age, all the best years of her life, passing, until she too became old, in looking after the children, carrying up brass cans of hot water, cooking meals, looking after Mrs Hawkesford (in her second childhood), first in Rodmell rectory and then in the end in a Brighton flat. In 1919 there were hundreds of Marys all over England. Next to the war memorial in Whitehall there should be another to the millions of daughters who gave their lives to looking after selfish parents and millions of Marys who gave their lives to looking after Mrs Hawkesfords.

In Southease, the next village to Rodmell, was another rector, the Rev. Mr Thomas. He had succeeded his father, and, when Mr Thomas junior died, the parish of Southease had had only two rectors in nearly 100 years. The number of his parishioners, men, women, and children, was well under fifty and the total size of Southease parish was 850 acres. Outside his services the rector had simply nothing to do. He was unmarried and lived in a pleasant rectory with a fair sized garden, looked after by his two antediluvian unmarried sisters. One of the sisters kept bees and sold honey, and to go into the rectory to buy honey from her was like walking into the sixteenth century and talking to someone who was unaware of the twentieth century or of a world outside the Southease rectory. The rector himself spent most of his time sitting in his study, which looked across the water-meadows to the railway line from Lewes to Newhaven and Seaford, and counting the number of trucks in the goods trains which he could see passing along the line. The great war of 1914-1918 was a landmark in the life of the rector of Southease, not because it launched a thousand ships and killed ten million men and destroyed European civilisation, but because it caused the longest goods trains which Mr Thomas had ever seen to pass along the railway line to Newhaven. This was because Newhaven became one of the Channel ports through which our army in France was supplied, and all day long for four years the rector watched from his study longer and longer goods trains pass backwards and forwards along the line and counted the number of trucks. Whenever I happened to meet him in Southease village he used to tell me of a train which he had seen with a record number of trucks. The only other interest in life which the rector seemed to have was the weather. He had the appearance and gave one the feeling of an unusually happy and contented man.

The country life of a Sussex village fifty years ago and the people who lived it have, as I said, now completely disappeared. They were probably nearer to Chaucer's England than to the England of 1963. In many ways it was a terribly hard life and an uncivilised society, both physically and spiritually. It was full of unhappy Mrs Hawkesfords, village women worn out by childbearing and domestic slavery, men of considerable brutality. It took ten to fifteen years before the villagers regarded one as other than a stranger—and all strangers were regarded with distrust and some hostility. But when they got to know you and allowed you to get to know them, you found that beneath the surface, side by side with the grimness and brutality, life was complex, with deep down sometimes happiness and sensitiveness to beauty. No writer has so clearly felt and recreated this as the countryman Hardy in his novels.

I never felt it in real life more intensely than when I got to know the carter on the Rodmell farm. In the early summer morning one heard him bring the horses up from the brooks and, after working them all day, he brought them slowly down to the fields in the evening. There is no doubt that he had a passion for his horses and that to have anything to do with them gave him intense pleasure. On Sunday afternoon, whenever it was fine, dressed in his Sunday clothes he walked through the churchyard and down the field to the watermeadows. There, leaning over a gate, he would stand for an hour or more in contemplation and there for a time I would sometimes join him. It is a lovely, profoundly peaceful place, with the great stretch of watermeadows lying in the circle of the downs. Our conversation was desultory, broken by long silences, and I have no doubt that he went there, as I did, instinctively to allow the beauty to seep soothingly into the soul. One day he came to me and asked me to make his will for him. He had several sons and one daughter and he wanted me to write out on a sheet of paper a statement, which he would sign in the presence of his children and of me, saying that he left everything to his daughter. I told him that this would not be a legal will and that he ought to go to a solicitor and sign a proper legal will. He refused to do this and said that if I would do what he asked, his sons would carry it out after his death. So I did do what he asked. I wrote out the statement and took it round to his cottage one Sunday morning. He, his sons, and his daughter were all there in their best clothes. I read aloud the document and he signed it and they all thanked me and we shook hands. When he died, everything went to the daughter without difficulty.

I must return to the spring and early summer of 1912. I had tried in February to get an extension of my leave, but, as recorded in *Growing*, the Ceylon Government were not prepared to grant it unless I stated 'the exact nature of the private affairs' on account of which I was applying for an extension. This on my part I was not prepared to do, and in April I had to make a decision either to go back to Ceylon and give up the possibility of marrying Virginia or to resign from the Ceylon Civil Service and start afresh in London in the hope that Virginia might decide to marry me. On 25 April I sent in my resignation and it was accepted by the Secretary of State on 7 May. I continued to write *The Village in the Jungle*, and in rather a desultory way, when staying for a week-end in May in Cambridge, I went to the Appointments Board to see whether there was any likelihood of my getting a job from which I could earn a living.

Then on 29 May I had lunch with Virginia in her room and we sat talking afterwards, when suddenly Virginia told me that she loved me and would marry me. It was a wonderful summer afternoon and we felt that we must get away from London for a time. We took the train to Maidenhead and I hired a boat and rowed up the river to Marlow and then we came back and dined at the riverside restaurant in Maidenhead. We both felt that in those ten hours from after lunch to midnight when we got back to Brunswick Square we had seemed to drift through a beautiful, vivid dream. First, after the intense emotion of Virginia's saying that she would marry me, the gentle rhythm of the row up the river. There is always to me something of the noiseless drift of dreaming in the gliding of the boat through the water of the river. Then the complete unreality of the brash restaurant and the blatant riverside crowd. As a rule it is disquieting to find oneself insulated and isolated in a crowd, in the herd, but not of it. But there are rare moments when this seems appropriate and comforting. In the restaurant and coming back in a crowded train, I think we both felt a strange happiness of being for a moment alone together in an empty universe.

Such moments are indeed only moments; they pass in a flash, and before one knows it one is again in and of the herd. Virginia and I were married on Saturday 10 August at St Pancras Register Office in a room which, in those days, looked down into a cemetery. In the ceremony before a Registrar one makes no promise 'to love and to cherish, till death us do part, according to God's holy ordinance', but in the St Pancras Office, facing the window and looking through it at the tombstones behind the Registrar's head, one was, I suppose appropriately, reminded of the words 'till death us do part'. Apart from the tombstones, our wedding ceremony was provided with an element of comic relief (quite unintended) characteristic of the Stephens. In the middle of the proceedings Vanessa interrupted the Registrar, saying: 'Excuse me interrupting; I have just remembered: we registered my son—he is two years old—in the name of Clement, and we now want to change his name to Quentin—can you tell me what I have to do?' There was a moment of astonished silence in the room as we all looked round sympathetically and saw the serious, slightly puzzled look on Vanessa's face. There was a pause while the Registrar stared at her with his mouth open. Then he said severely: 'One thing at a time, please, Madam.'

In the seven weeks between our visits to Maidenhead and our visit to the St Pancras Registrar Office we lived rather a hectic life. In those days we went continually to theatres, concerts, operas. We had a vast number of friends and acquaintances and so lived a very social life. I was taken off to be exhibited to many of Virginia's relations whom hitherto I had not met. The most interesting was Lady Ritchie, Aunt Anny as she was always called. Aunt Anny had been born in 1837 and was therefore seventy-five when I dined in the Ritchies' house in St George's Square, slightly oppressed and depressed by the solid Victorian gloom of their dining-room. She was Thackeray's eldest daughter and the sister of Virginia's father's first wife. At the age of forty she married her cousin Richmond Thackeray Ritchie, who was seventeen years younger than she. He was an extremely able, formidable man and, sitting at the head of the table, he seemed to me rather saturnine; he was Under Secretary of State in the India Office.

Aunt Anny was a rare instance of the child of a man of genius inheriting some of that genius. You can see it in her books, even in her now unread novels, but particularly in her autobiographical books. Her genius, like most things about her and in her, was a shade out of control. This erratic streak in her made her miss trains, confuse dates, and get the chapters of most of her novels so muddled that the last chapter was printed as the first (and nobody noticed it). This flightiness was absurd and, as Virginia records in her essay 'The Enchanted Organ', amused the great Charles Darwin, who said apologetically: 'I can't for the life of me help laughing.' But it—and still more she—was not entirely absurd. It was part of her great charm and of her flashes of genius and imagination. Virginia noted that 'she said things that no human being could possibly mean; yet she meant them'.

That evening in 1912 she sat at one end of the dining table, with Richmond at the other, looking very frail, living not entirely in the same world as we were living in, and suddenly from time to time saying one of these things which no human being could possibly mean, but which she meant. From time to time too Richmond from the opposite end of the table heard one of these strange pronouncements which obviously irritated him like a little thorn which had been for so many years domestically and matrimonially embedded in his mind, and he put her somewhat sharply in her place. The curious thing was that when I thought about what she had in fact said, the absurdity remained, but through the absurdity I seemed to see something imaginative, something which only Aunt

Anny had seen and which we could not quite get at, and Richmond's irritation irritated me. I think I must have shown her something of what I felt about her and about what she was saying, for in a letter which she wrote to Virginia some time later she said: 'I always feel glad when I think of your dear husband who belongs to the order of those to whom my heart goes out.' The first sentence of this letter is worth quoting, because it is a good example of her style and of some of her peculiarities which I have described above: 'My dearest Virginia, I meant to have a pretty card for you also, but only Nessa's butterflies flew off and yours posted itself as cards do, and there is only the outside wrapping to send with my love and blessing.'[1]

We went down and had luncheon at Wellington College with the headmaster, Virginia's cousin Will Vaughan. He was married to Madge, a daughter of John Addington Symonds. There were also present Symonds's widow and his biographer, Horatio Brown. The atmosphere of his luncheon party was curious; it was compounded of two opposite, antipathetic, and entirely unmixable elements. Will was the public school headmaster in excelsis, a product of Rugby and New College, breezy, his feet planted with no nonsense on the solid earth of the English public school, a liberal of course, but accepted as invincibly safe by the most conservative of conservatives. He was charming to me, treating me at once as a favourite prefect. Madge too was charming and Virginia was fond of her. But she, her mother, and Horatio Brown oozed the precious, incense laden, Italianate culture of Walter Pater and the eighties and nineties. I don't suppose anyone now reads Symonds, but he had a reputation in the last decade of the nineteenth century which still existed, in a rather decrepit state, in 1912. Symonds was a littérateur, lock, stock, and barrel. He lived in Venice and wrote a large number of books on Italian literature and history. Horatio, who seemed to me

[1] The following letter which she wrote to me is also characteristic; I had asked her to support the Adult Suffrage movement: 'O my dear Leonard What will you think of me. It seems to me ten thousand pities to give equal votes to unequal men I should like to give 100 to one man and ¼ of a vote to another I would give you a great many to you and to Virginia too and my love to her. I have a friend to tea at the Sesame at 4 o'c next Thursday and I have asked a charming Mrs. Kendall who writes plays Could you come there or *here* the following Thursday. We have had dear poor Blanche Cornish here for a month tell Virginia She has lost that dear Gerald who used to know Virginia and Nessa so well Yrs with affectionate sympathy and what is the word?—dissidence?—Anne Ritchie'

a kind of caricature pussycat littérateur, also lived in Venice. His relation to Symonds was that of the lesser to the greater fleas; besides the biography, he wrote books about Venice and literature and history, with titles like *Life on the Lagoons* and *Venetian Studies*.

Madge worshipped her father as so many daughters have since the time of Electra, in a way which was not fully understood until the second eating of the apple on the tree of knowledge by Sigmund Freud. She had the same kind of literary gift as her father and, when young, had followed in his footsteps with a book *Days Spent on a Doge's Farm*. She was rather intense, and the atmosphere of the Doge's Farm and Venetian lagoons would not mix with that of Wellington and Will, who treated her across the luncheon table much as Richmond had treated Aunt Anny across the dining table. I find few things more distressing than the note of matrimonial exasperation in one's host or hostess when they speak to each other.

Another visit we made was to Virginia's half-brother, Sir George Duckworth, Eton, Trinity College, Cambridge, married to Lady Margaret Herbert, very handsome, immensely kind and charming, and—it has to be admitted—a snob. He lived in a large house in largish grounds near East Grinstead, and he kept some Highland cattle in a field. We went down for lunch and there was one other visitor, Reginald Farrer. I was much amused to meet him again in such very different circumstances. For the last time I had seen him was when he appeared as an English Buddhist in Kandy, and, at the request of the Diyawadana Nilame, the Manager of the Temple, I opened the shrine and showed Farrer the famous relic, the Buddha's tooth.[1] He gave no sign of recognising me so I did not recall to him our meeting. I could see nothing of the Buddhist in him as I watched him in Dalingridge Place, rather a drawing-room pussycat, talking to the Lady Margaret.

I was glad when the tour of introductions ended. The children of Sir Leslie Stephen had, at the turn of the century, when their father died, broken away from the society into which they were born. That society consisted of the upper levels of the professional middle class and county families, interpenetrated to a certain extent by the aristocracy. But, although Vanessa, Virginia, and Adrian had broken away from it and from Kensington and Mayfair to live in

[1] See Volume 1, pp. 224-5.

Bloomsbury what seemed to their relations and old family friends a Bohemian life, there was no complete rupture; they still from time to time saw socially their Stephen and Duckworth relations and the old family friends. It was a social class and way of life into which hitherto I had only dipped from time to time as an outsider, when, for instance, I stayed as a young man with the Stracheys.[1] I was an outsider to this class, because, although I and my father before me belonged to the professional middle class, we had only recently struggled up into it from the stratum of Jewish shopkeepers. We had no roots in it. The psychology of the different strata of English society is extremely important in its effects upon the individual (or was fifty years ago). The Stephens and the Stracheys, the Ritchies, Thackerays, and Duckworths had an intricate tangle of ancient roots and tendrils stretching far and wide through the upper middle classes, the county families, and the aristocracy. Socially they assumed things unconsciously which I could never assume either unconsciously or consciously. They lived in a peculiar atmosphere of influence, manners, respectability, and it was so natural to them that they were unaware of it as mammals are unaware of the air and fish of the water in which they live. Now that I was going to marry Virginia and went round to see her relations, I began to see this stratum of society from the inside. I said in *Sowing* that I know that I am ambivalent to aristocratic societies, disliking and despising them and at the same time envying them their insolent urbanity. In a milder form there was the same ambivalence in my attitude to the society which I found in Dalingridge Place and St George's Square. I disliked its respectability and assumptions while envying and fearing its assurance and manners. I should, perhaps, add that the class stratum or strata which I have been writing about in this paragraph are now practically extinct; they were almost destroyed by the 1914 war and were finally wiped away in the 1939 war.

During the time that I lived in the same house as Virginia in Brunswick Square, and particularly in the months before we married, I became for the first time aware of the menace of nervous or mental breakdown under which she always lived. I had had no experience at all of nervous or mental illness and it was some time before I realised the nature and meaning of it in Virginia. It played a large part in her

[1] See Volume 1, pp. 119-23. I dipped into another, but different, section of the same social class when I used to lunch with Leopold Campbell in Manchester Square (Volume 1, pp. 113-15).

life and our lives and it was the cause of her death. If in the following pages I am to give an accurate and understandable account of our life from 1912 to 1941, when she committed suicide, it is necessary at this point that I should explain the nature of her illness. The doctors called it neurasthenia and she had suffered from it all her life. In the thirty years of our married life, we consulted a considerable number of nerve and mental specialists in and around Harley Street. I do not think that any of them knew the cause or—except superficially—the nature of the disease which they called neurasthenia. It was a name, a label, like neuralgia or rheumatism, which covered a multitude of sins, symptoms, and miseries. They knew the symptoms, or some of them, and they could prognosticate, within limits, what would alleviate and what would exacerbate the symptoms. Superficially the nature of the disease was clear and simple. If Virginia lived a quiet, vegetative life, eating well, going to bed early, and not tiring herself mentally or physically, she remained perfectly well. But if she tired herself in any way, if she was subjected to any severe physical, mental, or emotional strain, symptoms at once appeared which in the ordinary person are negligible and transient, but with her were serious danger signals. The first symptoms were a peculiar 'headache' low down at the back of the head, insomnia, and a tendency for the thoughts to race. If she went to bed and lay doing nothing in a darkened room, drinking large quantities of milk and eating well, the symptoms would slowly disappear and in a week or ten days she would be well again.

But if she did not take these drastic steps at once, if she ignored the symptoms and went on working and walking and going to parties and sitting up late, then suddenly the headache, the sleeplessness, the racing thoughts would become intense and it might be several weeks before she could begin again to live a normal life. But four times in her life the symptoms would not go and she passed across the border which divides what we call insanity from sanity. She had a minor breakdown in her childhood; she had a major breakdown after her mother's death in 1895, another in 1914, and a fourth in 1940. In all these cases of breakdown there were two distinct stages which are technically called manic-depressive. In the manic stage she was extremely excited; the mind raced; she talked volubly and, at the height of the attack, incoherently; she had delusions and heard voices, for instance she told me that in her second attack she heard the birds in the garden outside her window talking Greek; she was violent with the nurses. In her third attack, which began in 1914, this stage lasted for several months and ended by her falling into a coma for two days. During the depressive stage all her thoughts and emotions were the exact opposite of what they had been in the manic stage. She was in the depths of melancholia and despair; she scarcely spoke; refused to eat; refused to believe that she was ill and insisted that her condition was due to her own guilt; at the height of this stage she tried to commit suicide, in the 1895 attack by jumping out of a window, in 1915 by taking an overdose of veronal; in 1941 she drowned herself in the River Ouse.

This is, of course, a very summary account of extremely complicated mental reactions of a most sensitive and sophisticated mind. One or two things should be noted. The initial symptoms of fatigue which were, as I have said, in Virginia's case danger signals, were exactly the same, except in one or two particulars, as almost everyone experiences if they overtire themselves. Most people have had the experience of going to bed 'dead tired' and finding that, although they were half asleep before going to bed, they cannot sleep because their mind is 'racing'. With an ordinary person the fatigue and symptoms disappear as soon as he has had a night's rest. Virginia differed from the ordinary person only because the symptoms of fatigue appeared much more easily, were much more severe, and required, not a night's rest, but a week's rest to get rid of them. They differed, therefore, from the ordinary person's symptoms in degree rather than in kind. And this is true also in most respects of the symptoms in the later stages of an attack, even when she had passed from sanity to insanity; they differed mainly from the initial symptoms by becoming much more violent and severe. Even the delusions, the volubility, and the incoherence were exaggerations of the 'racing' thoughts.

All this is true, and because it is true, one might be inclined to say that 'insanity' of the kind which was a perpetual menace and terrifying curse in Virginia's life is solely a matter of degree, the degree of duration or violence of mental states which habitually, in certain circumstances, occur in everyone. In that case everyone is slightly and incipiently insane, and Virginia differed from ordinary 'sane' persons only because, when she had a 'breakdown', there was a great increase in the degree of intensity and duration of symptoms which occurred in her when she was 'sane' and occur in all other people, 'sane' or 'insane'. I do not think this view is correct. For nearly thirty years I had to study Virginia's mind with the greatest intensity, for it was only by recognising the first, most tenuous mental symptoms of fatigue that we could take in time the steps to prevent a serious breakdown. I am sure that, when she had a breakdown, there was a moment when she passed from what can be rightly called sanity to insanity. On one side of this line was a kind of mental balance, a psychological coherence between intellect and emotion, an awareness and acceptance of the outside world and a rational reaction to it; on the other side were violent emotional instability and oscillation, a sudden change in a large number of intellectual assumptions upon which, often unconsciously, the mental outlook and actions of everyone are based, a refusal to admit or accept facts in the outside world.

The human mind is so complex and so self-contradictory that one can never safely make any statement about it without qualification. In the previous paragraph I have seemed to maintain that there is generally and was in Virginia a definite line between sanity and insanity—that normally she was sane, but four times in her life passed over the line which divides the sane from the insane. This is partly true and partly untrue. When Virginia was quite well, she would discuss her illness; she would recognise that she had been mad, that she had had delusions, heard voices which did not exist, lived for weeks or months in a nightmare world of frenzy, despair, violence. When she was like that, she was obviously well and sane. But even then she was not well and sane in the way in which the vast majority of human beings are well and sane. If, when she was well, any situation or argument arose which was closely connected with her breakdowns or the causes of them, there would sometimes rise to the surface of her mind traces or echoes of the nightmares and delusions of her madness, so that it seemed as if deep down in her mind she was never completely sane.

For instance, one of the most troublesome symptoms of her breakdowns was a refusal to eat. In the worst period of the depressive stage, for weeks almost at every meal one had to sit, often for an hour or more, trying to induce her to eat a few mouthfuls. What made one despair was that by not eating and weakening herself she was doing precisely the thing calculated to prolong the breakdown, for it was only by building up her bodily strength and by resting that she could regain mental equilibrium. Deep down this refusal to eat was connected with some strange feeling of guilt: she would maintain that she was not ill, that her mental condition was due to her own fault—laziness, inanition, gluttony. This was her attitude to food when she was in the depths of the depressive stage of her insanity. But something of this attitude remained with her always, even when she appeared to have completely recovered. It was always extremely difficult to induce her to eat enough food to keep her well. Every doctor whom we consulted told her that to eat well and drink two or three glasses of milk every day was essential if she was to remain well and keep off the initial symptoms which were the danger signals of an approaching breakdown. Everything which I observed between 1912 and 1941 confirmed their diagnosis. But I do not think that she ever accepted it. Left to herself, she ate extraordinarily little and it was with the greatest difficulty that she could be induced to drink a glass of milk regularly every day. It was a perpetual, and only partially successful, struggle; our quarrels and arguments were rare and almost always about eating or resting. And if the argument became heated, even when she was apparently quite well, in a mild vague form the delusions seemed to rise again to the surface of her mind. Her hostility to the doctors and nurses which was very marked during the breakdowns would reappear. She would argue as if she had never been ill—that the whole treatment had been wrong, that she ate too much and lived a life too lethargic and quiet. Below the surface of her mind and of her argument there was, I felt, some strange, irrational sense of guilt.

Some pages back I referred to the ancient belief that genius is near allied to madness. I am quite sure that Virginia's genius was closely connected with what manifested itself as mental instability and insanity. The creative imagination in her novels, her ability to 'leave the ground' in conversation, and the voluble delusions of the breakdowns all came from the same place in her mind—she 'stumbled after her own voice' and followed 'the voices that fly ahead'. And that in itself was the crux of her life, the tragedy of genius. It was mental or physical strain and fatigue which endangered her mental stability; if she lived a quiet vegetative life, she was well and sane. But to tell her, as doctors did and I often had to tell her, that she must live a quiet, vegetative life, was absurd, terribly ironical. If she tired herself by walking too long and too far, if she sat up later than eleven two or three nights running, if she went to too many parties, the physical strain would very soon bring on the dangerous symptoms, the danger signals. As soon as they appeared, one could reasonably tell her that she must really stop and go to bed and do nothing for a few days, and, by continual vigilance and (to her) tiresome interludes of inanition, we were successful in dealing with this kind of strain. But the mental strain of her imagination or genius, of her own mind, was equally or rather more dangerous, and though you can tell a person like Virginia not to go for a walk or to a party, you cannot tell her not to think, work, or write. I have never known any writer work with such concentration and assiduity as she did. When she was writing a novel, she did the writing in the morning from ten to one, but she was thinking about it almost all day long. And she put the whole of herself into the writing and the thinking. Even with a review, she would write and rewrite it and rewrite it again from end to end five or six times, and she once opened a cupboard and found in it (and burnt) a whole mountain of MSS; it was *The Voyage Out* which she had rewritten (I think) five times from beginning to end. Thus the connection between her madness and her writing was close and complicated, and it is significant that, whenever she finished a book, she was in a state of mental exhaustion and for weeks in danger of a breakdown. In 1936 she only just escaped a breakdown when finishing *The Years*; in 1941 she wrote the last words of *Between the Acts* on 26 February, and twenty-three days later on 21 March she committed suicide.

When we married, I had no clear knowledge or understanding of all this, but I had become extremely uneasy about Virginia's health. It was obvious that exertion and strains which had no effect at all upon me were disastrous to her. She was at the time writing *The Voyage Out* and in March 1912 she read some of it to me. I thought it extraordinarily good, but noticed even then what a strain it was upon her. Then came the emotional strain of our engagement and she got a severe headache and insomnia and had to go for a time to a nursing home in Twickenham and rest there. Her doctor was Sir George Savage, a mental specialist at the head of his profession. He was also a friend of her family and had known her ever since her birth. I went to see him quite early on in 1912 and he discussed Virginia's health with me as a doctor and as an old friend. He was very friendly to me, but impressed me much more as a man of the world than as a doctor. In the next few months, I became more and more uneasy about one thing. We both wanted to have children, but the more I saw the dangerous effect of any strain or stress upon her, the more I began to doubt whether she would be able to stand the strain and stress of childbearing. I went and consulted Sir George Savage; he brushed my doubts aside. But now my doubts about Sir George Savage were added to my doubts about Virginia's health. There seemed to be more of the man of the world ('Do her a world of good, my dear fellow; do her a world of good!') in his opinion than of the mental specialist. So I went off and consulted two other well known doctors, Maurice Craig and T. B. Hyslop, and also the lady who ran the mental nursing home where Virginia had several times stayed. They confirmed my fears and were strongly against her having children. We followed their advice.

We were married, as I said some pages back, on Saturday 10 August 1912. Then we went off for a long meandering honeymoon. In those days I had the *wanderlust* almost perpetually upon me. I suppose it was partly due to Ceylon: during my last three years there in the Hambantota District I was continually on the move, never more than two weeks at a time sedentary in my bungalow, continually travelling on circuit, sleeping anywhere in tents or in the bare circuit bungalows. I had got into the habit of thinking that one could go anywhere anyhow at any time, and rather on that principle we wandered about, first in Provence and then into and all over Spain. It was very pleasant, but of course we occasionally got into difficulties staying in posadas off the beaten track and hiring mulecarts in out-of-the-way villages. I did not realise at the time that this kind of travelling was probably much too tiring for Virginia. Eventually we got to Valencia, and there by chance I found a Hungarian ship on the point of sailing to Marseille and willing to take us as the only passengers. Not being able to make ourselves understood in English, French, Sinhalese, or Tamil, and not understanding Hungarian, we did not realise that we should have dined at 6.30 p.m. and that after 7.30 it was contrary to the laws of the Medes and Persians, and of the Hungarians and Austrians, to give any food to a passenger. We went to bed hungry; the Mediterranean was extremely rough; the boat bucked and rolled, creaked and groaned. In the middle of the night I woke up and realised that I was not alone in my bunk; three large cats had joined me. At 7.30 in the morning I staggered up on to the deck and found the Third Officer who spoke English. I explained to him that I was very hungry and why. He took me up on to the bridge and had breakfast sent to me there; the first course was an enormous gherkin swimming in oil and vinegar. One of the bravest things I have ever done, I think, was to eat this, followed by two fried eggs and bacon, coffee and rolls, with the boat, the sea, and the coast of France going up and down all round me. From Marseille we took the train to Venice, where for a week or two we rested in a pension on the Grand Canal, experiencing for the first time its strange beauties and the wind which, whistling through its canals, can sometimes seem the coldest wind in Europe. And at the end of November we returned to London.

2
THE YEARS 1913 AND 1914

In December 1912, when we got back from our honeymoon, we went to live in Cliffords Inn in Fleet Street. It was still then the old Cliffords Inn, rather beautiful, our rooms incredibly ancient, also incredibly draughty and dirty, for fifty years ago in the City of London all day and all night long there fell a slow gentle rain of smuts, so that, if you sat writing by an open window, a thin veil of smuts covered the paper before you had finished a page. The City is—or rather was—one of the pleasantest of all London districts to live in. From Monday to Saturday morning there was something peculiarly exhilarating about it. It was not residential, and yet, with Fleet Street and the Temple and Fetter Lane and Gough Square at one's door, one felt that it had been lived in for hundreds of years by Chaucer, Shakespeare, Pepys, Johnson, Boswell. And though Fleet Street was one of the noisiest streets in London, in Cliffords Inn one heard only the incessant muted hum or rumble of the traffic. On Saturday morning and all through Sunday the whole place changed completely; it became a deserted city. There was practically no traffic and only an occasional solitary policeman or pedestrian. On Sunday you could walk—and we often did—for miles eastward through empty streets. No Londoner who has never lived east of Chancery Lane really knows what the essence of London is. I have lived in Kensington, Bloomsbury, Westminster, and the City—I would give the palm to the City.

I went back to Cliffords Inn in November 1941 after Virginia's death. I had been bombed out of Mecklenburgh Square and I took a flat in Cliffords Inn. They had pulled down the old building and put up in its place a great block of modern flats. I found it intolerable. I had a little box consisting of a sitting room and bedroom and all round me, above and below, to the right and to the left, were dozens of other people, each and all in his or her precisely similar little box—many of them journalists whom I knew, Francis Williams and Ritchie Calder and Hubert Philips. I felt as if I was being weighed down and suffocated by the sound and smell and weight of human animals all round me; it was a kind of andro-claustrophobia. I could not stand it for more than a few months. In April 1942 I got two rooms in my bombed house in Mecklenburgh Square patched up and moved in there. The first night of my return as I was letting myself in with my latchkey, a voice behind me said: What are you doing there?' I turned round and found that it was a policeman. When I said that I was going to sleep in my house, he told me that I would be the only person sleeping in the square as all the houses were uninhabitable. It was certainly an odd life, though I think he exaggerated when he said that all the other residents had had to move out. My two rooms had, of course, no glass in the windows, which were boarded up so that one had to have the electric light on day and night. The ceilings were down and the sparrows got in through holes in the roof and scrambled about all day long on the rafters above one's head. The water pipes had been so shaken by the bombings that every now and then there was no water in them or in the middle of the night one would suddenly burst and I would wake up to hear water cascading down the stairs. But I preferred it to Cliffords Inn.

As I have jumped forward in time to 1942, I may as well say something more about the house in Mecklenburgh Square during the great bombing. We had moved into it from Tavistock Square in 1939 on the very day of the outbreak of war. When in March 1924 we left Richmond and took 52 Tavistock Square, we had as subtenants on the ground floor and first floor a firm of solicitors; old Mr Pritchard was the senior and young Mr George Pritchard was the junior partner. They were extraordinarily nice people and, when we moved to Mecklenburgh Square, they came with us, again as sub-tenants occupying the ground floor and first floor. The house was not actually hit by a bomb, but bombs fell all round it and the house next door was completely destroyed by an incendiary bomb. All the ceilings of my house were blown down and all the windows blown out by bombs and a landmine; the front door and many of the other doors were blown off their hinges. The roof was so much damaged that, as I said, the sparrows came in and fluttered about the skeleton of the house. But all through the war Mr George Pritchard, now senior partner, imperturbably refused to budge. He sat at his desk day after day in a leather coat and hat—to protect himself from the cold and the dust and dirt which the sparrows, scrabbling on the rafters above his head, rained down upon him—and continued his 'business as usual'. It was comforting and reassuring to see him sitting there surrounded by the deed boxes and the papers.

But I must get back to 1912. Life in Cliffords Inn was extraordinarily pleasant. The old buildings, the rooms, the court were almost exactly the same as a Cambridge College and it was as though I had returned to live in the Great Court of Trinity. We felt wonderfully free. We had, of course, no servants; only a daily char came in and made the beds, swept up the smuts, and washed up the dishes. Every night we crossed Fleet Street and dined at the Cock Tavern. The Cock still remembered Tennyson; it had in its furniture and its food an air and flavour of considerable antiquity. It was a real old city eating house. One sat in wooden partitions and at night it was almost always pretty empty, only journalists from the dailies and lawyers from the Temple dropping in until quite late. Henry was a vintage head waiter, belonging to an era and tradition which, even in 1912, one felt was passing. Large, white faced, redheaded, he was incredibly solemn, slow, unruffled. It was a great day when at last he recognised one as a 'regular'. He would greet one with the ghost of the shadow of a smile, and, as one sat down, he would whisper confidentially: 'I can recommend the devilled bone tonight, Sir,' or: 'I am afraid I can't recommend the steak and kidney pudding tonight, Sir; it's not *quite* as good as usual.'

We both worked hard when we settled in to Cliffords Inn. Virginia was rewriting the last chapters of *The Voyage Out* for the tenth or, it may have been, the twentieth time. She finished it in February and I read it in early March and took it on 9 March to Gerald Duckworth, her half brother, who owned the publishing firm of Duckworth & Co., in Henrietta Street. Edward Garnett wrote an extremely appreciative reader's report on it and Gerald agreed to publish it. The terms of the agreement are interesting: the publishers agreed to pay the author

> on the published price of twelve out of thirteen copies sold the following royalties: 15% on the first 5,000 copies sold, 20% on all sales above 5,000.

There was to be no advance payment on account of royalties. The book was not actually published until 1915. It was held up for the two years because of Virginia's breakdown. They printed 2,000 copies, and fourteen years later, when in 1929 the Hogarth Press acquired the rights from Duckworth, there were still a few copies unsold. In the ten years before the Hogarth Press took the book over, 1919-1929, Duckworth sold 479 copies for which Virginia received in royalties £26 2s. 10d. The fate of *The Voyage Out* in its first fifteen years after publication shows what a long time it takes for a writer like Virginia to get any sale for her books or to make any money out of them. *The Voyage Out* had an extraordinarily good press; the reviewers were nearly all complimentary and she was recognised from the first as an important novelist. By 1929 she had published *To The Lighthouse* and *Orlando* and had established herself as a highly successful writer. 4,000 copies of *To The Lighthouse* were sold in the first year of publication and *Orlando* sold 4,000 copies in its first month. But it took fifteen years to sell 2,000 copies of *The Voyage Out*, as I said, and the earnings of the author from it in those fifteen years were less than £120. However as soon as an author really establishes himself, all his books sell. That is why when we in the Hogarth Press reprinted *The Voyage Out* in 1929, we sold 781 in the first year, though it had sold fewer than 500 copies in the previous ten years.

Meanwhile in 1913 Edward Arnold published my novel *The Village in the Jungle*. The book was not unsuccessful in its way. It had very good reviews. The first edition sold out at once and it was reprinted twice before the end of 1913 and again in 1925. Four editions of one's first book in twelve years sounds pretty good, but in fact the sound was a good deal better than the material reality. Arnold did not take a rosy view of the selling prospects of the book, and when the first edition sold out, he printed only a few hundred copies. Rather to his dismay, I think, he sold these immediately and had to reprint for the second time. By 1929 the book had sold 2,149 copies. My agreement with Arnold was less favourable for the author than Virginia's with Duckworth. I got 10% royalty on the first 1,000 sold and 15% thereafter, and as the price of *The Village in the Jungle* was 5s. while *The Voyage Out* was 6s., by 1929, though my book had sold a few more copies than hers, I had earned £63 3s. 0d. against her £110 to £120. As a publisher myself today, I am amused to find that in 1913 when I bought one of my own books (published price 5s.) from Arnold, he charged me 4s. and also 4d. for sending it to me in Brunswick Square. He was therefore charging the author 4s. 4d. for a book for which he would get from a London bookseller either 3s. 9d. or 3s. 4d.

I give these figures about the sales of the books which we wrote, partly because our earnings as writers had an important effect upon what we actually did in life, but also because they have a more general interest. Professional writers rarely reveal, even in autobiographies, accurately and in detail what exactly they earned by their books. I propose, off and on throughout this book, to give such figures in order to show the effect of our earnings upon our writing and our lives, and also because of the light which they shed upon the economics of the literary profession in the twentieth century. Consider for a moment the fate of these two novels *The Voyage Out* and *The Village in the Jungle*. They are two very different books, but both have survived. In the year 1961, forty-six years after the date of its first publication, 441 copies of *The Voyage Out* were sold in England at the published price of 10s. 6d. and the royalties paid amounted to £23 3s. 1d.—compare this with the 479 copies sold and royalties £26 2s. 10d. in the ten years 1919 to 1929. In the year 1961, forty-eight years after its first publication, *The Village in the Jungle* sold 610 copies at the published price of 7s. 6d. and the royalties paid amounted to £12 3s. 6d.[1]—compare this with the 770 copies sold and royalties £28 7s. 11d. paid in the ten years, 1919 to 1929.

In the years immediately following our marriage this kind of figures became of great practical importance to us. Virginia had a certain amount of capital invested in stocks and shares, theoretically worth about £9,000; it gave her an income of rather less than £400. In 1917 our expenditure was £697, in 1918 £717, and in 1919 £845. It was obvious therefore that somehow or other we must between us earn between £400 and £500 a year. In fact our financial position was a good deal darker or more precarious than these figures suggest. In 1915, when Virginia's mental breakdown was at its worst, we had nurses—sometimes four—in the house for months and she was visited continually by Harley Street doctors. The doctors' and nurses' bills must have been more than £500 for the twelve months. Any hope that we could earn this by writing books soon faded. Virginia had taken more than four years to write *The Voyage Out*. It took her six years to write her second novel *Night and Day*, which was published by Duckworth in 1919. The agreement was much the same as for the first book. Duckworth printed 2,000 copies and the published price was 9s. They reprinted 1,000 copies in 1920 and began to sell them at a published price of 3s. 6d. in 1923. When the Hogarth Press acquired the rights from Duckworth

[1] The reason why the royalties on the 610 copies are so small is because most of them were sold at export prices to Ceylon.

in 1929, they had sold 1,768 of the 9s. impression and 566 of the 3s. 6d., so that they still had over 500 copies unsold. Virginia had earned in royalties £119 3s. 11d. There was also an American edition published by Doran; 1,326 copies were sold in 1921 and Virginia received £27 13s. 7d. in royalties. The total, therefore, which she received in the first ten years, 1919 to 1929, for this book was £146 17s. 4d. The first book of hers to be published after *Night and Day* was *Monday and Tuesday*, a book of sketches and short stories in 1921. Up to the end of 1921 she had earned less than £100 on *The Voyage Out* and £108 on *Night and Day*. In the twelve years from 1909 (when she began to write *The Voyage Out* and £108 on *Night and Day*. In the twelve years from 1909 (when she began to write *The Voyage Out*) to 1921, therefore, she had earned by writing books say £205 or £17 1s. 8d. per annum.

My second novel *The Wise Virgins* was published in 1914 simultaneously with the outbreak of war. The war killed it dead and my total earnings from it were £20. By the end of 1921 *The Village in the Jungle* had brought me in £42, so that my income as a novelist had been £62 in 10 years, or £6 4s. 0d. per annum. It looked therefore as if Virginia and I could not count on earning more than £23 between us per annum by writing novels, and we must obviously make somehow or other by other means, say, £477 a year if we were to be certain of making both ends meet.

The attitude to money and financial security in different people is very curious. I am not, I think, a worrier by nature, at any rate about material things. If I am to tell the truth, the whole truth, and nothing but the truth, I must admit that I am, I think, a psychological worrier at the back of my mind, in the depths of my soul, or in the pit of my stomach (probably all three). I have always felt psychologically insecure. I am afraid of making a fool of myself, of my first day at school, of going out to dinner, or of a week-end at Garsington with the Morrells. What shall I say to Mr Jones, or to Lady Ottoline Morrell, or Aldous Huxley? My hand trembles at the thought of it, and so do my soul, heart, and stomach. Of course, I have learnt to conceal everything except the trembling hand: one of the consolations of growing old is that one learns to talk to Mr Jones and Lady Ottoline Morrell—one has learnt that even the dreariest dinner party or longest week-end does come to an end, that even the weariest river winds somewhere safe to sea. I have had to be extremely careful about money for long periods in my life, but I have never worried about it, probably because I learnt by experience as a child and a youth to be insecure and comparatively poor and not to worry about it.

Virginia's experience had been very different and had had a very different effect upon her. Her family belonged to the Victorian professional upper middle class which was financially as impregnably secure as (almost) the Bank of England. In their current account in the Westminster or Barclays Bank there was always a balance of hundreds of pounds, and both the heavens and justice would have fallen before that balance fell below zero. The consequence was that her father, Sir Leslie Stephen, K.C.B., author of the *History of English Thought in the 18th Century*, editor of *The Cornhill Magazine* and *The Dictionary of National Biography*, owner of a large house in Hyde Park Gate, another in Emperor's Gate, and another in St Ives, Cornwall, with capital invested in gilt-edged securities bringing him in dividends sufficient to maintain his whole family in comfort—the highest income tax which he ever paid was 1s. 3d. in the £ and it varied between 3d. and 8d. in the £ until a few years before his death at the age of seventy-two—this fortunate man, whose bank balance was virtually impregnable, never stopped worrying himself and his children about money. He lived in a perpetual fear of bankruptcy, convinced every Monday morning that he was being ruined by what were called by Victorian fathers and their women folk the household books. When his wife died in 1895, Vanessa, then aged sixteen, took over the running of the house in Hyde Park Gate, helped by Sophie, that perfect example of the devoted Victorian cook, whose letter I have quoted on page 32. For the next nine years, until Sir Leslie's death in 1904, every Monday morning Vanessa brought to him the household books in order that he might give her a cheque to cover the previous week's expenditure. Then for ten minutes or more he sighed and groaned[1] over the enor-

[1] Leslie Stephen in old age was much given to groaning audibly, like many distinguished Victorians, particularly if they were widowers. (I think Tennyson groaned freely and so did Watts, the painter.) Mr Gibbs was an old friend of the Stephen family and at more or less regular intervals used to come and dine with them at Hyde Park Gate. He had been tutor for six or seven years to the Prince of Wales, later Edward VII, and in spite or because of this was a bit of a bore—I think Mr Pepper in *The Voyage Out* has some of his characteristics. On the nights when Mr Gibbs came to dinner, towards ten o'clock, Leslie Stephen would start groaning and saying at intervals quite audibly: 'O why doesn't he go; O why doesn't he go!'

mous sums which they were spending on food, wages, light, coal—at this rate ruin stared them in the face and they would soon all be in the workhouse. 'Ruin staring us in the face' and 'the workhouse' were the economic nightmares which haunted so many wealthy Victorians. Yet Leslie Stephen was an extremely kind and affectionate man, and generous except on Monday mornings.

The cloud of impending bankruptcy and poverty, not to say positive starvation, which hung over her father and sister on Monday mornings had an effect upon the impressionable Virginia between the ages of thirteen and twenty-two. She never suffered from her father's obsession about ruin and bankruptcy; she was usually quite sensible about money, not worrying about it, and, when she had it, she enjoyed spending it. But every now and again she would get into a sudden panic about our finances, particularly in the first seven or eight years of our marriage when we had no regular or even probable means of earning the £400 or £500 which we needed to cover our expenditure. But the panic did not last and we took no immediate steps to find me a paid job. It was more or less understood that Virginia should go on writing novels and reviewing for *The Times Literary Supplement*; I decided to stop writing novels and to see what I could earn by journalism.

The first job which I took was a curious one. The second Post-Impressionist Exhibition, organised by Roger Fry, opened in the Grafton Galleries in the autumn of 1912. In Spain on our honeymoon I got an urgent message from Roger asking me whether I would act as secretary of the show on our return. I agreed to do so until, I think, the end of the year. It was a strange and for me new experience. The first room was filled with Cézanne water-colours. The highlights in the second room were two enormous pictures of more than life-size figures by Matisse and three or four Picassos. There was also a Bonnard and a good picture by Marchand. Large numbers of people came to the exhibition, and nine out of ten of them either roared with laughter at the pictures or were enraged by them. The British middle class—and, as far as that goes, the aristocracy and working class—are incorrigibly philistine, and their taste is impeccably bad. Anything new in the arts, particularly if it is good, infuriates them and they condemn it as either immoral or ridiculous or both. As secretary I sat at my table in the large second room of the galleries prepared to deal with enquiries from possible purchasers or answer any questions about the pictures. I was kept busy all the time. The whole business gave me a lamentable view of human nature, its rank stupidity and uncharitableness. I used to think, as I sat there, how much nicer were the Tamil or Sinhalese villagers who crowded into the veranda of my Ceylon kachcheri than these smug, well dressed, ill-mannered, well-to-do Londoners. Hardly any of them made the slightest attempt to look at, let alone understand, the pictures, and the same insane questions or remarks were repeated to me all day long. And every now and then some well groomed, red faced gentleman, oozing the undercut of the best beef and the most succulent of chops, carrying his top hat and grey suede gloves, would come up to my table and abuse the pictures and me with the greatest rudeness.

There were, of course, consolations. Dealing with possible purchasers was always amusing and sometimes exciting. Occasionally one had an interesting conversation with a stranger. Sometimes it was amusing to go round the rooms with Roger and a distinguished visitor. I have described in *Sowing* Henry James's visit. Roger came to the gallery every day and spent quite a lot of time there. We used to go down into the bowels of the earth about four o'clock and have tea with Miss Wotherston, the secretary, who inhabited the vast basement, and we were often joined by Herbert Cook who owned Doughty House, Richmond, and a superb collection of pictures. I saw so much of Roger that at the end of my time at the Grafton Galleries I knew him much better than when I first went there. His character was more full of contradictions even than that of most human beings. He was one of the most charming and gentle of men; born a double dyed Quaker, he had in many respects revolted against the beliefs and morals of The Friends, and yet deep down in his mind and character he remained profoundly, and I think unconsciously, influenced by them. Like his six remarkable sisters, he had a Quaker's uncompromising sense of public duty and responsibility and, though he would have indignantly repudiated this, ultimately the Quaker's ethical austerity. And yet there were elements in his psychology which contradicted all these characteristics. I was more than once surprised by his ruthlessness and what to me seemed to be almost unscrupulousness in business. For instance, we discovered, shortly after I took on the secretaryship, that when Roger had been preparing the exhibition and asking people to exhibit, owing to a mistake of his, they had been offered much too favourable terms—the figure for the Exhibition's commission on sales was much too low. When the time came to pay artists their share of the purchase amounts of pictures sold, Roger insisted upon deducting a higher commission without any explanation or apology to the painters. Most of them meekly accepted what they were given, but Wyndham Lewis, at best of times a bilious and cantankerous man, protested violently. Roger was adamant in ignoring him and his demands; Lewis never forgave Roger, and, as I was a kind of buffer between them, he also never forgave me.

There was another odd—and rather endearing—contradiction in Roger's psychology. He had been educated as a scientist both at Clifton and at Cambridge, and in many ways he had the scientific, careful, sceptical mind and methods. This was notably the case in that province of knowledge where he was a great expert, the science of the Kunstforscher. I once saw an interesting display of this. One evening when he and Virginia and I were at Clive Bell's flat, a well-known politician, who was something of a buyer of pictures, came in after dinner accompanied by a large canvas. He wanted Roger's opinion as to whether the picture was or was not a Poussin. Roger examined it with the greatest care, but refused to commit himself. The picture was placed on the floor against the wall and we all began talking about something else. The conversation was general, but I noticed that, as it went on, all the time at intervals Roger's eyes wandered to the picture. After about an hour, Roger suddenly said that he had made up his mind, that it was not a Poussin. He then gave his reasons at great length; he may or may not have been right, but the performance was extraordinarily convincing; it was an opinion based on expert knowledge and scientific investigation. This was the scientific side of Roger's mind, but there was another side which was amazingly credulous. He was really capable of believing anything, particularly the most extravagant assertions of the great quacks. He believed in the famous black box and sent a drop of his blood to America so that it might be put into the black box and all his ailments—and he always had a good supply of ailments—might be diagnosed thereby. Another characteristic example of his capacity to believe the unbelievable was the following. One evening when we were all sitting round the fire, he suddenly said with intense and gloomy seriousness: 'I am convinced that the future is not with man, but with the birds.' When some of us laughed, he was a little upset and explained at considerable length that he had read in some obscure authority that a curious development in the intestines of birds as compared with that of the human inside would inevitably lead in the course of evolution and the struggle for existence to the extinction of man and the survival of birds.

The quality of Roger's mind which produced this rather ridiculous credulity also produced his unflagging curiosity and the fertility of his thought and imagination. His mind was packed with information on almost every subject, so that he was also the most erudite of men. As he was, like me an indefatigable arguer, I found him a fascinating companion. Virginia and I went with him and his sister Margery for a month to Greece in 1932. They were wonderful travellers. Their knowledge was encyclopaedic. Roger always everywhere knew the most important thing which nobody else knew, e.g. the most perfect Byzantine building on the top of some formidable mountain far off the beaten track or a perfect moussaka only obtainable in one small dingy restaurant in an alley of Athens. He was sixty-six years old and not at all well. But his energy was terrific. We hired a large open car, driven by a chauffeur, and went to Delphi and all over the Peloponnese. The sun was very hot, but the winds (the chauffeur always called them draughts) that blew between the mountains were icy cold so that Virginia and I trembled and shivered under the blazing sun. The Frys, impervious to heat or cold, every now and again stopped the car, leapt out, and rapidly painted a picture. At the end of a strenuous sixteen-hour day, after dinner at eleven Roger would say to me: 'There's just time for a game of chess before we go to bed.'

One last picture of Roger in Greece. In 1932 the roads there were nearly all appallingly bad. We drove to Delphi by the long road which circled Mt Parnassus and was fairly good. Roger said that there was a marvellous monastery called Hosios Loucas and that there was a road to it direct from Delphi. The chauffeur said that the road was almost impassable and that it was terribly dangerous to attempt it. Roger was ruthless. The road, he said, is marked as a main road on the map and is obviously just as good as the road which we had driven over from Athens to Delphi. We stood in the Delphi street where outside every house the people were roasting the Paschal lamb on wooden skewers—it was Easter—and the chauffeur and Roger argued interminably. At last, just before it was time to go into the inn and have dinner, the Greek gave in: 'All right,' he said, 'but we shall all be killed.' About half an hour after dinner, they brought us a message to say that the chauffeur was outside and wanted to speak to us. Next minute we were back again all four in the street among the roasting lambs. The chauffeur, with a long face, told us that they had just brought two dead American young men into Delphi; they had tried to drive their car on Roger's 'main road' from Hosios Loucas and had ended upside down at the bottom of a ravine. He definitely refused to follow their example. Reluctantly and with unconcealed scepticism Roger gave way. So next day we drove back the same way all round Mt Parnassus to the cross-roads where Oedipus met and killed his father. From near there the road was indeed so bad that we got out of the car and, with Roger riding on a mule, we walked up to the monastery. It should be added that the face of Greece has greatly changed in the last thirty years. When I visited it again in 1961, I found that the road which the chauffeur refused to drive on was now a first class main road. When I reached Hosios Loucas by it, I found an hotel there and half a dozen omnibuses.

I must return to the Grafton Galleries, but only for a moment, for I handed my duties to Sydney Waterlow at the end of the year. My seven years as a civil servant in Ceylon had made me very much a political animal, and I have remained such ever since. Once one has been personally concerned with communal affairs and has felt personally responsible for them, one can never again escape a feeling of political responsibility. Consequently, as soon as I had resigned from the Ceylon civil service I began to look at the politics and economics of London and Britain—and very soon Europe—in the way in which I had looked at those of the Hambantota District and Ceylon. I had to study the details of the social system in which I was now going to live as carefully as I had studied that of the Tamils of Jaffna and the Sinhalese of Kandy or the Southern Province—to understand its merits and its defects. I had been so absorbed in the administrative problems of Ceylon and my district there that in England I was to a great extent politically both ignorant and uncommitted. In 1912 I was, I think, a liberal, but not a Liberal, and half way to socialism.

My first political experience made me complete my journey to the Left. Virginia had a cousin, Marny Vaughan, who, like many serious, middle class, maiden ladies of the Victorian era engaged in 'good works', and her particular good work was a Care Committee connected with the Charity Organisation Society. She induced me to join it. It was in Hoxton, in those days a typical London east end district, full of dreary depressed sordid streets, houses, and people. Our business was to help the poor, to dispense charity. I cannot remember exactly what kind of charity we proposed to dispense, whether it was hard cash or charity in kind. What happened was that, when the committee assembled, the secretary put before us a number of applications or recommendations for relief. Relief was given only if we were satisfied that the case was deserving, and usually in order to satisfy ourselves about this one of us was sent off to interview the applicant in his or her home. I made, I think, two visits of this kind. There was no doubt about the poverty in the east end of London in 1912; I would rather have lived in a hut in a Ceylon village in the jungle than in the poverty stricken, sordid, dilapidated, god-forsaken hovels of Hoxton. And the moment that I stood in their grim rooms and began to speak to the dejected inhabitants, whose voices and faces revealed nothing but the depths of their hopelessness, I realised my hopelessness and helplessness there. In the Ceylon jungle village there was still a place or excuse for government paternalism. Life and the people there were still simple and primitive enough to make a simple and primitive relationship between ruler and ruled possible. Even so I had resigned from the Ceylon Civil Service largely because I personally did not like being a ruler of the ruled. Having refused to remain the benevolent ruler of Silindu and Hinnihami in Beddegama, I was not going to try to play the part of benevolent father to Mr and Mrs Smith in a Hoxton slum. Besides, one only had to spend a quarter of an hour sitting with Marny Vaughan on a Care Committee and another quarter of an hour with the victim, Mr and Mrs Smith in the Hoxton slum, to see that in Hoxton one was confronted by some vast, dangerous fault in the social structure, some destructive disease in the social organism, which could not be touched by paternalism or charity or good works. Nothing but a social revolution, a major operation, could deal with it. I resigned from the Care Committee and the C.O.S.

Hoxton turned me from a liberal into a socialist, and this led directly to my next political step. At Cambridge I had known Theodore and Crompton Llewelyn Davies (because they were Apostles) although they were a good deal older than I was.[1] They

[1] See Volume 1, pp. 91 and 127.

belonged to a remarkable family. Their father had four sons and one daughter, all of them extremely intelligent, finely built, beautiful—they all had great personal charm, immense energy. Though they were almost fanatical in their integrity and high principles, they were, unlike so many exceptionally serious and good people, amusing and interesting, companionable and lovable. They were friends of the Stephen family and Virginia often saw Margaret Llewelyn Davies, the daughter. She was secretary of the Women's Co-operative Guild. To the vast majority of my readers the last sentence will convey little or nothing and it would have conveyed even less in 1912. Yet Margaret was one of the most eminent women I have known and created something of great value—and at the time unique—in the Guild. If she had been a man, her achievements would have filled probably half a page in *Who's Who*; though she lived to be over seventy, you will not find the name of Margaret Llewelyn Davies in any edition of it—the kind of fact which made—and makes—feminism the belief or policy of all sensible men.

I am writing an autobiography, not a political or social treatise, and I shall enter into political questions and problems as little as possible; but I shall have to say something about them when or where they affected my life. And strangely enough, the Co-operative Movement, the Guild, and Margaret did affect my life. The Co-operative Movement is a peculiar and enormous system of manufacture, retail trade and banking, based upon the consumers organised in retail Co-operative Societies and controlling through them retail trade, through the Co-operative Wholesale Societies wholesale trade and manufactures, and through Co-operative banks finance. It originated in 1844; it was a working class movement and in 1912 the membership of consumers' co-operative societies was overwhelmingly working class. The Women's Co-operative Guild or W.C.G. was an organisation of women members of Co-operative Societies. When I first knew it, it had a membership of about 30,000 and its objects were 'to educate its members, advance co-operative principles, and to obtain for women's interests the recognition which within and without the movement is due to them'. It sounds dreary and superficially it was dreary, for on its surface were the drabness and cheerlessness which, not without reason, infected the working classes and their institutions at the beginning of the twentieth century. In fact it was a unique and even exciting regiment of women whose energy and vitality were exhilarating. They were almost all of them working class women who had had little or no regular education, and they were organised, in the traditional working class way, in 'Branches'—i.e. the women members of a Co-operative Society, say the York Co-operative Society, formed a York Branch of the W.C.G. which was federated with all the other branches in the Guild which had its head office in London. Each branch held its weekly, fortnightly, or monthly meetings, and sent its delegate to the Annual Congress of the Guild, held in London or Manchester or some other big town.

The vitality and inspiration of the Guild—and also its organisation—were mainly due to Margaret. I think that what had primarily moved and shocked her was the grimness, hardship, narrowness of the lives to which most working class wives and mothers were condemned. Then when she got to know them individually and in the mass, she was deeply moved and exhilarated to find in them great strength and resilience of character, great potentialities, not merely as human beings, but also as political animals. She was that strange and usually inexplicable phenomenon 'a born leader'. Of course one could explain it by her immense energy and enthusiasm; by her laugh which was so characteristically Margaret, a deep contralto spontaneous laugh; by the feminine charm which was also so spontaneous and unconscious, and sometimes among her regiment of working women, her blue books, and Co-operative Stores so endearingly incongruous; and by her beauty, which remained even when she had grown fat and almost an old woman, the fresh English beauty of hair and eyes and skin marvellously united with a chiselled classical beauty of Greek features—nearly all the Llewelyn Davieses had this pure chiselled nobility of face, particularly in profile, which perhaps should be called Roman rather than Greek. But when one has catalogued all these charms and powers, one feels that there was something beyond them which made her glow in the co-operative drabness so that she was able to inspire thousands of uneducated women with her own passion, both for 'sweetness and light', and also for liberty, equality, and fraternity. This something can, I think, only be described as a kind of virginal purity of mind and motive which—I am afraid it sounds rather absurd, but is nonetheless true—made her a kind of Joan of Arc to her cohorts of Lancashire and Yorkshire housewives in her crusade against ignorance, poverty, and injustice.

When I first knew Margaret she was a middle-aged woman, but she still had the quicksilver eagerness of the young which remained with her until she was an old woman. I do not know why she never married—partly, I suppose, because, like thousands of other middle class Victorian virgins, she was devoted to and devoted her life to, her father,[1] partly because it would have been only a very superior young man whom the terribly serious, austere, dynamic young Margaret would not have scared away, and partly because it would probably have been only a super-superior, terribly serious, austere, and dynamic young man whom the young Margaret would have considered for one moment as a possible husband.

There is a peculiar contradiction in the Co-operative Movement and in everything connected with it. On the face of it it is one of the most depressingly drab and dreary creations of the human ant, and of the working class human ant in particular. Its embodiment seems to be the dingy Co-operative grocery store in some rain-sodden street in a hideous grimy northern industrial town. A great deal of the co-operative spirit which moves the vast co-operative machine is as drab and dreary as its material surface. And yet from its very beginnings in 1844, there has been working below this surface a passionate belief in a social ideal. The spirit and the contradiction—passion and imagination yoked to dreariness—can be traced back even to the strange man who invented the co-operative

[1] Not but what her father, the Rev. John Llewelyn Davies, was himself a remarkable man and worthy of some filial devotion. Born in 1826 he was an admirable scholar and a Fellow of Trinity College, Cambridge. A friend of Charles Kingsley and F. D. Maurice, he was, like them, a Christian Socialist and shared their austere sense of social responsibility. He was for twenty years Vicar of the small and remote Westmorland village of Kirkby Lonsdale and there too, of course, for the best twenty years of her life Margaret lived. When I knew him first, he was nearly ninety, and a few years later, when the time came for him to die, he was mentally and physically so strong that life refused to leave him. During the weeks of his struggle for death I used often to go up to Hampstead, where they lived, to see Margaret. A few hours before he died, she told me, though he was quite blind, he suddenly saw a cat and a large portrait of Mr Gladstone. But, though almost everything else in him was already dead, his clearness of mind and its tenacity of truth were such that he knew that his visions were hallucinations. The mystery of why a blind dying clergyman should know that he is seeing a non-existent cat and non-existent portrait of Mr Gladstone remains, unexplained either by the clergyman's God or even by Dr Freud.

system and movement, Robert Owen, who was accurately described as 'one of those bores who are the salt of the earth'.

This dichotomy of dreariness and inspiration, of deadness and life, extended, it must be admitted, to Margaret, for, like all fanatics, and the first prophet of co-operation, Owen, she could be a bore. But she not only saw the practical, material importance of consumers' co-operation and recognised the potentialities of the Movement and Guild as economic, political, and educational instruments for the working class; she saw, to some extent, that behind the unpromising multiplicity of Retail and Wholesale Societies there existed, thanks to Owen's stroke of imaginative genius, an immensely valuable method or principle of economics and social organisation.[1] Impressed by her enthusiasm, I embarked on a thorough study of the movement, both its principles and its practice. This study completed my conversion to socialism, but I became and have remained a socialist of a rather peculiar sort. To regard socialism as an end in itself in the way in which many socialists and all communists do has always seemed to me ridiculous mumbo-jumboism. But I do not think that in the modern over-populated world of large-scale industry and monopolies you can have a civilised society unless the community, in some form and by some method, exercises considerable control over the whole economic system. There are considerable disadvantages and dangers if that control is exercised by the state, and still more if it is exercised by the community organised as workers or producers. Owen seemed to me to have devised in the Co-operative Movement a system which, if extended and developed, would place large sections of the economy in the control of the community organised as consumers. The advantages of this form of socialism were that it could eliminate profit and class conflict and make some democratic control of the economic system possible.

I wrote a book, published in 1919, *Co-operation and the Future of Industry*, describing the Movement and its methods and its potentialities for the socialist. I still agree with the greater part of what I wrote in that book forty-five years ago, though my vision of a

[1] One of the first persons to see the significance of the Consumers' Co-operative Movement was Mrs Sidney Webb; her book published in 1891 and for long a classic, *The Co-operative Movement in Great Britain*, was a revelation both to co-operators and to people who had ignored and despised the movement.

socialist society based on consumers' control now sounds utopian, because the events of history have turned in the opposite direction. The view that everything which has not happened was always utopian, however, seems to me false—it is one of the commonest forms of stupidity after the event. At any rate, started off by Margaret I soon became a believer in the theory and principles of co-operation and have remained one ever since. But I decided that I must also see for myself how the principles and the machinery worked.

I began by going up to Newcastle in June 1913 to attend the annual congress of the Women's Guild. I was enormously impressed by this unofficial parliament of 650 working class women. In the eyes of a middle class person they were lamentably ignorant and most of them were completely uneducated except in what is called the hard school of life. But they showed an extraordinary native, intuitive understanding of their own ignorance and therefore of their own problems and, what was more unexpected, of the problems of the working class. They showed a passionate desire for education and it was clear that the Guild meant everything to them as an instrument of self education. When I wrote the words 'passionate desire' in the last sentence, I paused in hesitation. I think it is true that there was in those working women what may rightly be called a passion of desire for education and for other social or political ends, and when I got to know them much better than I did in 1913 I was often aware of it. But it would have been quite possible for a careless observer to miss the passion altogether, for it was almost always well below the surface. One of the most inveterate and gross vulgar errors is that women are more emotional than men and more flighty. Ten minutes with the 650 women in the hall at Newcastle would have proved to anyone how untrue this old error is. They were much more unemotional, stable, quiet, matter of fact than any similar male assembly. They were in fact a little too serious; I remember once at one of their congresses, when during a very serious debate on divorce there was a burst of laughter at something that one of the speakers said, a delegate rose and with a strong Yorkshire accent, shouted: 'Shame on you! Shame on you!'

There was, however, another characteristic both in individuals and in the congress generally which was remarkable; it was a kind of intensity of patience, learnt perhaps by those particular women over babies, saucepans and frying pans, and coppers. For instance, at

Newcastle one of the questions discussed was the proposal that there should be a 'fusion of labour forces', i.e. some sort of union between the Co-operative Movement, the trade unions, and the Labour Party. Many Co-operators and many of the women in the Congress were strongly opposed to this. Then one of the delegates spoke in favour of the proposal and I described her intervention at the time as follows:

> This Northern delegate, a typical working-class woman both in speech and appearance, spoke with passionate and yet restrained earnestness in favour of the resolution. She told with an eloquent simplicity, which made her speech a work of art, how, as a child, she had learnt from her father to believe that the one hope for the working classes was to forget their differences and to work together loyally for the same ideals and the same ends. Then she paused, and told the delegates that she did not wish her words to influence their votes; if they had come prepared to vote against the resolution they should do so; but then they should go home and think over what she had said, and, if it convinced them, they should return to Congress next year and vote in favour of the resolution. 'We can wait,' she said, 'we can wait. We women have waited years, thousands of years, even to be able to discuss things like this. We can wait.'

Later on I got to know many of these women well and the better I knew them the more they confirmed my first impressions. The Guild used to arrange week-end classes or short courses of lectures in London and big towns like Manchester and Leeds for their members, and I used to take classes or give lectures on subjects like taxation, international, affairs, or the colonial empire. Superficially there was no resemblance, either in mind, body, experience, or environment, between the wife of a Lancashire textile worker or Durham miner and a Sinhalese villager. Yet I think that the days, weeks, months, years I had spent talking to those strange, alien men and women in Kandyan hills or among the rice fields and jungles of Hambantota helped me to understand and get in touch with Mrs Barton and Mrs Harris. It is not true that the poor and primitive are more 'real' than the rich and sophisticated, that there is more 'reality' in the Congo or a coalfield than in Cambridge or Cavendish Square; but those who live, physically unprotected and mentally almost naked, close to and desperately vulnerable to the catastrophes of nature or the economic system, acquire a crystalline simplicity, a straight disillusioned look in the eye which are to me humanly and aesthetically attractive. In Ceylon I learnt, I think, after a long time to sit under a kumbuk tree by a village tank and talk to a villager or even an old village woman so that they would talk to me, and somehow or other this helped me to be able to talk to the women Co-operators. At any rate I was not unnaturally pleased and flattered when one of them, after being lectured by me for an hour on taxation, came up to me and said: 'You are the only *gentleman* whom we can always understand when you talk to us.'

In March 1913 I went for a fortnight to the North of England and Scotland, visiting Liverpool, Manchester, Bolton, Leeds, Glasgow, Sheffield, and Leicester. I had introductions to the officials of the Co-operative Societies in each of these towns and of the English and Scottish Wholesale Societies, and I had arranged with them to be taken over the stores and factories. I 'inspected' them as I would have inspected them if they had been in my district in Ceylon and I cross-examined the officials minutely on the structure of the Movement, the organisation of the societies, the way in which it worked and the way in which they worked it. It was my first experience of the industrialised towns of the North and of the strange race which inhabits them. The inhabitants differ as much from the southerner, the Londoner or the Sussex man, as the Tamil in the north of Ceylon differs from the Sinhalese in the south, or as the German who is born and bred in East Prussia differs from the Italian born and bred in Calabria. Large scale, highly developed, twentieth-century industrial civilisation, if it can be called civilisation, fills me with despair. The melancholy which descended upon me in Manchester grew blacker in Bolton and still blacker in Glasgow. I cannot believe that what used to be called 'the good life' can be lived by millions of men and women spending all their days in monotonous manual labour in order to produce parts or particles of salable articles of which some are necessary, some useful, but most of them ugly or shoddy, while in order to achieve this end these unfortunate people have to live in surroundings of grey and grimy ugliness and discomfort. This judgment is not refuted by the fact that these men and women are generally very nice people and no less civilised than those who live in Bermondsey or Brighton. It is just an inexplicable miracle that human nature can remain as nice as it is in a Manchester slum or a Ceylon village.

My rapid, but pretty thorough, look at the Co-operative Movement impressed me, but it also depressed me. Many of the societies were very well managed, and so on the whole were the Wholesale Societies which, in addition to manufacturing a vast number of things, from boots and soap to flour and mustard, controlled a very large wholesale and banking business. The Movement was still growing rapidly both in numbers of co-operators and in the volume and variety of their trade. I met several secretaries or managers of societies who were intelligent and efficient men, proud of and devoted to their own societies and to co-operation. That this vast organisation had been built up entirely by working class men and women was indeed something to be proud of—it was an amazing achievement. But from my point of view there was something wrong about the Movement as a whole, or rather something which filled me with doubt and suspicion. There was too often in the societies and their officials a narrow parochialism, a social and economic stuffiness, timidity, dreariness. 'The Co-op', product and emblem of the Movement, was more often than not a third-rate badly arranged grocery shop in one of those terrible side-streets of such sordid respectability that they ought to have a sign, not of NO ENTRY, but ABANDON HOPE ALL THOSE WHO ENTER HERE. Most of those who were engaged in the practical work of the societies, and still more of the rank and file co-operators, seemed quite content with co-operation provided it went on making and selling soap and other things at a low price and in an ever expanding circle. The possibilities in consumers' co-operation for economic revolution and social evolution, which had been perceived, if dimly, by Robert Owen and did inspire some of the men in the societies and women in the Guild, meant nothing at all to the vast majority. The Englishman, indeed the Briton—though I think the Englishman more than the Scot—is taught in every class to dislike and distrust the intellect and the intellectual. He likes to know what to do and he is very good at seeing how to do it; he hates to think—he does not want to know—why he does it or should do it. He has no use for theories or principles, being socially and politically a plain, practical man, a human species which is responsible for a great deal of good, but also for some of the worst human disasters. Nearly all co-operators that I came across were plain, practical men, and so were the trade unionists and working class members of the Labour Party with whom later on I worked.

That the Co-ops should make their own soap and mustard and sell them to millions of members is, I think, a very good thing, but that is not what I was primarily interested in. What attracted me in co-operation was its potentialities as a socialistic alternative to the profit-making capitalist system and as a means of applying some of the principles of democracy to the economic system. The Movement also had an educational side, nearly all societies spending a certain amount of money on organising educational classes or lectures. My two weeks tour of the northern societies had to some extent depressed me, but the enthusiasm of the Women's Guild and of some of the leading men in the North encouraged me, and for many years I did a good deal of work on the educational side of the Movement, trying to make the co-operators see the social potentialities of co-operation.

The most interesting experience I had trying to educate co-operators was during the 1914 war. I think it was the Co-operative Union which asked me to give a series of lectures on international government to a number of Lancashire and Cheshire Co-operative Societies. I spent some time going from society to society and giving a lecture in the evening to audiences ranging in numbers from thirty to forty to 100 or a little more. I was given what in labour organisations is called hospitality, i.e. someone put me up for the night. The hospitality was fascinating, for I had an extraordinary variety of hosts. At the end of my lecture tour, I felt that I had probably learnt a great deal more than I had taught—at any rate, I came back with a knowledge of the class structure of industrial society in the north of England which I had not had when I started out from Euston to Manchester. In Manchester I stayed with Mrs Eckhard who was the mother-in-law of Sydney Waterlow. I started therefore in the middle classes, for the Eckhards belonged to the well-to-do Manchester bourgeoisie. They lived in a large comfortable ugly Didsbury 'villa residence'. Mrs Eckhard was one of those immensely energetic, dominating Jewish matriarchs who amuse me and with whom I get on quite well provided that our meetings are not too long and the moment does not come when I have to show that even in the drawing-room, the dining-room, and the bedroom I want liberty, equality, and fraternity. What the horse power of her energy was may be shown by this: one day at lunch I said to her that her garden and house would be much improved if she cut down a large tree near her front door. She jumped up, abandoned our lunch, fetched an axe and saw, and we spent the rest of the afternoon felling her tree and sawing it up. Hot, dishevelled, and dirty I only just caught the train to take me to my evening lecture.

In Bolton and some of the other towns I stayed with working class families. They were extraordinarily nice to me. After the lecture we went back to my host's house and had an enormous high tea, usually fried fish with delicious rolls and cakes. In a Cheshire town, Macclesfield I think, I stayed with the local editor, a man and a family quite unlike anything which I had ever come across in the south of England. They seemed socially to be hybrid between the middle and working classes and much more alive and intelligent than a bourgeois or working class family in Sussex. When we got back from the lecture, the whole family sat in a large room and we drank quantities of tea and ate special plates of fried fish, and the fried plaice and the fire and the warmth and humanity of our souls produced an immediate understanding and intimacy between us. We sat until quite late at night and we talked and argued seriously about politics and classes and the war and education and what the children would do or wanted to do and we told old tales and laughed while every now and again Mrs Brown would say: 'Now really children you must go off to bed,' and the children would say: 'Now really, Mum, you have said that before.'

Finally at Oldham I stayed in a house such as I had never seen before and have never seen since; it belonged to a different world from that of Mr Brown of Macclesfield. In it lived Dame Lees, who was Mayor of Oldham and a very wealthy widow of a textile manufacturer. Miss Lees, the daughter, met me at the station, took me to the meeting, and after the meeting back to the house where I was to stay the night. Werneth Park stood in the middle of Oldham and was indeed a park, but it was exactly like the bleakest of public parks, consisting entirely of slabs of grass intersected by asphalt paths and low railings about 1½ feet high which in my childhood disfigured Kensington Gardens and practically all public parks in England. The house itself was very large, and every inch of every wall of every room, staircase, and landing (including the W.C.) was covered by heavily framed pictures. The pictures were all by R.A.s or A.R.A.s and must have cost Dame Lees thousands of pounds —when they were sold, if they ever were sold, they would, I suppose, have fetched a few hundreds. It is probable that in the heyday of the British Empire wealthy industrialists all over the north of England were papering their vast houses with pictures which they bought, like Dame Lees, for large sums at the annual exhibition of the Royal Academy in Burlington House. The effect of this miniature Royal Academy upon me was depressing and intimidating as Miss Lees led me into the Billiard Room apologising for the absence of the Mayor, her mother, who was ill in bed with a cold. In the Billiard Room, however, were cakes, biscuits, lemonade, and Lord and Lady Emmott. Lord Emmott, in dinner jacket and black tie, was the Mayor's son-in-law and had been Liberal M.P. for Oldham. The only relic of our conversation which I remember was Lord Emmott saying to me in a muted voice as we went up to bed: 'I had better show you the geography of the house', a euphemism used in those days by the upper middle classes for the W.C. But all our conversation was in the same key of muted respectability.

I must now retrace the footsteps of my memory to 1913 and explain how the Co-operative Movement affected my life, professionally and economically. In June, 1913, the *Manchester Guardian* published an article which I wrote for them about the Newcastle Congress of the Women's Guild. The Webbs, sitting in the centre of their Fabian spider-web, always kept an eager eye watching for some promising young man who might be ensnared by them. They read and were impressed by my article, and the result was an invitation to lunch, and on 12 July I ate my first of many plates of mutton in Grosvenor Road. The Webbs thought as well of me as they had thought of my article and they got me to join the Fabian Society at once. This led, as I shall explain, to my doing work for the Fabians and for the *New Statesman*, but before I deal with that I should like to say something about those two strange human beings, Beatrice and Sidney Webb.

I came to know them, I think, as well personally as anyone of my age could get to know them. Hundreds of people have poked their fun at the Webbs and they were so absurd that you could not caricature them for they were always caricaturing themselves. But behind the fantastic façade there were two human beings for whom I eventually acquired real affection. I do not think that Sidney ever felt much affection for anyone except Beatrice, but he liked me and I liked him. Beatrice, who was highly strung and neurotic, came to have a certain amount of affection for Virginia and me, and I had a real affection for her. But however long one knew them, one never got accustomed to their absurdities, to the ludicrous way in which they caricatured the Webbs. What astonished one again and again was that they were so intelligent and in many ways so quick in their perceptions and yet seemed to be quite unconscious of their own absurdities. I cannot resist giving one or two examples of this.

It was another lunch in Grosvenor Road and this time Virginia was with me—also the long lean bearded Noel Buxton, a Buxton of the Buxtons and in the cockles of his heart and the convolutions of his brain a Liberal of the Liberals, but still on the day of the lunch a Labour M.P. and later a Labour peer, Lord Noel-Buxton. The conversation drifted, if conversation with the Webbs can ever accurately be said to have drifted, into the subject of education. Beatrice said that she thought it would be a good idea if Education Authorities provided for the small children in government schools sets of 'municipal bricks' inscribed with the names of various organisations; in playing continually with these the children would more or less unconsciously 'learn their civic duties'. Beatrice was quite serious, but Virginia, who described the meal in her diary, said that 'even Sidney had his mild joke at her'. She also says, perhaps rather unfairly, that 'Noel Buxton obsequiously offered his son for the experiment. Rich men nowadays can be seen divesting themselves of particles of gold with a view to the eye of the needle'.

I am going to relate another conversation with the Webbs because it is the best thing which I ever heard them say, but it is possible that I may have related it somewhere before. I am not sure that other people have not recorded similar remarks by the Webbs, and it is probable that they did sometimes say to other people what they said that day to Virginia and me. At any rate I can vouch for the accuracy of what follows. In September, 1918, we boldly, if not recklessly, asked Beatrice and Sidney to come to us for a week-end at Asham and we were rather astonished and a little dismayed when they accepted. They arrived on a Saturday, and also Joris Young.[1] On Sunday afternoon the Webbs, Virginia, and I went for a walk across the bridge over the river to Southease and the down above Telscombe. Even a walk with the Webbs tended to become regularised or institutionalised and organised, like the municipal bricks, and

[1] George Young, who, when his father died, later became Sir George Young, Bart. He was a brother of Geoffrey Young and Hilton Young (Lord Kennet). For many years I saw a good deal of him as he joined the Labour Party and, having been in the diplomatic service, considered himself and was considered an authority on foreign affairs. He was a nice, absurd, cantankerous man. Desmond MacCarthy said truly (but not in fact originally) that Hilton Young was a sphinx without a riddle. There was a faint shadowy sphinxiness about Joris's face; it was rather like a very blurred, out-of-focus photograph of a sphinx—but there was not even a shadow of a riddle.

therefore on the way out I walked with Beatrice and Virginia with Sidney, and on the way back we changed partners. Sidney and I walked rather faster than the ladies and got a good way ahead of them; so we stopped on the top of a small hill just before we got to Asham and waited for them. When they came into view some distance away, Sidney said to me: 'I know what she is saying to your wife; she is saying that marriage is the waste paper basket of the emotions.' In the evening when we were at last alone I asked Virginia whether on the road from Southease to Asham Beatrice Webb had told her that marriage was the waste paper basket of the emotions. She said she had. As soon as Sidney and I had started off ahead of them Beatrice had asked Virginia what she intended to do now that she was married. Virginia said that she wanted to go on writing novels. Beatrice seemed to approve and warned Virginia against allowing her work to be interfered with by emotional relations. 'Marriage, we always say,' she said, 'is the waste paper basket of the emotions.'[1] To which, just as they came to the level crossing, Virginia replied: 'But wouldn't an old servant do as well?' 'We were entangled', Virginia writes in her diary, 'at the gates of the level-crossing when she remarked: "Yes, I daresay an old family servant would do as well." ' Virginia continues her account of her walk with Beatrice.

On the way up the hill she stated her position that one should wish well to all the world, but discriminate no one. According to her the differences are not great; the defects invariable; one must cultivate impersonality above all things. In old age people become of little account, she said; one speculated chiefly upon the possibility, or the impossibility, of a future life. This grey

[1] It is a curious fact that in Virginia's diary she records this conversation as follows: 'One should have only one great personal relationship in one's life, she said; or at most two—marriage and parenthood. Marriage was necessary as a waste pipe for emotion, as security in old age when personal attractiveness fails and as a help to work.' This shows how difficult it is to be certain of any accuracy in recorded conversations. I am absolutely certain that Sidney used the words 'waste paper basket of the emotions' in speaking to me, and I am almost certain that those were the words that Virginia agreed Beatrice used to her. But did Beatrice in fact say 'waste pipe' and not 'waste paper basket'? It is impossible now to know. Virginia was never an accurate recorder of what people said, and it is quite possible, if not probable, that when she came to write her diary, three days after the events, she dashed down (inaccurately) waste pipe. But it is, as I say, impossible now to know.

view depressed me more and more; partly I suppose from the egotistical sense of my own nothingness in her field of vision. And then we wound up with a light political gossip and chatter of reminscences, in which Mr and Mrs Webb did their parts equally and so to bed; and to my horror, in came Mrs W. early next morning to say Goodbye, and perched in all her long impersonality on the edge of my bed, looking past my stockings, drawers, and po. This has taken so long to write that we are now arrived at
Monday September 23rd
and so many things have accumulated that I can hardly proceed to that masterly summing up of the Webbs which I intended. I had intended to dwell upon the half carping half humorously cynical view which steals into one's description of the Webbs. I had meant to point out the good qualities which come from such well kept brisk intellectual habits, how open minded they showed themselves; how completely and consistently *sensible*. . . . Their horizon is entirely clear, unless, in the case of Mrs Webb, as the medium said, a cloud of dust surrounds them.

It should be added to complete a true picture of the Webbs, what I have rarely, if ever, seen properly recorded, that their mutual affection and devotion were unmistakably deep. When they stayed with us they brought with them all the paraphernalia for making tea, including kettle and spirit lamp. Very early in the morning, six o'clock I think it was, Sidney made tea in his room and carried it along to Beatrice, and he then read aloud to her until it was time to get up. And one vivid memory which I have of them is Sidney standing on the terrace at Asham, his little figure and beard silhouetted against the lovely line of downs and a flaming September sunset, explaining to us that they were in their sixties and therefore their expectation of life was now some four or five years, and 'I wish', he said, 'I could compound with'—here he characteristically used the correct technical insurance term—'the Almighty so that she and I would die at exactly the same moment'—Sidney always referred to Beatrice as 'she'.

One other reminiscence of the Webbs. One summer we went and stayed with them for a week-end at a house which they had taken for a month near Three Bridges. Bernard Shaw and Mrs Shaw were the only other week-end guests. Beatrice had a characteristic habit of classifying all her friends or acquaintances in a kind of psychological and occupational card index. Thus Virginia was 'the novelist', I was 'the ex-colonial-civil-servant'—and anything connected with novels which arose in conversation would be referred to Virginia, anything connected with Asia or Africa to me. Beatrice always treated Shaw as the generalised or universal artist and his department was therefore not only the arts generally but anything connected with the embellishment, non-utility side of life. A curious example of this habit of hers took place at lunch one day. There was on the table a vase in which were some flowers. The flowers were sweet peas or pinks—I have forgotten exactly what they were, but they were so common or garden that everyone in Europe except the Webbs would have known their name. Beatrice did not know their name, and as the question came within Shaw's sphere of knowledge according to the psychological-occupational card index, it was solemnly referred to him.

Perhaps as I have dealt with the Webbs here, not with chronological exactitude, I had better go on and deal with Shaw, whom I first met at the Webbs and who for many years was inseparably connected with them. One of the strangest things about him was that he was personally the kindest, most friendly, most charming of men, yet personally he was almost the most impersonal person I have ever known. He was always extremely nice to Virginia and me. If one met him anywhere, he would come up and greet one with what seemed to be warmth and pleasure and he would start straight away with a fountain of words scintillating with wit and humour. You might easily flatter yourself that you were the one person in Europe to whom at that moment the famous George Bernard Shaw wanted to talk, but if you happened to look into that slightly fishy, ice-blue eye of his, you got a shock. It was not looking at you; you were nowhere in its orbit; it was looking through you or over you into a distant world or universe inhabited almost entirely by G.B.S., his thoughts and feelings, fancies and phantasises. Writing this, I remember three more or less casual meetings with him which seem to me wonderfully characteristic. The first was at Golders Green; Virginia and I went to the cremation of H. G. Wells's wife. When we came out, Maynard and Lydia Keynes came up to speak to us. Lydia was in tears. Then Shaw came up and put his hand on Lydia's shoulder and made a kind of oration to her telling her not to cry, that death was not an event to shed tears upon. It was a kindly, even a beautiful and eloquent speech, and yet, though he knew Lydia well and certainly liked her, one felt that it was hardly addressed to this highly individual and warm-hearted woman, who had danced as Lydia Lopokova in Diaghilev's Russian Ballet and out of it into marriage with John Maynard Keynes, but rather to 'someone in tears', who indeed might have been any woman in tears.[1]

The second was in a Committee Room in the House of Commons. It was, I think, a Fabian Committee of which Webb was chairman and I was secretary. Shaw was sitting next to me; on committees he was just like the Shaw not on a committee; he loved to talk paradoxically and amusingly and at considerable length. If Webb was the chairman, G. B. S. was never allowed to get going; he was kept to the point or to silence, and it was usually to silence. On this afternoon, he had been allowed scarcely two sentences, and when the proceedings came to an end, he must have been bursting with words and ideas. He turned to the man sitting on his left, who was an M.P. and one of the dullest and stupidest men I have ever known, and began an extraordinarily brilliant and amusing monologue. I had to discuss some matter of business with Sidney Webb, who was sitting on my right, and, when I had finished, I found that Shaw's splendid display was still going on. Indeed the fireworks went on for another five or ten minutes; it was superb, but I don't think that the M.P. understood, let alone appreciated, a single one of Shaw's squibs, crackers, or rockets. But it made no difference to G. B. S.; it made no difference to him whether he talked to the dummy M.P. or the cleverest man in Europe—the ice-blue eye went through or over the M.P., fixed upon the universe of G. B. S.

The third occasion was in Kensington Gardens. One fine Sunday afternoon Virginia and I went for a walk in the Park and we had just crossed from Hyde Park into Kensington Gardens and were making for the Flower Walk when we met Shaw coming from the opposite direction. He stopped and immediately began to tell us about his

[1] The same scene is described—rather differently—by Mrs Bernard Shaw in a letter to T. E. Lawrence (in *Mrs G. B. S.* by Janet Dunbar, p. 289): 'The moment the coffin was shoved through the door into the furnace, and H. G. and the boys went round, G. B. S. trotted through another door into the garden and I took quite a little time to get quiet. Then we went into the yard to look for the car and found the rest of the congregation—mostly in tears (it was as bad as that). First thing I knew Lopokova flung herself into my arms sobbing and shaking. A tiny thing she is: she felt like a bit of thistledown that had been out in a rainstorm. Then Sydney Olivier, with red eyes, held out a shaking hand: and Virginia herself, looking very stately and calm, and remote, relieved me of Lopokova . . . G. B. S., of course, began to "behave badly" at once, making jokes to everyone, and finally—putting H. G. into his car—he actually got a sort of grin out of *him*.' (I have to thank Miss Dunbar for allowing me to quote this.)

voyage round the world in a 'luxury' liner from which he had just got back. For the next quarter of an hour or twenty minutes he stood in front of us in the characteristic G. B. S. attitude, very erect with folded arms, his beard wagging as he talked, and gave us a brilliant unflagging monologue, describing the ship, the passengers, his audiences, what he said to them, his triumphs. When the fountain of words at last died down and we parted, I found that we were the centre of a wide circle of fifteen or twenty people; they had recognised Shaw and had stopped to listen to his oration as though it were a public entertainment. And it struck me then that that was just exactly what it was. Although we were fond of him and he, I think, in his curious way really liked both of us, the sparkling display to which we had just listened might just as well have been addressed to the twenty strangers gaping at him as to us.

Though Shaw had, quite rightly, a very high opinion of Shaw, he was entirely without the pretentiousness and personal prickliness which nearly always make the great or still more The Very Important Person such an intolerable nuisance. Like the Webbs, he seemed never to resent or to be offended by anything which a younger person said or did to him. No one but Sidney and Beatrice Webb would have shown no resentment when in the heyday of the Fabian Society G. D. H. Cole treated them with the ruthless arrogance of brilliant and foolish youth. When about the same time I wrote *International Government* for the Fabian Society, I found that Shaw had written a preface for it, I insisted that the book should be published in England without Shaw's preface on the ground that, as a young man and writer, I wanted my book to be judged on its merits and defects; it should stand solely on its own legs, and not on those of a great man's preface. I agreed to the preface later appearing in an American and a French edition. Most great men would, I think, have felt some slight resentment or hurt at this treatment of what was a kind and generous act on his part. Many years later I found that the opposite was true of Shaw, for Sir Frederic Osborn showed me a letter written to him in 1917 by Shaw explaining why he should not write a preface to some book and adding:

> I think you will see, on consideration, that Woolf, the author of the Fabian Research Department's book on Supernational Organisation, to which I, as chairman of the Department, had to supply a preface, was quite right in insisting that the English edition should appear in the first instance without my preface.

In the war years, when Virginia and I, recently married, were each just beginning our literary careers, Shaw, H. G. Wells and Arnold Bennett were at the height of their powers and stood together at the zenith of the literary heavens. Of course there was Hardy—and, of course, Conrad and Galsworthy. But Hardy stood by himself, an Olympian surviving from a previous age. Galsworthy seemed to us and to all of our generation a second rate novelist and stuffy, respectable, reactionary. Conrad had been welcomed by all of us in our youth as a writer of great prose—though always, a little uneasily—but he too was 'respectable' and had no contact with or message for our generation. Shaw, Wells and Bennett were stars which formed a very different kind of constellation. We criticised them, and, being of a younger generation, naturally and healthily reacted against them in some directions—as, for instance, Virginia did against Bennett in *Mr Bennett and Mrs Brown*. But we understood them and respected them and to some extent they understood us; at any rate, as European civilisation began to break up under the attacks of the barbarians, we found ourselves always on the same side of the barricades with Shaw, Wells and Bennett.

It is the fate of even stars to fade or die. The red giants dwindle to white dwarfs or to dead black suns. The light of the three giants of 1917 has dimmed, particularly of Wells and Bennett. No doubt this is natural, right and proper, in the logic of time. But looking back over the last forty-five years I still see them as a remarkable trinity—not negligible men or writers. It was fascinating to see the three of them together with the sparks flying. I got to know Wells, as I shall explain later, during the war, and early on in our careers, when I was Literary Editor of the *Nation*, we were asked to dinner by Mrs Wells. We arrived at Whitehall Court punctually and found only H. G. and his wife, son, and secretary there. But soon the door opened and the maid announced Mr and Mrs Bernard Shaw, and a few minutes later it opened again and she announced Mr and Mrs Arnold Bennett. We had hardly met Bennett before, and I felt rather overwhelmed by the galaxy. Bennett did not put me at my ease. I had reviewed his novel, *Lord Raingo*, rather critically in the *Nation*. When we sat down to dinner, Bennett was on Mrs Wells's left and I was on her right with Mrs Shaw on my right; Virginia was at the other end of the table between Shaw and H. G. As soon as we had sat down Bennett fixed me with his eye, leant across, and said 'W-w-woolf d-d-does not l-l-like my novels.' I tried to expostulate that this was not the case, but several times during the dinner the minute gun was fired at me across the table: 'W-w-woolf d-d-does not l-l-like my novels.' The three great men were all personally rather formidable; what interested me, as the evening went on, was to see how dominating Shaw was. At intervals, through our conversation, one heard the fountain of his words going up at the other end of the table, and towards the end we were all dominated by Shaw. Arnold with his slow stutter had no chance of getting a word in and soon resigned himself to firing the minute gun at me. H. G. did not give way without a struggle, but he was no match for Shaw and the Shavian pyrotechnical monologue.

I have said that Shaw was extraordinarily charming and that I think he did, in his own way, like Virginia and me. The following letter which he wrote to Virginia seems to prove this. She had written to him with regard to some point when she was working on her life of Roger Fry:

My dear Virginia, 10th May, 1940.

I do not remember the occasion described by Roger; and I could hardly have dismissed art so summarily from consideration as a social factor as if I had just looked into it as a foreign subject for five minutes or so. As a matter of fact I am an artist to my finger tips, and always contend that I am a highly educated person because I had continual contacts with literature and art, including music, in my childhood, and found school and its Latin and Greek grind nothing but a brutalizing imprisonment which interfered disastrously with my real education. Now that I am nearly 84 I am more convinced than ever that an aesthetic education is the best available, and that the neglect of the aesthetic factor in science has deprived it of its claim to be scientific.

Probably what Roger heard me say was that nothing fundamental can be done by art until the economical problem is solved. I am fond of saying that 12 hours hunger will reduce any saint, artist, or philosopher to the level of a highwayman.

I think my first private meeting with Roger was also my first meeting with Elgar. We three lunched with Madame Vandervelde, then wedded to the late Belgian Socialist Minister. Elgar, who had enjoyed my musical criticisms when he was a student and remembered all my silly jokes, talked music so voluminously that Roger had nothing to do but eat his lunch in silence. At last we stopped to breathe and eat something ourselves; and Roger, feeling that our hostess expected him to contribute something, began in his beautiful voice (his and Forbes Robertson's were the only voices one could listen to for their own sakes) 'After all, there is only one art: all the arts are the same.' I heard no more; for my attention was taken by a growl from the other side of the table. It was Elgar, with his fangs bared and all his hackles bristling, in an appalling rage. 'Music,' he spluttered, 'is written on the skies for you to note down. And you compare that to a DAMNED imitation.'

There was nothing for Roger to do but either to seize the decanter and split Elgar's head with it, or else take it like an angel with perfect dignity. Which latter he did.

I have a picture by Roger which I will give you if you care to have it: a landscape.

I wish we could see more of you and Leonard; but we two are now so frightfully old that we no longer dare to offer our company as a treat to friends who are still in the prime of life.

There is a play of mine called Heartbreak House which I always connect with you because I conceived it in that house somewhere in Sussex where I first met you and, of course, fell in love with you, I suppose every man did.
always yours, consequently
G. Bernard Shaw

I must once more retrace my steps to the point at which I left my career a few pages back and the influence of the Webbs upon it. After my first lunch with them in Grosvenor Road they at once took me in hand and made me come up to a Fabian Society Conference for two days in Keswick. This too was the moment at which the *New Statesman* was being brought to birth and every week the Webbs had a *New Statesman* lunch on, I think, Monday. They invited me to one of the earliest, if not the first, of these. There for the first time I met Clifford Sharp, the editor; Jack (later Sir John) Squire, the Literary Editor; Robert Lynd, one of those impeccable journalists who every week for thirty or forty years turn out an impeccable essay (called in the technical jargon of journalism a 'middle') like an impeccable sausage, about anything or everything or nothing; John Roberts, the manager.

The name of Robert Lynd reminds me of an absurd incident which I cannot refrain from relating out of its order and I will therefore interrupt my account of luncheon with the Webbs by an account of a dinner with Rose Macaulay. Rose, whom we both liked very much, some time, I suppose, in the late twenties asked Virginia and me to dine with her. We thought it was just an ordinary dinner and that we should be alone with her or at most with one or two other guests. When the day came we printed all the afternoon, Virginia setting and I machining, and we got very late. We dashed off without changing, dishevelled and probably with traces of printer's ink still on our persons. To our horror we found a formal dinner party of ten to twelve people (in a restaurant just across the road from Rose's flat) all literary gents and ladies and all immaculate in evening dress. Though we loved Rose, it was the kind of party that both of us loathed, for the literary gent, who may be quite nice when he is in small numbers and in literary mufti, is a bore when he is in a formal herd and evening dress. Being the last to come and obviously having kept them all waiting, conscious of our dirt and dishevelment, we both lost our nerve. I sat by Mrs Lynd and Virginia on the other side of the table was between Robert Lynd and Conal O'Riordan, a prolific novelist who described himself with grim truth in *Who's Who* as a Man of Letters. I began badly; my hand trembled so that I could not eat my soup, and my spoon startled everyone by clattering threateningly upon my plate and splashing the soup perilously near to Sylvia Lynd upon the table cloth. I could think of nothing to say while the conversation began to hum and boom all round the table. Suddenly however it came to a stop in one of those complete silences which fall upon even a literary dinner party. And then in the deathly silence Virginia's beautiful clear voice was heard to say on the other side of the table: 'What do you mean by The Holy Ghost?' To which O'Riordan replied angrily: 'I did not say "Holy Ghost", I said "the whole coast".' I felt that Virginia had disgraced herself and that the whole table felt it too, but everyone tried to hide it by turning and talking animatedly to their neighbours. I turned to Mrs Lynd, and noticing, as I thought, that she had dropped her white napkin on the floor, leaned down and picked it up to give to her. Unfortunately I found that it was not her napkin, but her white petticoat which (wrongly) showed below her skirt. She took it badly and we slunk away as soon as we could after dinner.

To return to Grosvenor Road, it was the first of many *New Stateman* lunches which I have sat through in my life. At this one I was obviously asked by the Webbs for a purpose. They never, as far as I saw, ever interfered at all with Sharp and the editorial side of the paper. But they wanted to introduce me to the editor and his staff in order to give them a chance of employing me and me a chance of being employed by them. In this they were successful. Squire sent me books to review and in a year or two I was reviewing for him practically all the books published on the war, foreign affairs, and international questions. He used to send me enormous parcels of these kinds of books and leave it to me to decide whether to review them or not.

The editor, Clifford Sharp, was the exact opposite, in almost every characteristic, of his literary editor, Jack Squire. Jack was the best type of gay, casual, good tempered, generous Bohemian, a literary gent of the kind which has been indigenous round about Fleet Street since the eighteenth century. Sharp was a curiously chilly and saturnine man with a face or complexion which always looked to me as if it had recently been given a good rub with emery paper. He was unlovable—not a nice man. But, as time went on, I got to feel something towards him which might perhaps be called affection. It was the affection which one sometimes acquires for an old, mangy, surly, slightly dangerous dog. One is rather proud of being one of the few people whom he will—with a growl—allow to pat him gingerly on the head. He was by training an engineer, and he seemed to me to bring to human relations and politics, and so to journalism, the attitude of the engineer, of a sanitary inspector or super-plumber. When he stood in his room—I hardly ever saw him sit down—listening to what one had to say, there was about him an atmosphere of intellectual Jeyes' Fluid, moral carbolic soap, spiritual detergents—to such an extent that I sometimes had the illusion that he himself smelt strongly of soap and his room of disinfectants. Temperamentally and fundamentally he was a conservative of the Disraelian, Rule Britannia, 1878 vintage; but he was also, as the Webbs used to point out with quiet enjoyment, a collectivist. Indeed, collectivism and drainage—material or spiritual—were, I think, the only things Sharp believed in with any flicker of enthusiasm. He liked to think of himself as the hard-boiled tough, without sentimentality, without illusions, without emotions—the realist and no damned nonsense; and his face, particularly the eyes and nose, which made him look like a hooded falcon, helped him to sustain this character. In fact he had the sentimentality of those who make a fuss about being anti-sentimental.

After my first *New Statesman* lunch Sharp told me that he would like to consider articles by me and that I was to come and suggest subjects to him. As a beginner in journalism, I found his methods rather disheartening, until I came to know him better. He was one of those editors who believe in keeping his contributors up to the mark by a liberal use of cold water (perhaps another instance of his sanitation complex). I used to go to the office in Gt Queen Street and suggest an article to him. He would stand in front of the fireplace, his head thrust forward, fix me with a cold eye, and listen in complete silence. He then poured down my back several metaphorical buckets of cold water, and when he had convinced me that the subject suggested was silly and the way I proposed to treat it imbecile and that I had wasted a good deal of his valuable time, he would say: 'Well, Woolf, you may as well go off and see what you can do, I don't say it won't make an article.' I slunk off with my tail between my legs and gloomily wrote what seemed to me a depressed and depressing article. I then took it to Sharp dejectedly expecting him to reject it. He always did take it, and I do not think that it is the euphoria of memory and senility that makes me believe that occasionally he gave it and me a word of grim and tepid praise.

I have known a good many well-known editors: the famous Scott of the *Manchester Guardian*, Wickham Steed of *The Times*, Massingham of the *Daily Chronicle* and *Nation*, Sir Gerald Barry of the *News Chronicle* and *Week-end Review*, Sir Bruce Richmond of *The Times Literary Supplement*, Kingsley Martin of the *New Statesman*. As professional journalists go, Sharp was not a bad editor, though he was not in the very front rank. He performed the first duty of an editor, he impressed upon his paper an indelible character, a journalistic aroma which ultimately was the personal aroma of Sharp. It pervaded every corner of the paper, every article whether signed or unsigned. The way in which a real or 'good' editor pervades his paper is very remarkable; when you write for him his unseen presence broods over your pen or typewriter and unconsciously your thoughts and your words are infected by him. You become a ventriloquist's puppet. For a short time I used to write unsigned articles occasionally for Sharp in the *New Statesman* and for Massingham in the *Nation*. You could not find two men more different in temperament, style, and editorial methods, and, though, when writing for them, I was never conscious of being influenced by them, I know that my articles in the *Statesman* were in the image of Clifford Sharp and in the *Nation* in the image of H. W. Massingham. The image of Sharp was rather bleak and acrid, and to read—or write for—the *New Statesman* always seemed to me rather like sitting in a cold draughty room in which the fire was smoking a little. You might not like it; but at least the paper had a character of its own; it knew what it thought and said it in its own peculiar way—an important and by no means common journalistic merit.

Sharp ruined himself by drinking—a by no means uncommon journalistic failing. It is curious that, though I fairly often used to go and see him at the office latish in the day, when, according to all accounts, he was usually in an obviously drunken state, I had no idea that he drank until the final disaster. Journalism is a highly dangerous profession. Among its many occupational diseases is not only drink, but a kind of fatty degeneration of the mind. Only a few very strong minded men escape the latter disease, the nemesis of successful journalism. I have practised journalism, not unsuccessfully, for fifty years and have been an editor on three different papers. In 1924 I became Literary Editor of the *Nation*, practically a full time job, though I made conditions that I would only go to the office for two and a half days a week. Its effect upon me and my mind was, I am sure, bad, and I resigned after six years, because I felt that it was destroying what mind I had. I made up what mind it had left me never again to take a full time journalistic job.

There are two great mental dangers in journalism. The first is most virulent among editors. It creates a kaleidoscopic, chaotic, perpetual motion rhythm of the mind. As soon as you have produced one number of your paper, you have to begin thinking of and planning the next. Your mind gets into the habit of opening and shutting at regular intervals of twenty-four hours or seven days like the shells of a mussel or the shutter of a camera, and everything in your mind—and indeed in your life—gets to be determined and conditioned by this interval. What you wrote for or published in last week's or yesterday's issue was written or published for a moment of time, last week or yesterday; it is now dead and forgotten and now all that concerns you is what you are publishing or writing for this week or for today. Your mind thus develops a curiously feverish habit of regular and ephemeral opening and shutting. You become a shell fish or a camera, but, unlike them, you soon delude yourself into thinking that the opening and shutting of your mind and the contents of the mollusc or camera are of immense importance. Nearly all good editors—like the owners of some of them, the great newspaper owners—become megalomaniacs and suffer from the hallucination that they control and exercise great power. The hallucination of power corrupts as efficiently as power.

The second occupational disease of journalism is connected closely with the first, but it affects all journalists, not merely editors. What you write for a paper you write for a moment of time, the moment being a morning or an evening, a week, a month, or three months. Whatever the length of the moment, what you produce is written under the shadow of ephemerality; you write it not in the mould of eternity, but for consumption with the kipper or eggs and bacon at the breakfast table or to distract someone from falling asleep in a railway carriage. There is, however, writing which is quite different from this, 'serious' literature or the art of literature. Literature may be a novel or a history, an essay or a poem; it is written not with the eggs and bacon, but sub specie aeternitatis. It is incompatible with journalese. Of course, occasionally and incidentally a work of serious literature has got into a newspaper and nearly all modern serious writers write for the papers. But generally habitual or professional journalism destroys any ability to write literature. In the vast majority of journalists this does not matter, for they are journalists and not potentially artists. But every now and again a serious writer is destroyed or maimed by journalism.

This is, I think, a point which has become more and more important with the enormous growth of popular journalism and of the incomes of popular journalists during my lifetime. The temptation in journalism is terrific for the young man or woman who has to earn a living and yet wants to be and perhaps might be a serious writer. 'I will earn my living in Fleet Street,' they think, 'and write my masterpiece in the evenings and at week-ends.' But newspaper offices are paved with unwritten masterpieces. If you want to write a masterpiece in the evening, the last thing you should do during the day is to write journalism or indeed to have anything to do with writing. When I was Literary Editor of the *Nation*, young men and women from Oxford and Cambridge were continually coming to me for advice; they wanted to write masterpieces, usually novels, and their idea was to earn their living by journalism or in a publishing office; they wanted me to tell them how to start. My advice was: 'Don't. If you want to write a masterpiece in the evening, you have an infinitely better chance of doing so by being a cook or a gardener during the day than if you write second rate stuff or mess about with books and writing all day.' I do not think that any of them took my advice or that any of them has written a masterpiece.

There is another snare and delusion in journalism for the young writer. When you write for an editor and a paper, particularly when you write what is unsigned, but even if your name appears, in a curious way you escape responsibility. This often has a very bad, if not fatal, effect upon a would-be serious writer. I am thinking of a person like Desmond MacCarthy. I was given a good dressing down by *The Times Literary Supplement* reviewer of my book *Sowing* because I wrote in it that when we were young men at Cambridge we thought of Desmond as 'someone upon whom the good fairies appeared to have lavished every possible gift both of body and of mind', that he seemed to be 'in the making a writer, a novelist of the highest quality', and that 'as a writer he never achieved anything at all of what he promised'. The reviewer, who admittedly only met Desmond, middle-aged or elderly, entertaining aristocratic or non-aristocratic dinner tables with his entrancing conversation, says that this is complete nonsense, Desmond 'surely could never have been a novelist even of passable quality, for he lacked that power of organisation demanded by the novel, and indeed by even the shortest of short stories. This was manifest in his appearance, which, in the most engaging way, suggested a dishevelled bird just fallen out of the nest'. And not only did his middle-aged appearance show that he could never have written even a passable short story, 'his special gift for conversation' might also have revealed it to us in 1903.

The reviewer is mistaken and he arrives at his wrong conclusion by making a number of mistakes, large and small, on the way. First, he like many other people is really assuming that because a thing happened it and nothing else had to happen. Because Desmond never did write a novel, he never could have written a novel. This simplifies life, history, and people, and if it were true it would be unnecessary to write or review biographies or autobiographies. But there is no reason to believe it to be true and his own arguments are so bad that they tell against him. Take for instance his view that because Desmond looked like a dishevelled bird it proved that he could not write a passable novel. It is true that Desmond did look like a dishevelled bird when he was middle-aged and he knew it himself—hence his characteristic pen name Affable Hawk. But when I first saw Desmond—he was twenty-six and just returned from a Grand Tour of Europe—there was nothing of the dishevelled fledgling fallen from the nest about him; he looked like a superb young eagle who with one sweep of his great wing could soar to any height he chose. He not only looked it; the good fairies had lavished upon him every possible gift and particularly those gifts which every would-be writer and novelist would pray for. Why did he never fulfil his promises? Why did the splendid eagle degenerate into an affable hawk, a dishevelled fledgling? The answer is infinitely more complicated than the reviewer's superficial explanation.

It is infinitely more complicated because the human being is psychologically so infuriatingly complex that you can never explain his thoughts, actions, or character by trotting out a single superficial cause. One of the difficulties is that in the human mind the same element is at the same time both a cause and an effect. Thus in the case of Desmond it is probably true to say that 'his special gift of conversation' was a cause of his not writing novels, but it is also true that (1) it was an *excuse* for his not writing novels, and (2) his not writing novels was a cause of his special gift for conversation. One summer Desmond came to stay for a few days with us in the country at Asham House. He was slightly depressed when he arrived and soon told us the reason. His friend A. F. Wedgwood, the novelist, had recently died leaving a posthumous novel and Desmond had promised the widow to write an introduction and memoir of the author for the book. He had continually put off doing this; the book had been printed, was ready for binding, and was completely held up for Desmond's introduction; the publisher was desperate and desperately bombarding Desmond with reply paid telegrams. Desmond had sworn that he would write the thing over the week-end and post it to the publisher on Monday morning. He asked me to promise that next morning I would lock him up in a room by himself and not let him out until he had finished the introduction. And he told me then that he really suffered from a disease: the moment he knew that he ought to do something, no matter what that something was, he felt absolutely unable to do it and would do anything else in order to prevent himself from doing it. It did not matter what 'it' might be; it might be something which he actually wanted to do, but if it was also something which he knew he *ought* to do, he would find himself doing something which he did not want to do in order to prevent himself doing something which he ought to do and wanted to do.

Here, for instance, was a fairly common situation in Desmond's life; he is engaged to dine at 7.30 with someone whom he likes very much in Chelsea; he looks forward to the evening; at seven he is sitting in a room at the other end of London talking to two or three people whom he does not very much like and who are in fact boring him; at 7.05 he begins to feel that he ought to get up and leave for Chelsea; at 7.30 he is still sitting with the people whom he does not much like and is uncomfortably keeping them from their dinner; at eight they insist that he must stay and dine with them; at 8.05 he rings up his Chelsea friends, apologises, and says that he will be with them in twenty minutes.

I should add that that evening at Asham Desmond recovered his spirits and was in fine form. After we had gone to bed, we heard him for a short time walking up and down the corridor groaning: 'O God! God!' Next morning he was quite cheerful when I locked him in the sitting room. An hour later he thumped on the door and shouted: 'You must let me out, Leonard, you must let me out.' He had run out of cigarettes and I weakly let him out so that he could walk over to Rodmell, a mile away, and buy some at the village shop. I cannot remember whether when he left us on Monday or Tuesday morning, he had finished the introduction. I rather think he had not.

Now one of the several reasons why Desmond never fulfilled his youthful aquiline promise and never wrote that brilliant novel which in 1903 lay embryonically in his mind was that he thought he *ought* to write a novel and that the novel *ought* to be absolutely first class. Desmond was in many ways Moore's favourite apostle and Desmond loved and followed Moore with the purity and intensity of the disciple devoted to the guru or sage. He, as an impressionable young man, like all of us in the Cambridge of those days, took *Principia Ethica* as a bible of conduct. In Volume 1, pp. 91-5, I tried to describe and define this influence of Moore and his book upon us. The book told us what we *ought* to do and what we ought not to do, and, when one thought of those words, it was impossible not to see and hear Moore himself, the impassioned shake of his head on the emphasised words as he said: 'I think one *ought* to do that,' or 'I think one ought *not* to do that.' So when Desmond sat down to write, an invisible Moore, with the 'oughts' and 'ought nots', stood behind his chair. But both as a man and a writer his gifts were of a lyrical kind; they had to be given a free hand; his imagination would not work and so he could not write on a tight, intellectual rein.

The best, said the Greeks, is the enemy of the good. The vision of the best, the ghostly echoes of *Principia Ethica*, the catechism which always begins with the terrifying words: 'What exactly do you *mean* by that?', inhibited Desmond. When he wrote 'seriously', he began to labour, and the more he tinkered with what he wrote the more laboured and laborious it became. This brings me back to the point from which I started, the effect of journalism upon Desmond and writers like him. Journalism provided him with the easy way out of his difficult and complicated situation as regards writing a novel. He thought that he ought to write a novel—something serious—and as the habit grew upon him of not being able to do what he thought he ought to do, the habit of always doing something else in order to avoid doing what he ought to do, writing the weekly article for the *New Statesman* or *Sunday Times* became his refuge and shelter from his duty to be a great writer. (Of course, there was the further stage that, when the moment came at which he *ought* to begin writing the article, he had to find something else to prevent his doing so, and it was only a devoted and efficient secretary who managed somehow or other to get Affable Hawk's article, usually a few minutes after the very last moment, to an infuriated printer.)

But writing an article as a refuge for Desmond against doing what he ought to do, i.e. writing a novel, was only part of the story. In literature he had tremendously high standards, and, if he had ever been inclined to lower them, the memories of Cambridge, Moore, and *Principia Ethica* would have warned him off. To write a book, say a novel, as a serious artist, requires a good many qualities, by no means common, besides the ability to write. However sensitive you may be to praise or blame, you have to be at some point ruthless and impervious—and ruthless to yourself. The moment comes when the writer must say to himself: 'I don't care what they say about it and me; I shall publish and be damned to them.' And he has to accept responsibility, the responsibility for what he has written; he must strip himself artistically naked before the public and take the icy plunge. People like Desmond, once they begin to doubt whether what they are writing is really any good—and such doubts occasionally torture practically all good writers—cannot stay the course. They cannot force themselves through those despairing moments of grind in the long distance race before you get your second wind and they cannot face responsibility. Here again journalism is the refuge. Even *Principia Ethica* would allow one to lower one's standards in the *Sunday Times* or *New Statesman*, where one is writing not sub specie aeternitatis, but for a short weekend. And in any case the responsibility is not so much yours as the editor's. Journalism is the opiate of the artist; eventually it poisons his mind and his art.

Off and on over the years I saw a great deal of Desmond, walking and talking with him at all hours of day and night, watching him try to write and even occasionally working with him. I am sure that his psychology as a writer was more or less that analysed by me in the previous paragraphs. One can only add that the charm of the dead cannot be reproduced second-hand in words. One can only record the fact that Desmond was the most charming of men, the most amusing companion, and finally had about him in friendship the honesty and faithfulness which I associate with old sheep dogs.

When I had written this, I remembered that Virginia had once in her diaries, when after being ill she was for a time only able to write her novel for an hour a day, amused herself by writing short accounts of her friend's characters. I turned up what she had written about Desmond and this is what she said in January 1919:

How many friends have I got? There's Lytton, Desmond, Saxon: they belong to the Cambridge stage of life; very intellectual . . . I can't put them in order, for there are too many. Ka and Rupert and Duncan, for example, all come rather later . . . Desmond has *not* rung up. That is quite a good preface to the description of his character. The difficulty which faces one in writing of Desmond is that one is almost forced to describe an Irishman. How he misses trains, seems born without a rudder to drift wherever the current is strongest; how he keeps hoping and planning, and shuffles along, paying his way by talking so enchantingly that editors forgive and shopmen give him credit and at least one distinguished peer leaves him a thousand in his will . . . Where was I? Desmond, and how I find him sympathetic compared with Stracheys. It is true; I'm not sure he hasn't the nicest nature of any of us—the nature one would soonest have chosen for one's own. I don't think that he possesses any faults as a friend, save that his friendship is so often sunk under a cloud of vagueness, a sort of drifting vapour composed of times and seasons separates us and effectively prevents us from meeting. Perhaps such indolence implies a slackness of fibre in his affections too—but I scarcely feel that. It arises rather from the consciousness which I find imaginative and attractive that things don't altogether *matter*. Somehow he is fundamentally sceptical. Yet which of us, after all, takes more trouble to do the sort of kindness that comes his way? Who is more tolerant, more appreciative, more understanding of human nature? It goes without saying that he is not an heroic character. He finds pleasure too pleasant, cushions too soft, dallying too seductive and then as I sometimes feel now, he has ceased to be ambitious. His 'great work' (it may be philosophy or biography now, and is certainly to be begun, after a series of long walks, this very spring) only takes shape, I believe, in that hour between tea and dinner, when so many things appear not only possible, but achieved. Comes the daylight, and Desmond is contented to begin his article; and plies his pen with a half humorous half melancholy recognition that such is his appointed life. Yet it is true, and no one can deny it, that he has the floating elements of something brilliant, beautiful—some book of stories, reflection, studies, scattered about in him, for they show themselves indisputably in his talk. I'm told he wants power; that these fragments never combine into an argument; that the disconnection of talk is kind to them; but in a book they would drift hopelessly apart. Consciousness of this, no doubt, led him in his one finished book to drudge and sweat until his fragments were clamped together in an indissoluble stodge. I can see myself, however, going through his desk one of these days, shaking out unfinished pages from between sheets of blotting paper, and deposits of old bills, and making up a short book of table talk, which shall appear as a proof to the younger generation that Desmond was the most gifted of us all. But why did he never do anything? they will ask.

There is something of Desmond in Bernard in *The Waves*. ' "Had I been born," said Bernard, "not knowing that one word follows another I might have been, who knows, perhaps anything. As it is, finding sequences everywhere, I cannot bear the pressure of solitude. When I cannot see words curling like rings of smoke around me I am in darkness—I am nothing. When I am alone I fall into lethargy, and say to myself dismally as I poke the cinders through all the bars, Mrs Moffat will come. She will come and sweep it all up." ' That was true of Desmond; he had a tremendous zest for life and friends and phrases and also that streak of melancholia when he fell into despair alone in front of the dying fire. Then he wrinkled his forehead and groaned 'O God! God!', and left it in despair for one of the innumerable Mrs Moffats to sweep it all up. Of course, one of them came, for in 999,999 cases out of a million there is a Mrs Moffat to sweep it all up for the Desmonds of this world. His wife Molly was one of them all her life; but an incompetent Mrs Moffat, for she was much too charming, amusing, hesitant, and unsure of herself to be any good at sweeping up anything. She was one of those people whose minds go blank the moment they are faced by the slightest crisis; her vagueness and fluttering indecision must have been perpetually nourished by a lifetime of waiting for Desmond to return to dinner to which he had forgotten that he had invited several friends. The way that Molly's mind refused to work is shown by the following affectionate memory of her. One week-end she and W. B. Yeats were both staying at Garsington. On Saturday night after dinner the poet, as his way was, got off on one of his, to me boring, disquisitions about spirits, second sight, and mediums. He suddenly turned to Molly and said that he was sure that she was psychic and she must let him try to get her to 'see' things. Much against her will Molly at last gave in and said flutteringly that she could try. There were I suppose some ten or twelve people sitting around in the drawing-room, and poor Molly was seated in a chair next to Yeats who performed the usual ceremony of mumbo jumbo. There was a moment of complete silence, and then Yeats said: 'And now what do ye see, my dear?' Molly's mind went absolutely blank; she saw nothing and could not even think of anything which she might see. Yeats became agitated 'Come now, my dear, come now, ye must see something.' A long paralysing silence, and then Molly said miserably: 'Yes, I think I do see something—a frog.' Yeats was outraged.

To return for a moment to Desmond. Bernard has something of Desmond in him, even in the last speech where he sits alone in the restaurant and talks about phrases. But Bernard is not Desmond; none of Virginia's characters are drawn completely or photographically from life. The final heroic charge against death, 'unvanquished and unyielding', was not in Desmond. The last time I saw him, not long before he died, I walked away from him from the house in Gordon Square where we had had a Memoir Club meeting. It was 11 o'clock and a cold autumn night. He was suffering terribly from asthma and was racked by a sudden fit of it as we turned out of the Square. I made him wait while I ran off to find a taxi. When I put him into the taxi, he looked, not like an affable hawk or even a dishevelled fledgling, but like a battered, shattered, dying rook. At the corner of Gordon Square I suddenly saw him again as a young man walking with me on the hills above Hunter's Inn in Devonshire when we were on an Easter 'reading party' with Moore and Lytton. There are few things more terrible than such sudden visions of one's friends in youth and vigour through the miseries of age and illness. I left Desmond sitting in the taxi, affectionate, dejected, unheroic, because so obviously broken and beaten by asthma and by life; but brave in not complaining and not pretending and in still, when he could, making his joke and his phrase.

I have been led to say this about Desmond because I was discussing the effect of journalism on the would-be serious writer. In the two years and four months between my resignation from the Ceylon Civil Service in April, 1912, and the outbreak of war in August 1914 I had chosen my profession. I had become a writer of books, earning from them an average of six pounds per annum, and a freelance journalist with a completely unknown earning capacity and future before me. Then the shot was fired in Sarajevo which destroyed the civilisation and the way of life which I had known in the first thirty-four years of my life.

3

The 1914 War

On Saturday 1 August 1914, in the afternoon, I bicycled from Asham to Seaford to bathe in the sea, as I did on many fine days that summer. It was a hot day and I swam out to a diving raft moored some little distance from the shore. I dived a long dive into the sea and came up against a large man with a large red face who was swimming out from the beach. I apologised and he said to me, almost casually: 'Do you know it's war?' We swam side by side for a bit and he told me that he was a London policeman on two weeks holiday, and, although he had had only a few days of his holiday, he had that morning had a telegram recalling him to duty in London. 'It's war,' he said again dejectedly, as we swam towards the beach; 'otherwise they wouldn't have recalled me.' That was how I first learnt that the war was inevitable and that nineteenth-century civilisation was ending. On Sunday 2 August, and Monday 3 August, I walked to Lewes and back eight miles after tea to hear what the news might be, for it was still nineteenth-century civilisation for us at Asham with no car, no buses, no telephone, and no newspaper unless one walked into Lewes to get one. The spectacle of the outbreak of war and the death of civilisation as seen by me in Lewes was depressing. I stood about with some twenty or thirty other depressed persons outside the Post Office where short notices were posted up from time to time or at the railway station hoping to get somehow or other news of something definite. It came at last—we were at war, and I walked back the four miles to Asham.

It was, I think, the day that war broke out that Virginia and I walked from Asham to what is now Peacehaven and Telscombe Cliffs on the coast road between Newhaven and Brighton. The walk there and back was six or seven miles, beginning in the Ouse valley across the river, up through Southease on to the downs and then over the top of the down to the sea. That day now fifty years ago we passed, a quarter of a mile from Asham, Itford Farm, the house standing much as it did 500 years before and looking on to a valley which, except for the railway line, had changed little since 1414. In Southease we passed the church which stood there unchanged for 700 years, the farm which was unchanged since the eighteenth century, the rectory hidden by trees, and two or three cottages. After Southease across the down, the fields of stubble or uncut corn in the hollows, the shepherd and his great flock of sheep and his dog on the top or on the slopes, and no sign of human habitation all the way to the sea, except that one could just see a mile or more away above Piddinghoe a building known locally as Mad Misery Barn, a name which I always thought must be a corruption of Me Miserere. And when one got to the coast road overlooking the sea there were visible, looking east and west and north, only three or four houses, a few cottages, a largish farm house, and the Post Office which supplied teas as well as stamps.

In the tea room, we found, to our surprise and slight annoyance, Jack Pollock (the son of old Sir Fred),[1] who had been a young Fellow of Trinity when I was up at Cambridge, and Prince and Princess Bariatinsky. Jack Pollock some years later married the princess and still later, when old Sir Fred died, succeeded to the baronetcy. I do not know what that strange party was doing at Telscombe Cliffs greeting the great war with tea and cakes. But our meeting now in memory seems to me an appropriate part of the unreality, the dreamlike catastrophe of the August days of 1914.

I have described the walk in some detail because when I look back to it, I see that part of the civilisation which the war destroyed was the environment, the country and the country life, through which Virginia and I walked to the sea that day. Before the end of the war a company bought a stretch of land near Telscombe Cliffs Post Office and offered it for sale in building plots. They called it Anzac Cove, and, when this did not succeed, Anzac Cove was rechristened Peacehaven. Acre plots of land began to be sold and a rash of

[1] Sir Frederick Pollock, Eton and Trinity College, Cambridge, died at the age of ninety-two in 1937. He was an Apostle and I therefore got to know him when I was an undergraduate, but he was also a friend of the Stephen family. He was a strange, tough and stringy man of great and universal learning. He was Second Classic at Cambridge, Fellow of Trinity, Professor of Jurisprudence, a K. C., an authority on the history of law. When Virginia published a novel, she often received from him a letter of somewhat pedantic appreciation, pointing out minute errors about anything ranging from literature to seismology or ornithology. The last time I saw him was at a party on the stage of Sadler's Wells Theatre—he must have been about ninety. His toughness was shown by the fact that, at about the same age, he was knocked down by a boy on a bicycle. I was told that the nonagenarian was unhurt; it was the boy who died.

bungalows, houses, shops, shacks, chicken runs, huts, and dog kennels began to spread over Peacehaven and Telscombe Cliffs. It soon covered practically all the land between Newhaven and Brighton, smothering the fields and the downs, and beyond Brighton to Worthing and Littlehampton so that the south coast of England has become an almost unbroken chain of suburbs. This development seems to be, as I said, part of the destruction of the civilisation, the way of life, which existed in Sussex and vast stretches of England before 1914. There were tremendous evils in that way of life and much of the civilisation deserved destruction. But I don't see any point in destroying unless you put something rather better in the place of what you destroy. I can see nothing whatever to be said for Anzac Cove and Peacehaven, and for what they have put in place of what they destroyed around the Post Office and tea room at Telscombe Cliffs. No sane man would walk to Peacehaven from Asham today for on the way he would see lovely downs spattered with ugly buildings and, when he got there, he would find all round him, as far as the eye can see, miles of disorderly ugliness, shoddiness, and squalor. If one has to choose between the sheep and sheepdog, not to speak of the shepherd, of 1914 and the respectable devotees of T.V., football pools, and bingo who flock into the hideous houses which in 1963 are flung together higgledy piggledy in Peacehaven, then I am not sure that one should not prefer the civilisation of the sheep.

And now I must face the task of dealing with our life during the four years of war. Our life during those four years was dominated not only by the war, but also by Virginia's illness, and I must therefore begin with the illness. In the first chapter of this book I have given some account of the nature and symptoms of the neurasthenia, as the doctors called it, from which she suffered. As I explained there, I had had no experience of insanity or mental illness and it took me some time before I realised the seriousness of her symptoms and the razor edge of sanity upon which her mind was often balanced. I was already troubled and apprehensive when we returned from our honeymoon in the autumn of 1912. All through the first seven months of 1913 I became more and more concerned, for the danger symptoms or signals became more and more serious. In January and February she was finishing *The Voyage Out*, writing every day with a kind of tortured intensity. I did not know then what over the years we learnt bitterly by experience, that the weeks or months in which she finished a book would always be a terrific mental and nervous strain upon her and bring her to the verge of a mental breakdown. It was not merely the strain of the mental intensity with which she always wrote, the artistic integrity and ruthlessness which made her drive herself remorselessly towards perfection. She also suffered from what most people would say was a weakness or fault of character, but which was intricately entangled with her mental instability, an almost pathological hypersensitiveness to criticism, so that she suffered an ever increasingly agonising nervous apprehension as she got nearer and nearer to the end of her book and the throwing of it and of herself to the critics.

I have never kept a proper diary recording events and comment upon events, but for the last fifty years or more I have kept a skeleton diary in which I enter in a few lines a bare account of what I do each day. Very occasionally in times of crisis, when I want to make the record unintelligible to anyone but myself, I make my entries in cypher mainly composed of a mixture of Sinhalese and Tamil letters. My diary of the year 1913 shows very clearly the rapid progress of Virginia's illness and of my apprehension. From January to August I noted almost daily the state of her health, whether she could work, how she slept, whether she had sensations of headache; and in August I began to keep the diary in cypher.

The diary shows that after she finished the book and I had taken it to the publisher in March, she was continually suffering from bouts of intense worry and insomnia, and every now and again from the headache which was the danger signal of something worse. From time to time Sir George Savage was consulted, and some time in the spring it was at last definitely decided that it would not be safe for her to have a child. We spent most of our time in London in Cliffords Inn, but sometimes went for week-ends and holidays to Asham. In the first two weeks of July I became more and more alarmed. The symptoms of headache increased, she could not sleep, she would hardly eat anything. She could not work and became terribly depressed, and what was most alarming, she refused to admit that she was ill and blamed herself for her condition. I knew now that this irrational sense of guilt had been a symptom of her previous breakdown and had led to her jumping out of a window in an attempt to commit suicide. I realised in the first week of July when we were at Asham that one had to face the danger of suicide. I had undertaken to go to and speak at a Fabian Conference in Keswick on

22 July and Virginia insisted that I should go and that she was well enough to come with me. We went and it was the beginning of a nightmare which lasted for several months, one of those appalling nightmares which, because they belong to the world of reality and yet seem to be overlaid with unreality, have the double horror of the collapse of one's everyday life and, at the same time, of the most fantastic and devastating dream.

As soon as we got to the hotel at Keswick, Virginia became worse and went to bed and she remained in bed for the greater part of the two days of the conference. When we got back to London, I took her to see Sir George Savage. He said she must go at once to a nursing home in Twickenham and stay there for some weeks, remaining in bed. She had been to this nursing home several times before when there had been serious threatenings of breakdown. It was kept by a Miss Jean Thomas, who made a speciality of taking nerve or mental patients. She was somewhat emotional and adored Virginia, a combination which had its disadvantages, but old Savage thought well of her and Virginia liked her up to a point and was willing to go to her for a week or two.

It was at the interview with Savage that he made her a promise which led to catastrophe; he said that if she would agree to go to the nursing home for a week or two and rest absolutely in bed under Jean's directions, she could go away for a holiday in Somerset with me in August. We had more than once stayed at an inn in the little village of Holford in the Quantocks and we had planned to go and stay there for some weeks in August. Virginia went into Jean's nursing home on 25 July and she stayed there until 11 August. She appeared to be a good deal better and on 11 August we went down to Asham meaning to stay there until 23 August when we proposed to go to Holford. The nightmares closed in upon us again during those twelve days. It became clear that she was no better. She was terribly worried, full of delusions about her own mind, sleepless, eating hardly anything. I became convinced that at any moment she might fall into complete despair and try to kill herself; what would the position be if we were alone in a small inn in an isolated Somerset village? To go off there with her in her present state seemed to me to make a catastrophe almost inevitable.

On 22 August we went up to London on our way to Holford and stayed the night in Gordon Square with Vanessa. In the afternoon I went to Savage, explained the situation, and said that in my opinion it was terribly risky to take Virginia in her present state of mind to a small inn in the country. He rather pooh-poohed the danger and said that he thought that in any case we must go, for if she was in the state described by me, suddenly to tell her that she was not well enough to go away would throw her into despair and she would immediately try to kill herself. I had lost all confidence in old Savage and felt that I was in a hopeless quandary. When I got back to Gordon Square, I discussed the whole situation with Vanessa and with Roger, who happened to be there. They agreed with me that it was extremely dangerous to take Virginia to Holford. Roger suggested that he should take me at once to Dr Henry Head, a brilliant physician whom he knew well, and see what he would say. Head was a well-known consultant, a neurologist and an F.R.S. He was himself an intellectual and would understand a person like Virginia better than a man like Savage. We rang him up and he agreed to see me at once. I explained the situation and what I thought Virginia's mental condition was. He said that it was terribly risky to take her to Holford, but, as she had been told by Savage that she could go there, it would be still more disastrous suddenly to tell her that she was not well enough to go away. If we did that, she would almost certainly try to kill herself. I had better go with her as arranged next day to Holford and, of course, keep a continual and unobtrusive watch over her. It was possible that if I could get her to rest and eat there, she would begin slowly to mend. If I found that she got worse and more depressed, I must somehow or other get a friend to come down and stay as a second line of defence against an attempt at suicide. If then she still got worse and I felt that the situation was getting out of control, I must bring her back to town and try to induce her to come and see him (Head). I should write to him from time to time and keep him informed of how things were going on.

We went down to Holford on 23 August. Fifty years ago it was a remote, lovely little village at the foot of the Quantock hills. It contained the pleasant Alfoxton or Alfoxden House in which William and Dorothy Wordsworth lived in 1797 and 1798. And only a few miles away in the village of Nether Stowey is the house where Coleridge lived. Walking on the top of the Quantocks above Holford with Wordsworth he began to compose *The Ancient Mariner*, and Dorothy's entries in her Journal for 22 and 23 March are:

22nd.—I spent the morning in starching and hanging out linen; walked

through the wood in the evening, very cold.
23rd.—Coleridge dined with us. He brought the ballad finished. We walked with him to the Miner's house. A beautiful evening, very starry, the horned moon.

In 1913 the horned moon above Holford Combe was the same as Dorothy had seen in 1798 and I don't think that really there had been much change in Nether Stowey and Holford and the Coombe since the February night when the Wordsworths and Coleridge walked to the Miner's house. Certainly if they had walked into the Plough Inn and joined us at dinner, they would have found it much the same as they had seen it 115 years before.

It was primitive but extraordinarily pleasant. The people who kept it—I have forgotten their name—were pure Holford country folk. I knew them well as I had stayed there before. As the days went by, they saw what state Virginia was in and they behaved with the greatest kindness, sensitiveness and consideration. I don't suppose that today there is anywhere in Britain an inn such as the Plough was in 1913. The food was delicious, the most English of English food which could hold its own with the best cuisine of the world, but which people who for the past 150 years have despised all English cooking have never heard of. Nothing could be better than the bread, butter, cream, and eggs and bacon of the Somersetshire breakfast with which you began your morning. The beef, mutton, and lamb were always magnificent and perfectly cooked; enormous hams, cured by themselves and hanging from the rafters in the kitchen, were so perfect that for years we used to have them sent to us from time to time and find them as good as or better than the peach-fed Virginian hams which one used to buy for vast sums from Fortnum and Mason. As for the drink that they offered you, I do not say that you could compare it with, say, Ch. Margaux or La Romanée-Conti or Deidesheimer Kieselberg Riesling Trockenbeerenauslese, but they gave you beer and cider which only a narrow minded, finicky drinker would fail to find delicious.

For the first week at Holford Virginia was very up and down. She insisted that she was perfectly well; she slept badly; it was with the greatest difficulty that she could be persuaded to eat; she certainly suffered from various delusions, for instance that people laughed at her. I had veronal tablets and I gave her one when she could not sleep. After the first seven days she was definitely worse—more depressed. The strain for one person to look after her was considerable, for I had to be on the alert continually, day and night, and yet, if possible, not give her the feeling of being watched. I had arranged with Ka Cox (who later married Will Arnold-Forster), a great friend of both of us, that, if I found it absolutely necessary, I would wire to her to come and join us. After the first week I came to the conclusion that it was not safe for one person alone to look after Virginia and I wired to Ka. She arrived on 2 September. She was extremely good, but nothing could really be done. We lived the quietest possible life, walking a bit and reading. Things grew steadily worse and it became impossible to get Virginia to eat or to try to rest—the only things which might have done her good. After a few days both Ka and I agreed that it was not safe to go to Holford and that I must, somehow or other, induce Virginia to come up to London and see a doctor.

What happened then shows that the working of the human mind, ill or well, insane or sane, is extraordinary and unpredictable. I went to Virginia and said that I thought we should not go on any longer in Holford; that I thought she was ill and so did her doctor and we were convinced that if she ate well and tried to rest she would soon recover as she had several times before; that she was convinced that she was not ill, that her condition was due to her own faults, and that eating and resting made her worse. I suggested that we should return to London at once, go to another doctor—any doctor whom she should choose; she should put her case to him and I would put mine; if he said that she was not ill, I would accept his verdict and would not worry her again about eating or resting or going to a nursing home; but if he said she was ill, then she would accept his verdict and undergo what treatment he might prescribe.

At first Virginia objected to the whole idea, but after some argument she agreed. When I asked her what doctor she would go to, she amazed me by saying at once that she would go to Head. It seemed to me at the time a kind of miracle. It was to Head that I wanted her to go, but I had always anticipated insuperable difficulties to getting her agreement to consult him. She could not possibly have known that *I* had consulted him, and, had she known, in her then state of mind, it would naturally have influenced her against him. When she said that she would go to Head, I felt for a moment as if she had read my thoughts, had taken the thought out of my mind. I do not think that she did this in any sense of thought reading. We often knew instinctively what the other was thinking, as is so often the case when two people live together continually and intimately. But I have never felt that this is in any strict sense of the words thought transference. We thought so often about the same things at the same time, even without talking about them, and therefore often at a particular moment we could guess what at that precise moment was in the other's mind. It is probable that what influenced her to choose Head was that Roger used to talk about him as not only an intelligent doctor, but also an intelligent man—and the two things do not necessarily go together.

I wired to Head for an appointment and on Monday afternoon, 8 September, we took the train from Bridgwater to London. The journey had that terrible quality of the most real of real life and at the same time of a horrible dream, a nightmare. Virginia was in the blackest depair and there was, I knew, danger that she might at any moment try to kill herself by jumping out of the train. However, we reached London in safety and went to spend the night in Brunswick Square. Next day we went to see Head in the afternoon. I gave my account of what had happened and Virginia gave hers. He told her that she was completely mistaken about her own condition; she was ill, ill like a person who had a cold or typhoid fever; but if she took his advice and did what he prescribed, her symptoms would go and she would be quite well again, able to think and write and read; she must go to a nursing home and stay in bed for a few weeks, resting and eating.

We returned to Brunswick Square and then a catastrophe happened. Vanessa came and talked to Virginia, who seemed to become more cheerful. Savage had not known that we were seeing Head and a rather awkward situation had arisen about that. Head asked me to see Savage and explain how it had come about that I had brought Virginia to see him; he wanted me to arrange for him to have a consultation with Savage next day. I went off to Savage, leaving Ka with Virginia. I was with Savage at 6.30 when I got a telephone message from Ka to say that Virginia had fallen into a deep sleep. I hurried back to Brunswick Square and found that Virginia was lying on her bed breathing heavily and unconscious. She had taken the veronal tablets from my box and swallowed a very large dose. I telephoned to Head and he came, bringing a nurse. Luckily Geoffrey Keynes, Maynard's brother, now Sir Geoffrey, then a young surgeon, was staying in the house. He and I got into his car and drove off as fast as we could to his hospital to get a stomach pump. The drive, like everything else during those days, had the nightmare feeling about it. It was a beautiful sunny day; we drove full speed through the traffic, Geoffrey shouting to policemen that he was a surgeon 'urgent, urgent!' and they passed us through as if we were a fire engine. I do not know what time it was when we got back to Brunswick Square, but Head, Geoffrey, and the nurse were hard at work until nearly one o'clock in the morning. Head returned at nine next morning (Wednesday) and said that Virginia was practically out of danger. She did not recover consciousness until the Thursday morning.

The responsibility for the catastrophe was in no way Ka's; it was mine. At Holford I had always kept my case containing the veronal locked. In the turmoil of arriving and settling in at Brunswick Square and then going to Head, I must have forgotten to lock it. When I went to Savage, Virginia lay down on her bed and Ka quite rightly left her so that she might if possible get some sleep. My case was in the room and she must have found that it was unlocked and have taken the veronal. I suppose, as a truthful autobiographer, I ought to record two psychological bad marks against myself in connection with this catastrophe. Though I was the cause of it, I did not at the time and have not since felt the misery and remorse that many people would think I ought to feel. This was due partly to the general fact, recorded by me in Volume 1 (pp. 6 and 9-10), that I seem to be without a sense of sin and to be unable to feel remorse for something which has been done and cannot be undone—I seem to be mentally and morally unable to cry over spilt milk. In this particular case I felt that it was almost impossible sooner or later not to make a mistake of the kind. For the previous two months I had had to be on the watch day and night to prevent a disaster of this kind. No person by himself could really do this, and even after Ka came and we were two, it was not enough. This is shown by the fact that after the catastrophe, we had for weeks four trained nurses, so that there were always two in the room with Virginia day and night. The second psychological black mark—probably not unconnected with the first—is that, after that appalling day and night, when I went to bed at one in the morning, I immediately fell into a profound and peaceful sleep and did not wake up until seven hours later. This again confirms what I said in Volume 1 (p. 285) that the only really bad sleepless night I can remember to have had in my life was in the village of Kataragama in Ceylon.

As soon as Virginia regained consciousness, I was faced with the problem of what to do. In those days, if anyone was in Virginia's mental state, dangerously suicidal, it was customary to certify them. The procedure took place before a magistrate who, on a doctor's certificate, made an order for the reception and detention of the person either in an asylum or in a nursing home authorised to take certified patients. Doctors were naturally unwilling to take the risk of leaving a suicidal patient uncertified in a private house. I was against certification, but agreed to go and see some mental homes which took certified patients. I think I went to see two or three which Head or Savage recommended. They seemed to me to be dreadful, large gloomy buildings enclosed by high walls, dismal trees, and despair. I told the doctors that I was prepared to do anything required by them if they would agree to her not being certified. They agreed not to certify her, provided I could arrange for her to go into the country accompanied by me and two (at one time four) nurses. This meant that it was impossible to take her to Asham, because it could not accommodate two or four nurses and was in any case too remote.

George Duckworth came to our rescue and offered to lend me his country house, Dalingridge Place. George was Virginia's half-brother, being a son of her mother by her first husband, Herbert Duckworth. He was a man of the world or at any rate what I think a man of the world in excelsis should be. As a young man he was, it was said, an Adonis worshipped by all the great and non-great ladies. He was still terribly good looking at the age of forty-five. A very good cricketer, Eton and Trinity College, Cambridge; he knew everyone who mattered; was a friend and private secretary of Austen Chamberlain, and landed in the comfortable job of Secretary to the Royal Commission in Historical Monuments and a knighthood. Married to Lady Margaret Herbert, he built himself a large house, Dalingridge Place, near East Grinstead, which had every modern convenience for a gentleman's residence including some highland cattle. He was an extremely kind man and, I think, very fond of Vanessa and Virginia. He had at that time a London house as well as Dalingridge, but Dalingridge was in full working order with cook, parlourmaid, housemaids, and gardeners. So all we had to do was to go down there and settle in.

There were many things to clear up in London, for we still had Cliffords Inn and all our possessions were there. There was a great deal of packing which, at the best of times, is one of the dreariest occupations, and it was not until 20 September that we got away to

Dalingridge. I took four mental nurses with us and Ka came and stayed for a few days. For the next two months—until 18 November—we lived at Dalingridge.

I do not know what the present state of knowledge with regard to nervous and mental diseases is in the year 1963; in 1913 it was desperately meagre. After the catastrophe I practically gave up Savage as a serious doctor (though I still consulted him formally in order not to hurt or offend him) and went to Maurice Craig, the leading Harley Street specialist in nervous and mental diseases. He was a much younger and a more intelligent man and doctor than Savage, and he not only took charge of the case during its acute stage over the next two years, he also, for the rest of Virginia's life, remained the mental specialist to whom we went for advice when we wanted it. Over the years I consulted five neurologists or mental specialists, all at the head of their profession: Sir George Savage, Henry Head, Sir Maurice Craig, Maurice Wright, and T. B. Hyslop. They were all men of the highest principle and good will; they were all (or had been) brilliant doctors; I have no doubt that they knew as much about the human mind and its illnesses as any of their contemporaries. It may sound arrogant on my part when I say that it seemed to me that what they knew amounted to practically nothing. They had not the slightest idea of the nature or the cause of Virginia's mental state, which resulted in her suddenly or gradually losing touch with the real world, so that she lived in a world of delusions and became a danger to herself and other people. Not knowing how or why this had happened to her, naturally they had no real or scientific knowledge of how to cure her. All they could say was that she was suffering from neurasthenia and that, if she could be induced or compelled to rest and eat and if she could be prevented from committing suicide, she would recover.

The course of Virginia's illness vitally affected the course of our lives, and therefore from the autobiographical point of view I feel that I should deal with it in detail; but I also think that it ought to be of great intrinsic interest to describe the impact of illness or insanity upon such a remarkable mind as Virginia's Her mental breakdown lasted in an acute form from the summer of 1913 to the autumn of 1915, but it was not absolutely continuous. There were two insane stages, one lasting from the summer of 1913 to the summer of 1914 and the other from January 1915 to the winter of 1915; there was an interlude of sanity between the summer of 1914 and January

1915. There was one remarkable fact about the two insane stages which throws light upon the primitive and chaotic condition of medical knowledge about insanity in 1913. There was at that time apparently a type of insanity scientifically known as manic-depressive. People suffering from it had alternating attacks of violent excitement (manic) and acute depression (depressive). When I cross-examined Virginia's doctors, they said that she was suffering from neurasthenia, not from manic-depressive insanity, which was entirely different. But as far as symptoms were concerned, Virginia *was* suffering from manic-depressive insanity. In the first stage of the illness from 1914 practically every symptom was the exact opposite of those in the second stage in 1915. In the first stage she was in the depths of depression, would hardly eat or talk, was suicidal. In the second she was in a state of violent excitement and wild euphoria, talking incessantly for long periods of time. In the first stage she was violently opposed to the nurses and they had the greatest difficulty in getting her to do anything; she wanted me to be with her continually and for a week or two I was the only person able to get her to eat anything. In the second stage of violent excitement, she was violently hostile to me, would not talk to me or allow me to come into her room. She was occasionally violent with the nurses, but she tolerated them in a way which was the opposite of her behaviour to them in the first stage.

As a person with no medical training and with experience of only one case of mental illness, my opinion about the nature and symptoms of Virginia's case is probably of little value, but I watched and studied it intensively for months, and I have very little doubt that some of my conclusions were right. For instance, practically all Virginia's (insane) symptoms were exaggerations of psychological phenomena observable in a large number of people, and particularly in her, when perfectly sane. You can be quite sanely angry, but if you get so angry as completely to lose control of yourself, you may be insanely angry. Virginia's fits of violence against the nurses during both attacks were the result of insane anger of this kind. The same thing applied, I think, to the alternation between depression and excitement, the depressive-manic stages. Nearly everyone experiences this kind of alternation in ordinary sane life—and Virginia certainly did when she was quite well. When I was not in good spirits or grumpy as a child, my nurse used to say: 'You must have got out of your bed on the wrong side.' Everyone knows what getting out of bed on the wrong side means. You suddenly feel that the bottom has dropped out of your world and you have fallen into a pit of desolation, futility, and hopelessness, and it is when you yourself can see no reason for this misery and despair that they are at their worst. This mood again and again seems to follow or to be followed by a feeling of unusual well-being and happiness. You get out of bed on the right side and the day seems to be brighter, the sun warmer, the air more sparkling, the coffee more fragrant than it has been before. And there is no more a discernible reason for your happiness than there was for your depression.

My nurse, who had imbibed the traditional knowledge of the human mind that nearly all nurses have possessed since Odysseus's nurse Eurycleia 2,800 years ago burst into tears when she recognised the scar on his leg, used to call out to me when I was boisterously and unreasonably happy: 'Now then, Master Leonard, now then, you know there'll be tears before evening.' Sunt lacrimae rerum, said Virgil in one of the most beautiful and untranslatable of Latin hexameters. There always were, as my nurse and Virgil said, lacrimae rerum, tears before evening. The use of the word rerum, in the plural, by Virgil shows that tears were the same 2,000 years ago as they are today; 'tears for things', Virgil says, not for any particular thing—just tears before evening, as my nurse said.

In the first weeks at Dalingridge the most difficult and distressing problem was to get Virginia to eat. If left to herself, she would have eaten nothing at all and would have gradually starved to death. Here again her psychology and behaviour were only a violent exaggeration of what they were when she was well and sane. When she was well, she was essentially a happy and gay person; she enjoyed the ordinary things of everyday life, and among them food and drink. Yet there was always something strange, something slightly irrational in her attitude towards food. It was extraordinarily difficult ever to get her to eat enough to keep her strong and well. Superficially I suppose it might have been said that she had a (quite unnecessary) fear of becoming fat; but there was something deeper than that, at the back of her mind or in the pit of her stomach a taboo against eating. Pervading her insanity generally there was always a sense of some guilt, the origin and exact nature of which I could never discover; but it was attached in some peculiar way particularly to food and eating. In the early acute, suicidal stage of the depression, she would sit for hours overwhelmed with hopeless melancholia, silent, making no response to anything said to her. When the time for a meal came, she would pay no attention whatsoever to the plate of food put before her and, if the nurses tried to get her to eat something, she became enraged. I could usually induce her to eat a certain amount, but it was a terrible process. Every meal took an hour or two; I had to sit by her side, put a spoon or fork in her hand, and every now and again ask her very quietly to eat and at the same time touch her arm or hand. Every five minutes or so she might automatically eat a spoonful.

This excruciating business of food, among other things, taught me a lesson about insanity which I found very difficult to learn—it is useless to argue with an insane person. What tends to break one down, to reduce one to gibbering despair when one is dealing with mental illness, is the terrible sanity of the insane. In ordinary life, as her writings, and particularly her essays, show, Virginia had an extraordinary clear and logical mind; one of the most remarkable things about her was the rare combination of this strong intellect with a soaring imagination. There were moment or periods during her illness, particularly in the second excited stage, when she was what could be called 'raving mad' and her thoughts and speech became completely unco-ordinated, and she had no contact with reality. Except for these periods, she remained all through her illness, even when most insane, terribly sane in three-quarters of her mind. The point is that her insanity was in her premises, in her beliefs. She believed, for instance, that she was not ill, that her symptoms were due to her own 'faults'; she believed that she was hearing voices when the voices were her own imaginings; she heard the birds outside her window talking Greek; she believed that the doctors and nurses were in conspiracy against her. These beliefs were insane because they were in fact contradicted by reality. But given these beliefs as premises for conclusions and actions, all Virginia's actions and conclusions were logical and rational; and her power of arguing conclusively from false premises was terrific. It was therefore useless to attempt to argue with her: you could no more convince her that her premises were wrong than you can convince a man who believes he is Christ that he is mistaken. It was still more useless to argue with her about what you wanted her to do, e.g. eat her breakfast, because if her premises were true, she could prove and did prove conclusively to you that she ought not to eat her breakfast.

We lived at Dalingridge, as I said, until 18 November. At one time we had four nurses, two on duty in the day, and two at night. For some time Virginia was extremely violent with the nurses, but after about a month she became slightly better and it was possible to have only two nurses. It was one of the most perfect autumns for weather than I can ever remember, the gentle, windless, cloudless days of an Indian summer. There is, I think, not much to be said for the country round East Grinstead and to live in a Gentleman's Residence and a large garden belonging to someone else with someone else's servants, but four mental nurses of one's own, is not a pleasant experience. But there was a lawn and terrace at Dalingridge from which one had a magnificent view over the Sussex weald to the downs, and one could see the gap where Lewes lay and one knew that just through the gap there were the watermeadows of the Ouse valley and, in the hollow below the hill under the elm trees, Asham. When Virginia became calmer, I used to play croquet with her on this terrace after tea, and in the warm, peaceful, soft and sunny evening a kind of peace descended upon us as we looked towards the long hazy line of downs and the gap where Lewes lay. Virginia was anxious that we should leave Dalingridge and go and live at Asham.

After much consultation with doctors it was decided that it would be safe to go to Asham with two nurses in the middle of November, and this we did. We settled down and lived at Asham until August, 1914; early in the year I gave up Cliffords Inn. Virginia very slowly got better. In January it was considered safe to have only one nurse, and finally towards the end of February the last nurse went. Not that Virginia was fully recovered. She was still liable to moments of excitement and it was always difficult to get her to eat enough; she read, but was not able to work. I occasionally went up for a night or two to London and I once stayed for a week with Lytton at Lockeridge near Marlborough. When I was away Vanessa or Ka came to Asham and stayed with Virginia. Then in April it was decided that it was advisable that she should have a change and that we could safely go to Cornwall.

We went to St Ives and Carbis Bay for three weeks, staying in lodgings. It was in some ways a nerve-racking business: Virginia was not fully recovered; she was nervous of being with strangers; her delusions persisted not very far below the surface of her mind; there was still continual trouble about food and sleep. But Cornwall and St Ives had a nostalgic romance for her as it had for all her family. It was the romance of childhood which can give to places and memories a brilliance and glory unfading even when age has destroyed all our other illusions. Every summer when Virginia was a child the family went and stayed in Talland House, St Ives, and their time there remained in her memory as summer days of immaculate happiness. *To the Lighthouse* is bathed in the light of this happiness and, whenever she returned to Cornwall, she recaptured some of it. This happened to some extent in the weeks which we spent in Cornwall that April; memory calmed the jangled mind and nerves.

We returned to Asham on 1 May and for the next three months lived as far as possible a vegetative life. That Virginia was not fully recovered is shown by the fact that I still kept a daily record of whether she had a good, fair, or bad day and a good, fair, or bad night, whether she had had to take aspirin or veronal at night, and of similar facts about her health. She read, but did not write, and *The Voyage Out* still remained unpublished in the hands of Duckworth. In many ways 1914 and 1915 were years which we simply lost out of our lives, for we lived them in the atmosphere of catastrophe or impending catastrophe. I did a certain amount of work. I did some reviewing for the *New Statesman*, the *New Weekly*, the *Co-operative News*, and *The Times Literary Supplement*, and I began to write a book about the Co-operative Movement, which was commissioned by the Home University Library and, after a curious business with Williams & Norgate who commissioned it, was eventually published by Allen & Unwin under the title *Co-operation and the Future of Industry*. I seemed in process of becoming a kind of authority on the Movement, for I made a dash from Asham in July to Keswick for a night in order to open a discussion on the Co-operative Movement at a small Fabian Society conference. The Webbs were there and so was Bernard Shaw, who at one point gave me the only serious dressing down I ever had from him, my sin—a somewhat inadvertent sin—having been to use the word 'natives' of Indians.

Walter Lippman, then unknown, but later in life one of the most famous of American columnists, was also at the conference. We travelled down together from Keswick to Euston. I only saw him once or twice in my life again and I do not think that I had a premonition of his future eminence. But I liked him very much as a man and felt him to be both intelligent and sensitive, and we talked almost without stopping through the long hours of the train journey. Almost at once our talk became much more intimate than is usual with a new and casual acquaintance, so that I remember some of it as vividly after fifty years as if it had happened only a year ago. In June I had reviewed Freud's *Psychopathology of Everyday Life* in *The New Weekly* and before writing it I read *The Interpretation of Dreams*, which had been published the previous year. I am, I think not unreasonably, rather proud of having in 1914 recognised and understood the greatness of Freud and the importance of what he was doing when this was by no means common.[1] Somehow or other Lippman and I got on to the subject of Freud, psychoanalysis, and insanity. There are few things more unexpected and more exciting than suddenly finding someone of intelligence and understanding who at once with complete frankness will go with one below what is the usual surface of conversation and discussion.

Virginia and I planned to go away for a month or more in August to the Cheviot country in Northumberland and we engaged rooms in the Cottage Hotel in Wooler. When the war broke out, we hesitated for a moment, but in the end decided to go. On 7 August we travelled up to Wooler and stayed there until 4 September, when we moved on to Coldstream across the border. We stayed at Cold-

[1] People, among whom I include myself, so often quite honestly, but mistakenly, credit themselves with this kind of foresight that I turned up my review in order to see what in fact I had said about Freud. I quote the following, which is almost exactly what I would write about Freud today: 'One is tempted to say that he suffers from all the most brilliant defects of genius. Whether one believes in his theories or not, one is forced to admit that he writes with great subtlety of mind, a broad and sweeping imagination more characteristic of the poet than the scientist or medical practitioner. This wide imaginative power accounts for his power of grasping in the midst of intricate analysis of details the bearing of those details on a much wider field of details . . . his works are often a series of brilliant and suggestive hints. And yet from another point of view this series of hints is subtly knit together into a whole in such a way that the full meaning of a passage in one book is often to be obtained only by reference to some passage in another book. No one is really competent to give a final judgment upon even the *Psychopathology of Everyday Life* who has not studied the *Interpretation of Dreams* and Freud's more distinctly pathological writings.' And after saying that many people will say of Freud's books: 'Very interesting but too far fetched,' I say that one cannot discuss the justice of such a verdict in a short review, I can only state my opinion that 'there can be no doubt that there is a substantial amount of truth in the main thesis of Freud's book, and that truth is of great value'.

stream until 15 September, when we returned to London. It was strange and rather disturbing to be away from everyone whom we knew in a small hotel in Northumberland during those first weeks of war. The air of Wooler was always thick with false rumours. I must have heard almost at its source one of the most famous of these false stories which spread like a contagious disease over the whole country. For one evening a man came into the bar of the hotel and in some excitement told us all that he had just come by train from Newcastle, and, while he was waiting in the station, he saw trainload after trainload of Russian soldiers with fur hats and guns pass through on their way to the south and to France.

I am inclined to think that the Cheviots are the loveliest country in England. Mountains some distance away create in many places superb landscapes, as for instance in Greece or when you look to the Sierra Nevada across the great Spanish plain. But to live in mountains is like living with someone who always talks at the top of his, or it may be her, voice. For beauty in everyday life I prefer hills which only occasionally pretend to be mountains, for instance the South Downs of Sussex, or mountains like the Cheviots which usually pretend to be hills. The Cheviots never shout and never insist. They have a superb sweep, but there is an extraordinary stillness and peace in the beauty of their forms; and nowhere in the world is the light and colour of sky and earth more lovely than in this bit of England—due, perhaps, to its being such a narrow strip of land between two seas.

Early in September we moved on across the border and the Tweed to Coldstream. This is very different country from the Cheviots, but the border and Tweed valley are in their own peaceful way of great beauty. And I must recur to the great subject of food. We stayed in rooms kept by a woman appropriately called Miss Scott. The many English people who think that good cooking begins only on the other side of the English Channel will never believe that a meal at Miss Scott's could be compared with one in Touraine or Provence. But in its own very different way Miss Scott's cooking was perfect. I still remember the bread and scones, the porridge, the scotch broth, the trout, the mutton, the butter, milk, and cream. It deserved the three stars for cuisine which you will find appended in the Michelin Guide to many restaurants and to places like Montluçon and Vienne.

When we got back to London in the middle of September the

problem arose of where we should live. Virginia had barely recovered and it was obvious that any strain, mental or physical, was dangerous to her. I was convinced that she could not possibly, in her present state, stand the strain of London life, but she herself was always in favour of living in London. We spent several weeks looking at houses in London, Hampstead, Richmond, and Twickenham and we also went down to Asham for a time. Eventually we took rooms at 17 The Green, Richmond, temporarily, meaning to find a house in Richmond. We moved in on 16 October. In 1914, before the motor car had destroyed its beauty and peace, Richmond Green was a charming place to live in. No. 17 was an old substantial house on the east side; on the south was the lovely Maids of Honour Row and the old palace. We had a large, comfortable, well proportioned room on the first floor overlooking the Green.

The house was kept and the rooms let to us by a Belgian woman, Mrs le Grys. She was an extremely nice, plump, excitable flibbertigibbet, about thirty-five to forty years old. You never knew what was going to happen next in her house. Mrs le Grys had only one servant, a typical overworked 'skivvy' of fifty years ago, wild and grubby, perpetually slamming doors and dropping with a loud crash trays laden with plates, cups, and saucers. I remember two of Lizzy's feats. One morning when I was in my bath I heard cries on the landing: 'Fire! Fire!' Putting on a coat and pair of trousers, I went out and found smoke pouring out of a room on the floor above; a big screen in flames was flung out of the window on to the pavement in front of the house. Lizzy had put a large piece of newspaper 'to draw up the fire,' the newspaper had 'caught', things on the mantelpiece had 'caught', the screen had 'caught', even the wallpaper had 'caught'. It was a miracle that the whole hadn't 'caught'.

Having escaped death by fire, a few days later we barely escaped death by water, again thanks to Lizzy. We were awakened by a tremendous throbbing and thumping and drumming and the whole house began shaking; it sounded, as Virginia said, as if there were a motor omnibus on the roof trying to start. I jumped out of bed and rushed into the bathroom, which seemed to be the focus of the din. When I turned on the taps, steam burst forth in such volume that it seemed as if it must be the prelude to a volcanic eruption. In fact large pieces of pipe, rust, and dark red water erupted. Why the boiler in the basement did not blow up, I do not know, for Lizzy had contrived to light an enormous kitchen fire when there was no water in the pipes. After that Lizzy was given notice by Mrs le Grys and departed. In a way I was sorry to see her go, to know that I should never again see her grubby face and wild distracted eye or hear her breaking the crockery. I like to contemplate people who are the perfect prototypes of their class, even when the class is that of the nineteenth-century lodging house skivvy. If there is the platonic idea of the damp soul of a housemaid laid up in heaven, it will be the image of poor Lizzy's soul.

We settled down in Richmond and it seemed as if things were going well. We decided to try to find a house in Richmond and towards the end of 1914 we went to see Hogarth House in Paradise Road and fell in love with it. It was very beautiful. In 1720 Lord Suffield had built a large country house in a good sized garden; in the nineteenth century it had been sold and divided into two houses, one still called Suffield House and the other Hogarth House. Every room except one was perfectly proportioned and panelled; there was quite a good garden. There were the usual hitches, alarms and excursions, over the negotiations, but eventually early in 1915 I obtained a lease and we were to move in in March. Virginia's health seemed to have improved and she had begun to work and write again. I was doing a good deal of work for the *New Statesman* and had begun a book commissioned by the Fabian Society on international government. Then quite suddenly in the middle of February there was again catastrophe. Virginia had had some symptoms of headache and had not slept well, but this seemed no more serious than what had occasionally happened during the previous six months. But one morning she was having breakfast in bed and I was talking to her when without warning she became violently excited and distressed. She thought her mother was in the room and began to talk to her. It was the beginning of the terrifying second stage of her mental breakdown. It was, as I have said, completely different from, almost the exact opposite of, the first stage. I had to get nurses at once, and, although Mrs le Grys behaved admirably, it was obvious that we could not turn her house into a mental hospital. It was necessary to get Hogarth House ready for us to move into immediately, to take our furniture which was being warehoused and put it into the house and find servants. Annie, the cook, and Lily, the house parlourmaid, whom we had had at Asham, agreed to come, and early in March we moved into Hogarth House with four mental nurses.

The first fortnight was indeed terrifying. For a time Virginia was very violent with the nurses. The violence then subsided a little, but she began to talk incessantly. It is difficult now to remember accurately how long the various stages lasted, but I think in this stage she talked almost without stopping for two or three days, paying no attention to anyone in the room or anything said to her. For about a day what she said was coherent; the sentences meant something, though it was nearly all wildly insane. Then gradually it became completely incoherent, a mere jumble of dissociated words. After another day the stream of words diminished and finally she fell into a coma. I had a Richmond doctor, one of the best G.P.'s I have ever known, and the mental specialist, Maurice Craig, came down several times from London. They assured me, even when she was completely unconscious in the coma, that she would recover. They were right. When she came out of the coma, she was exhausted, but much calmer; then very slowly she began to recover. The number of nurses was reduced to two and then to one, and towards the end of the summer we went down to stay at Asham with the one nurse. By the end of the year she was well enough to do without nurses.

Quite apart from Virginia's madness, life in Hogarth House during the first six months of 1915 acquired a curious atmosphere of wild unreality. Strange, ridiculous scenes took place. Here is one, a kind of tragicomedy inserted in the tragedy. In the previous year when we were at Asham, we had engaged a house parlourmaid called Lily. Lily was one of those persons for whom I feel the same kind of affection as I do for cats and dogs. She was an extremely nice character, but temperamentally born to certain disaster. She was not feeble-minded, but simple-minded and she found it almost impossible to refuse anyone anything. When we wanted a servant at Asham we went to a Lewes agency and they gave us Lily's name and a reference to a convent at Haywards Heath. We took up the reference and a nun came out to see us. She told us that Lily had been seduced and had had an illegitimate child. She was not a Roman Catholic, but the convent had taken her in and cared for her and the child. The nun said that she was in many ways a very nice girl, but weak; if we took her as a servant, we ought to 'keep an eye on her'; she hoped that we would let the convent know how things went on, as they would look after the child.

People like Lily have characters which seem to me psychologically fascinating. She was pure English, in fact a regular Sussex country girl. In England and in Sussex villages, the young women, even when they have illegitimate children, never, of course, have tragic or complicated characters, though the author of *Tess of the D'Urbervilles* and *Jude the Obscure* was an English writer who thought otherwise. The squeegee of Church of England and the rural middle class, the Sunday school and the rector and the rector's wife, the squeegee of a religion and morality which have scarcely any standard of value except that of respectability or disreputability, had passed over and flattened poor Lily—she had passed from the category of respectability into that of disreputability; it and she were quite simple and that was the end of it. Unfortunately for her and for us it was not the end of it. If Lily had been born in the neighbourhood of Skvoreshchniki instead of Haywards Heath, she would have fitted, without any alteration except of name, into a Dostoevsky novel. If you had called her Marya Timofeyevna instead of Lily, you might have seen at once that she was just another Lebyadkin's sister or even a female village Myshkin. These 'sillies', as Tolstoy called them, are terribly simple and at the same time tragically complicated.[1] You could almost see this in Lily's face; she had a long, pale, weak, rather pretty, sad face. There was a gentleness in her voice and manners which was certainly unusual in country girls of her class in 1913. And in 1913 in Haywards Heath fate had marked her down for disaster no less certainly than it had marked down the House of Atreus for disaster nearly 3,000 years before in Mycenae.

This is how fate set to work in Hogarth House, Richmond. One night at three o'clock in the morning I was suddenly woken up by Annie, the cook, bursting into my bedroom and crying aloud: 'There is a soldier in the kitchen; there is a soldier in the kitchen—and Lily's there.' I went down to the kitchen in the basement and found that indeed a soldier—a sergeant—was there and Lily too in some disarray. When I opened the door, the sergeant dashed past me down the passage, through the door into the garden (by which he had apparently come into the house) and presumably over a wall into the street—leaving behind him in the kitchen his cane. I told Lily that she had better go up to bed and that I would talk to her in the morning. Our conversation in the morning was very distressing. It

[1] The strange psychology of the 'silly' is extraordinarily interesting. I wrote something about it in Volume 1, pp. 43-4 and 87.

was a moment at which Virginia was still terribly ill; it was essential that she should be kept completely undisturbed and unexcited. and one could not risk her being startled by soldiers dashing about the house and garden in the early hours of the morning. I told this to Lily and she was miserably contrite, saying that she had no excuse and had behaved abominably and had no right to expect to be kept on. I said that I thought I had better think the whole thing over, and, unless she objected, I must let the nuns know what had happened and consult them, as when I had engaged her they had asked me to keep in touch with them and let them know how she went on. She agreed to this and in fact seemed to be eager that I should consult the nuns. So I wrote to the convent and one of the nuns immediately came to Richmond to see me. She has a talk with Lily and then asked me not to dismiss her as she was full of remorse and had, the nun said, 'learnt her lesson'.

I agreed to this and so Lily remained. But she was very depressed and I was hardly surprised when she came to me after a few weeks and said that she should go and try to find another place. It was not because I had in any way reproached her after I had agreed to her remaining, she said, because I hadn't done so; it was that she reproached herself; 'Mrs Woolf was so good in taking me and now I keep on feeling that I have done her harm and I shall never again be happy here; it's better that I should go at once.' I said that I should be sorry if she went and that before finally deciding she ought to consult the nuns, and this she did. The nun wrote to me that she was very sorry, but she thought that Lily had better go as she had worked herself up into such a state of contrition and unhappiness that she would never settle down again with us in Richmond. So Lily left. There is no doubt that she was tragically sensitive and in Haywards Heath born to disaster. Yes, if she had been born in Skvoreshchniki, she might have been Lebyadkin's sister and I suppose that she would have been seduced and ruined by Stavrogin. Her ruin in Haywards Heath was different, being, as I have said, English and presided over by the Church of England, Roman Catholics, and rural middle class and regulated by me and the nun on the highest principles and with scrupulous decorum. Not that I think it made much difference to poor Lily. As far as I can remember, the nuns told me that they had found her another place, but that after a time they lost touch with her. We never saw or heard from her again. Her epitaph has been written by two poets, one of the seventeenth and the other of the eighteenth century. 'When lovely woman stoops to folly, and finds, too late, that men betray, what charm can soothe her melancholy?' 'There is no armour against fate.'

The year 1915 with its private nightmare dragged itself slowly to an end. Meanwhile the public nightmare of the war also dragged itself on, but became continually more oppressive and terrible. In the first year of the war I was so entangled in the labyrinth of Virginia's illness—the psychological struggle, the perpetual problems of nurses and doctors, the sense of shifting insecurity—that I do not think that I had time to consider my own personal relation to the war and the fighting. But as the year waned and the fighting waxed and Virginia gradually grew better, I was forced to consider my position. Of my five brothers the two youngest, Cecil and Philip, joined up from the first day of the war. They had a passion for horses and riding and had joined the Inns of Court regiment a year or two before 1914. They were actually in camp with the regiment somewhere near Dover when the war broke out and they went straight into the Hussars, being given commissions. Two other brothers, Harold and Edgar, joined up later and took commissions, one in the R.A.S.C. and the other in an infantry regiment. On the other hand many of my most intimate friends were Conscientious Objectors and claimed exemption before the Tribunals which were set up when conscription was introduced. Personally I was, in a sense, 'against the war': I thought, and still think, that it was a senseless and useless war for which the Austrian and German governments were mainly responsible, but which our government probably could have prevented and should never have become involved in. (In this it was unlike the war of 1939 which, as soon as Hitler came to power in Germany, was inevitable.) But I have never been a complete pacifist; once the war had broken out it seemed to me that the Germans must be resisted and I therefore could not be a Conscientious Objector.

My brothers, Cecil and Philip, were in 1915 in training with their regiment in Mayfield, north of Lewes, and they used to come over to Asham to see us from time to time. They were anxious that I should join up and they assured me that, if I did, they could get me into their regiment. I think that, if I had not been married, or even if Virginia had been well, I should probably have joined up, because, though I hated the war, I felt and still feel an irresistible desire to experience everything. When it became clear that sooner or later there would be conscription, I decided to let things take their course; if I were called up and put into the army, I would try to get a commission in my brothers' regiment. But the prospect was terribly disturbing. Virginia's state was still precarious; it was only with the greatest difficulty and by incessant watchfulness that she could be induced to live the kind of life which would allow her recovery to continue and consolidate.

When I saw that I should very soon be called up, I went to Dr Maurice Wright to consult him both as a doctor and a friend. He was the doctor to whom, when I returned on leave from Ceylon, I had gone to see whether he could cure me of my trembling hands.[1] He also knew everything about Virginia, for I had consulted him when she was at her worst. He was, moreoever, an exceptionally nice and very intelligent man. I was surprised to find him in the uniform of a colonel or it may even have been a brigadier. He was in fact head of the R.A.M.C. district which included Richmond and Surrey. I explained the situation to him and told him that I had come to him, rather as a friend than a doctor, to hear what he felt about it. He said that he thought it might be disastrous to Virginia if I were called up; he did not think that I was medically the kind of person who ought to be a private in the army and, having treated me unsuccessfully for a nervous disease, he could conscientiously give me a certificate to produce at my medical examination. He gave me the following certificate, with which, to tell the truth, I did not and do not entirely (medically) agree:

> Mr L. S. Woolf has been known to me for some years and has been previously under my care. Mr L. S. Woolf is in my opinion entirely unfit for Military Service and would inevitably break down under the conditions of active service. Mr L. S. Woolf has definite nervous disabilities, and in addition an Inherited Nervous Tremor which is quite uncontrollable.

In 1916 I was duly called up and on 30 May, with this certificate in my pocket, presented myself at Kingston Barracks. It was a curious experience. When I was taken in charge by a sergeant-major, thrust into a room with a dozen other sacrificial victims, and told to strip, I was back in my prep. school in the year 1892. We waited and waited for the doctor, shivering with nervousness and the winds which whistled through the continually opening and shutting door. At last I was examined by a very young doctor. Being naked I had left Dr Wright's letter in my coat, but I thought it ad-

[1] See Volume 1, pp. 63-4.

visable for the moment not to say anything—the less a new boy says, the safer for him. I was so cold and shivering by this time that the doctor could not well avoid noticing that my hands trembled more than those of the average private. He did not say anything to me, but took me off to a small room in which was sitting a doctor in the uniform of a captain. 'Here's a fellow with chorea, Sir,' he said. I only just stopped myself telling him that I was not suffering from St Vitus's dance. The captain made me hold out my trembling hand and began to cross-examine me. I told him I had a letter from Wright and he sent me to fetch it. Nothing was said to me and then after waiting an hour or so, I was told to go; eventually, much to my surprise, I was given exemption from every form of military service. What was even more surprising was that when I was called up again in the great comb-out of 1917, and thought that I should inevitably be sent to scrub floors and tables, at the very least, I was again given the same complete exemption.

We saw a good deal of my brothers Cecil and Philip during the first part of the war, when their regiment was stationed first at Mayfield and later at Colchester. It led to a curious incident which showed the thoroughness of the security system. I must begin the story by saying that in 1915 we let Asham for a time to a friend who was in the Foreign Office and had a brother-in-law who had a commission in an infantry regiment. One morning in Richmond the bell rang and I was told a gentleman wished to see me. A large man came into my room and presented a document showing that he was a Scotland Yard detective. He very politely said that he had to ask me a few questions. He then cross-examined me for about twenty minutes regarding Philip and Cecil, their movements and our meetings during the last twelve months. In doing so, he showed me that during the past months detectives had shadowed them; he knew, for instance, that on a certain day some weeks previously they had come from Colchester and had lunched with us in Richmond. After the twenty minutes of this, he suddenly stopped, smiled, and said that he spent a great deal of his time investigating mare's nests—'and this is another', he said. From what he told me then 'confidentially' and from what I heard later I found that the mare's-nest had arisen in the following way.

The brother-in-law of my lessee had gone down to Asham one day to stay for a week-end with his sister. One afternoon he went down through the fields meaning to cross the railway line to the river bank. In the 1914 war, unlike the 1939 war, the railway line between Lewes and Newhaven was guarded by sentries. Lieutenant X, as I will call him, was, of course, in uniform. He was stopped by a sentry and told that no one was allowed to cross the line. Lieutenant X pointed out that he was an officer and that the sentry had no right to stop him. The sentry demurred and the officer pushed past him and crossed the line. The sentry reported the matter and some weeks later a staff officer appeared and interrogated the shepherd and his wife, Mrs Funnell.[1] He asked them who the officer was who had been staying at Asham. Apparently they did not know about Lieutenant X, but they had often seen Cecil and Philip in uniform when they came over from Mayfield to lunch with us. So they said that if it was an officer in uniform, he must have been one of Mr Woolf's brothers. And that started the mare's-nest.

The war brought tragedy to Cecil and Philip. Occasionally there grows up between brothers a David and Jonathan affection. From their earliest years, when they were four and five years old—they were the two youngest in the family of nine brothers and sisters—there was this relation, this deep affection, between them. Temperamentally they were very different. Cecil was fundamentally a scholar, a gentle and cynical conservative; he had an exceptionally good mind and did brilliantly at Cambridge, finally getting a fellowship at Trinity just before the war. He was a historian and won his fellowship with an extremely learned dissertation, which was published under the title *Bartolus of Sassoferrato, his Position in the History of Medieval Political Thought*. Philip was much gayer, but also with a distinct vein of scepticism and cynicism; he was an artist and temperamentally revolutionary. He went up to Sidney Sussex, Cambridge, after leaving St Paul's, but he soon gave up Cambridge to become a painter, and he was at the Heatherly School of Art when the war broke out. In so far as it was possible they were inseparable and, as I said, joined the same regiment from the beginning of the war. Being cavalry, their regiment was for some time not sent to France, and, when they did go to France they were dismounted and sent into the trenches as infantry. Cecil was killed and Philip severely wounded and it was appropriate that the death of the one and the wounds of the other were caused by the same shell. The episode was characteristic of the 1914 war.

[1] See p. 38 above.

The Hussars were in the trenches in Bourlon Wood. They had the Irish Guards on their right and a line regiment on their left. It was one of the costly muddles and disasters of 1916. Like some others who went through the fighting of the 1914 war in France and Flanders, Philip very rarely spoke about his experiences, but he did once describe to me what happened to them in Bourlon Wood. They were forgotten, no orders coming to them all day. They were shelled mercilessly all day. Their left flank was uncovered, for the line regiment melted away in the afternoon. Bourlon Wood had been reduced to a cemetery of broken and blackened stumps of trees. The Irish Guards were still on their right, but a drunken Irish guardsman was staggering about in no man's land shouting and singing; though shells fell all round him he was unhit. Late in the afternoon, the strain began to tell on the men, and the major, as officers did in those days, left the trench and walked up and down in the open; this was supposed to inspire the men with confidence. A shell burst near the major and he was severely wounded. Philip and Cecil left the trench to bring him in, but a shell fell between them; it killed Cecil, and wounded Philip.

Philip was for a long time in hospital in Fishmongers Hall by London Bridge, and later in the country. He recovered and went back to the front and was in France until the end of the war. Only at the end when the German line broke were the Hussars mounted and, as cavalry, pursued the retreating Germans. In this pursuit Philip's regiment suffered heavy casualties and he himself had a very narrow escape from a booby trap, a mine laid for them by the Germans. The mine blew up in the middle of the regiment.

I do not think that Philip ever completely recovered from Cecil's death. He lived, no doubt, a happy life, for he married happily and had three children of whom he was extremely fond. But it was happiness with a reservation. After demobilisation he trained as a farmer and for a short time went to India as adviser on cattle-breeding to the Indian Government. Then Jimmy Rothschild, who had married one of our cousins, asked him to manage the Waddesdon Estate. Philip did this for over thirty years, and, when he retired, bought a farm and farmed on his own in Somersetshire. After the death of his wife, and when he was in his seventies, he committed suicide. I think that he just came to the conclusion that life offered him no longer anything worth the living. The contemplation of his life and death fills me with melancholy. For he was a most charming and intelligent man; everyone who knew him agreed about this. He was also, as I said, by temperament a gay and happy person. He had the catholic curiosity of mind, the passionate interest in men, women, and animals, in literature and art, in truth, which is one of the most effective means of keeping a man's life alive, of preventing him in middle age beginning the slow descent to the life of a sea-urchin or a cabbage. He did not, I must repeat, live an unhappy life, indeed it was in many ways happy, but he deserved to achieve so much more than he did in happiness and in other things. If the Everlasting *has* fixed his canon 'gainst self-slaughter, I think the Everlasting has in this made one of his many mistakes, but the thought that someone has been brought to the point of suicide fills me with melancholy and despair.

I must go back to our own life during the war. I soon became involved in activities which were directed towards understanding the causes of the 1914 war and of war in general and of finding ways, if possible, of making war less likely in the future. What started me on this was that in 1915 Sidney Webb asked me whether I would undertake a research into this vast question for the Fabian Society and write a report on it, which might or might not be published as a book. The report would, in accordance with the usual Fabian Society procedure, be made to a committee of which he would be chairman and of which Shaw would be a member. But the committee would be a mere formality; I should be completely free to proceed in my own way, say exactly what I liked, and, if the book were published, it would be over my name. The Society would pay me a fee of £100.

My friends, and Maynard especially, were discouraging; they thought that I should find the whole thing very boring and a waste of time. It is significant that all these highly intelligent people with whom I discussed the matter thought of the problem as simply and solely a question of arbitration—'I hear', one of them would say to me, 'that you're going to write a book on arbitration.' The main reason for this was that in the happy, innocent golden age before 1914 intelligent people did not worry themselves about international relations and the problem of preventing war—they left all that to professional politicians and diplomatists. There were, of course, wars, but they were either colonial wars, in which white men slaughtered yellow men, or brown men, or black men, or wars between second-rate white men or second-rate white men's states in the Balkans or South America. In 1914, although colonial warfare, like the sun, never set on the British Empire, and we had had a nasty time beating the Boers, it was sixty years since we had fought a European nation and 100 years since we had been involved in a world war. We had a vague memory that it was about 250 years since we had seen the face of a foreign solder on English soil—didn't Van Tromp once sail up the Thames in 1652 or 1653?—and that it was 848 years since Englishmen had heard 'the drums and tramplings' of a conquest. There were at rare intervals what the newspapers called a crisis, e.g. when a French colonel occupied a patch of African desert claimed by Britain; but the crisis and the French soon gave way when they heard us singing in the music halls:

> We don't want to fight, but, by Jingo, if we do,
> We've got the men, we've got the ships, we've got the money too.

Another rather vague recollection we had was of Hague Conferences, called by a somewhat foolish Tsar in the cause of peace, and that the conference had been asked to consider 'limitations of armaments, arbitration, and laws of war'. There were two conferences and we seemed to remember that they had confined their discussion to the laws of war and to arbitration and the principal result was the establishment of a permanent court of international arbitration at the Hague. That was why there was this vague idea among my friends and many other apparently well-informed people that the prevention of war was to all intents and purposes a question of arbitration.

I have often irritated people by saying that an intelligent person can become what is called an 'authority' on most 'questions', 'problems', or 'subjects' by intensive study for two or three months. They thought me arrogant for saying so, or, if not arrogant, not serious. But it is true. The number and volume of relevant facts on any subject are not many or great and the number of good or important books on it are few. If you have a nose for relevant facts and the trails which lead to them—this is essential and half the battle—and if you know how to work with the laborious pertinacity of a mole and beaver, you can acquire in a few months all the knowledge necessary for a thorough understanding of the subject.

In 1915 I worked like a fanatical or dedicated mole on the sources of my subject, international relations, foreign affairs, the history of war and peace. By 1916 I had a profound knowledge of my subject;

I was an authority. This is not retrospective vanity; I can give, at the risk of appearing vain and boastful, a little proof of it. Early in 1920, Massingham, a famous editor in those days, of the *Nation*, asked me whether I would take Brailsford's place, during his temporary absence, as leader writer on foreign affairs, I did this for three months, writing everything which the *Nation* published on foreign affairs. In the middle of October Massingham wrote to me: 'Brailsford is back from Russia, and will resume his work for the "Nation" next week, so I shall not call on you for a Leader or for Notes; but I want to say what a very high value I attach to your work for us. It has been faultless in manner and quality and of the greatest possible service. I do hope you will regard yourself as attached to the paper, and open to do work for it whenever there is special pressure in respect of foreign affairs.' And on 23 July, when in fact I was writing for Massingham, Clifford Sharp wrote to me asking me to write an article on foreign affairs for the *New Statesman*. Journalistically at any rate I had become an authority.

By the middle of 1915 I had completed my report and it was published immediately as a supplement to the *New Statesman*. It began by dealing with the causes of war and then examined the nature, history, and records of international law, treaties, international conferences and congresses, arbitration and international tribunals. My conclusion was that the first step towards the prevention of war must be the creation of 'an international authority to prevent war' and I examined the minimum requirements for such a league of states if it was to have any chance of success. Webb and I then drew up a formal international treaty for the establishment of such a supernational authority for the prevention of war, based upon my conclusions; this too was published as a supplement to the *New Statesman*. This was the first detailed study of a League of Nations to be published, the first working out and description of the structure which the Allied governments would have to agree to give it if it was to have any chance of preventing war or of making war less probable. During my work on this I became more and more convinced that the problem of an international authority and the prevention of war was part of a much larger problem—international government. It was commonly said or assumed that international government did not exist and could not exist among sovereign independent states; but a very little investigation convinced me that this was not true and that a considerable field of human relations had been subjected to various forms of international government. But practically no books existed on the subject and no attention had been given to it. I told Sidney Webb that I thought that it would be well worth while doing some serious work on it as it ought to throw important light on the whole field of international relations, including a League to prevent war. Webb agreed and the Fabians gave me a fee of £100 to write a second report.

I did an immense amount of work on this. You could not become an authority on international government in 1915 by reading books, because the books did not exist;[1] you had to go to what are called original sources. I had therefore to read Blue Books and White Books and annual reports dealing with such vast international organisations as the Universal Postal Union or the International Institute of Agriculture, and I had many interviews with civil servants and others who attended the conferences or congresses of these unions or associations as national representatives. It was perhaps from these interviews that I learnt most; I remember, in particular, the fascinating account of the problems of international government in the Universal Postal Union which the Post Office civil servant who represented Britain at the Union's Congress gave to me. It was he who told me the wonderful story of the bibles in Persia, which is worth telling again.

It was the rule of the Union that each country retains the sums which it receives from postal matter despatched from it. This on the whole works out fairly, but in 1906 Persia brought to the notice of the Union a case of considerable hardship. Persia is inhabited mainly by Muhammadans, Great Britain by Christians. The Christians of Great Britain and the U.S.A. have a passion for sending bibles to the Persian Muhammadans, but the Persian never sends his Koran to

[1] There were in fact only two books of any use, and one of these was simply a work of reference. One was an American book, *Public International Unions* by Professor Reinsch. The other was the Yearbook of L'Union des Associations Internationales, *Annuaires de la Vie Internationale*; this remarkable book was invaluable to me, because it contained a list of all international associations, from the great International Institute of Agriculture in Rome to the International Association for the Rational Destruction of Rats or the secret international conference of eighty-nine white slave traffickers which met in Warsaw in 1913 to consider 'an international agreement as to the future conduct of the trade' and which ended in the arrest of all eighty-nine representatives by the Warsaw police.

Britain or America. There were no railways in Persia, and the Persian government had to provide every year at vast expense strings of camels to carry the hundreds of foreign bibles to its subjects. The British and American governments retained all the large sums paid by their Christian subjects for postage on these bibles; the Persian government got nothing, and as Persians write few letters and send fewer parcels to foreigners, the Persians were being ruined by the Holy Bible. The justice and eloquence of the Persian plea had its effect upon representatives of the other nations at the Postal Congress and a new Article was added to the Convention of 1906 authorising Persia to levy a special duty on all printed matter sent by post into the country.

The two reports which I had written and our draft treaty were published by me in a book, *International Government*, in 1916. It had, I think, some effect; it was used extensively by the government committee which produced the British proposals for a League of Nations laid before the Peace Conference, and also by the British delegation to the Versailles Conference. My authority for this statement comes from Sir Sydney Waterlow, Philip Noel-Baker, who was secretary, and Lord Cecil, who was head of the League of Nations Section of the British Delegation. Sydney Waterlow was in the Foreign Office and in 1918 he was instructed to draw up a confidential paper on 'International Government under the League of Nations' for use by the British Delegation at Versailles. He gave me a copy. In the prefatory note he said: 'The facts contained in Part I are taken almost entirely from "International Government", by L. S. Woolf (1916). Where a mass of facts has been collected and sifted with great ability, as is the case with Mr Woolf's work, it would be folly to attempt to do the work over again, especially as time presses. My detailed descriptions of the various existing organs of international government are therefore for the most part lifted almost verbatim, with slight abridgements, from Mr Woolf's book.'

My work on this book led me by degrees into what are euphemistically called practical politics. Many people besides myself and the Fabians were early in the war convinced that it ought, if possible, to be transformed into a war to end war, and therefore it was essential that some sort of international authority— a League of Nations, as it soon began to be called—should be established after the war in order to settle international disputes, promote the growth of a system of international law, and so help to keep the peace.

Various groups of people of varying political complexion in Britain and other countries were formed to study the problems connected with the idea and to get the wider public to support it. In Britain the most important of these groups was the Bryce group, under the chairmanship of Lord Bryce, and in the United States the League to Enforce Peace.[1]

Goldsworthy Lowes Dickinson—Goldie, as his friends always called him—was one of the most active and influential of these workers. Goldie was a good deal older than I—eighteen years older—but I had known him well since my Cambridge days for he was an Apostle and one of the most popular of dons at King's. He was, I think, one of the most charming of men; he belonged to Roger Fry's generation, and it is curious to recollect how many of that Cambridge generation were remarkable for a particular variety of great, gentle, slightly melancholy, male charm. Roger himself had it, but Goldie had it in excelsis. The extraordinary gentleness of thought, speech, manner was an integral part of it and so was melancholy; these had their charm, but also their defects or dangers. Goldie wrote a number of books of great merit, notably *Letters from John Chinaman* and his books on war and peace; they were extremely good and brought him considerable reputation and influence, but to those who knew him intimately and affectionately they were disappointing, and the disappointment was not, it must be admitted, unexpected. There was a weakness, a looseness of fibre, in Goldie and in his thought and writing, which was subtly related to the gentleness and high-mindedness. He was very fond of Virginia and he came to see us or stay with us from time to time. Virginia too was very fond of him, though the thin vapour of gentle high-mindness sometimes irritated her; it was, no doubt, in such a moment of irritation that she wrote the following in her diary on 28 December 1935, an extract which some of his friends thought I was wrong to include in *A Writer's Diary* (p. 261):

> Goldie depresses me unspeakably. Always alone on a mountain top asking himself how to live, theorising about life; never living. Roger always down in the succulent valleys, living. But what a thin whistle of hot air Goldie lets out through his front teeth. Always live in the whole, life in the one: always

[1] Nearly all these groups published schemes for a League and in 1917 I published a book, *The Framework of a Lasting Peace*, giving the text of eight such schemes.

Shelley and Goethe, and then he loses his hot water bottle; and never notices a face or a cat or a dog or a flower, except in the flow of the universal. This explains why his high-minded books are unreadable. Yet he was so charming intermittently.

Goldie was the most active member of the Bryce group. He, Sir W. H. Dickinson, M.P. (afterwards Lord Dickinson), J. A. Hobson, Raymond Unwin, H. N. Brailsford, and I were active in starting the League of Nations Society and were on its Executive Committee. It was a propaganda body, its object being to get the public to understand the necessity for a League and for its establishment in the peace treaty after the war. There was another organisation, The League of Nations Association, formed about the same time and with much the same objects. But, as so often happens among the good and wise, the two organisations viewed each other with suspicion or misprision. The champions of the Association were Wickham Steed, Gilbert Murray, H. G. Wells, Lionel Curtis, and C. A. McCurdy, M.P. The Association thought us pacifist and pro-German, and we thought them much too violently the opposite. But as the end of the war and the making of a peace began to come in sight, it became obvious to us all and to both sides that it was absurd to have two rival organisations of this kind and that we ought to combine.

It was eventually decided that each of the two Executive Committees should appoint four representatives who should meet and try to work out a basis for agreement and amalgamation. The Society appointed as their representatives Goldie, W. H. Dickinson, Hobson, and myself, the Association appointed McCurdy, Steed, Murray, and Wells. We very wisely decided to dine together and this we did two or three times. Over food and drink we found agreement on the terms of amalgamation and on the rules and objects of the new organisation, which became the League of Nations Union.

At the first dinner I sat next to H. G. Wells, and we got on extremely well together, and this was the beginning of a friendship with him which was very pleasant and lasted until his death, though it was broken, as friendship with H. G. often was, by interludes of storm and stress. After the League of Nations Union business was over H. G. asked me to lunch at the Strand Palace Hotel, but when I met him there he whisked me off to Boulestin round the corner and I felt that he had promoted me. Over lunch he told me that he had come to the conclusion, as a result of the war and studying the

League of Nations idea, that a history of the world should be written from a new angle, 'plainly for the general reader'. He thought it should be done to a certain extent co-operatively by a few people who looked at history and politics from the same angle. Would I co-operate? He proposed to take a room in the Central Hall and meet once a week with the following friends: Gilbert Murray, Lionel Curtis, J. A. Spender, editor of the *Westminster Gazette*, John Hilton, William Archer, and myself. Archer had agreed to act as a kind of secretary, but our meetings would be entirely informal and friendly tea parties. I accepted his invitation and for some months on Wednesday afternoons we had the most enjoyable meetings. Those who came were usually H. G., Archer, Gilbert Murray, and myself; at first occasionally Spender and Hilton turned up. H. G.'s original idea was that we should all take our part in writing the great work and I think that he even got to the point of apportioning provisionally periods to some of us. But very soon the whole thing degenerated or blossomed into a friendly and to me most enjoyable tea and talk. The history of the world faded further and further away and we discussed everything in the world except its history. Our first meeting was on 30 October 1918, and we still met occasionally in February 1919, and then Wells got tired of it and told me that he was in fact writing the book on his own. I have as a memento of these many teas and talks a copy of *The Outline of History* inscribed to me by H. G.

I used to see H. G. from time to time and get affectionate cards from him and, when I edited the *International Review*, he very generously gave me *The Undying Fire* to serialise. But his temper was always uncertain for he was a terribly irritable little man, and you never knew when you might not unwittingly cause an explosion. I twice incurred his wrath. The first occasion was not very serious, but it was curious. Many Liberals and Labour people were greatly concerned at the atrocious proceedings in Ireland under the reciprocal violence of Black and Tans and rebels. But there were also some Conservatives who were horrified by the British government tolerating the behaviour of their forces, the Black and Tans, and one of these was Lord Henry Cavendish Bentinck, one of those curious Tory aristocrats who are always more liberal than the Liberals and continually vote against their own party. He was a brother of Ottoline Morrell's and I had met him at the Morrell's house. He formed a small society to agitate for 'peace with Ireland' and withdrawal of the Black and Tans. He asked me to join it and we used to meet, often in my office of the *International Review*. Except for Brailsford and, I think, Hobson, I cannot remember who were the other members. We were an ineffectual body but one day Henry Bentinck said that there was a young Conservative M.P. called Oswald Mosley, who had been in the 16th Lancers and had married Lord Curzon's daughter, but despite that was very advanced, was horrified by the Black and Tans, and would, if we approved, become treasurer of our society. We approved and at our next meeting Mosley appeared, a handsome young man in top hat and morning coat carrying a gold-headed walking stick. Mosley put new life into us and among other things it was decided that I should write to Wells and ask him to help further our objects. Back almost by return came a bitter, angry letter: the Irish were a set of nasty murderous thugs and they were getting all that they deserved.

H. G.'s second quarrel with me—I never really quarrelled with him—was more serious and more absurd. In 1932 I wrote in the *New Statesman* a review of his book *The Work, Wealth and Happiness of Mankind*; as with nearly everything he wrote, much of it was very good, and I gave it high praise. Unfortunately, I wrote among other things that some of the younger generation said that Mr Wells was a thinker who could not think; in this, I went on, they are wrong, Mr Wells thinks with his imagination. I immediately received a card from H. G., who was in the south of France, asking me to tell him who was the brilliant young critic who had said that he was 'a thinker who cannot think'. When I wrote the review, I remembered—or thought that I remembered—that A. L. Rowse had written the words in his book, *Politics and the Younger Generation*, which I had recently read. So when I got H. G.'s card I searched through Rowse's book, and to my astonishment could not find the quotation. I wrote to H. G. telling him this, namely that I had thought that I had read the words in Rowse's book, but that I was mistaken—the words were not in the book. H. G. exploded at once: 'It looks as though you wanted the thing said and hadn't the guts to say it as your own,' and I was told that I 'ought to do something in the way of public repudiation of that pseudoquotation.' I wrote the following letter in reply:

19 March, 1932

Dear Wells,

I am not quite sure whether your card is serious or not. If you have seen my review, I cannot believe that it is. I read your book with the greatest admiration and said so quite clearly in my review. That the result should be your falling foul of me is only one more curious instance of the danger of praising an author's work. Why if I wanted to say that you are a thinker who cannot think, I 'should not have the guts' to do so, I cannot imagine. I am not conscious of being in the least afraid of expressing such opinions as I have in print.

I suggested to the editor that I should write a letter to the *New Statesman* explaining what I had done and your objection, though it seems to me that the result would only be to make you look slightly ridiculous, which personally I have not the least desire to do. The editor himself did not seem to be at all anxious to have the letter. However if you want me to do so, I will. Perhaps you will let me know.

Yours
Leonard Woolf

H. G. replied that it would not mend matters if I wrote a letter to the *New Statesman* in order to make him look slightly ridiculous, and he sent me the following draft of the letter which he required me to send:

In a review of *The Work, Wealth & Happiness of Mankind* in the N. S. of (date) I said (quote the passage under discussion). I made the statement in order to enhance the credit of Mr. Wells with your readers and as a delicately indirect way of expressing my own admiration for his work. There was no word of truth in that statement, objection has been made to it, and I tender my sincere apologies both to Mr. Wells and to the rising young economist to whom, in the first excitement of being challenged, I ascribed it.

He added that this was the simple, honest way out for me. 'What else, in the name of decency, *can* you do?'

I replied that 'I have the greatest admiration for you as a writer (and thinker), but I cannot agree to your writing the letters which I send to the papers'. I had therefore written my own letter, explaining what had happened and had sent it to the *New Statesman*. However the editor then received a telegram from H. G. asking him not to publish my letter and later on H. G. wrote to me that he had decided that the incident should terminate without publication. 'I was acutely hurt and exasperated by what I thought was a stroke of ungenerous and disingenuous detraction from you, because you have always been of importance in my mind. It seems you didn't mean it. I begin to think you didn't and anyhow we are too much in the same camp to knock the paint off each other in the sight of our enemies.'

Meanwhile there was a curious and, to me, amusing development. At that time I was editor of the *Political Quarterly* and some weeks before the storm with H. G. blew up, A. L. Rowse had submitted to me an article on the House of Lords. I had accepted it, but returned the MS to him making suggestions for a few alterations. Now he returned the MS to me and, when I read it, there (now crossed out) was the fatal sentence about H. G. I told Rowse what had happened and asked him whether he had any objection to my sending the sentence to H. G. and telling him how I had seen and forgotten it in Rowse's unpublished article. Rowse told me that H. G. had written to him from France and asked him to lunch in the following week—and it would be very awkward if he now found that it *was* Rowse who had said that he was a thinker who did not think.

So I never told H. G. and for a year or more he did not really forgive me. Then one day Mary Hutchinson rang me up and asked us to dine, but added that H. G. would be there and had we quarrelled and would I rather not meet him? I told her that he had quarrelled with me, but not I with him—and I always liked talking to him. We arrived before him and when he came and had shaken hands with Mary, he walked over to me, took my hand in his and patted it gently two or three times, looking at me with a slightly sheepish smile. It was our first meeting since the storm.

Meanwhile the war went on. Apart from Virginia's illness, the four years of the 1914 war were the most horrible period of my life. The five years of the 1939 war were more terrible and they brought the suicide of Virginia, but at least things moved and happened and one was kept keenly alive by the danger of death continually hanging just above one's head. The horror of the years 1914 to 1918 was that nothing seemed to happen, month after month and year after year, except the pitiless, useless slaughter in France. Often if one went for a walk on the downs above Asham one could hear the incessant pounding of the guns on the Flanders front. And even when one did not hear them it was as though the war itself was perpetually pounding dully on one's brain, while in Richmond and Sussex one was enmeshed in a cloud of boredom, and when one looked into the future, there was nothing there but an unending vista of the same boredom. When the telephone rang on 2 December 1916, and they told me that Cecil had been killed in France, in the dull, static greyness of one's days it was as if one had suddenly received a violent blow on the head.

There was indeed one lightening of the darkness. In the last two years of the war Virginia's health slowly but firmly improved. She was able once more to work and she wrote steadily at *Night and Day* so that she gave me the completed MS to read in March 1919. Gradually too she was able, with cautious restraint, to live a social life. We began to see a large number of different people; among them were Philip and Ottoline Morrell, whom we got to know through Lytton. It was in 1917, I suppose, that we first went and stayed a week-end at Garsington. The house, Philip and Ottoline, the kaleidoscope of their friends and guests formed a framed picture of a society and life unlike any which I have ever met anywhere else in the real world; but in the world of fiction I recognised its counterpart, for the people in Crotchet Castle, Headlong Hall, Nightmare Abbey, and Gryll Grange would have felt quite at home and have fitted in beautifully at Garsington Manor. Garsington was a lovely Oxfordshire manor house with a lovely garden embellished with a swimming pool and peacocks. Ottoline was herself not unlike one of her own peacocks, drifting about the house and terraces in strange brightly-coloured shawls and other floating garments, her unskilfully dyed red hair, her head tilted to the sky at the same angle as the birds' and her odd nasal voice and neighing laugh always seeming as if they might at any moment rise into one of those shattering calls of the peacocks which woke me up in the morning at Garsington just as so often I had heard them blare in the jungles of Ceylon. She was, like the motley crowd which sat round her breakfast table or drifted about her garden, a fantastic hotchpotch.

Philip was a Liberal M.P., a supporter of Asquith as against Lloyd George, and politically and socially there was an aura of liberalism or even radicalism about him and Ottoline. They were leading members of that stage army of British progressives who can be relied upon to sign a letter to *The Times* supporting an unpopular cause or protesting against a pogrom or judicial murder. She was proud of having broken out of the ducal family and Welbeck, as a young woman, to study literature at Liverpool University under Walter Raleigh. She became a patron of artists and writers, proletarians and Bohemians and underdogs. In Bedford Square or Garsington you would meet the Duchess of Portland, the immaculate Lord Henry, and Lord Berners (who had a piano or harpsichord in his car), but these aristocrats were heavily outnumbered by the underdogs and scallywags, penniless and, in the eyes of the Duchess, mannerless intellectuals or C.O.s like Gertler, John Rodker, and Middleton Murry.

I was, however, always fascinated to watch for the moment—not so very rare—when the aristocrat, which was only just below Ottoline's proletarian façade, would suddenly show itself and some scallywag would be put in his place by the great lady, the daughter[1] and sister of dukes. I have seen this happen when someone 'presumed' or went a little too far at Garsington, but it was still more amusing to see her absolute self confidence and unselfconsciousness in public. For instance, one summer evening when we had been to see her in Bedford Square, she walked back with us to Tavistock Square. Her appearance was more than usually fantastic and eccentric; her hat, hair and clothes flopped and flapped around her; she looked like an enormous bird whose brightly and badly dyed plumage was in complete disarray and no longer fitted the body. Almost everyone turned to stare at her as she passed; and at one place where the road was up, and men were working in a trench, they looked up at her, roared with laughter, and whistled and cat called after her. She walked on absolutely oblivious and impervious.

The company of people whom one met at Garsington was, as I said, a strange hotchpotch. During the war there was a resident sediment of Conscientious Objectors, for Philip had a kind of farm and the Morrells, with their usual high-minded generosity, took on to it a number of C.O.s to whom the tribunals had given exemption from military service provided that they worked upon the land. The C.O.s lived either in the house or in neighbouring cottages. There were, therefore, at meals a more or less resident population of Lytton, Gerald and Fredegond Shove, Clive Bell, Mark Gertler, and Frank Prewett, a poet. Superimposed upon this literary and artistic stratum was a drifting, irregular procession of incongruous figures from high society and high politics. At one week-end mixed in with the intellectual underworld were a beautiful and brainless deb and Lord Balniel, at the beginning of a political career which has resulted in his being a trustee of an incredible number of national art galleries and museums.

There were, too, frequent irruptions of the Asquith family.

[1] To be accurate, I think that Ottoline was only a grand-daughter and sister of Dukes of Portland.

Margot, Lady Oxford, in particular used to appear suddenly at almost any time of the day or night. She was, as many reminiscences and her own autobiography show, a very English mixture of tomboy, enfant terrible, and great lady. What fascinated and eventually irritated or bored one was her indefatigable energy, her will which worked upon her environment like a psychological electric drill. It was quite impossible not to like her even when she was most intolerable—odi et amo. One afternoon at Garsington everyone, except Julian, Ottoline's daughter, and me, had gone off either to do their work or visit the Poet Laureate. I did not feel that I could bear the poetic pomposity of the Poet Laureate, so I stayed behind and played tennis with Julian. After a set or two she went indoors and I strolled about the garden. Suddenly Margot appeared. It was the moment of the great split in the Liberal Party between Lloyd George and Asquith, when L. G. had gone off with the swag and the two factions were locked in a deadly, catch-as-catch-can struggle. When Margot found that I was alone, I saw a gleam in her eye which warned me to be careful. She began walking me up and down the lawn, she on my left with her right hand resting on my right shoulder. It was obvious that Margot wanted something and it was not long before she showed her hand (on my shoulder) and what was in her mind. 'I know you are a very great friend of Maynard Keynes' was the prologue to what was in the hand and the mind. I was told all the details of L.G.'s perfidy and dishonesty, of his complete lack of principles, and she insisted upon the importance of brilliant young men like Maynard not being cajoled by the abominable wizard. She hoped that I would tell him what she had told me and use my influence to guide his footsteps on the right path—into the Asquith camp. Maynard was much amused when I told him what she had said.

Margot, I think, admired and genuinely was fond of Virginia. But she was one of those people who quite naïvely are always trying to get something out of one. She once rang Virginia up and asked her to lunch with her 'entirely alone' in Bedford Square next Thursday—they would be quite alone as she wanted to talk to Virginia about an important matter. Virginia went on the Thursday to find a luncheon party of twelve people. Nothing was said about the important question until Virginia got up to go and then Margot said could she come next Monday to tea with us. She came to tea and explained that she admired Virginia's writing more than anyone's.

'What I want you to do, Virginia', she said, 'is to write my obituary in *The Times*—I am sure that, if you offer to do it, they will jump at it—and I feel I would die happy if I knew that my obituary in *The Times* was written by you.' Virginia said that she thought that Bruce Richmond was in charge of the obituaries and she did not think that he would welcome an offer from anyone to write one of them. She would not commit herself. 'Think it over, think it over,' were Margot's final words. We often wondered whether she had asked Bruce Richmond to a solitary lunch (with ten other people) to discuss an important matter and had suggested that her obituary should be written by Virginia. If so, she was unsuccessful.

It would be unfair to Margot not to say that she was a giver as well as a taker. But her generosity was as peculiar as all her other actions. Just before the 1939 war she told Virginia that she had an original bronze reproduction of Houdon's famous statue of Voltaire. She explained that years ago she was walking in Paris with a friend of hers who was very much in love with her—though she was not in love with him. 'He took me into a shop selling antiquities and told me he wanted to give me a present; I must choose what I would most like to have in the shop. I decided to choose what seemed to me the most valuable and I took the Voltaire. And now, Virginia, I want to give it to you.' There seemed to be no reason and no explanation of why Margot should give Virginia the bronze Voltaire, and Virginia said that she really must not give it to her. But some time later, just after the beginning of the last war, when we were at Monks House, a Rolls drove up to the door and a chauffeur carried Voltaire into the house, a gift from her ladyship. The gift, the car, the chauffeur, the 100 miles journey to deliver the gift, the mystery of motive seemed to be characteristic of Margot.

The zenith of a Garsington week-end in late spring or early summer was Sunday afternoon; then, if the sun shone, a great convocation of young and old, of brilliant (and not so brilliant), of distinguished (and not so distinguished) men thronged the garden, strolling to and fro, sitting on chairs and seats, talking incessantly. It was not without significance that the company was almost entirely male. The only distinguished women whom I ever saw at Garsington were Margot, Katherine Mansfield, and Virginia; but there was always a galaxy of male stars, from ancient red giants like Yeats to new white dwarfs from Balliol and New College. The older generation would be there: Bertie Russell, Goldie Dickinson,

Bridges, Lytton, Maynard; and then early in the afternoon there would be an irruption from Oxford of undergraduates or young dons. The Oxford generations of the nineteen tens and nineteen twenties produced a remarkable constellation of stars of the first magnitude and I much enjoyed seeing them twinkle in the Garsington garden. There for the first time I saw the young Aldous Huxley folding his long, grasshopper legs into a deckchair and listened entranced to a conversation which is unlike that of any other person that I have talked with. I could never grow tired of listening to the curious erudition, intense speculative curiosity, deep intelligence which, directed by a gentle wit and charming character, made conversation an art. And out of the Oxford colleges of those years came, besides Aldous, L. A. G. Strong, David Cecil, Maurice Bowra.

It was in Garsington too that we first came across Katherine Mansfield and Middleton Murry. When we first got to know them, they were living together and I suppose that it was shortly after this that they married. There was an atmosphere about them then of what I can only describe as the literary underworld, what our ancestors called Grub Street. There was also a queer air of conspiracy about them; it was as if you caught them every now and then exchanging a surreptitious wink or whisper: 'There you see, didn't I tell you how hostile the world is to us.' I never liked Murry; there was a strong Pecksniffian vein in him which irritated and revolted me.[1] He was always ready to weep loudly and generously over the woes of the world, but the eyes reminded me of the crocodile's.

Katherine was a very different person. I liked her, though I think she disliked me. She had a masklike face and she, more than Murry, seemed to be perpetually on her guard against a world which she assumed to be hostile. Very soon after we first met she came and stayed an uneasy weekend with us at Asham. By nature, I think, she was gay, cynical, amoral, ribald, witty. When we first knew her, she was extraordinarily amusing. I don't think anyone has ever made me laugh more than she did in those days. She would sit very upright on the edge of a chair or sofa and tell at immense length a kind of saga, of her experiences as an actress or of how and why Koteliansky

[1] I once reviewed in the *Nation* a book of his simply by mixing up indiscriminately quotations from the book and quotations from Pecksniff. I defied anyone to disentangle them, and I do not think anyone ever did—but the Murry-Pecksniff paragraphs made perfect sense.

howled like a dog in the room at the top of the building in Southampton Row. There was not the shadow of a gleam of a smile on her mask of a face, and the extraordinary funniness of the story was increased by the flashes of her astringent wit. I think that in some abstruse way Murry corrupted and perverted and destroyed Katherine both as a person and a writer. She was a very serious writer, but her gifts were those of an intense realist, with a superb sense of ironic humour and fundamental cynicism. She got enmeshed in the sticky sentimentality of Murry and wrote against the grain of her own nature. At the bottom of her mind she knew this, I think, and it enraged her. And that was why she was so often enraged against Murry. To see them together, particularly in their own house in Hampstead, made one acutely uncomfortable, for Katherine seemed to be always irritated with Murry and enraged with Murry's brother, who lived with them and, according to Katherine, ate too much. Every now and then she would say sotto voce something bitter and biting about one or the other.

The relation between Katherine and Virginia was ambivalent. Virginia's first impression of her in 1917, when she came and dined with us, was dismay—dismay at the cheap scent, the 'commonness'—'lines so hard and cheap'. But before the end of the evening she noted that 'when this diminishes, she is so intelligent and inscrutable that she repays friendship'. A curious friendship, with some deep roots, did spring up between them. When they did not meet, Katherine regarded Virginia with suspicion and hostility and Virginia was irritated and angered by this, and supercilious towards Katherine's cheap scent and cheap sentimentality. But when they met, all this as a rule fell away and there was a profound feeling and understanding between them. I can show it best by quoting what Virginia wrote in her diary about Katherine's death on 16 January 1923, for it is terrifyingly frank, not only about Katherine, but also about Virginia:

> Katherine has been dead a week, and how far am I obeying her 'Do not quite forget Katherine' which I read in one of her old letters? Am I already forgetting her? It is strange to trace the progress of one's feelings. Nelly said in her sensational way at breakfast on Friday 'Mrs Murry's dead! It says so in the paper.' At that one feels—what? A shock of relief?—a rival the less? Then confusion at feeling so little—then, gradually blankness and disappointment; then a depression which I could not rouse myself from all day. When I began to write, it seemed to me there was no point in writing. Katherine won't read

it. Katherine's my rival no longer. More generously I felt, But though I can do this better than she could, where is she, who could do what I can't! Then as usual with me, visual impressions kept coming and coming before me—always of Katherine putting on a white wreath and leaving us, called away; made dignified, chosen. And then one pities her. And one felt her reluctant to wear that wreath, which was an ice cold one. And she was only thirty three. And I could see her before me so exactly, and the room at Portland Villas. I go up. She gets up, very slowly, from her writing table. A glass of milk and a medicine bottle stood there. There were also piles of novels. Everything was very tidy, bright, and somehow like a doll's house. At once, or almost, we got out of shyness. She (it was summer) half lay on the sofa by the window. She had her look of a Japanese doll, with the fringe combed quite straight across the forehead. Sometimes we looked very steadfastly at each other, as though we had reached some durable friendship, independent of the changes of the body, through the eyes. Hers were beautiful eyes—rather dog-like, brown, very wide apart, with a steady slow rather faithful and sad expression. Her nose was sharp, a little vulgar. Her lips thin and hard. She wore short skirts and liked 'to have a line round her' she said. She looked very ill—very drawn, and moved languidly, drawing herself across the room like some suffering animal. I suppose I have written down some of the things we said. Most days I think we reached that kind of certainty—in talk about books, or rather about our writing, which I thought had something durable about it. And then she was inscrutable. Did she care for me? Sometimes she would say so—would kiss me—would look at me as if (is this sentiment?) her eyes would like always to be faithful. She would promise never never to forget. That was what we said at the end of our last talk. She would send me her diary to read and would write always. For our friendship was a real thing, we said, looking at each other quite straight. It would always go on whatever happened. What happened, I suppose, was faultfindings and perhaps gossip. She never answered my letter. Yet I still feel, somehow, that friendship persists. Still there are things about writing I think of and want to tell Katherine. If I had been in Paris and gone to her, she would have got up and in three minutes we should have been talking again. Only I could not take the step. The surroundings—Murry and so on—and the small lies and treacheries, the perpetual playing and teasing, or whatever it was, cut away much of the substance of friendship. One was too uncertain. And so one let it all go. Yet I certainly expected that we should meet again next summer and start afresh. And I was jealous of her writing—the only writing I have ever been jealous of. This made it harder to write to her; and I saw in it, perhaps from jealousy, all the qualities I disliked in her.

For two days I felt that I had grown middle-aged, and lost some spur to write. That feeling is going. I no longer keep seeing her with the wreath. I don't pity her so much. Yet I have the feeling that I shall think of her at intervals all through life. Probably we had something in common which I shall never find in anyone else. (This I say in so many words in 1919 again and again.) Moreover I like speculating about her character. I think I never gave her credit for all her physical suffering and the effect it must have had in embittering her.

As the war went on, I became more and more entangled in politics. The Russian revolution in 1917 was a tremendous event for me and for all those whose beliefs and hopes had been moulded in the revolutionary fires of liberty, equality, fraternity. I suppose everyone is born either a little revolutionary or a little anti-revolutionary, just as in the placid bourgeois English society of 1881 the poet remarked that

> nature always does contrive
> That every boy and every gal,
> That's born into the world alive,
> Is either a little Liberal,
> Or else a little Conservative.

Born a year before the poet wrote *Iolanthe*, I was born a little Liberal and also—though I did not realise it for some time—a little revolutionary. I am on the side of Pericles and Tom Paine; I am instinctively against all authoritarians, aristocrats, or oligarchs from Xerxes and Lycurgus to Edmund Burke who held that 'a perfect democracy is the most shameless thing in the world' and 'nobility . . . the Corinthian capital of polished society'. The psychology of the really great revolutions, like those of 1789 and 1917, is curious. If you are on the side of Pericles and Tom Paine, and alive when society is shaken by one of these great political cataclysms, you feel a sudden exhilarating release—the feeling which the Conservative Wordsworth remembered to have felt in 1789:

> Bliss was it in that dawn to be alive,
> But to be young was very heaven!

The release is something real—release from the tyrannies, cruelties, injustices, which principalities, power, the social sclerosis of classes build up and so harden or ossify the arteries of society.

I have described in the first volume of my autobiography (Volume 1, pp. 102-8) how as young men of nineteen and twenty we felt ourselves to be part of, active agents in, a great social revolution:

> We were not, as we are today, fighting with our backs to the wall against a resurgence of barbarism and barbarians. We were not part of a negative movement of destruction against the past. We were out to construct something new; we were in the van of the builders of a new society which

should be free, rational, civilised, pursuing truth and beauty. It was all tremendously exhilarating.

The Dreyfus case, as I explained, seemed to us to be a turning point in this new struggle for liberty, equality, fraternity, and justice, and when at last the innocent man was reinstated, there was this tremendous feeling of release and exhilaration for those who stood on the side of truth and justice in this 'struggle between two standards of social and therefore of human value'.

The outbreak of the Russian revolution of 1917 produced the same feeling of liberation and exhilaration. In the long, grim history of despotisms the Tsarist régime of the nineteenth century must take a high place for savage, corrupt, and incompetent government. Even among the European royal families the Romanovs were distinguished for their unbalanced minds or feeble intellects, yet the Tsars exercised greater and more irresponsible power than even the German and Austrian Kaisers. Their ministers were second-rate men who ruled and were ruled by terror, for they administered a police state and were removed from office either by the whim of the Tsar or an assassin's bomb or bullet. The country was administered by an inefficient and frequently corrupt civil service, and the generals and admirals who mismanaged the army and navy were even worse than the civil servants. The horrifying barbarism of the aristocracy is shown by the fact that the mother of Turgenev, one of the most civilised and sophisticated of Russian writers—he died three years after I was born—had the right to flog her servants to death and exercised it. Though the government allowed Turgenev's mother freely to torture and kill her servants, he himself in 1852 was put under arrest for a month because he said publicly that 'Gogol was a great man'. The government attempted to rule by violence and terror, secret police and wholesale deportations to Siberia, the encouragement of anti-semitism and pogroms; they not unnaturally begat an opposition which came to rely upon similar methods of murderous terrorism.

One had not to be very far on the Left to dislike Tsarism and to feel that the régime which was responsible for Turgenev's mother, Red Sunday of 1905,[1] Siberia, pogroms, and that last infirmity of

[1] On 22 January 1905, a large body of strikers, led by the Government agent provocateur, Father Gapon, went to the Winter Palace in St Petersburg to present a petition to the Tsar and were massacred by the Tsar's troops.

ignoble minds, the 'Holy Monk' Rasputin, was indeed what was euphemistically called 'a blot on European civilisation'. Even a Liberal Prime Minister, Campbell-Bannerman, when the Tsar autocratically dismissed the Duma, was moved publicly to say: 'The Duma is dead; long live the Duma.'

The first activity connected with the Russian revolution in which I took part was curious. Twelve prominent Labour and Trade Union leaders, among whom were Ramsay MacDonald, Robert Smillie, the Miners' President, and Philip Snowden, on behalf of the United Socialist Council, summoned to meet in Leeds on 3 June 1917,

> Great Labour, Socialist *and* Democratic Convention
> *to hail the* Russian Revolution
> *and* to Organise *the* British Democracy
> *To follow Russia*

To this Convention I was invited to go as a delegate, but I am now not quite sure what body I represented—it must have been, I think, either my local Labour Party or the Fabian Society. At any rate on Saturday 2 June, I took the midnight train to Leeds. In the very early hours of a grey, chilly, windy summer morning, I came out of the Leeds central station in the distinguished company of MacDonald, Snowden, and other democrats. In the middle of the great war in all the large cities of England there were a number of violent and vociferous patriots who were always ready to throw stones at any democrat or socialist, or anyone who ventured to mention the League of Nations or, that dirtiest of all words, peace. Only a few weeks before I had been stoned in good company by a hostile crowd in Farringdon Street, a crowd of patriots who objected to us holding a Labour Party meeting in a hall there. Another crowd of hostile patriots soon surrounded us outside the Leeds railway station. They did not throw stones at us, but they booed us all the way to the Albert Hall where the Convention was held.

Labour conventions and conferences, on a large scale, are either very flat or very fizzy; the Leeds convention was one of the most enthusiastic and emotional that I have ever attended. All Labour people—indeed nearly all people in England—hated the Tsarist régime; they felt extremely uneasy when they remembered that they were fighting the war with that régime on their side, a war which we were fighting, according to President Wilson, because 'the world must be made safe for democracy'; and Mr Asquith was telling us that

We are fighting for the moral forces of humanity. We are fighting for the respect for public law and for the right of public justice, which are the foundations of civilization.

The convention was a kind of public sigh of relief at the lifting of this incubus in eastern Europe. The ecstatic meeting passed four resolutions. It is worth recalling them from the ironical ebb and flow of time and events. MacDonald, who exactly twenty years later was to end his political career widely discredited as the rather pitiful prisoner of his aristocratic and Tory allies, moved the first resolution: 'Hail! The Russian Revolution.' At one time I knew Ramsay fairly well and later on shall have more to say about him; here it is sufficient to say that he was in his element in 1917, a period of his career in which he was a rebel and pacifist in the political wilderness, addressing this immense sympathetic audience in Leeds. For he was a fine figure of a man, with a handsome face to satisfy a maiden's or a hairdresser's dream, with a golden bell-like bull-like voice which said nothing at such inordinate length and so persuasively that he could always get a Labour audience shouting with enthusiasm—at least until 23 August 1931, when most Labour people thought he had deserted them for the Londonderrys and the Tories.

The second resolution, proposed by Snowden, pledged 'ourselves to work for . . . a peace without annexations or indemnities and based on the rights of nations to decide their own affairs'. The third resolution was on Civil Liberty, proposed by Ammon, a trade unionist Labour M.P., and Mrs Despard. Mrs Despard was a well known suffragette. A very frail elderly lady, she had, I think, only recently come out of gaol; she was given a tremendous reception by the meeting. Clio, the cynical Muse of History, who presumably knows both the future and the past, if she listened to our resolution, must have smiled grimly at the irony of facts. For this is what we voted unanimously:

This Conference calls upon the Government of Great Britain to place itself in accord with the democracy of Russia by proclaiming its adherence to and determination to carry into immediate effect a charter of liberties establishing complete political rights for all men and women, unrestricted freedom of the press, freedom of speech, a general amnesty for all political and religious prisoners, full rights of industrial and political association, and the release of labour from all forms of compulsion and restraint.

Another frail figure received an enthusiastic welcome when he supported the resolution in the precise, clipped, aristocratic voice which, I always think, Bertie Russell must have inherited from his eighteenth-century Whig ancestors. I wonder how many of us who cheered Bertie and the resolution remembered what we had voted for when the democracy of Russia was embodied in first Lenin, Trotsky, and Dzerzhinsky, and later Stalin. Finally in the fourth resolution we called upon 'the constituent bodies at once to establish in every town, urban and rural district, Councils of Workmen and Soldiers' Delegates for initiating and co-ordinating working-class activity'.

The only other thing that I remember about this conference is a speech by Tom Mann. He belonged to a generation of trade unionists which has now completely died out. He worked on a farm from the age of nine to the age of eleven, and from eleven to fourteen in the mines; he was a socialist and agitator and general secretary of the A.S.E. He excelled in the peculiar style of oratory which had developed in the working class and socialist movements of the continent and of Britain. The great exponents of it were the French. At big Labour or trade union conferences during the nineteen twenties there were usually foreign 'fraternal delegates' each of whom made a short speech. A Frenchman who often came as a delegate—I cannot remember his name—was an amazing orator. He was a short bearded man, unimpressive to look at; he would stand absolutely motionless on the rostrum, his right hand held out in front of him with the first finger pointing straight up to the roof. Then for five minutes a liquid fountain of words would issue from him ceaselessly, but rising a little and falling a little in a kind of rhythm, and one was hypnotised into the optical and oral delusion that this fountain of words was issuing not from his mouth, but from the tip of that first finger of his right hand. Nobody knew what he was saying—I don't know that he himself knew—but we were all carried away by it; it reminded me of a canary singing in a cage or even sometimes of a Chopin mazurka.

In June, 1918, I went to a great Labour Party Conference in the Central Hall, Westminster, at which the question of whether or not to continue the 'party truce' was discussed. Suddenly the proceedings were interrupted by a strange figure walking on to the platform and embracing the chairman. It was Kerensky who had fled from Russia after his government had been destroyed by the Bolshevik revolution of November, 1917. He spoke to us for five minutes and he was given an ovation. He was another of these orators whose words rose and fell in an inexhaustible, almost visible fountain of emotional sound. I do not think his Russian meant anything more than the French of the fraternal delegate or than the English of Tom Mann. For it was in this style of oratory that Tom Mann excelled.

Looking back to 1917 after nearly half a century, with the knowledge and even perhaps wisdom which half a century gives us, it is easy to deride our hopes and enthusiasm, our oratory and resolutions in the Leeds Albert Hall. To me personally the forty-six years and my knowledge of what has happened in them have not brought me to repent or recant. I have always disliked and distrusted oratory and in the light of events I would wish to emend the wording of our resolutions. But if I could return to 1917 possessing the knowledge and experience of 1963 I would again welcome the Russian revolution and for the same reasons for which I originally welcomed it. Like the French revolution, it destroyed an ancient, malignant growth in European society, and this was essential for the future of European civilisation. The intelligent revolutionary knows, however, that all revolutions must disappoint him. There is nothing more violent than violence and it is true that more often than not if you draw the sword you will perish by the sword. The violence of the great revolutions becomes more and more violent and the civilised men who made the violent revolution almost always perish by revolutionary violence until in the end power is safely in the hands of savage, ruthless, fanatical dictators, Marats and Robespierres, Dzerzhinskys and Stalins. Nevertheless the destruction of the ancien régime in France and of the Tsarist régime in Russia was essential—and indeed inevitable, in the sense that, if you go on pouring water into a glass after it is full, it is inevitable that the water will overflow. That is why, if I could return to 1789 and 1917, I would still be on the side of the revolution—though I have no doubt that I should have been guillotined by Marat and liquidated by Stalin.

The year 1917, historically so important, is also remembered by me personally and autobiographically for two reasons. I helped to found the 1917 Club and Virginia and I started the Hogarth Press. The 1917 Club was a strange phenomenon. I do not really like clubs. I have been a member of only three in London during my life, the Trade Union, the 1917, and the Athenaeum. Most are terribly respectable, with the kind of male pomposity and public school unreality which I find irritating. That is why for years I refused to join one and only late in life became a member of the Athenaeum. I rarely go to it, and when I do enter its famous doors it is usually to go to the lavatory on my way to somewhere else. Indeed it sometimes seems to me that I pay twenty-two guineas a year for the privilege and glory of using its distinguished urinals six or seven times in the year—which works out at the rather heavy cost of round about three guineas a time.

If the Athenaeum is the nadir of respectability, my other two clubs were the zenith of disreputability. The snobbery which induced me in old age to join the Athenaeum inversely induced me, when a callow labour neophyte, to join the Trade Union Club. I did not use even its lavatory. My memory is that it had a room or two on the first floor of a dingy building in Holborn, that I looked in once and was so depressed by its melancholy gloom and smell of stale beer that I never went there again.

I do not remember in whose brain the idea of a left wing club originated in 1917. I rather think it started in a conversation between Oliver Strachey, Lytton's brother, and me. At any rate in April we were sounding all kinds of people about the idea and found everywhere enthusiastic support for it. We got together a kind of informal committee which met for the first time on 23 April and continued to direct affairs until the first general meeting of the club on 19 December. I have forgotten who all the people were who worked with us, but the following certainly were concerned in it with us: Ramsay MacDonald, J. A. Hobson, Mary Macarthur, a prominent woman trade unionist, and her husband, W. C. Anderson; H. N. Brailsford; Molly Hamilton (Mrs M. A. Hamilton), who became a Labour M.P. and wrote the life of MacDonald; Emile Burns who became a communist. By July we were looking at houses in Long Acre and elsewhere and eventually we took the lease of a house in Gerrard Street, in those days the rather melancholy haunt of prostitutes daily from 2.30 p.m. onwards. On 19 December, as I said, we held the first general meeting; I was elected to the committee and remained a member of it for a good many years.

The membership of the club during its first years was a curious mixture. It was mainly political and the politicals were mainly Labour Party, from Ramsay downwards. But there was also an element of unadulterated culture, literary and artistic, and during the first two or three years of its existence it was much used by culture, particularly at tea time, so that if one dropped in about four o'clock and looked round its rooms, one would hardly have guessed that it was political. Virginia was often there and there was a strong contingent of Stracheys, including Lytton and a retinue of young women and young men who often accompanied him. Years later the stage must have invaded and captured the club, for, when I had long ceased to use it, I was asked, as a founder of it, to come to a dinner to celebrate its foundation. Ramsay MacDonald presided and I sat at the high table, as it were, with him and some other aging politicians, while the active members seemed to be mainly actors and actresses and musicians. In its beginnings the stage gave us, I think, only one member, Elsa Lanchester, and music only Harold Scott.

It was at the club that I first got to know Ramsay MacDonald well, though during the war I also saw him a good deal in connection with the Union of Democratic Control. This therefore seems to be an appropriate place to say something about one of the most curious characters that I have known. When I first knew him, he was more or less in a political wilderness, partly because of his attitude towards the war and partly because he was not altogether trusted in his own party. He was M.P. for Leicester, but it must be remembered that he became chairman of the Parliamentary Labour Party only in 1922, five or six years after the time which I am writing about. In 1922 he had moved already to the right wing of the party, but in 1917 he was counted to be very much to the left, for he was a leader of the Independent Labour Party and the Union of Democratic Control.

I used to lunch with him now and again at the 1917 Club and was always amused to observe the acts which he would put on even for my benefit. For he was essentially an actor, the most egocentric and histrionic of men. I remember meeting him one Monday at the Club for lunch when he had come down straight from Lossiemouth and was going to the House in the afternoon for an important debate at which he was to make an important speech. We had met to discuss some political question connected, I think, with his speech.[1] Instead

[1] I think this is so because I remember a curious incident of that afternoon even today, forty-five years later. For after lunch Ramsay and I had a discussion with Charles Trevelyan and E. D. Morel, of the U.D.C., and Camille Huysmans, the Belgian labour leader who subsequently became Prime Minister. After our talk we all walked away together accompanying

of getting down to business he gave me a long account of how he had spent the Sunday walking on the Scottish hills; it was the set sentimental speech in the mellifluous voice of the orator who wants to draw tears from your eyes before he moves on to the thunderous peroration. It was typical of Ramsay that he should address it to my stony and sceptical ears over the dreary rissoles of the 1917 Club. As we walked away he told me that he had influenza and that his temperature was 102, but that he must go and make his speech. I think it was in fact probably true that he had travelled down in the night train from Scotland with a temperature of 102, had eaten his rissoles, had talked without stopping, and would go on and make his speech—all without turning a hair, for he had the kind of iron constitution which is the first and, when I think of the Prime Ministers I have known, perhaps the only necessary qualification or asset which a man must possess if he is to become Prime Minister.

I have never known a vainer and a more treacherous man than Ramsay. It was in 1916 that he asked me to come and see him one afternoon in his room in Lincoln's Inn Fields. He wanted me to write a regular article in the *Labour Leader* on the debates in parliament. I agreed to do it for a year. It was quite interesting, for I had a ticket for the Press Gallery in the House of Commons and only went to listen from time to time to important debates. After I had done it for some months, Ramsay asked me to come and see him again. He buttered me up for a bit, praising my articles, then he came round in a gyrating circle to the real point—couldn't I make it rather more *personal*, dealing with what the Labour M.P.s actually said, and particularly the leaders—and he talked so much about himself that he left me in no doubt that by leaders he meant leader. When Ramsay talked about himself, he seemed to ooze vanity and it was to me very interesting to compare his attitude to these articles with that of another Labour leader who at that time was very well known. Near me in Richmond lived a Durham miner called Tom Richardson,

Ramsay, I suppose, to the House. For I was walking ahead of the three others with Huysmans when in the middle of Trafalgar Square he told me that everyone in France realised that we were on the brink of military disaster, because Foch was completely incompetent being 'estropié à cause de prostate'. I had no idea what 'prostate' meant and made him explain. Huysmans knew everyone and was a highly intelligent man. I always remember his telling me this in Trafalgar Square because a few weeks later Foch routed the Germans.

who was M.P. for Whitehaven. Richardson himself was a pleasant man, but a typical rank and file miner Labour M.P. During parliamentary sessions he often had staying with him another miner M.P., Bob Smillie, President of the Miners' Federation of Great Britain. If there was any question or Bill important for Labour coming up in the Commons and I knew Smillie to be in Richmond, I used to go round in the evening to discuss it with him. He was the exact opposite of Ramsay. On the surface he was the dourest of Scots, with a granitic face, soul and mind. Not only did he never use two words if one sufficed; he never used one word if silence sufficed. Beneath the granite he was the nicest and most simple and genuine of men. He was extremely intelligent. If the question or Bill was some labour problem which he knew about and I did not, he would explain it carefully to me; if it was something which I knew about and he did not, he would take any amount of trouble to pick my brains until he really understood it. This impersonal objectivity, this passionate pursuit of the thing rather than passionate concern with the self is even rarer with politicians than most people.

I once came across a curious case in which this pursuit of truth and knowledge was combined with ruthless egotism in a leading trade unionist. Years later when I was secretary of the Labour Party Advisory Committee on Imperial Questions the T.U.C. asked Charles Buxton, who was chairman, and me to meet the trade union delegates to an I.L.O. Conference and advise them about a draft treaty on forced labour which they would have to deal with at the conference. When the delegates turned out to be the great Ernest Bevin and the great J. H. Thomas, I felt a good deal of dismay as we sat down at the table to go through the treaty clause by clause. Bevin was a ruthless man who notoriously despised and distrusted intellectuals and Thomas despised them in a flamboyant way peculiar to himself. I suppose it took an hour or more to go through the draft treaty and I do not think that Thomas listened to a single word that was said. But Bevin amazed me. He was just like Smillie. He knew nothing about what is now called colonialism or the facts about forced labour in colonies and he saw that Buxton and I did. He picked our brains clause by clause and continually asked us what line we advised him to take over every detail. Like Smillie, he was quick to see every point explained to him. But whereas when I left Smillie I always felt that, underneath the granite surface of the trade unionist, I had seen and felt a human being, when the door closed on Ernest

Bevin, I felt that, having picked my brains, he would ruthlessly dismiss and, if necessary for his purposes, or perhaps even if unnecessary, destroy me. And there was nothing gentle or genteel about destruction by Ernest Bevin. I was present at the famous Labour Party Conference in the charming Brighton Regency Pavilion when Bevin battered George Lansbury to political death. I happened to be on Bevin's side in that particular dispute and Lansbury, with his slightly lachrymose, self-righteous righteousness which worked as persistently and noisily as an automatic drill, always tended to make me feel uncomfortable or irritable. But there was something indecent in the cruelty, the sadistic enjoyment with which Bevin destroyed the poor man.

To return to Ramsay, one of his most marked characteristics was tortuousness of mind. One never felt that one quite knew what he was really at, why he was doing or saying what he was doing or saying. This uncertainty was not peculiar to me; people who worked closely with him in the Cabinet or the House of Commons, like Sidney Webb and Arthur Ponsonby, always said the same—if you ever got a glimpse of what was really in his mind, it was so convoluted and equivocal that you felt that you had got inside a mental maze.

Here is a strange example of his methods. In 1924 I wrote a memorandum on some foreign affairs question—I no longer remember what it was all about—which was to be discussed at the next meeting of the Labour Party Advisory Committee on International Questions. About a week before the meeting I got a letter from him asking me whether I would come and have a talk with him about the memorandum one afternoon in his room in the House of Commons. He was at the time both Prime Minister and Foreign Secretary. I was an insignificant member of the Party; the memorandum was about a more or less insignificant subject; if passed by the committee, it would have merely gone up as a recommendation to the Executive Committee of the Party—and almost certainly have died the usual death there. But I found Ramsay with a copy of the memorandum on the table in front of him; he must have read it line by line and word by word, for it was covered with notes[1] which he had written

[1] A curious thing happened with regard to these pencilled notes. The week after Ramsay gave them to me I reviewed a book on handwriting in which the author gave specimens of well known people's handwriting and explained how certain characteristics in the writing indicated certain characteristics in their psychology. One of the people he dealt with was Ramsay

on it in pencil. He then took me through the thing paragraph by paragraph by paragraph, arguing all the points minutely and carefully, and at the end he gave me his copy and asked me to consider what he had written there and what he had said. I was more than half an hour with him in the middle of an afternoon when parliament was sitting. He was at the time trying to combine the work of Prime Minister with the work of Foreign Secretary—an impossible job which no one dreamt of attempting again. Yet he must have given up at least an hour of his time to me and to this totally unimportant memorandum on a, for him, totally unimportant subject. I know that, as I sat opposite to him, I kept on thinking to myself: 'What on earth is going on in the tortuous maze of that mind?' I got, of course, a glimpse of his usual inordinate and jealous vanity; there was obviously some probably quite unimportant point in the memorandum on which, he felt, I ought to have consulted him, James Ramsay MacDonald, Prime Minister and Foreign Secretary. But there must have been, and I felt that there was, more to it than that. There was some inexplicable and for ever unascertainable worm in the labyrinth of his mind which caused him, with some satisfaction, to waste an hour of his time in a futile discussion with a futile intellectual over a futile memorandum.

Finally there was the curious streak of treachery in Ramsay. Some people in the Labour Party who knew him much better than I did, and therefore suffered much more from him, used to say that his instinct to double-cross and stab his friends in the back was derived from the traditional habit of the highland Scot to pursue secret feuds. I personally had a remarkable experience of this habit. In the last years of the war I got to know well Norman Angell and the group of young men—John Hilton, H. D. Henderson, and Harold Wright—who were tremendously influenced by his remarkable personality and his remarkable book, *The Great Illusion*. They ran a small monthly magazine, *War and Peace*, which propagated Angell's

MacDonald and he maintained that a trait in Ramsay's character was shown by the fact that he made casual dots on the paper on which he was writing. I mentioned in my review that I had a document covered with Ramsay's handwriting in which there were no casual dots and that I did not think there was in his character the trait alleged by the expert. The expert asked to see my document and as it was confidential, I allowed him to come to my office and look at it. He had to admit that there were no dots, but I do not think that he admitted being also wrong about Ramsay's character.

views; it was edited by Harold Wright and financed by the Rowntrees. They asked me to join the editorial board and, when Harold Wright was ill, I edited the paper for some months. When he recovered, he asked me what I thought of the paper and whether I had any ideas for its improvement. I said that I thought that, if Rowntree would finance it, it could be turned into an important international review[1] dealing with foreign affairs and problems of war and peace, with an advisory editorial board consisting of all the leading socialists and trade unionists in Britain and on the Continent. I had discussed this idea with Camille Huysmans and some other continental socialists; they were all enthusiastically in favour of it, but there had seemed no possibility of financing it.

Harold asked me to put my scheme in writing so that he could put it before the Rowntrees. I did this and he and I had an interview with Arnold Rowntree and his business manager, Bonwick. The Rowntree Trust was willing to finance the review, provided that I would get the leading Labour and socialist people to join the board and would undertake to edit the review. As Harold was in favour of my doing this, I agreed. I went to Huysmans and he undertook to get all the continental leaders, and in this he was successful. I went to Ramsay MacDonald, Arthur Henderson, the Webbs, Smillie, and the other British leaders and they all agreed to join the board. The Webbs were particularly enthusiastic and had me to lunch to meet Branting, an influential Scandinavian socialist, and other foreign labour leaders to discuss details. I got the support and consent of everyone in writing except Ramsay, though he had verbally agreed and told me that he thought well of the scheme. As he had not put anything in writing and July was waning with everyone soon going away for their holidays, I wrote him again. Two days later I lunched with him at the 1917 Club; the first thing which he said was that he had got my letter and would be delighted to join the board.

Two days later Arnold Rowntree asked me to come and see him. He told me that Ramsay had come up to him in the House and said that he understood that Rowntree was considering starting an international review supported by British and foreign labour leaders and edited by Leonard Woolf. He (Ramsay) would have nothing to do with it, and strongly advised Rowntree not to touch it; it was 'an

[1] I proposed to publish the review at first in English, but with the hope that eventually it would be possible to publish it also in French and German.

absurd idea'. I told Rowntree what Ramsay had said to me two days before. Rowntree said that unless Ramsay gave it his unreserved support, they would not go on with the idea, as otherwise he would do everything to wreck it, and would probably succeed. I went off and rang up Ramsay, but could not get hold of him; so I wrote him a stiff letter asking him what the devil he meant by saying one thing to me and another to Rowntree. I got a wonderful letter back in which the worm coiled and uncoiled and coiled itself again until it was impossible to straighten anything out, but in the last sentence he did tell me to go ahead and God speed you. But I knew now that, whatever God might do, Ramsay was determined not to speed me—and Arnold Rowntree knew it too. He decided that, in the teeth of Ramsay's hostility, they would not go ahead with the original idea, but they asked me to edit the *International Review*, which they were prepared to start, a straightforward review on the lines originally sketched by me, but without any socialist and labour support; rather reluctantly I agreed. The question remains: why did Ramsay stab me in the back? No one could possibly know the convolutions in Ramsay's mind, not even, I think, Ramsay; but incredible though it may seem to be, I believe that one reason was that he himself edited an insignificant paper called the *Socialist Review*. My review could not conceivably have damaged his, but it was safer to stab it in the back before it was born. And yet to give him his due, Ramsay was so convoluted and ambivalent that I should not be at all surprised if he did not with a genuine tear in his eye and a little choke in his superb voice tell me to 'go ahead and God speed you' at the very moment that, with practised and unerring skill, he was putting his thin little knife into my back and into the *International Review* in the lobby of the House of Commons. One certainly gets a great deal more pleasure from contemplating the psychology of a man like Ramsay than pain from the way in which he treats one.

What with Ramsay and the *Labour Leader* and the abortive editorial committee for the *International Review*, not to speak of the Co-operative Movement, I had become very much mixed up with the whole Labour Movement, both on its political and its trade union and economic sides. To this in the last year of the war, owing to Sidney Webb, was added an entanglement with the Labour Party and its machine which lasted for over twenty years. Already in 1917 the feeling that the war must end sometime, if not soon, began to creep over us, and there was also a feeling that, if, as we were told, the war was to make the world safe for democracy, the Left and the Labour Party ought to have something to say about what kind of new world should rise out of the ruins of the old world and its great war. The structure of the Labour Party was primitive, and it was decided that Webb and Arthur Henderson should draft for it a new constitution which would enable the party to appeal both to the trade unions and to individuals, and organise them effectively into a political force capable of competing with the Conservative and Liberal Parties. When they had finished their work and the new constitution was ready to be put before a Labour Party Conference, Sidney asked me to come and see him.

He told me that they were instituting a system of advisory committees which was a new invention and which he thought should be of very great importance politically. Those who voted Conservative or Liberal and those whom they elected to the House of Commons were overwhelmingly middle class; if you took a cross-section of them, you would find it contained individuals working in every kind of profession and business, who by education and occupation could provide expert knowledge on every kind of political problem. The position of the Labour Party was entirely different. The Labour electorate and the Labour M.P. were overwhelmingly working class and would remain so. By education and experience their knowledge was habitually limited to a narrow range of occupational and industrial conditions and problems. When the day came that 100, 200, or 300 Labour members were elected, the number among them who would have any real knowledge of finance, economics, education, international or imperial affairs would be dangerously small. Even on the Executive Committee, in which the policy of the Party on everything, from war and peace to income tax and infant schools, was determined, it was rare to find anyone with the elementary expert knowledge or experience necessary for advising or deciding. Webb proposed that the Executive Committee should set up four or five advisory committees consisting of experts appointed by the Executive and of any M.P.s who wanted to join a committee. The advisory committee would be authorised to consider any question or problem connected with its terms of reference, and to send to the Executive reports and recommendations. Sidney asked me whether I would become secretary of the advisory committee dealing with international and imperial questions; he himself was going to be chairman, at least for a time. I agreed to do this.

The committee soon after the war split into two, one on international and the other on imperial questions, and I remained the secretary of both for over twenty years. For all that time we met once a week regularly upstairs in a committee room of the House of Commons, and a few persons on each committee did an immense amount of work. Many of these, who had remarkable expert knowledge and experience, were habitually disappointed by the results of their labours, but I think we did influence the Party's policy occasionally in important ways and—what was even more significant—a small number of Labour M.P.s regularly attended our meetings and gradually became real experts on foreign or imperial affairs and policies. In many ways I much enjoyed the work, partly because I got to know a large number of different men and could observe intimately their relations to one another and sometimes their strange political and psychological antics; partly because I made many real and lifelong friends among them, and partly because I often got behind the scenes a fascinating view of that kaleidoscope of persons, politics, and policies which is a tiny corner in what we call history. Some of the details of this may be worth recounting, but I will not pursue them here, for they belong to the post-war world and therefore to my fourth volume if it should ever be written.

A few names should, however, be mentioned here. Charles Roden Buxton, a worthy member of the famous anti-slavery Buxton family, was chairman of both committees and did an enormous amount of work. Sir John Maynard succeeded Buxton as chairman of the Imperial Committee. He was a remarkable man; a retired Indian civil servant, he was the exact opposite of what many people would regard as the prototype of a high ranking Indian civilian; a first-rate administrator, he was a most intellectual progressive and progressive intellectual who devoted himself to promoting the prosperity and the freedom of what in those days were called 'subject peoples'. Two other ex-government servants, Norman Leys, who had been in the Kenya Health Service, and McGregor Ross, who had been head of the Kenya Public Works Department, devoted themselves to the cause of liberty, equality, and prosperity in Africa; Africans and African independence owe an immense debt to these two passionate, fanatical, and forgotten men. Drummond Shiels, who became Under-Secretary of State, and Arthur Creech Jones, who became Secretary of State for the Colonies, were also members to whom the new Africa and the new Asia owe a considerable debt. In international affairs an untiring worker was Phil Noel-Baker who crowned a distinguished political career by winning the Nobel Peace Prize in 1959. Finally in this list I mention with affection and respect Harry Snell, one of the Labour M.P.s who learned much from the advisory committees. I got to know him well and was very fond of him. He began life as a farm worker and became a groom, a ferryman, and a public-house potman. He ended life as a peer and Deputy Leader of the House of Lords. But he remained always a countryman, the intelligent, wary, simple, kindly Harry Snell. When he was Deputy Leader of the House of Lords he came to me one day and said that a certain young hereditary peer, with Labour sympathies, had made rather a mess of his maiden speech, partly from nervousness at being kept on tenterhooks before he could catch the Lord Chancellor's eye, and partly perhaps because he had fortified himself against the nervousness. Snell thought him a youth of promise and asked me to get him to join one of the advisory committees, encourage him to take it seriously, and become a serious politician. We did this, and our pupil became, unaware of our guidance, a distinguished politician. What the ancestors of the peer and the potman would have thought of this I do not know. Even the House of Lords has seen some things change a little through the ages.

In 1916 and 1917 I suddenly found myself once more immersed in Ceylon affairs. In 1915 rioting broke out in Kandy and lasted for two days; after it had stopped in Kandy, it broke out in Colombo where it was extremely violent. There were many casualties and much damage to property. Five provinces were placed under martial law and the army restored order. Martial law continued for several months and large numbers of people were tried and sentenced by Courts Martial, the judges being military officers. Eighty-three persons were condemned to death and sixty sentenced to life imprisonment. There is no doubt that many of these people were completely innocent of the offences with which they were charged. The Ceylon Government justified their actions by alleging that the riots were seditious. The Sinhalese maintained that there was no sedition at all or anywhere; no European was molested, no European property attacked; it was an exacerbated example of communal riots, indigenous in India and Ceylon. In this case economic questions had led to embittered feelings between the Buddhist Sinhalese and the Moslem Moormen which culminated in attacks by the Sinhalese upon the Moormen. The Government and the police had shown themselves weak and incompetent in the early stages and had so allowed the rioting to get out of hand.

The Sinhalese appointed two delegates to come to England and ask the British Government for an enquiry and revision of sentences: E. W. Perera, a Colombo advocate, and D. B. Jayatillaka (who later became Prime Minister of Ceylon and was knighted). They came to me and asked me to help them to get support for their demands. I went carefully into the evidence and came to the conclusion that the Sinhalese case was entirely correct and that there ought to be an enquiry and revision. For a year or more I worked closely with the two delegates and got to know them well. Jayatillaka was an exceptionally nice person and so was his wife; she used to come and dine with us and sing Sinhalese songs more beautifully than I had ever heard singing in Ceylon. The delegates and I did an immense amount of work in the press and House of Commons and at last in 1918 the Secretary of State for the Colonies agreed to receive a deputation on the subject.

Governments nearly always treat these kinds of deputation irritably and contemptuously, ignoring the evidence, particularly when the Government knows that it is in the wrong, but on 16 January 1918, in the Colonial Office I got a certain amount of cynical pleasure observing the antics of myself and my fellow deputies on one side of the table and of Under-Secretary of State for the Colonies, W. A. S. Hewins, M.P., and his permanent officials on the other. We were a motley gang, the Bishop of Lincoln, Gilbert Murray, Sir J. Rolleston, and I supported the Sinhalese. Sir V. Buxton introduced the deputation and I then made a speech. I began by saying that I knew something about Ceylon as I had been seven years in the Ceylon Civil Service. Hewins looked me up and down and then turned and said something, obviously a question, to his Permanent Under-Secretary. He looked at me with some misprision. We all did our best, but all we got from Mr Hewins was the inevitable and expected refusal. Who killed imperialism? I, said the imperialist, with my imperialism—and my Hewinses and my refusals.

And now I come to the fortuitous way in which we started the Hogarth Press and became publishers. In the last two years of the war Virginia's health became gradually more stable. She was writing again strenuously and regularly. She was at work on *Night and Day* and finished it at the end of 1918, and she also from time to time wrote short pieces like the *Mark on the Wall*. In 1917 and 1918 there was not a single month in which she did not have reviews in *The Times Literary Supplement*; many of these were reprinted in *The Common Reader* in 1925. She earned from these reviews £95 9s. 6d. in 1917 and £104 5s. 6d. in 1918. The routine of our life became pretty regular. We worked strenuously during the week. In addition to my political activities I was writing *Empire and Commerce in Africa*. Over the week-end we usually went for what we called a treat. It was a mild 'treat', a bus to somewhere up the river and a walk and tea in Hampton Court or Kingston perhaps. In those days—forty or fifty years ago—Richmond and Richmond Park, Ham, Kingston, Hampton Court were still very beautiful, and even on Saturdays and Sundays the beauty of trees and grass and river and willows was not yet obscured by hundreds of cars and thousands of people crawling like queues of blackbeetles and ants every week out of London in the morning, and having scattered their paper bags, ice-cream cartons, and beer bottles over the landscape, back again into London in the evening. Socially it was the prehistoric era in which one still had servants living in one's house. We had almost inherited from Roger Fry two: Nellie the cook, and Lottie the house-parlourmaid, who stayed with us for years. In 1917 they cost us in wages £76 1s. 8d. Though we had two servants and two houses our expenditure in 1917 was under £700. And we saw and entertained a good many people. They came out to lunch or dinner with us at Richmond and often stayed the night.

I have never known anyone work with more intense, more indefatigable concentration than Virginia. This was particularly the case when she was writing a novel. The novel became part of her and she herself was absorbed into the novel. She wrote only in the morning from ten to one and usually she typed out in the afternoon what she had written by hand in the morning, but all day long, when she was walking through London streets or on the Sussex downs or over the watermeadows or along the River Ouse, the book would be moving subconsciously in her mind or she herself would be moving in a dreamlike way through the book. It was this intense absorption which made writing so exhausting mentally for her, and all through her life she tried to keep two kinds of writing going simultaneously, fiction and criticism. After some weeks on a novel she would switch to criticism as a relief or rest, because, though she devoted great care and concentration to even a comparatively unimportant review, the part of her mind which she used for criticism or even biography was different from that which she used for her novels. The relief or relaxation which she obtained from this change in the angle of her mental vision was of the same kind as that obtained by a man whose work entails hard, concentrated thinking and who finds refreshment and relaxation for his mind in a hard, serious game of chess, because in the game he is using a different part of his mind and for a different purpose from what was required for his work.

As I have explained more than once in my autobiography, such wisdom as I possess is largely derived from the saws and sayings of my nurse who came from Somersetshire. One of the great truths which I learned from her was that all work and no play did irreparable harm to all humanity whom she and I recognised in a boy called Jack. The difficulty with Virginia was to find any play sufficiently absorbing to take her mind off her work. We were both interested in printing and had from time to time in a casual way talked about the possibility of learning to print. It struck me that it would be a good thing if Virginia had a manual occupation of this kind which, in say the afternoons, would take her mind completely off her work. Towards the end of 1916 we definitely decided that we would learn the art of printing. But that proved to be not at all an easy thing to do. The individual finds that very few actions are easy or simple for him, entangled as he is in the complicated machinery of life which, with him in it, is turned round and round and round by the colossal anonymous engine of twentieth-century society. When we went to the St Bride's school of printing down Bride Lane, Fleet Street, we learned that the social engine and machinery made it impossible to teach the art of printing to two middle-aged middle-class persons. Printing could only be taught to trade union apprentices, the number of whom was strictly limited.

This seemed to end our career as printers before it could begin. But on 23 March 1917, we were walking one afternoon up Farringdon Street from Fleet Street to Holborn Viaduct when we passed the Excelsior Printing Supply Co. It was not a very large firm, but it sold every kind of printing machine and material, from a handpress and type to a composing stick. Nearly all the implements of printing are materially attractive and we stared through the window at them rather like two hungry children gazing at buns and cakes in a baker shop window. I do not know which of us first suggested that we should go inside and see whether we could buy a machine and type and teach ourselves. We went in and explained our desire and dilemma to a very sympathetic man in a brown overall. He was extremely encouraging. He could not only sell us a printing machine, type, chases, cases, and all the necessary implements, but also a sixteen page pamphlet which would infallibly teach us how to print. There was no need to go to a school of printing or to become an apprentice; if we read this pamphlet and followed the instructions, we should soon find that we were competent printers. Before we left the shop we had bought a small hand-press, some Old Face type, and all the necessary implements and materials for a sum of £19 5s. 5d. The machine was small enough to stand on a kitchen table; it was an ordinary platen design; you worked it by pulling down the handle which brought the platen and paper up against the type in its chase. You could print one demy octavo page on it, and, I think, you could just squeeze in two crown octavo pages.

When the stuff was delivered to us in Richmond, we set it all up in the dining-room and started to teach ourselves to print. The Excelsior man proved to be right; by following the directions in the pamphlet we found that we could pretty soon set the type, lock it up in the chase, ink the rollers, and machine a fairly legible page. After a month we thought we had become sufficiently proficient to print a page of a book or pamphlet. We decided to print a paper-covered pamphlet containing a story by each of us and to try to sell it by subscription to a limited number of people whom we would circularise. Our idea was that, if this succeeded, we might go on to print and publish in the same way poems or other short works which the commercial publisher would not look at.

We set to work and printed a thirty-two page pamphlet, demy octavo, with the following title page:

Publication No. 1.

TWO STORIES

WRITTEN AND PRINTED

BY

VIRGINIA WOOLF

AND

L. S. WOOLF

HOGARTH PRESS
RICHMOND
1917

Virginia's story was *The Mark on the Wall* and mine was *Three Jews*. We even had the temerity to print four woodcuts by Carrington. I must say, looking at a copy of this curious publication today, that the printing is rather creditable for two persons who had taught themselves for a month in a dining-room. The setting, inking, impression are really not bad. What is quite wrong is the backing, for I had not yet realised that a page on one side of the sheet must be printed so that it falls exactly on the back of the page on the other side of the sheet.

We began to print *Two Stories* on 3 May in an edition of about 150 copies. We bound it ourselves by stitching it into paper covers. We took a good deal of trouble to find some rather unusual, gay Japanese paper for the covers. For many years we gave much time and care to find beautiful, uncommon, and sometimes cheerful paper for binding our books, and, as the first publishers to do this, I think we started a fashion which many of the regular, old established publishers followed. We got papers from all over the place, including some brilliantly patterned from Czechoslovakia, and we also had some marbled covers made for us by Roger Fry's daughter in Paris. I bought a small quantity of Caslon Old Face Titling type and used it for printing the covers.

We printed a circular offering Publication No. 1 for 1s. 6d. net and explaining that we in the Hogarth Press proposed to print and publish in the same way from time to time paper-covered pamphlets or small books, printed entirely by our two selves, which would have little or no chance of being published by ordinary publishers. We invited people to become subscribers to the publications of the Hogarth Press, either A subscribers to whom all publications would automatically be sent, or B subscribers who would be notified of each publication as it appeared. We sent this notice to people whom we knew or who, we thought, might be interested in our publications. I do not know how many people we circularised, but we published in July and by the end of the month we had practically sold out the edition for we had sold 124 copies. (The total number finally sold was 134.) I still have a list of eighty-seven people who bought the 134 copies and all but five or six of them were friends or acquaintances. There are some rather unexpected names among them, e.g. Charles Trevelyan, M. P., Arthur Ponsonby, M.P., Mrs Sidney Webb, and Mrs Bernard Shaw. The total cost of production was £3 7s. 0d., which included the noble sum of 15s. to Carrington for the woodcuts, 12s. 6d. for paper, and 10s. for the cover paper. The two authors were not paid any royalty. The total receipts were £10 8s. 0d., so that the net profit was £7 1s. 0d. Eventually forty-five people became A subscribers and forty-three B subscribers. Among the A subscribers was one bookseller, James Bain of what was then King William Street, Strand, and except for him every copy of our first publications was sold to private persons at the full published price. By 1923 the Press had developed to such an extent that we had become more or less ordinary publishers, selling our books mainly to booksellers at the usual discount, and we therefore gave up the subscriber system altogether.

We so much enjoyed producing *Two Stories* and its sale had been so successful (134 copies!) that we were induced to go on to something more ambitious. Katherine Mansfield and Murry were extremely interested in what we were doing, and Katherine offered us for Publication No. 2 a long short story which she had written, *Prelude*. When I look at my copy of *Prelude* today, I am astonished at our courage and energy in attempting it and producing it only a year after we had started to teach ourselves to print. For we printed only in the afternoon and even so not every afternoon; it is a sixty-eight-page book and we printed and bound it entirely with our own hands. The edition must have consisted of nearly 300 copies for, when it went out of print, we had sold 257 copies. Virginia did most of the setting and I did all the machining, though I did set when there was nothing to machine.

I did not machine *Prelude* on our small handpress; in fact, it would have taken much too long to do it page by page. I machined it on a large platen machine which printed four crown octavo pages at a time and which belonged to a jobbing printer called McDermott. McDermott had a small jobbing printing business in a street near The Green in Richmond. I got to know him in a curious way and we became great friends. While printing *Two Stories*, I one afternoon, when I took a proof of a page, found that there was something wrong with it which I could not get right and could not understand. None of the letters printed completely black, there were tiny white dots everywhere. My pamphlet gave me no help. I had noticed McDermott's printing business; it was called The Prompt Press. (When I got to know McDermott, I sometimes thought that he had called it The Prompt Press on the principle of 'lucus a non lucendo'.) After struggling with my page for hours, I took a proof, walked down to McDermott's shop, and boldly—but rather tremulously—went in. I explained to McDermott that I was trying to teach myself to print and that I had got into an inexplicable difficulty. I showed him my speckled proof and asked him whether he could tell me what was wrong. 'Wrong?' he said; 'it isn't on its feet, that's all; it isn't on its feet.' He explained to me that, in locking up type in the chase, you might get the whole page infinitesimally not flat on the imposing surface—it would be 'off its feet' and would not print evenly.

This was the beginning of a friendship which lasted as long as we were in Richmond. McDermott had for years been a compositor in a very large London firm of printers. They had printed *The Spectator* and McDermott was never tired of telling me stories of the editor, St. Loe Strachey, Lytton's cousin, and what a fuss he made about the 'colour'—i.e. the inking—of the paper; it had to be very black indeed, too black for McDermott's liking. He had always had a longing for independence, for a small jobbing business of his own; he saved up for years, and late in life bought the business in the street near The Green. He began with an old fashioned Albion press, on which he printed posters, and two large platen machines, one worked by power and the other by treadle. Just before I got to know him he had bought and installed a very large rotary machine.

He was an extremely nice man and he was very much interested in our—to him—rather eccentric and amusing printing antics. He came and looked at our outfit and at what we were doing, and said that I could, if I liked, borrow the chases for his big treadle platen machine, lock up four pages of *Prelude* at a time, carry them down to The Prompt Press, and machine them myself on his machine. This I did, a pretty laborious business, but not quite as laborious as it would have been to print the sixty-eight pages one by one. In the process I got to know McDermott and his business better and better. His large rotary press was really a white elephant; it was too large to be economical for the size of his business. It was continually going wrong; partly, I always suspected, because, having been a compositor all his life, he did not really understand machining and the kind of machine he had purchased. The result was that quite often, when I went down to print my own pages, I found him covered with oil and ink, pouring with sweat, and pouring a stream of the most hair raising language over his bloody machine. When that happened, instead of machining *Prelude* I spent the next few hours helping him to tinker at his bloody machine until I too was covered with oil and ink and pouring with sweat.

McDermott, I am sorry to say, produced one of the worst printed books ever published, certainly the worst ever published by the Hogarth Press. By 1919 we had become very friendly and he was eager that I should let him print a book for us. I had my doubts about this, because, though he was, of course, a first class compositor, he was a terribly impatient, slapdash worker, and in the other branches of printing was almost as much an amateur as I was. However, Virginia and I had discussed bringing out a book of her short stories and sketches, but had felt that it would be too much for us to print ourselves—and so, with considerable hesitation and certainly foolishly, I gave it to McDermott to print. It was bound in paper over boards with a woodcut design by Vanessa on the cover, and there were four woodcuts by her in the text. My greatest mistake was to allow him to provide the paper. He produced a nasty spongy antique wove and, ignorant as I was in those days about paper and printing, I had my doubts about it from the first. I went down and helped him to print the beastly thing. I have never seen a more desperate, ludicrous—but for me at the time tragic—scene than McDermott printing *Monday or Tuesday*. He insisted upon printing the woodcuts with the letterpress. The consequence was that, in order to get the right 'colour' for the illustrations, he had to get four or five times more ink on his rollers than was right for the type. His type was soon clogged with ink; but even that was not the worst: he got so much ink on the blocks and his paper was so soft and spongy that little fluffy bits of paper were torn off with the ink and stuck to the blocks and then to the rollers and finally to the type. We had to stop every few minutes and clean everything, but even so the pages were an appalling sight. We machined 1,000 copies, and at the end we sank down exhausted and speechless on the floor by the side of the machine, where we sat and silently drank beer until I was sufficiently revived to crawl battered and broken back to Hogarth House.

By having *Monday or Tuesday* printed for us by a commercial printer, we were, of course, abandoning the original idea of the

Press, which was to print small books ourselves. In fact we had been already in 1919 forced fortuitously to take a similar step, the first step on the path which was to end in our becoming regular and professional publishers. In 1918 we printed two small books: *Poems* by T. S. Eliot and *Kew Gardens* by Virginia. Of Tom's *Poems*, we printed rather fewer than 250 copies. We published it in May 1919 price 2s. 6d. and it went out of print in the middle of 1920. Of *Kew Gardens* we printed about 170 copies (the total sold of the first edition was 148). We published it on 12 May 1919, at 2s. When we started printing and publishing with our Publication No. 1, we did not send out any review copies, but in the case of *Prelude*, Tom's *Poems*, and *Kew Gardens* we sent review copies to *The Times Literary Supplement.* By 31 May we had sold forty-nine copies of *Kew Gardens*. On Tuesday 27 May, we went to Asham and stayed there for a week, returning to Richmond on 3 June. In the previous week a review of *Kew Gardens* had appeared in the *Literary Supplement* giving it tremendous praise. When we opened the front door of Hogarth House, we found the hall covered with envelopes and postcards containing orders from booksellers all over the country. It was impossible for us to start printing enough copies to meet these orders, so we went to a printer, Richard Madley, and got him to print a second edition of 500 copies, which cost us £8 9s. 6d. It was sold out by the end of 1920 and we did not reprint.

The expansion of the Press into something which we had never intended or originally envisaged can be seen in the following list of books published by us in the first four years of its existence:

1917.	L. and V. Woolf. *Two Stories*. Printed and bound by us.
1918.	K. Mansfield. *Prelude*. Printed and bound by us.
1919.	V. Woolf. *Kew Gardens*. 1st ed. printed and bound by us.
	T. S. Eliot. *Poems*. Printed and bound by us.
	J. Middleton Murry. *Critic in Judgment* Printed for us.
1919.	Hope Mirrlees. *Paris*. Printed and bound by us.
1920.	E. M. Forster. *Story of the Siren*. Printed and bound by us.
	L. Pearsall Smith. *Stories from the Old Testament*. Printed for us.
	Gorky. *Reminiscences of Tolstoi*. Printed for us.

The publication of T. S. Eliot's *Poems* must be marked as a red letter day for the Press and for us, although at the time when I began to set the lines

> The broad-backed hippopotamus
> Rests on his belly in the mud;

Although he seems so firm to us
He is merely flesh and blood.

I could not, of course, foresee the remarkable future of the author or the exact course of our long friendship with him. I do not remember exactly how or when we first met Tom, but it must, I think, have been in 1917, or even 1916. I bought a copy of *Prufrock* when it was published by The Egoist Ltd. in 1917, and it has the following inscription written on the cover:

Inscribed for Leonard Woolf (my
next / second } publisher)
with gratitude and affection
T. S. Eliot

Tom showed us some of the poems which he had just written and we printed seven of them and published them in the slim paper covered book. It included three remarkable poems which are still, I think, vintage Eliot: 'Sweeney among the Nightingales', 'Mr. Eliot's Sunday Morning Service', and 'Whispers of Immortality'. Professional compositors, indeed all professional printers, do not attend to the sense of anything which they print—or so I was told by McDermott, who also one day said to me that of all the millions of lines which he had set in his time he doubted whether more than a few hundred were worth reading. But as an amateur printer and also the publisher of what I was printing, I found it impossible not to attend to the sense, and usually after setting a line and then seeing it appear again and again as I took it off the machine, I got terribly irritated by it. But I never tired and still do not tire of those lines which were a new note in poetry and came from the heart of the Eliot of those days (and sounded with even greater depth and volume in the next work of his which we published, the poem which had greater influence upon English poetry, indeed upon English literature, than any other in the twentieth century, *The Waste Land*):

The host with someone indistinct
Converses at the door apart,
The nightingales are singing near
The Convent of the Sacred Heart,

And sang within the bloody wood
When Agamemnon cried aloud,
And let their liquid siftings fall
To stain the stiff dishonoured shroud.

When we first got to know Tom, we liked him very much, but we were both a little afraid of him. He was very precise, formal, cautious or even inhibited. One can feel this in the language of one of the first letters which he wrote to Virginia—in 1918—particularly in the first sentence:

Dear Mrs Woolf,

Please pardon me for not having responded to your note immediately—on Mondays I never have a moment up till late at night. And I was not furthermore quite sure of being able to come, as I thought my wife might be arranging to return on Friday morning, but I now hear that she is coming tomorrow.

I shall look forward to Friday with great pleasure.

Sincerely yours
T. S. Eliot

Rather nervously after the war we asked Tom to come for a weekend to Monks House, and this broke the ice. The reserve, even the language thawed, and by 1922 it was Dear Virginia and Dear Leonard instead of Dear Mrs Woolf and Dear Woolf. And the following is his letter accepting an invitation to tea, new style:

Be sure that Possums can't refuse
A tea with Mrs. Woolf on Tues.
And eagerly if still alive,
I'll come to Tea with you at five.
I'd like to come at half past four,
But have a business lunch before,
And feel responsibility
To do some work before my Tea.
But please don't let the kettle wait
And keep for me a cup and plate,
And keep the water on the bile,
A chair and (as I hope) a Smile.

Or this in 1937:

Thank you, Virginia, I WILL come to Tea on Tuesday the 4th May at 4.30 and I hope that Leonard will perhaps be in before I leave; anyway, it seems the only possibility between now and the end of May. But I don't see why you should be broadcasting without pay, unless you are appealing for a Good Cause (which is hard work at that): I should say that there was quite enough unpaid work to be had without adding broadcasting to it. To go to the Opera in a box is the only endurable way of going to the Opera: I have not been under such conditions for many a long year. Perhaps I shall go to Vienna and see if they have any cheap Opera there. I wish I might see you oftener, because as things are I seem to be degenerating into an Old Buffer. All my sports are getting to be Old Buffers' sports—e.g. I went to Wisbech last weekend, by way of the high table of Magdalene, to drink Port, and I have taken to the vice of Dining Clubs. It would not surprise me if I ended as a member of the Wine Committee of something or other; and this June I am to deliver the Prize Day Speech at Kingswood (Methodist) School. A respected citizen. And I have gone to live in Emperor's Gate. O dear. Am I a humbug? I envy you having finished an opus so recently as not to be expected to be working on a new one. I am trying to write a play, but it is very difficult, irritating when interrupted and tedious when not interrupted. O dear.

Your faithful
Tom

It was not until the end of 1922 that Tom gave us *The Waste Land* to read; we agreed to publish it; printed it ourselves and published it on 12 September 1923. That does not belong to this volume, but Tom was responsible for an interesting episode in our history as publishers which took place before the end of the war. He told us at the end of 1917 or the beginning of 1918 that Miss Harriet Weaver of *The Egoist*, which had published his *Prufrock*, was much concerned about a MS by James Joyce which she had. Both she and he thought it was a remarkable work, but it was indecent and there were grave doubts whether it was publishable in England. He asked us whether we could perhaps consider it for the Hogarth Press or at any rate have a talk with Miss Weaver about it. This we agreed to do and on Sunday 14 April 1918, Miss Weaver came to tea, bringing with her a large brown paper parcel containing the MS of *Ulysses* by James Joyce—though not the whole of *Ulysses* because Joyce was still writing it. She left the MS with us and we put this remarkable piece of dynamite into the top drawer of a cabinet in the sitting-room, telling her that we would read it and, if we thought well of it, see if we could get a printer to print it for us. The entry in my diary for the day is:

Miss Weaver to tea about Joyce's book and the Egoist, a very mild blueeyed advanced spinster.

And this is Virginia's entry:

But almost instantly Harriet Weaver appeared. Here our predictions were entirely at fault. I did my best to make her reveal herself in spite of her appearance, all that the editress of the Egoist ought to be, but she remained unalterably modest, judicious and decorous. Her neat mauve suit fitted both soul and body; her grey gloves laid straight by her plate symbolised domestic rectitude; her table manners were those of a well bred hen. We could get no talk to go. Possibly the poor woman was impeded by her sense that what she had in the brown paper parcel was quite out of keeping with her own contents. But then how did she ever come in contact with Joyce and the rest? Why does their filth seek exit from her mouth? Heaven knows. She is incompetent from the business point of view and was uncertain what arrangements to make. We both looked at the MS. which seems an attempt to push the bounds of expression further on, but still all in the same direction. And so she went.

We read the MS and decided that we would publish it if we could find a printer to print it. I showed it to William Maxwell of R. & R. Clark, Edinburgh, and to Clay, both very respectable printers of the highest rank. Neither of them would touch it and both of them said that no respectable printer would have anything to do with it, for the publisher and printer of it would certainly be prosecuted. All this took some time and it must have been in 1919 that we finally had to return the MS to Miss Weaver.

The publication of Maxim Gorky's *Reminiscences of Leo Nicolayevitch Tolstoi* in 1920 was also another milestone on the road of the Press towards ordinary, commercial publishing. I do not remember how we first came to know S. S. Koteliansky, always known as Kot, but I think that it must have been through Katherine Mansfield and Murry. In 1919 he came to us with a copy of the *Reminiscences*, just published in Moscow, which Gorky had sent to him, giving him the English translation rights. Kot suggested that he and I should translate it and the Hogarth Press publish it. We agreed to do this and thus began a collaboration between Kot and Virginia and me in translating Russian books. Our actual procedure in translating was that Kot did the first draft in handwriting, with generous space between the lines, and we then turned his extremely queer version into English. In order to make this easier and more accurate, we started to learn Russian and at one moment I had learned enough to be able to stumble through a newspaper or even Aksakov.

Gorky's book was a great success. We published it in July and had to reprint it almost immediately, and in the first year we sold about 1,700 copies. It was reprinted many times and is still selling forty years after publication. We serialised some of it in *The London Mercury*, and sold the American rights, so that at the end of 1920 Kot received nearly £50 which both he and we in those early days thought extremely satisfactory.

Kot was a fine translator from the Russian, and Lawrence and Katherine also at one time or another collaborated with him in translating. The translation of Bunin's *Gentleman from San Francisco*, a masterpiece or near-masterpiece, which he did with Lawrence and which we published in 1922, is magnificent. Gorky's *Reminiscences* is, I think, indisputably a miniature masterpiece of the purest water. Kot's English, which I had to turn into my English, was usually very strange, but it was also so vivid and individual that I was often tempted to leave it untouched. For instance, he wrote: 'She came into the room carrying in her arms a peeled-off little dog,' and on another occasion: 'she wore a haggish look'. If he was in doubt about a word, he sometimes looked it up in his dictionary and put all the variants into his translation, occasionally with curious results, e.g. 'he looked in the glass at his mug, dial, face'. One learned to the full Kot's iron integrity and intensity only by collaborating with him in a Russian translation. After I had turned his English into my English, we went through it sentence by sentence. Kot had a sensitive understanding of and feeling for language and literature, and also a strong subtle mind. He would pass no sentence until he was completely convinced that it gave the exact shade of meaning and feeling of the original, and we would sometimes be a quarter of an hour arguing over a single word.

The publication of Gorky was the beginning of our friendship with Kot which lasted thirty-five years, until his death in 1954. He was a remarkable and a formidable man. Physically he was a Jew of the Trotsky type, with a pelt of thick black bristly hair going straight up into the air off his high forehead. His eyes, behind thick glasses, looked at, through, and over you, sad and desperate, and yet with resigned intensity. When he shook hands with you, you felt that all the smaller bones in your hand must certainly have been permanently crushed to a fine powder. The handshake, which always reminded me of the Commendatore taking Don Giovanni by the hand in the last Act of Mozart's opera, was merely an unconscious symptom of Kot's passionate and painful intensity and integrity. I always had a secret hope that this devastating handshake meant that Kot liked one, and that those whom he didn't like didn't get it, and so it was worth while enduring the pain, having experienced what, I felt, one would have experienced if Elijah, Isaiah, or Jeremiah had shaken hands with one. For if you knew Kot well, you knew what a major Hebrew prophet must have been like 3,000 years ago. If

Jeremiah had been born in a ghetto village in the Ukraine in 1882, he would have been Kot. There are some Jews who, though their ancestors have lived for centuries in European ghettoes, are born with certain characteristics which the sun and sand of the desert beat into the bodies and minds of Semites. The heat of the desert burns their bodies until they are tempered like steel; it tempers their minds until they seem to be purified of all spiritual grit, leaving in mind and soul only pure, undiluted, austere, fanatical passion.

I am not saying that this is good or bad—I don't really know—but aesthetically it had a kind of austere beauty. In daily life it is also often extremely uncomfortable. Kot was not at all a comfortable man, but neither was Elijah nor Isaiah, I am quite sure. I have felt the same qualities of steely, repressed, purged passion, burnt into a Semite by sun and sand, in an ordinary Arab pearl diver from the Persian Gulf; he stood on the shore in Ceylon looking down on his dead comrade—he had died when diving for pearls at the Ceylon pearl fishery—and he made a long speech to the dead man's brother. It was in Arabic and I did not understand a word, and yet I understood every word. It was Isaiah and Jeremiah and Job—and Kot.

Kot was born in a Jewish village and his family, before the 1914 war, was well off, his father owning a mill. The fortunes of the Koteliansky family in the Ukraine are part of the terrible story of misery, death, and destruction which have swept over Jew and Gentile in central and eastern Europe since 1914. For centuries no doubt Jews, like the Kotelianskys in eastern Europe, suffered spasmodically from pogroms. Every now and then deaths by violence here or a rape there reminded them of what some people would call realities; for them it was something which the experience of two millennia had taught them to expect from God and from Governments, but in between these visitations or realities Jehovah more or less honoured his promise to Abram.

After 1914 families like the Kotelianskys were ruthlessly wiped off the face of the earth. Their village suffered the tramplings of more than three conquests, it was fought over first by the Austrians and Russians, then by the White Guards and a 'brigand' called, I think, Petlura, and finally by the Red Army. The Kotelianskys were well liked even by their Christian neighbours, and, when anti-Semitic armies were known to be approaching, the old grandmother was hurried away by her Christian neighbours into the comparative safety of their village. She died in the midst of one of these removals, and by the end of the fighting, when the Red Army finally established itself, Kot's parents and most of his brothers and sisters and their families had been liquidated by one side or the other. One brother did escape and soon after the war managed to reach Antwerp, and thence London and Canada.

Kot came to London with some kind of scholarship a few years before the 1914 war; he must have been nearly thirty. In 1914 he met D. H. Lawrence on a walking tour in the Lakes and they took to each other at once. Kot's passionate approval of what he thought good, particularly in people; his intense hatred of what he thought bad; the directness and vehemence of his speech; his inability to tell a lie—all this strongly appealed to Lawrence. When Kot approved of anyone, he accepted him absolutely; he could do no wrong and Kot summed it up always by saying of him: 'He is a real person.' This ethical accolade was given by him to a very few people. Lawrence, Katherine Mansfield, and Virginia were among the few who received it. When he said of someone: 'You see, he is a *real* person, yes, a *real* person,' you felt that you and he and that 'real person' had received some blessed vision or even sacrament of reality. Lawrence liked this kind of thing in Kot, just as he liked Kot's ruthless condemnation of people like Murry, and they became very fond of each other.

Kot's condemnations were terrific. If you said to him: 'Do you like such and such a book?' and he did not, he would say: 'It is hor-r-r-ible,' and the roll of his r's was like the roll of thunder on Mt Sinai. Or he would say of someone of whom he disapproved: 'A swindler, just a swindler'—and you felt that his vehemence had blown away all screens, disguises, veils, and uncovered the nakedness of some wretched sinner.

Kot once told me a little story which gives the flavour of his character and of his relations with the Lawrence circle. He went to stay for a weekend with Lawrence and Frieda near Chesham. It was only the second time that he had met Frieda and only his third meeting with Lawrence. At lunch Frieda began lamenting how much she missed her children. (She had left her husband and children to marry Lawrence.) Kot said: 'Frieda, you have left your children to marry Lawrence—and if you choose Lawrence, you must stop complaining about the children.' After lunch Frieda left them and Lawrence and Kot sat talking while outside the rain poured down in torrents. Suddenly the door opened and there stood a young woman with her skirt tucked up, in Wellington boots, soaking wet. She said: 'Lorenzo. Frieda has asked me to come and tell you that she will not come back.' 'Damn the woman,' shouted Lawrence in a fury, 'tell her I never want to see her again.' The young woman said nothing, but turned and went out into the rain.

The young woman was Katherine Mansfield, and it was the first time that Kot saw her. Later they became great friends. Katherine's feeling for him is clearly shown in her letters and journals; he was perhaps the only person whom she trusted and respected completely. And of Katherine Kot always said: 'She is a real person.' When I first knew Kot, he sat in a room at the top of a high building in Sicilian Avenue, and there sometimes when we were sitting, talking and Katherine was there, she would say to him: 'Now, Kot, howl like a dog.' And Kot would howl like a dog with such canine verisimilitude, with so melancholy and penetrating a howl, that from far off, even as far off as Russell Square, would come the answering howl of real dogs. This accomplishment had been acquired by Kot in the following way. When a young man in the Ukraine he had fallen in love with a woman living in a village about five miles from his home. He used once a week to go and see her, and then had to walk back the five miles late at night. The darkness, loneliness, silence terrified him, and he taught himself to howl like a dog because then the dogs in distant villages howled back in answer to him, and he felt that at any rate he was not entirely alone in a dark and hostile world.

The world in which Kot lived remained for him a dark and hostile world even in Acacia Road, St John's Wood, where for many years he lived alone. I went to see him there a few days before his death. Owing to the war and the aftermath of war I had not seen him for a long time, but, although obviously ill, he was the same as he had always been. My hand was crushed in the iron hand of the Commendatore. His hair was grey, his body flagging, but the spirit of Elijah, Isaiah, and Jeremiah remains to the end indomitable. Yes, Kot was a real person.

It is perhaps worth while recording the finances of the Hogarth Press in the first four years of its existence, during which we published the nine books listed on page 175. By the end of 1920 the total capital expenditure was £38 8s. 3d., on the printing machine, type, accessories, and a paper cutting machine. The following shows the net profit on each of the eight books:

	£	s.	d.
Two Stories	7	1	0
Prelude	7	11	8
Kew Gardens	14	10	0
Eliot's *Poems*	9	6	10
Murry's *Critic in Judgment*	2	7	0
Forster's *Story of the Siren*	4	3	7
Mirrlees's *Paris*	8	2	9
Stories from the Old Testament	11	4	5
Gorky's *Reminiscences*	26	10	9

In the first four years, therefore, the total net profit was £90, but this was without any charge for rent and overheads. We usually paid the author twenty-five per cent of the gross profits, and, where we printed the books ourselves, nothing was charged for printing and binding.

When the war ended, though the MS of *Ulysses* was in the cabinet in the drawing-room and I was on the point of buying McDermott's large platen printing machine from him for £70, we still had no idea of turning ourselves into an ordinary, commercial publishing business. But by 1924, if not indeed by 1922, we had, without realising it, done so. For in 1922 we published Bunin's *Gentleman from San Francisco*, Dostoevsky's *Stavrogin's Confession*, Virginia's *Jacob's Room, The Autobiography of Countess Tolstoy*; in 1923 *Tolstoy's Love Letters*, Goldenveizer's *Talks with Tolstoy*, Roger Fry's *Sampler of Castile*, Stephen Reynold's *Letters*, Forster's *Pharus & Pharillon*; in 1924 Freud's *Collected Papers* and the beginning of the Psycho-analytical Library, *Kenya* by Norman Leys, *The Rector's Daughter* by F. M. Mayor, Living Painters: *Duncan Grant*, *Seducers in Ecuador* by V. Sackville-West, *Early Impressions* by Leslie Stephen.

Ten years after we started printing *Two Stories* the Hogarth Press was a successful commercial publishing business. It remained for Virginia and me, and has always remained for me, a half-time occupation. I have little doubt that, if I had made it my full-time occupation, it would have become a bigger, fatter, and richer business. I have often heard it said by professional publishers and other people who know the book producing and book selling industry far better than I do that it would be quite impossible today to do what we did in 1917 to 1927, i.e. build up a successful publishing business from zero with no capital. Costs of production have increased to such an extent and publishing is so geared to large scale, best seller industry that today there is no place for the kind of books with which we began and which floated the Hogarth Press into prosperity. I see the added difficulties, but I am not convinced that the thing would not be possible in 1963. First, one would have to have, of course, the kind of luck which we had—to know or find a few writers, unknown but potentially of the first class. Secondly, one would have to start it, as we did, as a very part-time occupation, making one's living for the first years in other ways. Thirdly, one would have to refuse absolutely, as we did for many years, to publish anything unless we thought it worth publishing or the author worth publishing. I think that 'thirdly' is the most important of the three conditions of success. Most small publishers perish by trying to become too big too quickly. One reason why the Press survived was because for many years our object was, not to expand, but to keep it small. In business the road to bankruptcy is paved with what the accountant calls 'overheads' and too many publishers allow their 'overheads' to dictate to them the size of their business and the kind of books they publish. My theory was that the main object of a publisher, as business man, should be to keep his overheads as near to zero as possible, and, if he did that, he could forget about them and publish only what he wanted to publish. I still think that this had a good deal to do with the survival of the Hogarth Press.

The last year of the war was incredibly gloomy. Looking back on it I feel as if we lived in a perpetual fog. Only a few incidents emerge from the fog into my memory. Air raids became important. Bugles were blown and Virginia and I and Nellie, the cook, and Lottie, the housemaid, went down into the basement kitchen, and remained there while the anti-aircraft guns blazed away in Richmond Old Deer Park and sometimes the shrapnel fell rattling into the area.

One night when Desmond was staying with us there was one of the longest and most violent thunderstorms which I have ever lived through. It was impossible to sleep and Desmond and I sat talking and looking out of the window of his room on to the street. At about three o'clock in the morning a solitary horseman cantered down the empty street through the pouring rain while the lightning flashed and the thunder rolled around him.

At eleven in the morning of Monday 11 November 1918, I was writing in my room in Richmond when the maroons, as they were called, were fired. From this we knew that the armistice had been signed and the Great War had ended. Virginia celebrated the return of peace by going to the dentist in Harley Street and I restlessly followed her. We met in Wigmore Street and drifted to Trafalgar Square. The first hours of peace were terribly depressing. The Square, indeed all the streets, were solid with people, omnibuses, and vehicles of all kinds. A thin, fine, cold rain fell remorselessly upon us all. Some of us carried sodden flags, some of us staggered in and out of pubs, we wandered aimlessly in the rain and mud with no means of celebrating peace or expressing our emotions of relief and joy. Our emotions of joy and relief ebbed, our spirits flagged. All, or nearly all of us, decided at the same moment to go home, and at once it became impossible to go home, for the buses, the trains, the stations became a solid mass of people struggling to go home. Eventually we managed to get to Waterloo and some two hours later Richmond.

On the first page of this book I recorded that the one thing which I remember in my return from Ceylon after seven years to Europe is the chocolate creams in Marseille. It is a strange fact—I have no doubt, discreditable to me, some unsavoury juggling between my scruffy ego and sluttish id—that one of the chief things which I remember as connected with the return from those terrible four years of war to peace is chocolate creams. A good many Belgian refugees in the first year of the war settled in Richmond and a large florid Belgian woman opened a kind of delicatessen shop (as they were called in those days) and tea-shop some way up the hill near Richmond Bridge. As the war went on delicatessen became very thin on the ground and chocolate creams vanished. Some months after armistice day, Virginia and I, walking up Richmond Hill, looked into the shop and there upon the counter were slabs of chocolate cream bars. When I was a child, you could buy large fat bars of chocolate cream which cost, I think, a halfpenny the bar. Some were made by Cadbury and some by Fry, and if you were an addict of Cadbury, you regarded the Fry eater as a drinker of Musigny Vieilles Vignes regards the drinker of Australian Burgundy. I belonged to the Cadbury school and have remained an addict of chocolate cream in bars ever since (though I have not seen any for years). The Belgian chocolate cream bars were un-English, being thin and continental, but when we saw them, the world seemed to change just a little and we dashed into the shop and each bought three bars which was the maximum that Madame X allowed each customer to buy. We carried them back to Hogarth House and ate them silently, almost reverently. The Great War was at last over.

Downhill all the Way
1919–1939

The herd ran violently down a steep place
into the lake, and were choked.

St Luke, chapter 8

1
Peace In Our Time, O Lord

At the end of the third volume of my autobiography the great war of 1914 to 1918 had just ended, having in its four years killed 100 million men and caused 36 million casualties. It has been estimated that the direct cost of the war was about £60,000 million and its indirect cost about £50,000. It destroyed, I think, the bases of European civilisation. We, like everyone who lived through those years, had been profoundly influenced by them. When the maroons boomed on 11 November 1918, we were no longer the same people who, on 4 August 1914, heard with amazed despair that the guns had begun to boom. In 1914 in the background of one's life and one's mind there were light and hope; by 1918 one had unconsciously accepted a perpetual public menace and darkness and had admitted into the privacy of one's mind or soul an iron fatalistic acquiescence in insecurity and barbarism. There was nothing to be done about it, and so, as I recorded, Virginia and I celebrated the end of a civilisation and the beginning of peace by sitting in the lovely, panelled room in Hogarth House, Richmond, which had been built almost exactly 200 years before as the country house of Lord Suffield, and eating, almost sacramentally, some small bars of chocolate cream.

The last sentence seduces me into a digression, though what I am about to say is not really irrelevant on the first page of a volume of autobiography, for it is concerned with the impossibility of telling the truth, the extraordinary difficulty of unearthing facts. The moment one begins to investigate the truth of the simplest facts which one has accepted as true—about one's own life, for instance—it is as though one had stepped off a firm narrow path into a bog or quicksand—every step one takes one sinks deeper into the bog of uncertainty.

For instance, the above statement about Hogarth House is not true, though for years I believed it to be true. When in 1915 we took a lease of Hogarth House, it was part of a large eighteenth-century mansion which belonged to a lady living in Bushey. The mansion had been very ingeniously divided into two houses, one called Suffield House and the other Hogarth House. We were told at the time that the whole house had been built originally in 1720 as a country house for Lord Suffield and had been converted into two houses with two front doors in the nineteenth century. That it was built in 1720 was, I think, almost certainly true. That was, it seems to me, about the best moment for English architecture, at any rate for the medium-sized, aristocratic country house like the one which Lord Suffield did not build in Richmond in 1720. The interior of the original undivided house must have been perfect. All the rooms were panelled, the ones on the ground floor with a certain amount of chaste ornamentation; in the others the panels became progressively plainer as one went up from floor to floor. Every room was beautifully proportioned. Most houses and gardens are, like most of the people who make them or live in them, featureless, amorphous; the houses are closed boxes in which people live, the gardens open boxes in which people grow flowers or vegetables. Occasionally one comes across a house upon which those who built it or lived in it have imposed a character and form markedly and specifically its own, as though it were a person or a work of art. Hogarth House was one of these. All the rooms, even when we first saw them in the dirty, dusty desolation of an empty house, had beauty, repose, peace, and yet life. One felt at once that each of them only needed a table and chair, a bed or a bookcase to become the perfect cell in which a human being might eat and sleep, talk, read, or work. Perhaps the people who for 200 years had been doing just that in these rooms had left the aura of their lives in them, but more prosaically it was matter—bricks and mortar and wood—and the way in which they had been used 200 years before which gave to Hogarth House its extraordinary character of being the perfect envelope for everyday life. It was partly its combination of immense solidity with grace, lightness, and beauty. The electrician who had to take a wire through the inside wall of the drawing-room, told us that in all his experience he had never seen as thick an inside wall in a house. In the room itself one felt the security from anything like a hostile world, the peace and quiet, in this tremendous solidity of walls, doors, and windows, and yet nothing could have been more light and graceful, more delicately and beautifully proportioned than the room itself, its fireplace and great windows, its panelling and carved woodwork.

In the house before it was divided there was a great hall and a very beautiful staircase, and on the first floor a tremendously broad corridor. We lived in this house from 1915 to 1924. After the war, in 1920, the owner refused to renew our lease, but offered to sell us the whole property, i.e. both Suffield and Hogarth House. We bought it for £2,000, and at one moment we thought we might restore the two houses to their original condition as one great country house and live for the remainder of our lives in this magnificent Suffield House. But it was a project half serious and half a day dream. By 1924 we had abandoned it, for the house would have been much too large for us and we had decided that it was time to move back into London. So we sold what had once been Suffield House and moved to Tavistock Square.

But had it ever been Suffield House? Had it ever belonged to Lord Suffield? It is impossible to know, but what is quite certain is that no Lord Suffield built it as his country house in 1720, because the barony of Suffield was created in 1786. So much for the truth about the genealogy of a house. I recently discovered that when I bought Monks House, Rodmell, in 1919, what I was then told about its name and its genealogy was also quite untrue. As I recorded in a previous volume of my autobiography,[1] it was said to have been called Monks House, because in the fifteenth century it belonged to Lewes Priory and the monks used it for their 'retreats'. I said that I hope the story was true, but I rather doubted such legends about houses when there is no documentary evidence for them. Since writing that, I have examined the deeds for Monks House and find that the story is entirely untrue. The deeds go back to 1707 and record the names of everyone who lived in it (together usually with the names of all their sons and daughters) from 1707 to 1919, when I bought it from the heirs of Jacob Verrall. From 1707 to 1919 only three families owned and lived in it. In 1707 John Cleere or Clear, carpenter of Rottingdean, acquired it from James de la Chambre. From 1707 to 1796 it remained in the Clear family, passing from father to son. In 1779 John Clear, carpenter, great-grandson of the original John Clear, carpenter, inherited it, and left it, when he died in 1782, to his son James. (He left five guineas to each of his two sons, Edward and Thomas, and a guinea to his granddaughter Charity.) In 1796 James Clear sold it to John Glazebrook. All this time, from 1707 to 1796, the house was called Clear's.

From 1796 to 1877 the house was in the Glazebrook family,

[1] See above, p. 40.

thirty-three years in the hands of John Glazebrook and for forty-eight years in those of his widow, Mercy, and his son William, except for a short interval in 1829 when it was sold for £300 to Matthew Lower, publican, of Rodmell, who resold it for £300 back to William Glazebrook. The Glazebrooks must have been connected with the Clears and with the house already thirty years before they actually acquired it, for in a mortgage deed of 1765 the property is described as a messuage in the tenure of John Clear and John Glazebrook. The Glazebrooks were millers; John Glazebrook in 1749 bought the mill which was up on the down above Rodmell, and it remained in the family for 128 years, when the executors of William Glazebrook sold it to Jacob Verrall in 1877.

At the same time, in the same year, the executors also sold what is now called Monks House to Jacob Verrall. From 1796 to 1877 the house was called Glazebrook's except for a short interval when it was called Lower's. The first time that it was ever called Monks House in any document was when it was advertised for sale in 1919 on Jacob Verrall's death. The story that Monks House belonged to the Lewes monks in the fifteenth century is therefore just as false as the story that Suffield House was built by Lord Suffield in 1720.

It is rather depressing for an autobiographer starting on a fourth volume to find in this way that most of his facts are will-o'-the-wisps and that it is almost impossible to tell the truth. Facts about the houses in which one lives during the whole journey from the womb to the grave are not unimportant. The house—in which I include its material and spiritual environment—has an immense influence upon its inhabitants. Looking back over one's life, one sees it divided by events into compartments or chronological sections, e.g. I was at St Paul's School 1894 to 1899, I was in the Ceylon Civil Service 1904 to 1911, I lived through the war of 1914 to 1918 and the war of 1939 to 1945. I was married in 1912. All such momentous or catastrophic events moulded the form of one's life, disrupted or distorted its movement. But what has the deepest and most permanent effect upon oneself and one's way of living is the house in which one lives. The house determines the day-to-day, hour-to-hour, minute-to-minute quality, colour, atmosphere, pace of one's life; it is the framework of what one does, of what one can do, and of one's relations with people. The Leonard and Virginia who lived in Hogarth House, Richmond, from 1915 to 1924 were not the same people who lived in 52 Tavistock Square from 1924 to 1939;

the Leonard and Virginia who lived in Asham House from 1912 to 1919 were not the same people who lived in Monks House from 1919 to 1941. In each case the most powerful moulder of them and of their lives was the house in which they lived. That is why looking back over my life I tend to see it divided into sections which are determined by the houses in which I lived, not by school, university, work, marriage, death, division, or war.

When I bought Monks House in 1919 there was an auction of all its contents. It took place in the garden on a marvellous sunny day. All the village attended, including descendants of the long line of Glazebrooks who had already been moving about in the house and garden 155 years before. 1919 was a great fruit year in Sussex; the trees were laden with plums and pears and apples. The branches of an enormous apple-tree heavy with great red apples hung over the yew hedge along which we stood bidding or just watching the auction; and every now and again someone would pull a great red apple off the tree and eat it. There is nearly always something sad and sinister in the auction of the contents of a house, a kind of indecent exposure of the lives of dead men, women, and children. This is particularly the case when the auctioneer reaches those cold and comfortless attics in which in distant days servants slept on iron bedsteads. As the auctioneer's men carried the furniture, glass, and china, ornaments, pictures, and the accumulated odds and ends of a family's possessions on the Monks House lawn, it seemed at moments as though one were watching the disembowelling, not merely of a house, but of time. Old Jacob Verrall's[1] wife Lydia was, I think, a connection of the Glazebrooks and much of the furniture etc. must have belonged to them and to have been in the house for a century and more. Some of the old furniture and china was beautiful and was bought up at quite high prices by dealers. I bought three pictures painted on wood by a Glazebrook in the middle of the nineteenth century or perhaps a little earlier. They were painted in that curious stiff uncompromising style of the inn signboard of a hundred years ago. One was of a middle-aged man, very dark and bewhiskered, and another of a man holding a horse. The third was of four children heavily swaddled in hats and coats standing stiffly in a line in front of the house. They were, I am sure, the Glazebrook children of a hundred years ago. Their spirits, I almost felt and feel,

[1] I gave some facts about old Verrall and his wife above, pp. 41 and 42.

walk in the house, clattering up and down the narrow stairs, now deeply worn by the countless comings and goings of Clears, Glazebrooks, and Verralls. At the top of the stairs you can see the place where they had once put a small gate to prevent the children plunging downstairs. And once when a floorboard was taken up by a workman we found a tiny little wooden eighteen-century shoe; another time I found in the cellar a George III fourpenny piece which appeared to have been charred in a fire.

These little facts are not, I think, either unimportant or irrelevant. In the atmosphere of both houses, Monks House in Rodmell and Hogarth House in Richmond, there was something similar. In both one felt a quiet continuity of people living. Unconsciously one was absorbed into this procession of men, women, and children who since 1600 or 1700 sat in the panelled rooms, clattered up and down stairs, and had planted the great Blenheim apple-tree or the ancient fig-tree. One became a part of history and of a civilisation by continuing in the line of all their lives. And there was something curiously stable and peaceful in the civilisation of these two houses. In 1919 when we bought Monks House, Virginia was only just recovered or recovering from the mental breakdown which I have described in *Beginning Again*; in 1919 we still had six years of life in Hogarth House before we moved into London. Those six years were, I am sure, crucial for the stabilising of her mind and health and for her work, and I am quite sure that the tranquil atmosphere of these two houses, which was in their walls and windows and gardens and orchard, but also in the soothing, chastening feeling of that long line of quiet people who century after century had lived and died in them—I am sure that this tranquil atmosphere helped to tranquillise her mind.

At the end of 1919, then, we were the owners of two houses. Our expenses during the previous twelve months had been £845. We had been printing and publishing books in the Hogarth Press for two years, but the Press was still a hobby which we practised in our spare time. The three books which we published in 1919 were Virginia's *Kew Gardens*; T. S. Eliot's *Poems*, and J. Middleton Murry's *Critic in Judgment*—on which we made a net profit of £26 3s. 10d. Virginia had just begun her 'career' of a novelist. Her first novel *The Voyage Out*, had been published by Duckworth four years ago in 1915. Her second novel, *Night and Day*, had just been published, also by Duckworth, in October 1919. *The Voyage Out* had received high praise, and so did *Night and Day*, but to a less degree. Neither book was a success financially either for the author or publishers, for, as I have recorded elsewhere, nine years after it was published Duckworth had sold only 2,238 copies of *Night and Day*. Virginia's only other publications by the end of 1919 were *The Mark on the Wall*, which the Hogarth Press published in 1917, and *Kew Gardens*, which we published in May 1919. She did not begin to write her third novel, *Jacob's Room*, until April 1920, but she wrote some short pieces like *An Unwritten Novel* and did a certain amount of reviewing in *The Times Literary Supplement* and *Athenaeum*. Her earnings in 1919 from her writing, at the age of thirty-seven, were £153 17s. 0d. Virginia was forty years old before she earned a living wage by writing; if she had had to earn her living during those years, it is highly improbable that she would ever have written a novel.

By 1920 I had accumulated a considerable number of paid and unpaid occupations. I was editor of the *International Review* on a salary of £250. I did a good deal of freelance journalism, mostly for the *New Statesman*, but a certain amount for the *Nation* and the *Athenaeum*. I earned in 1919 £578, £262 by freelance journalism, £250 from my editorship, and £66 from my books. The *International Review* was a monthly financed by the Rowntrees; I had an office in Red Lion Court, Fleet Street, in which sat Miss Matthaei, Assistant Editor, and Miss Green, Secretary. I went to the office three or four days a week. We did a great deal of work. My idea was that the *Review* should cover the whole field of foreign affairs, international relations, and the problem of preventing war which centred in the inchoate League of Nations. My main object was to try to put before readers the facts without a knowledge of which it was impossible even to begin to understand the intricate problems of the international chaos created by the war. I therefore had two features in the paper which I thought of great importance. The first, which I wrote myself, was an 'international diary'; in it I dealt with the chief international events of the previous month. In order to produce this diary Miss Matthaei and I read French, German, Austrian, Italian, and Spanish daily papers. The second feature was, I think, something quite new in this kind of journalism. I had a section called 'The World of Nations; Facts and Documents'. It ran to thirty or forty pages and it contained all kinds of documents, and the kind of thing we published is shown by the contents of a single number, November 1919: (1) Message of Admiral Kolchak to the peoples of Siberia and instructions to military officers; (2) Declaration of the Ukrainian Government regarding Denikin; (3) The text of an Anglo-Persian Treaty; (4) The text of an alleged treaty between Germany and Japan which had been published in America but not in Britain; (5) A translation of the full text of the new German Constitution.

In my search for documents I had some curious experiences; the following was one of the most interesting. I do not remember how or when I first got to know Theodore Rothstein, a Russian Jew living in London. He is frequently mentioned in the diaries of Wilfrid Scawen Blunt, for in 1907 he was London Correspondent of the *Egyptian Standard* and worked closely with Blunt and Brailsford for Egyptian independence. When I knew him in 1919 he was unofficial ambassador of the unrecognised Bolshevik Government. He told me that, when the Bolsheviks first seized power, the London police arrested him and put him on a ship lying in the Pool just below London Bridge, meaning to deport him in it to Russia. Rothstein knew Lloyd George and had had 'off the record' communication with him on behalf of Lenin. He succeeded in getting a letter to the Prime Minister smuggled out of the ship, and orders were immediately given to the police to release the Russian 'ambassador'.

Rothstein was a short, stumpy, bearded, bespectacled revolutionary who looked like Karl Marx. He was the first of the many hundred per cent dyed in the wool, dedicated communists that I have had the misfortune to come across in the last forty-five years of my life. Communists, Roman Catholics, Rosicrucians, Adventists, and all those sects which ferociously maintain as divine or absolute truth, monopolistically revealed to them, an elaborate abracadabra of dogmas and fantasies, fill me with melancholic misery. The ruthlessness and the absurdity of the believers' beliefs reduce me to despair. What is the point, one feels, of any political, social, scientific, or intellectual activity if civilised people in the twentieth century not only accept as divine truth the myths dreamed by Palestinian Jews two or three thousand years ago or by German Jews a hundred years ago, but also condemn to Hell, death, or Siberia those who disagree with them?

Rothstein, as I said, was the first of these modern civilised savages, these communist fanatics, that I came across. Outside the circle of his Marxist religion he seemed to me a nice man and highly intelligent; inside the magic circle he was a cross between a schoolman and a dancing dervish. He would expound the gospel of Marxism-Leninism to me at great length in that dreadful jargon of meaningless abstractions which has become the language of communism and the excuse for the torture or killing of hundreds of thousands of human beings. Some time in 1919 he came to me and said that he had the full text of a number of speeches made by Lenin since his return to Russia. None of these very important speeches and statements of policy had been reported in the British or American press, and he was willing to give me translations of them if I would publish them in the *International Review*. I said that I would, and then I had my first experience of the behaviour of the real underground revolutionary.

The question was how the typescript of the translation of Lenin's speeches should be physically handed over by Rothstein, his agent, to me, the editor. Having had no experience of revolutionaries, secret agents, or spies, I naturally thought that it would be sent to me in the ordinary way through the post. Rothstein was horrified at such a crude and naïve idea. There was, he said, and in this he was correct, still operating a censorship, which was a legacy from the war, and if the authorities knew of the existence of verbatim translations of Lenin's speeches, they would refuse to allow publication; we must on no account allow the police to know that he was going to give them to me. The only way to defeat the police was for me to follow his instructions meticulously. On Wednesday afternoon I was to walk down the Strand towards Fleet Street, timing it so that I should pass under the clock at the Law Courts precisely at 2.30. I must walk on the inside of the pavement and precisely at 2.30 I would meet Rothstein under the clock walking from Fleet Street to Trafalgar Square on the outside of the pavement. He would be carrying in his right hand an envelope containing Lenin's speeches, and, as we passed, without speaking or looking at each other, he would transfer the envelope from his right hand to mine.

This elaborate procedure was carried out and I sent the speeches to the printer to be printed in the next issue of the *International Review*. I do not know how the police discovered that we were going to publish these documents or why the authorities thought that it would be dangerous for the British people to know what Lenin was saying—it seems rather fantastic to believe that a Secret Service man was always trailing Rothstein and saw him hand over the envelope to me outside the Law Courts. At any rate a few days later the police went to the printers, seized the documents and, I think, some type which had already been set, and forbade publication.

The British public were thus prevented from knowing what Lenin was saying in Russia at the historical moment when that knowledge was most interesting and politically important. This is one of the many instances of congenital stupidity in secret services and censorship which I have come across in my life and which, however often I come across them, fill me with innocent surprise. No intelligent person who went about his business in London in 1918 and 1919, who talked to the common man and knew what is called the climate of opinion, could possibly have thought that the number of people who would have been politically influenced by reading Lenin's speeches in the *International Review* would have exceeded the number of righteous men whom Abraham and the Lord found in Sodom. But once one begins to try to suppress some knowledge or some opinions, one loses all sense of proportion and relevance in one's obsession with the danger of ideas. In the end the only safe course for the worried, nervous policeman and the cloistered censor, sitting aloof in his office with the blue pencil in his hand, is to try to suppress all knowledge and all thought.

I do not think that I saw Theodore Rothstein many times after the fiasco with Lenin's speeches. It was not very long before he went back to Russia. I was told—I do not remember by whom or know with what truth—that he became a Commissar in Samarkand or some other remote province of the Soviet Empire. He was such a ruthless dogmatist and such a dedicated Leninist-Marxist that he must, I think, sooner or later have been liquidated in one of the great purges by some equally dedicated and ruthless comrade.

To someone like myself born in the comparative civilisation of the nineteenth century one of the horrors of life since 1920 is its senseless savagery. If one shuts one's eyes or one's mind, it is just possible to ignore the millions of Jews slaughtered in Hitler's gas chambers and the millions of unstigmatised persons killed in concentration camps and 'on the field of battle' during the 1939 war. But somehow or other the crowning point of barbarism seems to have been reached in the kind of doctrinal or racial cannibalism that has swept over the earth. The merciless savagery with which Spaniard treated Spaniard in the civil war, or Italian treated Italian under Mussolini, or German treated German under Hitler, or African is now treating African in the Congo, makes such outbreaks as the Armenian atrocities, which horrified Gladstonian liberals towards the end of the nineteenth century, appear insignificant. 'Dog does not eat dog' and 'a wolf does not make war on a wolf' are such ancient truths that they are proverbial, but in the twentieth century large-scale fratricide has been common among patriots, monarchists, republicans, fascists, nazis, socialists, anarchists in Germany, Italy, Spain and Africa. But the doctrinal cannibalism of communists since 1917, particularly in Russia, has been even more repulsive if only because of its scale. The liquidation in 1930 of the Russian kulaks—peasants numbering with their families five million persons—is one of the most dreadful stories in the whole of history.[1] And no one will ever know how many hundreds of thousands of Russians have been liquidated by Russians in the last forty years—in forced-labour camps, prisons, judicial murders, purges. When one reads that a million kulaks have been ruined or done to death because they were rather prosperous peasants, or 500,000 Russian communists have been killed by Russian communists because they were either right deviationists or left deviationists, or six million German Jews have been killed by German Christians because they were Jews, one cannot feel that each one of these persons was an individual like oneself, that every one of a million Russian peasants when he was suddenly driven out of his house and off his land to starve and die with his family in the snow, and each one of those hundreds of thousands of Russian communists when he felt himself rotting to death in the Siberian labour camp, and each of those six million Jews when he found himself being driven naked by the nazi guards into the gas chamber, suffered, before the final annihilation of death, the same agony which you or I would suffer if it happened to us.

I do not think that to say this is sentimental or here irrelevant. At any rate it has, I know, to me personally a peculiar and profound relevance. I have known as individuals and friends in London two Russians who went back to Russia and put their heads into the noose of Stalinist communism. I feel pretty certain that in each case the noose was pulled sooner or later and my friends were liquidated. If you had searched the world, you could not anywhere have found

[1] Sir John Maynard in *The Russian Peasant* says that 'it can only be compared for ruthlessness with the wholesale removals of population by the ancient monarchies, or the expulsion of the Moors from Spain or the Jews from Germany'.

two men more unlike each other than Theodore Rothstein and Prince Mirsky, the Russian Jew and the Russian aristocrat. Rothstein was, as I said, a mediaeval schoolman born into the twentieth century, a pedant and fanatic where the gospel of Karl Marx was concerned. He was, I think, by nature a gentle and civilised man, who loved talk and the intellectual pleasure to be derived from the intricate working of good brains. But he had been caught in the cruel inhuman machinery of communism. If he were not ruthlessly liquidated, he would himself have been a ruthless liquidator.

Let me leave Rothstein for the moment being shot by a comrade or shooting a comrade in one of those purges by which behind the iron curtain men build the perfect society. Let me turn to Prince Mirsky. Mirsky was a stranger man than Rothstein. I always felt that he was fundamentally one of those unpredictable nineteenth-century Russian aristocrats whom one meets in Aksakov, Tolstoy, and Turgenev. Sometimes when one caught in a certain light the vision of his mouth and jaw, it gave one that tiny little clutch of fear in the heart. It made one think of Turgenev's mother flogging the servant to death. I have known only a very few people with this kind of mouth; its sinister shape comes, I think, from the form of the jaw and arrangement of the teeth. There is always the shadow of a smile in it, but it is the baleful smile of the shark or crocodile.[1] Mirsky had this kind of smile. It may have had no psychological significance and he may well have had nothing cruel or sharklike in his character. In all our relations with him he seemed an unusually courteous and even gentle man, highly intelligent, cultivated, devoted to the arts, and a good literary critic. He had, at the same time, that air of profound pessimism which seemed to be characteristic of intellectual Russians, both within and without the pages of Dostoevsky. Certainly Prince Mirsky would have found himself spiritually at home in *The Possessed* or *The Idiot.*

One day Mirsky came to us in Tavistock Square and told us that

[1] One day when I was travelling by train along the south coast of Ceylon from Matara to Galle, on the platform of one of the stations through which we passed there were dozens of dead sharks. I had never seen anything like it in Ceylon and I do not know why they were there. On each dead face there was this sinister grin. Talking to Mirsky in a London sitting-room, as he suddenly turned his head to say something and there was a glint of teeth and smile, I was back in Ceylon twelve years ago in the railway carriage looking at the rows of dead, smiling sharks.

he was going back to Russia. This must have been in 1931. By that time one knew something of the kind of life (or death) that an intellectual might expect in the Russia of Stalin. It seemed madness, if not suicide, for a man like Mirsky voluntarily to return to Russia and put himself in the power of the ferocious fanatics who could not possibly have the slightest sympathy with or for him. We knew Mirsky well enough to say so. He was extremely reticent, shrugging it all off with some platitude, but he left us with the impression of an unhappy man who, with his eyes open, was going not half, but the whole, way to meet a nasty fate. We never saw him again.

The fate of Mirsky and Rothstein seems to me terribly typical of our time. Both of them, as I said, were almost certainly liquidated, which means that they were in some horrible way put to death, murdered. Even if they were not, they must have escaped by some accident, for thousands of men like them have been liquidated in Russia. Contemplating this and them, I feel the horror of the savagery of contemporary man in a way in which I do not feel it when I hear of the more horrible stories of the massacre of millions. I knew them as individuals, and it is as an individual that I feel their fate, this liquidation, this senseless torture and killing of two harmless individual human beings. For what after all could be more harmless than the slightly ridiculous bespectacled Rothstein spinning the endless web of the Marxian abracadabra or Mirsky endlessly discussing the magnificent absurdity of Tolstoy or the niceties in the torrential style of Dostoevsky? That Theodore Rothstein may have been himself potentially as cold-blooded a murderer as his cold-blooded murderers, or that Prince Mirsky may have been potentially as inhumanly cruel as so many other Russian aristocrats, does not contradict or make nonsense of what I have just written; it only underlines the senseless political and social stupidity of contemporary Europe. I have sat talking in Richmond with Rothstein and in Paris and Tavistock Square with Mirsky, and I know that what interested them and what gave them pleasure were things of the intellect and the arts, painting, music, and literature. In a world which had the slightest claim to civilisation, they would have lived and died civilised men, doing or suffering no public evil. As it was, their lives became hopelessly entangled in the wheels of an idiotic, barbarous social and political system, and the misery and death which they suffered (or which perhaps they caused) were inflicted on pretexts or for reasons which have no sense, no reality, no importance for the vast majority of the human race. Power and the struggle for power are of course realities involved in the machinery of communism and Soviet Russia in which Rothstein and Mirsky became fatally involved; but power is always the concern of a tiny minority. The Rothsteins and Mirskys and the thousands of anonymous victims of communism are sacrificed for words and phrases, tales 'told by an idiot, full of sound and fury, signifying nothing'.

I know that I am prejudiced against communism, which seems to me in some ways worse than nazism and fascism. *Corruptio optimi pessima*—the greatest evil is the good corrupted. The Hitlers and Mussolinis are just thugs or psychopaths, savages who in all ages have formed the scum of society; their imitators like Oswald Mosley rouse in me no emotion more serious than contempt. But communism has its roots in some of the finest of human political motives and social aspirations and its corruption is repulsive. The first time I met Mirsky was in Paris, in Jane Harrison's flat. Jane Harrison, the brilliant Newnham classical scholar, was one of the most civilised persons I have ever known. She was also the most charming, humorous, witty, individual human being. When I knew her she was old and frail physically, but she had a mind which remained eternally young. She liked Mirsky and enjoyed talking to him, and he, I felt, sat at her feet. That from that environment he should have been drawn into the spider web of Soviet Russia to be destroyed there fills one with despair, despair that communism, by *corruptio optimi*, again and again and again has 'lighted fools the way to dusty death'.[1]

I have reached the period in my autobiography in which our lives and the lives of everyone have become penetrated, dominated by politics. Happy the country and era—if there can ever have been one—which has no politics. Ever since 1914 in the background of our lives and thoughts has loomed the menace of politics, the canker of public events. (One has ceased to believe that a public event can be anything other than a horror or disaster.) Virginia was the least political animal that has lived since Aristotle invented the definition, though she was not a bit like the Virginia Woolf who appears in

[1] Since writing the above, I have been told by Malcolm Muggeridge, who saw a good deal of Mirsky in Moscow in 1932-3, that Mirsky just before the war was sent to a camp for ten years and either died or was shot there.

many books written by literary critics or autobiographers who did not know her, a frail invalidish lady living in an ivory tower in Bloomsbury and worshipped by a little clique of aesthetes. She was intensely interested in things, people, and events, and, as her new books show, highly sensitive to the atmosphere which surrounded her, whether it was personal, social, or historical. She was therefore the last person who could ignore the political menaces under which we all lived. *A Room of One's Own* and *Three Guineas* are political pamphlets belonging to a long line stretching back to *Vindication of the Rights of Women* by Mary Wollstonecraft, and she took part in the pedestrian operations of the Labour Party and Co-operative Movement. And by 'pedestrian' I mean the grass roots of Labour politics, for she had a branch of the Women's Co-operative Guild meeting regularly in our house in Richmond and we had the Rodmell Labour Party meeting regularly in Monks House, Rodmell.

The theme of politics and public events must therefore become more important and more persistent in this autobiography from 1919 onwards. It was not merely that I became more and more actively immersed in them. We lived our daily life and ate our daily bread in the shadow of recurring crisis and catastrophes. When peace at last came in 1918, it was, of course, like the break in the appalling sky which must have covered poor Noah's ark, a gleam of sun 'after the end of the hundred and fifty days' when 'the fountains of the deep and the windows of heaven were stopped and the rain from heaven was restrained'. Of course we welcomed the dove with the olive leaf in her beak. We put out a few flags and a few hopes hesitantly, apprehensively. Almost immediately the flags drooped, the olive leaf withered, the hopes faded. In the years 1918 to 1939 one impotently watched a series of events leading step by step to barbarism and war; the Versailles Treaty and the canker of reparations; the creation of Stalin's Russia, the iron curtain, and the cold war; the rise of fascism and nazism; the failure of the League of Nations; the menace of nuclear war; the Hitlerian Götterdämmerung.

In all this gloom the darkest spot seemed to me and to many other people, at any rate until Hitler came to power in 1933, Stalin's Russia. I have described in *Beginning Again* (above, pp. 150-55) how, when the Tsarist regime fell, we welcomed the 1917 revolution with the same kind of relief and elation which Wordsworth felt in 1789 in the first days of the French revolution. The disillusionment was all the greater. At first one was puzzled by the senselessness of the iron curtain—the shutting off of millions of civilised persons in the twentieth century from the rest of the world and from truth. Then gradually it became clear that the communist rulers of Russia were determined not only to keep their subjects in darkness and ignorance, but also, if possible, to keep the rest of the world in a state of fluid chaos. The foreign policy of the Soviet Government was always simple and consistent: they fished in troubled waters, but they were also continually trying to make the waters troubled so that they could fish. Hence the cold war.

Then still more gradually one became aware of the senseless barbarism of communist society behind the iron curtain. Here again, so far as I was concerned, a realisation of the truth only came gradually by personal experience, by knowing some insignificant individual caught and crushed in the inhuman machinery of the Soviet state—which according to Theodore Rothstein and Karl Marx ought to have withered away. I remember the shock of the first time when I caught a glimpse of this monstrous juggernaut crushing a little individual (and innocent) fly. I knew a young woman, whom I will call Jane, who married, in the early years of the Soviet regime, a Russian scientist employed in Russia. They lived in Leningrad and she was allowed to come for a few weeks every year and visit her mother in England. She always came to see me. I knew her well and she used to tell me about her life and her views with the greatest frankness. Jane was intelligent and had that spontaneous, generous political enthusiasm often characteristic of the young, and particularly the female young. She was a communist before she married her Russian, for she was one of the many intelligent young people on the political Left who in the early 1920s were depressed by the dreary record of German social democracy and were carried away by the promises of communists and communism. Every year for a year or two after her marriage the day used to come when Jane would burst into my room in the highest spirits and tell me of all that the communist regime was doing and was going to do for the 'toiling masses'. Eventually when a year had gone round and the day came for her visit, things had changed. She was depressed and worried, and admitted that she was anxious about the way things were going in Russia. According to her account, the idealistic asceticism which Lenin had imposed upon the party was breaking up. What had attracted her in communism and what she had found in Lenin's Russia was the selfless dedication of the leaders to the task of transforming

Russia into a society 'in which the free development of each is the condition of the free development of all'. Lenin was a ruthless man, and he created a ruthless party; but he was ruthless with himself and he insisted upon communists being ruthless with themselves. Their aim was socialism pure and undefiled, both in theory and in practice. Nearly all communists whom I have known have been very callow or very cunning. (Some of the most hoary old Marxists, like Rothstein, were really both at the same time.) Jane was as politically callow, when a young woman, as an unfledged sparrow. She married and went to Russia believing that the communists and she with them were out to build Utopia—the New Jerusalem and Cloud-Cuckoo-Land. After Lenin's death and the struggle for power which followed it, even Jane could see that idealism and a good deal of freedom were dying out of communism and the Soviet Republic. Something new had come in with Stalin and Stalin's men. Any clouds or cuckoos faded away, for the new rulers were tough and realists. They drove about in big cars and you had to be careful of what you said about them. Jane went back to Russia depressed and uneasy.

It must have been in 1936 that Jane returned to England from Russia for good and came to see me. She was in tears when she told me her wretched story. Her husband, she said, was a scientist, and a devoted scientist who took no part in politics. He was an extremely cautious man and, whatever he may have thought about the regime, never criticised it. One day he did not return home from his laboratory; he just disappeared. Some time later she received an official notification directing her to take some of his clothes and personal possessions to a certain government building. When she got there, she found a series of what looked like ticket offices each labelled with letters of the alphabet. She was told to hand in her husband's possessions at the ticket office labelled with the initial letter of his name. There were long queues of people, like herself, waiting to hand in bundles and suitcases at the various ticket offices. She was given a receipt for her husband's possessions. She never saw him again; eventually she received a letter from him from a labour camp in the Far East. When the time came for her annual visit to England, she was given her permit. In London she went to see Maisky, then the Russian ambassador, and consulted him as to what she should do; he strongly advised her not to return to Russia, and she took his advice.

Thus the enormous machinery of the Soviet state was used to disrupt the lives of these two little innocuous insects, Jane and her husband. And senselessly this two-handed engine at the door smote, and smote no more, so far as these two insects were concerned. It is this streak of senselessness in the savagery of communist, and indeed all authoritarian, states which repels and puzzles me. I am quite sure that Jane was speaking the truth when she said that her husband was entirely non-political and that the only possible reason for his liquidation was that one of his fellow-scientists, working in the same laboratory, who was arrested at the same time, was notoriously indiscreet in his criticism of the regime.

I got from Jane another glimpse of the grotesque nightmare of mutual fear in which, under the shadow of the secret police, both rulers and ruled lived in Russia. 1937 was the centenary of the great Russian poet Pushkin's death. Jane gave me a manuscript translation of a short book by Pushkin which had not been translated into English before, I think, or at any rate was not in print; as far as I can remember, it was autobiographical and extremely interesting. The translation, which was excellent, was by a Russian woman, a friend of Jane's. The suggestion was that the Hogarth Press should publish it in the centenary year. I was eager to do so, but instantly the menacing spectre of the Soviet Government and the secret police and Siberia rose up out of the manuscript to make us pause in Tavistock Square, London, W.C.1, in the year 1936. Jane explained the difficulty to me. Whether in fact to publish was a nice question, the nicety being for her friend the thinnest partition between life and death. For it to be known that someone in Russia was the translator of a book written by Pushkin over 100 years ago and now published in London might or might not be extremely dangerous for the translator. Whether it would lead to the liquidation of the translator or not would depend upon the amount of terror and fear obtaining at any particular moment among the rulers, secret police, and the ruled in Leningrad and Moscow. Jane had therefore arranged with her friend, that, if I decided that the Hogarth Press would like to publish, I should send her a telegram saying simply: 'Many happy returns'. If it was safe to publish, she would reply: 'Many thanks for good wishes'; if it was not safe, she would not reply. I sent off my wire and got no reply, and so the book was never published. It is interesting to compare this incident with the action of the London police with regard to Lenin's speeches which I have related above.

The idea that the publication of a translation of a book by Pushkin in London could have harmed in any way the Russian state or people was as fantastic as the idea that the publication of Lenin's speeches in the *International Review* would have done the slightest damage to the British state or people. But, as I said before, censorship of thought and opinion in the hands of a government and its police is a malignant canker which grows and grows, gradually destroying its environment, the mind of society. If there are dangerous thoughts, all thought may be dangerous; it is safer therefore to suppress as much as you can whether it be Lenin or Pushkin.[1]

The insistent pressure of politics, increasing rapidly as soon as war ended, caused me to stand rather halfheartedly for Parliament. It began in 1920. In those days there was a Combined English University Constituency which included all the English University universities other than Cambridge and Oxford; they elected two M.P.s. After the khaki election of December 1918, the Seven Universities' Democratic Association asked me whether I would consider becoming a candidate at the next election. It was not a prospect which filled me with any enthusiasm. As a secretary of the Labour Party Advisory Committees on International and Imperial Affairs, which after a time took to meeting in a Committee Room in the House of Commons, I got to know a good many Labour M.P.s who were members of my committees, and I saw from the inside the kind of life they had to lead. The hour-to-hour and day-to-day life of professional and business men in their offices and at their 'work' consists largely of time wasted in a vicious circle of unnecessary inaction or futile conversations. Nearly all important business is done effectively and expeditiously outside the office, which can be reserved mainly as a place in which one dictates and signs letters. (That is why during the last fifty years, whether as editor or publisher, I have always stipulated that I would spend the minimum amount of time 'in the office'.) The business life of a backbench M.P. in the 1920s seemed to me the acme of futility and boredom. He was, no doubt, a member of what was said to be the best club in London, but he had to be perpetually in it, endlessly doing nothing as he waited to record his vote at the next division.

[1] I suppose that the secret police were not merely afraid of Pushkin, but afraid that a Soviet citizen should know a British citizen.

This prospect of joining the melancholy procession of back-benchers through the lobbies of the House of Commons, as I said, did not appeal to me, and for some time I hesitated to become a candidate. However, eventually I agreed, and in May 1920 was adopted as a candidate. I agreed partly, and rather pusillanimously, because there was really no chance of my being elected. The sitting members were the Conservative Sir Martin Conway and the Liberal Herbert Fisher. I must admit that a second reason which induced me to stand was the prospect of standing against Herbert Fisher. Herbert was a first cousin of Virginia's, a man of great charm, both physical and mental, but also the kind of man whom in those days I thought it to be almost a public duty to oppose in public life. For he was the kind of respectable Liberal who made respectable liberalism stink in the nostrils of so many of my generation who began their political lives as liberals. Winchester and New College, Oxford; Trustee of the British Museum; Vice-Chancellor of Sheffield University; Warden of New College Oxford; he was chosen by Lloyd George, with his unerring instinct for political window-dressing, to be in 1916 Minister for Education (in those days called President of the Board of Education). I may have been prejudiced and unfair, but I thought the Fisher Education Act, which Herbert was responsible for, to be the sort of cowardly compromise which seemed to save the face of its author at the expense of his principles. When he was a Minister, we used to see him fairly often. He would come to us in Richmond, but he also sometimes stayed with Sir Amherst Selby-Bigge, Permanent Secretary at the Board of Education, at Kingston, which was three miles from us at Rodmell, and then he would walk over to see us. His conversation fascinated us; he was so nice, so distinguished, and so ridiculous that he might have walked straight into *Crotchet Castle*. His face and his mind had the gentle, pale, ivory glow, the patina which Oxford culture and innumerable meals at College high-tables give to Oxford dons. So quiet flows the life of the don that there is nearly always something innocent and childlike in his mind. Herbert, with all this academic innocence, suddenly found himself projected into the very centre of the world of action, the House of Commons, Downing Street, the Cabinet. L. G. and the Cabinet went to his head, and he was intoxicated by this 'life of action', though his intoxication, like everything else in him and the Fisher family, was a muted, genteel intoxication. He was obsessed by L. G. who was to him a cross between the superman and a siren, and by Downing Street, sitting in which he felt himself to be sitting bang on the hub of the universe.

About all this poor Herbert discoursed to us lyrically, but with just that touch of humour and restraint required by the good taste which with him was a characteristic both inherited from nineteenth-century ladies and gentlemen and acquired all over again in Oxford. He was never tired of telling us that we and everyone else who did not sit in Downing Street knew nothing about anything. He gave us a vision of the Prime Minister and the President of the Board of Education sitting in the Cabinet Room in Downing Street and receiving an unending stream of secret, momentous messages from every quarter of the earth, if not the remotest galaxies of the outer universe. When the Lloyd George government fell and Herbert went back to New College, he still continued to tell and retell nostalgically the fairy story of his days in Downing Street. And before I leave him in New College I cannot refrain from telling another little absurd story which Adrian Stephen, Herbert's cousin, once told me. Adrian went to stay for a week-end with the Fishers at New College. The Fisher household was run on extremely economic (to put it euphemistically) lines, which extended to the blankets. It was a bitter cold winter night and Adrian, who was six foot five inches in height, was given a very short bed with a single thin blanket. In the middle of the night he could stand it no longer; he managed to get the whole carpet up and put it over instead of under the bed, and then crept in under it. Unfortunately in the morning he found it impossible to get the carpet properly back in its place and he left his room in a state of chaos. He was not again invited to spend a week-end in New College.

I must return to the election of 1922 and my candidature. I propose to quote from my election address, because it shows where I stood politically a few years after the first great war ended, and also because, I think, my attitude was also that of those who at the time were considered to be on the Left in the Labour Party; we stood between the Labour Party Centre and the Communists and their Fellow Travellers, who were called the Extreme Left. (It has always seemed to me to be curious and confusing that communists are accepted, on their own classification, as Extreme Left; their political outlook and organisation is more like that of the Catholic clerical parties on the Continent, the old Centre Party in Germany, and the present Christian Democrats in Italy, and of the deceased Fascists and

Nazis, i.e. their correct classification is slightly to the Right of the Extreme Right.) Here then is my declaration of political faith in October 1922:

I am asking for your votes as a candidate adopted by the Seven Universities' Democratic Association . . . The Association is affiliated to the Labour Party, of which I have been a member for some considerable time . . . We have in this country two alternatives before us at this election: we can once more entrust the government of the country to one of the two political parties which, for the better part of a century, have separately or in coalition been in power, and which, therefore, are jointly and severally responsible for the social, political, economic, and international conditions in which we find ourselves today; on the other hand, we have an opportunity of making a break with the past and of entrusting the government to a party of new principles and of new men. I confess that one reason why I am a member of the Labour Party, and why . . . I ask you to support that Party with your vote, is this: that, looking round upon the political and economic conditions in London and Manchester, in Dublin, India, and Egypt, and remembering the graves in France and Gallipoli which were to be the price of a new world, I feel that this is no time for a mere reshuffle of the ancient Conservative and Liberal Pack and for entrusting power to one or other of the two parties whose political principles and practice are directly responsible for the disastrous situation in which the country finds itself today. A century of Conservative and Liberal Governments brought us war and a peace which has proved hardly better than war. There will be no change if the old men and the old methods are reinstated in Westminister, and if we want a change we must try a party with new principles and new men. I have no illusions with regards to governments and political parties, and I do not ask you to vote for me and for Labour on any promise that we will hang the Kaiser, or make Germany pay, or take five shillings off the income tax, or make everyone peaceful and prosperous. If the Labour Party is returned to power, it will make many mistakes; it will not succeed in carrying out all its principles or all its promises; it will disappoint very many of its supporters. But the Party has this great advantage over the two older parties: unlike them it has ideals and principles which are real and alive, based not only upon the possessions and privileges of classes or upon political doctrines which were dead before our grandfathers were born, but upon the generous hopes and vital needs of millions of ordinary men and women. It is these ideals, hopes, and needs which, if I were elected, I should endeavour to help the Labour Party to translate into details of the following practical policy . . .

There can be no economic recovery in this country, no beginning to build up an educated and prosperous community, unless there is a complete break with the dangerous and extravagant foreign policy which has been pursued equally by Conversative and Liberal Governments. This country must stand out in Europe and the world as a sincere supporter of a policy of peace and international co-operation. The pivot of its programme must therefore be (1) a real League of Nations, inclusive of all nations, the members of which undertake a definite obligation not to go to war; (2) disarmament, beginning with drastic limitation of naval and military armaments, coupled with a general guarantee against aggression; (3) an equitable settlement of the reparation problem and the promotion of good relations between France, Germany, and this country, as the first step towards economic recovery in Europe. This third point is urgent, and it is practicable. The policy which I would support is an offer by this country to France to relieve her of her debt to us in return for her consent (*a*) to fix reparation payments at a figure which Germany can reasonably be expected to pay, to confine such payments strictly to restoration of the devastated areas, and to grant a sufficiently long moratorium to enable German credit to be restored; (*b*) to revise the Treaty of Versailles and withdraw the armies of occupation.

I went on to say that I believed 'that the only hope for Europe consists in the gradual building up of a close understanding and co-operation between Britain, France, and Germany in a League of Nations', and that the policy outlined above was the first step towards such an understanding. I added four other steps which I considered essential: (1) recognition of the Russian Government and promotion of trade with Russia; (2) close co-operation with the U.S.A.; (3) 'complete abandonment of the policy of imperialism and economic penetration and exploration which has been pursued by us from time to time in the Near East, Mesopotamia, Persia, and China'; (4) 'It is essential that the promises of self-government made to India and Ceylon, and of independence to Egypt, should immediately be carried out with scrupulous honesty, and, further, that those methods in our government of the so-called backward races of Africa which are leading to their subjection and exploitation should be fundamentally revised'.

In home affairs I said that education was the subject of greatest importance and I set out an educational policy which would 'assure to all classes a complete equality of opportunity to obtain elementary, secondary, and university education' and which would produce 'an adequate staff of trained and certified teachers'. I pledged myself to a policy of economy on unproductive expenditure, a more equitable system of taxation, and 'a special graduated levy upon fortunes exceeding £5,000'. I ended my manifesto thus:

In this statement I have confined myself to the immediate and practical problems which will have to be faced by the next House of Commons. I believe in socialism and co-operation, but not in violent revolution; I believe that the resources of the community should be controlled by and in the interests of the whole community rather than small groups and classes. But the work of the next Parliament ought to consist neither in bolstering up the vested interests of the present economic system nor in immediately destroying it, but in laying the foundations of a real peace in Europe and of an educated democracy in this country.

I have given at some length this declaration of my political faith in October 1922 both for general, historical, and also for personal reasons. If a man has the temerity to write the story of his life, he should have a double aim: first, to show it and his little ego in relation to the time and place in which he lived his life, to the procession of historical events, even to the absurd metaphysics of the universe; secondly to describe, as simply and clearly as he can, his personal life, his relation, not to history and the universe, but to persons and to himself, his record in the trivial, difficult, fascinating art of living from day to day, hour to hour, minute to minute. I have reached the years in the story of my life which make the first aspect of my autobiography more and more insistent. I have been alive from November 1880 until November 1965; no period in the world's history has been more full of what are called great events, bringing disruption, disaster, cataclysms to the human race, than those eighty-four years. In the 1914 war there was a nasty poster the object of which was to shame the reluctant citizen into joining the army; it was of a cherubic child asking: 'What did you do in the great war, Daddy?' The question soon lost its meaning—its sting. But 'What did you do in the years between the two great wars?' is a vital question which anyone who took any part in public affairs must answer. The policy for which I declared in the election address was not popular in 1922; it was, and still often is, misrepresented. Looking back over what has happened since, I think that it was the only policy which might have saved Europe from fascism and nazism and from the horror and disaster which they brought upon the world.

I still have to deal with all this later in my passage through the years from 1919 to 1939; now I must return to the election. I rather enjoyed the election campaign, such as it was. The procedure for this peculiar constituency was that candidates made, at most, only one visit to each of the seven universities and made a speech in each. As far as I can remember I visited only Liverpool, Manchester, Durham, and Newcastle. In each I made a speech to what seemed to me a semi-public meeting of already convinced supporters. I do not think that I made a very good impression, partly because I did not always succeed in concealing the fact that I was not really very eager to be an M.P. In March 1921, when I went to Manchester, Virginia came with me. It is many years since I have been in that city, and in 1965 it may be a very different place from what it was when I knew it in the 1920s. In 1921, from the moment when I arrived at its grimy station to the moment when I departed from it, it filled me with a kind of exasperated despair. It was the City of Dreadful Night—'the street lamps burn amidst the baleful glooms'; a drizzle of sooty raindrops dripped remorselessly from the dirty yellow sky upon the blackened buildings and the grey crowds of melancholy men scurrying perpetually, like ants, this way and that way through the foggy streets. Through these streets an unending string of trams ground their way one behind the other; everywhere all the time one's ears were battered by the scraping and grating of their wheels and the striking of their bells. We stayed at the Queen's Hotel, as Virginia recorded in her diary, paying 18s. each for a bed, 'in a large square, but what's a square when the trams meet there? Then there's Queen Victoria like a large tea-cosy, and Wellington, sleek as a mastiff with paw extended'.

My spirits, depressed by the streets and sky, by Queen Victoria and the Duke of Wellington, were not raised by my constituents. I made two speeches to them, one before and one after dinner. They were extremely nice and extremely good people, many of them professors or lecturers, who had been conscientious objectors or had been arrested for keeping the flag of liberty flying in Manchester during the war. But, like Queen Victoria and the Duke, they were somewhat grey, depressed, low in tone. 'Old Mrs Hereford and Professor Findlay', Virginia noted, 'sat patiently looking at the tablecloth with nothing to say, like two old horses who have been working in the fields all day together.' When Mrs Findlay asked Virginia whether she was a politician and whether she did much organising work, Virginia said she listened. 'Mrs Findlay shook her head. Why was I there then?' There was, it must be admitted, no satisfactory answer to that question.

When I find myself in a strange city, at a loose end, waiting as one does eternally in strange cities for a boat, a plane, or an interview—when time seems to stop and the universe seems to have dwindled to an unending series of hotel corridors, lavatories, and lounges—I tend to go to the zoo. I am ambivalent about zoos: I have an uneasy feeling that one should not keep animals in cages, but I never get tired of watching animals anywhere. You can learn a great deal about the character of a country or city by going to its zoo and studying its arrangement and the behaviour of the animals. The London Zoo is an animal microcosm of London, and even the lions, as a rule, behave as if they had been born in South Kensington. I once saw a curious incident there when one of them did not. It was a warm summer day and the lions were in their outdoor cages. A stout, middle-aged middle-class lady was standing near the bars looking at a magnificent lion who was standing on the other side of the bars gazing over her head, as lions seem to do, into eternity. Suddenly he turned round, presented his backside to her, and pissed on her through the bars. 'Oh the dirty beast,' she said, 'Oh, the dirty beast,' wiping her face and blouse, half angry, half amused, and the tone of her voice was exactly as if some nasty little boy had done some dirty trick in the Earls Court Road.

I recall vividly two other zoos. When I was in Jerusalem in 1957, I had to go to the Foreign Office which seemed to me a long weary way out from the centre of the city. I started to walk back; it was hot and dusty, and I seemed to have got into a ramshackle suburb frequented by those unshaven, long-haired orthodox Jews, young men whose self-conscious, self-righteous hair and orthodoxy fill me with despair. When I saw a signpost directing me to the zoo, I made off for it at once. But I did not, as I had hoped, escape from the melancholy of the dreary streets and the moth-eaten anachronism of those ridiculous young men. I have never seen anywhere else so melancholy a collection of animals. The architecture of the zoo seemed to be a ramshackle replica of the surrounding streets, and long-haired monkeys gazed at one, it seemed to me, with the self-satisfaction of all the orthodox who have learned eternal truth from the primeval monkey, all the scribes and pharisees who spend their lives making mountains of pernicious stupidity out of molehills of nonsense.

I should add that the long-haired monkeys in the Jerusalem Zoo and the long-haired orthodox Israelis in the neighbouring streets are characteristic of only one side of contemporary Israel. When you enter Israel by Tel Aviv, buzzing with business as though it were a gigantic human hive, drive up the road to Jerusalem, or visit Haifa and Tiberias, you are exhilarated by the energetic exhilaration of the people who are everywhere living dangerously and happily wresting from the rocky earth and a ring of implacable enemies a new way of life in a strange land. These people, who form the immense majority of the population, are the exact opposite of the orthodox Jews in Jerusalem. It makes it the more lamentable that they should allow politics and therefore life in Israel to be continually influenced by orthodox Judaism. Again and again one has in life to say, with Lucretius, '*tantum religio potuit suadere malorum*'—how much evil religion has induced human beings to do! One is accustomed to see throughout history down to today the absurd delusions of savages promoted to divine truths and their morality and rules of conduct maintained for two or three thousand years as an excuse for protecting the vested interests of ignorance and injustice. To see this process once more repeated in modern Israel is horrifying. After all, the austere, bare monotheism which the ancient Hebrews developed made it comparatively easy for their Jewish descendants in modern times to shed the primitive beliefs and rituals and morality of the Pentateuch. Already two thousand years ago the writers of the books which we call *Job, Ecclesiastes*, and *Micah* had laid the foundations of a civilised morality and a sceptical, rational theism, from which by the process of time might come 'the religion of all sensible men'—agnosticism or atheism. It is deplorable to find the builders of the modern state in Israel making its laws conform to the belief that the creator of the universe, with its suns, planets, galaxies, atoms—old bearded Jehovah sitting up there on Mount Sinai amid the thunder and lightning and once in three thousand years showing his backside to a favoured Moses—that this omnipotent deity has enacted an eternal law, revealed to a handful of rabbis and ignorant men in Jerusalem, regulating the shaving and haircutting of males, the eating of pork and the slaughtering of sheep, and the use of trains and taxis on days which some people happen to call Saturday and others Samedi.

The other zoo which I vividly recall is in Colombo. Colombo is as different from Jerusalem as the Sinhalese are from the Israelis. My likes and dislikes are catholic, and I have remarked before in this autobiography that I see no reason why, because one likes claret, one should not also like burgundy; I like both, and I like both Israel, with its fierce sun, fiery rock, its furnace of human activity, and Ceylon, with its tropical 'lilies and languors', the gaily coloured kaleidoscope of flowers, trees, and cheerful, drifting crowds. Three years after I visited the Jerusalem Zoo I visited Ceylon. The plane which was to take me back to England was delayed somewhere in eastern Asia and I found myself in one of those exasperating predicaments in which one has nothing to do but wait indefinitely for someone to ring you up and say that you need wait no longer. I waited from eight in the morning, when my plane should have left, until twelve midnight, when it did. Half-way through the morning I went to the Colombo Zoo. It was a microcosm of Colombo, of the Sinhalese low country, of the Sinhalese way of life. It was 'full of trees and waving leaves', amid which, in the humid languorous heat, elephants, lions, leopards, bears lived their happy natural lives. I was watching a family of lions, father and mother, and three cubs, who were in a large open-air enclosure. The male was lying asleep up in one corner and the female was drowsing down in the other corner; the cubs were playing about. Suddenly one of the cubs went over and began to play with his father's tail. There was a low growl; the tail flapped angrily on the ground; the cub made another dart at it. The lion lifted his great head just off the ground and let out a blood-curdling snarl. The lioness rose up and slowly, threateningly went over to the lion and quite silently stood over him between him and the cub. The lion got up and slowly, sullenly walked over to the farthest corner where he flopped down to sleep again. The lioness shooed the cub back to her corner. It seemed to me what I might have been watching a domestic scene in a compound in one of those Sinhalese villages, a Sinhalese mother slowly, firmly shooing her child away from mischief and danger.

I must unfortunately return once more from the Colombo Zoo in 1960 to Manchester, Durham, and the election in 1922. When I went to meet my constituents and make a speech to them in Durham, the meeting was held in the room of a graduate. The audience was extremely small; indeed, in each of the universities the number of people who came to my meetings was very small. I was told by the chairman of the Durham meeting that many who would support and might vote Labour would not do anything openly which might connect them with the Labour Party, because that connection would be viewed with disapproval by the university authorities and would jeopardise their prospects of a good job after they had taken a degree. He said that this was to some extent due to political prejudice, but what was more important was the fact that the university relied for financial and other support in part upon the local wealthy Conservatives, often 'big business', and had to be careful not to offend or antagonise them. Theoretically and on the surface your religion, politics, or economics were as unimportant as the colour of your hair, but if you wanted to do well for yourself academically it was safer to conceal the fact that you were left of centre. I was told that this was more or less true of all the provincial universities in those bad old days.

I came, as was expected, at the bottom of the poll, Sir Martin Conway, Conservative, and the Right Honourable Herbert Fisher, Liberal, being elected. Conway was a curious man. He had been mountaineer and explorer and a Slade Professor, and in 1922 he was Director General of the Imperial War Museum. Shortly after the election I received the following letter from him:

It was only two days ago that I learned who you are—the author of *A Village in the Jungle*. That is a book which I read with extraordinary delight and which I treasure alongside of the *Soul of a People*. I am really sorry to have been put in opposition to a writer I so heartily admire. Of one thing, however, I am certain: the writer of such a book would have found the H. of C. a most unattractive place and would have been very unhappy there, especially if he had been obliged to associate intimately with the rank and file of the Labour Party—tho', of course, among them are some delightful souls, very lovable, but the bulk are not such.

I am venturing to send you a book of mine in kindly remembrance of our contest. Your late father-in-law was an honoured friend of mine, as you may guess.

Yours faithfully
Martin Conway

Sir Martin asked me to lunch with him in the House of Commons and I found him to be a pleasant, not very interesting man. His letter—and the attitude towards the Labour Party in the Universities—show clearly the social and political snobbery of those days. It amused me that the Slade Professor of Fine Arts should think that I must be such a sensitive plant that I would wilt unhappily in the company of the rough trade unionists of the Labour Party. As a matter of fact I knew a good many Labour M.P.s as Secretary of the Labour Party Advisory Committees and because for a time I was Parliamentary Correspondent of the *Labour Leader*. Of course, some of them were pretty tough, but I never found any difficulty in getting on with them.

In the period of my life of which I am now trying to tell the story—and indeed in the whole of my life after the year 1919—it has, as I have said, been dominated by politics and public events which are living and lived history. As I look back over the mental and physical chaos and kaleidoscope which has been my individual life from 1919 to 1965, I see that history ruthlessly divided it into four periods: (1) 1919 to 1933, the fourteen years of struggle for civilisation which ended with Hitler's rise to power; (2) 1933 to 1939, the six years in which civilisation was finally destroyed and which ended with war; (3) 1939 to 1945, the six years of war; (4) the post-war world. If I am to continue with the story of my life, I shall have to deal with the events of each of these four periods, the effect of each upon me and my life, and my reaction to each of them. But even in our cruel, mechanised, barbarous age, we have not yet become completely robots, puppets jerked through life by history, governments and computers. We still have, at any rate in Britain, some shreds of private life, which we can preserve unaffected by public events. It is to our private lives that I must now turn—to return later to politics in the kind of see-saw which must inevitably continue through the fourth volume of my autobiography. What dominates or moulds our private lives privately is, as I have said, the house in which we live. In each period of our living we are profoundly influenced, therefore, by both history and geography, by time and place. In my own case, war and peace and Stalin, Mussolini, and Hitler divided the twenty years of my life from 1919 to 1939 into the two periods 1919-1933 and 1933-1939, and the same twenty years were deeply divided for us into two other periods by two houses, Hogarth House in Richmond from 1919 to 1924 and Tavistock Square in Bloomsbury from 1924 to 1939. I must now deal with the period of six years in Richmond.

One must begin with Virginia's illness and her slow recovery from it, for we continued to live in Richmond mainly to protect her from London and the devastating disorientation which would threaten her from social life if we returned to live there. It was a perpetual struggle to find the precarious balance of health for her among the strains and stresses of writing and society. The routine of everyday life had to be regular and rather rigid. Everything had to be rationed, from work and walking to people and parties. Despite all our precautions, her diary shows how often in the first few years after the war she was ill or threatened with illness. The threat was almost always a headache, which was the warning signal of mental strain; the 'illness', if it came to that, was the first stage towards breakdown. We knew exactly what the treatment should be; the moment the headache came, she had to go to bed, and remain there comatose, eating and sleeping, until the symptoms began to abate. That was the cure; the difficulty was always to perform the actions which the cure required: unfortunately one does not sleep—or even eat—because one knows that sleeping or eating is the one thing which will cure one of a shadow across one's brain.

In 1921 and 1922 Virginia was continually beset with these attacks. For instance, in the 1921 diary there is an entry for 7 June describing how Tom Eliot came to tea and joined us in lamenting the Pecksniffian character of John Middleton Murry. The next entry in the diary is 8 August and I will quote it, because it shows so clearly what Virginia actually suffered in one of these threatening attacks:

> What a gap! How it would have astounded me to be told when I wrote the last word here, on June 7th, that within a week I should be in bed, and not entirely out of it till the 6th of August—two whole months rubbed out—These, this morning, the first words I have written—to call writing—for sixty days; and those days spent in wearisome headache, jumping pulse, aching back, frets, fidgets, lying awake, sleeping draughts, sedatives, digitalis, going for a little walk, and plunging back into bed again—all the horrors of the dark cupboard of illness once more displayed for my diversion. Let me make a vow that this shall never, never, happen again; and *then* confess that there are some compensations. To be tired and authorised to lie in bed is pleasant; then scribbling 365 days of the year as I do, merely to receive without agitation of my right hand in giving out is salutary. I feel that I can take stock of things in a leisurely way. Then the dark underworld has its fascinations as well as its terrors; and then sometimes I compare the fundamental security of my life in all (here Mrs Dedman interrupts for fifteen minutes) storms (perhaps I meant) with its old fearfully random condition. Later I had my visitors, one every day, so that I saw more people than normally even. Perhaps, in future I shall adopt this method more than I have done. Roger, Lytton, Nessa, Duncan, Dorothy Bussy, Pippa, Carrington, James and Alix—all these came; and were as detached portraits—cut out, emphatic, seen thus separately compared with the usual way of seeing them in crowds. Lytton, I note, is more than ever affectionate. One must be, I think, if one is famous. One must say to one's old friends 'Ah my celebrity is nothing—nothing—compared with this'.

This was, of course, a severe bout, and in the autumn and winter of 1921 she had recovered to her normal equilibrium which allowed her safely—but within limits—to work and live a social life. But during the first seven months of 1922 she was off and on continually unwell or threatened with headaches. In March she started a temperature which the doctors took seriously and sent us on a fairly long odyssey through Harley Street and Wimpole Street which gave us a curious view of medical science and the tiptop Harley Street specialists. We had at the time an extremely nice, sensible G.P., Dr Ferguson. He sent us first to a lung specialist who said that Virginia's symptoms were due to her lungs, which were in a serious state. When this was reported to Ferguson, he said it was nonsense; he had examined her lungs frequently and there was nothing wrong with them; we should ignore the diagnosis. He sent us off to a heart specialist, who said that Virginia's symptoms were due to her heart, which was in a serious state. We returned sadly to Richmond and Ferguson. I was told by him that the great man had diagnosed inflammation of the heart, a disease from which some famous man—I think it was the great Alfred Harmsworth, Lord Northcliffe—had just died. The disease was incurable and death imminent and inevitable. In his opinion, he said, this was nonsense; he had frequently examined her heart and there was nothing seriously wrong with it; we should ignore the diagnosis. We did so. We went, I think, to one more specialist, a distinguished pathologist who discovered that Virginia was suffering from the disease in which he specialised. He was wrong; we ignored his diagnosis and decided to forget about it and about Harley Street. She not only recovered from the three fatal and incurable diseases; the disquieting symptoms gradually disappeared.

At our last interview with the last famous Harley Street specialist to whom we paid our three guineas, the great Dr Saintsbury, as he shook Virginia's hand, said to her: 'Equanimity—equanimity—practise equanimity, Mrs Woolf'. It was, no doubt, excellent advice and worth the three guineas, but, as the door closed behind us, I felt that he might just as usefully have said: 'A normal temperature—ninety-eight point four— practise a normal temperature, Mrs Woolf'.

With regard to her writing, Virginia certainly never learned to practise equanimity. Like most professional writers, if she was well, she went into her room and sat down to write her novel with the daily regularity of a stockbroker who commutes every day between his house in the suburbs and his office in the neighbourhood of Throgmorton Street. Her room was very different from a stockbroker's office. She was an untidy writer, indeed an untidy liver, an accumulator of what Lytton Strachey used to call 'filth packets', those pockets of old nibs, bits of string, used matches, rusty paper-clips, crumpled envelopes, broken cigarette-holders, etc., which accumulate malignantly on some people's tables and mantelpieces. In Virginia's workroom there was always a very large, solid, plain wooden table covered with filth packets, papers, letters, manuscripts, and large bottles of ink. She very rarely sat at this table, certainly never when she was writing a novel in the morning. To write her novel of a morning she sat in a very low armchair, which always appeared to be suffering from prolapsus uteri; on her knees was a large board made of plywood which had an inkstand glued to it, and on the board was a large quarto notebook of plain paper which she had bound up for her and covered herself in (usually) some gaily-coloured paper. The first draft of all her novels was written in one of these notebooks with pen and ink in the mornings. Later in the morning or in the afternoon, or sometimes at the beginning of the next morning, she typed out what she had written in the notebook, revising it as she typed, and all subsequent revisions were made on the typewriter. A curious thing about her was that, although she was extremely sensitive to noise and was one of those people who 'jumped out of her skin' at a sudden noise or unexpected confrontation, she seemed usually, when writing, to acquire a protective skin or integument which insulated her from her surroundings. Her room tended to become not merely untidy but squalid. She reached the final stage of organised disorganisation and discomfort when we moved from Richmond to 52 Tavistock Square in Bloomsbury. At the back of the house was what had once been an immense billiard room. We used it as a storeroom for the Hogarth Press and there embedded among the pyramids and mountains of parcels, books, and brown paper sat Virginia with her disembowelled chair, her table, and her gas fire.

In the regularity of this routine of writing and in her disregard of her surroundings when writing one might not unreasonably have seen a measure of equanimity. Up to a point this was true; in some ways her attitude in writing and to her writing was extraordinarily controlled, dispassionate, coldly critical. In the process of her writing—of her artistic creation—there were long periods of, first, quiet and intense dreamlike rumination when she drifted through London streets or walked across the Sussex water-meadows or merely sat silent by the fire, and secondly of intense, analytical, critical revision of what she had written. No writer could possibily have given more time and intensive thought to the preparation for writing and to the revision of what she had written. Both these periods required and got from her dispassionate equanimity. But there were also for her two periods of passion and excitement. The first was in the moment of creation, in the whole process of actual writing. I think that, when writing, Virginia was almost the whole time writing with concentrated passion. The long strenuous intellectual process was over and would be called in again for revision; now emotion and imagination took control. And at moments, as I pointed out in *Beginning Again*,[1] genius or inspiration seemed to take control, and then, as she described how she wrote the last pages of *The Waves*, 'having reeled across the last ten pages with some moments of such intensity and intoxication that I seemed to stumble after my own voice, or almost after some sort of speaker (as when I was mad) I was almost afraid, remembering the voices that used to fly ahead'.[2] There was, of course, no place or possibility for Dr Saintsbury's 'equanimity' in this kind of emotional and imaginative volcanic eruption, the moment of artistic creation. But I think that whenever Virginia was actually writing a novel—or rather the first draft of a novel—her psychological state was in a modified degree that described above. The tension was great and unremitting; it was emotionally volcanic; the conscious mind, though intent, seemed to follow a hair's breadth behind the voice, or the 'thought', which flew ahead.[3] It was this terrific, persistent tension which, because it naturally produced mental exhaustion, made her writing a perpetual menace to her mental stability. And the moment that the symptoms of mental exhaustion began, she was unable to write.

In what I have written above, I have distinguished two markedly different—indeed almost antithetical—phases in Virginia's creative process. This swing of the pendulum in the mind between conscious, rational, analytic, controlled thought and an undirected intuitive or

[1] Above, page 17.

[2] *A Writer's Diary*, p. 169.

[3] I think that when she was revising and rewriting on a typewriter what she had written with pen and ink in the morning, her psychological state and her method were quite different. The conscious, critical intellect was in control and the tension was less. It was largely the same when she was writing criticism. I used to say that, when she came in to lunch after a morning's work, I could tell by the depth of the flush on her face whether she had been writing fiction or criticism.

emotional process almost always takes place where the mind produces something original or creative. It happens with creative thinkers, scientists, or philosophers, no less than with artists. Perhaps the most famous instance was recorded over two thousand years ago in Sicily when the problem in hydrostatics which Archimedes had unsuccessfully worked upon for days suddenly solved itself in his drowsing mind as he lay in his bath and he dashed out naked into the streets of Syracuse shouting: 'I have found it, I have found it!' Virginia, too, often 'found it' by the same kind of mental process and with the same excitement.

It was this excitement which was the sign and symptom of the mental strain of her writing and which was a perpetual menace to her stability. But there was also, as I have said above, a second period of passion and excitement through which she almost always had to pass in the process of writing a novel. This came upon her almost invariably as soon as she had finished writing a book and the moment arrived for it to be sent to the printer. It was a kind of passion of despair, and it was emotionally so violent and exhausting that each time she became ill with the symptoms threatening a breakdown. In fact, the mental breakdown which I described in *Beginning Again* occurred immediately after she had finished writing *The Voyage Out*, and the breakdown in 1941 which ended in her suicide occurred immediately after she had finished *Between the Acts*. And in 1936, when she had finished *The Years* and she had to begin correcting the proofs, she came desperately near a mental breakdown. On 19 April she wrote in her diary:

> The horror is that tomorrow, after this one windy day of respite—oh the cold north wind that has blown ravaging daily since we came, but I've had no ears, eyes, or nose: only making my quick transits from house to room, often in despair—after this one day's respite, I say, I must begin at the beginning and go through 600 pages of cold proof. Why, oh why? Never again, never again.[1]

The psychology of the artist in the final stages of creation and production is very interesting. Many writers have I think felt, but have not, like Virginia, recorded, the horror of facing those pages of 'cold proof' and, even more, the cold breath of criticism in the first days after publication. In *Beginning Again* I said that, in my opinion, one reason why Desmond MacCarthy never wrote the

[1] *A Writer's Diary*, p. 268.

novel which, when he was a young man, we thought he could write and which he intended to write, was that he could not face the responsibility of publication, the horror of the final day when the book and the author are handed over to the icy judgment of the reviewers and the public. However sensitive the serious author may be, the moment comes when he has to be ruthless with himself. He must coldly go through the weary waste of cold proof, put the last comma into the last sentence, deliver himself artistically naked to the public, take the icy plunge of publication. At that point he must have the courage to say to himself: 'Literary editors, reviewers, my friends, the great public—they can say what they like about the book and about me. Hippokleides doesn't care.'[1] Virginia was terribly—even morbidly—sensitive to criticism of any kind and from anyone. Her writing was to her the most serious thing in life, and, as with so many serious writers, her books were to her part of herself and felt to be part of herself somewhat in the same way as a mother often seems all her life to feel that her child remains still part of herself. And just as the mother feels acutely the slightest criticism of her child, so any criticism of her book even by the most negligible nitwit gave Virginia acute pain. It is therefore hardly an exaggeration to say that the publication of a book meant something very like torture to her.

The torture began as soon as she had written the last word of the first draft of her book; it continued off and on until the last reviewer, critic, friend, or acquaintance had said his say. And yet, despite her terrifying hypersensitivity, there was in Virginia an intellectual and spiritual toughness which Desmond lacked. It came out in the dogged persistence with which she worked at every word, sentence,

[1] I have the greatest admiration for Hippokleides—his story is in Herodotus. He became engaged to Kleisthenes's daughter, and at the feast to celebrate the engagement he got rather above himself and danced on his head on the table. When Kleisthenes, who was very grand, being Dictator of Sikuon, saw the legs waving in the air, he was outraged and said: 'O son of Tisandros, you have danced away your marriage'. To which Hippokleides replied: 'Hippokleides doesn't care'. His reply became a Greek wisecrack. How surprised Kleisthenes and, indeed, Hippokleides would be at the vagaries of immortality if they knew that the Dictator and hundreds of other 'great' men of his time are completely forgotten while Hippokleides, with his legs waving in the air above his head and his wisecrack, are still, 2,400 years later, recalled with approval and affection.

paragraph of everything she wrote, from a major novel to a trumpery—or what to almost any other writer would have seemed a trumpery—review. The consequence was that the moment always came when she stiffened against the critics, against herself, and against the world; ultimately she had the courage of her convictions and published, saying—not with much conviction—'Virginia doesn't care'. And that was why, unlike Desmond, she had published, when she died, seventeen books.

The psychology of human misery is curious and complicated. Several critics have expressed surprise and disapproval at the spectacle of Virginia's misery over blame or even the lack of praise. Max Beerbohm, for instance, 'had reservations' about her and disliked her diary. 'I have never understood,' he said, 'why people write diaries. I never had the slightest desire to do so—one has to be so very self-conscious.' (It is significant that Max thought that his not wanting to do something was a good reason or an excuse for his not understanding why other people wanted to do it and did it.) 'It was deplorable', he said, 'to mind hostile criticism as much as Virginia Woolf did.'[1] It was no doubt highly deplorable both ethically and from the point of view of her own happiness. But it and the writing of diaries is surely a little less difficult to understand than Max found them. The mother's instinct to resent criticism of her children is irrational and deplorable, but common and not entirely unnatural. Vanity explains part of it, but not, I think, all. Oddly enough there is mixed in with the vanity something which is almost the opposite of vanity in these cases, a kind of objective ideal. The mother wants the child to be perfect for its own sake, and Virginia, whose attitude towards her books was, as with so many serious writers, maternal, wanted her books to be perfect for their own sake. She was also abnormally sensitive, both physically and mentally, and it was this which helped her both to produce her novels and to be miserable when Mrs Jones or Max Beerbohm didn't like them. And I rather think it helped her once to hear the sparrows talking Greek outside her bedroom window.

When I remember how, owing to her health, Virginia always had to restrict her daily writing to a few hours and often had to give up writing for weeks or even months, how slowly she wrote and how persistently she revised and worked over what she had written

[1] See *Max*, by Lord David Cecil, pp. 483-4.

before she published it, I am amazed that she had written and published seventeen books before she died. There are today (in 1965) twenty-one volumes in the list of her publications. This is the more surprising because none of these books had been written by her before the age of thirty, and all her major works, except *The Voyage Out* and *Night and Day*, were written in the last twenty-one years of her life. In the period with which I am now concerned, our years at Richmond from 1919 to 1924, her writing was strictly rationed and often interrupted. They were years of crucial importance in her development as a novelist, for during them she revolted against the methods and form of contemporary fiction—pre-eminently the fiction of Galsworthy, Wells, and Bennett—and created the first versions of her own form and methods which ultimately and logically developed into those of *The Waves* and *Between the Acts*.

The process began with the 'short stories' which she collected and published in March 1921 in *Monday or Tuesday*. They were all written between the years 1917 and 1921 and were a kind of prelude or preliminary canter to *Jacob's Room* which was published in October 1922. *The Mark on the Wall* was the first sign of the mutation in method which was leading to *Jacob's Room*; it was published in July 1917, forming part of *Two Stories*, our first Hogarth Press publication, and was written at the end of 1916 or the beginning of 1917. It has been said by some critics that Virginia derived her method, which they call the stream of consciousness, from Joyce and Dorothy Richardson. The idea that no one in the arts has ever invented anything or indeed has ever had an original thought, since everything is always 'derived' from something else in an unending artistic House that Jack Built, is extremely common and has always seemed to me untrue—and if not untrue, unimportant. The merits or defects of *The Waves* remain unaffected whether they were or were not 'influenced' by Joyce's *Ulysses* or Dorothy Richardson's *The Tunnel*. But it is perhaps just worth while to point out that *The Mark on the Wall* had been written at latest in the first part of 1917, while it was not until April 1918 that Virginia read *Ulysses* in manuscript and January 1919 that she read *The Tunnel*.

In May 1919 we published in the Hogarth Press *Kew Gardens*. As I recorded in *Beginning Again* (above, p. 175), this thin little volume, which we had printed ourselves, had great importance for us, for its immediate success was the first of many unforeseen happenings which led us, unintentionally and often reluctantly, to turn the Hogarth Press into a commercial publishing business. But it was also a decisive step in Virginia's development as a writer. It is in its own small way and within its own limits perfect; in its rhythms, movement, imagery, method, it could have been written by no one but Virginia. It is a microcosm of all her then unwritten novels, from *Jacob's Room* to *Between the Acts*; for instance, Simon's silent soliloquy is a characteristic produced by the same artistic gene or chromosome which was to produce twelve years later Bernard's soliloquy in *The Waves* and twenty-two years later the silent murmurings of Isa in *Between the Acts*.

Virginia began to write *Jacob's Room* in April 1920; the period of eleven months between that date and May 1919, when *Kew Gardens* was published, had been one of rumination and preparation. She wrote little, and what she did write was journalism. It was for her a disturbed period, partly because of warning headaches and partly because of the publication of *Night and Day* in October. It is clear from the diary that 'the creative power' which, Virginia said, 'bubbles so pleasantly in beginning a new book' was simmering throughout those eleven months. By April 1920 the content, characters, form of *Jacob's Room* must have been in her mind in some detail, for she had already given the book its significant name. And she was conscious that the method of her experimental short stories, *The Mark on the Wall*, *Kew Gardens*, and *An Unwritten Novel*, must be adapted to produce a full-length novel. This is what she wrote in her diary on 26 January 1920 (*A Writer's Diary*, p. 23):

> Suppose one thing should open out of another—as in an unwritten novel—only not for ten pages but 200 or so—doesn't that give the looseness and lightness I want; doesn't that get closer and yet keep form and speed, and enclose everything, everything? My doubt is how far it will enclose the human heart—Am I sufficiently mistress of my dialogue to net it there? For I figure that the approach will be entirely different this time; no scaffolding; scarely a brick to be seen; all crepuscular, but the heart, passion, humour, everything, as bright as fire in the mist. Then I'll find room for so much—a gaiety—an inconsequence—a light spirited stepping at my sweet will. Whether I'm sufficiently mistress of things—that's the doubt; but conceive *Mark on the Wall*, *K. G.* and *Unwritten Novel* taking hands and dancing in unity.

On 6 November 1921, she wrote the last words of *Jacob's Room*; it was published in October 1922. The writing of this novel was the beginning of a period of great fertility. In the three years 1921 to

1924 she wrote *Mr Bennett and Mrs Brown* (published in 1924), and prepared or wrote the material included in *Monday or Tuesday* (published in 1921) and *The Common Reader* published in 1925). In 1922 she began *Mrs Dalloway* and was writing it all through 1923 and 1924. She began it as a short story and for a short time hesitated whether to expand it into a full-length novel. Early in 1923 she had decided upon its being a novel; she called it at first *The Hours*, but finally went back to the original title *Mrs Dalloway*.

Throughout these six years, 1919 to 1924, she was also writing a considerable amount of journalism, if one remembers how much work she was giving to her books and how limited was the total time she could devote to writing. Most of her journalism consisted of reviews in *The Times Literary Supplement* and, after 1923, in the *Nation*. Her attitude to her reviewing was not consistent. She looked upon it usually as a method of making money—at this time, indeed, it was almost her only way. As such she resented it and occasionally decided to give it up altogether. The following entry in her diary on 15 September 1920, shows this:

> I should have made more of my release from reviewing. When I sent my letter to Richmond,[1] I felt like someone turned out into the open air. Now I've written another in the same sense to Murry,[2] returning Mallock; and I believe this is the last book any editor will ever send me. To have broken free at the age of thirty eight seems a great piece of good fortune—coming at the nick of time, and due of course to L., without whose journalism I couldn't quit mine. But I quiet my conscience with the belief that a foreign article once a week is of greater worth, less labour and better paid than my work; and with luck, if I can get my books done, we shall profit in moneymaking eventually. And, when one faces it, the book public is more of an ordeal than the newspaper public, so that I'm not shirking responsibility. Now, of course, I can scarcely believe that I ever wrote reviews weekly; and literary papers have lost all interest for me. Thank God, I've stepped clear of that *Athenaeum* world, with its reviews, editions, lunches, and tittle tattle—I should like never to meet a writer again. The proximity of Mr Allison,[3] reputed editor of the *Field*, is enough for me. I should like to know masses of sensitive, imaginative, unselfconscious, unliterary people, who have never read a book. Now, in the rain, up to Dean, to talk about the door of the coal cellar.

[1] Bruce Richmond, editor of *The Times Literary Supplement*.

[2] J. Middleton Murry, editor of the *Athenaeum*.

[3] Wrongly reputed. He was advertisement manager of *The Times* and owner of the *London Mercury*. He had just bought a large house and farm in Rodmell.

But Virginia did not always hold this uncompromising view of her journalism and reviewing. She found that she could not go on for long periods uninterruptedly writing fiction and she relieved the strain by doing something which used another part of her brain or literary imagination. As the years went on, she discovered that reviewing performed this function admirably; it gave her the relief which some thinkers or writers find in chess or crossword puzzles.

I give below the figures of Virginia's earnings by her pen or typewriter in the years 1919 to 1924. They are interesting, I think, from a particular point of view, from the light which they throw on her work as a novelist and journalist, but also from a general point of view, the economics of the literary profession in the 1920s.

	Journalism	*Books*	*Total*
1919	£153 17 0	nil	£153 17 0
1920	234 6 10	£106 5 10	340 12 8
1921	47 15 1	10 10 8	58 5 9
1922	69 5 0	33 13 0	102 18 0
1923	158 3 9	40 0 5	198 4 2
1924	128 0 0	37 0 0	165 0 0

Virginia was forty-two years old in 1924. Jane Austen died at the age of forty-two, Emily Brontë at the age of thirty, Charlotte Brontë at the age of thirty-nine; all three were famous novelists and had written best-sellers at the time of their deaths. By the age of forty-two Virginia had already published three major novels: *The Voyage Out, Night and Day*, and *Jacob's Room*. All three had been widely recognised as novels of great merit, and even genius; they had been published in America as well as in Britain; but their sales were small in both countries. Thus the total which she earned from her books, including the American editions, in the six years, ending with 1924 was £228, or £38 per annum; indeed her total earnings, from books and journalism, during the period were only £1,019, or £170 per annum.

Many people, including even many writers and publishers, will be surprised at these miserable figures. Having for fifty years observed, as writer, editor, and publisher, the rise and fall of many literary reputations and incomes, I know that there is nothing particularly unusual in them. Nothing can be more erratic and fickle than literary reputations and earnings. In 1963, i.e. forty years after 1924, these three novels earned in royalties in Britain alone

£251—£22 more than all Virginia's books, including the three novels, had earned in Britain and America during the six years. There must be many best-sellers of the year 1924 which did not sell a copy or earn their authors a penny in the year 1963. I shall later on give from time to time the figures of Virginia's sales and earnings; here I will give only one other fact to show how sudden and unpredictable are the movements in the market where writers sell their wares. Five years after 1924, the year in which Virginia earned £38 by her books, she earned £2,063 by her books. This astronomical increase after the six years of complete stagnation was due partly to *Mrs Dalloway*, published in 1925, and *To the Lighthouse*, published in 1927, but still more to *Orlando*, which was published in 1928.

The development of the Hogarth Press was bound up with the development of Virginia as a writer and with her literary or creative psychology. When we moved from Hogarth House, Richmond, to 52 Tavistock Square on 13 March 1924, the Hogarth Press had published thirty-two books in the seven years of its existence. I give below the complete list of books published in each of these seven years, for it shows the scale and quality of the development. I have marked with an asterisk the books which we printed with our own hands.

1917	**Two Stories* by Leonard and Virginia Woolf
1918	*Prelude* by Katherine Mansfield
1919	**Poems* by T. S. Eliot
	**Kew Gardens* by Virginia Woolf
	Critic in Judgment by J. Middleton Murry
1920	**Story of the Siren* by E. M. Forster
	**Paris* by Hope Mirrlees
	Gorky's *Reminiscences of Tolstoi*
	Stories from the Old Testament by Logan Pearsall Smith
1921	*Monday or Tuesday* by Virginia Woolf
	**Stories from the East* by Leonard Woolf
	**Poems* by Clive Bell
	Tchekhov's Notebooks
1922	*Jacob's Room* Virginia Woolf
	Stavrogin's Confession by Dostoevsky
	The Gentleman from San Francisco by Bunin
	Autobiography of Countess Tolstoi
	**Daybreak* by Fredegond Shove
	**Karn* by Ruth Manning-Sanders

1923 **Pharos and Pharillon* by E. M. Forster
**Woodcuts* by Roger Fry
Sampler of Castile by Roger Fry
**The Waste Land* by T. S. Eliot
**The Feather Bed* by Robert Graves
**Mutations of the Phoenix* by Herbert Read
**Legend of Monte della Sibilla* by Clive Bell
**Poems* by Ena Limebeer
Tolstoi's Love Letters
Talks with Tolstoi by A. V. Goldenveizer
Letters of Stephen Reynolds
The Dark by Leonid Andreev
When it was June by Mrs Lowther

The above list shows, that though we started the Hogarth Press in 1917, it was only in 1920 that we began—with Gorky's *Reminiscences of Tolstoi* and Logan Pearsall Smith's *Stories from the Old Testament*—to have books printed for us by commercial printers and so to become ourselves commercial publishers. The four books published by us in 1917, 1918, and 1919 were all printed and bound by ourselves,[1] and the production, such as it was, was entirely that of the hands of Leonard and Virginia Woolf. Until 1920 the idea of seriously becoming professional publishers never occurred to us. The Hogarth Press was a hobby, and the hobby consisted in the printing which we did in our spare time in the afternoons. A second object, which developed from the first, was to produce and publish short works which commercial publishers could not or would not publish, like T. S. Eliot's poems, Virginia's *Kew Gardens*, and Katherine Mansfield's *Prelude*. We were able to do this without financial loss, because we printed and bound the books ourselves in the dining-room or basement of Hogarth House and had no 'overheads'. Our first step up or down into professional publishing was the result of the sudden success of *Kew Gardens*. As I explained in *Beginning Again* (above, p. 175), when we were suddenly overwhelmed with orders for the book from booksellers, we decided to have a second edition printed for us commercially. This brought us

[1] On the title-page of our first book, *Two Stories*, we put 'Written and printed by Virginia Woolf and L. S. Woolf' and the imprint was Hogarth Press, Richmond. Later on our usual imprint on books printed by ourselves was 'Printed and published by Leonard and Virginia Woolf at The Hogarth Press' and on books printed for us by a commercial printer 'published by Leonard and Virginia Woolf at The Hogarth Press'.

into contact with all the big and many of the small booksellers, both wholesale and retail, and it was not difficult to learn the not very complicated customs and structure of the book trade. *Kew Gardens* showed me that we could, if we wished, publish a book commercially and successfully.

When, therefore, Koteliansky brought us Gorky's *Reminiscences of Tolstoi* and suggested that we should publish it, we were faced with a difficult decision. He translated some of it to us and we saw at once that it was a masterpiece. If we published it, we should have to print at least 1,000 copies, a number which we could not possibly manage ourselves. We took the plunge and had 1,000 copies printed for us by the Pelican Press for £73. It was our first commercial venture.[1] It was an immediate success and we had to reprint another 1,000 copies before the end of the year. Kot and I translated it and I do not think that I have ever got more aesthetic pleasure from anything than from doing that translation. It is one of the most remarkable biographical pieces ever written. It makes one hear, see, feel Tolstoy and his character as if one were sitting in the same room—his greatness and his littleness, his entrancing and infuriating complexity, his titanic and poetic personality, his superb humour. The writing is beautiful; every word and every sentence are perfect, and there is not one superfluous word or sentence in the book. I got immense pleasure from trying to translate this ravishing Russian into adequate English.

The success of Gorky's book was really the turning point for the future of the Press and for our future. Neither of us wanted to be professional, full-time publishers; what we wanted to do primarily was to write books, not print and publish them. On the other hand, our three years' experience of printing and publishing had given us great pleasure and whetted our appetite for more. In 1920 I felt in my bones that the Hogarth Press, like the universe and so many things in it, must either expand or explode or dwindle and die; it was too young and too vigorous to be able just to sit still and survive. And we were impelled by another very powerful motive for keeping the Press in existence. Publishing our *Two Stories* and Virginia's *Kew Gardens* had shown us, and particularly Virginia,

[1] In 1919 we had had Middleton Murry's *Critic in Judgment* printed for us by a small printer, my friend McDermott, but he and I had really printed it together, and we printed only 200 copies. Virginia and I bound it.

how pleasant it is for a writer to be able to publish his own books. As I have said more than once, Virginia suffered abnormally from the normal occupational disease of writers—indeed of artists—hypersensitiveness to criticism. The publisher of her first two novels was her own half-brother, Gerald Duckworth, a kindly, uncensorious man who had considerable affection for Virginia. His reader, Edward Garnett, who had a great reputation for spotting masterpieces by unknown authors, wrote an enthusiastic report on *The Voyage Out* when it was submitted to Duckworth. Yet the idea of having to send her next book to the mild Gerald and the enthusiastic Edward filled her with horror and misery. The idea, which came to us in 1920, that we might publish ourselves the book which she had just begun to write, *Jacob's Room*, filled her with delight, for she would thus avoid the misery of submitting this highly experimental novel to the criticism of Gerald Duckworth and Edward Garnett. So we decided to allow the Press to expand, if it could, into a proper publishing business, publish a book of short stories by Virginia, *Monday or Tuesday*, in 1921, and to ask Gerald to abandon his option on *Jacob's Room* so that it could be published by the Hogarth Press.[1]

This decision to allow the Press to expand and become professional, respectable, and commercial was bound up with another major decision. Lytton Strachey was considerably intrigued by what he considered to be our eccentric publishing and printing antics. Having, in his usual way, poured a good deal of icy water over the head of the Press and down our backs, he began to warm up a little when we told him that we thought we should have either to kill the Press or expand it into a regular publishing business, which would mean employing someone to work with us. He suggested and was soon urging that we should take Ralph Partridge into the Press. In 1920 Ralph was a unit in a strange *ménage à trois* which inhabited a very pleasant old mill-house in Tidmarsh. It belonged to Lytton, who had just become famous by the publication of his *Eminent Victorians* in 1918. With him lived Carrington, a young woman with one of those mysterious, inordinately female characters made up of an infinite series of contradictory characteristics, one

[1] Gerald agreed to this and later we purchased from him the rights in and stock of *The Voyage Out* and *Night and Day* so that all Virginia's books became Hogarth Press publications. The Press also bought from Edward Arnold the rights in my book, *The Village in the Jungle*.

inside the other like Chinese boxes. She was the apotheosis of the lovely milkmaid who is the heroine of the song: 'Where are you going to, my pretty maid?' She had a head of the thickest yellow hair that I have ever seen, and as, according to the fashion of the time among art students at the Slade, it was cut short round the bottom of her neck, it stood out like a solid, perfectly grown and clipped, yew hedge. She had the roundest, softest, pinkest damask cheeks and large, China blue eyes through which one was disconcerted to glimpse an innocence which one could not possibly believe really to exist this side of the Garden of Eden—in 1920 in the Berkshire house of the author of *Eminent Victorians*. She was a painter, having studied at the Slade, and she habitually wore the rather sacklike dresses which in the early 1920s were worn by artistic young women and can still be seen in the works of Augustus John. For some reason unknown to me she was universally called Carrington, which was her surname; I never heard anyone call her by her Christian name and I am not quite certain whether it was or was not Doris. I liked her very much, for she was charming when we stayed at Tidmarsh or when she came to us, and always very affectionate. But she was a silent woman and rarely took part in any general conversation. It was impossible to know whether the Chinese boxes were full of intricate psychological mysteries or whether in fact they were all empty. Carrington was devoted to Lytton, running his house for him and waiting hand and foot upon him and everyone staying in the house, like a perfect housekeeper and a dedicated cook, parlourmaid, and housemaid.

Ralph Partridge was the third member of the trinity living in Lytton's house in Tidmarsh. He was a very large, very good-looking, enormously strong young man. At Oxford he had been a first-class oar and would have got his Blue if he had not suddenly taken against rowing. He fought as a commissioned officer through the 1914 war. I am not quite sure how he got to know Lytton; I think it was through Carrington with whom in 1920 he was very much in love. Ralph was an interesting character; on the surface he was typical public schoolboy, Oxford rowing Blue, tough, young blood, and on the top of this he was a great he-man, a very English Don Juan. But behind his façade of the calm unemotional public school athlete there was an extraordinary childlike emotional vulnerability. An incident made me think that Ralph's emotionalism was in part hereditary.

He once asked us whether he could bring his father to dinner with us, as he was much concerned about him and thought that conversation with us might take his mind off his worries. His worries were curious. He was, like his son, a very large man, with a surface of rugged imperturbability. He was a retired Indian civil servant. He lived in the country and Ralph from time to time went down and spent a weekend with him. Some weeks before, Ralph in his father's study had casually opened the door of a small safe and found lying in it a loaded revolver. Thinking this very strange, he asked his father why he kept a loaded revolver in an unlocked safe. At first his father tried to shrug the whole thing off, but eventually admitted that he was desperately worried. His story was this. When in India, he had bought a considerable number of shares in an Indian company. After his retirement, when he had to make out his income tax returns, for some reason or other, he had got it into his head that he was not liable to pay income tax on the dividends paid in India by an Indian company and he had not included them in his returns for many years. Then suddeny he became aware that the dividends had always been part of his income liable to income tax. He had defrauded the revenue! He wrote to the Commissioners of Inland Revenue explaining what he had done and asking them to let him know what he should now do. His letter was acknowledged and then silence from the Commissioners. He wrote again with the same result, and then a third time with the same result. He then loaded his revolver and decided that, if he did not hear from the Commissioners in ten days' time, he would commit suicide. Ralph, having induced him to hand over the revolver, wrote to the Commissioners of Inland Revenue to inform them that, if they did not reply to his father's letters, his father would shoot himself. Almost by return a letter informing him of the total tax he must pay on the undeclared dividends. Poor Mr Partridge was saved from self-slaughter and some years later died from natural causes.

I do not think that Ralph, in a fairly long and certainly happy life, probably ever came near to suicide or even to the contemplation of it. But beneath the rather ebullient, hail-fellow-well-met, man of the world façade there was a curious stratum of emotionalism not unlike Mr Partridge's. He was easily moved to tears. He was, as I said, very much in love with Carrington. She was the classic female, if there has ever been a classic female—if the male pursued, she ran away; if the male ran away, she pursued. These tactics, applied to

Ralph, drove him into almost hysterical craziness. We decided that drastic steps must be taken. We asked Ralph whether he really, seriously wanted to marry Carrington, and he said that he did. I explained to him the phenomenon of the classic female, and told him that he must go to Carrington and put a pistol at her, not his head; he must say to her that she must marry him at once or let him go—if she said no, he would go off altogether. She gave in and married him.

Lytton as I said, was eager that we should take Ralph into the Hogarth Press, first as an employee on trial, and with the prospect of ultimately becoming a partner. Eventually we agreed, and on 31 August 1920, the Press acquired its first paid employee. Ralph was not a full-time employee; he came and worked two or three days a week; he was paid a salary of £100 and fifty per cent of the net profits. For the year 1920 his earnings were £56 6s. 1d. and for 1921, £125. The first thing we had to do was to teach him to print, for his main work, at the start, was to help us with the printing. As soon as he was able to set up a page of type and machine it, we decided to develop that side of our activities: in November 1921. I bought a Minerva printing machine for £70 10s. 0d and 77 lb of Caslon Old Face 12 pt. type for £18 9s. 5d. By 1923, i.e. exactly five years after its birth, the total capital invested in the Press was £135 2s. 3d.—all of it for printing machines, type, and materials. The Minerva machine was a formidable monster, a very heavy, treadle, platen machine, and, after treadling away at it for four hours at a stretch, from two to six in the afternoon, as I often did, I felt as if I had taken a great deal of exercise.

When the printing machine was delivered, we had it put in the corner of the dining-room, but, when McDermott saw it there, he shook his head and said it was much too dangerous—the machine was so heavy that if we worked it there, it would probably go through the floor on to the cook's head in the kitchen. So we had to have it all dismantled again and erected in a small larder at the back of the house in the basement. The invasion of the larder was not popular with Nellie and Lottie, the cook and the house-parlourmaid, but at least it was safer for them to have it there than over their heads in the dining-room.

The effect of Ralph's joining the Hogarth Press can be seen in the rapid expansion of our list to six books in 1922 and thirteen in 1923. Four in the 1922 lists were printed for us commercially.

Virginia's *Jacob's Room* was our first major work, a full-length novel, 1,200 copies of it were printed for us by R. & R. Clark Ltd. of Edinburgh. This was the beginning of our long connection with one of the biggest and best of British printers and with their remarkable managing director, William Maxwell. Willie Maxwell was inside and outside a Scot of the Scots; he was a dedicated printer and a first-class business man. The moment he saw our strange, unorthodox venture into publishing, he became personally interested in it, and he took as much trouble over printing 1,000 copies for us as he did in later times over printing 20,000. When he came on his periodical business visits to the London publishers, busy though he was, he would usually find time to come out and see the Hogarth Press in Richmond. *Jacob's Room* was published in October 1922 and began at once to sell fairly briskly, and I had a second impression of 1,000 copies printed by Clark. By the end of 1923 we had sold 1,413 copies; the cost of printing and publishing up to that date had been £276 1s. 6d. and the receipts had been £318 6s. 0d., so that our publisher's profit was £42 4s. 6d. We thought that we had done extremely well. It is true that Virginia Woolf, the publisher, had to some extent swindled Virginia Woolf, the author. As the whole thing was an experiment, a leap into the darkness of publishing in which we had practically no experience, and as Ralph had just come into the Press with a half share of the profits, we agreed that Virginia should not be paid a royalty, but should be paid one-third share of the profits. On the 1,413 copies sold she was paid £14 1s. 6d.

The three other commercially printed books which we published in 1922 were Russian; they came to us through Kot, and either Virginia and I collaborated with him in the translation of them. All three were remarkable. Two of them had just been published in Russia by the Soviet Government and came to Kot through Gorky: *Stavrogin's Confession* contained unpublished chapters of Dostoevsky's novel *The Possessed* and *The Autobiography of Countess Sophie Tolstoi* had been written in 1913 by Tolstoy's wife. The other book, Bunin's *Gentleman from San Francisco*, is one of the greatest of short stories. These books, which I still think to be beautifully printed and bound, were very carefully designed by Virginia and me, and they were unlike the books published by other publishers in those days. They were bound in paper over boards and we took an immense amount of trouble to find gay, striking, and beautiful papers. The Dostoevsky and the Bunin were bound in very gay patterned paper which we got from Czechoslovakia, and the Tolstoy book in a very good mottled paper. We printed, I think, 1,000 of each of the three books and published the Bunin and Tolstoy at 4s. and the Dostoevsky at 6s. Each of them sold between 500 and 700 copies in twelve months and made us a small profit, and they went on selling until we reprinted or they went out of print.

The big expansion of the Press took place in 1923, in which year we published seven books printed by ourselves and six printed for us. *Pharos and Pharillon* by E. M. Forster, which we printed ourselves, was a terrific undertaking. It was an eighty-page demy octavo volume and we printed between 800 and 900 copies. Virginia, Ralph and I set it up, and Ralph and I machined it. It was only just possible to print four pages at a time on the Minerva printing machine, so that Ralph and I between us had to treadle twenty two runs of over 800 pages a run. The first edition sold out in less than a year; the receipts, at a published price of 5s., were £135 10s. 11d., and our expenditure £90 19s. 0d., so that the book showed a profit for the Press of £44 11s. 11d. We at once had a second edition reprinted for us, crown octavo, and published it in paper covers at 3s.

The three of us must have done a tremendous amount of printing in the years 1921 and 1922 in order to produce the crop of our hand-printed books published in 1923. For they included *The Waste Land*, thirty-seven pages, and Robert Grave's *The Feather Bed*, twenty-eight pages crown quarto; a large book of Roger Fry's woodcuts, which was not easy printing for amateur novices; two crown quarto books of poetry by Herbert Read and Clive Bell, the latter being illustrated and decorated by Duncan Grant; and a small book of poems by Ena Limebeer. We bound the woodcuts and Ena Limebeer's poems ourselves, but the other books were too large for us to tackle ourselves and we had them bound for us by a commercial bookbinder.

The Hogarth Press, in these early days, met with a rather chilly welcome, or rather cold shoulder, from the booksellers. If you compare the thirteen books which we published in that year with any thirteen similar books from other publishers, you will find that all of ours have something more or less unorthodox in their appearance. They are either not the orthodox size or not the orthodox shape, or their binding is not orthodox; and even worse, what was inside the book, what the author said, was in many cases unfamiliar and therefore ridiculous and reprehensible, for it must be remembered that, if you published forty-two years ago poetry by T. S. Eliot, Robert Graves, and Herbert Read and a novel by Virginia Woolf, you were publishing four books which the vast majority of people, including booksellers and the literary 'establishment', condemned as unintelligible and absurd. Conservatism is the occupational disease in all trades and professions, and the booksellers suffer from it like everyone else. In 1923 we had no travellers and in a very desultory way we took our books round to the more important booksellers ourselves in order to get subscription orders before publication. It was a depressing business, though no doubt salutary and educative for an embryonic publisher. There were a few booksellers, like the great Mr Wilson of Bumpus, James Bain of King William Street, Lamley of South Kensington, Goulden and Curry in Tunbridge Wells, the Reigate bookshop, who were immediately interested in what we were trying to do and did everything to help and encourage us. But they were the exception. The reception of *Jacob's Room* was characteristic. It was the first book for which we had a jacket designed by Vanessa. It is, I think, a very good jacket and today no bookseller would feel his hackles or his temperature rise at sight of it. But it did not represent a desirable female or even Jacob or his room, and it was what in 1923 many people would have called reproachfully post-impressionist. It was almost universally condemned by the booksellers, and several of the buyers laughed at it.

Most human beings will never move unless a carrot is dangled in front of their noses, and, like the donkey, they must have precisely that kind of carrot which they and their fathers and fathers' fathers back to the primal ass have always recognised as the only true, good, and respectable carrot. Our books forty years ago were not recognised by the trade as the right kind of carrot, either internally or externally. But looking at them today any bookseller would admit that they are extremely well-produced books and that their jackets are admirable. Within ten or twelve years the binding of books in gay, pretty, or beautiful papers over boards was widely adopted for all kinds of books, particularly poetry. Time or the rise and fall of reputations have justified our judgment of the inside of these books. Only three out of the thirteen, Ena Limebeer's *Poems*, Mrs Lowther, and Reynold's letters, would not be recognised today as important books by important writers, and even for these there is still something to be said. As for the other ten, there are few publishers who in 1965 would not be very glad to have them on their lists.

In 1922 a storm blew up in the Hogarth Press, the kind of crisis which, during the next twenty years, was to recur with depressing regularity. After two years' experience it was clear to us that our arrangement with Ralph was not turning out successfully. He worked only two or three days a week, and that rather erratically. It was an impossible arrangement if we were to publish, as we did in 1923, twelve books in the year, and ourselves print half of them. We wanted Ralph to become full time, a professional publisher. This he would not do, though he was enthusiastic about the Press and with tears in his eyes and voice, maintained that nothing would induce him to give it up.

The truth was—as I suspected at the time and now see clearly looking back to 1923—that we were trying to do what is practically impossible, enjoy the best of two contradictory worlds. The success of the Press was forcing it to become a commercial publishing business. My experience in Ceylon had taught me (I think immodestly) to be a first-class business man, but I was not prepared to become a professional publisher. The Press was therefore a mongrel in the business world. We ran it in our spare time on lines invented by myself without staff and without premises; we printed in the larder, bound books in the dining-room, interviewed printers, binders, and authors in a sitting-room. I kept the accounts, records of sales, etc., myself in my own way, which was from the chartered accountant's view unorthodox, but when it was challenged by the Inland Revenue and I took my books to the Inspector of Taxes, he agreed that they showed accurately the profit or loss on each book published, the revenue and expenditure of the business, and the annual profit or loss, and for many years the Commissioners accepted my accounts for the purpose of assessing income tax.

The organisation and machinery of the Press were amateurish; it was, so far as Virginia and I were concerned, a hobby which we carried on in afternoons, when we were not writing books and articles or editing papers. We did not expect to make money out of it. But at the same time we were already committed to publish full-length, important books, not only for Virginia herself, but also for writers whom we considered important. We felt to these writers and their books the responsibility of the commercial publisher to the author, we had to publish their books professionally and competently. Our idea in 1922 was to get someone like Ralph who would work full time in the Press under me and earn his living from it, while Virginia and I would continue to work at it in our spare time as a by-product of our life and energies.

The last sentence shows what a very curious type of business we were trying to create and that the position of the young man who was to work under me would not be easy—nor would it be easy to find the right young man. I have never been an easy person to work with. I emphasise the words 'work with'. My experience in the Ceylon Civil Service proved that I get on much better with subordinates than with equals or superiors in business. In practical affairs I am in many ways a perfectionist—a character for which in the abstract, or when I see it in other people, I have no great admiration. I have a kind of itch or passion for finding the 'right' way of doing things, and by 'right' I mean the quickest and most accurate and simplest way. In 1923 I was still young enough to be hot tempered and allergic to fools.

By the middle of 1922 it was clear to us that Ralph, from our point of view, would not do. As it was, I was becoming a full-timer and he a part-timer, whereas we wanted the exact opposite. We found ourselves sitting uncomfortably on the horns of a dilemma—and the same situation would build itself up again and again from time to time over the following years. Shall we give up the Press altogether or shall we make one more attempt to find a manager or a partner who will help us to run this commercial hippogriff on the lines on which we want it to develop? We were then (and more than once again in the future) very much inclined to give the whole thing up and leave ourselves free of responsibility to pursue our other activities. On the other hand, we were urged from the outside to develop the Press and naturally were rather flattered by this. James Whittall, a cultured American, put out feelers and we considered him as a possible partner. But more surprising was a direct offer from the great publishing house of Heinemann to take us into a kind of partnership or 'association'. We had several talks with Whittall and, invited by the managing director of Heinemann, I went and had an interview with him on 27 November 1922. He offered to take over the whole business management of the Hogarth Press, distribution, accounting, advertising, and, if we wanted it, printing and publishing. We should be left complete autonomy to publish or not to publish any book we liked.

We turned down Whittall and we turned down Heinemann. We liked Whittall very much personally, but we came to the conclusion that he was too cultured for us and for the Press. We did not want the Press to become one of those (admirable in their way) 'private' or semi-private Presses the object of which is finely produced books, books which are meant not to be read, but to be looked at. We were interested primarily in the immaterial inside of a book, what the author had to say and how he said it; we had drifted into the business with the idea of publishing things which the commercial publisher could not or would not publish. We wanted our books to 'look nice' and we had our own views of what nice looks in a book would be, but neither of us was interested in fine printing and fine binding. We also disliked the refinement and preciosity which are too often a kind of fungoid growth which culture breeds upon art and literature; they are not unknown in Britain and are often to be found in cultivated Americans. It was because Whittall seemed to us too cultured and might want to turn the Hogarth Press into a kind of Kelmscott Press or Nonesuch Press that we turned him down. I am, of course, aware that many people would have thought—and some would still think—it ludicrous for us, and particularly Virginia, to talk of anyone being too cultured. The myth of Virginia as queen of Bloomsbury and culture, living in an ivory drawing-room or literary and aesthetic hothouse, still persists to some extent. I think that there is no truth in this myth. Her most obvious fault, as a person and as a writer, was a kind of intellectual and social snobbery—and she admitted it herself. There is also sometimes a streak of incongruous archness in her humour which is almost ladylike and very disconcerting. But her novels, and still more her literary criticism, show that she had not a trace of the aesthete or hypercultured. One has only to compare her attitude towards life and letters, towards art and people, with that of writers like George Meredith or Henry James or Max Beerbohm, to see that, although she was a cultured woman, the roots of her personality and her art were not in culture and that she had a streak of the common-sense, down to earth, granitic quality of mind and soul characteristic to many generations of her father's family.

We turned down Heinemann for the simple reason: *timeo Danaos et dona ferentes*, I fear the Greeks, especially when they offer me gifts. We felt that we were really much too small a fly to enter safely into such a very large web. So there we were with two pretty heavy albatrosses hanging round our necks—the Hogarth Press and Ralph Partridge. Lytton and Ralph put forward various proposals which we could not agree to, and sometime in 1922 we more or less agreed to part. Then a curious thing happened. In November 1922 we were in the midst of our negotiations and conversations and hesitations, and on the 17th of that months we met Whittall in the 1917 Club to discuss Heinemann's offer with him. While waiting for him, a young woman came in and began talking to a man who was sitting near us. She is described in Virginia's diary as 'one of those usual shabby, loose, cropheaded, smallfaced bright eyed young women'. It was impossible not to overhear the conversation. She told the man (who, I think, was Cyril Scott, the composer) that she was sick of teaching and had decided to become a printer. 'They tell me,' she said, 'that there's never been a woman printer, but I mean to be one. No, I don't know anything about it, but I mean to be one.' Virginia and I 'looked at each other with a wild surmise', and when the young woman went out, Virginia followed her and brought her back to our table. There we told her what we were doing with the Press and arranged that she should come and see it for herself and discuss possibilities.

Some days later on a Sunday afternoon the young woman, whose name was Marjorie Thomson, accompanied by a friend, came and had tea with us at Richmond in order to see what we were doing and discuss her possible employment. This was the first time I met Cyril Joad, for the friend was Joad, who was to become famous later as Professor C. E. M. Joad, the highbrow radio star. Cyril was a curious character; high minded, loose living and loose thinking, he inhabited a kind of Platonic or Aristotelian underworld. He was one of those people whom I dislike when I do not see them and *rather* like when I do see them. He was in fact a selfish, quick-witted, amusing, intellectual scallywag. He told us that he was going to marry Marjorie in a few months' time, and in a few months' time, Marjorie told us that she had married him. They lived together for some time, not I think very happily, in the Vale of Health, but the marriage was one of the many figments of Professor Joad's fertile imagination.

Marjorie had a nice face and a nice character. She belonged to what Virginia called the underworld, and it was, I suppose, looked at from certain altitudes, both socially and intellectually an underworld, a twentieth-century mixture of Bohemia and Grub Street; a certain number of its inhabitants could always be met in the 1917 Club in Gerrard Street. Marjorie had a bright, if somewhat shallow, mind, and as soon as she saw what we were doing in the Press, was anxious to join us. With Professor Joad's benediction, it was agreed that she should come to us on 1 January 1923, on a salary of £100 and a half share of the profits, Ralph leaving the Press finally in March. This, then, was the position of the Press when in March 1924 we moved from Hogarth House, Richmond, to Tavistock Square in Bloomsbury, and a new phase with rapid development began for our publishing. I will deal with this in the next chapter.

Our energy in the last four years of our life in Richmond was considerable. With no staff, to publish thirteen books (seven printed by ourselves) in a year would, I think, have been considered by many people a full-time job. I kept all the accounts myself and did a good deal of the invoicing. This in itself was no light labour. For instance, *Jacob's Room* was published on 27 October 1922, and by the end of 1923 it had sold 1,182 copies on over 200 orders. Each of these orders was entered by me in a serial number book and in a ledger; the invoices were made out either by me or by Ralph; and the books were packed and despatched by Virginia, Ralph, and me. This was our spare-time occupation almost always confined to the afternoon. During the same twelve months of 1923 Virginia was writing *Mrs Dalloway*, preparing *The Common Reader*, and earning £158 by reviewing. My own major occupation or occupations had become more complicated and variegated.

I wrote *Empire and Commerce in Africa* in 1918 for the Fabian Society. It is a formidable book of 374 pages, and I did a great deal of intensive reading for it. It is, I think, one of the earliest studies of the operations of imperialism in Africa. In 1920 Philip Snowden asked me to contribute a volume to the Independent Labour Party's 'Social Studies Series'. In the early 1920s there was a triumvirate of Labour Party leaders, Ramsay MacDonald, Arthur Henderson, and Philip Snowden. Snowden, whom I never knew as well as I knew the other two, was a curious man. He was lame and gave one the impression of being embittered by pain, though in ordinary conversation it was a rather gentle embitterment. I was an active member of the I.L.P., which in those days was the left wing of the Labour Party, and we were inclined to believe that Snowden was the most advanced or progressive of the triumvirate. In this we were very much mistaken. In *Beginning Again* (above, pp. 157-163) I have dealt with Ramsay; he was an opportunist who genuinely confused the highest political principles with the personal interests of James Ramsay MacDonald; he was neither on the Left nor on the Right, he was always bang on the Centre, and the Centre was James Ramsay MacDonald. In those early days I underestimated Henderson, thinking him to be what he looked like and what his political pet-name of Uncle Arthur seemed to indicate—a rather stuffy, slow-going and slow-thinking professional politician. He was something more and a good deal better than that. He was a man of some political principle and political understanding, a rare phenomenon among Cabinet Ministers anywhere. He was still capable of genuine and generous feelings for what he thought politically or socially right, and the desiccation of years in the trade union movement and the Labour Party had not dimmed or dulled these feelings. On the surface these were concealed behind a slow, watchful, slightly suspicious stare from hooded eyes, not uncharacteristic in those days of the British working man. Henderson's calibre was shown by his work as President of the League of Nations Disarmament Conference in 1932 and his behaviour to the great rat race of 1931 when Ramsay and Snowden temporarily destroyed the Labour Party. He had been himself chairman of the Labour Party before 1919, and the history of the party, Britain, and even Europe might well have been different and less catastrophic if he and not Ramsay had been leader and Prime Minister in the 1920s.

Snowden, the third member of the triumvirate, was quite unlike Henderson—and indeed quite unlike Ramsay. He came, I think, from the lower middle class and had been a subordinate civil servant and journalist. He was really an old-fashioned Liberal, which meant that by the time that I knew him he was in most things, from my point of view, about as progressive as a member of the Junior Carlton Club whose political faith was limited to support of the Crown, the Church, and free trade. He was one of those very honest, unimaginative, conservative—fundamentally, reactionary—politicians who drift into a left wing, progressive, or even revolutionary party, and do a good deal of harm politically. That he and Ramsay were leaders of the Labour Party in the crucial years from 1919 to 1931 was a disaster not only for the party but also for Britain, for their leadership inevitably landed them and all of us in the barren wilderness of the 1930s and the howling wilderness of the war. The most dangerous thing for a boat in a stormy sea is to find herself with no rudder; thanks to Ramsay and Snowden, that was the condition of the Labour Party in the years which followed the 1914 war. Though the upper ranks of the party have always been full of intellectuals, Labour has always shared the general British suspicion and misprision of the intellect and of those who use it in everyday life. As an unredeemed and unrepentant intellectual I was only too well aware of the widespread feeling that intelligence, unless camouflaged by silliness or stupidity, is dangerous and discreditable, and I never felt comfortable with Snowden who was a very British Briton and did not, it seemed to me, like me or my intellect. I was surprised when he asked me to write a volume for the I.L.P. series. I wrote a short book with the title *Socialism and Co-operation*, for which I was paid £25.

I have always been a heretical socialist, and, since very few heresies ever become orthodoxies, this book was even more futile than most of my books. Yet I still think that what the book said is both true and important, though neither the true-blue capitalist nor the true-red socialist nor even the pinkish trade unionist will have anything to do with it. The gist of my argument was that, in the modern world, socialism, i.e. the ownership or control of the means of production by the community, is not an end in itself, but an essential means to a prosperous and civilised society, and that the ownership and control should be based not on the state or the organised producers, but on the organised consumers. The curse of the capitalist system is that it produces states of mind in individuals and classes which contaminate society by inducing a profound, instinctive conviction that the object and justification of everyone's work, trade, profession, in fact of nine-tenths of a person's conscious existence from youth to senility, are and should be money, i.e. the personal interests of the individual. The machinery of communal economics and production is organised not to produce what the community wants or needs to consume but in order to provide either profit or a salary or wage or just 'work' for individuals. Marxist socialists and all those variegated 'packs and sets' of communists and socialists who, since Marx, 'ebb and flow by the moon', because they start from the exploitation of the worker, have unconsciously accepted the psychology of capitalism; both in theory and, where they have the opportunity, in practice, they organise society in the interest of the producers, not the consumers, the economic system being geared to and judged by its ability to provide work, wages, and salaries, competition for the profits between different classes of worker being substituted for competition between capitalists. This process had, of course, been enormously encouraged because in Europe trade unionists and trade unionism have been a dominating influence in all socialist parties, and the trade unionist, as a trade unionist, is concerned not with what he produces and its consumption but with 'work', which the production provides for him, and the amount of money which he can make out of it.

The importance of the British co-operative movement and system is that they have proved that efficient control of large-scale production and distribution by consumers is possible. I argued that it was possible and desirable to develop and extend this system into consumers' socialism, i.e. the control of the industrial system by the community organised as consumers, and that this would not only revolutionise the whole economic system but also the social psychology of capitalism and of socialism based upon production and the interests of the producers.

I think that the nature of social or economic organisation has an immense effect upon social psychology for good or ill. I will give a trivial example which, nevertheless, always seems to me to throw light upon our civilisation and upon the barbarous psychology which it has bred in us. If you stand at any bus stop in London and observe what happens to the queue of consumers, i.e. of the people who wish to use the bus to get from one place to another in London, you will note a strange thing about this simple industrial or economic operation. The buses drive up very often in conglomerations of three, four, or even five, all of the same number, i.e. all going to the same place—the first bus being full, the second half-full, and the two or three others empty. They dash off almost immediately and the slightest hesitation on the part of anyone in the queue will leave him behind to wait a long wait for another conglomeration of buses. The explanation of this is that the system of transport by bus in London is not organised primarily with the object of transporting the public as rapidly and comfortably and efficiently as possible from one place to another, i.e. in the interests of consumers, but for three entirely different objects: first, for what is known as a schedule, i.e. the timetable which says that the bus must leave a particular garage at a particular time and arrive at another garage at a particular time; secondly, to provide work for the drivers and conductors, i.e. to provide the highest possible wage under the best possible working conditions for the producer; thirdly, to obtain from the public the maximum amount in fares so that, while paying the highest possible wages, the whole business can be run at a profit, or at least not a loss. The interesting fact is that this barbarous system is accepted as rational, inevitable, and civilised, not only by the management, the major and minor bureaucrats who direct London Transport, not only by the workers and employees, but even by the underdogs in the queue, the cringing consumers. And members of the Labour Party and the trade unions will welcome this system as socialism, provided that it is controlled at the top by a Transport Board instead of a Board of Directors.

The psychology of trade unionism and the psychology of capitalism, which spring from the same social postulates, and are complementary like the positive and negative in electricity, are so firmly established in modern society that to most people the idea that the object of industry should be consumption, not production or profit, seems Utopian and even immoral. I never imagined, therefore, that my argument in favour of socialism controlled by consumers would cut any ice in the Labour movement. But even in politics, where reason is so suspect and so unwelcome, I have an absurd, pig-headed feeling that one ought to use one's reason. However, I propose to leave the account of my political activities to the next chapter and to return now to my other occupations in the years 1919 to 1924.

Between 1921, when *Socialism and Co-operation* was published, and 1931, when *After the Deluge*, Vol. 1, was published, I did not produce any book, partly because I was so much occupied by journalism, publishing, and politics, and partly because I was ruminating and slowly writing *After the Deluge*. But in 1921 I had one incident connected with my writing which amused Virginia and me. In that year we published in the Hogarth Press a book of three short stories by me, *Stories from the East*, and one of them, 'Pearls and Swine', said Hamilton Fyfe in a review in the *Daily Mail*, 'will rank with the great stories of the world'. Mr Henry Holt, a literary agent, on the strength of this review wrote and asked me whether I would let him have the story for America. I did not do so, and months later in 1922 he wrote to me again, asking whether I would let him deal with the story, which 'ought to have netted you anything up to a couple of hundred pounds for serial rights. Possibly more'. This time I sent the book—I don't think that up to this time he had read the story—and told him that he could try his hand. When he read the story, it was obviously a bit of a shock to him, being a good deal too plain spoken for the two hundred pound bracket in the United States of America. He wanted me to tone it down a bit—he called this euphemistically 'a few artistic alterations'—and send it to the great American literary agent, Ann Watkins, who had already expressed an interest in it. I replied that I 'cannot bear to contemplate rewriting anything which I wrote a long time ago', but that he could deal with the story and Ann Watkins himself. This he did. Ann Watkins also thought the story a masterpiece, but was also obviously horrified by it and the idea of offering it to the American market. 'The realism, the vivid picture quality of "Pearls and Swine", she wrote, 'is so great as to be terrific. It is as powerful a story as I have read in a long time. . . . But there are only about two magazines in America that I think would touch it. You see, we here in the States are still provincial enough to want the sugar-coated pill; we don't like facts, we don't like to have to face them. It seems to be a characteristic of the American people. And where we won't face them in our politics, in our domestic problems, in our personal lives—why in the devil should we be forced to face them in fiction? I think, fundamentally, our demand of the author is that he entertain us with his wares. We veer from the shocking, the revolting— the truth. But holy, suffering cats! how Woolf can write! I should like nothing better than to represent him in the American market. But I should like to represent him only if in so doing I can be of profit to both him and myself.'

Mr Holt was much impressed and wrote to me: 'I wish I could make you realise the tremendous commercial significance of this'. He wanted me to settle down to writing something suitable for the great American market—'I may never again', he said, 'have patience to bully a man into making several thousand a year, so, for the last time, *do think it over.*' I do not think that I answered this letter, and then one afternoon a car stopped at the gate of Monks House, and out of it stepped Mr and Mrs Holt. He said that he wished to talk to me alone while Mrs Holt would talk to Virginia. It took me the better part of an hour to get rid of him. He said that I must devote myself to writing stories with him as my literary agent, and that, if I did, he would guarantee that I would make £3,000 a year. I said that I didn't want to write stories and in any case I could never think of plots for them. Eventually we went in and joined the ladies over a cup of tea. Virginia recorded the following conversation: ' "He sells everything—he'll be selling me next," she says, very arch. Mr Holt half winked and cocked his head. "Little woman, little woman," said Mr Holt. "He's the straightest boy that ever lived," said Mrs Holt, not without emotion.' At last they drove away, and some days later I got a letter from Mr Holt in which he gave me the outline of a plot for a short story which I should write, and he assured me that, if I would do so and send it to him, he would get me a large sum of money for it. I did not write Mr Holt's story and I do not think that I ever heard from him again.

I have told in *Beginning Again* how it came about that I started and edited the *International Review* for the Rowntrees. It did not last very long, for Arnold Rowntree had, I think, underestimated the costs and loss involved in financing a monthly review dealing with international affairs. When it came to an end, Rowntree asked me to write regularly sixteen pages on international affairs for the *Contemporary Review*, which was also a Rowntree paper. I did this in 1920 and 1921 for the noble fee of £250 per annum. From the great newspaper proprietors, like Lord Northcliffe and Lord Beaverbrook, down to the humble sub-editor or reporter, and the still more humble writer for the highbrow weeklies, monthlies, and quarterlies, it is almost impossible for the journalist and the owners of journalists not to believe that what they write or what they hire other people to write has great influence and importance. In general, the bigger the journalistic bug, the bigger his delusion about his influence and importance. I have no doubt that no one who writes for papers ever completely sheds this delusion and that I myself still nourish in my unconscious a secret and sheepish hope, if not belief, that a few people will be influenced by what I write. But I think that my early journalism—writing for the *New Statesman* and for the *Nation* and editing the *International Review*—rapidly disillusioned me. In writing, it seems to me, one just has to cast one's bread upon the waters, resigning oneself to the fact that nothing will ever return to you except so many pounds per thousand words,[1] and the soggy bread will sink without a trace. Certainly one would have had to be

[1] 'No man but a blockhead ever wrote except for money,' said Johnson.

very artless or very sanguine to think that many people read or anyone minded sixteen pages on international affairs in the *Contemporary Review*. I found it a depressing job, and was not sorry to hand it over to George Glasgow in 1921.

In 1920 and 1921 I still did quite a lot of reviewing and article writing for the *New Statesman* and the *Nation*, earning from the *New Statesman* £65 7s. 0d. in 1920 and £44 4s. 0d. in 1921, and from the *Nation* £81 8s. 0d. in 1920 and £40 14s. 0d. in 1921. The large sum of £81 which I earned from the *Nation* in 1920 was due to the fact that, as I recorded in *Beginning Again* (p. 134), for three months during that year I temporarily took H. N. Brailsford's place as leader writer on the paper. The *Nation* was owned by the Rowntrees, the Quaker chocolate and cocoa kings of York, and was edited by H. W. Massingham, one of the most famous editors of his time. In 1922 Brailsford became editor of the *New Leader* and Massingham asked me to take his place on the staff of the *Nation*. I accepted and landed myself in a tangle of events and a journalistic career which lasted for eight years. Initially my duties when I took over Brailsford's job were to go to the *Nation* office in Adelphi Terrace every Monday morning and arrange with Massingham what I should write for next Saturday's paper. Practically always it consisted of the first leader on some political subject, three or four notes on political subjects, and occasionally a review. Massingham was a strange, rather disquieting person. He was a small neatly dressed, quiet spoken man whose face had the look of one of those small, brindled, reserved mongrels who eye one with motionless suspicion—the expression of eye and mouth always fills me with apprehension. In 1922 he was sixty-two years old and had edited the *Nation* for fifteen years. All his life he had been a pillar of both liberalism and Liberalism and his whole journalistic career had been on Liberal papers; before editing the *Nation* he had been editor of the *Daily Chronicle*. The *Nation* was supposed to be, and had been, a Liberal weekly supporting the Liberal Party, and Arnold Rowntree, the head of the Rowntree clan, was a Liberal M.P. These facts are important for an understanding of what happened in the next twelve months and of the entanglements in which to my surprise I found myself. For Massingham had in the years just before 1922 drifted further and further from the Liberal Party and had become gradually a supporter of the Labour Party whereas the Rowntrees remained Liberals.

I did not realise any of this when I first stepped into Brailsford's shoes. It was a peaceful office with the gentle, deaf H. M. Tomlinson as literary editor and Miss Crosse one of those highly geared, super-efficient secretaries who are themselves capable of editing and often, *de facto* but not *de jure*, do edit the paper. Then there was a band of very distinguished, veteran Liberals, old friends of Massingham's, who formed the staff of the paper, J. A. Hobson, J. L. Hammond, and H. W. Nevinson. In their company I felt very much the new boy and they were so high-minded—the particular brand of high-mindedness seemed to be peculiar in those days to Liberals who lived in Hampstead and Golders Green—that I always felt myself to be a bit of a fraud in their company. Hammond and Hobson were two charming men; I liked them very much and I became a friend of both; to many people Nevinson was a great charmer, but he was altogether too noble for my tastes. I don't like knights *sans peur et sans reproche*—they, like mongrels, make me uneasy. These three with Massingham and Tomlinson used to lunch together on Mondays and I often used to join them.

Before the lunch I had had my talk with Massingham and decided with him what I was to write. I never felt that I really understood Massingham. He was always extremely nice to me and I got on with him very well, both in work and over the lunch table, but I do not think that I ever got more than a fraction of an inch below the surface. The routine of Monday morning was that he invariably asked me to suggest the subject of my article and notes and left it to me to tell him what I proposed to say. I do not remember him ever not accepting my subject or line of policy, and his comments and suggestions were always very few. But though he said very little when we were talking as professionals on the week's job, there is no doubt that he was a first-class editor in that somehow or other he impressed his personality on those who wrote for him and what they wrote. The consequence was that the paper too had a personality, a flavour, a smell of its own, and this got into what one wrote when one was writing for it. I was never conscious of writing differently in the *Nation* and the *New Statesman* and in my own books—I never felt Massingham looking over my shoulder or breathing down my journalistic back—but if I reread what I had written for him, I was startled to get a faint whiff of Massingham and Massingham's *Nation*.

His editorial and political personality and odour or aura were complex and fascinating. First, he was extremely high-minded; the political aura of the *Nation* in 1922 was still that of Gladstonian liberalism impregnated with sophisticated or civilised non-conformity. Secondly, he was a gentle man, on the side of culture and quiet, of sentiment, if not sentimentality; the *Nation* again reflected this, being pacific, humane, with occasionally a tear—some people said a crocodile's tear—in its eyes and voice. Thirdly, he was a bitter and violent man, with a peculiar bitterness of which I will say more in a moment; the *Nation* had an undercurrent of aggressive acerbity and sudden bursts of intemperance.

I found the study of his public and private character and its extraordinary contradictions absorbing. After we had decided what I should write, we nearly always had for ten minutes or more a general conversation on the political situation. It was a time of continual crisis: Lloyd George's fatal adventure in the Middle East, the Conservative revolt against him, and the break up of the coalition government. I suppose that Massingham must have been in pre-war years a fervid supporter of Lloyd George's, but when I knew him, he hated him with an almost crazy violence and bitterness. He was, as I said, a gentle, quiet-spoken man, but nine Mondays out of ten he would begin a tirade against L. G. He never raised his voice, but out of his mouth poured a kind of commination recital against L. G. and, frequently linked to him, J. P. Scott, editor of the *Manchester Guardian*. I do not know why he had conceived such violent hatred of the immaculate Scott, the journalistic pillar of liberalism, but he astonished me by his venomous and grotesque accusations. I could scarcely believe that I was not dreaming a mad dream when I heard him more than once accuse these two spotless Liberals of a homosexual passion for each other.

Not much has been written about the psychology or psychopathology of political beliefs and emotions. I can remember only two books of any importance. The distinguished psychoanalyst Edward Glover in *War, Sadism and Pacifism* maintained that one had to be peculiarly sadistic and bloody-minded to be a pacifist or even a supporter of the League of Nations, and *Personal Aggressiveness and War* by Evan Durbin and John Bowlby was another original book on more or less the same subject. When I first read Dr Glover's book, I thought that his own unconsciousness was not altogether unconcerned with his finding such very discreditable motives for pacifism in the unconscious of the pacifist, but I have no doubt that there was a good deal of truth in his main thesis. I am sure that if one could look deep into the minds of those who are on the Left in politics (including myself), Liberals, revolutionaries, socialists, communists, pacifists, and humanitarians, one would find that their political beliefs and desires were connected with some very strange goings on down among their ids in their unconscious.

At any rate, watching and listening to Massingham on a Monday morning, I often felt that something like this could only explain the conflict in his character, his gentle high-mindedness and absurd verbal violence. Down below he was, I think, a man of strong feelings which might range from the milk of human kindness to hatred and bitterness. It is also possible that he had the diffused dissatisfaction and grudge against the universe that small men often have, though I may be wrong about this and indeed about his stature. At any rate, as Freud insisted in *Civilization and its Discontents*, to be even a moderately civilised man is not only difficult but also extremely painful. If you have to be as high-minded all the time as a Liberal of Golders Green or Welwyn Garden City, editing or writing for the *Nation*, in 1922, you had to be suppressing all the time some very violent and curious instincts which might, I think, have surprised and shocked even the editor of the *Nation* had he found them in his unconscious mind. Nineteen hundred years before Freud wrote *Civilization and its Discontents* Horace said *naturam expellas furca, tamen usque recurret* (you may drive nature out with a fork, but she will always return)—and we now know that she returns in strange and very different forms. I have no doubt that the strain of being so civilised caused the explosions of Massingham's verbal violence.

His queer, secretive, complex character had, I am sure, much to do with causing the curious situation in which I found myself involved about a year after I joined his staff. The Rowntrees, proprietors of the paper, were, as I said, Liberals and the *Nation* had been, and was still supposed to be, a Liberal paper. But in fact, when I joined it, it was to all intents and purposes a Labour paper. Massingham had become bitterly hostile to the Liberals and Hammond, Hobson, Nevinson, like Brailsford, Noel and Charles Buxton, who before the war had been active and distinguished Liberal intellectuals, had all drifted into the Labour Party. Massingham never told us exactly what happened behind the scenes between him and the Rowntrees. I am inclined, knowing him and them, to believe that Arnold Rowntree treated him very well, allowing him a great deal of latitude, but warning him that the Rowntrees could not agree to the paper becoming a mere Labour Party organ. All through 1923 the divergence between their political views increased and suddenly there was an explosion or showdown.

I had been told nothing of what was going on, and I was astonished when one morning Massingham told me that the Rowntrees had decided that they could not go on financing the paper as it was, and that they had decided to sell it, but would give him first option to buy it. Massingham said that he knew someone who would put up the money, and he asked me whether I would agree to continue on the staff under a new proprietorship; Hammond, Hobson, Nevinson, and Tomlinson had all agreed to stand by him. I said I would.

There followed weeks of unpleasant doubt and mystery. He was understood to be hard at work raising the money, but he told us nothing. At one moment he went off to the South of France to deal with the man who was to supply most of the money, and we were left to carry on with the editing of the paper. We met for dejected lunches and speculated gloomily on what could be happening. Then Massingham returned, but told me nothing definite. I was astonished when Maynard Keynes in March 1923 told me that he and some others had acquired an interest in the *Nation*, the Rowntrees also still retaining an interest. Hubert Henderson was to be editor and Maynard asked me to become the literary editor. I went to Massingham and explained to him what had happened. I said that if he was going to acquire the *Nation* or was going to be editor of a new weekly, I would continue with him, but, if there was to be no weekly edited by him, I would accept Maynard's offer, provided that he had no objection to my doing so. He said that he had failed to raise the money to purchase the *Nation* and there was no immediate prospect of his editing a new weekly so that I had no longer an obligation to him and I must be free to accept Maynard's offer. This I did, but I insisted upon the following two conditions, which were accepted by Maynard and by Hubert: (1) I would do the work in my own time, though I would normally come to the office on Mondays, Tuesdays and the morning of Wednesdays; (2) I should be autonomous in my part of the paper, though the editor would have the right to object to and require the removal of anything which I had passed, but, if he did, I would then have the right to insist that Maynard should arbitrate between us. Maynard only once had to arbitrate between us during the seven years in which I was literary editor. I had given a book to review to David Garnett, then at the beginning of a distinguished literary career, but not yet, I must admit, a very skilful reviewer. When Hubert read his review in proof, he said that it was not good enough and required me not to print it. I insisted that Maynard should arbitrate, as the review, though not very good, did not merit rejection, Maynard agreed with me and the review was published.

The events, such as they were, of my seven years' work on the new *Nation*—which became, of course, a Liberal paper, for Maynard and Hubert were both Liberals—belong to the next chapter and I will leave to that chapter too my political activities on the Labour Party committees and the Fabian Society. In the four years 1920 to 1923, as Virginia's health grew more stable, our social life increased and became more and more of a problem. Our taste in human beings was pretty much the same, but we did not always agree about the best way of seeing them. Virginia loved 'Society', its functions and parties, the bigger the better; but she also liked—at any rate in prospect—any party. Her attitude to this, as to most things, was by no means simple. The idea of a party always excited her, and in practice she was very sensitive to the actual mental and physical excitement of the party itself, the rise of temperature of mind and body, the ferment and fountain of noise. Sometimes she enjoyed it as much in the event as in anticipation, and sometimes, of course, owing to her peculiar vulnerability to the mildest slings and arrows of (not very) outrageous fortune, she would leave a boring party in despair as if it were the last scene of Wagner's Götterdämmerung with Hogarth House and the universe falling in flames and ruin about her ears. Of one of these catastrophic depressions in August 1922 she wrote in her diary: 'No one ever suffered more acutely from atmosphere as I do; and my leaves drooped one by one; though heaven knows my root is firm enough. As L. very truly said, there is too much ego in my cosmos'.

She not only enjoyed society, the kaleidoscope of human beings, conversation, the excitement of parties, she was through and through a professional novelist, and all this was the raw material of her trade. This dual sensitivity to the most trivial meetings with her fellow human beings meant that society and parties were a great strain on her mental health and she herself was well aware of this.

The following is another extract from her diary in the summer of 1922: 'Clive came to tea yesterday and offered me only the faded and fly blown remnants of his mind. He had been up late. So had I—at the pictures. For my own part, all my strings are jangled by a night out. Dissipation would rot my writing (such as it is, I put in, modestly). Words next day dance patterns in my mind. It takes me a week to recover from Lady Colefax—who by the way invites me for Friday.'

Virginia always thought she was going to enjoy a party enormously before she went to it and quite often she did. I did not share her optimism, nor, therefore, ever quite so keenly her disappointments, and, though I sometimes enjoyed parties, I never felt the exhilaration which they sometimes gave to her. When we were still living in Richmond, she wrote in her diary that she and I were becoming celebrities and that I denied this, but then I had not, as she had, gone to Logan Pearsall Smith's tea-party in Chelsea or to the week-end with Ottoline Morrell at Garsington. I did occasionally go to Logan's tea-parties where one drank Earl Grey's china tea amid china, furniture, pictures, books, and human beings, not easily distinguishable from one another or from the tea with its delicate taste and aroma, for they were all made, fabricated, collected in accordance with society's standards of sophisticated culture and good taste. Earl Grey has never been my cup of tea, nor was Logan.

I occasionally went to Garsington, but not as often as Virginia. Garsington, its week-ends and Ottoline and Philip, have been described, with or without venom, in many memoirs and novels, and I have myself had something of a say in *Beginning Again* (above pp. 143-7), and I do not propose to say much more about this interesting phenomenon. It was an interesting phenomenon, both from a human and from a social point of view. The ingredients and therefore the flavour and taste of Garsington altered a little when peace came. The C.O.s—Conscientious Objectors—whom Philip and Ottoline had so generously harboured during the war, of course, drifted away. The C.O.s, being pacifists, were, for the reasons which I have explained above in dealing with Massingham's virulence, more quarrelsome and cantankerous than the average man or woman. At week-ends they formed an unquiet, disquieting, turgid sediment beneath the brilliant surface of very important people, the distinguished writers, cabinet ministers, and aristocrats who sat down to breakfast, lunch, and dinner.

Ottoline is almost always described in the setting of Garsington, but she functioned just as characteristically in the large house in Bedford Square. In the 1920s there were three great London hostesses with would-be salons to which the literary gents and ladies were admitted and, if distinguished, welcomed—Lady Colefax, Lady Cunard, and Lady Ottoline Morrell. The social historian of the period would have studied in these salons the antics of some limited and not uninfluential sections of British society—a way of life, a collection of human subspecies, and even a form of influence which have, I suppose, completely died out of London and Britain. The three salons differed a good deal from one another. Of Lady Cunard's I could only speak second-hand, from Virginia, for I never went there myself. Sybil Colefax was the most professional of the three, an unabashed hunter of lions.

Ottoline's Bedford Square was even more a salon than her Garsington. It existed in four forms: you might be invited to a lunch, a tea, a dinner, or to an evening party after dinner, and the last might be very large or fairly small. At all of them the pudding would certainly contain plums, distinguished or very distinguished persons, and the point of the pudding was, it seemed to me, not so much in the eating as in the plums—the bigger the better. In the pudding of society I am not too fond of plums. Nothing is more enjoyable than 'society', if by the word one means the gathering together round a table or a fire or in a garden of congenial, intelligent, and amusing people, and the enjoyment comes from the play and interplay of character and the congenial, intelligent, and amusing conversation, and is enhanced by pleasant or beautiful rooms and houses, good food, and good wine. This kind of society and its enjoyment is only possible if the number of people gathered together—the party—is strictly limited, indeed small enough to make it possible for the conversation to become at any moment general. Both Virginia and I were very fond of this kind of society, and party, and we always contrived to get a good deal of it in Richmond, Rodmell, and later in London.

The society of the professional hostess, of Ottoline in Bedford Square, is entirely different. As a study of human behaviour, both of hostess and guests, it always fascinated me. The psychology of the hostess may contain all or any of the following ingredients: enjoyment of the enjoyment of her guests; a kind of artistic creativeness—the art of hostess-ship; the love of the exercise of power and prestige; the passion of the collector of anything from stamps to human beings. The ingredients in the hospitality of Lady Colefax in Argyll House were quite different from those of Lady Ottoline Morrell in Bedford Square. Sibyl gave me the impression of an armour-plated, electroplated, or enamelled woman, physically and mentally. The range of her feelings behind this metallic façade seemed to be extremely limited; but façades are façades, and behind hers there may, of course, have been a tremulous sensitiveness. Indeed I was often startled and shocked to observe the expression of the eyes in that mask of her hostess face; far behind and deep down below they gave one a glimpse of misery, anguish. But the surface was always hard, polished, plated, professional. Every morning Sibyl wrote her illegible notes or sat at her telephone collecting men and women, ranked solely for their fame or footing, their power or prestige. Her main motives were, I think, pleasure in power and prestige and the delights of collecting—'I must add Walter Lippmann and André Gide to my collection'.

The hostess psychology of Ottoline was quite different. I do not think that she had a very strong passion for collecting, although, as with all professional hostesses, it did exist in her. She was, too, not very much moved by power and prestige; as a Cavendish-Bentinck and sister of the Duke of Portland, she assumed unconsciously, like all aristocrats, that she had a peculiar right and relation to both, and therefore need not trouble about them. She was highly sexed and got some sexual satisfaction as a by-product of the art of hostess-ship. She also got aesthetic satisfaction from the practice of the art, for her aesthetic emotions were strong and persistent, if erratic and sometimes deplorable. The house and garden at Garsington were lovely, and Ottoline gave both an artistic finish, and she gave the same to the rooms in Bedford Square. Her own taste was for disorderly flamboyance, as her dress and hair showed, but she knew and respected what the world and the élite thought to be the right thing in books, pictures, music, houses, rooms, furniture, and persons. The compromise between good taste and her own tastes gave a peculiar and sometimes incongruous aspect to her rooms and a strange and sometime ludicrous flavour to her parties. Her reactions to what is great in art were strong, untrustworthy, and embarrassing; for instance, I have heard her gush over the beauties of Keats at the breakfast table of a Garsington week-end to five or six silent, gloomy, cynical, sophisticated members of the literary élite.

But she had a real gift for and pleasure in the art of hostess-ship which was unknown to Sibyl. She wanted to know, to have intimate relations with intelligent, imaginative, creative people, and to create herself the best possible surroundings in which these strange men (with an occasional woman) might flourish socially and enjoy one another's society and conversation. There is no doubt that in this she was to some extent successful.

If you want to know what a particular period was like, the nature of its society and classes, the kind of people who lived in it, you can learn something from the way in which the people met and entertained one another formally. The *Symposium* gives one a vivid and startling glimpse, not only of Athens in the fifth century, but of Socrates, Alcibiades, and Aristophanes, just as Petronius makes one suddenly see through Trimalchio's dinner-party a glimpse of what it meant to be a vulgar rich man or a slave girl in the time of Nero. Most of those whom I met in Ottoline's Garsington and Bedford Square or Sibyl's Argyll House are as dead as Socrates and Trimalchio, and the society of the 1920s is almost as dead as that of Athens in the fifth century B.C. or of Rome in the first century A.D. If I describe one or two parties at Sibyl's and Ottoline's, it may give a glimpse of what they and we and a section of London society were like in the third decade of the twentieth century.

First a trivial picture of Sibyl, the insensitive professional hostess, and the failure of her art. In *Beginning Again* (above, pp. 119-20) I described how, just before the 1914 war, I met for the first time the famous Walter Lippman, then unknown, how we travelled down from Keswick to London talking intimately the whole time, and how much I liked him. Not long before the 1939 war Sibyl came to see us and for some reason which I have forgotten I must have mentioned this. I also said that in the intervening twenty-five years I had hardly seen Lippmann. Lady Colefax, the pro, jumped on me. Walter Lippman would be in London next week; would I come and dine and meet him on Thursday? I knew that at a dinner in Argyll House I should have no chance of the only kind of conversation which I wanted to have with Lippmann, and I therefore refused. But Sibyl, as a hostess, was a ruthless Lady Bountiful, and I was not allowed to get off. She would get Lippmann to come and meet me at six one evening, if I would not come to a meal, and she would ask no one else. I foolishly agreed. We met unhappily and, under the inhibiting eye of Sibyl, had nothing to say to each other.

The second picture was at a top-notch, grand evening party at Argyll House. It was a fine, warm summer evening; the large room was full of Sibyl's top-notch lions, political and literary mainly, together with a sprinkling of lesser lights and the stage army of well-fed and well-dressed men and women whose only distinction was that they were habitually asked to this kind of London party. The doors which led from the large room into the garden were open, and the guests strolled about the garden, which was lit by garlands of fairy lamps. There is a certain beauty in this kind of scene, enhanced by the fact that among the strollers under the fairy lamps are the Prime Minister and half the Cabinet, Mary Pritchard, Margot Asquith, the editor of *The Times*, Max Beerbohm, and Augustus John. Everything seemed to be going as it should, when suddenly there came a social catastrophe of the kind which often happened in Argyll House. We were all summoned into the large room and seated down to hear a recital by a distinguished French pianist. She was led up to the piano by Sibyl and began to play. She had played only a few bars when two or three people came in from the garden talking loudly, obviously unaware of what was happening in the room. The pianist crashed her hands on the notes, got up, and walked to the end of the room, where she sat down, saying in a loud voice and a thick foreign accent: 'I do not play to accompany people talking'. It is a queer sensation to sit in such a company of 100 to 150 persons, in full evening-dress, all in awkward silence and all obviously feeling rather uncomfortable. No one moved, no one talked. After what seemed a long time Sibyl got up and walked over to where Arthur Balfour was sitting and had a longish conversation with him. Then he got up, went to the irate pianist, bent over her, and obviously pleaded with her. He was successful and led her gracefully amid applause to the piano.

Ottoline, as I said, treated her lions differently, and the atmosphere of her Bedford Square zoo was much more ramshackle and informal than that at Argyll House. I can, perhaps, best give its flavour by describing a tea-party there. I did not often go to these parties, and it was characteristic of Ottoline that she insisted that I should come to this one, because, she said, one of the Georgian poets whom I had never met was coming and she was quite sure I would like him. His name, I think, was Ralph Hodgson and Ottoline thought I would like him because he was a strong silent man who had written a poem about a bulldog and also a poem about a bull. When Virginia and I arrived, the poet of the bull and the bulldog was there, strong and silent, together with Yeats and James Stephens, who had written a very successful book, *The Crock of Gold*. It was an uneasy party. Yeats sat in the place of honour, but was grumpy and silent, and Virginia was commandeered, much too obviously, by Ottoline to go over and sit next to him and talk him, if possible, into a better mood. James Stephens was one of those Irish Irishmen, the stage Irishman who never stops talking with the soft brogue which makes one think despairingly of the indomitable soft rain falling upon the lakes of Killarney. Being also what I call a literary gent, he used to fill me alternately with depression and irritation, and I think that he probably had much the same effect upon Yeats. On this occasion he was in full spate, with a whimsical, poeticised fantasy about insects, whom he continually referred to as 'the little craytures'. When he made a more than usually absurd statement about 'the little craytures', before I could stop myself, I said in a loud voice: 'Nonsense'. Ottoline frowned upon me and the party became still stickier. However, nothing stopped Stephens talking, and the other Irishman, the great man, thawed bit by bit under the skilful and soothing ministrations of Ottoline and Virginia. The party began to go in the way in which Ottoline liked parties to go—intimate, intense, and rather intensive talk about books and writers and the arts generally. It was this kind of conversation which made Bedford Square so different from Argyll House. And it was characteristic of a Bedford Square party that it was suddenly deflated, broken up, exploded. For the door opened and in came the Duchess of Portland. She was obviously not expected by Ottoline and she looked upon us all as if we were 'the little craytures'. She sat down on a sofa next to Ottoline and began to talk to her about something which only concerned herself. Silence fell upon us little craytures; even Stephens was left without a drone or a buzz, for a Duchess of Portland is capable of silencing the voice even of the cicada. After a minute or two Ottoline got up and took her sister-in-law out of the room. They stood outside the door and the sound of their voices in inaudible conversation seemed to be going on interminably. When at last we heard the front door close behind the Duchess, the party rather despondently broke up.

The kind of party which I have just been describing, presided over by a professional hostess, is formal, public entertainment in which social pleasure is very deliberately offered and pursued. I have never

1 The author and Virginia, 1912

2 The Stephen family on the brink of the workhouse: Leslie Stephen, Lady Albutt, Mrs Stephen, Gerald Duckworth, Sir C. Albutt, Vanessa, Virginia and Adrian.

3 George Duckworth, Stella Duckworth and J. W. Hills

4 Roger Fry in Greece

5 The author and Virginia at Asham House, 1914

6 G. E. Moore at Asham House, 1914

7 Asham House, 1914

8 The author and G. E. Moore at Asham House, 1914

9 The author and Adrian Stephen at Asham House, 1914

10 The author and G. Lowes Dickinson at Asham House, 1914

11 Lytton Strachey and W. B. Yeats in the garden at Gower Street

12 T. S. Eliot

13 Sunday afternoon at Garsington, 1921: David Cecil, L. P. Hartley, Virginia, and Anthony Asquith

14 The road to Telscombe: spring, summer, autumn, winter

15 The author and Sally

16 Virginia and Dadie Rylands at Monks House

17 Virginia and Lytton Strachey at Garsington, 1921

18 T. S. Eliot at Monks House

19 Mitz, the marmoset, in Rome

20 Duncan Grant and Vanessa Bell at Cassis, 1930

21 The author, Sally and Virginia in Tavistock Square

22 The author and John Lehmann at Monks House

23 Monks House, Rodmell (back view)

24 Monks House, Rodmell

25 Rodmell village

26 The author and Nehru

27 Maynard Keynes and Kingsley Martin at Rodmell

28 Virginia (*photo: Man Ray*)

29 The author at Monks House

30 Group at Sissinghurst: Ben, Virginia, Vita and Nigel

31 Monks House, the author in the sitting room

32 The garden—view to Mt Caburn

33 Monks House in summer

34 Monks House in winter

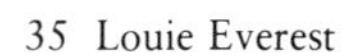

35 Louie Everest

36 Trekkie Parsons

37 Monks House: the garden in the evening

38 Monks House: the lean-to greenhouse

39 In Israel, 1957: Trekkie by the Sea of Galilee

40 The author by the Sea of Galilee

41 In Israel, 1957: Mr and Mrs Fernando, the author and Trekkie

42 In Ceylon, 1960: meeting the elephant

43 In Ceylon, 1960: Catamaran

44 In Ceylon: Anuradhapura

45 Receiving an Honorary Degree, Sussex University: Dr W. G. Stone, the author, Dame Marie Rambert

46 Malcolm Muggeridge interviewing the author, September 1966

47 Thanking for the £1000: John Betjeman, The Hon. David Smith, and the author after the presentation of the 1965 W. H. Smith Annual Literary Award

48 Mrs Sutherland and the author at the Psycho-analysts dinner, October 1966

49 The *New Statesman* Board of Directors: Kingsley Martin, the author, V. S. Pritchett, John Freeman, Gerald Barry, John Morgan (Secretary) and Jock Campbell (Chairman)

The pleasures of old age:
50 Cats—father and son 51 Gardening

The pleasures of old age: 52 Dogs 53 bowls
54 People: Peter Cochrane, Janet Cochrane, Ian Parsons, Alison Cochrane, Louise Cochrane and Trekkie

The pleasures of old age:
55 Writing

56 Typewriting

found that kind of pleasure very pleasurable. On the other hand, as I have said, both Virginia and I enjoyed society, if private, informal, intimate. As Virginia's health improved and civilisation began to penetrate to Rodmell in the form of a bus and other amenities, we became more and more social in that kind of way, and the number of our friends and acquaintances grew rapidly. We saw them at Richmond, but we also had them for weekends to Monks House. Our week-ends at Monks House were the antithesis of week-ends at Garsington. We had room for only one guest, and it was still pretty primitive and uncomfortable, so that one could only have those with whom one was already very intimate or with whom one could soon become very intimate. Among the former were Lytton Strachey and Morgan Forster, and among the latter T. S. Eliot.

In the years 1920 to 1923 Tom Eliot stayed with us several times in Rodmell and he used to come and dine with us at Richmond. It was in these years that our relations with him changed deeply, from extreme formality to the beginning of a real intimacy. But I do not think it was merely that we got to know him better. I think that Tom himself changed inside himself to some extent—to the extent perhaps that anyone ever can change inside himself after his first good cry on leaving his mother's womb and seeing the cruel light of day and the face of nurse and doctor. There was from the first a dichotomy in Tom, which, when he stayed with us on 19 September 1920, Virginia noted in his face; 'The odd thing about Eliot,' she wrote, 'is that his eyes are lively and youthful when the cast of his face and the shape of his sentences are formal and even heavy. Rather like a sculpted face—no upper lip; formidable, powerful; pale. Then those hazel eyes, seeming to escape from the rest of him.' He was so inhibited, those sentences were so formal and heavy that, although—or rather because—I had seen so much in his poetry and in those eyes which seemed to escape from him, the week-end left me with a feeling of disappointment. In conversation it was his brain that was disappointing, so much more rigid and less powerful than I had expected from the poems, and with so little play of mind. He was himself aware of this and disappointed in himself, for, in describing a week-end with Ottoline in Garsington, he said: 'And I behaved like a priggish pompous little ass'. I do not think that it was just conceit that made us think that we had something to do with changing Tom, with loosening up the pomposity and priggishness which constricted him, with thawing out the essential warmth of his nature which, when we first knew him, seemed to be enclosed in an envelope of frozen formality. How inhibited he was then can be seen from an absurd incident which happened at one of his very early visits to Monks House and in which I remember for the first time breaking the ice. He was walking with Virginia and me across the fields down to the river. I suddenly wanted to make water and fell behind to do so. Neither of my companions saw what I was doing, but I suppose it was very obvious what I was doing. Anyhow, when I caught them up again, I felt that Tom was uncomfortable, even shocked. I asked him whether he was and he said yes, and we then had what gradually became a perfectly frank conversation about conventions and formality. Tom said that he not only could not possibly have done what I did, that he would never dream of shaving in the presence even of his wife.

About literature, even about his own writing, even in those early days of knowing him, he was easy and unreticent—and always very interesting. During his visit, Virginia one evening tackled him about his poetry and told him that 'he wilfully concealed his transitions'. He admitted, this, but said that it was unnecessary to explain; explanation diluted facts. He intended to write a verse play in which the four characters of Sweeney would appear. What he wanted to do was to 'disturb externals'; he had had a kind of personal upheaval after writing *Prufrock*, and this altered his inclinations, which had been to 'develop in the manner of Henry James'.[1]

Tom had a great opinion of Virginia as a critic. Some ten years after this early visit to Rodmell, he came to us one day and said that he had just written some poetry which he would very much like us to criticise seriously. What he would like would be to send us each a typescript of the poems; we should read them and then come in after dinner one evening and each in turn criticise them—and he might ask one or two other people—Mary Hutchinson, for instance—to come as well. We agreed, and he sent us a typescript of what eventually was published as *Ash-Wednesday*. Then one summer evening we went round to his house after dinner and found Mary Hutchinson and McKnight Kauffer there. We all sat solemnly on chairs round the room and Tom began the proceedings by reading the poem aloud in that curious monotonous sing-song in which all poets from Homer downwards have recited their poetry. Then each in

[1] Some of the above is recorded in Virginia's diary.

turn was called upon to criticise. The order was, I think, Mary, I, Virginia, Kauffer. It was rather like an examination, not of the examinee, but of the examiners, and Mary, Kauffer, and I didn't do any too well—in fact Tom dismissed rather severely some of the things that some of us said. Virginia passed with flying colours. She told Tom that he had got into the habit of ending lines with a present participle; he had done it with great effect at the beginning of *The Waste Land*, and he was doing it again in this poem. She thought he should beware of it becoming a habit. Tom said that she was quite right and that what she said was very useful. I still have the original typescript copy which he gave to me and I have compared it with *Ash-Wednesday* as published. The two versions are not the same, but the present participles remain in the lines. The printed version is:

> Here are the years that walk between, bearing
> Away the fiddles and the flutes, restoring
> One who moves in the time between sleep and
> waking, wearing . . .

In the original typescript the three lines read:

> Here are the years that walk between, bearing
> Away the fiddles and the flutes, restoring
> One who walks between season and season, wearing . . .

In the book as published, there are six sections, in the typescript there are only five; presumably section VI was written after our critical seance. Tom did not alter very much in the first five sections; there are two main differences between the two versions. In the typescript each section has a title which is not in the printed book and the final version of section V is much longer than the original. The following are the titles of the sections:

I. PERCH'IO NON SPERO; II. JAUSEN LO JORN; III. SOM DE L'ESCALINA; IV. VESTITA DI COLOR DI FIAMMA; V. LA SUA VOLUNTADE.

The gradual growth of our intimacy with Tom can be traced in Virginia's diary. In February 1921 he dined with us at The Cock in Fleet Street and Virginia wrote: 'pale, marmoreal Eliot was there last week, like a chapped office boy on a high stool, with a cold in his head, until he warms a little, which he did. We walked back along the Strand. "The critics say I am learned and cold," he said. "The truth is I am neither." As he said this, I think coldness at least must be a sore point with him.' A month later she was wondering whether we would ever get to the stage of Christian names: 'But what about Eliot? Will he become Tom? What happens with friendships undertaken at the age of forty? Do they flourish and live long? I suppose a good mind endures, and one is drawn to it and sticks to it, owing to having a good mind myself. Not that Tom endures my writing, damn him.' By the end of the year we were calling him Tom and Virginia noted with regret that she was no longer frightened of him.

The first time Virginia met Vita Sackville-West (Mrs Harold Nicolson) was in December 1922, and the first entry in her diary describing Vita is rather critical. We saw something of Harold and her during the next year, but it was not until 1924 that we got to know them well. At that time they lived partly in London and partly in a very pleasant house, Long Barn, near Sevenoaks, and not far from her ancestral home, Knole. We stayed with them there, and Virginia began to see a great deal of Vita. There was a curious and very attractive contradiction in Vita's character. She was then literally—and so few people ever are literally—in the prime of life, an animal at the height of its powers, a beautiful flower in full bloom. She was very handsome, dashing, aristocratic, lordly, almost arrogant. In novels people often 'stride' in or out of rooms; until I saw Vita, I was inclined to think that they did this only in the unreal romantic drawing-rooms of the novelist—but Vita really did stride or seem to stride.

To be driven by Vita on a summer's afternoon at the height of the season through the London traffic—she was a very good, but rather flamboyant driver—and to hear her put an aggressive taxi driver in his place, even when she was in the wrong, made one recognise a note in her voice that Sackvilles and Buckhursts were using to serfs in Kent 600 years ago, or even in Normandy 300 years before that. She belonged indeed to a world which was completely different from ours, and the long line of Sackvilles, Dorsets, De la Warrs, and Knole with its 365 rooms had put into her mind and heart an ingredient which was alien to us and at first made intimacy difficult.

Vita was, as we used to say to her, only really comfortable in a castle, whereas a castle is almost the only place in which I could not under any circumstances be comfortable. When compared to the ramshackle informality of our life and rooms in Hogarth House and Monks House, Vita's Long Barn, with its butler, silver, Persian rugs, Italian cabinets, and all other modern conveniences, seemed to us a house and a way of life of opulence and grandeur. In their own way—which happens not to be my way[1]—both the house and the way of life had considerable charm and beauty. Later Vita's passion for castles led her to buy the great tower and ruined buildings of Sissinghurst. As the thousands of people who every year visit Sissinghurst know, she restored a good deal of the castle and created a garden of very great beauty.

In the creation of Sissinghurst and its garden she was, I think, one of the happiest people I have ever known, for she loved them and they gave her complete satisfaction in the long years between middle age and death in which for so many people when they look out of the windows there is only darkness and desire fails. But there was another facet in her character; she was, in many ways, a very simple person, and it was this side of her which emerged both in her poem, *The Land*, and in her passion for gardening, though combined with the opulent magnificence of the Sackvilles and Knole it produced something at Sissinghurst which could not exactly be called simple. It was this simplicity, when combined with other things in her character, which made one fond of her, the other things her own affectionate nature and her honesty and generosity. The scale of Sackville generosity in those days was to some extent, I think, influenced by the crazy munificence of Vita's mother (described in her book *Pepita*) who in her life had dissipated several million pounds without leaving herself nothing to show for it. Lady Sackville lived eccentrically at Rottingdean and Vita used from time to time to drive over to see her. On the way back she used to look in upon us at Monks House and we always went out to her car to see the presents which Lady Sackville had showered on her. The scale of her munificence can be seen in the fact that one day on the back seat of the car was a gigantic porcelain sink in which were piled about 150 green figs. I don't know why Lady Sackville had given Vita a porcelain sink, but the figs came about in this way. She took Vita for a drive to the famous fig garden in Worthing; she asked Vita whether

[1] Virginia, on the whole, liked rather more than I did the conventional opulence of the life and habitations of the wealthy English upper classes. But returning from a week-end at Long Barn, after describing the 'opulence', she added: 'Yet I like this room better perhaps; more effort and life in it, to my mind, unless this is the prejudice one has naturally in favour of the display of one's own character'.

she would like to take back some figs, and, when she said yes, insisted upon buying for her the entire crop of ripe figs.

I find some difficulty in determining exactly when what is called Bloomsbury came into existence. In *Beginning Again* (above, pp. 9-13) I treated it as having come into existence in the three years 1912 to 1914. I should now prefer to say that in those three years a kind of ur-Bloomsbury came into existence. Of the thirteen members of Old Bloomsbury, as we came to call it, only eight at that time actually lived in Bloomsbury: Clive and Vanessa in Gordon Square and Virginia, Adrian, Duncan Grant, Maynard Keynes, and myself in Brunswick Square, with Saxon Sydney Turner in Great Ormond Street. It was not until Lytton Strachey, Roger Fry, and Morgan Forster came in to the locality, so that we were all continually meeting one another, that our society became complete, and that did not happen until some years after the war. First the war scattered us completely and then Virginia's illness, by banishing us to the outer suburb of Richmond, made any return to our day-to-day intimacy impossible. But as Virginia's health improved and it became possible for us to go up to London more often to parties and other meetings, what archaeologists might call a second period of ur-Bloomsbury began. For instance, in March 1920 we started the Memoir Club and on 6 March we met in Gordon Square, dined together, and listened to or read our memoirs.

The original thirteen members of the Memoir Club, identical with the original thirteen members of old Bloomsbury, were all intimate friends, and it was agreed that we should be absolutely frank in what we wrote and read. Absolute frankness, even among the most intimate, tends to be relative frankness; I think that in our reminiscences what we said was absolutely true, but absolute truth was sometimes filtered through some discretion and reticence. At first the memoirs were fairly short; at the first meeting seven people read. But as time went on, what people read became longer and, in a sense, more serious, so that after a few years normally only two memoirs were read in an evening. They were usually very amusing, but they were sometimes something more. Two by Maynard were as brilliant and highly polished as anything he wrote—one describing his negotiations with the German delegates and in particular, Dr Melchior, in the railway carriage at Trèves after the 1914 war, and the other about Moore's influence upon us and our early beliefs at Cambridge—and these were after his death published, exactly as they were originally read to us, under the title *Two Memoirs*. Some of Virginia's were also brilliant, and Vanessa developed a remarkable talent in a fantastic narrative of a labyrinthine domestic crisis. The years went by and the Club changed as the old inhabitants died and the younger generation were elected. The last meeting took place, I think, in 1956, thirty-six years after the first meeting. Only four of the original thirteen members were left, though in all ten members came to the meeting.

These meetings meant for us going up to Bloomsbury from Richmond, with late nights, staying in London or midnight train journeys back to Richmond. And we were sucked into other parties both in and outside Bloomsbury. In order to give a more concrete idea of one of these parties in ur-Bloomsbury and of Virginia's social excitement which I have referred to when she found herself at one, I will quote from Virginia's diary the description of a fancy-dress party to which we went in Gordon Square in the first week of January 1923:

> Let the scene open on the doorstep of number 50 Gordon Square. We went up last night, carrying our bags and a Cingalese sword. There was Mary H. in lemon coloured trousers with green ribbons, and so we sat down to dinner; off cold chicken. In came Roger and Adrian and Karin; and very slowly we coloured our faces and made ready for number 46. It was the proudest moment of Clive's life when he led Mary on one arm and Virginia on the other into the drawingroom, which was full, miscellaneous, and oriental for the most part. Suppose one's normal pulse to be 70: in five minutes it was 120: and the blood, not the sticky whitish fluid of daytime but brilliant and prickly like champagne. This was my state and most people's. We collided, when we met; went pop, used Christian names, flattered, praised, and thought (or I did) of Shakespeare. At any rate I thought of him when the singing was doing. Shakespeare I thought would have liked us all tonight . . . My luck was in though and I found good quarters with Frankie [Francis Birrell] and Sheppard and Bunny [David Garnett] and Lydia [Lopokova]—all my friends in short. But what we talked about I hardly know. Bunny asked me to be his child's godmother. And a Belgian wants to translate me. Arnold Bennett thinks me wonderful and . . . and . . . (these, no doubt, were elements in my hilarity). Jumbo [Marjorie Strachey] distorted nursery rhymes: Lydia danced: there were charades: Sickert acted Hamlet. We were all easy and gifted and friendly and like good children rewarded by having the capacity for enjoying themselves thus. Could our fathers? I wearing my mother's laces, looked at X's Jerboa face in the old looking glass—and wondered, I daresay no one said anything very brilliant. I sat by Sickert and liked him, talking, in his very workmanlike but not at all society manner, of printing and Whistler; of an operation he saw at Dieppe. But can life be worth so

much pain, he asked. 'Pour respirer,' said the doctor. 'That is everything.' 'But for two years "after my wife's death" I did not wish to live,' said Sickert. There is something indescribably congenial to me in this easy artists' talk; the values the same as my own and therefore right: no impediments: life charming, good and interesting: no effort: art brooding calmly over it all: and none of this attachment to mundane things, which I find in Chelsea. For Sickert said, why should one be attached to one's body and breakfast? Why not be satisfied to let others have the use of one's life and live it over again, being dead oneself? No mysticism, and therefore a great relish for the actual things—whatever they may be—old plays, girls, boys, Proust, Handel sung by Oliver [Strachey], the turn of a head and so on. As parties do, this one began to dwindle, until a few persistent talkers were left by themselves sitting in such odd positions . . . And so, at 3, I suppose, back to No. 50 to which Clive had gone previously.

It was parties like this and our increasing sociability in London which made the question of whether we should stay on in Richmond or immigrate to Bloomsbury more and more urgent. Already in 1922 Virginia was eager for the move. She had begun to feel imprisoned, secluded, and excluded, in Richmond. If she lived in London, she said, 'I might go and hear a tune, or have a look at a picture, or find out something at the British Museum, or go adventuring among human beings. Sometimes I should merely walk down Cheapside. But now I'm tired, imprisoned, inhibited.' This was, of course, true, but I had been against a move, solely because I feared the result on Virginia's health. It had become much more stable, but it could never be neglected or ignored, and nothing was more dangerous for it than the mental fatigue produced by society and its social pleasures. She was one of those people who drained herself, exhausted herself mentally, both passively and actively, not only at a party but in any kind of conversation or social intercourse. In Richmond it was possible to keep some control over our social life and, at a danger signal, to shut outselves off from it for a time. I feared that this would prove impossible in London.

However, in the middle of 1923 I became converted to the idea, for the disadvantages of staying on in Richmond seemed to outweigh the dangers of moving to Bloomsbury. I had to count the cost both of Virginia's growing feeling of being cabined and confined and, as our engagements in London increased, the increasing strain and fatigue of catching crowded trains or buses in order to keep them. So I gave way and in November we began to search Bloomsbury for a house. The usual alteration of joy and disappointment and despair in house hunting lasted for two months, but on 9 January 1924, we acquired from the Bedford Estate a ten-year lease of 52 Tavistock Square. On 13 March following, we moved into it.

2
Downhill To Hitler

Fifty-two Tavistock Square, eventually destroyed in 1940 by one of Hitler's earliest bombs, was a very pleasant house, built, I suppose, by a Duke of Bedford, as speculative builder, early in the nineteenth century. It had four storeys and a basement. We put the Hogarth Press into the basement and ourselves occupied the flat on the second and third floors; the ground and first floors were already let to a firm of solicitors, Dollman and Pritchard. The firm actually consisted of old Mr Pritchard and his son, young Mr George, and a strange staff. First there was old Mr Pritchard's sister, who had, I believe, been matron in a large London hospital but now acted with immense efficiency as a kind of head clerk. Then sitting by himself in a room on the first floor was a most sophisticated Irishman, who had lived a good deal of his life in Paris and spoke perfect French. Finally there were two or three girl clerks. One would have to live many lives and travel a long way to find again as good tenants as the firm of Dollman & Pritchard; we got so friendly with the partners and all the staff that when we moved in 1939 from Tavistock to Mecklenburgh Square, we took the firm with us. Old Mr Pritchard, in looks, in speech, and in character, came straight out of Dickens, belonging to the year 1850 rather than 1924 and to the long line of angelic old men in the great Victorian's novels. The Pritchards were so absurdly generous that, when I employed them as solicitors, I found the greatest difficulty in persuading them to charge me anything.

I have lived practically all my life in London, but I am again and again surprised by its curious, contradictory character, its huge, anonymous, metropolitan size and its pockets of provincial, almost village life—also the congenital conservatism of Londoners, so that if you scratch the surface of their lives in 1924 you find yourself straight back in 1850 or even 1750 and 1650. In the fifteen years I lived in Tavistock Square I got to know a gallery of London characters who themselves lived in a kind of timeless London and in a society as different from that of Fleet Street, Westminster, Kensington, or Putney—all of which I have known—as Sir Thomas Bertram's in Mansfield Park must have been from Agamemnon's behind the Lion Gate in Mycenae. There was still in it a strong element of Dickensian London. There was a perfect Dickens character not only at the top, but also at the bottom of Dollman & Pritchard, solicitors. When at five or six o'clock the business closed its doors and their rooms were empty, the front door was pushed open and in sidled Mrs Giles. She wore, as Kot would have said, a haggish look; indeed, she always reminded me of one of those wizened, skinny, downtrodden, grimy women of the Dickensian underworld. She was the Platonic image of the London char laid up, not in heaven. but in an attic in Marchmont Street, London, W.C.1. She spoke the language of the Dickensian cockney. And when she was in a room by herself, she talked as, I am quite sure, Dickens's gaunt old women spoke when they were outside his novels—a language which would have been quite impossible in a Victorian novel. It was terrifying. When just before dinner I used to take my dog out into the Square garden for a run, as I passed through the hall, I used to hear Mrs Giles talking to herself as she cleaned Mr Pritchard's front room. It was a monotonous stream of the foulest language which I have ever heard. Some of it was just pure, disinterested swearing for the sake of swearing, but every now and again it turned into a particularised hymn of hate, the most horrible, obscene accusations against the various members of the firm. I cannot attempt to explain this strange phenomenon. There was little or no bitterness in Mrs Giles's voice—it was not so much vituperation as a monotonous threnody, a lament for the horrors of Mrs Giles's life—and all the Mrs Giles's lives—in Marchmont Street.

I used to take my dog for a run in the Square three or four times a day and I therefore walked in it far more often than any other resident, and I soon got to know the Square keeper very well. After a year or two I was elected to the Square Committee. We were a statutory body, and here again I found myself back in the London of Dickens. The use and government of Tavistock Square were regulated by by-laws which dated, I think, from about 1840. The Square Committee, which administered the by-laws, consisted of three persons annually elected by householders resident in the Square and each householder was entitled to a key admitting him into the garden. One by-law laid it down that no manservant or maidservant should be allowed in the Square and another prescribed what games children should be permitted to play there. The Square keeper was another type of nineteenth-century cockney. The square was for him the centre of a large village, bounded on the north by the Euston Road, on the east by the Grays Inn Road, on the south by Russell Square, and on the west by Tottenham Court Road. Within those boundaries few things happened, at any rate of a discreditable nature, which he did not learn, and, when I got to know him well, which he did not recount to me at great length. He knew by sight almost all those whom he counted to be true inhabitants of this Bloomsbury village and he had an extraordinary knowledge of the private lives of very many of them. Many of his stories were libellous and most of them were, I think, true. He was a sardonic, poker-faced, disillusioned man who noted and described, without heat or any sign of moral indignation, the frailties and rascalities of human nature in the rich, the poor, and the police between Tottenham Court Road and Grays Inn Road.

The police were not popular either with my friend or with the poor in Bloomsbury. Their chief victims, according to the Square keeper, were prostitutes, barrow-boys, and eating-house keepers. There was a regular tariff which the first two paid in order to pursue their business in peace. It was almost impossible for restaurant keepers not to break the law occasionally, and many of them insured against the consequences by providing free meals for any policeman from whom trouble might be expected.

I had one absurd brush with a policeman which at the time seemed to me to confirm my friend's view of the force. One Sunday night about eleven Virginia and I were walking down Francis Street towards Tavistock Square, returning from an evening with Vanessa in Fitzroy Street. Towards us came a large woman about thirty to thirty-five years old, rather drunk and staggery. Some way behind her also walking towards us came a policeman. Two men on the opposite side of the road began to jeer at her. She stopped and let loose a volley of abuse about 'bullocks' balls' across the road at them. They replied, but, catching sight of the approaching policeman, bolted down a side street, dropping in their haste a bottle of beer with a crash on the pavement. The policeman came up to the woman and began to hector her. She was in no yielding mood, and it seemed to me that he was deliberately trying to goad her into doing something which would justify an arrest for being drunk and disorderly. I suddenly lost my temper and dashed in between them, telling her to stop talking and to leave things to me. I told the policeman that he must have seen that it was the two men who had started the whole thing—why had he done nothing to them and begun to hector the woman? An argument began and I suddenly realised that we were already surrounded by a small crowd which murmured its support of me and the woman against the policeman. I gave my name and address to the policeman and told him that, if he prosecuted the woman, he would have to call me as a witness. The woman, finding that she was supported, then turned on the policeman and began to abuse him. The delighted crowd increased and things began to look rather unpleasant, so I turned to a rather sensible looking man who had been standing by my side and asked him to take the woman away before she got into more trouble. He and I induced her to go and I then had once more to face the policeman. Finding that everyone was against him, he was suddenly deflated and apologetic, assuring me that he never meant to charge the woman. We parted almost amicably and, as the crowd broke up, I saw Lydia standing on the outskirts under a gas lamp, gazing with amazement at me and the policeman.

Fifty-two Tavistock Square was, as I have said, divided into three parts: the top inhabited by Virginia and me, the middle by Dollman & Pritchard, and the basement by the Hogarth Press. There were four rooms in the basement. The Press used the large room, which had once been the kitchen, as its office, occupied, when we moved in, by our only employee, Marjorie Joad. We printed in what had been the ancient scullery. Then there was a small room at the back, and behind that the old billiard room, which I have described on page 223.

Virginia was such a bad sleeper and so disturbed by noise that, although she habitually used earstoppers, when we first came to Tavistock Square, she thought that, if she slept upstairs in the flat, the noise of the traffic would keep her awake. The first night, therefore, we had her bed put in the small room at the back of the basement and she started to sleep there. But in the middle of the night she was awakened by several rats scampering round her bed on the floor, and she had to retreat up to the flat for good.

The rats were the harbingers of much trouble and of a legal case which I had to bring in the High Court of Justice. The rats came from a large open space, full of old bricks and rubble, which fronted Woburn Place and stretched from the back of Tavistock Square to Russell Square. The Imperial Hotel Company had acquired this site and were clearing it in preparation for building what was eventually the Royal Hotel. The result was a vast number of displaced refugee rats who could be seen in the middle of the day searching the dustbins in the area and who invaded the basement of nights. With the help of a London County Council inspector who looked after vermin, we got rid of the rats, but the building of the hotel caused us a great deal of trouble. While the building operations were actually going on, the noise during the day was pretty bad, and we had double windows put into our main sitting-room, which looked straight into the area of devastation and the scaffolding, in order to keep out the creaking of the cranes, the clanking of lorries, the cries and curses of the builders.

But our troubles really began only after the vast hotel was finished. At the back was a long ballroom the windows of which were immediately below the windows of our sitting-room. When in the evening these windows were open and a jazz band was playing full blast from eight to twelve, the Bedlam of noise, funnelled into our room even with the double windows closed, made life impossible. I wrote to the Imperial Hotel Company complaining, and got back a sympathetic letter from the secretary, promising steps to mitigate the noise. The only possible mitigation was by closing the hotel windows and I think they gave orders that this should be done, but even if their dance began with closed windows, someone always opened them half-way through the evening, letting Bedlam loose into our sitting-room. I went round to see the secretary, who was very friendly, especially when he found that I had known his famous brother, E. C. Bentley, the author of *Trent's Last Case*. (E. C. Bentley and G. K. Chesterton had been members of a debating society to which I belonged, when a boy at St Paul's, as I related in *Sowing*, Volume 1, p. 57.) But in the end I had to take legal action, which turned out to be an interesting experience.

I employed Mr Pritchard as my solicitor. We eventually won our case, and it is, I think, the only serious case which, in my experience, has been taken to court, has been won, and has cost the plaintiff not one single halfpenny—we recovered all our costs. But the proceedings made me realise, as I had not before, the precariousness and helplessness of the individual in modern life. It was essential to prove that the noise was legally 'a nuisance', a nuisance which anyone or everyone would find intolerable, not just a noise which some hypersensitive person would object to. So I went round and canvassed all the residents whose rooms in Tavistock Square and

Upper Bedford Place looked on to the back of the hotel, to get them to come and give evidence that the noise was a nuisance to them. Every man and woman whose windows were near the hotel windows said that the noise made life intolerable to them in the evenings when there was a dance band playing, and that they would give evidence, but in the end, when it came to the point, not one single person would do so—they all cried off. The reason was that they all had short leases and were frightened of their landlord. The rumour was that their landlord, the Bedford Estate, was in some way interested in the hotel operations and was going to sell more property to the hotel company, and that, if any one took action against the company, he would probably find that he could not get a renewal of his lease.

Whether there was any ground for the rumour or for their fears, I do not know. The important point was that these people believed the rumour and, because of their fear, were prepared without resistance to allow 'them'—an impersonal company and an impersonal landlord—to make their lives a burden to them. The tyranny of these impersonal or personal 'thems' has of course always been a terrifying menace hanging over the lives of ordinary people. 'They' used to be kings, aristocrats, classes, and churches, and it was thought at one time that liberty, equality, and fraternity would abolish them, but 'they' have continued to exist and flourish under other names. In 1965 in a Sussex village a man, with a wife and three children, who has worked all his life until the age of forty on a farm in the village in which he was born, becomes ill and unable to do heavy farm work. He receives legal notice to leave the house, which is required for the man who is to take his place on the farm. There is no other house available for him, but the Rural District Council will find him lodgings, separating him from his wife and family, who will be 'accommodated temporarily in an institution'. In the country, of course, the working classes have always lived in tied cottages and, completely in the power of 'them', in the shadow of fate and eviction. But here in Tavistock Square in the 1920s were middle-class people living under the same kind of menace.

Despite the fact that it became clear that no one would give evidence on my side, I decided to go it alone, for I knew that I had a very strong, if not impregnable, case. For I had up my sleeve a sentence in one of the company's letters to me which in fact admitted that the noise was legally a nuisance. I was convinced that, when they were confronted in court with that letter, they would be unable to plead that the noise was not a nuisance, and that the only question would be what steps we could force them to take in order to 'abate' the nuisance. We were encouraged by the fact that, when the case was put down for hearing, they more than once applied for an adjournment. Eventually they came to us and asked us to agree to a settlement out of court. After some haggling it was settled that judgment should be entered against them, the terms being that the offending windows would always be screwed up if a band was playing and that all our costs would be paid by the Company. Mr Pritchard managed to get from them every penny of our costs. On the whole the nuisance was satisfactorily abated, though every now and again someone would forget to screw up the windows and our room and ears would be filled with din of jazz music. An irate telephone message from me to the hotel would then be required in order to get the nuisance once more abated.

Throughout my life I have always said to myself—and often to other people—that one should change one's occupation every seven years. The first person to discover this important truth appears to have been an ancestor of mine some thousands of years ago, for it is recorded in the twenty-ninth chapter of the book of Genesis that Jacob agreed to serve Laban for seven years for his daughter Rachel, and when Laban swindled him with Leah instead of Rachel, he agreed to work another seven years for Rachel. The number seven has, of course, for ages had some mystical attraction for human beings, connected perhaps with the seven days of the week and the seven stars of the Pleiades. It is possible that the mystical nature of the number had something to do with Jacob's offer to serve seven years for a wife and twice seven years for two, though his fiddling with the ringstraked and speckled goats, so practical and ingenious, showed that he was a pretty tough and hardheaded man. I do not think that I am much influenced by the mysticism of numbers or anything else. My feeling about what should be the length of time of an occupation is based on observation of myself and other people: no matter how interesting and complicated a profession or business or occupation may be, after about five years ninety per cent of it tends to become stereotyped and automatic, and after another two years ninety-nine per cent is performed with skill and efficiency, but as routine and habit and with about as much thought and originality as the spider has in the last 700,000 years given to its occupation of spinning, with great skill and efficiency, its web. And when that happens, it is time, I (unlike the spider) think, to make a change.

Throughout my life, to quite a considerable extent, I have taken my own advice and septennially changed my occupation. I began with the Ceylon Civil Service in 1904 and resigned from it in 1911 after seven years. For 1915 to 1923—about eight years—I earned a living mainly by journalism, writing for the *New Statesman*, editing the *International Review*, on the staff of the *Nation*. When the *Nation* changed hands in 1923 I was offered and accepted the post of literary editor. At the end of 1930, after rather over seven and a half years, I resigned. As I explained in *Beginning Again* (above, p. 94) my work as literary editor revealed to me the corroding and eroding effect of journalism upon the human mind, and I have never after 1930 taken a paid job—I have earned my living from the Hogarth Press, from my books, and from occasionally writing articles or reviews.

But for the first seven years in Tavistock Square the diurnal pattern of our lives was in the main drawn for us by my job on the *Nation*. Our offices were in Great James Street, a pleasant building dating from 1720. Every week I spent two or two and a half days in the office, but I also did a considerable amount of work at home, for I wrote a weekly article of about 1,200 words, called 'The World of Books'. For this article I had to read, on an average, two or three books, and I also had to read a rain of articles and poems with which journals like the *Nation* are perpetually deluged. No one who has not been an editor and/or a publisher can have any idea of how badly how many people can write—and what is even more astonishing than the number and badness of the writers and writings is the belief or even hope that such lamentable stuff could be accepted and printed. It was just the same in the Hogarth Press as it was on the *Nation*: manuscripts poured in upon us and quite a number of them were fatuous and sometimes ludicrously fatuous. Indeed, when they were sufficiently fatuous, they sometimes acquired a quality of such sublime craziness or profound stupidity that we seriously considered starting a 'Hogarth Worst Books of the Year Series' in which we could publish some of them. The number of people who today 'seriously' write books, articles, and poems must be colossal, and I doubt whether one in a hundred thousand of the manuscripts which they produce is ever published. Certainly it was extraordinarily rare to get an unsolicited manuscript which one could accept for the *Nation* or the Hogarth Press. One is inclined to believe that this universal itch of writing is a disease of universal education and the twentieth century—until one remembers that nearly two thousand years ago Juvenal noted it in its Roman form, *cacoethes scribendi*.

As literary editor I was responsible for getting the 'middles', which was the name given to the two or three articles of a literary or general non-political nature, the reviews of books, and regular articles on plays, pictures, music, and science. I doubt whether any weekly paper has ever had such a constellation of stars shining in it as I got for the *Nation*. Here are some of the writers who wrote articles or reviews for me in the first few months of my editorship: Bertrand Russell, G. Lowes Dickinson, Gorky, Augustine Birrell, Roger Fry, E. J. Dent, Walter Sickert, T. S. Eliot, Virginia Woolf, E. M. Forster, Lytton Strachey, Osbert Sitwell, Richard Hughes, Stella Benson, Robert Graves, V. Sackville-West, Arnold Toynbee. Many of these were in 1923 and 1924 unknown young men and women. In the last year of my editorship most of them were still writing for me and they had been joined by other writers, e.g. Aldous Huxley, L. B. Namier, and Raymond Mortimer.

The literary side of the *Nation* benefited by my running the Hogarth Press, and the Hogarth Press benefited by my being literary editor of the *Nation*. In the Press we were interested in young, unknown writers whose work might not attract the publishing establishment. A journal like the *Nation* puts into one's hand a very wide net and all sorts of literary fishes, large and small, swim into it. All sorts of literary fish, some the same as and some different from the *Nation*'s shoals, swam in and out of the Hogarth Press in Tavistock Square. It was possible to help the budding (and sometimes impecunious) Hogarth author by giving him books to review and articles to write; and, if one came across something by a completely unknown writer which seemed to have something in it, one could try him out with articles and reviews before encouraging him to write a book. Thus Tom Eliot, Virginia, E. M. Forster, Robert Graves, Vita Sackville-West, William Plomer came to the *Nation* via the Press, and Edwin Muir was an example of the reverse process in this shuttle service. Somewhere or other I saw a poem of Muir's which I thought very good, so I wrote and asked him to let me see some more. He sent me a few and I published one of them. I got him to come and see me and this began a friendship which lasted to his death. I offered to give him regular reviewing, and from the middle of 1924 for a long time almost every week he had a review in the *Nation*. In 1925 the Hogarth Press published his *First Poems*, in 1926 *Chorus of the Newly Dead*, in 1926 his first book of criticism *Transition*, and in 1927 his novel *The Marionette*. Nearly forty years later we published his autobiography (originally published by Harrap, but considerably enlarged for us) and his last book, *The Estate of Poetry*, was published by us posthumously in 1962.

I look back on this forty years' connection with Edwin Muir with great pleasure and some sadness. We printed his poems in 1925 with our own hands and he was the kind of author and they were the kind of poems for whom and which we wanted the Press to exist. *Chorus of the Newly Dead* was not a book which in 1926 and ordinary publisher would have looked at. We made it a sixteen-page book, bound in a stiff paper cover, for which we charged 2s. 6d. As we printed and bound the edition of 315 copies ourselves, the actual cost was negligible, i.e. £6 4s. 7½d. In the first year we sold 215 copies, and after paying the author £3 18s. 11d., the Hogarth Press had made a profit of £7 17s. 0d. Muir was a real, a natural poet; he did not just 'write poetry', the sap of poetry was in his bones and veins, in his heart and brain; that is why, as with practically all real poets, the form and substance of his poetry changed and developed all through his life as he and his mind changed, hammered upon by the grim reality of living. The form and substance of *First Poems* and *Chorus of the Newly Dead* are tremendously different from those of his later poems—so different that, as he tells us in his autobiography, when he reread *Chorus of the Newly Dead* thirty years after he had written the book, the Edwin Muir of 1926 seemed quite strange to the Edwin Muir of 1954. When he reread, he says, the three lines

> that ghostly eternity
> Cut by the bridge where journeys Christ
> On endless arcs pacing the sea.

they seemed 'so strange to me that I almost feel it was someone else who wrote them; yet that someone was myself'. He was an admirable critic. He was so sensitive, intelligent, and honest minded that, as a serious critic, he always had something of his own worth saying even about masterpieces buried long ago under mountains and monuments of criticism. But even in the ephemeral and debased form of criticism, reviewing, he was remarkable. For a long time he used to review novels for me in the *Nation*, a mechanised, mind-destroying occupation for most people. For him it never became mechanical and his mind's eye was as clear and lively after a year of it as when he began.

Edwin's wife, Willa, was also what Koteliansky called a real person and an original writer whose books the Hogarth Press published. They both came from Orkney. An aura of gentleness, soft sea, air, the melancholy of remote islands set in turbulent seas surrounded them. All this is too in Edwin's autobiography which we published in 1954. He was the most uncomplaining and unselfpitying of men. I said that I looked back upon my friendship with him with some sadness—the sadness comes from a feeling that life dealt rather hardly with him.

The main interest of my work on the *Nation* came from the people with whom my work brought me into contact. Many of them became my friends. But they were often merely strange adventures, the absurd comedies or tragi-comedies of real life which always astonish and fascinate me. I will give some examples. One afternoon there walked into my room at the *Nation*, Roy Campbell, whose poetry at that time was creating something of a stir. I knew him only slightly. He was dressed in or swathed in one of those great black cloaks which conspirators wear in operas and melodramas and he had a large black sombrero. He sat down, scowled at me, and then said in the peculiar voice which the villain always used in old-fashioned melodramas: 'I want to ask you whether you think I ought to challenge Robert Graves to a duel'. Experience as editor or publisher soon teaches one that authors, like Habbakuk, are capable of anything, but I was so astonished by what I heard that I could only gasp: 'But why?' 'Why?' he said, 'Why? Don't you remember the review he wrote of my book, the review you yourself published two weeks ago?' It was true that Robert had reviewed Campbell's book, but it had never struck me that there was anything in it to drive the most hypersensitive writer into lunacy. For the next quarter of an hour I had a lunatic conversation persuading Campbell that the laws of honour and chivalry obtaining in Great James Street in 1926 did not require him to fight Robert Graves.

Not long after this business I had trouble with another reviewer, Richard Aldington. I do not remember how I came across this disgruntled man, who was almost as prickly as Roy Campbell. He became a regular reviewer for me, the kind of reviewer who is a godsend to literary editors. He could and would write me a good review of almost any book which I sent him—never a very good and never a bad, always a good review. One day he came to me with a face almost as gloomy and threatening as Campbell's. He said that in the last issue of the *Nation* I had had a review by a Mr X—did I know that Mr X had run off with his (Aldington's) wife? I said that I did not know this and mumbled that I was sorry to hear it. 'And are you going to employ Mr X as a reviewer?' said Aldington louringly. I said that Mr X had written quite a fairly good review and that I would certainly send him more books from time to time if he continued to do well. I was immediately presented with a formal ultimatum. Unless I gave an undertaking never to employ Mr X again, Aldington would never again write a review for me—he could not write in the same paper as the man who had run off with his wife. I said that I did not think this reasonable; as a matter of editorial principle, I did not think it right to give an undertaking to A not to send books to X to review merely because in a private capacity X had run off with A's wife. A angrily left me and I do not think that I ever saw him again.

The strangest of all the incidents which came out of the *Nation* was the case of Mr Y. It began one morning when I was working at home and I received a telephone message from the office saying that a Mr X had called and wanted urgently to see me—he could disclose his business only to me. I told them to tell him that, if he came round to Tavistock Square at once, I would see him for a few moments. Twenty minutes later there appeared a small gentle-voiced man in sandals. He told me the following. He was a New Zealander and when a youth had become a great friend of another youth, Mr Y. Mr Y had been a good deal more affluent and of a higher class in their native land than Mr X—his father was an architect. As young men, the two of them acquired a passion for the works of Samuel Butler, who from 1859 to 1864 had owned and run a sheep farm in the province of Canterbury, New Zealand. They conceived the idea of starting a Samuel Butler museum and they wrote to Festing Jones, Butler's friend and the high priest of his memory, asking whether he would send them some relics of Butler. He sent them a few things which became the nucleus of their museum.

Some time before his call on me Mr X came to England and became a shop assistant in John Barker in High Street, Kensington. After a bit Mr Y followed him and they set up house together in Kensington. They wrote to Festing Jones and he asked the two young men to dinner. Mr Y decided that he must have a dress suit for the occasion and Mr X got into some trouble by borrowing one from John Barker. After this their financial position was precarious and Mr X earned a living by going abroad from time to time to Belgium and Holland, where, walking from small town to small town, he gave readings or recitations of English prose and poetry. Then another catastrophe befell them. Mr Y wrote some extremely indecent poems which he wanted to get printed in order to send them, as Christmas cards, to his friends. So he went to the policeman who stands at the gates of the House of Commons and asked him whether he could recommend him a printer. The policeman gave him an address of a printer in Whitechapel. Mr Y handed the printer the manuscript and asked him whether he would give him an estimate for printing a small number of copies. This printer, I discovered later, had been fined for printing the indecent poems of D. H. Lawrence, and, presumably on the principle of once bitten twice shy, he handed the poems over to the police. The police prosecuted Mr Y for publishing obscene poems and he was convicted and given three months.

Mr X wanted to appeal against the conviction and sentence, but had no money; he had been told by someone that I might be sympathetic and help him to raise the money for solicitor's and counsel's fees. I went into the whole thing carefully and came to the conclusion that it was a monstrous business. I do not think that Mr Y had ever intended to publish these poems in the usual sense of publication; to send them to his friends for Christmas was to be more or less of a joke; but the magistrate held that his handing the manuscript to the printer was technically and legally 'publication'. But to give a first offender three months' imprisonment for this seemed to me gross injustice. I knew Mr Y by sight, for he was a well-known figure in the streets of London, and as soon as I realised from Mr X's description who he was, I saw how prejudice would corrupt the incorruptible British magistrate or judge before whom he might appear. For Mr Y dressed himself in a long robe with skirts to the ground and he wore his hair so long that it hung beneath his shoulders.

I had a talk with Jack Hutchinson, the K.C., about it; he too thought the sentence to be monstrous and was willing to appear in the Appeal Court for a very moderate fee. So I went to a solicitor who lodged an appeal and I began the dreary business of sending round the hat to possible sympathisers. I got donations from seven publishers and more than twenty writers. In the end the solicitor's bill was £91 7s. 0d. and Mr X spent £12 4s. 0d. so that I had to raise rather more than £100—it cost me personally over £50. The result was extremely unsatisfactory.

The appeal was heard by Lord Chief Justice Hewart and two other judges. In *Sowing* I wrote the following sentences, to which some people have taken exception, but which I still stand by:

> I have always felt that the occupational disease of judges is cruelty, sadistic self-righteousness, and the higher the judge the more criminal he tends to become. It is one more example of the absolute corruption of absolute power. One rarely sees in the faces of less exalted persons the sullen savagery of so many High Court judges' faces. Their judgments, *obiter dicta*, and sentences too often show that the cruel arrogance of the face only reflects the pitiless malevolence of the soul.

I dare say that in private life Gordon Hewart, 1st Baron Hewart, Lord Chief Justice of England, was a nice man, a good husband and father, a good club man,[1] a pleasant man to play a round of golf with. I watched him 'doing justice' in the Appeal Court for the better part of a day and he seemed to me—and still seems to me—a typical example of a High Court judge suffering from the occupational disease of sadistic, vindictive self-righteousness. His treatment of the unfortunate Mr Y was disgraceful. One side of his judicial behaviour interested me greatly. In Ceylon for three years I had to do a considerable amount of work as judge and police magistrate and I noticed in myself a curious psychological phenomenon against which one had to be on one's guard if one wanted to be absolutely unprejudiced and just. If one had tried three or four cases one after the other in which one had found the accused guilty, one tended to be over-lenient to the next case, particularly if one had had a moment of slight hesitation in finding the last man guilty. And vice versa, if one had found four accused in four cases not guilty one after the other, one had to be very much on one's guard against being unconsciously over-severe to or prejudiced against the accused in the next case.

I was interested to detect the same mental process in the Lord

[1] It is worth recording that in *Who's Who* the late Lord Hewart used to list his clubs as follows: Athenaeum, Beefsteak, Garrick, Reform, Savage, United Service; Hadley, Littlestone, Moor Park, South Herts, and Woking Golf.

Chief Justice, who, however, took no steps to counteract his bias. In the case which he tried before Mr Y's the accused had been convicted of housebreaking. You only had to look at him to see that he was an old lag. The evidence against him was overwhelming; he had many previous convictions. He appealed upon a tenuous technical point and his counsel made a very clever speech. Hewart set aside the conviction, smacking his judicial lips over the absolute justice of British justice—'the appellant has been extremely lucky in having a counsel to put a difficult case so ably. We are giving the accused, whose record is a bad one, another chance and we hope that he will take it in order to amend his ways . . .' When I heard this, I felt in my bones that British justice having been so magnanimous to the old burglar would probably take it out on Mr Y. It did. Jack Hutchinson made a good speech and showed to any unbiased person that the sentence was monstrously excessive in relation to the offence. But Hewart made it pretty obvious that he was against Jack and did not like Mr Y. As soon as the case was closed he turned to the judge on his right and to the judge on his left and muttered something to each in turn. The judge on his right was the equivalent on the bench to the old lag, the burglar, whom we had seen in the dock. He had sat on the bench for so long that he administered justice like a machine and therefore mechanically agreed with the Lord Chief Justice. The other on the left was sitting for the first time in the Court of Appeal; I cannot remember his name, but he was a comparatively young man and I knew him to have a reputation for being civilised. He was obviously arguing with Hewart. The three went into a huddle and after a bit the young judge got up and walked round to stand between Hewart and the old judge so that he could put his view more audibly to the old man, as it seemed to me. It was fascinating to watch the, to me, of course, inaudible judicial argument. Hewart was obviously determined and impatient, and at last the young judge with what seemed to me a shrug walked back to his seat. Hewart rejected the appeal with the same self-righteous self-satisfaction with which he had allowed the appeal of the burglar.

Not all the work on the *Nation* was as interesting as this. In fact, after about five years of it, I began to grow rather restive. To be on the editorial side of a journal like the *Nation* is a curious occupation. There is first one's relations with one's immediate equals and superiors. The editorial staff in Great James Street consisted of Hubert Henderson, the editor, Harold Wright, assistant editor, and myself, literary editor. As I have already explained I had made it a condition that within the literary half of the paper I should enjoy practical autonomy. But of course autonomy in that kind of occupation must be relative and limited. I knew Hubert Henderson and liked him. I suppose that in politics in the broadest sense our outlook had a good deal in common. The world is still deeply divided between those who in the depths of their brain, heart, and intestines agree with Pericles and the French revolution and those who consciously or unconsciously accept the political postulates of Xerxes, Sparta, Louis XIV, Charles I, Queen Victoria, and all modern authoritarians. Hubert and I were both on the side of Pericles, but in our interpretation of what liberty, equality, and fraternity meant, or ought to mean, we differed pretty deeply and pretty often. That he voted for the Liberal and I for the Labour Party was in the 1920s not without significance. I thought, and still think, that Liberals after 1914 ought to have realised that Liberalism, like patriotism, is not enough, and that the great problem was to develop an economic liberalism and liberal socialism.

Hubert's articles in the first part of the paper naturally, therefore, often seemed to me extremely able, but conscientiously to hit the bull's-eye on the wrong target. He, on the other hand, regarded a good deal of what I was doing in the other half of the paper with some misprision. Like many liberal intellectuals, he mistakenly prided himself on being culturally an 'ordinary person', a good philistine, with no use for highbrows. This was an amiable delusion, but the result of it was that he had to convince himself that what he called Bloomsbury was impossibly highbrow and that there was far too much Bloomsbury in the literary section of his paper. This worried him more than it did me, for temperamentally, particularly in business and practical affairs, I tend to go my own way and do not worry. Moreover, in my experience there was almost always a pretty deep gulf between the political and literary editors of left-wing weekly papers, like the *Nation* and the *New Statesman*. The cultural scission or schism which, rather to my amusement, I found every now and again opening on a Wednesday morning between me on the one side and Hubert and Harold Wright on the other seemed to me no wider or more catastrophic than that which I had observed between the literary editor of the *New Statesman*, Jack Squire or Desmond MacCarthy, and the editor, Clifford Sharp.

Though this kind of thing did not worry me, it was one example of a good deal of work on the *Nation* which I found more and more boring. In the editorial rooms of weekly newspapers there is or was an unending struggle for space. As soon as the number of pages or columns in the next issue has been settled, the number of pages or columns to be assigned to the editor, the literary editor, and the assistant editor has to be settled. This too often led to a violent struggle for space between politics and literature. Whether the editor should sacrifice a page in which he wanted an article on the Revolution in Bulgaria by Arnold Toynbee to me for an article on John Donne by T. S. Eliot, or vice versa, might well entail a stubborn conflict. This kind of thing is bound up with one side of journalism which, as I have said before, corrodes and erodes the editorial mind. The moment you as editor send back to the printer, say on Wednesday afternoon, the last page proof corrected for the issue of 1 January you have to begin to think of what you are going to put in the issue of 8 January, and you have to get that question practically settled by next Monday morning. You are perpetually thinking in terms of articles, notes, reviews, authors, and titles in relation to pages, columns, lines, and words, and the scale of time against which you think of a revolution in Bulgaria or John Donne, of Hitler's Nuremberg Laws or the behaviour of the crowd at the Derby, is five, or at most seven, days. The editorial mind thinks kaleidoscopically in a framework of a few hours or days, but the human mind should, I think, every now and again think steadily *sub specie aeternitatis*. But eternity to the editor of *The Times* is twenty-four hours and to the editor (and literary editor) of the *Nation* seven days.

Every now and again I have an intense desire for solitude, to shut the door, pull down the blinds, and to be entirely alone for a day or two. When the desire comes upon me, even if Shakespeare or Montaigne knocked at the door, I should pretend to be out. The frame of mind is connected, I think, with a desire occasionally to think of things *sub specie aeternitatis*, the eternal frame of eternity, not the eternity of twenty-four hours or seven days. To live perpetually in a kaleidoscope of which the kaleidoscopic changes are always more or less the same bores and depresses me. After four years as literary editor of the *Nation* I already began to feel that I had had enough of this kind of journalism and talked to Maynard about giving it up. He wanted me to stay on and eventually I agreed provided that it was arranged that I spent less time in the office, my salary being reduced from £400 to £250. I went to the office only on Tuesdays and Fridays; in fact, I did practically the same work as I had done before—I do not know how I contrived to get through it in less than two full days at the office. But I continued to do this for another three years. In 1929 I told Maynard that I could not stand any more of it and resigned early in 1930.

My resignation from the *Nation* was made possible by our financial situation which was revolutionised in the years 1928 to 1931. From 1924 to 1928 our income only just covered our expenditure and we had to be very careful about both. I propose to give some exact and detailed figures; the private finances of people seem to me always interesting; indeed they have so great an effect upon people's lives that, if one is writing a truthful autobiography, it is essential to reveal them. Here, at any rate are a few figures:

Income in £'s

	LW	Hogarth Press	VW	Other	Gross Income	Tax	Net Income	Expenditure
1924	569	3	165	310	1,047	126	921	826
1925	565	73	223	404	1,265	114	1,151	846
1926	499	27	713	419	1,658	144	1,514	962
1927	352	27	748	369	1,496	183	1,313	1,193
1928	394	64	1,540	347	2,345	268	2,077	1,117
1929	357	380	2,936	323	3,996	859	3,137	1,120
1930	383	530	1,617	345	2,875	796	2,079	1,158
1931	258	2,373	1,326	411	4,368	1,376	2,992	1,224
1932	270	2,209	2,531	321	5,331	1,278	4,053	1,153
1933	263	1,693	1,916	327	4,199	1,262	2,937	1,187
1934	202	930	2,130	353	3,615	1,086	2,529	1,192
1935	208	741	801	458	2,208	683	1,525	1,253
1936	263	637	721	477	2,098	683	1,415	1,230
1937	271	77	2,466	524	3,184	315	2,869	1,122
1938	365	2,442	2,972	570	6,349	2,462	3,887	1,116
1939	778	350	891	802	2,821	974	1,849	1,069

Some explanation of these figures is necessary. First as regards expenditure. At the end of the 1914 war I invented a system with regard to our finances which we found both useful and amusing and which we kept going until Virginia's death. At the end of each year I worked out in detail an estimate of expenditure for the coming year. This was to provide for only the bare joint expenses of our common life together; it therefore covered rents, rates, upkeep of houses, fuel and lighting, food, servants, garden, upkeep of car (when we got one), doctors and medicine, an allowance to each for clothes. At the end of the year I worked out what the actual expenditure had been and also the total actual combined income, and then the excess of income over expenditure was divided equally between us and became a personal 'hoard', as we called it, which we could spend in any way we liked. For instance, when we decided to have a car, I bought it out of my 'hoard', and if Virginia wanted a new dress which she could not pay for out of her allowance, she paid for it out of her hoard. The amount of our hoards varied enormously as time went on. To take an example, the above figures show that at the end of 1927 we each got £60, but at the end of 1929 we each got £1,008.

The revolutionary increase in our income was due first to the sudden success of Virginia's books and secondarily to the Hogarth Press. In January 1925 Virginia was forty-two years old. She had already published three novels *(The Voyage Out, Night and Day,* and *Jacob's Room)* and a book of short stories *(Monday or Tuesday).* In 1924 her income from her books was £37, £21 from her English and £16 from her American publishers; she earned £128 by journalism, so that her total earnings for 1924 were £165. In 1925 she published *Mrs Dalloway* and *The Common Reader* with the Hogarth Press in England and Harcourt, Brace in America. These two books brought her in during the two years 1925 and 1926 £162 in England and £358 in America. In England *Mrs Dalloway* sold 2,236 copies and *The Common Reader* 1,434 copies in the first twelve months. In 1927 *To the Lighthouse* was published and was distinctly more successful than any of her previous books, at any rate in England, where the Hogarth Press sold 3,873 copies in the first year, and she earned from her books in that year £270 in England and £275 in America. That meant that at the age of forty-seven, having written for at least twenty-seven years and having produced five novels, Virginia for the first time succeeded in earning as much as £545 from her books in a year—the most that she had ever made before was £356 in 1926.

The turning-point in Virginia's career as a successful novelist came in 1928 with the publication of *Orlando*. In the first six months the Hogarth Press sold 8,104 copies, over twice as many as *To the Lighthouse* had sold in its first 12 months, and Harcourt, Brace sold 13,031 copies in the first six months. In America Mr Crosby Gaige published a limited edition of 872 copies about a week before the Harcourt, Brace edition was published. The effect upon Virginia's earnings as a novelist was immediate. In 1928 she earned from her books £1,434 (£556 in England and £878 in America) and in 1929 £2,306 (£761 in England and £1,545 in America). In 1929 *A Room of One's Own* was published and in 1931 *The Waves*. In the first six months *A Room of One's Own* sold 12,443 copies in England and 10,926 in America and *The Waves* sold 10,117 copies in England and 10,380 in America. Virginia's earnings from her books were in 1930 £1,294 (£546 in England and £748 in America), in 1931 £1,266 (£798 in England and £468 in America), and in 1932 £1,795 (£554 in England and £1,241 in America). In 1932 *The Common Reader Second Series* was published and in the first six months sold 3,373 copies in England and 3,271 in America. Then in 1933 came *Flush*. This was a great success. The Hogarth Press sold 18,739 copies in the first six months and Harcourt, Brace 14,081 in America, where it was an alternative selection of The Book of the Month Club.

Virginia finished writing *Flush* in January 1933 and immediately began to work seriously on *The Years*, which she first called *The Pargiters*. It took her four years to write *The Years*, and no major book of hers was published between 1933 and 1937. Her earnings from books during those four years were as follows:

	England	America	Total
1933	£1,193	£1,253	£2,446
1934	301	778	1,079
1935	214	297	511
1936	158	476	634

The Years was published in March 1937 and was much the most successful of all Virginia's books. It was the only one which was a best-seller in America. Harcourt, Brace sold 30,904 copies and in the Hogarth Press we sold 13,005 in the first six months. Virginia's earnings from books for the years 1937, 1938, and 1939 were as follows:

	England	America	Total
1937	£1,355	£2,071	£3,426
1938	1,697	1,275	2,972
1939	193	254	447

These figures may seem too dull and detailed to many people, but autobiographically and biographically they are important. The facts behind them had economically a considerable effect upon our lives. After 1928 we were always very well off. In the next ten years our income was anything from twice to six times what it had been in 1924. Neither of us was extravagant or had any desire for conspicuous extravagance; we did not alter fundamentally our way of life, because on £1,000 a year we already lived the kind of life we wished to live, and we were not going to alter the chosen pattern of our life because we made £6,000 in the year instead of £1,000. But life is easier on £3,000 a year than it is on £1,000. Within the material framework which we had chosen for our existence we got more of the things which we liked to possess—books, pictures, a garden, a car—and we did more of the things we wanted to do, for instance travel, and less in the occupations which we did not want to do, for instance journalism.

But the statistics of Virginia's earnings as a writer of books have from another point of view still greater interest and importance. They throw a curious light on the economics of a literary profession and on the economic effect of popular taste on a serious writer. *Orlando, Flush,* and *The Years* were immeasurably more successful than any of Virginia's other novels. *The Years*, much the most successful of them all, was, in my opinion, the worst book she ever wrote—at any rate, it cannot compare, as a work of art or a work of genius, with *The Waves, To the Lighthouse,* or *Between the Acts. Orlando* is a highly original and amusing book and has some beautiful things in it, but it is a *jeu d'esprit*, and so is *Flush*, a work of even lighter weight; these two books again cannot seriously be compared with her major novels. The corollary of all this is strange. Up to 1928, when Virginia was forty-six, she had published five novels; she had in the narrow circle of people who value great works of literature a high reputation as one of the most original contemporary novelists. Thus her books were always reviewed with the greatest seriousness in all papers which treat contemporary literature seriously. But no one would have called her a popular or even a successful novelist, and she could not possibly have lived upon the earnings from her books. In 1932 Mrs Leavis, rather a hostile critic, wrote:

> The novels are in fact highbrow art. The reader who is not alive to the fact that *To the Lighthouse* is a beautifully constructed work of art will make nothing of the book. . . . *To the Lighthouse* is not a popular novel (though it has already taken its place as an important one), and it is necessary to enquire why the conditions of the age have made it inaccessible to a public whose ancestors have been competent readers of Sterne and Nashe.[1]

[1] *Fiction and the Reading Public*, by Q. D. Leavis, p. 223.

Mrs Leavis exaggerates. It is not true, as the subsequent history of *To the Lighthouse* shows, that the 'common reader' who does not bother his head about 'beautiful construction' or indeed works of art, can make nothing of the book. There is no reason to think that *Tristram Shandy* was more 'accessible' to the eighteenth-century common reader than *To the Lighthouse* is to the twentieth-century common reader. Mrs Leavis in another passage even more strangely asserts that *To the Lighthouse* is more highbrow art and less accessible to the ordinary person than Henry James's *Awkward Age* and *The Ambassadors*. But it is, of course, true, as I have shown above by the statistics that up to 1928 Virginia, although widely recognised as an important novelist, was read by a small public. The fate of her books after 1928, however, points to a conclusion quite different from, and more interesting than, Mrs Leavis's. Take, for instance, the sales of *To the Lighthouse* after 1928 and up to the present date. By 1964 the book had sold 113,829 copies in Britain and 139,644 copies in America. It is selling more today than it has ever sold since its publication in 1927. For instance, in 1964 it sold 10,142 copies in Britain and 13,060 in America and in 1965 22,340 in Britain and 21,309 in America. A book which sells 43,649 copies a year thirty-nine years after publication cannot be said to be unpopular or un-understandable by ordinary people.

A graph of the sales of Virginia's books and of her reputation since 1920 suggests that, so far as original writing is concerned, the law with regard to literature is the exact opposite of Gresham's law by which bad money drives out good. Nearly all artists, from Beethoven downward, who have had something highly original to say and have been forced to find a new form in which to say it, have had to pass through a period in which the ordinary person has found him unintelligible or 'inaccessible', but eventually, in some cases suddenly, in others gradually, he becomes intelligible and is everywhere accepted as a good or a great artist. In Virginia's case she had to write a bad book and two not very serious books before her best serious novels were widely understood and appreciated. And in her case the good drove out the bad. In the years 1963 and 1964, when *To the Lighthouse* sold annually 23,000, the sales of *The Years* and *Orlando* were negligible. In America they were out of print, and in Britain *Orlando* sold 641 in 1963 and 509 in 1964, *The Years* 213 in 1963 and 470 in 1964. But *The Waves*, the most difficult and the best of all her books, sold 906 in 1963 and 1,336 in

1964, and *Mrs Dalloway*, another difficult and the most 'highbrow' of her books, sold 8,242 copies in 1963 (2,306 in Britain and 5,936 in America) and 10,791 in 1964 (2,098 in Britain and 8,693 in America).

In *A Writer's Diary* I published extracts from Virginia's diary which show her engrossed in the day-to-day work of writing these books. She uses these pages as Beethoven used his Notebooks to jot down an idea or partially work out a theme to be used months or years later in a novel or a symphony. While writing a book, in the diary she communes with herself about it and its meaning and object, its scenes and characters. She reveals, more nakedly perhaps than any other writer has done, the exquisite pleasure and pains, the splendours and miseries, of artistic creation, the relation of the creator both to his creation and his creatures and also to his critics and his public. Her hypersensitivity—the fact that criticism tortured her mind like the dentist's drill on an exposed nerve—has seemed to many of her posthumous critics extraordinary and highly discreditable. She herself agreed with her critics that it was highly discreditable.[1] No doubt it was partly due to the fact, which I have noted before, that 'there was too much ego in her cosmos', and an excess of egoism is discreditable. It was also partly due to her attitude to her work, her art, her books. The vast majority of people

[1] On May 17, 1932, Virginia wrote in her diary: 'What is the right attitude towards criticism? What ought I to feel and say when Miss B. devotes an article in *Scrutiny* to attacking me? She is young, Cambridge, ardent. And she says I'm a very bad writer. Now I think the thing to do is to note the pith of what is said—that I don't think—then to use the little kick of energy which opposition supplies to be more vigorously oneself. It is perhaps true that my reputation will now decline. I shall be laughed at, pointed at. What should be my attitude—clearly Arnold Bennett and Wells took the criticism of their youngsters in the wrong way. The right way is not to resent; not to be longsuffering and Christian and submissive either. Of course, with my odd mixture of rashness and modesty (to analyse roughly) I very soon recover from praise and blame. But I want to find out an attitude. The most important thing is not to think very much about oneself. To investigate candidly the charge; but not fussily, not very anxiously. On no account to retaliate by going to the other extreme—thinking too much. And now that thorn is out—perhaps too easily.' The word 'thorn' here has a kind of special meaning. We used to say that Virginia was continually picking up mental thorns—worries which she could not get rid of—particularly from criticism. She would come to me and say: 'I've got a thorn', and we would discuss the thing until we had got the thorn out.

work for about eight hours a day, and during those eight hours apply less than fifty per cent of their attention or concentration to the work. Out of the sixteen hours of her waking day I should reckon that Virginia normally 'worked' fifteen hours and I should guess that she dreamed about it most of the time when she was asleep. Her work was her writing, and when she was actually writing, her concentration was 100, not fifty, per cent. But unlike most people, she was almost always at her work even when she was not working. Practically every afternoon, when at Rodmell, she would walk for an hour, two hours, or even more. All the time on the downs, across the water-meadows, or along the river bank, in the front or at the back of her mind was the book or article she was writing or the embryo of a book or story to be written. It was not that she did not see or feel her surroundings, the kaleidoscope of fields, downs, river, birds, a fox or a hare—she saw and felt them with intensity, as her conversation and the extraordinarily visual imagery of her writing show; but at the same time, at the back or just below the surface of her mind there seemed to be a simmering of thoughts, feelings, images connected with her writing and every now and again this simmering would rise to the surface or boil over in the form of a conscious consideration of a problem in her book or the making of a phrase or the outline of a scene to be written next morning.

Moreover, though she enjoyed intensely for their own sake the sights and sounds of her walk, these too were, I think, almost always registered as to some extent the raw material of her art. The same is true of all the activities of her life. For instance, as I have said before, no one could possibly have enjoyed society or parties more than she did; on the surface she was carried away by them and so more often than not was a great 'social success'. And yet I do not think that that second sight, that second layer in her mind, was ever entirely quiescent; there the scene, the dinner-party, the conversation, her own feelings were continually registered and remembered as the raw material of her art. This is shown by the fact that she so often described parties in considerable detail in her diary.[1]

[1] The following is an example written on 26 May 1932: 'Last night at Adrian's party. Zuckerman on apes. Dora Chapman sitting on the floor. I afraid of Eddy (Eddy Sackville-West) coming in—I wrote him a sharp but well earned letter. Adrian so curiously reminiscent—will talk of his school, of Greece, of his past as if nothing had happened in between: a queer psychological fact in him—this dwelling on the past, when there's his present

This unremitting intensity with which she worked upon whatever she was writing, when combined with her sensitiveness to all sensations and impressions, was perhaps to some extent a cause of her vulnerability, the intensity of her feeling about criticism of it. Even when she had reached the dangerous pinnacle of success, established as an important writer, she never showed the slightest sign of that fatal occupational disease of the successful writer, the feeling of being a very important person. On the contrary, the more successful she became, the more vulnerable she seemed to become, with a kind of humility and uncertainty which were the exact opposite of the assurance and importance one felt in the great men of their day, like Wells, Bennett, Galsworthy, and Shaw,[1] and even in many of the smaller fry.

The implacable intensity of concentration upon her writing and her almost pathological fear of the exposure of publication combined to produce the exhaustion and despair which assailed her in the interval between finishing a book and publishing it. All the books, from *Jacob's Room* to *The Years*, induced one of these dangerous crises. I have already referred to them and I do not propose to record in any detail the effect of each, great though it was, upon Virginia herself and upon our day-to-day life. The exact nature of them can perhaps best be seen in what she wrote on 23 December 1932, when she had just finished *Flush*, a book which she wrote very easily and never took too seriously:

[1] But characteristically not in Hardy.

---

and his future all round him: D. C. to wit and Karin coming in late, predacious, struggling, never amenable or comforting as, poor woman, no doubt she knows: deaf, twisted, gnarled, short, stockish, baffled, still she comes. Dick Strachey. All these old elements of a party not mingling. L. and I talk with some effort. Duncan wanders off. Nessa gone to Tarzan. We meet James and Alix on the door. Come and dine, says James with the desire strong in him I think to keep hold of Lytton. Monkeys can discriminate between light and dark: dogs can't. Tarzan is made largely of human apes. . . . Talk of Greece. Talk of Spain. Dick was taken for a ghost. A feeling of distance and remoteness. Adrian sepulchral, polite, emaciated, elongated, scientific, called Adrian by Solly; then in come rapid small women, Hughes and I think his wife. We evaporate at 11.20: courteously thanked for coming by Adrian. Question what pleasure these parties give. Some, presumably, or these singular figures wouldn't coagulate.'

I must write off my dejected rambling misery—having just read over the 30,000 words of *Flush* and come to the conclusion that they won't do. Oh what a waste—what a bore! Four months of work and heaven knows how much reading—not of an exalted kind either—and I can't see how to make anything of it. It's not the right subject for that length: it's too slight and too serious. Much good in it but would have to be much better. So here I am two days before Christmas pitched into one of my grey welters.

Her major works, by increasing the strain, only increased that 'dejected rambling misery' and the 'grey welter'. The moment she sent back the corrected proofs of *The Waves* to the printer she had to go to bed with a dangerous headache. When the book was published and before she had any criticism of it, whether from Hugh Walpole, John Lehmann, or anyone else, she wrote in her diary: 'I have come up here, trembling under the sense of complete failure—I mean *The Waves*—I mean Hugh Walpole[1] does not like it—I mean John L. is about to write to say he thinks it bad—I mean L. accuses me of sensibility verging on insanity'. And months later she said that she still felt her brain numb from the strain of writing *The Waves*.

How near these strains from writing and publishing brought her at any moment to breakdown and suicide is shown frequently in her diary. For instance, early in July 1933 the worrying over revising *Flush* and her excitement over beginning to write *The Years* brought on a headache, and she recorded on 10 July: 'And then I was in "one of my states"—how violent, how acute—and walked in Regents Park in black misery and had to summon my cohorts in the old way to see me through, which they have done more or less. A note made to testify to my own ups and downs: many of which go unrecorded though they are less violent I think than they used to be. But how familiar it was—stamping along the road, with gloom and pain constricting my heart: and the desire for death, in the old way, all for two I dare say careless words.'

Although her day-to-day mental health in general became stronger and more stable through the 1920s and 1930s, the crises of exhaustion and black despair when she had finished a book seemed each time to become deeper and more dangerous. We had a terrifying time with *The Years* in 1936; she was much nearer a com-

[1] She noted herself later that, though Hugh said that it was 'unreal' and that it beat him, John 'loved it, truly loved it , and was deeply impressed and amazed'. And she adds about herself: 'My brain is flushed and flooded. . . . Lord what a weathercock—not a wave of emotion is in me.'

plete breakdown than she had ever been since 1913. There are two gaps in her 1936 diary, one of two months between 9 April and 11 June and another of four months between 23 June and 30 October. They were filled with an unending nightmare. For the first three months of the year Virginia was revising the book and, as she revised it, we sent it to the printer to be put into galley proofs. We did this—getting galley instead of page proofs—because Virginia was in despair about the book and wanted galleys so that she would be free to make any alterations she wished in proof. But at the beginning of May she was in such a state that I insisted that she should break off and take a complete holiday for a fortnight. We drove down into the west country by slow stages, stopping in Weymouth, Lyme Regis, and Beckey Falls on Dartmoor, until we reached Budock Vean in that strange primordial somnolent Cornish peninsula between Falmouth and Helford Passage, where the names of the villages soothe one by their strangeness—Gweek and Constantine and Mawnan Smith. As a child Virginia had spent summer after summer in Leslie Stephen's house at St Ives in Cornwall—the scene of *To the Lighthouse* is St Ives and the lighthouse in the book is the Godrevy light which she saw night by night shine across the bay into the windows of Talland House. No casements are so magic, no faery lands so forlorn as those which all our lives we treasure in our memory of the summer holidays of our childhood. Cornwall never failed to fill Virginia with this delicious feeling of nostalgia and romance.

I thought that for Virginia's jangled nerves I might find in Cornwall the balm which the unfortunate Jeremiah thought—mistakenly—he might find in Gilead to salve the 'hurt of the daughter of my people'. That was why I drove west and stayed in Budock Vean, and revisited Coverack and the Lizard and Penzance, and went on to stay with Will and Ka Arnold-Forster in that strange house, Eagle's Nest, perched high up on the rock at Zennor a few miles from St Ives. As the final cure, we wandered round St Ives and crept into the garden of Talland House and in the dusk Virginia peered through the ground-floor windows to see the ghosts of her childhood. I do not know whether, like Heine, she saw the Doppelgänger and heard the mournful echo of Schubert's song: 'Heart, do you remember that empty house? Do you remember who used to live there? Ah, someone comes! Wringing her hands! Terrible! It is myself. I can see my own face. Hi, Ghost! What does it mean? What are you doing, mocking what I went through here all those years ago'.

I drove back by easy stages to Rodmell and then to London. Virginia seemed to be a good deal better, and, as a further precaution, she took another twelve days' complete holiday at Rodmell. She started to work on the proofs again on 12 June, but almost at once it became clear that she had not really recovered. After nine or ten days we decided that she must break off altogether and take a complete rest. In fact, on 9 July we went down to Rodmell and stayed there for three and a half months. Virginia did not write at all, did not look at her proofs, and hardly ever moved out of Rodmell. Once a week I drove up to London for the day and it was a pretty strenuous day. I used to leave Rodmell at eight and get to Tavistock Square about ten, where I dealt with the Hogarth Press business. In the afternoon I went to the House of Commons for a meeting of the Labour Party Advisory Committee. This meant that quite often I did not leave London until nearly seven so that I did not get back to Rodmell until close on nine. Virginia did not accompany me on these weekly expeditions. She spent her time reading, drowsing, walking. Towards the end of October she seemed very much better and we decided that I should read the proofs of *The Years* and that she would accept my verdict of its merits and defects and whether it should or should not be published. It was for me a difficult and dangerous task. I knew that unless I could give a completely favourable verdict she would be in despair and would have a very serious breakdown. On the other hand, I had always read her books immediately after she had written the last word and always given an absolutely honest opinion. The verdict on *The Years* which I now gave her was not absolutely and completely what I thought about it. As I read it I was greatly relieved. It was obviously not in any way as bad as she thought it to be; it was in many ways a remarkable book and many authors and most publishers would have been glad to publish it as it stood. I thought it a good deal too long, particularly in the middle, and not really as good as *The Waves*, *To the Lighthouse*, and *Mrs Dalloway*.

To Virginia I praised the book more than I should have done if she had been well, but I told her exactly what I thought about its length. This gave her enormous relief and, for the moment, exhilaration, and she began to revise the proofs in order to send them back to the printer. She worked at them on and off from 10

November until the end of the year, sometimes fairly happy about the book and sometimes in despair. 'I wonder', she wrote in her diary, 'whether anyone has ever suffered so much from a book as I have suffered from *The Years*'; I doubt whether anyone ever has. But—how often in my life I have gratefully murmured Swinburne's lines—'even the weariest river winds somewhere safe to sea'. She revised the book in the most ruthless and drastic way. I have compared the galley proofs with the published version and the work which she did on the galleys is astonishing. She cut out bodily two enormous chunks, and there is hardly a single page on which there are not considerable rewritings or verbal alterations. At last on 31 December the proofs were returned to the printer. The book was published in March of the following year, and, as I have said, at once proved to be the greatest success of all the novels which she had written.

Virginia was a slow writer. It took her four years to write *The Years* and there was an interval of six years between *The Waves* and *The Years*. Yet she was comparatively a prolific writer. She wrote nine full-length novels, two biographies, and there are seven volumes of literary criticism; in addition to this there must be at least 500,000 words of her unpublished diaries. As a novelist her output was greater than that of Fanny Burney, Jane Austen, the Brontës, George Eliot, Thackeray, or in modern times Joyce and E. M. Forster. This is a remarkable fact when one thinks of the psychological handicaps and difficulties which I have described in the previous pages. It was to a great extent due to her professional, dedicated, industriousness. Neither of us ever took a day's holiday unless we were too ill to work or unless we went away on a regular and, as it were, authorised holiday. We should have felt it to be not merely wrong but unpleasant not to work every morning for seven days a week and for about eleven months a year. Every morning, therefore, at about 9.30 after breakfast each of us, as if moved by a law of unquestioned nature, went off and 'worked' until lunch at 1. It is surprising how much one can produce in a year, whether of buns or books or pots or pictures, if one works hard and professionally for three and a half hours every day for 330 days. That was why, despite her disabilities, Virginia was able to produce so much.

Thus, although she was in such a desperate state about *The Years* all through the last six months of 1936, she already had simmering in her mind *Three Guineas* and the biography of Roger Fry. Indeed on 28 January 1937, exactly one month after sending back the proofs of *The Years* to the printer, she began to write *Three Guineas*; she finished the first draft on 12 October 1937, and began to write *Roger Fry* on 1 April 1938. But already in August 1937 a new novel, which was to become *Between the Acts*, was simmering in her mind and she began to write it, under its first title *Poyntz Hall*, in the first half of 1938. In 1938 we published *Three Guineas* and in 1940 *Roger Fry*. On 26 February 1941, she finished *Between the Acts* and, as had happened four years before, she fell into the depths of despair. On 28 March she drowned herself in the Ouse.

I must return to the subject of our income. I said that the sudden, large jump upwards in our income which began in 1928 was primarily due to the sudden success of Virginia's books. But I also said that it was due secondarily to the Hogarth Press and I will deal now with the development of this curious publishing business. When we moved from Richmond to Tavistock Square in March 1924, the Press, though it had published thirteen books in the previous twelve months, was still a very amateurish affair. It had one employee, Marjorie Joad. 1924 was again a year of considerable expansion and we had three publications which in particular were to have a great influence upon our future as publishers.

In 1924 Vita asked us whether we would like to publish a longish short story which she had written, *Seducers in Ecuador*. At that time she had already published some poems and two or three novels with Collins and Heinemann. *Seducers* was a curious little story which no ordinary publisher would have looked at. We made a very pretty little book out of it and published it at 4s. 6d. just before Christmas. When we sold out the edition of 1,500 copies we did not reprint. At that time Harold was still in the diplomatic service and in 1925 he was appointed to the British Legation in Teheran. Vita went with him and she wrote a good travel book about Persia, *Passenger to Teheran*, which we published in 1926. She followed this up with *Twelve Days* in which she described an adventurous journey across the Bakhtiari mountains to the Persian oil-fields, and we published this book in 1928. Next year she brought us the manuscript of *The Edwardians*. This was a novel about Knole, the Sackvilles, and Edwardian Society with the most aristocratic capital S, written from the inside of not only Knole, but also Vita. Inside Vita was an honest, simple, sentimental, romantic, naïve, and competent writer.

When she let all this go off altogether in a novel about high life, she produced in *The Edwardians* a kind of period piece and a real best-seller. Both Virginia and Vita had been warned by friends and friendly publishers that it was madness to have their books published by such an amateurish, ramshackle concern as the Hogarth Press, which had not the machinery to deal with a best-seller or even a seller. I have always been doubtful about this 'machinery' of publishing and was pleased to find that the machinery of the Press stood up to the strain of a best-seller. We sold nearly 30,000 copies of *The Edwardians* in the first six months, and by the end of a year the press had made a profit of nearly £2,000 on it. It has gone on selling for years.

Novels by serious writers of genius often eventually become best-sellers, but most contemporary best-sellers are written by second-class writers whose psychological brew contains a touch of naïvety, a touch of sentimentality, the story-telling gift, and a mysterious sympathy with the day-dreams of ordinary people. Vita was very nearly a best-seller of this kind. She only just missed being one because she did not have quite enough of the third and fourth elements in the best-selling brew. We published *The Edwardians* in 1930 and *All Passion Spent*, which she wrote in less than a year, in 1931. This was, I think, the best novel which she ever wrote, though there was rather more than a touch of sentimentality in it. It did very well, though not as well as *The Edwardians*, selling about 15,000 copies in the first year—it still sells thirty-five years after it was first published—and showing a profit of about £1,200. After this book the springs of Vita's invention and imagination which she required for novel writing began to run dry. She produced a fascinating and very amusing book, *Pepita,* a biography of her terrible mother and extraordinary grandmother, which we published with great success in 1937. But I had grave doubts about her two novels, *Family History* and *The Dark Island*, and then she brought us the manuscript of a novel which we felt we could not publish.

The relation of author and publisher is never an easy one. The publisher is, at the best of times, an ambivalent and often not very competent business man, wobbling between profits and art for art's sake; the writer has something of the same kind of wobble and is often convinced that the reason why his book is not a best-seller is because his publisher is an incompetent, profit-making shark. Vita was an ideal author from the publisher's point of view; she never complained when things went wrong and was extraordinarily appreciative of the publisher if they went right. This made it all the more unpleasant to have to tell her that we thought her novel not good enough for us to publish. We knew, too, that we should lose her as an author, because there were many reputable publishers who would publish this novel in order to get her 'on their list'. It was characteristic of her that she was not in the least bit hurt or resentful and the whole thing made no difference to her relationship with us.

By 1924, seven years after it started, the Hogarth Press, still with practically no employees, no capital invested, and no overheads, had on its general list already two potentially best-sellers, Vita and Virginia. But we were not merely a one- or two-horse shay. With courageous wisdom or reckless folly, we took on a considerable number of new authors and new books. There were 34 books announced in our 1925 lists and we had published all of them in 1926. In the next five years we published novels by William Plomer, Edwin Muir, F. L. Lucas, C. H. B. Kitchin, Alice Ritchie, F. M. Mayor, Svevo, and Rilke. The first six of these were first novels. Two of the six, which did quite well when published, are now forgotten, but are, I still think, remarkable, *The Rector's Daughter* by F. M. Mayor and *The Peacemakers* by Alice Ritchie. A little later, in the early 1930s we published Christopher Isherwood's *Mr Norris Changes Trains*, new novels by Ivan Bunin, and Laurens van der Post's first novel *In a Province*. In general publishing we also branched out into art with a classic, *Cézanne* by Roger Fry, in 1926, and very strongly into politics, economics, history, and sociology. This last category was directly connected with my own activities. In the 1920s I wrote *After the Deluge*, Vol. 1, and *Imperialism and Civilization*. But I also became more and more occupied with practical politics in the Labour Party and Fabian Society and this is reflected in the large number of political books which we published, among which some of the most important were *The End of Laissez-Faire* (1926) and *The Economic Consequences of Mr Churchill* (1925) by Maynard Keynes, the remarkable books on imperialism in Africa by Norman Leys, and Lord Olivier's *White Capital and Coloured Labour*.

I said above that there were three publications in 1924 which had a considerable influence on the development of the Press. The first was Vita's book. The second was a series, the Hogarth Essays, which we started in 1924 with three volumes, *Mr Bennett and Mrs*

Brown by Virginia, *The Artist and Psycho-Analysis* by Roger Fry, and *Henry James at Work* by Theodora Bosanquet. This series consisted of pamphlets, a form of publication which nearly all publishers fought (still fight) shy of because they always involve a good deal of work and a loss of money. I was eager to have a series of pamphlets in which one could have essays on contemporary political and social problems as well as on art and criticism. These essays, published at between 1s. 6d. and 3s. 6d., were surprisingly successful. In the first series in 1924, 1925, and 1926, we published nineteen essays, bound in stiff paper with a cover design by Vanessa, and among the authors were T. S. Eliot, Robert Graves, Edith Sitwell, J. M. Keynes, E. M. Forster, J. A. Hobson, Vernon Lee, Bonamy Dobrée, and Herbert Read. None of them sold a large number of copies, but every one of them, when they went out of print, had made a profit. This encouraged me to start in 1930 another series, Day to Day Pamphlets, devoted entirely to politics, bound in paper, and published at 1s. or 1s. 6d. In the nine years between 1930 and 1939 we published forty pamphlets, and among the authors were Harold Laski, H. N. Brailsford, W. H. Auden, H. G. Wells, Sir Arthur Salter, C. Day Lewis, A. L. Rowse, and Mussolini. This series also paid its way. It was significant of the political climate in the 1930s that the two best-sellers were Mussolini's *The Political and Social Doctrine of Fascism* and Maurice Dobb's *Russia Today and Tomorrow*, an excellent, though rather rosy, view of Soviet Russia and communism by a Cambridge don.

The pamphlet is not a commodity which it is easy to sell in Britain. Every now and again if you publish one by the right person at the right moment on some controversial subject, it will be a best-seller. We printed 7,000 copies of *The Economic Consequences of Mr Churchill* by Maynard and they sold out at once, but in the general run when we were publishing regularly four or five every year, we did well if we sold over 2,000 copies. Societies like the Fabians which regularly published pamphlets found the same difficulties in selling them. The principal obstruction is the trade. The pamphlet is an awkward and troublesome kind of book to sell, and most bookshops will not look at them. The railway bookstall, which is the right place to market them, also dislikes them, not without reason, as they are not nearly as lucrative as newspapers or that vast range of lurid or alluring publications on whose covers are portrayed murder and rape or the superfeminised female form in every stage of dress or nudity. The result is that the British have never acquired the habit of reading pamphlets. This is a great pity. The pamphlet is potentially an extraordinarily good literary form from both the artistic and the social or political point of view. Those which we published by T. S. Eliot, Roger Fry, Virginia, Maynard Keynes, J. A. Hobson, were remarkable and would never have been written if we had not had this series. All the others were, I think, well worth publishing. Our experience showed us that there is a potential market for the pamphlet. The potentiality never becomes actuality because all avenues of sale between publisher and purchaser are closed or obstructed. And so the habit of writing and reading pamphlets cannot establish itself.

However, these pamphlet series were sufficiently successful to pay their way. They showed us how valuable from the business point of view a series is to a publisher. If one gets a series started successfully with good books, it makes it possible subsequently to publish in the series successfully other books which, if published on their own, however good they might be, would almost certainly have made a substantial loss. In the next few years we started four other series: Hogarth Lectures on Literature, Hogarth Sixpenny Pamphlets, Hogarth Living Poets, and Hogarth Letters. The Living Poets and the Lectures were highly successful. I was over-optimistic about the other two. They contained some interesting and amusing essays, for instance, *A Letter to Madan Blanchard* by E. M. Forster, *A Letter to a Sister* by Rosamond Lehmann, *A Letter to a Grandfather* by Rebecca West. But it was impossible to sell enough of them at 6d. and 1s. to make both ends meet.

The third publication of the Press in 1924 which was to have a considerable effect on its future was a strange one. The publication was announced in our autumn list as follows:

COLLECTED PAPERS. By Sigmund Freud, M.D.
Vol. I. Early Papers and the History of the Psycho-Analytical Movement.
Vol. II. Clinical Papers and Papers on Instinct and the Unconscious.

The Hogarth Press has taken over the publications of the International Psycho-Analytical Library, and will in future continue the series for the International Psycho-Analytical Press. It has obtained the right to publish a complete authorised English translation of Professor Freud's collected papers. These papers are of the highest importance for the study of Psycho-Analysis; they have been translated into English by experts under the supervision of Dr Ernest Jones. The Collected Papers will be published in four volumes. Vol.

III, containing 'Five Case Histories', and Vol. IV, containing 'Metapsychology. Dreams', will be published in the course of next year.

The price of Vols. I, II, and IV will be 21s. each, of Vol. III 30s., and of the complete set four guineas.

That was the beginning of our connection with Freud and the Institute of Psycho-Analysis which has lasted until the present day. It came about in the following way. In the decade before 1924 in the so-called Bloomsbury circle there was great interest in Freud and psycho-analysis, and the interest was extremely serious. Adrian Stephen, Virginia's brother, who worked with Sir Paul Vinogradoff on mediaeval law, suddenly threw the Middle Ages and law out of the window, and, with his wife Karin, became a qualified doctor and professional psycho-analyst. James Strachey, Lytton's youngest brother, and his wife also became professional psycho-analysts. James went to Vienna and was analysed by Freud, and he played an active part in the Institute of Psycho-Analysis, which, largely through Ernest Jones, had been founded in London and was in intimate relations with Freud and the Mecca of psycho-analysis in Vienna, being itself a branch of the International Association of Psycho-Analysis.

Some time early in 1924 James asked me whether I thought the Hogarth Press could publish for the London Institute. The Institute, he said, had begun the publication of the International Psycho-Analytical Library in 1921 and had already published six volumes, which included two of Freud's works, *Beyond the Pleasure Principle* and *Group Psychology and the Analysis of the Ego*. They had also signed an agreement with Freud under which they would publish his *Collected Papers* in four volumes. The Institute had hitherto been their own publisher, printing and binding their books in Vienna and having them 'distributed' by a large London publishing firm. They did not find this system satisfactory and they wished to hand over to a publisher the entire business of publishing the International Psycho-Analytical Library in which they hoped regularly to publish a considerable number of important books by Freud and other analysts.

The idea seemed to me very attractive and I drew up an agreement which the Institute accepted. It was agreed that we should take over the books which they had already published, and publish all future books in the Library. For a fledgling inexperienced publisher this was a bold undertaking. The four volumes of Freud's *Collected*

Papers were a formidable work, for each of them ran to over 300 pages and it meant putting a good deal of capital into them. In fact, one of the most distinguished of the large London publishers, who heard what I was about to undertake, gave me a friendly warning that I should be risking too much. The *Collected Papers* was from the start one of the most successful of our publications. I circularised a large number of universities, libraries, and individuals in the United States and had almost at once a good sale in America as well as in Britain. The Institute had bought outright from Freud the rights for £50 for each volume and we bought the rights in the four volumes from the Institute for £200, but as soon as the books began to make a profit, we began to pay a royalty to Freud. The sale of these four fat volumes (we added a fifth later) has gone on steadily for over forty years. The fact that it was started successfully by a publisher with no staff and no 'machine' throws a curious light upon the business of publishing. The longer my experience of the business, the more convinced I have become that the ideas of most authors and indeed many publishers with regard to the efficacy or necessity of what is called the publisher's 'machinery' for selling books is largely delusion, though this applies only to 'serious' books, not to that branch of large-scale industry and mass production, the best-seller racket, in which books have to be sold by the same methods as beers. You may be able to sell a million copies of Mr X's *Women and Wine* or Miss Y's *Wine and Women* by the pressure cooker of large-scale advertising and the mysterious machinery of the colossal publisher, but it is doubtful whether you will sell ten copies of Freud's *Collected Papers*, T. S. Eliot's *The Waste Land*, or Virginia Woolf's *The Waves* by these methods.

Publishing the Psycho-Analytical Library for the Institute was always a very pleasant and very interesting experience. In the next forty years we published nearly seventy volumes in it. In the process I learnt a good many curious things about the art of publishing. For instance, we had in the Library a book by Professor Flügel called *The Psycho-Analytic Study of the Family*. I do not believe that any publisher who saw this book in manuscript or in print or in our list in 1924 would have thought that it had the slightest chance of being a best-seller, and I feel sure that very few of my readers in 1967 have ever heard of it. Yet this book has been a steady seller for over forty years, selling hundreds of copies yearly. It has practically never been advertised and no advertising would have materially influenced its sale. Its aggregate sale must be considerably greater than that of nine out of ten of the much advertised best-sellers that it has long outlived. It is an original book, an almost unknown classic in its own peculiar field, a publisher's dream. It sold steadily in Britain year after year, and year after year twice a year there came a large order from an American bookseller, because it was a 'set book' in an American college.

The greatest pleasure that I got from publishing the Psycho-Analytical Library was the relationship which it established between us and Freud. Between 1924 when we took over the Library and his death in 1939 we published an English translation of every book which he wrote, and after his death we published his complete works, twenty-four volumes, in the Standard Edition. He was not only a genius, but also, unlike many geniuses, an extraordinarily nice man. The business connected with his books, when we first began to publish them, was managed by his son Martin, and later after his death by his son Ernst and daughter Anna. They all seemed to have inherited the extraordinarily civilised temperament of their father which made every kind of relationship with him so pleasant.

The publication of the Standard Edition of the Complete Psychological Works of Freud, which we began in 1953, was one of the most difficult and delicate business operations which I have ever put through. The Internationaler Psycho-analytischer Verlag had already in the 1920s published the *Gesammelte Schriften* of Freud in Germany, Austria, and Switzerland, and after the war in 1942 the complete works in German (*Gesammelte Werke*) were published in London. I was most anxious to publish a complete edition in English and in the 1940s discussed the possibility several times with Ernst Freud. There seemed to be insuperable difficulties. Financially an English edition was not feasible unless it could be sold in the United States as well as in the British Commonwealth, but Freud's American copyrights were in such a tangled and chaotic condition that the moment we began definitely to face the problem there seemed to be no way of acquiring all the rights or even of being quite sure of who controlled them. Freud had been incredibly generous and casual with his copyrights. The outright sale of his English rights in the four volumes of *Collected Papers* for £200 was a good example of his generosity; his casualness is shown by the fact that he once simultaneously sold the American rights in one of his books both to the Hogarth Press and to another publisher. In America he had given the copyright in many of his books to his translator and friend, Dr Brill. This—quite apart from the difficulty of discovering who owned the American rights in several of the other books—presented us with an extremely delicate problem. We had been lucky enough to be able to arrange that, if we did ever succeed in publishing the complete works, the edition would be edited and translated by James Strachey, assisted by his wife, Alix. James has, in fact, accomplished this colossal task in thirteen years, and the twenty-four volumes are a monument to his extraordinary combination of psycho-analytical knowledge, brilliance, and accuracy as a writer and translator, and indomitable severity both to himself and to his publisher. I doubt whether there is any edition of technical scientific works, comparable to this one in size, which can compare with it in the high standard of translation and editing.

What made the task of our approach to Dr Brill, and after his death to his heirs and executors, doubly delicate was that we had to obtain their consent first to our publishing in America translations of the works in which they held the American rights, and second to our using not Dr Brill's translations but James's. For a long time every attempt to find a way through the maze of copyrights and overcome the other difficulties failed, but eventually, largely owing to Ernst Freud's tact and perseverance, an agreement with the Brill executors made publicaion in America possible.

I only once met Freud in person. The Nazis invaded Austria on 11 March 1938, and it took three months to get Freud out of their clutches. He arrived in London in the first week in June and three months later moved into a house in Maresfield Gardens which was to be his permanent home. When he and his family had had time to settle down there, I made discreet enquiries to see whether he would like Virginia and me to come and see him. The answer was yes, and in the afternoon of Saturday 28 January 1939, we went and had tea with him. I feel no call to praise the famous men whom I have known. Nearly all famous men are disappointing or bores, or both. Freud was neither; he had an aura, not of fame, but of greatness. The terrible cancer of the mouth which killed him only eight months later had already attacked him. It was not an easy interview. He was extraordinarily courteous in a formal, old-fashioned way—for instance, almost ceremoniously he presented Virginia with a flower. There was something about him as of a half-extinct volcano, something sombre, suppressed, reserved. He gave me the feeling which only a very few people whom I have met gave me, a feeling of great gentleness, but behind the gentleness, great strength. The room in which he sat seemed very light, shining, clean, with a pleasant, open view through the windows into a garden. His study was almost a museum, for there were all round him a number of Egyptian antiquities which he had collected. He spoke about the Nazis. When Virginia said that we felt some guilt, that perhaps if we had not won the 1914 war there would have been no Nazis and no Hitler, he said, no, that was wrong; Hitler and the Nazis would have come and would have been much worse if Germany had won the war.

A few days before we visited him I had read the report of a case in which a man had been charged with stealing books from Foyle's shop, and among them one of Freud's; the magistrate fined him and said that he wished he could sentence him to read all Freud's works as a punishment. I told Freud about this and he was amused and, in a queer way, also deprecatory about it. His books, he said, had made him infamous, not famous. A formidable man.

I must return now to the Hogarth Press and its fortunes. The figures of our income which I have given above on page 291 show that from 1929 to 1939 the Press contributed on an average £1,100 to our income. During those eleven years I had to revolutionise the organisation of the business. By 1930 we had a clerical staff of three bookkeepers and shorthand typists. We had a representative who travelled our books: Alice Ritchie was, I think, the first woman to travel for a publisher and some booksellers did not like the innovation. She was not only a very good traveller, but also a very good and a serious novelist. The question of the higher command continued to cause us great difficulty and we never found a satisfactory solution. I was determined not to treat publishing as a means of making a living and I was determined not to become a full-time publisher. The choice, therefore, lay between taking a partner or employing a manager competent enough to be responsible for the everyday running of the business so that I could treat it as a part-time occupation.

We started off with the first alternative. From 1924 to 1932 there entered and left the Press a succession of brilliant and not quite so brilliant young men. They entered as managers and potential partners. As I have already said, I think we were trying to get the best of two contradictory worlds and were asking these brilliant young men to perform an impossible feat, namely to publish best-sellers with the greatest professional efficiency for an amateur publisher in a basement kitchen. I still think that the technical efficiency of the Hogarth Press in the years 1924 to 1939 was extremely high, much higher in matters of importance than that of many—I almost wrote most—large and small publishing firms. For instance, for all those years, when we were publishing from twenty to thirty books a year, selling in the first six months of their existence anything from 150 to 30,000 copies, we practically never—I think that I could truthfully say never, but no one would believe me—ran out of bound copies and were unable to supply an order. This was the result of meticulous daily, sometimes hourly, supervision, checking, organisation. Professional publishers will probably politely disbelieve me or at any rate will say (privately) that such a record is impossible for any large publishing business. I am sure that they are mistaken. In a previous part of my autobiography (*Growing*, Volume 1, pp. 199-201) I related my experience with regard to business organisation in the government offices of Ceylon. Every head clerk in every kachcheri to which I was appointed, when on my first day in the office, I told him that 'every letter received in this kachcheri after this week must be answered on the day of its receipt unless it is waiting for an order from me or from the G.A.', threw up his hands in horror and despair, and said that this was much too big a kachcheri and received daily far too many letters to make this possible. The head clerk was mistaken and after six months he had to admit it. Whether ten letters or 100 or 1,000 are received daily, they can all be answered on the day of receipt, provided that there is an automatic routine and meticulous checking. It is the same with books. For the efficiency of publishing it is most important that the decision to reprint or rebind for every book on the list should be made at the right moment and for the right quantity so that there is always in stock an adequate number of bound copies to supply the demand (while, at the same time, the publisher, for his own sake, does not print or bind more copies than he can sell). This may seem a fatuously simple and self-evident truism. But a very little knowledge of what goes on behind the scenes will prove how often in practice the truism is neglected. But in ninety-nine cases out of a hundred in which a bookseller has to be told that a book cannot be supplied because it is 'printing' or 'binding', the failure was avoidable and was due to bad organisation and slovenly supervision. I should perhaps add that all this amounts to, including the truism, often overlooked even by publishers, is that a publisher cannot have an efficient publishing business unless the business has an efficient publisher.

The Hogarth Press was from 1924 to 1939, I repeat, an extremely efficient publishing business, though its methods were in most ways unorthodox. The business side during those years was managed by me and the succession of young men. The first young man to enter and leave the basement in Tavistock Square—and by no means the least brilliant—was G. W. H. Rylands, universally known as Dadie. We were aiming very high when we took Dadie into the Press and began to turn him into a publisher. Not unnaturally he did not stay long in the basement. When he came to us he was only twenty-two; a scholar of Eton and King's, he had just taken a degree and had written a fellowship dissertation. It was from the first understood that, if he got his fellowship at King's, we should lose him, for he would return to Cambridge to become a don. We treated him rather badly, for almost at once we went off for a week or two, leaving him alone in charge of the Press and of a strange, elderly shorthand typist, who, seeing that he was out of his depth and not very happy, tried to cheer him up by feeding him on sandwiches. Dadie, of course, got his fellowship and, much to our regret, left us for a distinguished career in the university, the arts, and the theatre. We published two books of poetry by him, *Russet and Taffeta* (1925) and *Poems* (1931), and *Words and Poetry* (1927), a very original book of literary criticism based on the dissertation which won him his fellowship.

Dadie was followed by Angus Davidson, who stayed with us from 1924 to 1929; he is now very well known as a translator of Italian books. He was followed by a very young man, Richard Kennedy, a nephew of Kennedy, the architect. Richard was too young to be a manager, and we now had, in addition to the clerical staff, a general manager. In 1931 he left us and John Lehmann entered the Press. His appearance on the scene was to have considerable effect upon the Press and its fortunes. Unlike the other young men, he took publishing very seriously and became a highly efficient professional publisher. His first term of work with us was short and not very successful, largely owing to my fault. Poor John, like Dadie a product of Eton and Cambridge, only twenty-four years old when he came to us, was put into a small, dark, basement room, from which he was expected, under my supervision, to 'manage' the publication of twenty-two books to be published by us in the spring of 1931. These twenty-two books included Vita's *All Passion Spent* (selling 14,000 copies in the first six months), Virginia's *The Waves* (selling 10,000), a first novel *Saturday Night at the Greyhound* by John Hampson (selling 3,000), and two masterpieces by Rainer Maria Rilke, very difficult publishing propositions thirty years ago, the *Duino Elegies* and *The Notebook of Malte Laurids Brigge*. We published these twenty-two books—and another eighteen in the autumn season of 1931—with a staff consisting of one traveller and four or five in the office. John, Virginia, and I, as well as the 'staff', were expected to be able to take a hand at any and everything, including packing—indeed, we all became expert packers. To pack and despatch 4,000 or 5,000 copies of a book before publication, as we did in the case of *All Passion Spent* or *The Waves*, is a very formidable business, but I do not think that in those days we ever failed to have all our books delivered on subscription orders in the shops well before the publication date. On the top of this John began to help us with the printing. I am not a person who bears even wise men gladly (sometimes and in some ways I bear fools more gladly), and it is not surprising that John soon found the Hogarth Press too much of a good or a bad thing, and left us in September 1932. He returned to us six years later and was Partner and General Manager in the Press until 1946. But that is part of a different story, a different world and phase of my life from that of 1930; it cannot be dealt with here, for it is part of the story of the war years.

John was a young man of twenty-four when he came to the Press in 1931; I was fifty-one and Virginia forty-nine. We were well aware that the worst menace of middle age is emotional and mental sclerosis which makes one insensitive to anything in any generation later than one's own. Both as publishers and private persons we wanted, if possible, to keep in touch with the younger generation or generations. In taking John into the Press we had had great hopes that he would help us to do this. A scholar of Eton and Trinity College, Cambridge, a poet himself and the friend of Virginia's nephew, Julian Bell, and the younger generation of Cambridge poets and writers, he seemed to have all the qualities and contacts which we were looking for. In this respect he did not disappoint us and in the two years during which he was with us he helped us to bring into the Hogarth Press some of the best writers of his generation.

The younger generation of the late 1920s and early 1930s was remarkable in quality and quantity. As is usual with the young who have something of their own to say, they were in revolt against their fathers (and mothers, uncles, and aunts). In *New Signatures*, which we published in 1932 and which was and still is regarded as that generation's manifesto,[1] Stephen Spender wrote in his poem 'Oh Young Men':

> Oh young men oh comrades
> it is too late now to stay in those houses
> your fathers built where they built you to build to breed
> money on money . . .
> Oh comrades step beautifully from the solid wall
> advance to rebuild, and sleep with friend on hill
> advance to rebel . . .

The rebellious youth of the 1930s were nearly all poets, and their knock on the door of *New Signatures* was poetic. Of the nine poets, five were at Cambridge, Richard Eberhart, William Empson, Julian Bell, A. S. J. Tessimond, and John Lehmann; three at Oxford, W. H. Auden, C. Day Lewis, and Stephen Spender; the ninth was William Plomer. Like most young poets, they took a pretty black view of the past, the present, and the future; it might be said of them, to quote Empson, that they 'learnt a style from a despair' (though every now and again, particularly with Julian, in the best tradition cheerfulness would break through). Despair has always been the occupational disease of young poets, but the nine poets of *New Signatures*, it must be admitted, had more reason than most for gloom and foreboding. They looked out upon a world which had been first devastated by war and was now being economically devastated by peace. What could be more grey and grim than the dole and unemployment; the communism of Stalin, the purges, the kulaks, and the Iron Curtain; the tawdry fascism of Mussolini and the murderous nastiness of Hitler and his Nazi thugs? And when

[1] 'The little book was like a searchlight switched on to reveal that, without anyone noticing it, a group of skirmishers had been creeping up in a concerted movement of attack' (*The Whispering Gallery* by John Lehmann, p. 182). 'The slim blue volume, No. 24 in the Hogarth Living Poets Series, which had caused so much fuss to assemble, came out in the spring of 1932, created a mild sensation then, and has since been taken to mark the beginning, the formal opening of the poetic movement of the 1930s' (*Journey to the Frontier* by Peter Stansky and William Abrahams, p. 77).

they looked from the present toward the future, they could only look forward to dying in another inevitable and futile war. 'Who live under the shadow of a war,' sang Stephen, 'What can I do that matters?' 'A cold wind blows round the corners of the world,' sang William Plomer; 'it blew upon the corpse of a young man, Lying in the street with his head in the gutter Where he fell shot by a revolutionary sniper. . . . He was rash enough to go out for a breath of fresh air. . . . Shot through the stomach he took time to die.'

It was John who brought *New Signatures* to us. Through his sister Rosamond he had got to know Stephen Spender and the Oxford poets. Then through his first book of poems, *A Garden Revisited,* which we had published in 1931, he got to know Michael Roberts, who had been a scholar at Trinity senior to John. He and John devised *New Signatures* and Roberts edited it. In fact, before John came to the Press, we had already published a good deal of work by the rebellious poets of *New Signatures*. Five years before, in 1926, we had published William Plomer's remarkable first novel, *Turbott Wolfe*. In 1929 and 1930 we had published two anthologies, *Cambridge Poetry 1929* and *Cambridge Poetry 1930*. They were anthologies of poetry written, selected, and edited by Cambridge undergraduates. Four of the five Cambridge poets of *New Signatures*—Julian, John, Eberhart, and Empson—were included in these two volumes: We had even penetrated into Oxford, for already in 1929 we had published Cecil Day Lewis's first book of poems, *Transitional Poem*. However, it was not only the emergent poets whom John helped us to keep in touch with. It was through him, via Stephen Spender, that one of the most remarkable and strange of the emergent novelists came to the Hogarth Press, Christopher Isherwood. In 1932 we published *The Memorial*, in some ways his best novel, and in 1935 the brilliant *Mr Norris Changes Trains*.

After John left us and until he returned to us in 1938, I tried the other alternative. We made no further attempt to find a partner, I ran the Press by myself in my own way, with a woman manager. In many ways this worked very well, but it had, from our point of view, great disadvantages. It meant a tremendous amount of work and much more time devoted to the business of publishing than I wanted to devote to it. It also meant that we were closely bound to the business in Tavistock Square and it was impossible to get right away from it for any length of time. Virginia felt this tie to be very irksome, and we were always on the point of throwing the whole thing up or of trying once more to find the ideal partner. But we drifted on, as one does, when something which one has oneself started in life without much thought of the future or of the consequences takes control of one. That did not mean that we let the actual business of the Press drift; we took it very seriously and energetically, and we continued to publish a considerable number of books of every sort and kind. For instance, in 1935, three years after John left us, we published twenty-five books. These included *Mr Norris Changes Trains* by Christopher Isherwood, *Grammar of Love* by Ivan Bunin, *An Autobiographical Study* by Freud, *Requiem* by Rilke, *A Time to Dance* and *Collected Poems* by C. Day Lewis, together with a great variety of books on politics, education, literature, biography, and travel.

I will leave the Hogarth Press now in its basement in Tavistock Square in our own hands and with us in its hands until the year 1938. It had, as I have said, materially added to our income. We were now very comfortably off, for in ten years from 1930 to 1939 our average annual income was over three times what it had been when we came to Tavistock Square in 1924. And, as I have also said before, we did not alter the framework of our lives. We lived in the same houses—in Tavistock Square and Rodmell—with the same servants and in the same 'style'. This is shown by the fact that what we spent on that day-to-day framework of living, on house, food, servants, etc., hardly altered—for instance, whereas in 1924 our income was £1,047 and our expenditure £826, in 1934 our income was £3,615 and our expenditure £1,192.

Yet there was one thing which, as Virginia often remarks at the time in her diary, had a great and immediate effect upon the quality and tempo of our life, and the change was directly due to our being able to spend money. In July 1927 we bought a second-hand Singer car for £275. I suppose that the nineteenth-century scientific revolution—in particular electricity and the internal combustion engine—have changed the world—one will probably soon have to say the universe—much more profoundly than anything else which has happened since God rather foolishly said: 'Let there be light'. That God's remark about the light has been the primal cause of infinitely more evil and misery than of good and happiness is certainly true. When one thinks of the two world wars and the destruction of Hiroshima, or even when one compares the car-infested streets of

London in 1966 with its humanly inhabited streets which I remember in 1886, one has to say the same about science and the inventions which have given us a Singer car and an aeroplane. Certainly nothing ever changed so profoundly my material existence, the mechanism and range of my every-day life, as the possession of a motor car. Even as an individual, I sometimes think how pleasant the tempo of life and movement was when the speed limit was about eight miles an hour, and I curse the day when I acquired a licence to drive motor vehicles of all groups. But those moments of nostalgic pessimism are rare and unreasonable. There is no doubt whatever that, as an individual, purely as an individual, I have enormously increased the scope and pleasures of living by the six cars which I have owned and driven in the last forty years.

The most important change and the greatest pleasure came, and still comes, from a holiday 'touring' on the Continent—I do not think that anything gave Virginia more pleasure than this. She had a passion for travelling, and travel had a curious and deep effect upon her. When she was abroad, she fell into a strange state of passive alertness. She allowed all these foreign sounds and sights to stream through her mind; I used to say rather like a whale lets the seawater stream through its mouth, straining from it for its use the edible flora and fauna of the seas. Virginia strained off and stored in her mind those sounds and sights, echoes and visions, which months afterwards would become food for her imagination and her art. This and the mere mechanism and kaleidoscope of travel gave her intense pleasure, a mixture of exhilaration and relaxation.

Before 1928 and the Singer car we used to go abroad, travelling as English people had done for the last hundred years, comparatively slowly, by boat and rail to some place where one would probably settle down for a week or two. Like so much of life before the motor car and the aeroplane, the tempo was slow. One got into the train at Victoria in the afternoon, crossed Paris from the Gare du Nord to the Gare de Lyon in the evening, and woke up to the entrancing moment when one saw the dawn over the Rhône valley and ate one's first *petit déjeuner*. A few years after the end of the 1914 war, when it again became possible to visit France as a civilian, we saw once more out of the carriage window the dawn break over the Rhône valley, for we were on our way to Cassis. In those days Cassis was a small fishing-village between Marseille and Toulon; it had one small hotel, the Cendrillon, at which we stayed. It is almost impossible to believe today that places like Cassis really did exist forty years ago on any European coast, warmed by the sun and looking upon the blue waters of the Mediterranean or other oarless sea. For it was a pretty, quiet village lying along a restful bay. There was a small resident colony of multi-racial artists, the ominous harbingers of civilisation who could already be found infecting the Mediterranean from Almeria to Rapallo. You would usually find three or four visitors, most probably English, at the Cendrillon. Otherwise Cassis still belonged to the people of Cassis. Looking back upon it today, its chief characteristic seems to have been its quiet. It was indeed so quiet that men might have risen up at the voice of a bird. The voice of the motor car was rarely heard in it. People sat in the café and talked or were silent for many hours; or down by the water they leaned against a boat and talked or just looked out across the bay. In the evening the men played boules.

The first time we went to Cassis was, I think, in March. In the mornings we used to go out and sit on the rocks in the sun and read or write. You were alone, the only sounds the water lapping on the rocks or the gulls crying. If you walked up through the wood over the headland to the east, when you came out of the wood on the other side, you had a view of the long line of sandy coast all the way to La Ciotat, Sanary, and Toulon. It was open, flat country, with scarcely a house to be seen until you got to Sanary. Twenty-six years later I was staying in Sanary and visited this stretch of country again, but the country itself had disappeared—it had disappeared under an unending sea of houses and villas, those hideous little villas which the French build all along the Mediterranean coast. I drove from Sanary to Cassis. A stream of perpetual motion, of moving cars nose to tail and tail to nose, ran on both sides of the dusty road between the unending sea of villas. Cassis itself was submerged in cars and villas. Down by the bay the earth was black with human beings; one's ears were deafened by the voice of the loudspeaker and innumerable transistors. The rocks were littered with bottles and paper bags. The scene is the same from Torremolinos to Rapallo, from Ostende to Brest, and from Deal to Land's End.

In the 1920s, as I said, Cassis was a quiet place and, liking quiet, we returned to it. In those days there lived in Cassis one of those curious Englishmen whose complicated characters seem so English and so un-English. Colonel Teed had been Colonel of the Bengal Lancers. When I first met him, I thought: what a perfect Colonel of the Bengal Lancers! A great horseman, the perfect English cavalry officer! I was quite right, but he was also something entirely different, something which one would not have expected to find in the perfect cavalry officer, for beneath the immaculate surface of the colonel of a crack Indian regiment Teed was fundamentally an intellectual who liked artists and intellectuals. He was also a charming man. When he retired from the Bengal Lancers, he bought Fontcreuse, a vineyard, with a lovely house a mile or two from the centre of Cassis. There he made excellent wine. We got to know him, and when Vanessa followed us to Cassis, she liked the place so much that she entered into an agreement with Teed which allowed her to build a villa on his land free of charge and live in it rent-free for ten or twenty years (I forget the exact figure), after which the villa would become Teed's property.

Vanessa and Clive and Duncan Grant used to spend much of their time in the Cassis villa, and this was an added inducement for us to return there. Teed let us have a room in Fontcreuse and we usually had our meals with the Bells at the villa. It was a pleasant way of life, so pleasant that at one moment we began to buy a villa for ourselves near Fontcreuse; it was called a villa, but was in fact a small, rather tumbled-down whitewashed house. But we did not complete the purchase. The procedure for an Englishman at that time to buy a house in Provence was an unending labyrinth; weary of the interminable business, we began to realise that our commitments in England, the Hogarth Press, writing, politics, made it extremely improbable that we should ever be able to spend much time in Cassis. So the project lapsed.

I am telling this because it explains why we tended, when we could snatch a few weeks from London and Rodmell, to make for Cassis. And in March 1928, under the new dispensation, we set out in our old Singer car to drive there. It opened to one a new way of life. In the old way of travel one was tied to the railway; as one moved through a country, one followed the straight steel parallel lines, one had no contact with the life of the road, the village, and the town. In Ceylon I had become accustomed to travel freely and lightly, on a horse or on foot, along empty roads, paths or game-tracks. I know nothing more exhilarating than starting out in the early morning, just before sunrise, through the jungle or along the straight empty road or the village path for some distant village, an all-day journey with all the day before one. Something of that wonderful feeling of liberation comes—or came—to one when one drove out of Dieppe and saw the long, white, empty road—roads in France, even the *routes nationales*, were in those days empty—stretching before one all the way to the Mediterranean. It is only of this kind of travel, the travel by road, that Montaigne's saying, which I have quoted so often, is really true—it is not the arrival, but the journey which matters.

Our first journey by road on the Continent to the Mediterranean and back was in parts an adventure. It was in 1928 and we crossed from Newhaven to Dieppe on 26 March and for the next six days we rattled along at about 100 miles a day in the old Singer car through Burgundy, and then down the Rhône valley through Vienne, Valence, Montélimar, and so to Provence, through Carpentras and Aix to Cassis. It is the journey, not the arrival, that matters! There are few things in life pleasanter than this long journey south along the white roads through the great avenues of trees and the villages and towns. The slower the better—it is the journey that matters. Even to recall and repeat the names of the towns through which we passed gives me—writing today in a grim grey February day in Sussex—intense pleasure. It is extraordinary how vividly the name of a place will recall to one from years ago the vision of it. I have only to murmur to myself Angunakolapelessa and it brings to me from fifty years ago quite clearly the vision of that small Sinhalese village; I can feel again the whip of heat across my face from the village path; I can hear again the hum of insects across the scrub jungle; I can smell again the acrid smell of smoke and shrubs. So with the names of those towns upon the road to Provence; each recalls the continual change of sound and sights and smells as one journeys south. And there are two particular moments in this journey. The first is at a bend in the road near Montélimar where you suddenly see that the country before you has changed completely—you have left northern Europe and central Europe for the south, you are in Mediterranean Europe. The second is when, after 700 miles of straight Roman roads, your road climbs a hill and from the top of it you see the Mediterranean sea, and at the sight of it I shout, like Xenophon's Greeks: 'Thalassa! Thalassa!'

We stayed for a week in Cassis at Fontcreuse, the Bell family being now established in their villa, and then we set off for Dieppe. I still in those days regarded travel much as I did in my district in Ceylon; I assumed that one could go on in a leisurely way anywhere, knowing one's eventual destination, but not thinking very much of what from day to day lay before one. I therefore mapped out what I thought would be a pleasant route through the centre of France, country which I had never been through. In fact, being fairly ignorant of geography, a subject which as a classical scholar I was never taught at school, I was completely unaware that the centre of France consisted of the massif central, the very formidable mountains of the Cévennes and Auvergne. I was also unaware that in early April one might run into heavy snowstorms on the top of these mountains. So I drove to Tarascon and, after sleeping there, started to drive through Alais and Florac to St Flour and Aurillac. I was rather dismayed later on in the morning to find myself confronted by a formidable, black mountain up which the road began to climb. We climbed and climbed; it grew blacker and blacker both on the earth and in the sky. The clouds seemed to descend upon our heads and we ran into a tremendous snowstorm. The scenery, such as one could see of it, reminded me of Wagner and Covent Garden, those absurdly melodramatic Valkyries' Rocks and Brünnhilde's cave. So Wagnerian was everything that I was hardly surprised when, driving at about fifteen miles an hour and peering through the snowstorm, I saw ahead of me suddenly the side of the mountain open into a long tunnel lit by electric lamps. So we passed through the Massif du Cantal, and, when we issued from the tunnel on the other side, it was into bright sunshine. Despite the sun, our troubles had not ended, and my drive from the Cantal to Dieppe was rather a nightmare. I had really only just learned to drive a car and knew very little about either its inside or its outside. I had not realised that the tyres were very worn and the roads very bad. In the 500 miles from the Cantal to Dreux, where at last I succeeded in buying new tyres, we punctured on an average every twenty-five miles. It seemed to me that there was hardly any road in France on which I had not grovelled in the mud changing wheels.

Such hazards of travel do, however, bring their compensations in curious meetings. On the day we passed through the Cantal in a grim, black, Wagnerian Auvergne hamlet of a few cottages I punctured immediately outside a cottage from which a man came out and offered to repair a tyre. It was raining hard and we went into the cottage and sat talking to the family. A girl of sixteen was sitting at a table writing a letter. The letter was to a 'pen-friend' in Brighton. The girl had never been more than twenty miles from her home, but there is an international organisation that organises these international pen-friends—and there she sat perched on the top of the mountain in the centre of France writing to a girl, whom she had never seen and never would see, who lived ten miles from us in Sussex. She showed us a photograph and the letters of her Sussex pen-friend, the daughter of an omnibus driver in Brighton. In half an hour we were on terms of warm friendship with the whole family. The internationalism of the savagely nationalistic world of the 1920s was remarkable.

To drive in a leisurely way through a foreign country, keeping one's ears and eyes open, is one of the best ways of getting a vision of both international politics and human nature. I had a curious example of this in 1935. Vanessa was in Rome where she had taken a house and studio for six months. We planned to spend the whole of May abroad, our idea being to drive through Holland, Germany, and Austria to Rome and to stay there for ten days or so. In 1935 people were just beginning to understand something of what Hitler and the Nazis were doing in Germany. I had only once been to that country: Virginia and I had stayed for a week in Berlin with the Nicolsons when Harold was still in the Diplomatic Service and in the Berlin Embassy. By 1935 Harold had abandoned diplomacy for politics—he was an M.P.—and journalism, but when I told him my plans for driving to Italy by way of Germany, he said that he had heard that the Foreign Office had advised Cecil Kisch of the India Office that it was inadvisable for Jews to travel in Germany. He thought it would be as well for me to consult someone in the F.O. It seemed to me absurd that any Englishman, whether Jew or Gentile, should hesitate to enter a European country. I remembered Palmerston's famous speech: *'Civis Romanus sum . . .'* and how he mobilised the British fleet and blockaded Greek ports on behalf of the British subject Don Pacifico, a Jew born in Gibraltar, in order to recover £150 damages done to this British subject's house in Piraeus. Surely, I thought, the British government in 1935 would insist that the Nazis and Hitler treat an English Jew as they would any other British subject. However, at that time I knew Ralph Wigram of the F.O.; he lived in Southease, the next village to Rodmell; so when we went down to Monks House, I rang him up and told him what Harold had said. Wigram said that he would rather not discuss the matter over the telephone and would come round and see me.

When Wigram appeared, I found his attitude rather odd. He said that it was quite true that the F.O. advised Jews not to go to Germany, and officially he had to give me that advice. But privately as a friend, he could say that he thought it nonsense, and that I should not hesitate to go to Germany. The only thing which I ought to be careful about was not to get mixed up in any Nazi procession or public ceremony. He also gave me a letter to Prince Bismarck, Counsellor at the German Embassy, and advised me to go and see him. So off I went to see Bismarck in the rather oppressive mansion in Carlton House Terrace. Bismarck was extremely affable—of course, my distinguished wife and I must go to Germany. There would be no difficulty of any sort, and he would give me an official letter which would ensure that all government servants would give me assistance if I needed it. He gave me a most impressive document in which Prince Bismarck called upon all German officials to show to the distinguished Englishman, Leonard Woolf, and his distinguished wife, Virginia Woolf, every courtesy and render them any assistance which they might require.

The sequel was amusing, for a marmoset made it quite unnecessary for me to use Bismarck's letter to protect me from the Nazis' anti-Semitism. At that time I had a marmoset called Mitz which accompanied me almost everywhere, sitting on my shoulder or inside my waistcoat. I had acquired her from Victor Rothschild. Victor and Barbara were then living in Cambridge. One hot summer afternoon we drove to Cambridge, dined with them and drove back to London after dinner. We dined in the garden and a rather rickety marmoset which Victor had bought in a junk shop and given to Barbara was hobbling about on the lawn. She climbed up on to my lap and remained with me the whole evening. A month later Victor wrote to me saying that they were going abroad for some time, and, as the marmoset seemed to have taken to me and I to the marmoset, would I look after her while they were away? I agreed and Mitz arrived in Rodmell. She was in very bad condition and I gradually got her fit. She became very fond of me and I of her, and when the Rothschilds returned to Cambridge I refused—much to their relief—to hand Mitz back to them.

Mitz was a curious character. I kept her alive for five years, which was a year longer, the marmoset keeper at the Zoo told me, than the Zoo had ever been able to keep a marmoset. She was eventually killed by a terrible cold snap at Christmas when the electricity failed for the whole of a bitter cold night at Rodmell. During the day she was always with me, but the moment it became dark in the evening she left me, scuttled across the room into a large birdcage which I kept full of scraps of silk. She rolled herself into a ball in the middle of the silk and slept until the next morning—the moment the sun rose, she left the cage and came over to me. She was extremely jealous, a trait which I on occasions took advantage of to outwit her. She was always quite free in the house, but I had to be careful not to let her get out into the garden at Rodmell by herself, for, if she did, she would climb up a tree and refuse to come down. When this happened, I usually succeeded in getting her back by climbing a ladder and holding out to her a butterfly net in which I had put the lid of a tin with a little honey on it. She was so fond of honey that usually she could not resist it and then I caught her in the net.

Late one summer afternoon on a Sunday, when we were just going to get into the car to drive back to London, she escaped into the garden at Rodmell and climbed about thirty foot up a lime-tree at the gate. When I called to her to come down, I could see her small head among the leaves watching me, but she would not budge. I tried the butterfly net trick, but not even the honey would tempt her. So I got Virginia to stand with me under the tree and I kissed her. Mitz came down as fast as she could and jumped on my shoulder chattering with anger. We successfully played the same trick on her another time when she got away into a large fig-tree and I could not dislodge her. She was rather fond of a spaniel which I had at the time and in the cold weather liked to snuggle up against the dog in front of a hot fire. She would eat almost anything. Meal-worms and fruit were regular articles of her diet. She once caught and ate a lizard and the Zoo keeper told me that in the open-air cage their marmosets would sometimes catch and eat sparrows. Mitz had a passion for macaroons and tapioca pudding. When given tapioca, she seized it in both hands and stuffed her mouth so full that large blobs of tapioca oozed out at both sides of her face.

I took Mitz with me when on 1 May 1935, we crossed from Harwich to the Hook of Holland. At that time I had a Lanchester 18 car with a Tickford hood so that, by winding the hood back, one could convert it from a closed-in saloon to a completely open car. Most of the day Mitz used to sit on my shoulder, but she would sometimes curl up and go to sleep among the luggage and coats on the back seat. For eight days we toured about all over Holland. Whenever I go to Holland, I feel at once that I have reached the apotheosis of bourgeois society. The food, the comfort, the cleanliness, the kindliness, the sense of age and stability, the curious mixture of beauty and bad taste, the orderliness of everything including even nature and the sea—all this makes one realise that here on the shores of the dyke-controlled Zuider Zee one has found the highest manifestation of the complacent civilisation of the middle classes. I have felt something of the same thing in Sweden and Denmark, but I do not think that the Scandinavians have ever reached quite the heights of domestication and complacency attained by the Dutch. It is, of course, easy and, particularly since 1847 and the Communist Manifesto, fashionable to pick holes in bourgeois civilisation or savagery, and I am sure that I should soon feel suffocated if I had to live my life in the featherbed civilisation of Delft or The Hague. Yet there is in fact a great deal to be said for it and for a short time it is very pleasant to feel that one is in a really civilised country from which nature has been expelled by something more efficacious than a fork. At any rate I prefer the tradition of comfortable civilisation in the Netherlands to that of Teutonic sentimental savagery across the border.

Mitz was a great success with the Dutch; wherever we went little groups of people would surround the car and go into ecstasies about 'the dear little creature'. On 9 May we crossed the frontier from Roermond into Germany near Jülich. Immediately I had my first distasteful taste of Nazism. When I went into the Customs office there was a peasant just ahead of me who had a loaded farm-cart. The Customs officer was sitting at a desk and behind him, on the wall was a large portrait of Hitler. The peasant did not take his cap off and the officer worked himself up into a violent tirade against the insolence of a swine who kept his cap on in front of the Führer's image. I do not know whether this exhibition was mainly for my benefit, but I felt with some disquiet that I had passed in a few yards from civilisation to savagery, and that perhaps it was just as well that I had Prince Bismarck's letter in my pocket.

The Customs man passed me through without abuse and I drove on to Cologne and from Cologne to Bonn. On the autobahn between these two towns I became more and more uneasy. We seemed to be the only car on the road, and all the way on both sides of it at intervals of twenty yards or so stood a soldier with a rifle. When I reached what must have been more or less the centre of Bonn, I turned a corner and found myself confronted by an excited German policeman who waved me back, shouting that the road was closed to traffic as the Herr Präsident was coming. I tried to find out from him whether there was any road open on which I could drive to Mainz, but he was too excited to do anything but shout that the Herr Präsident was coming.

I turned back and parked the car and we went to see Beethoven's house in order to revive our drooping spirits. Then we had a cup of tea and considered the situation. We were on the right bank of the Rhine and it seemed to me that if the Herr Präsident—whom I wrongly thought was Hitler; he was in fact Goering—was coming to Bonn on that bank, then the road to Mainz on the left bank must be open to traffic. What I had to do was to find a bridge over which I could drive to the left bank. Leaving the tea shop, I stopped a man and asked him how I could do this. He was an extremely kindly German, and he got into the car and guided me across the river. There we were faced by an inexplicable and disturbing sight. On each side of it the main road was lined with uniformed Nazis and at intervals with rows of schoolchildren carrying flags. There were flags everywhere and the singing of Nazi songs. One had to drive extremely slowly as the Nazis were drawn up so as to leave only a narrow strip for traffic. It seemed to me that these regimented crowds were obviously waiting for the Herr Präsident, but, if so, what on earth did it mean? Why were the roads on the right bank closed to traffic so that he could come safely to Bonn by them, if in fact these stormtroopers and schoolchildren were waiting to greet him on the main road, open to traffic, on the left bank?

At any rate, we had run straight into the kind of situation which Wigram had warned us to avoid. Here we were closely penned in by what, looking down the road ahead, seemed to be an unending procession of enthusiastic Nazis. But we soon found that there was no need for us to worry. It was a very warm day and I was driving with the car open; on my shoulder sat Mitz. I had to drive at about fifteen miles an hour. When they saw Mitz, the crowd shrieked with delight. Mile after mile I drove between the two lines of corybantic Germans, and the whole way they shouted 'Heil Hitler! Heil Hitler!' to Mitz and gave her (and secondarily Virginia and me) the Hitler salute with outstretched arm.

This went on, as I have said, for mile after mile, and eventually I could stand it no longer. I decided to turn off the road, go down to the river, and find a hotel where we could stay the night. On the bank of the Rhine, which seems to me one of the few really ugly rivers in the world, at a place called Unckel, we found a very large hotel. We were the only guests, and we had a curious experience there which threw an interesting light on the view which some Germans took of Hitler and the Nazis in 1935. We dined in an immense, long dining-room. We sat at a table at one end and at the other end the proprietor and his wife had their dinner. There was no other diner and a solitary waiter waited upon us. Towards the end of dinner the proprietor came over and asked us whether we had been satisfied. After some desultory conversation, I asked him whether he knew what the explanation was of the Herr Präsident, the closed and open roads, and the lines of expectant Nazis. He immediately shut up and said that he knew nothing about that, but he did not leave us and, after some rambling conversation, asked me where we came from. When I said from Tavistock Square in London, he suddenly changed into a completely different person: he saw that to an Englishman who lived in Tavistock Square it was safe for him to say anything.

His lamentable tale came pouring out of him. He had been a waiter for many years on the banks of the Thames at Richmond. Then he had returned to Germany in order to marry; he himself would have liked to go back to England, but his wife could not speak English, so he became manager of the Unckel hotel. Before the Nazis appeared on the scene, it was a pleasant and prosperous place; it was always full of young people, for students used to come up the river from Bonn and enjoy themselves. A short time before Hitler began to dominate the scene, our melancholy host had been offered the managership of a London hotel, actually in Tavistock Square itself—there were tears in his eyes as he told us this. He wanted to accept, but his wife could not face a great foreign city in which she would not be able to speak a word of the language. So he refused. Then the Nazis came into power and life in Unckel became hell. 'If one says a word of criticism,' he said, 'one is in danger of being beaten up. It is all processions and marching and drilling. And my business is ruined, for the students in Bonn are kept so busy marching and drilling that they hardly ever now come up the river from Bonn. *Und nun bin ich ins Gefängnis* (and now I'm in prison). They will never let me out; it's impossible to get out of this country.' Here the waiter, who had been standing and silently listening, burst out: 'I'm going to get out. It's terrible here—I'm going to get out—Oh, yes, one can—I shall go to America—that's the place to live in.'

Next day we left the manager, his wife, and the waiter in tears, and drove through Mainz and Darmstadt to Heidelberg, and from Heidelberg through Stuttgart and Ulm to Augsburg, and from Augsburg through Munich to the Austrian frontier, and so to Innsbruck, where on 12 May snow was falling. We did not enjoy this; there was something sinister and menacing in the Germany of 1935. There is a crude and savage silliness in the German tradition which, as one drove through the sunny Bavarian countryside, one felt beneath the surface and saw, above it, in the gigantic notices outside the villages informing us that Jews were not wanted.

Not that we had any difficulty anywhere. We forgot about Bismarck's letter, for Mitz carried us through trumphantly in all situations. Pig-tailed schoolchildren, yellow-haired Aryan Fräuleins, blonde blowsy Fraus, grim stormtroopers went into ecstasies over *das liebe, kleine Ding*. What was it? Where did it come from? What did it eat? No one ever said a sensible word about Mitz, but, thanks to her, our popularity was immense. In Augsburg in a traffic jam a smiling policeman made cars get out of the way for her and for us. It was obvious to the most anti-Semitic stormtrooper that no one who had on his shoulder such a 'dear little thing' could be a Jew.

As we approached the Austrian frontier, I told Virginia that I proposed to show Bismarck's letter to the Customs officers in order to see what effect it would have. When I drew up at the barrier, the usual scene took place. As soon as the officer saw Mitz on my shoulder, he shouted to his wife and children to come out and see '*das liebe kleine Ding*'. We were soon surrounded by two or three women, four or five children, and several uniformed men. The usual '*Achs*!' and '*Os*!', the usual gush of gush and imbecile questions. I thought that we would never get away, but eventually they calmed down and passed us through without any examination of anything. At the last moment, shaking hands all round, I presented Prince Bismarck's letter. The effect was instantaneous and quite different from that of Mitz, the marmoset. The chief officer drew himself up, bowed, saluted, clicked his heels together, drew all the uniformed men up in line, and, as we drove away, they all saluted us.

Next day we crossed the Brenner and drove down through Italy to Rome, staying a night at Verona, at Bologna, and at Perugia. How different in those menacing days was the Fascism of the Italians from the Nazism of the Germans! Beneath the surface of Italian life the vulgar savagery of Mussolini and his thugs who murdered Rosselli was, no doubt, much the same as that of Hitler and Goering; but whereas German history has never allowed civilisation to penetrate for any length of time, either widely or deeply, into the German people, Italian history has been civilising the inhabitants of Italy so deeply and so perpetually for over 2,000 years that no savages, from Alaric and his Germanic hordes to Mussolini and his native Fascists, have ever been able to make the Italians as uncivilised as the Germans. In 1935, therefore, whether Jew or Gentile, you did not require either a marmoset or a Prince Bismarck to protect you from the native savages.

The native savages of Italy delighted in Mitz in the same childish way as those of Holland, Germany, and Austria. It is perhaps interesting, from the anthropological and historical angles, to recall the reactions of the people of Holland, Germany, Austria, Italy, and France to Mitz in 1935. In twenty-five days I spent in the first four countries dozens of Dutch, Germans, Austrians, and Italians spoke to me about Mitz. They all made one or two of five or six standard remarks or asked one or two of five or six standard questions. The remarks and questions were banal, childish, or sometimes incredibly silly. Mitz was mistaken for practically every existing small animal including a rat and a bat. On Sunday 26 May, I crossed the frontier into France at Ventimiglia and had *déjeuner* at Menton, intending to drive on and spend the night at Aix. The Sunday traffic along the Riviera road was so abominable that after Nice I decided to turn north and drive by the unfrequented minor roads to Draguignan and so to Aix. When we got to Draguignan, we had had enough of it, and we decided to stay there for the night.

The stretch of country which runs north of the Riviera road from Grasse to Draguignan is grey and grim; Draguignan itself and its inhabitants are rather grey, grim, and chilly. The woman in the hotel, when she saw Mitz, gave her a chilly reception and refused to allow me to bring her into the hotel. We had at last, after travelling 2,469 miles on the continent of Europe, reached a country in which a marmoset was not a dear, little thing. I left Mitz for the night locked up in the car on the road in front of the hotel. Next morning, as soon as I got up, I went out to see that she was all right. She was sitting on the steering wheel and a soldier was standing on the pavement watching her through the window. I took her out and fed her and the soldier watched and talked to me about her. He was an ordinary soldier, and he talked about her in an adult, intelligent way—he was the first man, woman, or child who had done so in 2,469 miles and he was also the first Frenchman who had talked to me about Mitz. The reaction of the man in the street to a marmoset sitting on the steering wheel of a car teaches one something, I think, about the intellectual tradition, even the civilisation, of the country to which he belongs. There are a good many things which I do not like in the French tradition, but its scepticism and respect for intelligence seem to me admirable.

I must now say something about my writing and my political activities in the years between the wars; the two occupations were closely connected; they were complementary attempts, the one theoretical and the other practical, to understand and to help to solve what seemed to me the most menacing problems left to us by the war in a devastated and distracted world. There were in fact two vast, oecumenical problems which threatened, and still threaten, mankind and are interrelated: first, the prevention of war and the development of international government; secondly, the dissolution of the empires of European states in Asia and Africa which seemed to me inevitable and which would cause as much misery to the world as war unless the Governments of the great imperial powers recognised the inevitability, and deliberately worked for an orderly transference of power to the native populations, educated for self-government by their rulers. I had already begun to think and write about these two questions before 1920. In *International Government* I had shown that in fact the relations of states had for long been regulated or not regulated by a system partly of complete anarchy and partly of rudimentary international government, and I had argued that war could not be prevented in the complicated modern world unless some kind of League of Nations system could be established under which the relations of sovereign states would to some extent be controlled by law and order, by international government. I continued to write about this, editing for instance *The Intelligent Man's Way to Prevent War* in 1933, but, as I shall explain more fully in a moment, between 1920 and 1939 I became engrossed in a much wider and more fundamental subject of which the problem of preventing war was only a part. As regards imperialism, I lectured on this subject and I wrote two things specifically about it: *Imperialism and Civilisation* in 1928 and *The League and Abyssinia* in 1936.

But as a writer, during the twenty years between the wars, and even beyond that for another fourteen years until 1953, I devoted myself to a single subject, doing a great deal of work upon it and writing three books, *After the Deluge* Vol. I (1931), *After the Deluge* Vol. II (1939), and *Principia Politica* (1953) which was really intended to be the third volume of *After the Deluge*. There are 1,000 pages in these books and, I suppose, about 300,000 words. To all intents and purposes they have been a complete failure, but, though like most people I would rather succeed than fail—whether in a game of chess or bowls or in one's life work—in many ways I do not regret them. No doubt owing to the delusion of parentage, I see in my offspring merits invisible to other people. I still think that the subject of these volumes is of immense importance to the historian, the philosopher, the psychologist, and the politician, and that it has very rarely been posed and faced in the way I tried to pose and face it, and I still think that there are a certain number of words out of the 300,000 written by me which contribute something of truth and importance to the subject. As this is an autobiography of my mind as well as of my body, I propose to say something about this.

A good deal of mythological nonsense has been written about the impact of the 1914 war upon left-wing intellectuals, a pack or sect to which, I suppose, I have always belonged. The myth is that pre-war liberals all over Europe believed in the inevitability of progress and the complete rationality of man, the political animal, and that, as the war destroyed the foundations of their political beliefs, they became completely disorientated and exploded. Most intellectuals, dead or living, about whom I have known anything, have resembled Diogenes and the author of *Ecclesiastes* rather than Mr Chasuble, Tom Pinch, and Mr Micawber rolled into one innocent and imbecile optimist. I, like nearly all of them, have never believed that progress is inevitable or that man is politically rational. I was born, as I have recorded, in 1880 into a comfortable, professional middle-class family in Kensington. We had been affluent while my father was alive; his death made the position of the family for many years economically precarious. But in Kensington and Putney, as St Paul's School and Trinity College, Cambridge, life was lived in an atmosphere of social stability and security. The battle of Waterloo was fought eighty-five years before I went up to Cambridge; the Crimean war had been fought nearly thirty and the Franco-German war nearly ten years before I was born. There were some signs that European civilisation might develop more widely and quickly on the basis of liberty, equality, and fraternity in the twentieth century. Despite colonial wars and rivalry, and despite the endemic danger to Europe from the confrontation of the Triple and the Dual Alliance, to be moderately optimistic about the social and political future of the world was in 1900 not unreasonable.

Moderate optimism was, I think, the attitude of most intellectuals and intelligent people—not of course synonymous—during my lifetime up to the year 1914. The war was a tremendous shock to intellectuals, as it was to the world and all its inhabitants. When Austria invaded Serbia and Germany Belgium, it was one of the great turning-points in human history. There was no longer any place for 'moderate optimism'; as far as I was concerned, it seemed to me that events had proved that in the modern world war and civilisation were incompatible, and that, when the war ended the supreme political problem was to find means, if possible, for preventing war. That meant that one must find the chief causes of war and one must discover methods to destroy or counteract those causes. As in all cases of political action, to do this required the use of reason. To find the causes of social or political phenomena you have to use your reason to analyse a series of complicated situations or events; to find means of influencing or altering the series of events requires a constructive use of reason. To say this does not mean that one believes that human beings always act rationally. If you say to a man: 'If you walk over that precipice, you will fall 300 feet on a hard rock and almost certainly kill yourself', you are using reason analytically and constructively to explain the truth about a situation, cause and effect and the result of future action, to an individual. You do not imply any belief that *he will* use his reason and so avoid falling over the precipice. The problems of history and society are subject to precisely the same laws of reason and unreason, cause and effect. It is as simple as that, though unfortunately in history, the simplicity is delusive because of the immense complication of historical situations and events, and therefore of their causes and effects. Moreover, individuals are rather more rational about walking over precipices than states and governments

When I began to consider the history of war in Europe in the light of analytic reason, it seemed to me, as it did to many other people, that war would sooner or later be inevitable unless there was at least a rudimentary system of international law and order which would provide for the peaceful settlement of international disputes. That was the theme of my book *International Government*, in which I drew the outline of the structure and functions of a League of Nations. But I never thought or said that a League of Nations, even an effective League, was the only thing necessary to prevent war. No large conglomeration of civilised human beings has ever been able to exist anywhere in comparative peace and prosperity without a system of law and order, without some kind of government whose power to enforce the law against the individual law-breaker rests ultimately upon some kind of force. To say that does not mean that one believes that one only had to have laws, courts, and police to produce law-abiding individuals and a peaceful and civilised government and state. All this is also true of international society in which the units are independent sovereign states.

Ruminating on these matters I had come to three conclusions: first, that in the twentieth century science and industry made war and civilisation incompatible; secondly, that without some kind of League system war would be practically and eventually inevitable; third, that war was part of a much wider social phenomenon and problem, namely the government of human beings and what I call communal psychology. It was this third conclusion which led me into spending the next twenty years in writing three books. My mind led me down this path in the following way. When I wrote *International Government*, I did a good deal of reading and thinking about the wars of the eighteenth and nineteenth centuries and about the development of international government. The more I read and thought, the more interested I became in certain historical facts.

I found that historians accepted it as a fact that the principalities and powers, the captains and the kings, the governments and statesmen who 'made war' on one another had always done so for certain 'objects', and apparently the common people who fought and died in the armies of these rulers accepted these objects until the moment of either final victory or final defeat. It seemed to me curious that, when one examined and analysed these 'objects' for which wars had been fought in Europe ever since the revolutionary and Napoleonic wars, one found that they consisted apparently of beliefs and desires, and that the objects, the beliefs and desires, for which we fought the 1914 war appeared to be precisely the same as those for which our ancestors had fought in 1815 at Waterloo—indeed, they were not very different from those for which, according to Herodotus, the soldiers and sailors of Sparta and Athens fought against Xerxes at Marathon, Thermopylae, and Salamis 2,400 years ago. The revolutionary armies towards the end of the eighteenth century fought for liberty, equality, and fraternity and went into battle singing the Marseillaise; the Napoleonic army fought its way to the walls of Moscow for the same objects and, according to Schubert's famous song, in defeat struggled back to France through the snows of Russia and Poland still singing the Marseillaise. If you open the pages of Herodotus, written, I repeat, over 2,000 years before, and read the wonderful speech in which the Greek unsuccessfully tries to explain to Xerxes—sitting on the shores of the Hellespont and reviewing his mighty fleet—tries unsuccessfully to explain to him what it means to be a Greek and a free man and why one Greek will beat three Persians because he is fighting for—you will find that to all intents and purposes the Greek is saying that he is fighting for liberty, equality, and fraternity. And when in August 1914 the British Government, through the voices of the Prime Minister, Henry Asquith, and the Foreign Secretary, Sir Edward Grey, good liberals echoing the voices of Themistocles and Leonidas, Mirabeau and Lafayette, told us that we were fighting to protect the rights of small nations, the freedom of Serbia and Belgium, from aggression by the Great Powers Germany and Austria, were not statesmen and history once more proclaiming that governments and individuals were fighting a war for liberty, equality, and fraternity?

It seemed to me that, if one wanted to understand the causes of war and perhaps discover some means of preventing it, one must investigate more closely these statements of historians, generals, and prime ministers that wars are fought by nations for objects like liberty, equality, and fraternity. If the statements are true, wars are fought for beliefs and desires, for, if you are called upon and agree to fight for liberty, it means that you believe liberty to be so good and you desire it so deeply that you are prepared to fight and die for it. Moreover, if these beliefs and desires really do influence or cause communal actions like war, then they can accurately be described as communal beliefs and desires. If in 1914 the British answered Kitchener's appeal and joined up because they believed Asquith's appeal to fight for liberty, then it is true that there was a general acceptance in the community of the belief about and the desire for liberty and also a general agreement that these communal beliefs and desires should lead to communal action in war.

Such communal beliefs and desires connected with war seemed to me part of something much wider which I called communal psychology. For according to historians and statesmen communal action is almost always influenced or determined by communal beliefs and desires. For instance, they would hold that the communal belief that political equality was desirable and that it was unattainable unless every adult male had a vote determined the communal action in Britain which produced the Reform Acts of 1832, 1867, and 1884. Again, according to history, the political and economic beliefs and desires of a German Jew enunciated in his book *Das Kapital* in 1867 and in the Communist Manifesto became fifty years later the communal beliefs and desires which caused the Bolshevik revolution and has subsequently led to the spread of communism and the emergence of communist governments all over the world. Again, the paranoid beliefs and desires of a disgruntled Austrian corporal about Germans and Jews became the communal beliefs and desires of Nazism and the Third Reich which produced the second great war and the murder of over five million Jews in concentration camps and gas chambers.

I thought, and still think, that there are some very important and very strange things implied in these beliefs of historians and politicians regarding communal psychology. In every case they imply that some social end or situation is desirable or not desirable and that it can be attained or prevented by certain communal action. If this be true, it means that communal action or the events of history can be and are determined partly by emotional judgments of value—this or that is desirable or not desirable—and partly by reason, the convincing of large numbers of people that something, which is communally desirable, can only be attained by some specific communal action.

Though this is always assumed to be true both in theory or in practice—whether in Thucydides's history of the Peloponnesian war, Gibbon's *Decline and Fall*, a meeting of the Cabinet in 10 Downing Street, or of the Praesidium in the Kremlin—there are practically no serious studies by sociologists, psychologists, or historians of how this process of interaction between communal beliefs and desires and communal actions works or indeed of whether in fact it does work. I decided that, though I was not a professional sociologist, historian, or psychologist, I would try to do as an amateur what the professionals had left undone. In 1920 I had finished and published my book *Empire and Commerce in Africa* and in that year I began to read for and study this problem of communal psychology. Though the subject was vast and complicated, my object could be stated clearly and simply. I proposed to study intensively the years 1789 to 1914 and to try to discover what the relation between the communal beliefs and desires regarding liberty, equality, and fraternity and communal action had been during those years, i.e. what, if any, had been the effect of those communal beliefs and desires not merely upon war and peace but upon historical events generally. I had no idea in 1920 that I should be working and writing on this subject for the next thirty-three years.

I worked at it, it is true, continually for those thirty-three years but I had so many other occupations that I spent a good deal less than half my time upon these books. It was not until 1931 that I published the first volume of *After the Deluge*; it was concerned with democracy and democratic psychology as they developed in the eighteenth century and in the American and French revolutions. Eight years later I published *After the Deluge*, Vol. II, which dealt with the communal psychology of the years 1830-1832, the effect of the communal beliefs and desires regarding liberty, equality, and fraternity on the historical events of those years. 1939, the year of its publication, brought down upon Europe and the world the second great war. The years in which the first two volumes had been published had turned out to be between the deluges. I intended to write a third volume, but obviously it could not be entitled *After the Deluge*, Vol. III. It was Maynard Keynes who said to me that what I was really trying to do in these volumes was to analyse the principles of politics and I ought to call the third volume *Principia Politica*. I followed his advice, but it took me a long time to write the book, and *Principia Politica* was not published until 1953.

These three volumes have been, as I have said, to all intents and purposes a failure. The first of the three was published as a Penguin and I occasionally still get a letter of appreciation from some unknown person which faintly stirs in me the pleasure of authorship. All three on the whole had an unfavourable press, and *Principia Politica* was received with derision by the Oxford professional historians who do so much reviewing and who rapped me over the knuckles for having the effrontery to be a member of 'Bloomsbury' and use a title which recalled the works of Newton, Bertrand

Russell, and G. E. Moore.

I find it quite difficult to be certain in my own mind as to what 'in the bottom of my heart' is my real attitude towards my own books and criticism of them. My disappointment at the reception and fate of these books has been fairly deep, though not very prolonged. No doubt I was considerably annoyed by reviews which dealt at length with 'Bloomsbury' and the title of the book but never so much as mentioned what the book was attempting to do. No one likes to spend twenty-three years of his life and nearly 300,000 words on something which is invisible to a Fellow of All Souls or Magdalen. I still think that there is a little more in them than was seen by the professional historians who reviewed them. In 1953 at the age of seventy-three, however, I had to make up my mind whether I should carry on with my original intention and plan to write a fourth and even a fifth volume. I decided not to do so. The three volumes were a failure and I was not prepared to spend another five or ten years and another 200,000 words with the same result. I was, as I say, disappointed, but I do not think that the hurt went very deep or was prolonged. It is interesting, I think, to observe the attitude of different writers (and of oneself) to their writings. I have produced about twenty books, and, like most writers, I probably have, in the pit of my stomach, a better opinion of them than other people. But I am not really much concerned about them and people's opinion of them, once they have been published, and I do not feel the slightest interest in their fate after my death. It is here that I find the attitude of so many writers, good or bad, very strange. They seem to regard the fate of their books as if it were the fate of themselves and they seem to see in the book shops and libraries an unending struggle between mortality and immortality. I could never quite understand Virginia's feeling about her books and their reputation in the world. She seemed to feel their fate to be almost physically and mentally part of her fate. I do not think that she had any belief in life after death, but she appeared to feel that somehow or other she was involved in their life after death. Being so intimately a part of herself, a hurt to them was felt as a hurt to her, and her mortality or immortality was a part of their mortality or immortality.

The crux of the matter is perhaps there, in the immortality of the soul! The difference in the attitude of different writers to their work probably depends upon whether or not deep within them, even unconsciously, they still believe that they may be immortal. I suspect that Virginia, though she did not believe in life after death, did believe in her life after death in *The Waves*, and not merely in the life of *The Waves* after her death. Even if I had written *The Waves* or *Hamlet*, I do not think I could possibly have felt like that. I cannot believe that death is anything but complete personal annihilation. I cannot, therefore, feel any *personal* interest or involvement in anything of mine after I have been annihilated. I should like to know what happens on the day after my death, e.g. what horse wins the Derby if I die the day before Derby day, and I should like to know what happens to my books after my death, but as I shall never know either, annihilation makes it all one for me. The fate of my books, even before my death, loses some of its importance for me, and this in turn diminishes both the pleasure in success or the pain of failure.

And now I must leave books and theory, and say something of the practice of politics. As a practical politician, I worked mainly in the Labour Party and the Fabian Society, but before I deal with that side of my life, I must mention two other political activities. The first was journalistic. In 1930 I helped to start the *Political Quarterly*. The main credit for successfully launching this journal and for its still being successfully published today, thirty-six years later, must go to Professor William A. Robson. Willie Robson's enthusiasm and pertinacity succeeded in getting enough capital to start the journal—by no means an easy task—and an admirable group of writers to write for it. He and Kingsley Martin were the first joint-editors, and the Editorial Board consisted of A. M. Carr-Saunders, T. E. Gregory, Harold Laski, Maynard Keynes, Sir Arthur (later Lord) Salter, Sir E. D. (later Lord) Simon, and myself. It was, as the names show, Left Wing politically, but of irreproachable respectability. It proclaimed its object as 'to discuss social and political questions from a progressive point of view; to act as a clearing-house of ideas and a medium of constructive thought'. Its standard was from the beginning extremely high and has remained so for thirty-six years. A journal of this kind cannot be popular; it is written very largely by experts for an elite, for Members of Parliament and civil servants in the arena of practical politics, and in the academic arena by experts for experts in sociology, politics, law, and history. It can only succeed, indeed it can only justify its existence, by providing ideas for or influencing the ideas of a comparatively small number of 'men at the top'.

When Kingsley became editor of the *New Statesman*, I took his place as joint editor with Willie Robson on the *Political Quarterly*, and for some time during the war I was sole editor and even to some extent its publisher. I continued to be an editor until 1959 and remained on as literary editor until 1962. Having been for over thirty years editorially responsible for it, I am necessarily not an unprejudiced witness regarding its merits and influence. Practically all journalists, from the great Press Lords down to the humblest reporter, suffer from the grossest delusions about the 'influence' of the newspaper which they own, edit, or write for. The megalomania probably increases as you go up from the humble reporter through the pompous editor to the paranoiac owner. I am not sure that the evidence, such as it is, does not point to the fact that the larger the circulation of a paper, the less influence it has upon the opinions of its readers, or even that the influence of every paper is in inverse proportion to the number of copies sold or to the number of people who buy or read it. Certainly the millions who read the popular press seem to be singularly impervious to its propaganda, particularly political propaganda, for vast numbers must vote Labour who habitually read anti-Labour dailies. I do not know whether this should be a subject for rejoicing among the angels in heaven or the Left Wing intellectuals on earth. It depends upon what is the explanation of this curious phenomenon. If the millions who read the popular dailies are interested only in sport, battle, murder, and sex, and therefore are inoculated against the opinions of the proprietor and editor, there is not much reason for rejoicing; but if large numbers have learnt to doubt whether the Northcliffes and Beaverbrooks of the twentieth century are good political advisers to follow, I should feel faintly encouraged.

I feel some encouragement too when I contemplate the other end of the scale where are journals of small circulation like the *Political Quarterly*. There is no doubt that, if their standards, both journalistic and intellectual, are high, they can have considerable influence. The reason is that they are, as I have said, written by experts for experts, or, from another point of view, they are professional or trade papers. The *Political Quarterly* is partly a technical paper in which the professional politician, the administrator, or the civil servant can find information and ideas of the greatest importance to his work and unobtainable elsewhere. No one reads the popular dailies for serious ideas, and practically no one takes their ideas seriously; their main function is entertainment, to titillate the universal desire for sex, violence, gambling, and the royal family. No one reads an article by Professor Robson on local government or by Sir Sydney Caine on the common market for entertainment or for any form of sexual or monarchical titillation, but they may be absorbed and fascinated by the ideas. That is why we were able to start the journal with a capital of a few hundred pounds and we have been able to go on for thirty-six years without having to raise any more capital. It is perhaps also the reason why its influence has been much larger than its circulation.

I have said that I dislike journalism and editorship, because as soon as one has finished off one number, one has to begin to think about the next. This applied to the editorship of the *Political Quarterly*, but as there were three months instead of seven days, as with the *Nation* and *New Statesman*, between each issue, the perpetual turning of the wheel was longer and slower. On the whole I enjoyed my work on it, because I was extremely interested in the ideas with which it dealt and was working with people pursuing the same objects. I also enjoyed the second by-product of my political activities. In 1938 I was appointed a Member of the National Whitley Council for Administrative and Legal Departments of the Civil Service, and I remained a member for the next seventeen years.

The nature of the work of the Whitley Council for the Civil Service is not widely known. It consisted, so far as I was concerned, of sitting three of four times a year on arbitration cases. I found the work extremely interesting and even sometimes amusing, and also exasperating. The British Civil Service does not strike, and an elaborate procedure has been devised in the Whitley Council system for the peaceful settlement of economic disputes, i.e. for determining scales of payment and conditions of employment without resort to strikes or lock-outs. In 1938 the staff side of the Civil Service was organised in the Civil Service Clerical Association, which was in fact the civil servant's trade union. Any claim by a class or section of the Service for higher pay or improved conditions was made to the Treasury through the Clerical Association and negotiations then began between the Treasury and the Association. If agreement was reached, well and good, but if, after a time, the two sides could not agree, the claim was remitted to arbitration. The arbitration tribunal consisted of a permanent chairman, who was a lawyer appointed by the government, and two other arbitrators drawn from two panels. One panel was appointed by the Treasury, and consisted mainly of Directors of banks or railway companies; the other consisted of persons nominated by the staff side, by the Clerical Association. The Association had asked me to agree to serve and had nominated me for their panel.

As Assistant Government Agent in the Hambantota District of Ceylon for nearly three years, I had a fair amount of judicial experience, for as Police Magistrate and District Judge I had had to try both criminal and civil cases. To try any kind of case in a judicial capacity I find extraordinarily fascinating. The fascination to me consists largely in the curiously complicated state of mind into which you, as a judge, have to get, if you are to be a good judge. Your mind, like Caesar's Gaul, has to be divided into three parts, and yet, like Gaul, maintain its unity, First, your mind must work intellectually with great quickness and concentration upon the facts, for the first essential is that the judge should understand and interpret the facts, which are often connected with spheres of life and activities of which the judge has no previous experience. (In Civil Service arbitration cases one was continually having to understand and interpret very complicated facts about the details of work or occupations of which one was quite ignorant before one began to try the case.) I thoroughly enjoy this kind of intellectual problem. Secondly, no one can be a good judge unless he can combine, with this quick intellectual understanding of facts, an intuitive sensitiveness to human witnesses and their evidence. Often it is only by hearing and, as it were, feeling a witness that you can accurately interpret and assess the value of his evidence.[1] The third requisite of a

[1] This is well understood and theoretically admitted in British Courts of Appeal, though not always honoured in practice by Appeal Court judges. In Ceylon I learned by experience that, where there was a direct conflict of evidence, often suddenly some small thing, almost impossible to describe accurately—a gesture or movement of the witness perhaps—would reveal to one where the truth lay. Of course, one may have deluded oneself, though there were cases in which I would have staked my life on the accuracy of my judgment. The Appeal Court judge did not always agree. I still remember after fifty years a case in which a villager suddenly appeared in the kachcheri hauling along a man and a cow, claiming loudly and passionately that it was his cow and that the man had stolen it. There was a complete conflict of evidence and suddenly one of the witnesses said something in such a way that I was absolutely convinced that the cow had been stolen. I gave my verdict accordingly and it was set aside in appeal. I am certain that thus the thief obtained the cow, and after my death, if I find myself in heaven, the first thing I

good judge is, perhaps, in some ways the most difficult—it is complete and unfailing impartiality. Complacent prejudice is the occupational disease of judges. It can make the judge incapable of understanding and interpreting the facts or of judging the character of a witness and the value of his evidence. On the bench one has to be perpetually on one's guard against oneself, to prevent one's previous beliefs and prejudices interfering with one's acceptance or rejection of facts and arguments. But still more necessary is it consciously to watch and thwart one's own instinctive prejudices for and against persons. A woman enters the box oozing feminine charm—how difficult it is to regard her and her evidence exactly as one does the next witness who fills one with physical repulsion. And it requires an even more ruthless act of will against oneself to force oneself to judge with complete impartiality the value of the evidence of a man whose appearance you dislike.

This point is to me so interesting that I cannot resist saying a word or two more about it. The behaviour of Lord Hewart in the Court of Appeal, described by me on pages 287-8, is a good example of judicial injustice caused, in part, by the judge allowing his prejudice against a man's appearance to make him give a grossly inequitable judgment. I once watched an even worse exhibition of prejudice by Mr Justice Avory at the Old Bailey. I had been summoned as a juror and was waiting in court for the next case while Avory tried a working class woman for stealing a piece of luggage at Victoria Station. There was no doubt about the facts. She had been convicted several times of the same offence: she loitered on a railway station platform and walked off with the most likely looking suitcase of some first-class passenger. There was nothing against her character except this inveterate habit of pinching first-class passengers' luggage. She was not attractive to look at, but I was convinced by everything she did and said that, apart from this habit, she was an exceptionally nice person. If ever there was a case of a criminal whose crime was in the eyes of God and medical science not a crime, but a symptom of mental or emotional disorder which might well be curable, there it stood in the dock facing us all in the dingy court, including Mr Justice Avory and the jury. I say that it might well have been curable because I happened to have had per-

---

shall do is to ask Saint Peter whether my judgment was correct. I am sure that he will answer: 'Yes'.

sonal knowledge of a similar case in a very different walk of life from that of the North Country working-class woman being tried by Avory. I knew a young man, born into a hightly respectable professional family, himself in a first-class professional post after a successful university career. Suddenly he was arrested for precisely the same offence as this woman, and it was discovered that he had habitually for some time stolen luggage at railway stations. Like her, normal and law abiding in every other way, he had this uncontrollable compulsion to steal suitcases from railway station platforms. He had the good fortune to be tried by an intelligent and sympathetic judge and he was discharged on condition that he took psychiatric treatment. He did so and was completely cured, ending his life as a respected member of a learned profession.

Very different was the treatment which the working-class woman received from Mr Justice Avory. The indignation which I felt while I watched and listened to him as he summed up rises again in me today. He was an exquisitely elegant man in his wig and gown and immaculate lace, and behind the icy ruthlessness of his pitiless summing up against her I felt the righteous indignation of the first-class passenger confronting the thief who had stolen his suitcase. The jury rightly found her guilty and Avory gave her the maximum sentence. Justice had been done, but—

> A man may see how this world goes with no eyes. Look with thine ears: see how yond justice rails upon yond simple thief. Hark in thine ear: change places; and, handy-dandy, which is the justice, which is the thief?

But I must return to the Civil Service Arbitration Tribunal. There, of course, there was no 'simple thief' before us, but, handy-dandy, much the same attitude was required, if one was to be a good arbitrator, as was necessary if one was to be a good High Court judge in the Old Bailey. The procedure was that, when one was chosen from the panel to try some case, one received the detailed claim by the Association or, in some cases, a trade union, and the answer by the Treasury, both in writing. Then on the day fixed for the hearing the three arbitrators heard both sides and any witnesses that they wished to call. When I first became an arbitrator, the case for the staff side was almost always conducted by W. J. Brown, Secretary of the Civil Service Clerical Association. A very able and rather flamboyant man, he was a first-class advocate, and, as he had considerable experience and was meticulous in mastering every detail in the most complicated claim, the case of the staff side was always admirably presented to the court whenever he appeared. I was often greatly interested and amused by the psychological display when William John Brown, who had been educated in the Salmestone Elementary School, Margate, and the Sandwich Grammar School, and had begun his career as a boy clerk in the Civil Service, on one side, confronted a young Treasury official in the Administrative Class, educated at Winchester and New College, Oxford, on the other. Winchester and Oxford were often no match for Margate and Sandwich.

The work was often very interesting. The occupational diversity of the hundreds of thousands of persons—or is it millions?—employed by the state is amazing, and the arbitrators almost always had to get a detailed knowledge of the work of claimants in order to determine what should be a fair wage or salary for the work which they did. In the course of my service on the Tribunal I learned all about the hourly work of the cohort of women who clean out the government offices in Whitehall, foresters in the north of Scotland, the men who talk down aeroplanes at certain airports in fog, and a small and peculiar class of men in the secret service. In order to try the last case, the Tribunal had to be indoctrinated and de-indoctrinated (if that was the correct word) by an army officer. Though this infinite variety made the whole business much more interesting for the arbitrator, the longer I served on the Arbitration Tribunal, the more crazily irrational the whole industrial structure of the Civil Service appeared to me. The Service was divided into classes, e.g. administrative, executive, clerical, and there were a certain number of subclasses and grades. But throughout this enormous business each of the hundreds of government occupations had, on the face of it, a scale of pay and conditions of employment peculiar to itself. On the other hand, the Civil Service Clerical Association, the organized scientific workers, and the trade unions claimed that throughout government employment similar work should entitle the worker to similar pay, and the Treasury agreed. The consequence is that, if 502 workers in occupation A receive a 5 per cent increase in the scale of their pay, 5,003 workers in occupation D will probably claim a similar increase on the ground that their work is similar to that of occupation A. I should guess that about eighty per cent of the claims which I had to try in my seventeen years on the Tribunal were of this kind. This meant that one had to listen to a detailed exposition of the exact nature of the work in each occupation and then judge whether they were sufficiently similar to justify a similar scale of pay. And one knew that if one assimilated the scale of, say, D to that of A, it was quite probable that the increase of the scale of D would provoke a claim from occupation E and occupation F to a similar increase.

The inevitable result of this system is an unending chain reaction of claims, a successful claim in one part of the Service setting off one or more claims somewhere else. The amount of wasted time and money in negotiations and arbitrations must be considerable. I am sure that much could be done to rationalize the structure of the Civil Service in this respect, though to do so would require courage and determination. If, as was proved again and again on the Tribunal, the work and conditions of occupations A to E, for instance, are so similar that the Tribunal has to give them the same scale of pay and conditions of employment, then those who work in the five occupations should all be recruited into one large government service Division, divided into Classes, each with its fixed scale of pay. This rationalisation and reclassification of government employment ought to be done by a Special Commission. It might not be possible to apply the new classification and pay structure to people already in government employ, but it could be applied to all recruits after a certain date. I do not suppose that it would ever be possible to rationalise the whole government service, from top to bottom, in this way; there would always be some occupations so peculiar that their pay and conditions could not be assimilated to any other. But there would not be a great number, and the vast majority of government employees could equitably and efficiently be recruited as, say, a member of Class IV of Division X in the Civil Service. If they were, the work of the Civil Service Arbitration Tribunal would dwindle.

My exit from the Tribunal after seventeen years amused me. Though I was on the panel nominated by the staff, I always considered that, as a member of the Tribunal, I had to be completely impartial. And on the whole, I think, we all of us were pretty impartial. Our decisions were nearly always unanimous. On two or three occasions only I found myself in a minority of one; once the chairman and I were on one side, and the Treasury arbitrator on the other. The written statements of the Treasury case were nearly always admirable and the statement of claims by the Civil Service Clerical Association were usually good, but the claims from other bodies were sometimes set out badly. In 1954 one of the big unions put in a claim for a large number of government employees; the statement of claim put in by them seemed to me perfunctory, slovenly; it asked for an increase in the scale of wages, but did not even take the trouble to give the existing scale. When we three arbitrators met before going into the court room, I said that I thought the statement extremely bad and I suggested that the chairman might gently draw the attention of the claimants to the deficiencies. The other two agreed and the chairman made the mildest of protests. The secretary of the union, who had come to conduct the case, was enraged and refused to continue before us—so we all trooped out astonished rather than dismayed. Arbitrators were appointed to the panels for four years, and hitherto when my four years' term had come to an end, I had always been renominated and reappointed. When shortly after this incident my four-year term came to an end, I was not renominated.

When one comes to the practice of politics, anyone writing about his life in the years 1924-39 must answer the crucial question: 'What did you do in the General Strike?' Of all public events in home politics during my lifetime, the General Strike was the most painful, the most horrifying. The treatment of the miners by the government after the Sankey Commission was disgracefully dishonest. If ever there has been right on the side of the workers in an industrial dispute, it was on the side of the miners in the years after the war; if ever a strike and a general strike were justified, it was in 1926. The actions of the mine-owners and of the government seemed to me appalling and when the General Strike came, I was entirely on the side of the workers. There was, of course, really nothing one could do, and one watched appalled the incompetence of those who had called and were conducting the strike. Then when the failure of the strike was inevitable, I was rung up one morning by R. H. Tawney, who asked me to come round and see him in Mecklenburgh Square, When I got there, he told me that he was going to try to get as many well-known people as possible to sign a statement publicly calling upon the government to see that there was no victimization when the strike was over, He asked me whether I would be responsible for collecting the signatures of as many prominent writers and artists as possible. I agreed and for the next few days organised a company of young people who bicycled round London collecting signatures. It was the kind of job which I find depressing, because I cannot really believe in the efficacy of what I am doing. However, we worked hectically, and only one person refused when asked to sign. This was John Galsworthy. The young woman who bicycled up to Hampstead and received a pretty curt refusal became Principal of Somerville College and a D.B.E.

In the general practice of politics my main activities were in the Fabian Society and the Labour Party. For many years I was elected a member of the Executive Committee of the Fabian Society, for ten years I was chairman of the Fabian International Bureau, and for even longer was a member of the Colonial Bureau. I do not like to think of the innumerable hours of my life which I have spent on this kind of work. It was mainly committee work. I do not enjoy committees and I am not a good committee man unless I am chairman or secretary; as an ordinary member, I tend either to become exasperated by what seems to me inefficiency and waste of time or to sink into a coma from which at long intervals I rouse myself to sudden, irritated energy. My attitude to the Fabian Society was, I think, always slightly ambivalent. When I first knew it, it was pre-eminently a creation of Sidney and Beatrice Webb. They meant it to be and they made it an instrument for the political education of the labour movement and ultimately of the Labour Party. By what they understood as 'research', by committees, reports, pamphlets, books, and conferences, the Society fed the labour movement with facts and theories, with ideas and policies. I was mainly interested politically in international affairs and in colonial and imperial problems. When, at the end of the 1914 war, Asquith, Lloyd George, and the ruthless logic of history had sterilised and emasculated liberalism and had irrevocably destroyed the Liberal Party, and when Labour was just emerging as the only political alternative to conservatism and the Tory Party, both among the leaders and the rank and file of the labour movement there was a profound and almost universal ignorance of international and imperial facts and problems. The rank and file were predominantly working class and trade unionist, and were naturally concerned with the industrial and economic aspects of politics of which their knowledge and interests alone made them acutely aware. Even their middle-class leaders and instructors, like the Webbs, before the 1914 war ignored and were ignorant of international and imperial problems. As I have recorded elsewhere, when I first knew Sidney, if an international question cropped up, he would say: 'It's not my subject', and that seemed to mean that it was no business of his and could be left to some other expert. After I had written *International Government* and *Commerce in Africa* for the Fabian Society, the Webbs treated me more or less as the Fabian and Labour Party 'expert' in international and imperial questions. In the Society Sidney turned over to me or consulted me about such questions and he had me appointed secretary of the Labour Party Advisory Committees on International and Imperial Affairs.

My work in the Society helped my work in the Labour Party and vice versa, though I always felt that the Advisory Committee work was potentially the more important, since it brought one directly in contact with the Executive Committee of the Labour Party and the Parliamentary Party. During the 1920s I did a good deal of work for the Fabian Society, but I did not take much part in its internal politics, though I watched them from a distance with some amusement. At the beginning of the decade, as I have said, the Society was still mainly the creation of the Webbs, who still, spiritually and materially, moved on the face of its waters. But the younger generation, in the person of G. D. H. Cole and his wife Margaret, were already knocking at the door—and there was no gentleness or consideration when Douglas and Margaret Cole knocked on any door. I have always thought that the way in which Sidney and Beatrice behaved when they heard that ominous knocking was a perfect example of how age should face with understanding and dignity the menace of the younger generation. When Douglas married Margaret in 1918, both were under thirty years of age; he was an extraordinary able product of Oxford University and she of Cambridge University. They did not suffer either fools or the opposite of fools gladly; they knew exactly what they wanted in life and in the Fabian Society, and they were determined to get it with the ruthlessness and arrogance of vigorous youth confronted by distinguished and static age. There was no gentleness in their opposition to the Webbs, but Sidney and Beatrice treated them and their views with the greatest consideration and never showed the slightest sign of resentment.

But this kind of thing was not very good for the work of the Fabian Society and between 1920 and 1930 it gradually went downhill. Indeed, it had got into such a miserable state that in 1931 the more active members hived off and started the New Fabian Research Bureau. Douglas Cole was honorary secretary, Clem

Attlee, chairman, and Hugh Gaitskell, assistant secretary. I was a member of the Executive Committee and ran the International Section. We did a considerable amount of work, producing pamphlets and reports. But after nine years, negotiations opened with the Fabian Society and we hived back again. The hiving back really meant that we, the New Fabian Researchers, took control of the Fabian Society. As far as I was concerned, I was elected a member of the Executive Committee and served on it for many years and I was also chairman of the International Bureau.

I did a good deal of work for the Fabian Society, but much more for the Labour Party. For nearly thirty years I was secretary of the two Advisory Committees each of which met in the House of Commons on alternative Wednesdays. The present General Secretary of the Labour Party (1966) has given me an opportunity of examining the reports which these two committees made to the Executive Committee and the Parliamentary Party. I knew that we had done a great deal, but I must say that I was amazed at the quantity and scope of our work. We simply bombarded the leaders of the Party and the active politicians with reports, briefs, recommendations, policies covering every aspect, question, or problem of international and imperial politics. As a civil servant, an editor of journals dealing with the theory and practice of politics, and a publisher who specialised to some extent in the publication of political books, I have learned—at the cost of infinite boredom and much mental torture—a great deal about political writers and historians, and how they deal with their subjects. Nearly everyone thinks that he can think, and most people today think that they can write what they think; in fact, the ability to think even among professional thinkers, and to write even among professional thinkers, and to write even among professional writers, is extremely rare; and I should put most political writers and historians at the bottom of the class. It is therefore extraordinary to find that the quality of the reports of these committees is in general extremely high; most of them are succinct and to the point, written clearly by experts for ordinary people, full of facts, expressing views and proposing policies with a sense of sober responsibility.

I will deal first with the imperial committee. Today, in the year 1966, imperialism and colonialism are among the dirtiest of all dirty political words. That was not the case forty-seven years ago at the end of the 1914 war. The British and French Empires were still going strong and still adding to their territories, either unashamedly or, rather shamefacedly and dishonestly, by the newly invented mandate system, which some people recognized as a euphemism for imperialism. The vast majority of Frenchmen and Britons were extremely proud of their empires and considered that it was self-evident that it was for the benefit of the world as well as in their own interests that they ruled directly or dominated indirectly the greater part of Asia and Africa. It was still widely accepted that God had so ordered the world that both individuals and states benefited everyone, including their victims, by making the maximum profit for themselves in every way, everywhere and everywhen. In the second volume of my autobiography, *Growing*, I recorded my experience as an imperialist empire builder for seven years in the Ceylon Civil Service and how gradually it made me dislike imperialism with its relation of dominant to subject peoples.[1] It was one of the main reasons why in 1911 I decided to resign from the Civil Service. The 1914 war and my work on *International Government* and *Empire and Commerce in Africa* increased my dislike of the imperialist system. It seemed to me certain that the revolt of the subject peoples— 'peoples not yet able to stand by themselves under the strenuous conditions of the modern world', as the Covenant of the League describes them—which had begun in Japan and was now rumbling in China, India, Ceylon, and the Near East, would spread through Asia and would soon reach Africa. In the modern world this was one of the most menacing political problems, and the world's peace and prosperity in the future depended upon accelerating the transfer of power from the imperialist states to their subject peoples in the ramshackle territories called colonies, dependencies, protectorates, and spheres of influence throughout Asia and Africa.

The importance of the Labour Party Advisory Committee on Imperial Affairs consisted for me in the fact that it enabled me, as secretary, to try to get the party and its leaders to understand the complications and urgency of what was happening in remote places and among strange peoples about whom they were profoundly and complacently ignorant. When it came down to day-to-day practical politics in the 'twenties and 'thirties of the twentieth century, there were in this field two main questions which it was essential to deal with: first, the demand for self-government in India and its reper-

[1] Volume 1, pp. 235, 298, 300.

cussions in Burma and Ceylon; secondly, the methods of government and economic exploitation in the British African 'possessions'. Between 1918 and 1939 the Advisory Committee did an immense amount of work upon these two questions and I was very lucky to have several members who not only agreed with my view of their importance but had a profound and practical knowledge of them. I propose to say something about what we aimed at and accomplished in each case.

First as regards India. Between 1924 and 1931 we sent twenty-three reports and recommendations on India to the Executive Committee and Parliamentary Party. We had on our committee four members with a wide and detailed knowledge of India, Major Graham Pole, H. S. L. Polak, G. T. Garrat, and above all Sir John Maynard. They closely followed events and we relied greatly upon them and their intimate knowledge of Indian conditions. John Maynard, who became chairman of the committee, was as I wrote in *Beginning Again* (p. 165), a very remarkable man. After a distinguished career in the Indian Civil Service he retired in 1927. He was for five years Member of the Executive Council of Governor Punjab. When he joined the Labour Party and the Advisory Committee he was well over sixty; at that age most people have lost any ability, if they ever had it, of admitting into their mind even the shadow of a new idea, and, after over forty years as a civil servant in India, he ought to have developed a sunbaked shell of impermeable conservatism. When one first met him, one might easily mistake him for the typical topgrade British civil servant, neat, precise, reserved, reticent, with an observant, suspicious, and slightly ironical gleam in his eye. He may have been to some extent all of this, and yet at the same time he was the exact opposite. For he was one of the most open-minded and liberal-minded men I have ever known—he was also personally one of the nicest—and to add to all his other gifts, after a life spent in administration, at the age of seventy-five he wrote one of the best books on Soviet Russia ever published, *The Russian Peasant and Other Studies*. Graham Pole, a Labour M.P. from 1929 to 1931, had a considerable knowledge of India and was an indefatigable member of the Advisory Committee; he was convinced that immediate steps should be taken to give self-government to India. Polak had the same equipment and outlook as Graham Pole, and he was an intimate friend of Gandhi.

Among the Labour leaders inside and outside Parliament there was very little knowledge or understanding of the Indian situation. In the highest regions Ramsay MacDonald posed as the expert in chief, having been a member of the Royal Commission on Indian Public Services in 1912 and having written two books on the 'awakening' and government of India. He was not entirely ignorant of the situation and took an interest in what we were doing on the committee, occasionally speaking to me or writing to me about our memoranda and recommendations. He professed to be, as usual, upon what I considered to be the side of the angels— in favour of self-government, but, as usual, he was entirely untrustworthy—I always mistrusted Ramsay, and particularly when he brought me the gift of agreeing with me. It was almost the inevitable sign that he would find some reason for doing the opposite of what he had agreed with you ought to be done. The only other front rank Labour leader who knew anything about India was Clem Attlee, but his interest in and knowledge of it only began in 1927, when he was a member of the Indian Statutory Commission. After becoming Secretary of State for the Dominions in 1942 and Prime Minister in 1945, he played a prominent part in the final events which brought independence and Dominion status to India and Pakistan in 1947.

The perpetual tragedy of history is that things are perpetually being done ten or twenty years too late. When in the last days and hours before the outbreak of the 1914 war, that monstrously unnecessary war, Grey and some of the other European statesmen were trying frantically to put forward proposals to stop it and the general staffs were taking frantic measures to make it inevitable, one of the Foreign Secretaries—I think it was the Austrian—to whom Grey had desperately telegraphed one more proposal which would have involved stopping Austrian mobilisation, plaintively replied that events had once more outstripped and outdated the proposal. This outstripping and outdating of the proposals, policies, and acts of governments and statesmen by events is the perpetual story of human history. Over and over again the oncoming of some horrible and unnecessary historic catastrophe—some war or revolution or Hitlerian savagery— is visible and a voice is heard in the wildnerness saying to the kings and presidents and prime ministers: 'If you want to prevent this catastrophe you must do X'. Then all the kings, presidents, and prime ministers, the governments, establishments, powers, and principalities shout in unison: 'This is the voice of Thersites, and Jack Cade, and Jacques Bonhomme, of Danton and

Marat, of Bakunin and Karl Marx, of bloody revolutionaries, Bolsheviks, Left Wing intellectuals, and Utopians. We conservatives are the only realists—it is fatal to alter anything except the buttons on a uniform or what makes no matter—but to do X would be the end of civilisation.' Ten, twenty, fifty years later, when it is ten years, twenty years, fifty years too late, when events have outstripped and outdated X which would have saved civilisation, then at last with civilisation falling about their ears, the realists grant X. This was the history of the French revolution, of Home Rule and Ireland, of war and the League of Nations.

It was also the history of British governments and India between 1920 and 1947. During the 1914 war the British government had declared that it would co-operate with Indians in order to establish self-government in India. The White Paper, the Round Table Conference, and the India Act of 1935 were the steps by which British conservative and imperialist patriots sought honourably to dishonour this promise. What they gave with one hand—niggardly reforms—they took away with the other—the massacre at Amritsar, the Rowlatt ordinances, the cat-and-mouse imprisonments and releases of Gandhi and Congress leaders. The vicious circle of repression and sedition, sedition and repression—the implacable legal violence of an alien government and the murderous, illegal violence of native terrorists—established itself. At each stage the demands of Congress for self-government and Dominion status were met by such grudging and contemptible dollops of self-government that any politically conscious Indian could only conclude that once more the tragedy of freedom would have to be acted out in India—the alien rulers would release their hold on the subject people only if forced to do so by bloody violence.

Of course, no one can be sure of any What Might Have Been in history. But I have no doubt that if British government had been prepared in India to grant in 1900 what they refused in 1900 but granted in 1920; or to grant in 1920 what they refused in 1920 but granted in 1940; or to grant in 1940 what they refused in 1940 but granted in 1947—then nine-tenths of the misery, hatred, and violence, the imprisonings and terrorism, the murders, floggings, shootings, assassinations, even the racial massacres would have been avoided; the transference of power might well have been accomplished peacefully, even possibly without partition. At any rate all through the crucial years between 1920 and 1940 the

Advisory Committee urged the Executive Committee and the Parliamentary Party, and the Labour Governments of 1924 and 1929, to do everything in their power to meet the demands in India for self-government and Dominion status. Our memoranda, written by Maynard, Graham Pole, and Polak, continually explained to the Excutive and Parliamentary Party the complicated and fluctuating situation, and the bewildering kaleidoscope of demands, proposals, reports, White Papers, negotiations, Bills and Acts. If we accomplished nothing else, we at least for the first time did something to educate our masters; we got a few Labour leaders to take an interest in and understand what was happening in India. Our recommendations were clear and consistent: at the crucial moments of the White Paper, the Round Table Conference, and the Act of 1935, we insisted that the government's offers or concessions were totally inadequate. The Party accepted our recommendations and came out publicly in favour of immediate steps to establish Dominion status.

All political parties make promises or announce policies generously when they are not in power which they regret, ignore, and repudiate when they obtain the power to carry them out. In my twenty-five years' service as secretary of the Imperial Advisory Committee I had splendid opportunities of often seeing that Labour governments and politicians were not immune from this change of heart or mind; in my own personal involvement with the Indian question, I have three vivid recollections of particular incidents, and one is closely connected with such a change of mind. It was during the war, when Attlee was Deputy Prime Minister and Secretary of State for Dominion Affairs in the Churchill Government. Something had occurred with regard to India which the Advisory Committee considered of immense importance. The exact point I do not now remember, but the Committee felt that something should be done which the Labour Party by its declared policy was morally and politically bound to stand for. In view of Attlee's position and his knowledge of the Indian problem and of the Party's declared policy since 1927, the committee decided that Charles Buxton and I should go and see him and put the case as the committee saw it and the desirability of doing everything possible in this case to follow the lines of our declared policy. Attlee gave us an interview in No. 11 Downing Street. Charles and I sat on one side of a table and the Deputy Prime Minister on the other side. I was not an intimate friend of his, but I had worked with him quite a bit, particularly on the New Fabian Research Bureau; Charles Buxton knew him much better. But we had a very frigid reception. He listened to what we had to say and then dismissed us. I felt that somehow we had committed or were thought to have committed something rather worse than a political indiscretion by bringing this inconvenient reminder into the Holy of Holies of power. I almost felt a slight sense of guilt as I slunk out of Downing Street past the policeman who during the war examined your credentials before allowing you to enter it.

My second vision of an incident with regard to the long-drawn-out tragedy of India is very different. It was in 1931, just after the Round Table Conference had ended. A Labour M.P., James Horrabin, said that Gandhi wanted to meet a few Labour people and discuss with them what his future action should be; Horrabin asked me to come in the evening of 3 December to his flat for this purpose. It was a curious party, consisting of Gandhi and some ten or fifteen Labour people—who we all were, I cannot now remember, but my recollection is that we were nearly all of us 'intellectuals', not first-line politicians. Everyone has seen photographs of that strange little figure, the Mahatma Gandhi, and he has been described again and again; what seemed to me remarkable about him was that, unlike most people, he was in life almost exactly like the photographs of him. He was, I suppose, one of the few 'great men'—if there are such people—that I have met. I do not think that, if I had met him in Piccadilly or Calcutta or Colombo, I would have recognised his greatness; but sitting with him in Horrabin's room, I could not fail to feel that he was a remarkable man. At first sight he presented to one a body which was slightly inhuman, slightly ridiculous. But the moment he began to talk, I got the impression of great complexity—strength, subtlety, humour, and at the same time an extraordinary sweetness of disposition.

Gandhi said that he was not going to talk much himself. He had asked us to come because he felt that the end of the Round Table Conference had left him personally in a difficult position and he was not at all clear what line he should follow when he got back to India. He wanted us each in turn to tell him how we saw the situation and what we thought his immediate course of action should be. Then one after the other round the room each said his piece—I cannot say that I found my piece very easy or illuminating. When we had all said our say, there followed one of the most brilliant intellectual pyrotechnic displays which I have ever listened to. Gandhi thanked us and said that it would greatly help him if his friend Harold Laski, who was one of us, would try to sum up the various lines of judgment and advice which had emerged. Harold then stood up in front of the fireplace and gave the most lucid, faultless summary of the complicated, diverse expositions of ten or fifteen people to which he had been listening in the previous hour and a half. He spoke for about twenty minutes; he gave a perfect sketch of the pattern into which the various statements and opinions logically composed themselves; he never hesitated for a word or a thought, and, as far as I could see, he never missed a point. There was a kind of beauty in his exposition, a flawless certainty and simplicity which one feels in some works of art. Harold's mind, when properly used, was a wonderful intellectual instrument, though as years went by he was inclined to take the easy way and misuse it both for thinking and writing.

My third vision connected with India is in Artillery Mansions in Victoria Street and another famous Indian, Shri Jawaharlal Nehru. It was in February 1936 that I received a letter from Nehru saying that he would very much like to have a talk with me: would I come in the afternoon of Monday and see him in Artillery Mansions, where he was staying? He had just been elected President of the All India Congress. I went to keep my appointment on a cold, grey, foggy, dripping, London February afternoon. I knew Artillery Mansions well, for at one time my sister, Bella, had a flat there. It fills me with despair whenever I see it—even on a bright spring day. It must rank among the greatest masterpieces of Victorian architectural ugliness; but it is not only horribly ugly, it is a monument of dark, gloomy inconvenience. It is one of the many human habitations over which I have always felt the inscription should be: 'Abandon hope all ye who enter here'.

It was no bright spring day when I went to see the future Prime Minister of India; it was, as I said, one of those dirty yellow, pea-soup, dripping London February days which make the heart sink. My heart sank as I climbed the dark staircase to Nehru's flat. The door of the flat was open, and, as nothing happened when I rang the bell, I walked in. The doors of all the rooms were open and the rooms were barely furnished. Hesitatingly I looked into a room from which came the sound of conversation; in it were three chairs and a table, Nehru, and another Indian. Nehru told me to come in and sit down, and the quite private conversation between the two went on for five or ten minutes as if I had not been there. My experience in Ceylon had taught me that the European custom of domestic privacy is unknown to Asiatics. In Asia houses and rooms often have no doors, and, no matter what may be happening in a room, all kinds of extraneous people will probably be wandering aimlessly in and out of it.[1] Eventually the Indian left and I had a conversation for about half an hour with Nehru. We talked in the bare room with the door of the room open and the door of the flat open and, as it seemed to me, all the doors in the world open. This is not calculated to give one a sense of privacy and comfort on a cold February afternoon in London. I liked Nehru very much as a man; he was an intellectual of the intellectuals, on the surface gentle and sad. He had great charm, and, though there was a congenital aloofness about him, I had no difficulty in talking to him. It was a rather strange and inconclusive conversation. I had thought and still think that he had intended to discuss politics and, in particular, imperial politics from the Labour angle with me. And in a vague way we did talk politics, the problems of India and Ceylon; but it was pretty vague and somehow or other we slipped into talking about life and books rather than the fall of empire and empires. After about half an hour I got up to go and Nehru asked me where I was going. I said that I was going to walk to the House of Commons to attend a Labour Party Advisory Committee there and he said that he would walk with me as he would like to go on with our conversation. When we got down into the extraordinary sort of gloomy well outside the front door of the Mansions, we found waiting a press photographer who wanted to take a photograph of Nehru. Nehru

[1] I saw a curious example of this when I revisited Ceylon in 1960. I was taken by Mr Fernando, the head of the Civil Service, to see the Prime Minister, Mr Dahanayake. The previous Prime Minister had only a short time before been assassinated. Mr Dahanayake was living in a large house, the gates of which were guarded by two soldiers carrying rifles who stopped us and examined our papers and credentials with the greatest care before admitting us. But the large compound at the back of the house was separated from other compounds only by a low unguarded fence through which any would-be assassin could easily have come unseen. And I had a long conversation with the Prime Minister in an open, unguarded room and, while we talked, all kinds of people wandered vaguely in and out of it. I remember thinking at the time how very different the precautions would have been if I had gone to see the Prime Minister in Downing Street although it was nearly 150 years since a Prime Minister had been assassinated in England.

insisted upon my being included in the photograph, which is reproduced here as plate 26. The gloom of Artillery Mansions, of London on a February afternoon, of life in the middle of the twentieth century, as it weighed upon the future Prime Minister of India and the Honorary Secretary of the Labour Party Advisory Committee on Imperial Affairs, and on their dingy hats and overcoats, is observable in the photograph. We then walked on up Victoria Street to the House of Commons, talking about life and literature on the way. We parted at the door to the central lobby and I never saw Nehru again.

There was another subject which the Imperial Advisory Committee spent even more time on than that of India—imperialism in Africa, the government of British colonial territories and the treatment of their native inhabitants in Africa. In knowledge and experience of this kind of imperial question the committee was exceptionally strong. In Norman Leys and MacGregor Ross we had two men who had spent many years of their lives as government servants in Kenya. Among other members were W. M. Macmillan, Director of Colonial Studies in the University of St Andrews, who had been educated and was subsequently a Professor in South Africa; Norman Bentwich, who had been in the Palestine Government and was Professor in Jerusalem; Lord Olivier, who had been in the Colonial Office, a colonial governor, and Secretary of State for India; T. Reid, who had been twenty-six years in the Ceylon Civil Service; Arthur Creech Jones, M.P., who became Secretary of State for the Colonies in 1946; Drummond Shiels, M.P., who was Parliamentary Under-Secretary of State for India in 1929 and Parliamentary Under-Secretary of State for the Colonies 1929-31. And in the chair we had Charles Roden Buxton, who came of a family which, ever since the abolition of the slave trade, had a hereditary interest and concern in the protection of the rights of subject peoples in the colonial empires.

As soon as the committee got to work I began to put before it memoranda on the government of the colonial empire and on its future. It was soon decided that we should produce for the Executive Committee a detailed report on the political and economic conditions and government in the British African colonial territories, together with, if possible, a detailed long-term policy which we could recommend for adoption by the party. In the next few years we spent a great deal of time and thought on this. As we gradually worked out a policy, the drafting of it was left to Buxton and me. The final report was a formidable document, but it was adopted in its entirety by the Executive Committee and published in a pamphlet under the title *The Empire in Africa: Labour's Policy.*

Rereading the pamphlet today, it seems to me remarkable that such a document should have been published over forty years ago and that the principles and policy in it should have been adopted by a political party which was on the point of being returned to power and therefore responsible for the government of the empire. The pamphlet dealt in detail with three subjects: (1) land and labour in our African possissions, (2) government and self-government, (3) education. It pointed out that Britain was pursuing two completely different and contradictory administrative policies in her east-and west-coast African possessions. On the west coast the policy was to preserve native rights in land, prevent its sale to Europeans, and promote a native community of agriculturalists and the growth of native industries; on the east coast the policy was to sell or lease immense areas of land to European syndicates or individuals, to help them to develop the country through 'hired' or forced native labour, and to confine the native population not working for Europeans to 'reserves'. Labour maintained that the east-coast system had deplorable results and that the right policy for the future was to treat land as the property of native communities so that there should be no economic exploitation of the native by the European, and the native should be given the opportunity of developing the economic resources of land as a free man and for the benefit of the native community. As regards self-government, the declared policy was ultimately the establishment of native representation on Legislative Councils and the gradual transfer of responsible government to these Councils. In order to train Africans to govern themselves, the government must educate them for self-government by making primary education accessible for all African children, by the provision of training colleges for teachers, technical colleges, universities, and experimental and model farms.

When our private or public world is overwhelmed by deserved or undeserved misfortune no one is more silly or infuriating than the self-satisfied person who says to us: 'I told you so'. I do not wish to seem to be saying here: 'We told you so'. But nothing is more important than that people should realise that the inveterate political conservatism of human beings—and pre-eminently of the ruling castes and classes—has produced an unending series of unnecessary historical horrors and disasters, ever since the Lord began it by trying to prevent Adam and Eve from learning the truth about the badly devised universe and world which He ill-advisedly had just created. I have lived nearly half a century since the end of the war, watching go by what must have been probably the most senselessly horrible fifty years in human history. When a hundred years hence the historian can calmly and objectively survey what we have seen and suffered, he will almost certainly conclude that fundamentally the most crucial events of the period were the revolt in Asia and Africa against European imperialism and the liquidation of empires. It has been a process of slow torture to millions of ignorant human beings—misery and massacre in Asia from India to China, Indo-China, Korea, Vietnam, and Indonesia; anarchy, massacre, and misery in Africa from Algiers and Mau Mau in Kenya to the Congo and Rhodesia. And the objective historian in 2066 will also, I feel sure, conclude that a very great deal of this misery and massacre would have been avoided if the imperialist powers had not blindly and doggedly resisted the demands of the subject peoples, but had carried out their own principles and promises by educating and leading them to independence.

At any rate for twenty years the Advisory Committee persistently pressed upon the Labour Party Executive the necessity for forestalling events by preparing and promoting self-government throughout Britain's colonial empire. We were not concerned with pious promises or generalisations. We continually put before the Executive detailed practical proposals to meet the actual situation throughout Asia and Africa, whether in India or the Far East, in Kenya or Rhodesia. Again and again the Executive accepted our recommendations and publicly announced them to be the Party's policy either in official pamphlets, drafted by us, or by resolutions passed at annual conferences.

I have said above that it is characteristic of politicians and political parties to announce policies and make promises when in opposition and to forget or repudiate them when in power. Between 1919 and 1939 there were two Labour governments; the first lasted nine months, the second two years, and neither commanded a majority in the House of Commons. Obviously this meant that the time was too short, the programme too crowded, and the voting strength in the House too small for the government to take major steps in the carrying out of Labour's colonial policy. Nevertheless, the record of Ramsay MacDonald's government in Asia and Africa seemed to me and a good many other people very disappointing by failing to carry out its promises in cases where it could have done so. An incident connected with the Advisory Committee, which I have already referred to, will show what I mean. In 1930 in Ramsay's second government Sidney Webb was Secretary of State for the Colonies and Drummond Shiels, a Scottish Labour M.P., was Under-Secretary. Sidney was in politics curiously ambivalent; he must have been born half a little conservative and half a little liberal. He was a progressive, even a revolutionary, in some economic and social spheres; where the British Empire was concerned, he was a common or garden imperialist conservative. Shiels, a medical man by profession, had been an assiduous member of the Advisory Committee and had, I think, learnt a great deal from it. There was nothing of the wild revolutionary about him; he was a hard-headed, liberal-minded, unsentimental Scot, and he was a convinced believer in the necessity for putting into practice the colonial policies worked out by the Advisory Committee and adopted by the Party. He used from time to time to ask me to come to the Colonial Office and discuss things with him. He was dismayed by Sidney's conservatism and his masterly inactivity whenever an opportunity arose to do something different from what Conservative governments and the Colonial Office Civil Servants had endorsed as safe, sound, and 'progressive' for the last half-century.

Towards the end of 1930 the Advisory Committee decided that an opportunity had occurred for trying to get Sidney to implement a small part of the Labour Party's policy. In those days the budgets of Crown Colonies had to be 'laid on the table' of the House of Commons and approved by the Secretary of State. I kept my eye on them so that any important point with regard to a budget might be discussed by the Advisory Committee. I brought the Kenya 1930 budget before the Committee when it was laid on the table of the House. The Committee considered that the proposed expenditure on education and communications was grossly unfair to the natives. The amount to be voted for the education of white children was enormously higher per head than that for the education of African children; the proposed expenditure on roads to serve the white settlers' estates was far higher than that proposed for roads serving the native reserves. On the other hand, the taxation of Africans was proportionally much more severe than that of the settlers.

The Committee decided that Charles Buxton and I should ask Sidney Webb to see us, and that we should point out to him that this discrimination against the African was absolutely opposed to the Labour Government's policy with regard to the education of Africans and promotion of African agriculture, and that the Secretary of State for the Colonies should insist upon a revision of the budget. Sidney, who was now Lord Passfield, for some strange reason asked us to meet him at the House of Lords instead of at the Colonial Office. We had an absurd meeting with Sidney in the red and gold Chamber of the House of Lords, which was, of course, completely empty except for the tiny Secretary of State for the Colonies and the humble chairman and secretary of the Advisory Committee sitting one on either side of him. We got, as I had expected, nothing out of Sidney, who was an expert negotiator and had at his fingers' ends all the arguments of all the men of action for always doing nothing.

This kind of thing, which often happened, made one wonder whether the immense amount of work which these Advisory Committees did was of any use at all. From time to time, off and on, one or other of the most active members would come to me and say that they had had enough of it, that we did an immense amount of work. pouring out reports and memoranda which the Executive Committee accepted, which became 'Party policy', and were then never heard of again. I tried to mollify and console them by recommending to them the rule by which I regulated my life and its hopes and fears: 'Blessed is he who expects nothing, for unexpectedly he may somewhere, some time achieve something'. The two Advisory Committees of which I was secretary did occasionally achieve something, though nothing commensurate with the amount of work we did. We spread through the Labour Party, and to some extent beyond it, some knowledge of the relations between the imperialist powers and the subject peoples of Asia and Africa, and even some realisation of the urgent need for revolutionary reform so that there would be a rapid and orderly transition from imperialist rule to self-government. And within the Labour Party—particularly in the Parliamentary Party—the committees did a useful educational job. When Drummond Shiels became Under-Secretary of State for the Colonies in 1929 and Arthur Creech Jones became Secretary of State for the Colonies in 1946, they were far better equipped for their jobs than most M.P.s who get ministerial office, and they both of them did very good work in the Colonial Office. They would, I am sure, have agreed that they had learnt a great deal from the Advisory Committee; the same is true of many rank and file Labour M.P.s who reached the rank of Minister.

Much of what I have said about the Imperial Advisory Committee applied to the International Advisory Committee. As I have said before, in 1919 the ignorance of foreign affairs in the Labour movement was almost as deep and widespread as the ignorance of imperial affairs. Like its sister committee, the International Committee performed a useful educational function in the Parliamentary Party, and even outside it. It was, perhaps, in membership rather stronger than the Imperial Committee. Until 1937 Charles Buxton was chairman, and two 'experts' in foreign affairs, Philip Noel-Baker and Will Arnold-Forster, did a great deal of work on it. In the 1920s both Ramsay MacDonald and Arthur Henderson kept in close touch with our work and the upper political stratum in the Party always treated the International Committee with rather more respect than the Imperial Committee. For instance, in June 1937, Ernest Bevin attended a meeting and developed to us the points which he had made in an important speech at Southport. There were twenty-three members present, and all, including Bevin, agreed that a memorandum should be sent to the Executive urging that a constructive peace policy should be put forward in the House of Commons by the front bench. The policy should be that the muddled pacts against aggression recently made by the government should be brought together into a uniform system, and it should be made clear that there would be an instant retort in event of any further act of flagrant aggression by Hitler.

In the terrible years between 1919 and 1939 everything in international affairs was dominated by the emergence of fascism in Europe and the menace of another war. To make up one's mind what seemed to be the right foreign policy and, where passions and prejudices became more and more violent, to keep cool and have the courage of one's convictions was a difficult, often an agonising business. Even today it is difficult to write truthfully and objectively about those years and the part which one played in them, for the passions and prejudices persist and distort history.

I propose first to give an account of my own attitude during those twenty years and then describe the trend of opinion and policy, as I saw it, in the Advisory Committee and the Labour Party. Like most people on the Left who had some knowledge of European history and of international affairs, I thought that the Versailles Treaty, particularly in the reparation clauses, was punitively unjust to the German people, that it would therefore encourage militarism and desire for revenge in Germany. In this way it had sown the seeds of a second world war. I accepted Maynard's arguments in *The Economic Consequences of the Peace.* It seemed to me disastrous that, instead of supporting and encouraging a pacific, democratic Social-Democratic German government, France and to a lesser extent Britain did everything calculated to weaken and discredit it. The final folly, which played into the hands of the German nationalists and militarists, was the occupation of the Ruhr.

This attitude towards Germany and France was condemned at the time by many people as pro-German. It is still today condemned by some as pro-German and short-sighted; the subsequent history of Hitler, the Nazis, and the 1939 war shows, they say, that the Versailles Treaty was far from being too harsh; it was too mild; the Allies should have made a recrudescence of German militarism impossible by subjecting Germany to a modern version of the treatment by which 2,000 years ago Rome settled Carthage. The real question in this dispute and argument is: which was the cart and which the horse in the years 1919 to 1924? What we said was that, if you demand impossible sums in reparations and unjustly penalise Germany, you will cause economic chaos, you will encourage the revival of German militarism and a demand for a revision of the treaty. Here you have sown the seeds of a future war. At least the course of history followed exactly as we had prophesied.

From 1920 to about 1935 I thought that the international policy of the British Government, and therefore of the Labour Party, should be based on the League of Nations; the aim should be to build it up into a really efficient instrument of international government, a system for developing co-operation between states, the peaceful settlement of disputes, and collective security and defence against aggression. At every opportunity I put before the Advisory Committee proposals for implementing this policy. In 1927 Will Arnold-Forster and I drafted a Convention for Pacific Settlement which I put before the Advisory Committee; it was intended to close a gap in the League system as laid down in the Covenant. I received the following characteristic letter from Ramsay MacDonald:

House of Commons January 17th, 1927

My dear Woolf,

I have been reading a very admirable memorandum put up by you and Arnold Forster regarding a Convention for Pacific Settlement. I think it is really a good piece of work, although one may see the possibility of filling certain detailed proposals, the idea and the general line laid down, seem to me to be excellent. I hope something will be done with it.

Yours very sincerely,

J. Ramsay MacDonald

The cryptic and ungrammatical second sentence is, I think, one of Ramsay's usual backdoors of escape which would enable him, if necessary, when the time came, to sabotage the damned thing with a clear conscience. I rather think that in fact that was precisely what he did do later on when Henderson put our draft before the League of Nations.[1]

All through the 1920s the Labour Party maintained this policy that the strengthening of the League and the collective security system was the only effective way of preventing another war. For seventeen out of those twenty years a Conservative government was in power, first under Baldwin and then under Neville Chamberlain; neither of these statesmen believed in a League policy or attempted to use or develop the League as an instrument of peace as between the major powers. In this they were supported by the great majority of conservative politicians, though the curious incident of the Peace Ballot and the Hoare-Laval abortive agreement in 1935 makes it probable that a considerable majority of the rank and file conservatives disagreed with their leaders and would have supported a League policy. The two crucial tests of the League and collective security came in 1932 when Japan attacked China and in 1935 when Italy attacked Abyssinia. In both cases Baldwin with his Foreign Secretaries, Sir John Simon and Sir Samuel Hoare, contrived that the League's collective security system with full sanctions against the aggressors should not be operated.

By 1935 I had personally become convinced that Baldwin and the French statesmen who thought and acted as he did had finally destroyed the League as an instrument for deterring aggression and

[1] I think this document was what was called 'The General Act', that it was put by Henderson before the General Assembly of the League of Nations and adopted; and then Ramsay refused to allow Henderson to ratify it. Mr Philip Noel-Baker confirms this.

preventing war. The rise of Hitler to power, his withdrawal from the League, his adoption of compulsory military service, followed by his reoccupation of the demilitarised Rhineland showed the precariousness of the international situation and the necessity to take steps to meet the menace of war from Nazi Germany. I wrote several memoranda to the Advisory Committee urging that the new situation required a new policy: the League was to all intents and purposes dead and it was fatal to go on using it as a mumbled incantation against war; the only possibility of deterring Hitler and preventing war was for Britain and France to unite with those powers, including the U.S.S.R. if possible, who would be prepared to guarantee the small powers against attack by Hitler. I also pointed out that, if the Labour Party was going to support new security agreements against fascist or Nazi aggression in place of the obligations under the League Covenant, 'mere negative opposition to a policy of rearmament would be sterile and ineffective'; if the Party really meant to commit itself to a policy of resisting any further acts of aggression by Hitler, then it committed itself to the corollary that Britain must make itself strong on land and sea and in the air to defeat Hitler.

These memoranda for the first time provoked a deep division of opinion in the Advisory Committee. But this was only part of a widespread disagreement, a profound, uneasy, often concealed ambivalence which for many years had permeated the Labour movement. There was within it a very strong pacifist element, derived in part from the traditional internationalism of the Labour and Socialist movements of the nineteenth century, and in part from the strong Liberal contingent which, with the break up of the Liberal Party after the war, had joined the Labour Party. To oppose armaments in general and to vote against the Service estimates in particular was traditional policy. This may or may not have made sense when the pacifists and their parties were opposing the jingo or imperialist policies of Conservative governments which made the armaments necessary. But when the pacifist Labour people (and surviving Liberals) accepted the obligations of the League Covenant and its collective security system, they were faced by an entirely different situation. How could they agree to commit Britain to join with other members of the League in resisting any act of aggression by military means, if necessary, and at the same time refuse to provide the armaments which alone could make such military resistance feasible? There were some Labour pacifists who, when confronted with this dilemma, logically took the view that the obligation under the Covenant to use force to resist aggression could only lead to world wars and should be repudiated. But there was a far larger number who never faced the dilemma and whose policy therefore contained a profound and dangerous inconsistency. The dilemma and the disagreement were for years habitually and discreetly ignored or glossed over. But as the menace of Hitler and another war became more manifest, the divergence of view within the Party rose to the surface. The show-down came at the Labour Party Conference in Brighton in 1935. George Lansbury had been Leader of the Parliamentary Party since 1931; he was one of those sentimental, muddle-headed, slightly Pecksniffian good men who mean so well in theory and do so much harm in practice. He was a convinced believer in the desirability of having the best of two contradictory worlds, of undertaking the obligation under the League to resist aggression without providing the arms which would be required for the resistance. At the Conference Ernest Bevin, who took the view—with which I agreed—that, if you were going to fight against Hitler or any other aggressor, you must have arms with which to fight—rose in the pretty Regency Pavilion and made the most devastating attack upon the unfortunate Lansbury that I have ever listened to in a public meeting. As I said in *Beginning Again* (above, p. 160), he battered the poor man to political death—Lansbury afterwards resigned the leadership—and, although I was politically entirely on the side of Bevin in this controversy, I could not help shrinking from the almost indecent cruelty with which he destroyed the slightly lachrymose, self-righteous Lansbury.

The Advisory Committee was, as I said, divided, like the Party, on this question. There was a majority in favour of the League system of collective security and armaments adequate for resisting aggression. But there was a minority consisting of some who took the pacifist view and, with their eyes open, opposed rearmament and of some who, as it seemed to me, shut their eyes to the dilemma, inconsistently combining support of resistance to aggression with opposition to rearmament. In consequence there was never unanimity on the Committee for my memoranda; the Committee always decided to forward them to the Executive Committee without any positive recommendation. A (to me) sad result of this disagreement was Charles Buxton's resignation of the chairmanship of the Advisory Committee. He was essentially what Pericles, Aristotle, and Theophrastus would have called a 'good man' both in public and in private life. He was really mentally and emotionally a nineteenth-century non-conformist Liberal of the best type and therefore never completely at home in the twentieth-century Labour Party. A gentle man, he was on the side of civilisation, hating violence of all kinds, regarding it as a first duty to devote oneself unselfishly to the public good. It was characteristic of him that he joined the Quakers and tried to translate the ethics of the Friends into political terms. It was a curious trait in this kind of nineteenth-century Liberal often to develop a not altogether rational attachment to some foreign nation, nationality, or race. There were pro-Turks, pro-Americans, pro-Boers, pro-Bulgarians, and in the twentieth century pro-Germans. In the Balkan wars of 1912 and 1913 Charles became a pro-Bulgarian, and in 1914 he and his brother Noel went to the Balkans on a mission the object of which was to keep Bulgaria out of the war. A Turk tried to assassinate them and shot Charles through the lung. The Versailles Treaty made him what was called a pro-German in the grim years of peace, and I do not think that in the 1930s, when Hitler and the Nazis came to power, he could bring himself to face the facts and the terrible menace of war and barbarism from Germany. He necessarily took the extreme pacifist view, and, as the majority on the committee held the views which I did, he resigned the chairmanship. He and I had worked together on both Advisory Committees for many years, and it was sad to see him go, though our political disagreement made no difference to our personal friendship.

My views on this subject involved me in a curious incident in 1938. When Hitler invaded Austria in March, I was convinced that the last glimmer of hope of preventing war was drastic action on the part of Britain and France, and that this would require a dramatic change of policy by the Labour Party. The evening after the invasion I was at a meeting or party at which several Labour people were present—inevitably discussing the situation. I said that I thought that the Executive Committee and the Parliamentary Party ought to have a joint meeting and instruct the Leader of the Parliamentary Party to make a formal public statement on their behalf as follows: The danger of further aggression by Germany and of war was so acute that the Labour Party considered that drastic action was necessary on the part of Britain and France to warn Hitler that any further aggression would be resisted; with a view to this the Party would be willing to enter a coalition government under Mr Winston Churchill pledged to forward this policy and would agree to an immediate introduction of conscription and rearmament. Over the week-end I was rung up by someone who had heard what I said; he told me that my arguments had convinced him and others and they thought it important to try to get the Labour leaders to take action along the line which I had suggested—would I come and discuss what we might do with a few people on Tuesday? I was dining out on the Tuesday, but after dinner I left my party and went round to Wansborough's flat in Russell Square. There I found Douglas Jay, Tommy Balogh, and, I think, Hugh Gaitskell and Evan Durbin; there may have been one or two others. After some discussion it was decided that we should try to get hold of one or two of the leaders and induce them to put my proposition before a joint meeting of the Labour Party and T.U.C. which was to be held later in the week. One of us—I forget who it was—undertook to see A. V. Alexander, who seemed to be one of the most likely leaders to put forward the policy, and I agreed to talk to Phil Noel-Baker. Alexander agreed with our arguments and proposals and half promised to come out publicly in favour of it at the conference if he could get support beforehand within the Parliamentary Party. I could not get hold of Phil, because he was at a meeting of the International in Paris. The whole thing fizzled out: Alexander could get little or no support and drew back. Nothing was done—and the herd, Europe and the world, continued downhill all the way under Hitler's direction and 'ran violently down a steep place' into war.

I must leave the subject of politics. The years 1930 to 1939 were horrible both publicly and privately. If one was middle aged or old and so had known at least a 'sort of a kind' of civilisation, it was appalling impotently to watch the destruction of civilisation by a powerful nation completely subservient to a gang of squalid, murderous hooligans. My nephew, Quentin Bell, who was twenty years old in 1930, has recently described what it felt like to be a young man alive in those years:

> Who but we can recall the horror of that period? Of course, it was not continuous: we had our gaieties, our moments of hope, of exhilaration, of triumph even. Nevertheless, they were years of mounting despair: unable to compound our internecine quarrels, unable to shake the complacency of a torpid nation, we saw the champions of tyranny, war and racial persecution

winning a succession of ever easier victories. In those twilight days it was bloody to be alive and to be young was very hell.

To the middle aged, i.e. to those who were already going downhill all the way to old age or death, it was often in those twilight days bloody to be alive and very hell to be no longer young. In 1938 I wrote a play, *The Hotel*, about the horrors of the twilight age of Europe, the kind of hush that fell upon us before the final catastrophe. It was published in 1939 and was republished by the Dial Press in America in 1963. I can best explain how I came to write it by quoting the introduction which I wrote for the American edition of 1963:

> It is a long time since I wrote this play, *The Hotel*, and it seems even longer. It was written and published in England just before the 1939 war, and Hitler and Stalin and Mussolini—the nazis, communists, and facists—finally destroyed the world in which it was written. That, after all, is what the play is about; what it prophesied has happened. Looking about us today, we can say with Stanovich: 'The ceiling's down; the clock's smashed; and there's no door. There's no back to the hotel and no boiler room, and the wind coming through is fair cruel. . . . What a place! What a place!'
>
> That, perhaps, is all the author can say about the play in an introduction to its publication, after more than twenty years, in America. It was written in the tension of those horrible years of Hitler's domination and of the feeling that he would inevitably destroy civilization. There is, however, one small point which I can add as author; I had written a play before I wrote *The Hotel*. But for a long time I had wanted to write one in which the scene would be the entrance hall of a hotel, with the revolving door through which a string of heterogeneous characters would have their entrances and their exits. It is a scene in real life which always seems to me infinitely dramatic. And then one day in 1938 I suddenly saw that my hotel on the stage might be both realistic and symbolic, the *Grand Hôtel du Paradis* which had become the *Grand Hôtel de l'Univers et du Commerce*, with Peter Vajoff, the proprietor, standing in front of the fire—and with bugs in the beds.

I was forty in 1920 and sixty in 1940. The twilight was in one's private as well as in public life. Death is, according to Swinburne, one of the three things which 'make barren our lives'; 'death is the enemy'. If one does not oneself die young, the moment comes in one's life when death begins permanently to loom in the background of life. Parents, brothers, and sisters, who were parts of one's unconscious mind and memories, die; the intimate friends of one's youth die; our loves die. Each death as it comes, so inevitable of course, but always so unexpected and so outrageous, is like a blow on the head or the heart. Into each grave goes some tiny portion of oneself.

This erosion of life by death began for Virginia and me in the early 1930s and gathered momentum as we went downhill to war and her own death. It began on 21 January 1932 when Lytton Strachey died of cancer. This was the beginning of the end of what we used to call Old Bloomsbury. Lytton was perhaps the most individual person whom I have ever known. His father was a Strachey and his mother a Grant; he came, therefore, on both sides from one of those distinguished upper middle-class families of country gentlemen who in the nineteenth century found their professional and economic home in India or the army. The mixture of Strachey and Grant blood in Lytton's family produced remarkable results; I gave some account of it in *Sowing* (Volume 1, pp. 119-23). It consisted of ten sons and daughters, all of whom were extremely intelligent and many of them intellectually remarkable. Lytton was unquestionably the most brilliant. He had an extremely subtle and supple mind, with a tremendously quick flicker of wit and humour continually playing through his thought. Everything about him—his mind, body, voice, thought, wit, and humour—was individually his own, unlike that of anyone else. His conversation was entrancing, for his talk was profounder, wittier, more interesting, and original than his writing. This was one of the reasons why his books, brilliant and successful though they were, slightly disappointed the expectations of many who had known him as a young man of twenty. He had a tremendous reputation among the intellectuals as an undergraduate at Cambridge and we thought that he might well become a great Voltairian historian or biographer. He never achieved that, though *Eminent Victorians* and *Queen Victoria* are much more remarkable than they are currently and momentarily judged to be, and they obviously had a considerable influence on biography and history in the twenty years which followed their publication.

Lytton's personal influence on his own generation and those which immediately followed it at Cambridge was also very great. His personality was so strong that he imposed it, intellectually and even physically, upon people, especially the young. You could tell who saw much of him, for they almost inevitably acquired the peculiar Strachey voice which had a marked rhythm and, in his case, a habit of rising from the depths in the bass to a falsetto squeak. Lytton repelled and exasperated some people, particularly the dyed in the wool, athletic, public school Englishman, with no (but O so much) nonsense about him. By public school standards he did not look right, speak right, or even act right, and, apart from such major vices, he had the lesser faults of arrogance and selfishness. He would therefore often exasperate even his most intimate friends —but only momentarily and superficially. Fundamentally he was an extremely affectionate person and had (in life and conversation, though not always in his books) a great purity of intellectual honesty and curiosity. That was why his death shocked and saddened us so painfully: it was the beginning of the end, for it meant that the spring had finally died out of our lives.

After Lytton's death Carrington tried unsuccessfully to commit suicide. It was clear that sooner or later she would try again. Ralph asked us to come down to Ham Spray and see her; he thought we might be able to do some good. On 10 March I drove down with Virginia in the morning. It was one of the most painful days I have ever slowly suffered. The day itself was incongruously lovely, sunny, sparkling. I remember most vividly Carrington's great pale blue eyes and the look of dead pain in them. The house was very cold; she gave us lunch and tea and we talked and she talked quite frankly about Lytton and his ways and his friends. At first she seemed calm and cowed—'helpless, deserted', as Virginia said, 'like some small animal left'. There was a moment when she kissed Virginia and burst into tears, and said: 'There is nothing left for me to do. I did everything for Lytton. But I've failed in everything else. People say he was very selfish to me. But he gave me everything else. I was devoted to my father. I hated my mother. Lytton was like a father to me. He taught me everything I know. He read poetry and French to me.' We left after tea, and just before we got into the car Virginia said to her: 'Then you will come and see us next week—or just as you like?' And Carrington said: 'Yes, I will come, or not'. Next morning she shot herself.

Two years later Roger Fry died, as the result of a fall in his room. Roger belonged, of course, to an earlier Cambridge generation than we did—he was fourteen years my elder, but he was an integral part of Old Bloomsbury and of our lives. I have tried to describe his character in *Beginning Again* (above, pp. 65-9) and I will not repeat myself here. From 1920 until his death fourteen years later he was indeed, as I have said, part of our lives. Living in Bernard Street, just round the corner from Gordon Square where the Bells lived and

Tavistock Square where we lived, he was in and of Bloomsbury. With his death again something was torn out of our lives.

On 18 July 1937, death struck again when Vanessa's son, Julian, was killed driving an ambulance in the Spanish civil war. The story of Julian's life and death has been told at length, and with great skill, sympathy, and understanding, by two Americans, Peter Stansky and William Abrahams, in their book *Journey to the Frontier*. It would be silly of me to try to do in a page what they have done so well and fully in so many. I saw him at close quarters grow from a rampageous youth and finally man—he was twenty-nine when he was killed. His mother and father, Vanessa Stephen and Clive Bell, were extraordinarily dissimilar in mind, temperament, and looks, and there was, I think, an unresolved discord in Julian's genes the effect of which could be traced in his character, mind, and life. I have never known any child make so much noise so cheerfully, and he never quite grew up: there was still something of the child, riproaring round the sitting-room in Gordon Square, in the young man of twenty-five driving a car or having a love affair. He was an extremely attractive and lovable person and highly intelligent, but, like all ebullient and erratic people, he could at moments be exasperating. Virginia was devoted to him and so was I. His death and the manner of it, a sign and symptom of the 1930s, made another terrible hole in our lives.

Finally—a very different death—just before the war, on 2 July 1939, my mother died. She was then an old woman of eighty-seven or eighty-eight; but in many ways she never grew old. She still retained an intense interest and curiosity in all sorts of things and persons, and was physically very active. Being short and fat and impulsive, and unwilling to accommodate herself to the limitations and infirmities of old age, she was always tripping over a footstool in her room or the curb in the street and ending with a broken arm or leg. At the age of eighty-seven she did this once too often, for the broken limb this time led to complications and she died in the London Clinic. I described her character at some length in *Sowing* (Volume 1, pp. 16-19); of her nine surviving children, four, in mind and body, were predominantly Woolfs, my father's family; two were predominantly de Jonghs, my mothers family; and two were half and half. I was very much my father's and very little my mother's son, and there were many sides of my character and mind which were unsympathetic to my mother; I had no patience with her invincible, optimistic sentimentality, and my unsentimentality, which seemed to her hardness and harshness, distressed her. There was no quarrel or rift between us, and I always went to see her once a week or once a fortnight up to the day of her death—but, though she would never have admitted it even to herself, I was, I think, her least-loved child. But there is some primitive valve in our hearts, some primeval cell in our brains—handed down to us from our reptilian, piscine, or simian ancestors, perhaps—which makes us peculiarly, primordially sensitive to the mother's death. As the coffin is lowered into the grave, there is a second severance of the umbilical cord.

With my mother's death we reached the beginning of the second war and, therefore, the end of this volume. I will actually end it with a little scene which took place in the last months of peace. They were the most terrible months of my life, for, helplessly and hopelessly, one watched the inevitable approach of war. One of the most horrible things at that time was to listen on the wireless to the speeches of Hitler, the savage and insane ravings of a vindictive underdog who suddenly saw himself to be all-powerful. We were in Rodmell during the late summer of 1939, and I used to listen to those ranting, raving speeches. One afternoon I was planting in the orchard under an apple-tree iris reticulata, those lovely violet flowers which, like the daffodils, 'come before the swallow dares and take the winds of March with beauty'. Suddenly I heard Virginia's voice calling to me from the sitting-room window: 'Hitler is making a speech'. I shouted back: 'I shan't come. I'm planting iris and they will be flowering long after he is dead.' Last March, twenty-one years after Hitler committed suicide in the bunker, a few of those violet flowers still flowered under the apple-tree in the orchard.

The Journey not the Arrival Matters
1939–1969

1
Virginia's Death

The second of the great world wars through which I have lived began on 3 September 1939. Twenty-five years before, the great war of 1914 on a summer day in August had come upon us, upon our generation and indeed upon all the generations of Europe, historically and psychologically, a bolt from the blue. It was as if one had been violently hit on the head, and dimly realised that one was involved in a dreamlike catastrophe. For a hundred years a kind of civilisation seemed to have been spreading over and out of Europe so that an Armageddon had become an anachronistic impossibility or at least improbability. There had been wars and we still prayed automatically on Sundays to a very anachronistic God to deliver us from 'battle' as from murder and sudden death, from the 'crafts and assaults of the devil' and from 'fornication, and all other deadly sins'; but the wars were local or parochial wars and millions of people had lived and died without hearing the drums and tramplings of any conquest, or had had the remotest chance of standing 'on the perilous edge of battle'.

The psychology of September 1939 was terribly different from that of August 1914. People of my generation knew now exactly what war is—its positive horrors of death and destruction, wounds and pain and bereavement and brutality, but also its negative emptiness and desolation of personal and cosmic boredom, the feeling that one is endlessly waiting in a dirty, grey railway station waiting-room, a cosmic railway station waiting-room, with nothing to do but wait endlessly for the next catastrophe. We knew that war and civilisation in the modern world are incompatible, that the war of 1914 had destroyed the hope that human beings were becoming civilised—a hope not unreasonable at the beginning of the twentieth century. The Europe of 1933 was infinitely more barbarous and degraded than that of 1914 or 1919. In Russia for more than a decade there had ruled with absolute power a government, a political party, and a dictator who, on the basis of a superhuman doctrinal imbecility, had murdered millions of their fellow-Russians because they were peasants who were not quite so poor as the poorest peasants; the communists, being communists, were continually torturing and murdering their fellow-communists on such grounds as that they were either right deviationists or left deviationists. In Italy there were established a government and dictator who, with a political doctrine purporting to be the exact opposite of Russian communism, produced, much less efficiently, exactly the same results of savage stupidity. In Germany the same phenomena had appeared as in Russia and Italy, but the barbarism of Hitler and the Nazis shows itself, in the years from 1933 to 1939, to be much nastier, more menacing, more insane than even the barbarism of Stalin and the communists.

In many ways, therefore, the last years of peace before war broke upon us in 1939 were the most horrible period of my life. After 1933 as one crisis followed upon another, engineered by Adolf Hitler, one gradually realised that power to determine history and the fate of Europe and all Europeans had slipped into the hands of a sadistic madman. When one listened on the air to the foaming hysteria of a speech by the Führer at some rally, whipping up the savage hysteria of thousands of his Nazi supporters, one felt that Germany and the Germans were now infected with his insanity. As the years went by, it became clear that those in power in Britain and France would offer no real resistance to Hitler. Life became like one of those terrible nightmares in which one tries to flee from some malignant, nameless and formless horror, and one's legs refuse to work, so that one waits helpless and frozen with fear for inevitable annihilation. After the Nazi invasion of Austria one waited helpless for the inevitable war.

It was this feeling of hopelessness and helplessness, the foreknowledge of catastrophe with the forces of history completely out of control, which made the road downhill to war and the outbreak of war so different in 1939 from what they had been twenty-five years before. A few facts connected with this foreknowledge and despair are worth recollecting. In the year before the outbreak of the war I was asked by Victor Gollancz, Harold Laski, and John Strachey to write a book for the Left Book Club. I wrote a book to which I gave the title *Barbarians at the Gate*. I began by quoting 'words written about twenty-five centuries ago' by Jeremiah, 'the father of communal lamentation', lamenting the destruction of a civilisation by barbarians, who have burnt incense to strange gods, filled Jerusalem with the blood of innocents, and burnt their sons with fire for burnt offerings unto Baal—'therefore, behold the days come that this place shall no more be called Tophet, nor The valley of the son of Hinnom, but The valley of slaughter'. I went on to point out (nearly thirty years ago) the difference between 1938 and 1914, for 'when you opened your newspaper in those days, you did not read of the wholesale torture, persecution, expropriation, imprisonment or liquidation of tens of thousands or hundreds of thousands of persons, classified or labelled for destruction as social-democrats, communists, Jews, Lutheran pastors, Roman Catholics, capitalists, or kulaks'. I insisted that the ultimate threat to civilisation was not so much in this barbarism of the barbarians as in the disunity among the civilised, and I made the correct and sad prophecy:

> 'It is practically certain that economics, a war, or both will destroy the Fascist dictators and their regimes. But that does not mean that civilisation will automatically triumph over barbarism.'

I have one amused recollection connected with that book. When I sent in the MS, I received a troubled letter from Victor; the three editors liked the book very much, he said, but they were worried about my criticism of the Soviet Government and communism, would I consider toning it down? I replied that I was willing to consider any precise and particular criticisms or suggestions for alterations, but I was not prepared to modify my views on the grounds of expediency. In the end it was decided that we should all four meet and discuss the MS in detail face to face. I met the editors in Victor's office after dinner on 24 July 1939. They were much upset by my criticism of the Russian communists and their government and pressed me to modify it. The modifications which they asked for would, I felt, be dishonest, from my point of view, for they would obscure what, in my opinion, was the truth about authoritarianism in the Russia of Stalin. The barbarians were already within the gates both in Moscow and Berlin; to conceal or gloss over the truth in the communist half of Europe would make disingenuous nonsense of my book. I refused to budge, and the discussion went on for two or three hours, becoming more and more difficult, as warmth increased on their side of the room and frigidity on mine. The book was published unaltered and unmodified, and I can console or even congratulate myself that today, if they were alive—alas, all three are dead—my three editors would agree with everything which I wrote.

That evening when I got up to go, I felt that I had not ingratiated myself with my three friends, all of whom I liked very much, both in private and public life. There was a slight cloud, slight tension in the room, but I am glad to remember that, before I went out, an absurd little incident entirely dispersed them. On the wall opposite to where I had been sitting was a picture which through the long, rather boring and exasperating, argumentative discussion I had frequently looked at with pleasure and relief. In gratitude to the painter, when I said good-night to Victor, I asked him who had painted it and added that I had got a great deal of pleasure by looking at it. I could not have said anything to give Victor more pleasure or more effectively relieve the tension, for the painter was his wife. I left the room, not under a cloud, but in a glow of good-will and friendship.

To return to the psychology of the years before the war, one only gradually became aware of the savage barbarism of the Nazis in Germany and of the inevitability of war, but I still remember moments of horrified enlightenment. When a Jew shot a German diplomatist in Paris, the Government instigated an indiscriminate pogrom against Jews throughout Germany. Jews were hunted down, beaten up, and humiliated everywhere publicly in the streets of towns. I saw a photograph of a Jew being dragged by storm troopers out of a shop in one of the main streets in Berlin; the fly-buttons of the man's trousers had been torn open to show that he was circumcised and therefore a Jew. On the man's face was a horrible look of blank suffering and despair which from the beginning of human history men have seen under the crown of thorns on the faces of their persecuted and humiliated victims. In this photograph what was even more horrible was the look on the faces of respectable men and women, standing on the pavement, laughing at the victim.[1]

As I recorded in *Downhill all the Way,*[2] when I drove through Germany in 1935, 'we did not enjoy this; there was something sinister and menacing in the Germany of 1935. There is a crude and savage silliness in the German tradition which, as one drove through the sunny Bavarian countryside, one felt beneath the surface and

[1] I feel something peculiarly terrible in the static horror of that photograph, the frozen record of the victim's despair and the spectators' enjoyment. Even more horrible and haunting is a photograph, published after the war, of a long line of Jews, men, women and children, being driven naked down a path into a gas chamber. Here again one sees visually before one the barbarism of the human race in the middle of the twentieth century.

[2] See above, p. 330.

saw, above it, in the gigantic notices outside the villages informing us that Jews were not wanted.' In 1935, however, Hitler had been in power only two years, and one felt only vaguely 'this crude and savage silliness' beneath the surface. There was in fact something much more savage and sinister beneath the surface, and in the next few years one occasionally caught a glimpse of it. For instance, just before the war Adrian Stephen learnt that a German friend of his was in grave danger from the Nazis, and, with influential support behind him, he went to Berlin to try to get his friend out of Germany. He conducted some very strange and complicated negotiations in the course of which he saw something of what the Nazis were doing and meant to do, and also of the desperate plight of their victims. The account of his experiences still further opened one's eyes—one looked into the abyss. As a result of that vision of the German brutality, when war had actually come and one had to face the possibility, if not probability, of invasion, Adrian told us that he would commit suicide rather than fall into German hands, and that he had provided himself with means of doing so; he offered to Virginia and me, who would certainly have been among the proscribed, a portion of this protective poison. I gather from Harold Nicolson's memoirs that he and Vita provided themselves with a similar 'bare bodkin', so that they might make their quietus in order to avoid the fate which would be theirs if they fell into German hands. Here again is terrible evidence of the difference in savagery between the Europe of 1939 and 1914. For here in 1939 were five ordinary intelligent people in England, coolly and prudently supplying themselves with means for committing suicide in order to avoid the tortures which almost certainly awaited them if the Germans ever got hold of them. It is inconceivable that anyone in England in 1914 would have dreamt of committing suicide if the Kaiser's armies had invaded England.

In writing an autobiography covering the years 1939 to 1945 one should, I think, try somehow or other objectively to face the facts about the horrible savagery of Hitler and the Germans. There was something insane in Hitler's genocide; in his writings, recorded conversation, and acts; in the conception and the execution of his colossal plan for killing in cold blood millions of human beings merely because they belonged to a race or religion which he did not like—Jews, Poles, or gipsies. But this sadistic nightmare of an insane megalomaniac was and could be executed only by hundreds, by thousands of ordinary sane Germans. They killed in various ways, but mainly by driving into lethal gas chambers six or seven million human beings with the greatest efficiency and the most appalling cruelty. The doctors who performed their disgusting experiments and operations on their victims, the commandants and guards who year after year starved and tortured millions of their fellow-citizens in the German concentration camps, seemed to be infected with Hitler's sadistic insanity. One hears occasionally quite casually of facts which show how widespread among the Germans was this inhuman cruelty. A Dutchman, a manual worker, told me that, when the Germans occupied Holland, he had to work for them on an airfield. On a railway line near by they loaded Jews into cattle trucks to be taken off to Germany, where they were destroyed. One day he saw a small child, frightened and crying, pull away from his mother so that she could not get up into the truck. A German guard caught hold of the child by one leg and flung him, as if he were a sack of corn, up into the air and over the side so that he fell onto the floor of the truck. The Dutchman told me that he could never forget the sight; it haunted him; it made him hate all Germans.

'It made him hate all Germans'—the sentence haunts me, just as the face of the well-dressed woman in the photograph laughing at the tortured face of the Jew with his fly buttons torn open and the bewildered faces of the naked women and children in the other photograph being driven down the narrow valley by the German uniformed guards into the death chamber haunt me. The callous cruelty, the pitilessness, the dreadful senselessness of those persecutors and murderers, and the hatred of all Germans which they generated in the Dutchman are the stigmata of the world in which I have lived since 1914. I feel the hatred welling up in myself, and yet I hate the hatred, knowing it to be neither rational nor objective. There is an old well-worn tag which says that one cannot condemn a nation, and there is some truth in it. Yet the scale of German cruelty and barbarism under Hitler in the years from 1933 to 1945 is so colossal that it seems to be different in quality or kind from the barbarism of other European peoples.

These horrible events and their effect upon personal and communal psychology in the world in which I have had to spend my life seem to me of profound importance; to understand them is also profoundly important. To understand them, at least to some extent, one must, I think, consider the nature and history of cruelty.

Montaigne in one of his essays writes:

> Amongst all other vices there is none I hate more than cruelty, both by nature and judgement, as the extremest of all vices. But it is with such a yearning and fainthartednesse, that if I see but a chickins neck pulled off, or a pigge stickt, I cannot chuse but grieve, and I cannot well endure a seelie, dew bedabled hare to groane, when she is seized upon by houndes.

I agree with Montaigne, there is nothing more horrible in human beings than human cruelty. But it is not just a question of liking or disliking or tolerating a vice or a virtue. I am writing these words in September 1967; it is four hundred years ago that Montaigne wrote the sentence quoted above—he may well have been sitting in the tower on the wall of his château in Montaigne on a September morning of 1567 when he wrote it. He was, I think, the first person in the world to express this intense, personal horror of cruelty. He was, too, the first completely modern man; he was pre-eminently a man of the Renaissance, that movement in the minds of men and therefore in history which created a new civilisation, modern civilisation which began in the Renaissance of the fourteenth century and was destroyed in 1914. An integral part in that new civilisation was the revolution in man's attitude to man. Before the Renaissance in all previous civilisations the individuality of the individual human being was only dimly realised and counted for little or nothing in the ethics and organisation of society; men, women, and children were not individuals, were in no sense 'I's', they were anonymous, impersonal members of classes or castes. In the middle of the fourteenth century this medieval attitude towards human beings, which was the basis of medieval society, began to give way to an uneasy awareness of the individuality of the individual. Montaigne was the first completely modern man in his intense awareness of and passionate interest in the individuality of himself and of all other human beings.

The combination in Montaigne of intense hatred of cruelty and intense awareness of individuality is not fortuitous. There is no place for pity or humanity in a society in which human beings are not regarded as individual human beings, but as impersonal classified pegs in a rigidly organised society. It is only if you feel that every he or she has an 'I' like your own 'I', only if everyone is to you an individual, that you can feel as Montaigne did about cruelty. It is the acute consciousness of my own individuality which makes me realise that I am I, and what pain, persecution, death means for this 'I'. For me 'death is the enemy', the ultimate enemy, for it is death which will destroy, wipe out, annihilate me, my individuality, my 'I'. What is so difficult to understand and feel is that all other human beings, that even the chicken, the pig, and the dew bedabled hare, each and all have a precisely similar 'I' with the same feelings of personal pleasure and pain, the same fearful consciousness of death, that destroyer of this unique 'I'. In the civilisation which developed from the Renaissance the ultimate communal ideal was defined in the famous liberty, equality, fraternity of the French Revolution. But those words only translate into social and political terms the consciousness of universal individuality and the right of everyone to be treated as an individual, a free fellow-human being. The development of a civilisation—its beliefs, ideals, and institutions—is a long and oscillating process. In the years between the life of Montaigne and the 1914 war there was a continual ebb and flow in the struggle for the emergence of the individual, for the right of everyone to be treated equally as an 'I'—even the baited bull and the hunted hare. By 1900 a civilised society, based upon individuality and liberty, equality and fraternity, had established itself with some firmness in only a few places, but taking the world as a whole nearly everywhere the movement of events and in men's minds seemed, despite oscillations, to be in the direction of Montaigne and Erasmus, Voltaire and Tom Paine.

Born in 1880 and bred in the bourgeois Kensington house and the 'liberal' atmosphere which derived from my father's sensibility, his extreme physical and moral fastidiousness, I very early came to understand and feel in my bones and recognise in events the various manifestations of this civilisation and of the counter-revolution still fighting bitterly against it. The spectrum of this civilisation stretched from political and social democracy at one end to humanitarianism and the Society for the Prevention of Cruelty to Animals at the other. What it means, and what it meant to me personally, and how its various manifestations are deeply rooted in our attitude to individuality and individuals can best be shown by a few examples of great oecumenical events and personal egocentric experiences which profoundly influenced or affected me.

First what some people may think a trivial and sentimental recollection, but an incident which to me is of great importance carrying me back to Montaigne and the essential nature of civilisation. It happened to me years ago when I was a boy and had not yet read the passage quoted above from Montaigne. My bitch had five puppies and it was decided that she should be left with two to bring up and so it was for me to destroy three. In such circumstances it was an age-old custom to drown the day-old puppies in a pail of water. This I proceeded to do. Looked at casually, day-old puppies are little, blind, squirming, undifferentiated objects or things. I put one of them in the bucket of water, and instantly an extraordinary, a terrible thing happened. This blind, amorphous thing began to fight desperately for its life, struggling, beating the water with its paws. I suddenly saw that it was an individual, that like me it was an 'I', that in its bucket of water it was experiencing what I would experience, and fighting death as I would fight death if I were drowning in the multitudinous seas. It was I felt and feel a horrible, an uncivilised thing to drown that 'I' in a bucket of water.

From the blind puppy struggling in the bucket of water to thousands of men, women, and children struggling for life in the mountains of Asia Minor. In 1894 one of those savage and senseless internecine massacres, epidemic among human beings, broke out in the Ottoman Empire. Turks and Kurds, encouraged by the Ottoman Government, began a systematic looting and destruction of Armenian villages and the slaughter of the inhabitants. The motives were religious, racial, and economic—which means that they were senseless, uncivilised, and inhuman. To kill a man and his wife, to rape his daughter and then kill her, because they pray in a church instead of a mosque, talk Armenian instead of Turkish, and are slightly (or thought to be slightly) more prosperous than you are, is senseless and barbarous, and the motives given above are labels which conceal a deeper and darker part of the human mind. The man who massacres can only do this if he regards his victims not as individuals like himself but as non-human pawns or anonymous ciphers in the fantasy or nightmare world of friends and foes, good men and evil men, in which he thinks he lives and which he therefore creates—or, of course, if he is just a plain common or garden sadist.

The campaign against Armenian massacres, like the antislavery movement of the early nineteenth century, was an example of a sudden mass movement against barbarism. It was led in England by Gladstone. That strange, Jesuitical, passionate, human man was eighty-five years old and had retired from politics, but he came out of his retirement and in a series of great public speeches denounced the massacres and their instigators as a disgrace to civilisation and called upon the Disraeli Government to intervene and stop them. I was fourteen years old at the time and it was my first profound political experience. Gladstone's campaign had a tremendous effect upon all kinds of different people, among whom was Mrs Cole, the headmistress of the school to which my sisters went and which in its kindergarten first introduced me to school and the stirrings of sex.[1] Mrs Cole was either the apotheosis or the caricature of the Victorian female teacher, depending upon the angle from which you observed her. She dominated the school and everyone in it, including her husband, who looked like the Prince Consort. Appropriately and, I think, deliberately she looked slightly like Queen Victoria. She was a short dumpy woman with thick shiny black hair, parted in the middle, and drawn back tightly and smoothly to a bun at the back. She was always dressed in black silk but somewhere or other on her person was a flounce or flower of bright pink. On her head, even when she was in the house, there was always a black bonnet with two long broad black ribbons attached to it. A woman of immense energy, mental and physical, she was perpetually whizzing about the house up and down stairs, in and out of classrooms, with the two black ribbons billowing out behind her. She addressed everyone, including whole classes and her flabby husband, in tones and vocabulary of cooing endearment—but there was an iron will under the velvety voice.

Mrs Cole became obsessed with the horrors and barbarism of the Armenian massacres. She descended like a whirlwind of black silk ribbons on her friends and acquaintances, imploring them to call upon the British Government to stop the massacres, beseeching them to give money to the Armenian Fund and woollen socks, stockings, and mittens to the starving and freezing survivors. The terrible stories and Mrs Cole's passionate indignation had a great effect upon me: for the first time I had, I think, a vague feeling or dim understanding of the difference between civilisation and barbarism. I could almost see the helpless Armenians being bayoneted by the Turkish soldiers and the women and children fleeing and floundering through the snowdrifts. And I had a shadowy feeling—as I had about the puppy in the bucket—that each of these victims was a person, like me an 'I'.

[1] See Volume 1, p. 31.

Thirdly, to the puppy drowning in the bucket and to the massacred Armenians I must add the tragic figure of Captain Dreyfus. I have already in *Sowing*[1] said something about the Dreyfus case as a key event in the history of our times, a symbol of the eternal struggle between barbarism and civilisation. Here I am concerned with the revelatory effect upon me which it shared with the puppy and the Armenians. If you look up Dreyfus in the current edition of the famous French dictionary *Petit Larousse*, published over seventy years after the obscure Captain Dreyfus was convicted by a court-martial of espionage and condemned to life imprisonment, you will find the following entry:

> Dreyfus (Alfred), officier français, né à Mulhouse (1859-1935), Israélite, accusé et condamné à tort pour espionnage (1894), il fut gracié (1899) et réhabilité (1906), après une violente campagne de révision (1897-1899) dénaturée par les passions politiques et religieuses. Ses adversaires étaient groupés dans la ligue de la Patrie française, ses partisans dans celle des Droits de l'homme. L'affaire avait divisé la France en deux camps.

These few lines give with admirable exactitude the bare bones of the Affaire: they put in the forefront that Dreyfus was Israélite—a Jew; an innocent man, he was accused and convicted of espionage; five years later he was given a free pardon, and, seven years later, after a terrific campaign for revision, he was retried, found to be innocent, and reinstated. The case divided France into two camps, for the battle against and for Dreyfus was fought with intense bitterness, between, on the one side, the army, Church, and conservatives and, on the other, the liberals and radicals.

It took a considerable time before people living outside France became aware of the Dreyfus case and its importance, and so it was several years after the Armenian massacres that I had my second political revelation from Paris. For some time after the conviction in 1894 one accepted the fact that a French officer had been convicted and sentenced for espionage, but by 1899 and the second court-martial one had become convinced of Dreyfus's innocence and one saw what his case involved for the future of France and of civilisation. It seemed in those days a terrible thing that the vast power of the State, the army, the Roman Catholic Church, and the press, concentrated in the hands of Cabinet Ministers, generals, cardinals, bishops, and editors, should deliberately be used by them to

[1] Volume 1, pp. 96-7, 102-3.

conceal and pervert the truth in order to ensure the conviction and life imprisonment of a man for a crime which they knew he had not committed. Occasionally in history some solitary figure in some tragic scene is transfigured and becomes a symbol of innocence or sin, of compassion or cruelty, of victory or defeat, of civilisation or barbarism. The Israelites three or four thousand years ago, in their passionate preoccupation with sin, invented such a symbolic scene in which the priest

> shall lay both his hands on the head of the live goat and confess over him all the iniquities of the children of Israel, and all the transgressions in all their sins, putting them on the head of the goat, and shall send him away by the hand of a fit man into the wilderness; and the goat shall bear upon him all their iniquities unto a land not inhabited: and he shall let go the goat in the wilderness.

The most famous of all such symbolic scenes took place nearly two thousand years ago in Jerusalem and is itself connected with the obsession of the Jews with sin and of the Christians and their churches who have absorbed and developed this obsession. The man accused before Pilate and condemned to be crucified between the two thieves is transfigured as the son of God, the symbol of innocence, salvation, civilisation, while the barbarians hissing and shouting, cry: 'Crucify him! His blood be on us and on our children.' And, as I pointed out in *Sowing,*[1] the scene of the formal degradation—a kind of crucifixion—of Dreyfus acquired the same kind of symbolic import—Dreyfus is brought into the huge square formed by detachments of all the regiments; the general says to him: 'Alfred Dreyfus, you are unworthy to bear arms. In the name of the French People we here degrade you'. Dreyfus raises his arms and cries: 'Soldiers, I am innocent! It is an innocent man who is being degraded, Vive la France! Vive l'Armée!'; a sergeant tears off from Dreyfus's uniform the insignia of his rank and breaks his sword, while the crowd hiss and shout: 'Kill him! Kill him!'

Because of all this Dreyfus had an even greater effect upon me than the drowning puppy and the massacred Armenians. The case was symbolic in two different ways, and to watch the interminable, fluctuating struggle was doubly agonising. There was first involved the impersonal, general principle of justice. People differ a great deal in their feeling about justice in the abstract. To many people it seems

[1] Volume 1, p. 103.

to mean little or nothing; others—and I am one of them—agree with the man, whoever he was, who said: '*Fiat justitia, ruat coelum*'. My father, as I recalled in *Sowing*,[1] thought that a perfect rule of conduct for a man's life had been laid down by the prophet Micah in the words 'do justly and love mercy'. I think that I too have always felt intensely about this. I get a keen kind of aesthetic pleasure in a complicated case in which perfect justice is done; on the other hand, injustice of any kind or to any person is extraordinarily disturbing and painful. An unjust law or a miscarriage of justice hurts and jars me like a false quantity or a discord in the wrong place, or a bad poem, picture, or sonata, or the stupidity of the overclever, or the perversion of truth. In all these cases the pain is impersonal, though it is no less acute for being that. But in cases like that of Dreyfus there is a second element which fills one with horror and despair. It is not merely that the impersonal principle of right or wrong, justice or injustice, is involved; Socrates condemned to death in Athens, Christ crucified in Jerusalem, Calas[2] condemned and tortured to death by the Church in France, Dreyfus condemned in Rennes and tortured in Devil's Island—in all these cases a person, an individual, faces us with the terrible, accusing, symbolic cry, addressed to God or to man, to society, to civilisation: My God! My God! why hast thou forsaken me? Dreyfus was not merely an anonymous unit among anonymous units, soldiers, officers, captains, Jews, like me and like the puppy—and Socrates, Christ and Calas—he was an 'I', an individual, and it was as this 'I' that a civilised society regarded him, his innocence or his guilt, his punishment and sufferings: not to do so is the negation of civilisation.

[1] Volume 1, p. 13.

[2] The case of Calas, falsely accused by the Roman Catholics of having murdered his son in order to prevent him renouncing Protestantism, was in every respect the Dreyfus case of the eighteenth century. Voltaire, in his passionate plea for the right of the individual to justice, did exactly what Zola did 140 years later, and the dead Calas was 'rehabilitated' in 1765 just as the living Dreyfus was 'rehabilitated' in 1906. Voltaire made the Calas judicial murder a test case of civilisation. To quote Theodore Besterman in *Voltaire Essays*: 'His cry of indignation echoed round the world and finally triumphed . . . For the first time and for good since the day on which Voltaire opened his arms to the Calas family . . . social injustice has been on the defensive: and it will remain on the defensive so long as men retain Voltaire's gift of indignation' (Mr Besterman's last sentence is, I think, over-optimistic).

I am insisting on this because it is essential to an understanding of the difference between the political and historical climate of 1939 and that of 1914; it also explains why people of my generation regarded with despair the world which Stalin, Mussolini, and Hitler had made, why so many people watched the war inevitably coming and entered it with a strange mixture of misery, calmness, and resignation. We knew that in Russia, Italy, and Germany there were hundreds of Calases, thousands of Dreyfuses. The world had reverted to regarding human beings not as individuals but as pawns or pegs or puppets in the nasty process of silencing their own fears or satisfying their own hates. It was impossible even for that most savage of all animals, man, to torture and kill on a large scale peasants, fellow-socialists, capitalists, Jews, gipsies, Poles, etc. if they were regarded as individuals; they had to be regarded as members of an evil and malignant class—peasants, deviating socialists, capitalists, Jews, gipsies, Poles, The world was reverting or had reverted to barbarism.

Personally I had felt this deeply and bitterly all through the last two years before war broke out. There was the horrible ambivalence towards Chamberlain's shameful betrayal of Czechoslovakia. Chamberlain always seemed to me the most coldly incompetent, most ununderstanding, unsympathetic of the British statesmen who have mismanaged affairs during my lifetime. But when one stands on the very brink of war suddenly, when one has practically abandoned hope, there is a shift in the kaleidoscope of events to peace instead of war, one cannot but feel an immense relief, release, and reprieve, even though at the same time one feels that the steps which have led to the avoidance of war ought not to have been taken, being shameful and morally and politically wrong. I suffered from this ambivalence all through the Munich crisis, for though the relief was extraordinary, I was convinced that by abandoning Czechoslovakia to Hitler we were only postponing war and that when it came we should have to fight it under conditions far more unfavourable to us than if we had Czechoslovakia and Russia as allies.

When the Polish crisis started, I felt that the end was coming. We went down to Monks House for the summer on 26 July but on 17 August, just seventeen days before we were actually at war, we had to move from Tavistock Square to the house which we had taken in Mecklenburgh Square; so we had to be driving backwards and forwards between Rodmell and London. The air of doom and calm resignation both inside one and outside one is what I chiefly remember of those days. The appearance of sandbags, the men digging trenches, the man on the removal van taking our furniture from Tavistock Square to Mecklenburgh Square and as an ex-soldier, receiving his call-up notice (I shan't be here tomorrow, Sir)—all with this quiet, dull, depressed, resigned sense of doom.

I suppose that, from the beginning of human history, men and women, the nameless individuals, have always faced the great crises and disasters, the senseless and inexorable results of communal savagery and stupidity, with the calm, grim, fatalistic resignation of the furniture removal man and all of us in Rodmell and London in August and September 1939. It is a kind of sad consolation to think that it must have been almost exactly like this in Athens in August and September 480 B.C. Ten years before, the horrors of war and invasion had swept down upon the Athenians with the Persian armies within a few miles of Athens. All the men of military age were called up, ten thousand infantry—'I shan't be here tomorrow, Sir'—and the Persian army was defeated and the war ended with the battle of Marathon. It answered to our war of 1914-18. Then the great army and fleet of Xerxes began again in 480 B.C. just as Hitler began again in 1939. All the men of military age were once more called up—'I shan't be here tomorrow, Sir'. The Persian armies swept down after the fall of Thermopylae (as France fell in 1940) and the whole population of Athens was evacuated to Salamis and other islands, just as the population of the East End of London was evacuated to Rodmell and other villages in 1939. Every Athenian who had been above the age of fourteen or fifteen in 490 must have remembered vividly in 480 the horrors and terrors of the first war and invasion. The young men once again drafted into the Greek army or navy, the old men and women ferried across from the Piraeus to Salamis were each and all of them individuals, as we were in London, waiting for the blitz. And I am sure each of them was feeling the same depressed resignation which Virginia and I felt driving up to London or watching a gang of Irish labourers digging, with incredible slowness and indolence, a bomb shelter in Mecklenburgh Square.

We were in Rodmell on Sunday 3 September when war was declared. The people evacuated from Bermondsey arrived and we helped to settle them into the cottages hurriedly prepared for them. They were typical Londoners and nearly all of them were horrified by our cottages and outraged and enraged at being asked to live in them. Most of them within a week or two had packed up and left us; they preferred to face the risk of Hitler's bombs to life in a Sussex village. The strange first air raid of the war—it was, of course, a false alarm—came to Rodmell on a lovely autumnal or late summer day. It came, I think, just after or before breakfast and I walked out onto the lawn which looks over the water-meadows to Lewes and the downs. It was absolutely still; soft, bright sunshine with wisps of mist still lying on the water-meadows. There are few more beautiful places in England than the valley of the Sussex Ouse between Lewes and Newhaven, the great sweep of water-meadows surrounded by the gentle, rounded downs. On a windless summer morning the soft sparkle of the sun on the meadows and downs, and every now and again the narrow ribbons of white mist lying upon them, give one an extraordinary sense of ageless quiet, King Arthur's 'Island valley of Avilion'—though one could never describe our water-meadows as a place

> Where falls not hail, or rain, or any snow
> Nor ever wind blows loudly.

It is curious that this Ouse valley should be so visually connected in my mind with peacefulness and beauty while I listened to the first air-raid sirens of the 1939 war, for, during the next six years, as soon as the phoney war ended and the real war began, it was over the peaceful water-meadows and above our heads over Rodmell village that again and again I watched the many strange phases of the war in the air being fought. Perhaps this is the best place to say something about how the air fighting actually affected us in the Sussex countryside.

The first sight of German planes which we saw was very odd. The real air war began for us in August 1940. On Sunday 18 August, Virginia and I had just sat down to eat our lunch when there was a tremendous roar and we were just in time to see two planes fly a few feet above the church spire, over the garden, and over our roof, and looking up as they passed above the window we saw the swastika on them. They fired and hit a cottage in the village and fired another shot into a house in Northease. This first experience of active warfare surprised me in one respect. I had always thought that I should be frightened under fire. The German planes just above my head, I was glad to find, left me perfectly calm and cold, the whole incident seeming to be completely unreal, and in fact in all the many 'incidents' of the kind which took place in subsequent years I never myself felt or saw anyone else feeling fear. Though between 1940 and 1945 I must have seen hundreds of German planes and many of them dropping bombs or fighting British planes, except in this incident I never saw or had real evidence of a German plane firing bullets at people or buildings on the ground, but very early in the war I had an experience with regard to the alleged machine-gunning by a German airman which taught me never to believe stories of 'incidents', even by eye-witnesses. It is worth recording.

In those distant days newspapers were delivered in villages like Rodmell by men or girls riding bicycles. There were two delivering in Rodmell whom I knew well. One was a man whom I will call Tom and the other was a girl of about 17 whom I will call Mary. One day I realised that it was several weeks since I had seen Mary and her bicycle, and a day or two later I met Tom in the village street. 'What has happened to Mary, Tom?' I said; 'I haven't seen her for a long time.' 'Haven't you heard?' said Tom. 'She was machine-gunned by a German plane, and I saw it happen. I was riding on the Ringmer road and Mary was riding about two hundred yards ahead of me. Suddenly a German plane swooped down, flew just above our heads along the line of the road, and fired a burst at Mary. She was badly wounded and it still in the hospital.' Here, I thought, at any rate is an authentic case of a senseless and brutal German 'atrocity'. About three months later I met Mary walking along a street in Lewes. I congratulated her on her recovery, but as soon as she began to talk about her experience, I found that the story told by Tom was entirely untrue. There had been no German plane and no shooting and the incident had taken place not in Ringmer but in the Lewes street where we were talking. Mary had been walking up the street during an air raid and when she was immediately opposite the Co-op store a bomb fell on a house not many yards away. The blast shattered the window of the shop and Mary was badly cut by the flying glass. I find it extremely difficult to understand Tom's behaviour in inventing, as he must have done, a completely false story. I knew him quite well and often talked to him; once when he was ill and in hospital, I went to see him and we talked about all kinds of things for half an hour or more. He never gave the slightest sign of 'talking tall' or of lying. I am inclined to think that by the time he told me that he had seen Mary shot on the Ringmer road, he really believed that he had. Yet he must at the same time have known that she was in Lewes hospital having been badly cut by flying glass from the shattered Co-op window. 'There's fevers of the mind as well as body', as Mrs Gamp remarked, and in wartime they show themselves in the wild way in which people invent stories of what they have heard or seen.

To return to bombing and to what did happen, some time in 1940 there were German planes over Rodmell one day and Virginia and I were standing in the garden when we heard the swishing of bombs through the air overhead and then the dull thuds of explosions towards the River Ouse. The bombs were aimed at and missed the cement works, but one or two of them hit and breached the river bank. There happened to be quite a high tide at the time and the river poured through the gap and flooded the fields. Then some days later there was an abnormally high tide with a strong wind, and a great stretch of river bank gave way. The whole Ouse valley was flooded and a great lake of water now stretched from the bottom of my garden to Lewes on the north and almost to Newhaven on the south. We had reverted to the conditions of the early nineteenth century before the river banks were built up. In those days whenever there was heavy rain and a high tide the whole valley was under water.

Early in the war I joined the fire service. My duties consisted of taking my turn patrolling the village at night and also helping to man a pump. The pump was a beautifully primeval machine which was mounted on a small truck. Four firemen, yoked like horses, pulled the truck to the (presumably) blazing building on which we hoped to direct a stream of water through long hoses. We used in practice to rush this strange contraption up and down the village street and play the water on some house or cottage. We were only once called out in earnest; about ten o'clock one night in March 1941, during a raid, a German bomber dropped a shower of incendiary bombs which just missed the village and fell all over the fields on the south of it. One of them hit a haystack a few hundred yards beyond the last house on the road to Newhaven. We rushed our pump to the spot, but the heat of the burning stack was so terrific that we could not get anywhere near it with our length of hose. So we rang up the professional fire engine in Lewes; when it arrived it was as impotent as we were, for by the time they arrived two other stacks had caught and even the professionals could do nothing. It was a curious sight typical of the way in which in the second world war people in Sussex faced battle, murder, and sudden death. Though there was an air raid in progress, half the village turned out and stood on the main road watching the burning ricks. Scattered over the fields there were numbers of little 'flames upturning' where the bombs were burning themselves out. We—twenty or thirty men, women, and children—the firemen, and the fire engines stood on the road in the tremendous glare of the fire. Suddenly came the drone of a plane and a German bomber flew low over our heads. I think everyone expected a bomb or two, but nobody moved. The plane plugged away and some minutes later we heard the thud of its bombs dropped on Newhaven. The ricks burnt themselves out, the fire-engine returned to Lewes, and the village of Rodmell retired to bed.

A few nights after this I was patrolling the village about three o'clock in the morning and the siren sounded an air-raid warning. Some time later a German bomber flew over the village, and when it was almost immediately overhead there was a tremendous crash about a hundred yards ahead of me. I rushed to the spot, which was a large building at the top of the village. This strange building had been built by a speculative builder as a warehouse in the middle of the nineteenth century when it was thought that the railway from Lewes to Newhaven, shortly to be constructed, would run through the village. The speculation missed fire when the railway was built on the other side of the river. The warehouse remained empty and derelict for years, but after the 1914 war was converted into flats. I expected to find the building half-demolished, but I could find no sign of anything wrong with it. As I walked round it a head appeared out of a window and a female voice said: 'It's all right, sir. The noise was caused by our cat; he jumped into an empty tin bath which was outside at the top of the steps and he upset it so as it went clattering down with him into the yard.'

One more curious Rodmell incident. I was playing a game of bowls with Virginia, her niece, and a young man one summer afternoon. I was just about to play a shot when a plane came overhead and the young man said to me: 'That's an odd plane; what is it?' I looked up and there very low down flying slowly was an old-fashioned-looking plane. I was more interested in my shot, and said casually: 'O, that must be a Lysander'. I played my shot, and as I did so there was the noise of splattering on the leaves of the great chestnut tree near by and I realised at once that it was the noise of bullets. I looked up again at the plane, which was circling slowly over the garden, and saw the swastika on it. The bullets did not come from the plane, but from a searchlight unit on the down above the village. We lay on the grass while more bullets spattered overhead. The plane circled round and then very very slowly flew off across the water-meadows. As we watched it, it came down in the brooks about two miles away. We heard later that the German pilot was a mere boy; he was taking mail in an antediluvian plane from France to the Germans in the Channels Islands. Losing his way, he had mistaken Sussex for Jersey. Some of the bullets hit his plane, but he himself was unwounded.

When the Battle of Britain and the bombing of London in earnest began, one watched daily in Rodmell the sinister preliminaries to destruction. First the wail of the sirens; then the drone of the German planes flying in from the sea, usually to the east of Rodmell and Lewes. On a clear fine day one could see the Germans high up in the sky and sometimes the British planes going up to meet them north of Lewes. There was very little fighting in the air immediately over the Ouse valley for the Germans flew regularly in a corridor more to the east. I saw only two incidents. A British Hurricane was shot down in a field near the river and I saw a German plane shot down into the water-meadows near Lewes. In the latter incident I felt strongly the spectacular or visual unreality—and also it must be admitted a strange beauty—in modern warfare. It was again on a lovely, windless, sunny autumn afternoon and there was considerable air activity all round us during a raid. I walked out on to the lawn overlooking the water-meadows to watch what was happening. Suddenly a German plane came flying low over the downs towards Lewes pursued by a British fighter. The fighter gained on the German and there was the sound of firing. Suddenly the German plane went straight up into the air, turned over upside down in a great slow loop, and, as the British plane shot by underneath it, fell into the meadows. A column of smoke rose absolutely straight into the windless sky.

When the night bombings of London began we were still living during the week in Mecklenburgh Square; but when the house was made uninhabitable by bombs, which fell in the square and in the street behind it, we had to live in Rodmell. We were in Mecklenburgh Square in one of the earliest night raids. We did not go into the shelter which had been built in the centre of the square though we had a look at it. We thought it better to die, if that were to be our fate, in our beds. There was a good deal of noise, but nothing that night fell very near to us. I wanted to see Kingsley Martin about something and at ten o'clock next morning Virginia and I walked round to the *New Statesman* office in Great Turnstile just south of Holborn. There was no sign of the blitz until we turned out of Gray's Inn into Holborn. It was the first sight we had of the aftermath desolation of an air raid. One got accustomed, or almost accustomed, to seeing it, as the war went on; but seen for the first time, it had a strange impact on one. The first thing one noticed was the litter of glass from the windows all the way up Holborn. Then the silence—no traffic and very few people about. The holes in the façade of the street where a building had been destroyed, like a tooth missing in a mouth. A smell of burning. We went down the narrow alley and into the *New Statesman* building. It seemed to be entirely empty. My recollection is that it was intact but there was a good deal of water about. I went along to Kingsley's room and there standing by himself with his hat in his hand in the empty room was a man who said to me in a plaintive voice: 'I have come to see Mr Kingsley Martin'. His look and tone of voice seemed to imply that I had caused the desolation and the absence of Mr Kingsley Martin. 'So have I,' I said, 'but he does not appear to be here.' He gave me a nasty look and left the room.

In the latter part of 1940, when we were living permanently in Rodmell, it was during the mass raids on London a sinister thing to listen every night to the drone of the German planes flying inland. In the hour or more of silence which followed, it was horrible to know that London was being bombed and burnt. Then the silence was broken by the drone of the returning planes. There was one strange incident connected with these night raids. Very often after the raiders had flown in to London, it seemed as if one plane had been left behind to fly round and round the Ouse valley. It did this until just before the other German bombers returned, when it dropped bombs, as it seemed, erratically anywhere in the water-meadows or on the downs. The curious manoeuvres of this lone wolf went on for some time and then suddenly stopped. I knew a stonemason in Lewes who, during the war, was one of those monitors of the skies who kept a check on and reported all planes entering the section of heaven for which he was responsible. When I met him one day, some time after the German raids had stopped, I asked him whether they had noticed this lone wolf of a bomber and whether he had any explanation of its curious behaviour. He said that the spotters were convinced that the lone wolf was a coward who habitually dropped out of his squadron in order to avoid the terrors which awaited him over London. They believed that his sudden disappearance was due to his having been 'executed' by his fellow-airmen; they probably shot him down into the Channel on their way back one night.

I must now leave these tales of the war and return to our daily life in 1939 and 1940. All through the last months of 1939 and the first of 1940 we divided our time between Mecklenburgh Square and Monks House. Virginia was working very hard—too hard in fact. She had begun both *Roger Fry* and *Between the Acts* in the first half of 1938 and was still writing them all through 1939. She enjoyed writing *Between the Acts*, but the life of Roger became a burden to her. It was a book which I do not think she ought to have undertaken, but she had been overpersuaded by Margery Fry to do it. The orderly presentation of reality, which remorselessly imposes its iron pattern upon the writer who rashly tries to discern and describe it in the infinite kaleidoscope of facts, was not natural to Virginia's mind or method. Four times in her life she forced herself to write a book against her artistic and psychological grain; four times the result was bad for the book and twice it was bad for herself. She said herself that she wrote *Night and Day* as a kind of exercise; she had a shadowy *Jacob's Room* in her mind, a novel which would break the traditional mould of the English novel, which would have a new form and method, because she felt that the traditional form and method did not allow her to say what she wanted to say. Before she broke the mould, she thought she ought to prove that she could write a novel classically in the traditional mould.

The second time was *The Years*. In 1932 after *Orlando* and *Flush* she decided to write a 'family novel', a form of fiction popular at the time. When she began to write it in 1932 with the title *The Pargiters* (which marked it as a family novel) she wrote in her diary:

> It's to be an Essay-Novel, called *The Pargiters*—and it's to take in everything, sex, education, life etc.

and she added:

> What has happened of course is that after abstaining from the novel of fact all these years—since 1919—and *N. & D.* is dead—I find myself infinitely

delighting in facts for a change, and in possession of quantities beyond counting, though I feel now and then the tug of vision, but resist it. This is the true line I am sure, after *The Waves—The Pargiters*—this is what leads naturally on to the next stage—the essay novel.

There was another thing which perhaps to some extent influenced her in this determination to write 'a novel of fact'. She was oversensitive to any criticism, and one of the things most often said against her as novelist was that she could not create real characters or the reality of everyday life. I think that in 1932, beginning *The Years*, at the back of her mind was the desire or determination to prove these critics wrong.

The third time was the biography of Roger Fry, which she began to write six years after she had begun *The Years*. Being a biography, it was far more concerned with the facts and determined by facts than a novel—it was fact, not fiction. When I first read it I thought there was a flaw in it, and as Virginia recorded in her diary on 20 March 1940,[1] walking over the water-meadows I tried—no doubt too emphatically—to explain to her what I felt about it. Like everything of hers, it had things in it which could only have been hers and very good they were, but the two parts of the book did not artistically fit together and she allowed the facts to control her too compulsively so that the book was slightly broken-backed and never came alive as a whole. Roger's sister Margery, Vanessa, and his friends and relations generally disagreed with me, but I still think I was right. There is something a little dead about *Roger Fry: A Biography*. Virginia herself, in the passage from her diary quoted above, in 1932 said that *Night and Day* was dead. In the third factual book, *The Years*, there is again something radically wrong. The 'factual' novel, the facts, got out of control, the book became inordinately long and loose. I have described in *Downhill all the Way*[2] the terrible time we had when *The Years* was finished and Virginia was faced with the proofs. She tried to regain control of the facts and the novel, to eliminate the length and the looseness, by drastic cutting, but the operation was not really successful, the Bed of Procustes was unable to turn the book into a masterpiece; it is a psychological and familial chronicle rather than a history, and, like

[1] *A Writer's Diary*, p. 328.

[2] See above, pp. 299-302.

Night and Day and *Roger Fry*, was slightly dead even at the moment of birth.

Virginia was an intellectual in every sense of the word; she had the strong, logical, down to earth brain which was characteristic of so many of her male Stephen relations: her grandfather, James Stephen of the Colonial Office; her father, the author of *History of English Thought in the 18th Century* and *Hours in a Library*; her uncle, James Fitzjames, the High Court judge; and her brother Thoby. It was not that she could not handle facts or had the weakness in induction or deduction which men so often, without much evidence, consider peculiarly feminine. Her reviews, and indeed these factual books themselves, show this. But she could deal with facts and arguments on the scale of a full-length book only by writing against the grain, by continually repressing something which was natural and necessary to her peculiar genius—she shows this in the passage quoted above when she writes: 'I feel now and then the tug of vision, but resist it'. The result is a certain laboriousness and deadness so different from the quicksilver intensity of the novels in which the tug of vision was not resisted. It is even easier to see the difference if one compares *A Room of One's Own* with *Three Guineas*, the fourth of her factual books. In *A Room of One's Own* there is no shirking of facts and arguments, but they are subjected to and illuminated by vision, and the book tingles with life; *Three Guineas*, in comparison, is oppressed by the weight of its facts and arguments.

In all these cases this forcing herself to write against the grain, to resist her own genius, added to the mental and physical strain of writing a book, the exhaustion and depression which nearly always overwhelmed her when the umbilical cord was severed and the MS sent to the printer. The most desperate example of this was what happened between the writing and the printing of *The Years*.[1] There is no doubt that the biography of Roger exhausted her in much the same way. She finally finished the book (there was nearly always a final finish with her books) on 9 April and it was at last off her hands with the corrected proofs returned to the printers on 13 May. But it had been a terrible grind in many ways. She said that she had 'written every page—certainly the last—ten or fifteen times over'. At first, with the relief of getting the book off her hands and being able

[1] See above, pp. 299-302.

to go back to fiction and vision in *Between the Acts*, she seemed to be less worried and more optimistic than she usually was when her book was on the threshold of publication.

The umbilical cord which had bound *Roger Fry: A Biography* to Virginia's brain for two years was, as I said, finally cut when she returned the proofs to the printer on 13 May 1940; 319 days later on 28 March 1941, she committed suicide by drowning herself in the River Ouse. Those 319 days of headlong and yet slow-moving catastrophe were the most terrible and agonising days of my life. The world of my private life and of English history and of the bricks and mortar of London disintegrated. To drag the memory of them out of one's memory, as I must do now if I am to continue publicly to remember, is difficult and painful. The reluctant recollection of protracted pain is peculiarly painful. The excitement in the moment of catastrophe, the day-to-day, hour-to-hour, minute-to-minute stimulus of having to act, produce an infallible anodyne for misery. I am always astonished to find that one instantly becomes oblivious of the most acute pain if one has to concentrate on anything else, even on a triviality. While one concentrates on crossing a crowded street, in London, the consciousness of the torture of toothache or of being crossed in love is completely obliterated. But there are no distractions or alleviation in one's recollection of misery.

Virginia's loss of control over her mind, the depression and despair which ended in her death, began only a month or two before her suicide. Though the strains and stresses of life in London and Sussex in the eight months between April 1940 and January 1941 were for her, as for everyone living in that tormented area, terrific, she was happier for the most part and her mind more tranquil than usual. The entry in her diary for 13 May, already published in *A Writer's Diary* (p. 331) gives the atmosphere of those violent days and the ambivalence of her mood and mind so vividly that I must quote it here.

'I admit to some content, some closing of a chapter and peace that comes with it, from posting my proofs today. I admit—because we're in the third day of "the greatest battle in history". It began (here) with the 8 o'clock wireless announcing as I lay half-asleep the invasion of Holland and Belgium. The third day of the Battle of Waterloo. Apple blossom snowing the garden. A bowl lost in the pond. Churchill exhorting all men to stand together. "I have nothing to offer but blood and tears and sweat." These vast formless shapes further circulate. They aren't substances: but they make everything else minute. Duncan saw an air battle over Charleston—a silver pencil and a puff of smoke. Percy has seen the wounded arriving in their boots. So my little moment of peace comes in a yawning hollow. But though L. says he has petrol in the garage for suicide should Hitler win, we go on. It's the vastness, and the smallness, that makes this possible. So intense are my feelings (about Roger); yet the circumference (the war) seems to make a hoop round them. No I can't get the odd incongruity of feeling intensely and at the same time knowing that there's no importance in that feeling. Or is there, as I sometimes think, more importance than ever? I made buns for tea today—a sign my thraldom to proofs (galleys) is over.'

A few days later when there was an appeal to join the Home Guard 'against parachutists' I said that I would join, and there was rather 'an acid conversation' because Virginia, though she saw that I was 'evidently relieved by the chance of doing something', was against it, feeling 'gun and uniform to me slightly ridiculous'. She admitted that her nerves were harassed under the strain of looming uncertainty. But we discussed again calmly what we should do if Hitler landed. The least that I could look forward to as a Jew, we knew, would be to be 'beaten up'. We agreed that, if the time came, there would be no point in waiting; we would shut the garage door and commit suicide. 'No', Virginia wrote, 'I don't want the garage to see the end of me. I've a wish for ten years more, and to write my book, which as usual darts into my brain . . . Why am I optimistic? Or rather not either way? Because it's all bombast, the war. One old lady pinning on her cap has more reality. So if one dies, it'll be a common sense, dull end—not comparable to a day's walk, and then an evening reading by the fire . . . Anyhow, it can't last—this intensity, so we think—more than ten days. A fateful book this. Still some blank pages—and what shall I write on the next ten?'

What she wrote was much the same kind of thing which anyone who kept a diary would have to write in the ten days of a great catastrophe of history, the death and destruction of a civilisation. In the ten days when heaven and civilisation, the country where one was born and bred and lived, one's private life and banking account, are falling about one's head, when one is contemplating suicide by asphyxiation in a damp and dirty garage after breakfast, one continues to cook and eat one's eggs and bacon for breakfast. Greeks were doing that, I feel sure, in Thebes and Athens 2,304 years ago when Alexander the Great and his armies were destroying the civilisation of Homer, Pindar, Sophocles, and Plato and every house except one in the city of Thebes—it was characteristic of one of the great conquerors, the great destroyers of civilisation, the inhuman pests of human history, that Alexander

> The great Emathian conqueror bid spare
> The house of Pindarus, when temple and tower
> Went to the ground,

and he sold all the inhabitants as slaves. It must have been the same when, 1,558 years ago in Rome the Romans were eating the equivalent of our eggs and bacon and Alaric, the Goth, was on the point of capturing and sacking their city. It must have been the same with the millions of victims of Jenghis Khan, and of the Turks when Constantinople fell in 1453, and of the drums and tramplings of all conquests from the Egyptian and Sumerian to that of Hitler.

Moore and Desmond MacCarthy came and stayed with us for the weekend of 18 May. It was the last time that I was to see Moore. Desmond and Moore together, the one talking, talking, the other silent in the armchair, were inextricably a part of my youth, of the entrancing excitement of feeling life open out in one and before one. I could shut my eyes and *feel* myself back in 1903, in Moore's room in the Cloisters of Trinity or the reading parties at the Lizard or Hunters Inn. With the eyes open we were older. I myself either have never grown up or was born old, for I have always had the greatest difficulty in feeling older. My 'I', that particle indestructible except by death, which answered to that particle in the drowning puppy, seems to me exactly the same in the child in Lexham Gardens, the undergraduate in Moore's room in Trinity, the middle-aged man of 1940, even the old man writing his memoirs. It is easy to feel the stiffness in one's knees, and it is of course only delusion that one does not feel it in one's heart and brain.

Moore was older. The extraordinary purity and beauty of character and of mind were still there, the strange mixture of innocence and wisdom. The purity, moral and mental, was the most remarkable of Moore's qualities; I have never known anything like it in any other human being. It was as though Socrates, Aristotle, and the Pure Fool—the Reine Tor is it?—had grown inextricably entangled in the same mind and body. Bertrand Russell in the second volume of his Autobiography writes of that other Cambridge philosopher Wittgenstein: 'He was perhaps the most perfect example of genius as traditionally conceived, passionate, profound, intense and dominating. He had a kind of purity which I have never known equalled except by G. E. Moore.' There was a streak of aggressive cruelty in Wittgenstein—I once saw him so brutally rude to Lydia Keynes at luncheon, when he was staying with Maynard, that she burst into tears. Moore had the passion, the profundity, the intensity, and the purity, but he seemed to be completely without cruelty and aggression. Age had blunted the passion and softened the intensity. It had chiselled away some of the beauty of his face. He told me that a little time before his visit to us he had a strange and alarming black-out which, he felt, had left its mark on him. But the luminous purity of mind and spirit was in him at the age of sixty-seven in Rodmell just as it was forty years before when I first saw him in Trinity.

Age had left its mark too upon Desmond; both his face and his mind were age-beaten. Asthma and the erosion by the incessant little worries of life had to some extent dimmed and depressed him, but every now and again memory, which could make an artist of Desmond, and his amused devotion and affection for Moore, inspired him so that the years fell away and one again felt to the full the charm of his character and his conversation.

There we sat in May 1940, Moore, Desmond, Virginia, and I in the house and under a hot sun and brilliant sky in the garden, in a cocoon of friendship and nostalgic memories. At the same time the whole week-end was dominated by a consciousness that our little private world was menaced by destruction, by oecumenical catastrophe now beginning across the Channel in France. It was, of course, a week before the capitulation of the Belgians, but the German offensive had been in operation for ten days, the tension was unrelieved and one's memories of unremitting defeat in the terrible first years of the 1914 war left one inevitably with premonition of disaster, so that even hope was a kind of self-indulgence and self-deception. The restless foreboding of those days was broken for me by a strange, grim incident which I always in memory connect with them. There lived in Rodmell at that time a working-class man whom I will call Mr X. I knew the whole family very well. The youngest son, now about eight or nine years old, had been injured at birth and was completely 'retarded'. He could not speak or feed himself and could hardly walk. As is so often the case, his mother adored him and devoted her life to looking after him, which indeed was a full-time job. Some years before the eldest son had come to me and asked me to try to persuade Mrs X to send the boy to a mental home, as he and the rest of the family thought that his mother was ruining her life by immuring herself with the child. They had tried to argue with her, but she would not listen to them; he thought that she might listen to me. She did listen to me, but what I said had no effect upon her.

The eldest son, Percy, was in 1940 called up for service in the army, and one evening he came to see me. He said his regiment was leaving in a day or two for France, and he was very much worried about his mother, who was really destroying her health and all happiness by her devotion to the youngest son. He would embark for France much relieved if I would make another attempt to persuade Mrs X to send the child to a home. This time I was successful and I went to the Medical Officer, who already knew about the case, and asked him to get the boy into a home. He did so, and at first everything went well; but after about two weeks Mrs X came to me and said that the boy was being starved and ill-treated, was getting very ill, and must be given back to them. Then one morning Mr and Mrs X appeared in my garden dressed in their Sunday clothes. They had hired a taxi and asked me to accompany them to the Medical Officer and demand the child.

There followed some painful hours. I agreed to go to the M.O. provided that they left the business to me and did not start abusing him and the Home for starving the boy. They promised, but within five minutes of our being shown into the M.O.'s room Mrs X was making the wildest accusations against him, the Home, and the nurses. The M.O. behaved admirably; he rang up the Home and arranged that if we went there immediately, the boy would be handed over to us. I do not think that I have ever had a more unpleasant pilgrimage in my life than that to the Home and back to Rodmell, sitting in the taxi with the unfortunate parents. The boy was delivered to us wrapped in blankets. He was obviously ill and a week or ten days later he died. There was an inquest, at which Mrs X repeated her accusations against the nurses and everyone connected with the Home, but the verdict was death from natural causes.

This kind of tragedy, essentially terrible, but in detail often grotesque and even ridiculous, is not uncommon in village life. At the time its impact upon me was strong and strange; somehow or other it seemed sardonically to fit into the pattern of a private and public world threatened with destruction. The passionate devotion of mothers to imbecile children, which was the pivot of this distressing incident, always seems to me a strange and even disturbing phenomenon. I can see and sympathise with the appeal of helplessness and vulnerability in a very young living creature—I have felt it myself in the case of an infant puppy, kitten, leopard, and even the much less attractive and more savage human baby. In all these cases, apart from the appeal of helplessness, there is the appeal of physical beauty; I always remember the extraordinary beauty of the little leopard cub which I had in Ceylon, so young that his legs wobbled a little under him as he began jerkily to gambol down the verandah and yet showing already under his lovely, shining coat the potential rippling strength of his muscles. But there is something horrible and repulsive in the slobbering imbecility of a human being. Is the exaggerated devotion of the mother to this child, which nearly always seems to be far greater than her devotion to her normal, attractive children, partly determined by an unconscious sense of guilt and desire to vindicate herself and her child? It is rather strange that I have twice been asked to interfere in a case of this sort. I once had a secretary who came to me and asked me to speak to her sister just as Percy had asked me to speak to his mother. The sister had a very highly paid post as buyer of dresses for one of the large Oxford Street stores. She had an imbecile son and, like Mrs X, devoted the whole of her domestic life to him. He was fifteen, physically strong, and occasionally violent. She refused to send him to a Home and I was asked to try to persuade her to do so. I failed, but in this case not long afterwards the boy's behaviour became so alarming that it was no longer possible for his mother to keep him at home.

To return to our daily life in May and June 1940, before the bombing of London began, it slipped into a regular routine. Virginia, having got rid of *Roger Fry,* settled down to writing *Between the Acts* or *Pointz Hall* as she still called it. It went well and on the whole she was quite happy about it. By 31 May she was within sight of the end, for she had already written the passage about 'scraps, orts and fragments', which in the printed book is only thirty-five pages from the end. In order to give her uninterrupted quiet for writing the novel, we divided our time between Rodmell and London. Every two weeks we went up to Mecklenburgh Square and stayed there for four days. That ensured Virginia ten days out of every fourteen in which she could write uninterruptedly in Rodmell.

The four days in London were always pretty hectic. My main business was the Hogarth Press. John Lehmann had come into the Press as a partner in 1938 and he was, to all intents and purposes, a managing director. It was a difficult time already for the Press, and it became much worse when the blitz started. In order to relieve the strain on the staff, we had them one by one to spend a weekend with us at Rodmell. In my bi-weekly four days in Mecklenburgh Square, in addition to the hours which I spent with John over the Hogarth Press business, I used to go to the House of Commons for the Labour Party Advisory Committees, of which I was still secretary, and to the Fabian Society where I was still a member of the Executive Committee and chairman of the International Bureau. We also crammed as much social life as possible into our four days, having many of our friends to dinner. For instance, in the two London visits of 21-24 May and 4-7 June we saw T. S. Eliot, Koteliansky, William Plomer, Sybil Colefax, Morgan Forster, Raymond Mortimer, Stephen Spender, Kingsley Martin, Rose Macaulay, and Willie Robson.

There was in those days an ominous and threatening unreality, a feeling that one was living in a bad dream and that one was on the point of waking up from this horrible unreality into a still more horrible reality. During the months of the phoney war, when everything seemed to be for the moment inexplicably suspended, there was this incessant feeling of unreality and impending disaster, but it became even stronger during the five weeks between Hitler's invasion of Holland and Belgium and the collapse of France. There was a curious atmosphere of quiet fatalism, of waiting for the inevitable and the aura of it still lingers in the account of our days in London which Virginia gives in her diary. For instance, in the first week in June, with the great battle raging in France, Virginia and I with Rose Macaulay and Kingsley Martin sat talking after dinner until 2.30 in the morning. Kingsley, 'diffusing his soft charcoal gloom', prophesied the defeat of the French and the invasion of Britain within five weeks. A Fifth Column would get to work; the Government would move off to Canada leaving us to a German Pro-Consul, a concentration camp, or suicide. We discussed suicide while the electric light gradually faded and finally left us sitting in complete darkness.

Then quickly came the collapse of the French and the retreat of the British to Dunkirk. In Rodmell Dunkirk was a harrowing business. There was not merely the public catastrophe, the terrible suspense with Britain on the razor's edge of complete disaster; in the village we were domestically on the beaches. For Percy, who had come to me about his mother only a few days ago, and Jim and Dick and Chris, whom I had known as small boys in the village school and watched grow up into farm workers and tractor drivers, were now, one knew, retreating like the two grenadiers of the Napoleonic wars, driven back to the Dunkirk beaches. There presumably they were waiting and we in Rodmell waited. On 17 June Percy suddenly appeared in the village; his story was the soldier's story which, with an infinite series of variations, has been told again and again ever since, and before, Othello 'spake . . . of hairbreadth 'scapes i' the imminent deadly breach'. It was not the less moving—partly because Percy was still badly shaken by his experiences; everything was still shockingly vivid to him, and it eased his mind somewhat to describe it vividly to someone else. He described the retreat through Belgium, the Belgian woman who gave him bread for nothing—'no French woman would do that—a nasty gabbling, panicky lot the French'—an abandoned jeweller's shop which they looted—he took some rings and two watches—the rings fell out of his pocket in the sea at Dunkirk, but he pinned the watches to the inside of his coat and got them safely back to England—they were strafed incessantly by German planes on the beaches and 'the bullets were like moth-holes in my coat'; there were no British planes; when they had to pass a pill-box, the officer made the men take off their boots and crawl past it and he then went himself and flung a grenade into it—he saw his cousin lying dead on the beach and also another Rodmell chap who used to live up the village street—on the beach a chap showed him a silk handkerchief which he had bought for his 'joy lady' and, as he did so, a bomb fell and killed the man. Percy still has the silk handkerchief—he swam out to sea to a small boat, *The Linnet*; when he got near it, they shouted to him: 'Say, chum, can you row?' and when he said that he could, they pulled him into the boat—they rowed for five hours before they saw the English coast, and they were so exhausted that, when they at last landed, they did not know or ask where they were and they did not know whether it was night or day. Actually he landed at Ramsgate, got lifts to somewhere on the Eastbourne road, and walked through the night to his sister's cottage in Rodmell. She, in that early morning, looking out of her kitchen window, saw a soldier whom she did not recognise at first, hatless, his tunic bloody and full of holes, his boots in rags, lying exhausted outside the front door. His morale was pretty low; he thought we were beaten—we had no arms or planes; yet he soon recovered, returned to his regiment, and fought until the end of the war, ending up in the army of occupation in Germany and marrying a very nice German girl from Hamburg.

Friday 14 June, the Germans took Paris, and we spent the day incongruously—or from another point of view appropriately—with history being made so catastrophically across the Channel—for we took a journey from the present into the past. Virginia had never been to Penshurst, the magnificent Elizabethan mansion in Kent which has remained in the Sidney family ever since the time of the romantic Sir Philip Sidney, who wrote *Arcadia* and was killed at the battle of Zutphen in Holland nearly four hundred years ago. We had more than once been on the point of making an expedition with Vita Sackville-West to see the house on a day when it was open to the public. And this is what we did on Friday 14 June. Penshurst is an epitome of English history with its vast banqueting hall and its vast clutter of pictures, furniture, utensils—some of them beautiful, but many appallingly ugly—which the great aristocratic families accumulate in their castles and mansions through the centuries. It was amusing to visit Penshurst with Vita who had the blood of all these owners of Elizabethan castles—including probably the Sidneys'—in her veins and seemed always to have a castle or two of her own hanging about her. We went through the rooms and the bric-à-brac, all of which, no doubt, is well worth seeing, but I left with that rather oppressive feeling of passing through centuries of history mummified or more modernly preserved in deep freeze.

When we came out from the immense banqueting hall into the open air, Vita said that she must go round and see the owner of Penshurst, Lord de L'Isle and Dudley, for he would never forgive her if he found out that she had been to Penshurst without seeing him. She rang the bell and was admitted through the front door of what seemed to be a small villa-ish annexe to the great house. Some minutes later she came out and said that Lord de L'Isle insisted that we too must come in. I have rarely felt anything to be stranger and more incongruous than the spectacle of the heir of all the Sidneys sitting in his ancestral mansion. He was an elderly gentleman, obviously in poor health, sitting in a small ugly room. Whether my scale of values had been distorted by looking at all the 'treasures' accumulated over four centuries in the great house, I do not know, but Lord de L'Isle and Dudley seemed to me to be having his tea in a room furnished by Woolworth, the only luxury being a small bookcase full of Penguins. He was a nice, but melancholy man, complaining to Vita and that he sat in his room most of the time and saw very few people, his only distraction being an occasional visit to Tunbridge Wells for a rubber of bridge.

There was something historically absurd and touching, ironically incongruous and yet, in that particular moment of history, appropriate in the spectacle of Vita and Lord de L'Isle and Virginia and me sitting together in that ugly little room. Vita was in many ways an extremely unassuming and modest person, but below the surface, and not so very much below, she had the instinctive arrogance of the aristocrat of the ancient regime, and above the surface she was keenly conscious of the long line of her ancestors, the Sackvilles, Buckhursts, and Dorsets, and of the great house of Knole a few miles away in Kent. Her ancestor, Thomas Sackville, Lord Buckhurst and Earl of Dorset, Lord High Treasurer of England, might well have driven over from Knole to visit Lord de L'Isle's ancestor, Sir Philip Sidney, at Penshurst four hundred years ago. He would not have taken either Virginia's or my ancestors with him, for Virginia's ancestors were labouring as little better than serfs in Aberdeenshire and mine were living 'despised and rejected' in some continental ghetto. Thomas Sackville would have been received in state in the enormous banqueting hall, with the great fire burning in the centre of the hall, and he would have been given a mighty feast on plates of gold or silver, and wine or mead in golden cups from silver flagons. In 1940 the descendants of the Scottish serf and the ghetto Jew, on payment of 2s. 6d. each, visited the banqueting hall and the sitting-rooms and bedrooms, with their accumulation of ancient furniture, pictures, silver, and china (which must now be worth hundreds of thousands of pounds), while Lord de L'Isle, the owner, and the descendant of Thomas Sackville, sat in a poky little room drinking tea from rather dreary china. I felt that in that room history had fallen about the ears of the Sidneys and the Leicesters, the Sackvilles and the Dorsets, while outside, across the Channel, in France, history was falling about the ears of us all.

The collapse of our world continued three days later when the Pétain Government in France asked for an armistice with the Germans and on 4 July came the harrowing incident of our attack upon the French fleet. It was then, however, that we, like so many other people, had that strange sense of relief—almost of exhilaration—at being alone, 'shut of' all encumbrances, including our allies—'now we can go it alone', in our muddled, makeshift, empirical English way. Then the bombing began. My first experience of public behaviour during an air raid was in the House of Commons. I was in a Committee Room attending a meeting of the Labour Party Advisory Committee when the sirens started. We all had to go down into the basement, ministers, M.P.s, officials, cleaners, and general public. For a quarter of an hour we stood or sat about rather solemn and self-conscious. One soon learned not to be solemn and self-conscious in the blitz. I hated air-raid shelters and only once went into one at night, the shelter constructed in Mecklenburgh Square, during a particularly heavy bombing. I hated the stuffiness and smell of human beings, and, if a bomb was going to get me, I preferred to die a solitary death above ground and in the open air. Like so many convinced and fervent democrats, in practice I have never found human beings physically in the mass at all attractive—there is a good deal to be said for solitude whether in life or in death. When death comes, I should choose, as some wild animals do, to go off and meet it alone—but not in an air-raid shelter or underground. I think that I felt the physical oppressiveness of human beings in the mass most heavily when, in the worst days of the blitz, I passed through Russell Square Underground Station at night on my way to or from my house in Mecklenburgh Square. It was used, like the other Underground Stations, as a dormitory and air-raid shelter by dozens of men, women, and children, on mattresses wrapped in sheets and blankets and lying side by side all the way down the platform as if they were sardines in a gigantic tin.

One missed something, of course, by not congregating with one's fellows when the bombs fell. Everyone felt the extraordinary blossoming of the sense of comradeship and good-will which settled upon us in London during the blitz, and the falling of bombs loosened our tongues. Queer little scenes and conversations, under those conditions, engraved themselves upon one's memory. For instance, one day, driving up from Rodmell to Mecklenburgh Square, we ran into a nasty air raid in Wimbledon. When we reached the Common, the bombs began to fall unpleasantly near us, and when I saw a 'pillbox' not far from the road, we left the car and took shelter in it. It was the usual large, square room with a cement floor and slits for guns in the thick walls. It was already inhabited. In one corner was a young woman typist who had been bombed out of her lodging and was now 'temporarily' living in the pillbox with a small suitcase containing all her possessions. In the other corner was a family consisting of husband, wife, and child. They had a camp bed, two chairs, several boxes, pots and pans, china and cutlery, and a Primus stove. They were having a cup of tea and we and the young woman were invited to join them. In two minutes we were all chatting happily like old friends. The man was a printer, originally from the North of England. Three weeks before he had taken a job with a printing firm in Wimbledon and with great difficulty had managed to find himself a small house. The first night he moved in a bomb fell in front of the house, blew out all the windows and blew off half the roof. The family was intact, but he could not find a lodging, so he moved into the pillbox. He was a typical printer, and printers, I had learned by experience, are or were typical of the working-class élite, the trade unionist, skilled worker. A year before he had been living a stuffy, petit bourgeois[1] life behind lace curtains in some dreary, respectable back street. The war and the bombs seemed completely to have changed his outlook on life. He had not quite reached the stage of wisdom in the Old Testament's 'Let us crown ourselves with rosebuds, before they be withered' and 'Let us eat and drink; for tomorrow we shall die', but he seemed to have accepted Christ's recommendation in the New Testament: 'Take therefore no thought for the morrow: for the morrow shall take thought for the things of itself. Sufficient unto the day is the evil thereof.' And so deserting the best parlour and the lace curtains, he was living, more

[1] Karl Marx was hopelessly wrong in believing that the bourgeoisie would be destroyed by the proletariat. On the contrary, as in so many other fields, in the class struggle and the world of economics the victors are absorbed and swallowed up by the vanquished as if they had fallen into a social jelly or quicksand. As soon as the workers lose their chains they adopt the food, clothes, habits, mentality, ambitions, and ideals of the middle classes. From Russia downwards there is no dictatorship of the proletariat, but always merely a dictatorship of the bourgeoisie under another name. Engels was the only leading Marxist who saw this and had the honesty to admit it (up to a point) when he wrote: 'The English proletariat is becoming more and more bourgeois, so that the most bourgeois of all nations is apparently aiming ultimately at the possession of a bourgeois aristocracy and a bourgeois proletariat *as well as* a bourgeoisie. For a nation which exploits the whole world this is, of course, to a certain extent justifiable.'

or less contentedly, a kind of nomad existence in a machine-gun emplacement on Wimbledon Common.

Early in August the German mass raids began on London, and almost every night their bombers roared over our heads at Rodmell on the way to London. I still had to pay the rent of 52 Tavistock Square; there was now no chance of anyone taking over the last year of my lease, for many people were leaving London in order to escape from the blitz. I was in correspondence with the Bedford Estate: I had asked them whether they would remit or reduce my rent as the house was empty and I had moved to Mecklenburgh Square. Then one day I received a letter from the Estate saying that the matter had now been settled, for the house had been completely destroyed the previous night. The next time I was in London, I went round to see the ruins of the house which we had lived in for fifteen years. It was a curious and ironic sight, for on the vast conical heap of dust and bricks precisely and meticulously perched upright upon the summit was a wicker chair which had been forgotten in one of the upper rooms. Nothing beside remained except a broken mantelpiece against the bare wall of the next-door house and above it intact one of Duncan Grant's decorations.

On 10 September I drove up to London, but found that it was impossible to get into the house in Mecklenburgh Square. The police had cordoned off the Square after evacuating the inhabitants. The neighbourhood had been badly bombed the night before and there was an unexploded bomb in the ground in front of our house. The Hogarth Press had come to a standstill. There was nothing to do but drive back to Rodmell and wait until they exploded the bomb. But three days later I drove up for the day again in order to meet John Lehmann and discuss what we should do about the Press. The bomb had been exploded and our house was in a dreadful state, all the windows blown out, doors hanging on one hinge, and the roof damaged. It was soon still further wrecked by the terrible havoc caused by a land mine which fell at the back, killing several families and blasting all our rooms in reverse direction from the previous bombing.

The Hogarth Press premises in the basement and our flat on the third and fourth floors were uninhabitable. All the windows had been blown out; most of the ceilings had been blown down, so that, in most places, you could stand on the ground floor and look up with uninterrupted view to the roof while sparrows scrabbled about on the joists of what had been a ceiling; bookcases had been blown off the walls and the books lay in enormous mounds on the floors covered with rubble and plaster. In the Press books, files, paper, the printing-machine and the type were in a horrible grimy mess. The roof had been so badly damaged that in several places it let the rain in and the water-pipes in the house had been so shaken by the blast that occasionally one burst without warning and sent a waterfall down the stairs from the third floor to the ground floor.

In those days the Press printed many of its books with the Garden City Press, Letchworth, Herts., and they nobly came to our rescue. They offered to give us office accommodation within the printing works for our staff if we evacuated them to Letchworth. We accepted gratefully and for the remainder of the war the entire business of the Hogarth Press was carried on from Letchworth; all our staff agreed to stay with us and migrate to Hertfordshire. The next five years they spent uncomplainingly in lodgings in a strange town away from their homes and friends. John Lehmann continued to live in London and his mother's house on the Thames, continually travelling to Letchworth to supervise and manage the publishing business. I only occasionally took the long, tedious (in wartime) journey from Lewes to Letchworth and back in the day. On one of these journeys I saw the grimmest London devastation of the blitz. I caught an early train from Lewes to London Bridge. When I walked out of the station I found that half the city had been destroyed during the night. There was no traffic, no buses or taxis. I started to walk to King's Cross and got to Cannon Street all right, but as soon as I started to walk from Cannon Street, though I knew every street there, I completely lost my way. Half the streets had disappeared into smouldering heaps of rubble and were unidentifiable. What was most extraordinary and sinister was the silence. There was no traffic, since most of the streets were blocked with the debris of buildings; there were hardly any pedestrians. There were many fire-engines and firemen still playing their hoses on burning ruins and every now and again I met a policeman. A pall of smoke hung just above one's head and everywhere there was an acrid smell of burning. Every now and again, too, through the smoke and above the ruins I caught a glimpse of St Paul's, and, though half the time I did not know exactly in what street I was, I steered a roughly north-western course by the Cathedral and so eventually found myself in the Farringdon Road and so by comparatively unblitzed street to

King's Cross.

Having lived through the two world wars of 1914 and 1939, I can say that my chief recollection of war is its intolerable boredom. In this respect the first was, I think, worse than the second, but the second was bad enough. It took me about seventeen hours to get from Rodmell to Letchworth and back, and owing to the bombing one was always waiting hours for trains which never came or in trains which could not move because a bomb had fallen on the line ahead of one. More than once I have sat in the train for four hours or more on the journey from Victoria to Lewes which normally took an hour; the main line had been bombed and we had to trickle half-way round Surrey and Sussex in order eventually to reach Lewes via Horsham and Brighton. And having eventually reached Lewes bored and hungry, one found the town in pitch darkness, the last bus gone, no taxis, and nothing for it but to face a four-mile walk in the rain. If I ever prayed, I would pray to be delivered, not so much from battle, murder, and sudden death, but rather from the boredom of war.

Having settled the Hogarth Press in the Letchworth Garden City Press, we then had to consider what to do with our private goods and chattels scattered over the floors of the rooms in Mecklenburgh Square. Something had to be done to rescue them from the wind and rain which swept over them through the shattered windows. Eventually I managed to arrange for their removal to Rodmell. But there was not only the furniture which filled six or seven rooms; there were thousands of books, a large printing machine, and a considerable quantity of type and printing equipment. I succeeded in renting two rooms in a Rodmell farmhouse and a large storeroom in another Rodmell house. Into these and into every spare space in my own house we stacked the mountains of books, furniture, and the equipment of the kitchen chaotically mixed up with the equipment of the printing room.

In a large ground-floor sitting-room of Monks House the thousands of books which we had had in London were piled on tables, chairs, and all over the floor. I had always had a passion for buying and accumulating books, and so had Virginia, but she had also inherited her father's library. This was the kind of library which, in the spacious and affluent days of Queen Victoria, a distinguished gentleman, who edited the *Dictionary of National Biography* and was an eminent critic and essayist, was apt to acquire. There upon his shelves in complete editions of ten, twenty, thirty, or forty volumes, often pompously bound in calf, stood the rows of English and French classics. Now they were piled into the sitting-room in grimy, hopelessly jumbled heaps. They led one day to one of those trivial, but unexpectedly pleasant, incidents that occasionally mitigated the menace and monotony of the war. In the years before the invasion of France large numbers of troops were being trained in the South of England and there was an unending succession of regiments on troop marches through Rodmell. They often camped in my field and quite often I used to put up the officers in one of the bedrooms and in a garden room. One day in the late summer there was a Lancashire regiment in my field, but I had seen nothing of the officers. In the late afternoon I was on a ladder gathering figs from a large fig-tree when I heard someone call to me. I looked down and there stood a very swarthy subaltern. He wanted to borrow something off me and I took him into the house. The door of the room in which the books were piled was open, and, when he saw them, he rushed into the room in the greatest excitment, seized on a book, and, though it was the *Novum Organum* of Francis Bacon, began to read it. One has learned to expect the vagaries of human beings to be infinitely unpredictable, but I must say that I was slightly surprised to see an unknown Lieutenant in an English regiment become engrossed in the *Novum Organum*. My visitor, who spent practically the whole of the next two days with me, was a very interesting and amusing man. He was a Pole belonging to the landowning class. Before the war he was in the Diplomatic Service, and, when it broke out, he was in the Polish Embassy in Washington. He wanted to fight against the Germans and managed to reach England. I forget how exactly the wheels of Polish politics revolved around Sikorski and Anders, but I think that my Lieutenant did not like them, and so somehow or other he contrived to obtain a commission in an English regiment. He gave one the impression of being what is called a tough customer, and in a tight corner I should have preferred to have him on my side rather than against me. But he also had a passion for literature, learning, books, and reading. He had been unable to read and had hardly seen a book for months, and the sight of the mountain of my books had the same effect upon him as the sudden sight of a spring of pure cold water would have upon a man dying of thirst. For the next forty-eight hours he sat in my house from early morning until midnight, devouring book after book, forgetting the war and his regiment. We had our meals in the kitchen and sat long over them discussing love and life and death and politics and literature. It was one of those rare, unexpectedly pleasant and exhilarating interludes in the claustrophobia of war, this sudden, fleeting appearance in one's life of an entirely sympathetic stranger. He and I, completely different in birth, nationality, education, and experience, had come together from the ends of the earth for a moment of time—forty-eight hours—but, under the shadow of death and disaster, sitting over our meagre war rations, we talked as if we had known each other for a life-time, finding that the world and the universe presented the same delightful, horrible, and ridiculous face to both of us.

My Lieutenant and his regiment disappeared into the fog of war at the end of the two days and, though I remembered with pleasure his toughness, eagerness, and intelligence, I never expected to see him again. But a year or two after the end of the war, one summer day I was in the garden and there suddenly into it came my Polish Lieutenant, in civilian clothes and accompanied by a very pretty young woman. He had survived the war, and, remembering me and my books, determined to come and see me again if he possibly could. Once more we talked for an hour or two and then once more he disappeared into Europe. I have never seen him again, and I hope that he has survived the peace in Poland as he survived the war.

One other incident connected with the regiments which camped in my field showed how international some of our regiments became in the war. One day when (I think) a Kent regiment was camped in my field I put three or four officers up in a room which contained a large bookcase full of translations of Virginia's books into almost every European language. In the afternoon I went into the room to see whether the officers had everything they needed. I found only one subaltern sitting in a chair and reading a book. To my astonishment the book was a Czech translation of *Flush*. The Lieutenant was a Czech and he had been astonished and delighted to find in a house in Sussex a book in his native language.

I must return to chronology, to the chronological narrative of this autobiography. The return is to August or September 1940—and perhaps this is the point at which I might for a moment digress about autobiographical digressions, and make, not an excuse or defence, but an explanation. Some critics of the previous volumes of this autobiography have complained of my digressions, my habit of 'not sticking to the point', and one or two have politely suggested that the cause is old age, garrulous senility. 'A good old man, sir, he will be talking; as they say, "When the age is in, the wit is out".' I would not deny the explanation or indictment, but I also digress deliberately. Life is not an orderly progression, self-contained like a musical scale or a quadratic equation. For the autobiographer to force his life and his memories of it into a strictly chronological straight line is to distort its shape and fake and falsify his memories. If one is to try to record one's life truthfully, one must aim at getting into the record of it something of the disorderly discontinuity which makes it so absurd, unpredictable, bearable.

Looking back from Virginia's suicide in March 1941 to the last four months of 1940, I have naturally often asked myself why I had no forebodings of the catastrophe until the beginning of 1941. What was the real state of her mind and her health in the autumn and early winter of 1940? I thought at the time and still think that her mind was calmer and more stable, her spirits happier and more serene, than was usual with her. If one is in the exact centre of a cyclone or tornado, one finds oneself in a deathly calm while all round one is the turmoil of roaring wind and wave. It seemed as if in Rodmell in those last months of 1940 we had suddenly entered into the silent, motionless centre of the hurricane of war. It was a pause, only a pause, as we waited for the next catastrophe; but we waited in complete calm, without tension, with the threat of invasion above our heads and the bombs and bombing all round us. It was partly that we felt physically and socially cut off, marooned. We had been bombed out of London. After November one had to hoard one's petrol and it was no longer possible to go to London by car. Travel by train became more and more tedious.

All this meant that for the first time in our lives Virginia and I felt we were country dwellers, villagers. And also for the first time we became completely servantless in the Victorian sense. In London before the war we had reduced our establishment to one, a cook, the strange, silent, melancholy Mabel. When the bombing of London began she had come down to us at Rodmell, but, though a typical country woman from the West of England, she disliked the country and hated being away from London. After a few weeks of Rodmell, she could stand it no longer and decided that she preferred the bombs of London. She left us for good to live with her sister and work in a canteen. To be thus finally without servants, without any responsibility for anyone beside ourselves, gave us an additional feeling of freedom and of the dead calm in the centre of the hurricane.

The calm came partly from the routine which established itself, the pleasant monotony of living. We worked all the morning; got our lunch; walked or gardened in the afternoon; played a game of bowls; cooked our dinner; read our books and listened to music; and so to bed. Virginia's diary shows clearly that this life gave her tranquillity and happiness. On 12 October she wrote:

> How free, how peaceful we are. No one coming. No servants. Dine when we like. Living near to the bone. I think we've mastered life pretty competently.

And two days later the following long entry gives the depth of her mood and its background (I published it in *A Writer's Diary*, but I quote it here because it is so relevant):

> I would like to pack my day rather fuller: most reading must be munching. If it were not treasonable to say so, a day like this is almost too—I won't say happy: but amenable. The tune varies, from one nice melody to another. All is played (today) in such a theatre. Hills and fields; I can't stop looking; October blooms; brown plough; and the fading and freshening of the marsh. Now the mist comes up. And one thing's 'pleasant' after another: breakfast, writing, walking, tea, bowls, reading, sweets, bed. A letter from Rose about her day. I let it almost break mine. Mine recovers. The globe rounds again. Behind it—oh yes. But I was thinking I must intensify. Partly Rose. Partly I'm terrified of passive acquiescence. I live in intensity. In London, now, or two years ago, I'd be owling through the streets. More pack and thrill than here. So I must supply that—how? I think book inventing. And there's always the chance of a rough wave: no, I won't once more turn my magnifying glass on that. Scraps of memoirs come so coolingly to my mind. Wound up by those three little articles (one sent today) I unwound a page about Thoby. Fish forgotten. I must invent a dinner. But it's all so heavenly free and easy—L and I alone. We raised Louie's wages to 15/0 from 12/0 this week.[1] She is as rosy and round as a small boy tipped. I've my rug on hand too. Another pleasure. And all the clothes drudgery, Sybil drudgery, society drudgery obliterated. But I want to look back on these war years as years of positive something or other. L gathering apples. Sally barks. I imagine a village invasion. Queer the contraction of life to the village radius. Wood bought enough to stock many winters. All our friends are isolated over winter fires. Letters from Angelica, Bunny etc. No cars. No petrol. Trains uncertain. And we are on our lovely free autumn island. But I will read Dante, and for my trip through English

[1] Louie, since 1932, lived in one of two cottages owned by me in Rodmell. She 'did' for us, coming at eight and washing up, making the beds, and cleaning the house—she still does in 1969.

literature book. I was glad to see the C.R. all spotted with readers at the Free Library to which I think of belonging.

Another entry in her diary (2 October), which I reprinted in *A Writer's Diary* (p. 353), gives vividly her mood that autumn, a kind of quietism and open-eyed contemplation of death. Death was no longer, as it is for all of us all our lives, the end of life, seen always a long way off, unreal, through the wrong end of the telescope of life, but now it was something immediate, extraordinarily near and real, hanging perpetually just above our heads, something which might at any moment come falling with a great bang out of the sky—and annihilate us. 'Last night,' she wrote, 'a great heavy plunge of bomb under the window. So near we both started.' Her immediate reaction was: 'I said to L.: I don't want to die yet.' And then there follows an extraordinarily vivid description of what it would feel like to be killed by a bomb:

> Oh I try to imagine how one's killed by a bomb. I've got it fairly vivid—the sensation: but can't see anything but suffocating nonentity following after. I shall think—oh I wanted another ten years—not this—and shan't for once be able to describe it.

Death, I think, was always very near the surface of Virginia's mind, the contemplation of death. It was part of the deep imbalance of her mind. She was 'half in love with easeful Death'. I can understand this, but only intellectually; emotionally it is completely alien to me. Until I began to grow old, I hardly ever even thought of death. I knew that it is the inevitable end, but fundamentally I am a complete fatalist. It is in part perhaps due to the Jewish tradition, the sceptical fatalism that undermines even Jehovah in *Ecclesiastes* and deep down in *Job*; and later in nearly two thousand years of persecution and the ghettoes of Europe the Jews have learnt that it is a full-time job to fight or evade life's avoidable evils, the wise man does not worry about the inevitable. I would accept the risk of immortality, if I were offered it, but I do not worry about my inevitable death. As one grows old, one is forced to think of it, for it grows nearer and nearer; the time comes when you see that people are surprised to see that you are still alive, when you know that, if you plant a tree in your garden, you will not be alive to stand beneath its branches, or, if you buy a bottle of claret 'for laying down', you will probably die before it has matured. I have reached this stage when 'I shan't be there to see it' is not academic, for one knows it is the day after tomorrow. Horace's *pallida mors*, pale death, is sitting on the horseman's shoulder. But I do not think that I am boasting or deceiving myself when I say that, though I resent imminent death, I do not worry about it. It is fate, the inevitable, and there is nothing to do about it.

Virginia's attitude to death was very different. It was always present to her. The fact that she had twice tried to commit suicide—and had almost succeeded—and the knowledge that that terrible desperation of depression might at any moment overwhelm her mind again meant that death was never far from her thoughts. She feared it and yet, as I said, she was 'half in love with easeful Death'. Yet in those last months of 1940 with death all round her, when the crash of the falling bomb was quite near us, 'I said to L: "I don't want to die yet".' The reason was that she was calmer and happier than usual. This was largely due to the ease and contentment of her writing. It is strange and ironical that *Between the Acts*, which was so soon to play a great part in her breakdown and suicide, caused her so little trouble and worry in the actual finishing of it. 'Never had a better writing season. P.H.' (i.e. *Between the Acts*) 'in fact pleases me,' she wrote in her diary on 6 October 1940. On 5 November, 'I am very "happy" as the saying is, and excited by P.H.' And when she finished the book on 23 November, she wrote:

> I am a little triumphant about the book. I think it's an interesting attempt in a new method. I think it's more quintessential than the others. More milk skimmed off. A richer pat, certainly a fresher than that misery *The Years*. I've enjoyed writing almost every page.

It is significant that, on the morning when she finished *Between the Acts*, she was already thinking of the first chapter of her next book. As was always the case with her, before she had finished a book she already had in her mind some outline of the theme and form of another. The book which was to follow *Between the Acts*, and which she did not live to write, was to be called *Anon*, a 'fact supported book'; 'I think', she wrote, 'of taking my mountain top—that persistent vision—as a starting point.' So the last months of 1940 passed away for Virginia in a real—and yet false—tranquillity. One amusing incident, characteristic of Virginia's immaculate feminism, which—particularly with regard to *Three Guineas*—has been castigated by many male critics, but which I personally feel to have been eminently right, happened in November. Morgan Forster asked her whether he might propose her for the London Library Committee. But years ago Morgan himself in the London Library itself, meeting Virginia and talking about its organisation or administration, had 'sniffed about women on the Committee'. Virginia at the time made no comment, but she said to herself: 'One of these days I shall refuse.' So now on Thursday, 7 November 1940, she had some quiet satisfaction in saying No. 'I don't want to be a sop—face saver,' she wrote in her diary. Many people think this kind of thing petty, trivial. I don't agree: I think something of profound social importance is uncovered in this obvious triviality. One of the greatest of social evils has always been class subjection and class domination. The struggle to end the subjection of women has been bitter and prolonged; it was not by any means over in 1940, nor in 1968 either. The male monopoly and vested interest can be seen of course in a small way—in the all male Committees of institutions like the London Library. In 1940 Virginia had already been a member of the Library for about forty years. She was eminently fitted to be a member of the Committee and so were many other women who were members of the Library. There is no doubt that, if they had been men, many of them would have been elected to the Committee. It was fantastic that before 1940 none of them had been elected and that Morgan could sniff at the idea of a woman on the Committee. And the spectacle of the male committee suddenly anxious to elect one woman—'a sop, a face saver'—in order to show their sexual open-mindedness is by no means uncommon. The egalitarian sees in these trivialities a real social significance.[1]

[1] An interesting example of the complacent male monopoly occurred twenty-seven years after this in the Royal Horticultural Society. The administrative organ of this large, affluent society is a large Council. The Council is elected by the members at an annual general meeting, but, as everyone with experience of annual general meetings and committees knows, the committees or councils of institutions like the London Library and the Royal Horticultural Society are nearly always self-reproducing. The ordinary members are quiescent and acquiescent and do not propose people for election; the committee, if there are three vacancies, proposes exactly three names for election and they are automatically elected. In the year 1967 the Council of the R.H.S. was entirely male, and when Lady Enid Jones and some others wrote to *The Times* protesting against the absence of female Councillors, the President, Lord Aberconway, defending the Establishment, seemed to imply that, all through the many years of the society's existence, the officers and Council had searched for a female horticulturist worthy to sit with them on

In Virginia's diary for the last two months of 1940 there is evidence of her tranquillity. There is, however, one exasperated and slightly unbalanced entry which might be thought to contradict this, but in fact Virginia all her life at any moment might have suffered this kind of short and sharp spasm of exasperation. Only hindsight could read something abnormally serious into this outburst. It is however a curious outburst. On 28 November I gave a lecture (I do not remember on what) to the Workers' Educational Association. Like everyone else, we were often asked—Virginia would have said pestered—to do this kind of thing. On 29 November Virginia wrote in her diary:

> Many many deep thoughts have visited me. And fled. The pen puts salt on their tails; they see the shadow and fly. I was thinking about vampires. Leeches. Anyone with 500 a year and education is at once sucked by the leeches. Put L and me into Rodmell pool and we are sucked—sucked—sucked. I see the reason for those who suck guineas. But life—ideas—that's a bit thick. We've exchanged the clever for the simple. The simple envy us our life. Last night L's lecture attracted suckers.

It was only in the first days of 1941 that the deep disturbance in her mind began to show itself clearly. I shall continue to quote from her diary because her own words are more revealing and authentic than my memory. The entry for 9 January is again strange, showing her preoccupation with death:

> A blank. All frost. Still frost. Burning white. Burning blue. The elms red. I did not mean to describe, once more, the downs in snow; but it came. And I can't help even now turning to look at Asheham Down, red, purple, dove blue grey, with the cross[1] so melodramatically against it. What is the phrase I

[1] The stone cross on the Rodmell church is visible from the window of our sitting-room silhouetted against the down.

---

the Council—and had failed to find one. This is surprising when one remembers the many famous names of women horticulturists, e.g. Miss Jekyll, Vita Sackville-West, Mrs Earle. Perhaps it was still more surprising that within a few months Lord Aberconway and the Council succeeded in unearthing a woman fit to serve. Lord Aberconway, at the annual general meeting, went out of his way to compliment the society and Mrs Perry on the fact that she would be the first 'lady member'; he added: 'It is my further personal hope . . . that before long we may decide that a second lady may be the most suitable candidate to fill a vacancy on the Council.' The patronising, complacent dictatorship of the male horticulturist in 1968 seems to me some justification of Virginia's contemptuous irritation with Morgan and the London Library in 1940.

always remember—or forget? Look your last on all things lovely. Yesterday Mrs Dedman was buried upside-down. A mishap. Such a heavy woman, as Louie put it, feasting spontaneously upon the grave. Today she buries the Aunt whose husband saw the vision at Seaford. Their home was bombed by the bomb we heard early one morning last week. And L is lecturing and arranging the room. Are these the things that are interesting? that recall: that say Stop, you are so fair? Well, all life is so fair at my age. I mean, without much more of it I suppose to follow. And t'other side of the hill there'll be no rosy blue red snow.

Then round about 25 January, I think, the first symptoms of serious mental disturbance began to show themselves. She fell into what she called a 'trough of despair'. It was a sudden attack and it lasted ten or twelve days. There was something strange about it, for, when it passed off, she said herself that she could not remember why she had been depressed. It did not appear to be connected with her revising *Between the Acts*—indeed, on 7 February she noted that she had been writing with some glow. Nevertheless, I am sure that what was about to happen was connected with the strain of revising the book and the black cloud which always gathered and spread over her mind whenever, a book finished, she had to face the shock of severing as it were the mental umbilical cord and send it to the printer—and finally to the reviewers and the public. I did not at first realise quite how serious these symptoms were, though I at once became uneasy and took steps which I will describe later. One thing which deceived me was the suddenness of this attack. For years I had been accustomed to watch for signs of danger in Virginia's mind; and the warning symptoms had come on slowly and unmistakably; the headache, the sleeplessness, the inability to concentrate. We had learnt that a breakdown could always be avoided, if she immediately retired into a hibernation or cocoon of quiescence when the symptoms showed themselves. But this time there were no warning symptoms of this kind. The depression struck her like a sudden blow. Looking back over what happened I can now see that once before there had been an even more sudden mental disturbance, a sudden transition from mental stability to disorder. In that case it was even more catastrophic. I described what happened in *Beginning Again*.[1] It happened early in 1915 when we were staying in lodgings on Richmond Green. Virginia seemed to have recovered from the terrible breakdown which had lasted for the better part of a year.

[1] See above, pp. 123-4.

One morning she was having breakfast in bed and I was sitting by the bedside talking with her. She was calm, well, perfectly sane. Suddenly she became violently excited, thought her mother was in the room, and began talking to her. That was the beginning of the long second stage in a complete mental breakdown.

I think it must have been about the middle of January that I began to be uneasy about Virginia and consulted Octavia Wilberforce. Octavia was a remarkable character. Her ancestors were the famous Wilberforces of the anti-slavery movement; their portraits hung on her walls and she had inherited their beautiful furniture and their fine library of eighteenth-century books. Her family was closely connected with Virginia's, both have their roots in the Clapham Sect. Octavia had been born and bred in a large house in Sussex, a young lady in a typical country gentleman's country house. But though she was always very much an English lady of the upper middle class, she was never a typical young lady. *Illi robur et aes triplex circum pectus erat*—oak and triple brass were around her breast—in all the important things of life. She was large, strong, solid, slow growing, completely reliable, like an English oak. Her roots were in English history and the English soil of Sussex, and, in her reserved way, she was deeply attached to both. She was already a young lady when she decided that she must become a doctor. It was a strange, disquieting decision, for in Sussex country houses in those days young ladies did not become doctors; they played tennis and went to dances in order to marry and breed more young ladies in more country houses who would breed still more young ladies in still more country houses. Octavia's idea was not thought to be a good one by her family, and she received no encouragement there. Another difficulty was that her education as a young lady was not the kind which made it easy for her to pass the necessary examinations to qualify as a doctor. But her quiet determination, the oak and triple brass enabled her to overcome all difficulties. She became a first-class doctor in Brighton.

Octavia practised as a doctor in Montpelier Crescent Brighton, and lived there with Elizabeth Robins. It was in 1928 that we got to know them. Virginia had been awarded the Femina Vie Heureuse prize, and one afternoon in May we went to the French Institute in Cromwell Road for the ceremony of the prize giving. After Hugh Walpole's speech and the presentation of the prize, the usual brouhaha began, and 'little Miss Robins, like a red-breast, creeping out', introduced herself to Virginia. She had known Leslie Stephen and the whole Stephen family when Vanessa and Virginia were small children. She had the gift of vivid visual memory and of vividly describing what she saw down the wrong end of the telescope of memory long ago and far away. She described Virginia's mother so that one saw her for the first time a living woman, a very different figure from the saintly dying duck of her husband's memories and even of Mrs Cameron's photographs: 'she would suddenly say something so unexpected from that Madonna face, one thought it *vicious*'. We asked Elizabeth to dinner with us in London and later went to see her in Brighton—and so we got to know Octavia.

Elizabeth was an even more remarkable woman than Octavia. She was born in Kentucky in 1862, a young lady belonging to the old slave-owning American aristocracy of the South. She did in Kentucky what Octavia was to do later on in Sussex; with extraordinary strength of mind and determination she broke the fetters of family and class, the iron laws which prescribe the life and behaviour of young ladies whether they be the Greek Antigone 600 years before Christ in Thebes or 2,500 years later Elizabeth in Kentucky, U.S.A., and Octavia in Lavington, Sussex. Elizabeth decided that she must become an actress, an unheard-of thing for a young lady in a Southern State, daughter of a banker and grand-daughter of a very formidable grandmother. The family was adamant and her father whisked her away to the Rocky Mountains in the hope that there she would forget all about the stage. But her will was as rocky as the mountains and her family had to give way. She went on the stage, toured America, came to London, and became a famous actress. She was the first actress to play the parts of the great heroines of Ibsen's plays, Hedda Gabler, Hilda in *The Master Builder* and Nora in *A Doll's House*. I think that she must have been a great actress. She was sixty-six years old when I first knew her and she was ninety when she died. But even when she was a very old woman, there was something magnetic in her when she spoke about the great characters of Shakespeare or Ibsen, and I felt the same passionate dedication to her art that is so noticeable in another great actress, Peggy Ashcroft, and in the great Russian ballerina, Lydia Lopokova. Her talents or genuis, however, were not confined to the stage. At the height of her career she threw up everything and set off by herself to the frozen wilderness of Alaska in search of her beloved brother Raymond. He was a strange, gifted, wayward character; he had the same mercurial vitality that she had, and he also suffered from the curious psychological kink, which I have known in two other men, occasionally all through his life an irresistible impulse would come upon him to run away from his life, to disappear. On this occasion he joined the gold rush to the mining camps in Klondyke—and after that complete silence.

Elizabeth, as I said, set off entirely by herself to find him. By that time she had become not only a distinguished actress but a well-known figure in the literary society of London. For such a young woman to start off entirely by herself for a mining-camp almost in the Arctic Circle was a dreadful, impossible thing to do in 1900. Her friends were horrified, but Elizabeth was fearless and indomitable. She disappeared into the snows of Alaska, but she found Raymond and stayed with him in the wild mining-town until she got ill and had to return to London. She did not return to the stage, but wrote a best-selling novel with an Arctic Alaskan background, *The Magnetic North*. She was a gifted writer, a fairly prolific novelist; she also wrote two vivid autobiographical works, *Raymond and I*, which described her odyssey in search of her brother, and *Both Sides of the Curtain*, which told of her life on the stage and of the many distinguished men and women whom she had known.

It was in 1908 that the friendship between Octavia and Elizabeth began. When we first got to know them, they were living, as I said, in Brighton. Elizabeth also owned a lovely Sussex farmhouse surrounded by a good deal of grazing land in Henfield. She had lived there until 1927 when she turned it into a Home of Rest for overworked professional women, a charitable trust over which Octavia presided medically and administratively. I give these details and those that follow because of the part which Octavia and Elizabeth played in the last months of Virginia's life and because afterwards my friendship with them led to my being concerned with their affairs and their relationship and also with the Backsettown Trust.

Octavia's relation to Elizabeth was that of a devoted daughter. If you had searched the earth from Kentucky in the United States to Lavington in Sussex, you would never and nowhere have found two other women more different from each other than they were. Elizabeth was, I think, devoted to Octavia, but she was also devoted to Elizabeth Robins; when we first knew her, she was already an elderly woman and a dedicated egoist, but she was still a fascinating as well as an exasperating egoist. When young she must have been beautiful, very vivacious, a gleam of genius with that indescribably female charm which made her invincible to all men and most women. One felt all this still lingering in her as one sometimes feels the beauty of summer still lingering in an autumn garden. She was not an easy companion, for she had that vampire nature which some old people develop which enables them to drain the strength and vitality of the young so that the older they grow the more invincible, indefatigable, imperishable they become. After the war, when she returned from Florida to Brighton, a very old and frail woman, she used every so often to ask me to come and see her and give her advice on some problem. I would find her in bed, surrounded by boxes full of letters, cuttings, memoranda, and snippets of every sort and kind. In stamina I am myself inclined to be invincible, indefatigable, and imperishable, and I was nearly twenty years younger than Elizabeth, but after two or three hours' conversation with her in Montpelier Crescent, I have often staggered out of the house shaky, drained, and debilitated as if I had just recovered from a severe attack of influenza.

She was so much an individual and so complex that it is impossible to paint a complete and satisfactory portrait of her, but it is worth recording one strange habit of hers. I do not think that throughout her life of ninety years she can ever have destroyed a single letter, document, or scrap of paper which concerned her or even merely passed through her hands. In her will she named Octavia and me as her executors, and we found literally mountains of letters and documents in the house in Montpelier Crescent and in dozens of trunks stored in a furniture depository. I will give one example of her squirrel or jackdaw hoarding habit. When the bombing became severe in the war, her brother Raymond induced her—much against her will—to come to the U.S.A. and stay in Florida. One day in Florida she bought a dozen bottles of soda water from a store; her letter ordering them and the receipt for what she paid for them were filed with all the other myriad documents of the utmost importance and of no importance all. Later on she returned the empty bottles and ordered another dozen; the second dozen was sent together with an account which did not allow for the returned dozen. She wrote a letter pointing out the omission and a corrected account was sent to her and paid by her. All these documents were filed, docketed, brought to England at the end of the war, and stored in a Brighton depository.

I feel that what I have written in the previous paragraphs will give to those who never saw or heard her a one-sided and inaccurately unfavourable picture of Elizabeth. It gives no idea of the charm and lovableness which age and egoism had not destroyed. Virginia fascinated her and I think she was fond of both of us. In the summers before the war, when we were in Rodmell for August and September, Octavia would from time to time bring Elizabeth to see us, and we would sit under the chestnut-tree in the garden talking. Elizabeth was an incorrigible talker. She had the gift, which is not uncommon among Irish women and women from the Southern States of America, of telling old tales of their youth poetically, romantically. Elizabeth had a beautiful voice; as an actress she could both be and act herself; the child in the Deep South, in the long white house, the languorous heat, the soft opulent life, the all-enveloping family with the adored, dominating, devouring grandmother. Virginia and I were entranced by this saga.

In the summer of 1939 and the first half of 1940 we saw Elizabeth and Octavia in this way from time to time and sometimes went to see them in Brighton. In the later part of 1940 Elizabeth was induced to go to America, but we still saw Octavia. She had, to all intents and purposes, become Virginia's doctor, and so the moment I became uneasy about Virginia's psychological health in the beginning of 1941 I told Octavia and consulted her professionally. The desperate difficulty which always presented itself when Virginia began to be threatened with a breakdown—a difficulty which occurs, I think, again and again in mental illnesses—was to decide how far it was safe to go in urging her to take steps—drastic steps—to ward off the attack. Drastic steps meant going to bed, complete rest, plenty of food and milk. But part of the disease was to deny the disease and to refuse the cure. There was always the danger of reaching the point when, if one continued to urge her to take the necessary steps, one would only increase not only the resistance but her terrible depression. Food in any case was a problem owing to rationing and shortages, and Octavia, who ran a farm at Henfield with a herd of Jersey cows, in January and February used to come to tea with us once a week bringing with her milk and cream.

Twelve days after Virginia's 'trough of depression' the mood had passed away and she wrote in her diary: 'Why was I depressed? I cannot remember'. That was on 7 February, and on 11 February we went to Cambridge for two nights and visited the Hogarth Press at Letchworth. Virginia seemed to enjoy this—the usual round of a visit to Cambridge, seeing Pernel Strachey, Principal of Newnham, and dining with Dadie Rylands in King's. Then we had a round of visitors: Elizabeth Bowen for two nights, Vita Sackville-West, and Enid Jones. Again Virginia seemed to enjoy a good deal of this, and I was less uneasy. Something of the state of her mind may, perhaps, be shown by the fact that on 26 February she recorded the following in her diary:

> Yesterday in the ladies' lavatory at the Sussex Grill in Brighton I heard: 'She's a little simpering thing. I don't like her. But then he never did care for big women. (So to Bert.) His eyes are so blue. Like blue pools. So's Gert's. They have the same eyes. Only her teeth part a little. He has wonderful white teeth. He always had. It's fun having the boys . . . If he don't look out he'll be court martialled.'
>
> They were powdering and painting, these common little tarts, while I sat behind a thin door, p—ing as quietly as I could.
>
> Then at Fuller's. A fat smart woman in red hunting cap, pearls, check skirt, consuming rich cakes. Her shabby dependant also stuffing. Hudson's van unloading biscuits opposite. The fat woman had a louche large white muffin face. T'other was slightly grilled. They ate and ate. Talked about Mary. But if she's ill, you'll have to go to her. You're the only one . . . But why should she be? . . . I opened the marmalade but John doesn't like it. And we have two pounds of biscuits in the tin upstairs . . . Something scented, shoddy, parasitic about them. Then they totted up cakes. And passed the time o'day with the waitress. Where does the money come from to feed these fat white slugs? Brighton a love corner for slugs. The powdered, the pampered, the mildly improper. I invested them in a large house in Sussex Square. We cycled. Irritated as usual by the blasphemy of Peacehaven. Helen has fallen through. I mean the house I got her with X, the day X lunched her with Vita: and I felt so untidy yet cool; and she edgy and brittle. No walks for ever so long. People daily. And rather a churn in my mind. And some blank spaces. Food becomes an obsession. I grudge giving away a spice bun. Curious-age, or the war? Never mind. Adventure. Make solid. But shall I ever write again one of those sentences that give me intense pleasure? There is no echo in Rodmell—only waste air . . . I spent the afternoon at the School, marbling paper. Mrs D discontented and said: There's no life in these children, comparing them with Londoners, thus repeating my own comment after that long languid meeting at Chavasses. No life: and so they cling to us. This is my conclusion. We pay the penalty for our rung in society by infernal boredom.

There are ominous signs in this entry. She had just finally finished *Between the Acts* and had given it to me to read. I saw at once now the ominous symptoms and became again very uneasy. After the entry in her diary on 26 February, quoted above, there are only two entries before she committed suicide on 28 March, one on 8 March of which I printed part in *A Writer's Diary* and the last on 24 March. I now give the unpublished portion of the 8 March entry and the final entry of 24 March, since they show, I think, very clearly the state of her mind in those last days:

Sunday, March 8th

. . . Last night I analysed to L. my London Library complex. That sudden terror has vanished; now I'm plucked at by the H. Hamilton lunch that I refused. To right the balance, I wrote to Stephen and Tom: and I will write to Ethel and invite myself to stay; and then to Miss Sharp who presented me with a bunch of violets. This to make up for the sight of Oxford Street and Piccadilly, which haunts me. Oh dear yes, I shall conquer this mood. It's a question of being open sleepy, wide eyed at present: letting things come one after another. Now to cook the haddock.

March 24th

She had a nose like the Duke of Wellington and great horse teeth and cold prominent eyes. When we came in she was sitting perched on a three-cornered chair with knitting in her hands. An arrow fastened her collar. And before five minutes had passed she had told us that two of her sons had been killed in the war. This one felt was to her credit. She taught dressmaking. Everything in the room was red brown and glossy. Sitting there I tried to coin a few compliments. But they perished in the [?] sea between us. And then there was nothing.

A curious seaside feeling in the air today. It reminds me of lodgings in a parade at Easter. Everyone leaning against the wind, nipped and silenced. All pulp removed.

This windy corner and Nessa is at Brighton and I am imagining how it would be if we could infuse souls.

Octavia's story. Could I englobe it somehow? English youth in 1900.

Two long letters from Shena and O. I can't tackle them, yet enjoy having them. L. is doing the rhododendrons.

Shena was Lady Simon of Wythenshawe. Octavia's story refers to a vague scheme of Virginia's. Whenever Octavia came to see us, Virginia tried to get her to 'tell the story of her life' and she had this vague idea of perhaps making it into a book. It is clear therefore from this entry that even four days before her suicide she could be thinking of writing another book. On the other hand there are signs of deep disturbance in these last entries. There is a note in my diary on 18 March that she was not well and in the next week I became more and more alarmed. I am not sure whether early in that week she did not unsuccessfully try to commit suicide. She went for a walk in the water-meadows in pouring rain and I went, as I often did, to meet her. She came back across the meadows soaking wet, looking ill and shaken. She said that she had slipped and fallen into one of the dykes. At the time I did not definitely suspect anything, though I had an automatic feeling of desperate uneasiness. On Friday 21 March, Octavia came to tea and I told her that I thought Virginia on the verge of danger. On Monday 24 March, she was slightly better, but two days later I knew that the situation was very dangerous. Desperate depression had settled upon Virginia; her thoughts raced beyond her control; she was terrified of madness. One knew that at any moment she might kill herself. The only chance for her was to give in and admit that she was ill, but this she would not do. Octavia had been coming to see us about once a week, bringing cream and milk. These visits were, so far as Virginia was concerned, just friendly visits, but I had told Octavia how serious I thought Virginia's condition was becoming and from our point of view, the visits were partly medical. On Wednesday 26 March, I became convinced that Virginia's mental condition was more serious than it had ever been since those terrible days in August 1913 which led to her complete breakdown and attempt to kill herself. The terrifying decision which I had to take then once more faced me. It was essential for her to resign herself to illness and the drastic regime which alone could stave off insanity. But she was on the brink of despair, insanity, and suicide. I had to urge her to face the verge of disaster in order to get her to accept the misery of the only method of avoiding it, and I knew at the same time that a wrong word, a mere hint of pressure, even a statement of the truth might be enough to drive her over the verge into suicide. The memory of 1913 when the attempted suicide was the immediate result of the interview with Dr Head haunted me.[1]

Yet one had to take a decision and abide by it, knowing the risk—and whatever one decided, the risk was appalling. I suggested to Virginia that she should go and see Octavia and consult her as a doctor as well as a friend. She agreed to this and next day I drove her to Brighton. She had a long talk with Octavia by herself and then Octavia came into the front room in Montpelier Crescent and she and I discussed what we should do. We stood talking by the window and suddenly just above the roofs of the houses a German bomber flew,

[1] See above, pp. 107-8 and 109-12.

almost as it were just above our heads, following the line of the street; it roared away towards the sea and almost immediately there was a crash of exploding bombs. We were so overwhelmed by our problem and so deep in thought and conversation that the sight and sound were not at the moment even consciously registered, and it was only some time after I had left Brighton and was driving back to Lewes that I suddenly remembered the vision of the great plane just above our heads and the crash of the bombs.

It seemed possible that Octavia's talk had had some effect upon Virginia and it was left that she would come and see Virginia again in Rodmell in a day or two. We felt that it was not safe to do anything more at the moment. And it was the moment at which the risk had to be taken, for if one did not force the issue—which would have meant perpetual surveillance of trained nurses—one would only have made it impossible and intolerable to her if one attempted the same kind of perpetual surveillance by oneself. The decision was wrong and led to the disaster. The next day, Friday 28 March, I was in the garden and I thought she was in the house. But when at one o'clock I went in to lunch, she was not there. I found the following letter on the sitting-room mantelpiece:[1]

[1] Later on I found the following letter on the writing block in her work-room. At about eleven on the morning of 28 March I had gone to see her in her writing-room and found her writing on the block. She came into the house with me, leaving the writing block in her room. She must, I think, have written the letter which she left for me on the mantelpiece (and a letter to Vanessa) in the house immediately afterwards.

Dearest,

I want to tell you that you have given me complete happiness. No one could have done more than you have done. Please believe that. But I know that I shall never get over this: and I am wasting your life. Nothing anyone says can persuade me. You can work, and you will be much better without me. You see I can't write this even, which shows I am right. All I wish to say is that until this disease came on me we were perfectly happy. It was all due to you. No one could have been so good from the very first day till now. Everyone knows that.

V.

You will find Roger's letters to Mauron in the writing-table drawer in the Lodge. Will you destroy all my papers?

The following is the letter which she wrote to Vanessa:

Sunday

Dearest,

You can't think how I loved your letter. But I feel that I have gone too far this

Dearest,

I feel certain that I am going mad again. I feel we can't go through another of those terrible times. And I shan't recover this time. I begin to hear voices, and I can't concentrate. So I am doing what seems the best thing to do. You have given me the greatest possible happiness. You have been in every way all that anyone could be. I don't think two people could have been happier till this terrible disease came. I can't fight any longer. I know that I am spoiling your life, that without me you could work. And you will I know. You see I can't even write this properly. I can't read. What I want to say is I owe all the happiness of my life to you. You have been entirely patient with me and incredibly good. I want to say that—everybody knows it. If anybody could have saved me it would have been you. Everything has gone from me but the certainty of your goodness. I can't go on spoiling your life any longer.

I don't think two people could have been happier than we have been.

V.

When I could not find her anywhere in the house or garden, I felt sure that she had gone down to the river. I ran across the fields down to the river and almost immediately found her walking-stick lying upon the bank. I searched for some time and then went back to the house and informed the police. It was three weeks before her body was found when some children saw it floating in the river. The horrible business of the identification and inquest took place in the Newhaven mortuary on 18 and 19 April. Virginia was cremated in Brighton on Monday 21 April. I went there by myself. I had once said to her that, if there was to be music at one's cremation, it ought to be the cavatina from the B flat quartet, op. 130, of Beethoven. There is a moment at cremations when the doors of the crematorium open and coffin slides slowly in, and there is a moment in the middle of the cavatina when for a few bars the music, of incredible beauty, seems to hesitate with a gentle forward pulsing motion—if played at that moment it might seem to be gently propelling the dead into eternity of oblivion. Virginia agreed with me. I had always vaguely

---

time to come back again. I am certain now that I am going mad again. It is just as it was the first time, I am always hearing voices, and I know I shan't get over it now. All I want to say is that Leonard has been so astonishingly good, every day, always; I can't imagine that anyone could have done more for me than he has. We have been perfectly happy until the last few weeks, when this horror began. Will you assure him of this? I feel he has so much to do that he will go on, better without me, and you will help him.

I can hardly think clearly any more. If I could I would tell you what you and the children have meant to me. I think you know.

I have fought against it, but I can't any longer.

Virginia.

thought that the cavatina might be played at her cremation or mine so that these bars would synchronise with the opening of the doors and the music would propel us into eternal oblivion. When I made the arrangements for Virginia's funeral, I should have liked to arrange this, but I could not bring myself to do anything about it. It was partly that, when I went to old Dean at the top of the village, whom we had known for nearly a quarter of a century, to get him to make the arrangements, it seemed impossible to discuss Beethoven's cavatina with him, and impossible that he could supply the music. But it was also that the long-drawn-out horror of the previous weeks had produced in me a kind of inert anaesthesia. It was as if I had been so battered and beaten that I was like some hunted animal which exhausted can only instinctively drag itself into its hole or lair. In fact (to my surprise) at the cremation the music of the 'Blessed Spirits' from Gluck's *Orfeo* was played when the doors opened and the coffin disappeared. In the evening I played the cavatina.

I buried Virginia's ashes at the foot of the great elm tree on the bank of the great lawn in the garden, called the Croft, which looks out over the field and the water-meadows. There were two great elms there with boughs interlaced which we always called Leonard and Virginia. In the first week of January 1943, in a great gale one of the elms was blown down.

2

The Hogarth Press

When the war broke out, the Hogarth Press was in a flourishing condition. A year before, in 1938, it had suffered a revolutionary change in its constitution and management. I had taken John Lehmann into partnership. This was effected by Virginia formally selling her fifty per cent interest in the Press to him; John and I then entered into a partnership agreement which gave us equal rights in the business, though he was to undertake the day-to-day management of it. In 1931, at the age of twenty-four, without publishing experience, he had come to us as manager, but as I related in *Downhill All The Way*,[1] the venture was not a success and he left us in 1932. In the six years between his leaving us as manager and returning to us as a partner I ran the Press on my own in my own way with a woman manager, and I gave up the idea of finding a partner. Both Virginia and I got a great deal of enjoyment out of these six years of publishing on our own in our own peculiar way. If one cares for books and literature, as we did, there is real pleasure in finding good writers and personally publishing their works. We had, I think, a remarkable list in those six years. We began the publication of Rilke's poetry in Leishman's translations: *Poems* in 1934, *Requiem* in 1935, *Sonnets to Orpheus* in 1936, and *Later Poems* in 1938. The following are some of the other books published by us during the period: Freud's *An Autobiographical Study* (1935) and *Inhibitions, Symptoms and Anxiety* (1936); Isherwood's *Mr Norris Changes Trains* (1935) and *Lions and Shadows* (1938); Ivan Bunin's *Grammar of Love* (1935); Laurens van der Post's *In a Province* (1934); Bertrand Russell's *The Amberley Papers* (1937); Vita Sackville-West's *Pepita* (1937); Virginia's *The Years* (1936) and *Three Guineas* (1938).

From my point of view the business was financially very successful. We never considered it in any way as a means of making a living. I had always treated it as a half-time, or, more strictly, quarter-time occupation and we deliberately fought against its expansion into a larger scale business: We were determined to publish

[1] See above, pp. 314-17.

only books which we thought worth publishing and our aim was to limit our list to a maximum of round about twenty new books a year. This was by no means easy. We were often offered books which, as the saying is, 'any publisher would like to have on his list', but which we refused because they would have swelled our list more than we wanted to see it swell. Our interest in the business of writing and publishing books also led us into continually having ideas for new books or series, and, when our enthusiasm induced us to get the books written, this from time to time made our list longer than we liked. For instance, a year before John came to us I started a series which I called World-Makers and World-Shakers. It was a series of short biographies for young people which would attempt to explain history to them through the lives of great men and women, and at the same time present history from a modern and enlightened point of view. I had hoped to get the books used in schools. The hope was not fulfilled, and, though we sold out the edition of the four books which we published, we never got the sale we wanted and did not go on with the venture. This was partly due to the fact that we were so soon overwhelmed by the war and the difficulty of getting paper. But I still think that the idea was a good one, and our first four books were extremely interesting. They were: *Socrates* by Naomi Mitchison and R. H. S. Crossman; *Joan of Arc* by V. Sackville-West; *Mazzini, Garibaldi and Cavour* by Marjorie Strachey; and *Darwin* by L. B. Pekin.

I said above that the Hogarth Press was by 1935 a successful business financially. In the three years before John came into it my income from it was annually over £1,000. For a quarter-time occupation this was satisfactory, but in fact Virginia and I did not need (or want) to make £1,000 a year by publishing. We made enough from writing to live the kind of life we wanted to live without bothering about money. We knew the kind of life we wanted to live and we would not have altered it however much money we might make. We were much better off in 1935 than we had been in 1925, but in fact fundamentally we had not altered our way of life. It is extremely pleasant to have plenty of money, particularly for anyone who has previously had little or none. There are two reasons why it is pleasant: first, if you have plenty of money you need no longer think about money; secondly, you can make yourself physically comfortable. We found that it works in mysterious, and often unexpected, ways. For instance, the Victorian domestic system, in which we were both brought up, assumed that one's comfort depended upon having servants living in the house, and we still had a cook and house parlourmaid in the nineteen-twenties. But it is really much more comfortable not to have servants living in, provided that you have enough money to organise your physical life without them. It was only when we had become comfortably well off that we dispensed with the comfort of a cook. We bought the kinds of things which make it easy 'to do for yourself'. And we bought two cottages in the village. In one we put a gardener, Percy, and in the other a young married woman, Louie Everest.

Percy and Louie were both remarkable people, descendants of a long line of agricultural workers and with their roots deep in Sussex. Percy, who is now dead, lived in my cottage and cultivated my garden for twenty-five years; Louie is still living in my cottage and working for me after thirty-six years. I liked Percy very much, though he was the most pigheaded man I have ever known. When he had been with me for over twenty years he got cataract in both eyes and some years later went into hospital for an operation. If he had had the operation, it would almost certainly have been successful, but for some unexplained reason two days before the operation was to take place, in the middle of the night Percy got very angry, said that he would not have the operation at all, and must leave the hospital immediately. He made the nurses summon his wife; she arrived early in the morning in a taxi and took him home. His sight became worse and worse and in the last years of his life he was completely blind. He might have come out of a novel by Balzac or perhaps Zola or a tale of Maupassant—very, very English, a character not uncommon in rural England from the time of Shakespeare. It is strange that, though he was so English, I think of three French novelists in whose pages one might have met him, but no English writer. One only has to write that, and of course immediately Hardy and his gallery of yokels rise up before one. But Percy and many of the other Sussex agricultural workers whom I have known could not have come out of the Wessex novels. There was an element of grim, granitic tragedy not very far below the surface in them which is very different from the fatalistic tragedy indigenous to the softer and gentler Dorsetshire. They would, as I said, have found themselves more at home in Brittany and Normandy with the peasants of Zola or Maupassant.

Percy's wife, who came from a different class from his, her father having owned a milling business in East Anglia, inherited over £10,000 from an aunt. Having become well-to-do rentiers, they hardly altered their way of life, for they continued to live in my cottage and Percy went on working as my gardener until he went blind. They then bought a house in Lewes.

Louie, as I said, is a no less remarkable character than was Percy. Her native intelligence is extraordinary and she has that rare impersonal curiosity which the Greeks recognised as the basis of philosophy and wisdom. I, as her employer, have known her in daily life for thirty-six years, and, though she is shrewd, critical, and sceptical, I have never heard a complaint from her, and she is, I think, the only person whom I have ever known to be uniformly cheerful and with reason for her cheerfulness.

It was due to Percy and Louie, as I said, that we were able to live in comfort without servants when we were in Rodmell, and it was only when we became more or less affluent that we could afford Percy and Louie. The annual income of £1,000 from the Hogarth Press was part of the affluence, but by 1938 we did not need it. The day-to-day running of the Press had, after three years of it, become a burden. In those days I edited the *Political Quarterly*, was a member of the Civil Service Arbitration Tribunal, was secretary of two Labour Party Advisory Committees, and did a good deal of work in the Fabian Society. I did a certain amount of reviewing and every now and again acted as editor of the *New Statesman* when Kingsley Martin wanted to go off abroad. What I most wanted to do was to write books, but I found it difficult to get the time to do this. Though I reckoned the Press to be for me a quarter-time occupation, it was the most exacting and insistent of all my activities. It tied us to the basement in Tavistock Square in a way which was irksome to both of us, for it meant that, as is always the case with a one-man business, it made it very difficult to get completely away from it for any length of time.

By 1938, therefore, we had slipped back into the rather absurd position in which we had wobbled from 1923 to 1932. Should we give the whole thing up or should we try once more to get someone to come in with us and take on the day-to-day management of the business? When John Lehmann reappeared out of the blue, or rather out of the continent of Europe, and called upon us, it became clear that, despite his abrupt leaving of the Press in 1932, bygones had become bygones and he was anxious to return to it. In his two volumes of autobiography he has given his own account of his return, of the seven years of partnership with me, and of his second abrupt withdrawal in 1945. Everyone's vision of the past is more or less distorted by his own personal emotions and prejudices, and my recollection of what happened to the Press in those troubled years from 1938 to 1945 differs, not unnaturally, in some respects from John's. He says that we first offered to sell the Press outright to him, but that he could not raise the money. We were always talking of giving the whole thing up, but I do not think that we ever seriously thought of selling it outright to him in 1938. It was always a question of a partnership and we had no difficulty in agreeing on its terms.

If we brought to John the Hogarth Press, with all that it had published in its twenty-one years of existence, John brought to us and to the Press *New Writing*. *New Writing* was, justifiably, the apple of John's eye, his publishing ewe lamb. It was a good lamb, of which he was justifiably very proud. In 1932, when he was with us as manager, we published in the Hogarth Living Poets Series, Vol. 24, a slim volume edited by Michael Roberts, *New Signatures*, and we followed this in 1933, the year after he left us, by publishing *New Country*, an anthology of 'Prose and Poetry by the Authors of *New Signatures*', also edited by Michael Roberts. *New Signatures*, the conception of which was due to Roberts and John, was a landmark in modern poetry. It contained the work of nine poets. We had already published something of six of them before 1931: C. Day Lewis, Julian Bell, Empson, Eberhart, William Plomer, and John Lehmann himself principally in two volumes of Cambridge Poetry. Roberts and John brought in three new poets: Auden, Stephen Spender, and A. S. J. Tessimond. In *New Country* Michael Roberts threw a still wider net, for, in addition to the original nine, he included among others Christopher Isherwood (whose novel *The Memorial* we had published in 1932), John Hampson (whose novel *Saturday Night at the Greyhound* we had published in 1931), Rex Warner, and Edward Upward. These two volumes which Roberts edited were, as P. Stansky and W. Abrahams remarked in *Journey to the Frontier*, 'taken to mark the beginning, the formal opening of the poetic movement of the 1930s', for they included all the protagonists except one (Macneice) in that movement: Auden, Spender, Isherwood, and Day Lewis.

When John left the Press in 1932, he went to live in Vienna and he got to know the works and in some cases the persons of the younger generation of writers in Austria, Germany, and France. This gave him the idea of a 'magazine in England round which people who held the same ideas about fascism and war could assemble without having to prove their doctrinaire Marxist purity. Why not a magazine to which the writers of *New Signatures* and *New Country* could contribute, side by side with writers like Chamson and Guilloux, and other "antifascist" writers from other countries?'[1] The project of a magazine had to be abandoned, but in its place Allen Lane and The Bodley Head agreed to publish *New Writing*, a book in stiff covers which was to appear twice a year. Isherwood, Spender, Plomer, Rosamond Lehmann, and Ralph Fox gave their advice and support. *New Writing* was published for some years by The Bodley Head and was then transferred to Lawrence & Wishart. By 1937 John's contract with Lawrence & Wishart was coming to an end and they had 'lost interest in *New Writing*',[2] so that in 1938 he was looking for a new publisher. His entry into the Hogarth Press as a partner solved his difficulties, for we welcomed both him and his ewe lamb, *New Writing*.

We began the publication of *New Writing, New Series, No.* 1 in autumn of 1938; its title-page announced that it was 'edited by John Lehmann with the assistance of Christopher Isherwood and Stephen Spender'. Two more numbers were published in the spring and autumn of 1939, but when war came with paper rationing and all its doubts and difficulties for the publisher, it was impossible to continue on the old scale. It did, however, continue in various metamorphoses and under different names until the end of the war. First it became *Folios of New Writing*, shrinking to 159 pages from the 283 pages of the last number of *New Writing*. Later it became *Daylight* in 1941, which became *New Writing and Daylight* in 1942.

These volumes were a cross between a literary magazine and ordinary hard-covered books of short stories, poetry, literary criticism, and politics. They tended, as time went on, to become not only a miscellany, but a miscellaneous miscellany. But at the time when they were first published they were remarkable and valuable. The status of contributors and the standard of their contributions were extraordinarily high. A wide range of British writers of the

[1] *The Whispering Gallery* by John Lehmann, p. 232.

[2] Ibid. p. 309.

older and younger generations appeared in the list of contributors, both those who had already appeared in Hogarth Press lists and several new names which have since become distinguished. It is always pleasant to praise famous men and here are some of them who contributed to these volumes: Auden, Isherwood, Spender, Day Lewis, Macneice, V. S. Pritchett, George Orwell, Henry Green. Before the war cut us off from the continent of Europe many foreign writers leavened the miscellany, some of them well known, e.g. Bertolt Brecht and Jean-Paul Sartre.

The war years were a publishing nightmare for the Hogarth Press, as indeed they were, I suppose, for all publishers. The blackest spot in the nightmare, perpetually preying on our minds, was the shortage and rationing of paper. Having taken John and his ewe lamb *New Writing* into the fold of the Press, we were determined not to allow it to die of starvation and we used a considerable portion of our exiguous paper ration to keep it and its successors going, if diminished in size, until the end of the war. Practically all successful publishers live financially, to some extent, upon books published by them which have become major, minor, or minimal classics. The best-seller, that precarious carrot dangling perpetually before the yearning eyes and nose of even the least asinine of publishers, is extremely exciting and pleasant when one does get hold of one, but few publishers live by best-sellers. It is the books, often very slow selling to begin with, but which establish themselves and go on selling steadily for ten, twenty, thirty and more years, which keep the business rather more than solvent and allow the publisher to sleep peacefully of nights. Virginia's *To the Lighthouse*, which sold in Britain a total of 7,000 copies in its first five years of existence, but in 1967, forty years after it was first published, sold over 30,000 in the year, is a very good example of this kind of book. The Hogarth Press, when the war broke out, had in our list a considerable number of such books which went on selling year after year and had to be continually reprinted. They included all Freud's works, and indeed a large proportion of the psycho-analytical books on our list, all Virginia's books, Vita Sackville-West's, and Rilke's poetry. It was essential, if possible, to keep these books in print, and we had to earmark some of our paper ration for this purpose.

We were left with very little paper for new writers and new books. We did manage to do something. We cut down our list drastically; for instance, there are only six books announced in our list for 1941, spring and summer. The standard of what we did publish was, however, pretty high. Between 1939 and 1945 we published Virginia's *Between the Acts, A Haunted House,* and *Death of the Moth*. We began the publication of Henry Green's novels with *Party Games* and William Sansom's short stories and novels with *Fireman Flower*. We published books of poetry by Rilke, Robert Graves, Cecil Day Lewis, William Plomer, Hölderlin, Terence Tiller, Vita Sackville-West, Laurie Lee, and R. C. Trevelyan. One of the surprises of the war, which I do not think any publisher foresaw when it broke out, was that, as it dragged on, you could sell anything which could be called a book because it was printed in ink on paper bound in a cover. By 1945, owing to the shortage of paper, and so of books, provided he could print a book the publisher could sell it, apparently in any quantities. What was even more surprising was that one found that one could sell all one's old stock. Novels, biographies, even poetry which had been left high and dry and unsalable before the war were snapped up by booksellers, and apparently by readers, as if they were best-sellers. By the end of the war the Hogarth Press, at any rate, had scraped the last book from the barrel and was left with no unsold stock.

At the end of the war my partnership with John Lehmann came to an end. I have to deal with this because it had an influence upon the future of the Press and of my life. John has given his account of what happened in the second volume of his autobiography[1] and I naturally see the facts in a slightly different form, because I saw and see them in a different perspective of prejudice. But apart from the personal question, what happened is, I think, of general and serious importance because our disagreement was fundamentally over the problem and feasibility of the small publisher.

During the war John acted as General Manager as well as a partner. I left him a very free hand, and, considering that we were both what I should call prickly characters, things went on for the most part pretty smoothly. We had two or three rather violent disagreements. They arose because John wished to alter the term of our partnership agreement that no book should be published unless both partners approved its publication. I could not agree to this alteration, because the rule seemed to me essential for two partners running a small publishing business with a list of very carefully

[1] *I Am My Brother*, pp. 310-16.

chosen books. But that was not really the kernel of our disagreement—the kernel was that John wished to 'expand' and I did not. The blessed word 'expansion' has been the death of most small publishers. John in his autobiography ingenuously explains the motives for this kind of dangerous expansion. After the war, he says, 'I realised that it would be essential to run The Hogarth Press in a different way: to expand in order to carry a proper staff; to have the opportunity to train managers who could take as much as possible of the complex and time-wasting detail off my hands'.[2] But this 'expansion' is a euphemism; what it really means is that you have to publish more books in order to pay for an increase in your staff and an increase in your overheads; and because you publish more books, you again increase your overheads and staff, and you then have once more to 'expand', i.e. to increase the number of books you publish in order to meet the increase in staff and overheads—and so on *ad infinitum*, or bankruptcy or a 'take-over'. And behind this circular process is another which John and many another small publisher have ignored at their peril. This kind of expansion entails not only an increasing number of books published and of expenditure on staff and overheads, but also a need for more and more capital. The small publisher who in this way has expanded into a big publisher only too often finds that he may be big, but he no longer controls his publishing business—those who have supplied the capital are now master in his house.

There are in the world of today, I think, two possible ways of publishing books. One is the large-scale business with a large office in central London, a large staff, large overheads, a large invested capital. The iron laws of figures and finance will bind the hands and soul of the publisher: he will have large overheads and he must ever aim therefore at a large and ever larger turnover, which will require a large and ever larger list of books and authors. In this type of business the number of books published by you must be largely determined by the amount of capital invested in your business, the size of your overheads, and the scale of your general expenditure, for it is uneconomic to publish ten books if your business and expenditure are geared to publish a hundred. Naturally the financial urge to 'expand', to increase your turnover and therefore the number of books you publish, is powerful and persistent. In a well-

[2] Ibid. p. 311.

established business with efficient directors and an efficient machine the process, within limits, is logical and may be profitable. If you are selling a million cakes of soap at a profit and you increase production to two million, you will probably increase your profit absolutely and proportionally, provided that you can sell the two million. In large-scale business what applies to soap applies to books. But not completely. The trouble with books is that the proviso is much more uncertain than it is in the case of soap. Every cake of soap is exactly the same, but unfortunately for the publisher every book in his list is unlike every other. If you publish 150 books at a profit in 1968, and you add 50 more in 1969 making 200, under the influence of your overheads, you are gambling on the assumption that the additional 50 will sell at least as well and as profitably as the original 150. But, as I have remarked before, the road to bankruptcy is paved with overheads—and books which do not sell. The big, established publishing business, with adequate capital and a long list of successful books still selling regularly, can weather its losses and its overheads. The small 'expanding' publisher has no back list of successful 'bread and butter books' to balance his losses and overheads and is perpetually harassed by the need to raise more capital. It is not surprising that very few of these small, 'expanding' publishing businesses survive expansion.

In his autobiography John writes: 'In the late Summer' (of 1945) 'I finally decided that Leonard and I had reached a point of no return: if our partnership remained the same, with each of us able to veto any project the other proposed, not only would The Hogarth Press come to a standstill, but my own career would finally be frustrated'. I had, in the summer of 1945 and when the war came to an end, no idea that we had come to 'a point of no return'—a point and a cliché which temperamentally I am inclined habitually to ignore. We had had, as I said, disagreements, but fewer than, knowing John, I had confidently expected. In the six years of our partnership I had never actually vetoed the publication of a book which John wished to publish, so that the picture of the Press grinding to a halt, with two frustrated partners unable to agree upon a book to publish, was slightly hyperbolical, if not hysterical.

Although John had decided on this point of no return in the summer of 1945 and had made up his mind to end the partnership, he did nothing for several months and gave me no hint of his intentions. I was therefore extremely surprised to get a letter from him one Saturday morning at the end of January 1946 giving me formal notice that he would terminate the partnership. According to our partnership agreement if either partner gave notice to the other of his decision to terminate the partnership, the partner receiving the notice had an option of buying out the partner who gave the notice. By return of post I formally informed John that I would exercise my right to buy him out.

I received John's letter at breakfast, and, when I had finished my kipper and coffee, I had made up my mind on what I should do about the Hogarth Press. Before lunch I had succeeded in settling its future satisfactorily. I have never been confronted more suddenly and unexpectedly by a major crisis in my affairs and have never succeeded so quickly, completely, and satisfactorily in solving it. Luck was on my side, because, when I saw the possibility of the solution, the means to solve it was almost on my doorstep. To be exact, it was exactly a mile and a half from Rodmell in the village of Iford, in which lived Ian and Trekkie Parsons. In the last three years of the war we had become intimate friends, as I shall relate in a further chapter. In the last year of the war, when Ian was with the Air Force in France, Trekkie stayed with me in Rodmell, and I had helped to negotiate the lease of the house for them in Iford into which they moved as soon as Ian was demobilised.

Ian was a director in Chatto & Windus, the other directors being Harold Raymond, Norah Smallwood, and Piers Raymond. I explained to Ian how John had put his pistol at my head and at the heart of the Hogarth Press, and I asked him whether he and his three co-directors would buy John's share in the Press for the sum which I should have to give John in order to buy him out. My only stipulation was that the Press should retain its independence and not be absorbed in or controlled by Chatto, and that my general policy with regard to the kind of books which we had published and with regard to expansion would be maintained. I would continue to take an active part in what is known as the editorial side of the publishing business; production, sales, distribution, and accounting would be carried out by Chatto & Windus on a commission basis.

Chatto was a moderate-sized publishing firm, but was large-scale compared to the Hogarth Press. It was one of the few remaining big publishing business in which the directors seemed to have a policy with regard to books and their publication similar to my own, and there were few, if any, books in our list which Chatto would not have been glad to publish, and vice versa. I felt certain that there would be no disagreement about the kind and quantity of books which the Press would publish. There was no question of a take-over or financial control; the Press was in no need of capital and our common object would be not to 'expand', but to maintain the peculiar character, quality, and scale of Hogarth publications. Ian accepted my proposal on the spot and the transaction was put through easily and quickly. Later the Hogarth Press became a limited company, and I became a director of it and, for a time, of Chatto & Windus Ltd.

It is nearly always wrong to believe that events have proved one right, and there is a nasty, smug, ill-conditioned satisfaction in saying: 'I told you so', even if it is true that you did tell him so. I did tell John so more than once, and I have the nasty, smug satisfaction of believing that events have proved me right. John went off and started his own publishing business as John Lehmann Ltd. and he proceeded to carry out the programme of publication which, according to him, I had prevented him adopting in the Hogarth Press. His connection with John Lehmann Ltd. lasted for only seven years, and since 1952 he has ceased to be a publisher. This is, I think, a loss both to the art of publishing and to himself. He is immensely energetic; he has a flair for some aspects of the business of buying and selling (not too common among publishers); he has tastes and talents which should have made him a very good publisher. That all these qualities have not brought him the reward which they deserve has been due to two things: he takes life and himself much too seriously, never having learned that nothing, including 'I', *sub specie aeternitatis*, matters, and he is much too certain that he is right and the other fellow (even Leonard Woolf) is wrong—a dangerous generalisation.

On the other hand the Hogarth Press still exists, having celebrated its half-century of existence last year (1967). I do not think that I over-estimate my achievement or its value, for I do not rate either very high. But in the twenty-three years since John left the Press it has retained its independence and maintained the character, scale, and quality of its publications. One can see this in the books announced in our spring and autumn lists of the years 1955 and 1965, ten and twenty years respectively after John left us:

1955

FICTION

Flamingo Feather by Laurens van der Post
A Contest of Ladies by William Sansom
No Coward Soul by Noel Adeney
The Honeymoon and a Religious Man by Richard Chase

TRAVEL

A Rose for Winter by Laurie Lee

POETRY

Poems 1906 to 1926 by Rainer Maria Rilke
Riding Lights by Norman MacCaig

BIOGRAPHY

Sigmund Freud: Life and Works by Ernest Jones
Letters to Frau Gudi Nolke by Rainer Maria Rilke
Raymond and I by Elizabeth Robins

POLITICS

The Civil Service, edited by Professor William Robson

MISCELLANEOUS

Men and Gardens by Nan Fairbrother
The Dark Eye in Africa by Laurens van der Post
Thomas Hardy's Notebooks by Evelyn Hardy

PSYCHO-ANALYSIS

Clinical Papers and Essays by Karl Abraham
Clinical Papers and Essays on Psycho-Analysis by M. Balint
The Psychology of the Criminal Act and Punishment by Gregory Zilboorg
Selected Contributions to Psycho-Analysis by John Rickman

1965

FICTION

A Case Examined by A. L. Barker
Throw by Anthony Bloomfield
It's A Swinging Life by Johannes Allen
Voyage by Laurette Pizer
The Ulcerated Milkman by William Sansom

BIOGRAPHY

Family Sayings by Natalia Ginzburg
Mandate Memories 1918-1948 by Norman and Helen Bentwich
Living and Partly Living by Jiri Mucha
Apprentice to Power: India 1904-1908 by Malcolm Darling

LITERATURE
Virginia Woolf and Her Works by Jean Guiguet
The Collected Essays of Virginia Woolf
Contemporary Writers by Virginia Woolf
Essays on Literature and Society by Edwin Muir
Living with Ballads by Willa Muir

POETRY
Measures by Norman MacCaig
The Year of the Whale by George Mackay Brown

MISCELLANEOUS
The House by Nan Fairbrother

PSYCHO-ANALYSIS
A Psycho-Analytical Dialogue: The Letters of Sigmund Freud and Karl Abraham
Neuroses and Character Types by Helene Deutsch
Collected Papers on Schizophrenia by Harold F. Searles
Normality and Pathology of Childhood by Anna Freud
Psycho-Analytic Avenues to Art by Robert Waelder
The Maturational Process and the Facilitating Environment: Studies in the Theory of Emotional Development by Donald W. Winnicott
Psychotic States by Herbert A. Rosenfeld
The Self and the Object World by Edith Jacobson

For a publishing business which publishes so few books the Hogarth Press has in recent years won a remarkable number of prizes and awards. Miss A. L. Barker is one of the best British short story writers, and she won both the first Somerset Maugham award and the 1962 Cheltenham Festival of Literature Award. We have twice had books which won the W. H. Smith & Son £1,000 Literary Award: *Cider with Rosie* by Laurie Lee, published in 1959, and the third volume of my autobiography, *Beginning Again*, published in 1964.

One of the greatest—and most difficult—achievements of the Press was the *Standard Edition of the Complete Psychological Works of Sigmund Freud* in 24 volumes. We began the publication of this work in 1953 and completed it in 1966. Many years before 1953 I had tried to prepare for an English translation of the monumental German complete edition and had discussed it with Ernst and Anna Freud. The difficulties were so great that for the time being they seemed insuperable and it did not look as if they could ever be overcome. It was obvious from the first that financially the project would be impossible unless we could get the American as well as the British market. But the copyright in the various books was in such a tangled state that it looked as if nothing would ever untangle them. In Britain all Freud's works after 1924 had been published by the Hogarth Press, and I thought that we might be able to come to an arrangement with the publishers of books published before 1924 for their inclusion in the Standard Edition. But the American copyrights were chaotic; some of the books had been poorly translated and we tried unsuccessfully to get the copyright owners to allow us to get them retranslated. In other cases it was doubtful who in fact owned the copyrights. If it had not been for Ernst Freud these dreary problems of law and persons would never have been solved. After the war he went to the U.S.A. and with tact and patience settled the legal and delicate personal questions. This enabled me at last to go ahead with negotiations with the copyright holders to include their property in the Standard Edition. We had no difficulty with the few English publishers, but in America it was a long and delicate business. At last all was settled successfully and it was possible to go ahead with publication by the Hogarth Press and the Institute of Psycho-Analysis. We took the bold—and eventually profitable—decision not to try to get an American publisher, but to sell the English edition in the U.S.A.

All the twenty-three volumes—the twenty-fourth volume contains the index—were translated by James Strachey. Anna Freud collaborated and he had the assistance of Alix Strachey, his wife, Alan Tyson, and Angela Richards. We—and everyone else—owe an immense debt to James. His translation of these twenty-three volumes is a marvellous work and rightly brought him the Schlegel-Tieck translation prize in 1966. I doubt whether any translation into the English language of comparable size can compare with his in accuracy and brilliance of translation and in the scholarly thoroughness of its editing. In October 1966 the Institute of Psycho-Analysis gave a great banquet to celebrate the completion of the work, and Anna Freud, James, and I made speeches. I do not find psycho-analysts in private life—much as I have liked many of them—altogether easy to get on with, because they so often cannot conceal the professional fact that they know or seem to know not only what one is thinking, but also what one is not thinking. To stand up in evening-dress and make a speech to several hundred psycho-analysts I found an intimidating experience, partly because they would know (1) what I was thinking, (2) that I was not thinking what I thought I was thinking, (3) what I was really thinking when I was not thinking what I thought I was thinking.

James Strachey died suddenly in April 1967 before the completion and publication of the index in the twenty-fourth volume. Today, 26 August 1968, when I am writing this *The Times* reports the death and contains the obituary of his sister Philippa Strachey. She was ninety-six and the last survivor of the ten brothers and sisters whom nearly seventy years ago I first saw gathered in deafening, furious, hilarious argument around the supper table in Lancaster Gate.[1] I feel I must pause for a moment here to say a word in remembrance of James and Pippa. Practically all the five sons and five daughters of Sir Richard and Lady Strachey were remarkable people. They were nakedly and unashamably intellectuals. Each was a person in his or her own right—a rare thing; they were so individual as to appear strange, eccentric, disconcerting to many people. They were extremely intelligent and amusing; in the realm of ideas they were emotionally violent, but in human relations, though affectionate, they were, I think, fundamentally rather cold and reserved. I knew James when he was a boy at St Paul's and when he came up to Trinity, Cambridge. All his life he was to some extent over-shadowed by the greater brilliance, achievements, and fame of Lytton. In similar fraternal cases—not uncommon—more often than not the less successful brother is embittered and, consciously or unconsciously, bears a grudge against his more distinguished brother in particular, and even against the world in general. I never saw the slightest trace of this in James. He was devoted to Lytton and delighted in his success. He confronted the world with a façade of gentle, rather cold, aloofness and reserve, but behind this was a combinatin of great sense and sensibility. Unlike Lytton, he had no originality or creativeness, but his editing of Freud shows both the power of his mind and delicacy of his understanding.

When, as an undergraduate at Cambridge, I first met Pippa Strachey, she was a young woman of twenty-nine. She had her full share of the Strachey mind—extremely intelligent, enthusiastic and highly critical, effervescing with ideas. Unlike her sisters, Dorothy, Pernel, and Marjorie, she was physically attractive and she faced life and human beings with a charming spontaneous warmth which was

[1] See Volume 1, pp. 122-3.

rare in the Strachey family. I have never known anyone more profoundly and universally a person of good-will than she was, but she was entirely without the congenital vice of so many good-willers—sentimentality. She wore no coloured glasses when she looked at life and people; her attitude was compounded of clear-sightedness, affection, tolerance, amusement, and scepticism. She seemed able to make everything possible and amusing. She once enlisted her friends, including myself, for classes in Lancaster Gate in which she taught us to dance Scottish reels. Though her pupils included such unpromising material as myself and Sir Ralph Hawtrey of the Treasury, it was a great success, and when it was considered that we were proficient, a large dance was given in the Strachey drawing-room at which the crowning point was a display by Pippa's pupils. She devoted her life to women's service as secretary of the society which eventually became the Fawcett Society. In that work she showed that she possessed great administrative ability as well as a strong intellect. With those abilities, if she had been a man, she would almost certainly have attained very high office. That she accepted without complaint the injustice of her own fate, while devoting her life to fighting against the injustices in the fate of others, was an essential part of the charm of her character. It was, too, an essential part in my affection for her.

To return to the Hogarth Press, it has remained a small, independent publishing business with a list deliberately limited to a maximum of round about twenty books a year, though in many years we have published fewer than twenty. We have never published a book for any reason other than a belief that it deserved to be published, a belief which, of course, may have been sometimes mistaken. We have never expanded, never published a book under the financial pressure of expenditure and overheads. We have never been in want of capital, for, as I have explained in *Beginning Again* and *Downhill all the Way*,[1] the total capital invested in the Press after five years of existence was £135 2s. 3d., and even that was on account of the printing, not the publishing. By that time the publishing was financed by the profits, and, as the Press has year after year from 1917 to 1968 always made some profit and I have never allowed it to 'expand', the problem of finding capital never arose—the Press found its own capital.

[1] See above, pp. 183-4, 238.

John Lehmann in his autobiography implies that he and the war 'turned The Hogarth Press into a moderately valuable property'.[1] This is an amiable and natural characteristic delusion for which there is no evidence. The Press was probably a more profitable business and a more valuable property before than after the war—this was probably also true of all publishers. I do not think that the war was good financially for any publisher—except that it enabled us all to sell unsalable sheets and volumes; the Hogarth Press, apart from this, suffered the loss of two of its best-selling authors, Virginia and Vita. John adds that at the end of the war he thought that 'it would certainly be possible to find the capital for expansion'. But, I repeat, up to that date no one had really put a penny into the business, other than the original £136 2s. 3d. which I spent on the printing-machine, type, etc.; I never had to 'find capital' and never have since then; the business, because it grew slowly and successfully, found its own capital. When John became a partner he did not put any money into the Press, and when Ian paid me for a half-share in the business the money did not go into the Press as capital, but into my pocket so that I could buy John out.

In the twenty-three years since John left us the Press may be said to have pursued the even tenor of its ways not unsuccessfully. The kind of book it publishes and the kind of author whom it publishes have not altered. We publish rather fewer books in 1968 than we did in 1938. This is mainly due to the fact that, although I still play an active part and go up to the office about once a week, the active part is rather passive; i.e. I am content with the good fat fish in the net or the good young fish who swim into it, and I no longer go out on the high seas on the lookout for adventure and the unrecognised genius. This, of course, is the sclerosis which commonly attacks an established and successful publisher. The Hogarth Press, by its nature and history, is peculiarly vulnerable to it. It was from a business point of view always an anomalous creature, depending for its birth and existence for many years on Virginia and me. It remains to a large extent today a personal product, and one result of its happy connection with Chatto & Windus is that inevitably there has come into the business no one who might be the personal successor to me. When I die, therefore, the Hogarth Press will almost certainly also die as an entity. I do not regret this. I deplore the fact that

[1] *I Am My Brother*, p. 311.

I shall have to die and be annihilated; I should like to live personally for ever. But if I am, as I feel sure I shall be, annihilated, I take no interest in the little odds and ends of me—my books, the Press, my garden, my memory—which might persist for a few years after my death.

I cannot finally leave the subject of the Press and its burial in my grave without returning for a moment to the question whether it would be possible to do today what we did in 1917—create a flourishing publishing business, with no capital and no staff, out of nothing. I am often told by people with a great deal more experience of publishing than I have that what we did in 1917 was a personal fluke and that today it would be quite impossible for Virginia and me or anyone else to accomplish it. I am not convinced that this is the case. It is true that the business and therefore the art (if there is an art) of publishing have changed enormously in the last fifty-one years; we live, so far as the economic, industrial, and financial system is concerned, in a megalithic age. Everywhere the domination of finance and industry by gigantic companies, with vast capital and enormous turn-overs, becomes more common and more intense. Owing to take-overs and amalgamations publishing is now dominated by big business, it is said, and only these new publishing dinosaurs and megatheriums can hope to make a profit, let alone publish efficiently. Sprats, like the Hogarth Press, have no hope of survival unless they give themselves to be swallowed up by Leviathan, the huge whale or the gigantic shark.

I am not, as I said, entirely convinced by these arguments. It would be more difficult, of course, today to do what we did in 1917. We had some fortuitous and lucky advantages. In Virginia's books we had an enormous potential asset; they were the economic rock upon which in the 'twenties the economic fortunes of the Hogarth Press were profitably based. Many of our closest friends were writers who were to become distinguished or even famous. I do not think it is conceited to say that both Virginia and I were quite good at spotting literary talent or even genius in unknown young writers, and the fact that I was literary editor of the *Nation* during the early years of the Press gave me frequent opportunities to spot them. Again I do not think it is a delusion of conceit which makes me believe that I am a good man of business. I had learned a great deal about the management of an office, about business and finance, in my seven years in Ceylon. As I explained in *Growing*, I owed much to Ferdinando Hamlyn Price, who taught me to be a good man of business.[1] Later in Ceylon my experience for two and a half years as head of a district was invaluable. I was responsible for the revenue and expenditure of the district and for the accounts. And I knew what I was doing as an accountant, for I had had to pass an examination in accounts before I could be promoted to administer a district. As Assistant Government Agent of Hambantota, in addition to the ordinary business connected with Government revenue and expenditure, I was responsible for running a fair-sized industry, the manufacture, sale, and distribution of salt, which was a Government monopoly. I am, by nature, a good businessman, and up to a point enjoy administration and organisation and accounts and figures and dealing with all sorts and kinds of people. After the administration, business, and finances of a Ceylon district, running the Hogarth Press seemed to be child's play and a spare-time occupation. The knowledge of business which I gained from my experience in Ceylon was thus of great value to us in the early days of the Press, particularly when events forced us to allow it to develop into a serious publishing business. It enabled me to understand and control its finances and so consciously to adopt the policy of limiting its operations and so resisting the fatal lure of expansion.

The advantages enjoyed by us, which I have just described, were, of course, the foundation of the development and success of the Hogarth Press. It would be rare for anyone at any time who wanted to start as a publisher to find that he had up his sleeve such, and so many, good writers as Virginia and the other authors whom we published during the first five years of the Hogarth Press. Let me recall their names in the order in which they appeared on our lists from 1917 to 1922: Virginia and Leonard Woolf, Katherine Mansfield, T. S. Eliot, J. Middleton Murry, E. M. Forster, Hope Mirrlees, Logan Pearsall Smith, Gorky, Bunin, Dostoevsky, and in the next two years we published books by Roger Fry and V. Sackville-West and the *Collected Papers* of Freud. This is a remarkable constellation of stars, a formidable list of publications. It is also probably rare for intellectuals like myself to take the trouble to become good businessmen. But I am not so foolish as to believe that our advantages could not occur again. There is no reason to believe that it is impossible that tomorrow or tomorrow or tomorrow there

[1] Volume 1, pp. 199-202.

may not be a circle of young, unknown, brilliant writers whom someone might begin to publish on a small scale as we did in 1917. And there is no reason why he should not succeed as well as we did, provided he is a good businessman and is determined to limit his operations, refusing to listen to the John Lehmanns singing their siren song about expansion which can lure one so easily on to the Scylla of the take-over or the Charybdis of bankruptcy.

3

1941–1945

After Virginia's death I continued to live in Rodmell. Many of my friends, I think, felt that I ought not to remain alone there; they offered to come and stay with me or asked me to stay with them. It is no good trying to delude oneself that one can escape the consequences of a great catastrophe. Virginia's suicide and the horrible days which followed between her disappearance and the inquest had the effect of a blow both upon the head and the heart. For weeks thought and emotion were numbed. My mind was haunted by certain phrases of Claudio in *Measure for Measure:*

> To lie in cold obstruction and to rot

and

> to reside
> In thrilling region of thick-ribbed ice.

They applied, not to the dead, but to the living, to me. I remained where I was, for, in fact, there was nothing else to do. You cannot escape Fate, and Fate, I have always felt, is not in the future, but in the past. I have my full share of the inveterate, the immemorial fatalism of the Jew, which he has learned from his own history beginning 3,428 years ago—so they say—under the taskmasters of Pharaoh in Egypt, continuing 2,554 years ago in the Babylonian captivity when Nebuchadnezzar was king in Babylon, and so on through the diaspora and the lessons of centuries of pogroms and ghettoes down to the lessons of the gas chambers and Hitler. Thus it is that we have learned that we cannot escape Fate, because we cannot escape the past, the result of which is an internal passive resistance, a silent, unyielding self-control.

So I continued to live in Rodmell. I had nowhere to stay in London, for bombs had made the house in Mecklenburgh Square uninhabitable. The scaffolding or skeleton of my life remained the same. Work is the most efficient anodyne—after death, sleep, or chloroform—for pain, whether the pain be in your great toe, your tooth, your head, or your heart. To work and work hard was part of the religion of Jews of my father's and grandfather's generations. In the ghetto for hundreds of years, I imagine, you had to work hard to keep alive, and long before that when Adam heard the voice of the Jewish God walking in the garden in the cool of the day, he heard it say: 'In the sweat of thy face shalt thou eat bread, till thou return unto the ground; for out of it wast thou taken: for dust thou art, and unto dust shalt thou return.' I doubt whether there is any great difference in the genes and chromosomes of the various tribes, races, and nationalities that have inherited and desolated the earth, but their ways of life, their laws and traditions and customs, the fortuitous impact and the logic of events and history have gradually moulded the minds and characters of each so that often they differ profoundly from one another. There is, I think, or there was, a tradition consciously or even unconsciously inculcated in Jews that one should work and work hard, and that work, in the sweat of one's brain as well as of one's face, is a proper, even a noble, occupation for all the sons of Adam. I think that my father had absorbed this tradition and instinctively obeyed it, and that, young as I was when he died, I had observed it and again, in my turn, instinctively obeyed it. In the ordinary sense of the words, I doubt whether I have a 'sense of duty', but I have always felt the urge, the necessity, to work and work hard every day of my life.

I worked immensely hard at school—both at my prep school and at St Paul's—and there for the first time I came up against a tradition exactly opposite to mine with regard to the ethics of work. It was at school that I first, and very soon, heard the word 'swot'—'he's a bloody' or 'he's a dirty swot'. The word 'swot' derives from the word 'sweat', and so appropriately carries us back to the voice of the Jewish God walking in the garden in the cool of the evening. The tradition of the English public school was in my youth, and had been for a hundred years and more, the aristocratic tradition which despised work and the worker. It had spread all through the educational system. Even the masters at my prep school in Brighton and at St Paul's—most of them had been themselves educated in public schools—despised the dirty swot and often showed their contempt for him. It was only cricket and football, not work, which a gentleman took seriously. I very soon observed the difference in values between my attitude to the swot and that of the other boys and the masters in my prep school in Brighton when I went there in 1892 at the age of twelve. I kept my knowledge to myself, but, being by nature stiffnecked and pigheaded, I went my own way and worked tremendously hard all through my school days. Being fairly good at games, I escaped much of the odium of being a swot, until, when one reached the top forms in St Paul's, one was high enough in the establishment to be able to work without indignity.

During the remainder of my life, after school and the university, I have never ceased to work long hours and intensively. In Ceylon I normally worked a twelve-hour day, and in the six and a half years that I was there I had—apart from the weeks when I was ill with typhoid—only about four weeks' holiday. In the fifty-seven years since my return to England I have worked no less hard and persistently. I do not claim this as a merit, but state it as a fact. Both Virginia and I looked upon work not so much as a duty as a natural function or even law of nature. Except when we were officially 'on holiday', we each every day retired to our respective rooms and worked from 9.30 to 1, and it was as natural and as inevitable that we should do so as that we should go to bed and sleep each night. In London in the afternoon almost always I worked in the Press or on some political committee, and if we were in in the evening, I would usually read a book for review or in connection with what I was writing. Virginia's working day was as long as, perhaps longer than, mine. What she was writing or going to write was rarely not in the centre of her mind. She was continually thinking about the book she was writing or was going to write, or she was living, observing, or absorbing the raw material for them. She also did an immense amount of reading either for her essays or for reviewing; she read the books intently and intensively and there are still in existence an immense number of notebooks full of the notes which she made methodically as she read. I should say that in an ordinary normal day of twenty-four hours we each of us slept for eight and worked ten or twelve hours.

I continued to work even harder and longer after Virginia's death. I was writing *Principia Politica* with unconscionable slowness. Then there was the Hogarth Press; I had an almost daily correspondence with John Lehmann and frequently met him in London for discussion and decisions, and I occasionally went to Letchworth to see the staff there. In 1931 I had become joint editor of the *Political Quarterly* with Willie Robson; when the war came, Willie went into the Ministry of Fuel and Power and had to give up his editorship. From 1940 to 1946 I was sole editor and, under war conditions, this was no easy business. A more or less 'learned' or rather expert journal like the *Political Quarterly* presents a completely different editorial problem from a weekly like the *Nation* or *New Statesman* or, I should think, still more a daily paper. The trouble which faces the editor of the weekly every Monday morning is that he has too much material and too little space; the nightmare which perpetually haunts the editor of the quarterly is that he will find himself with too much space and too little material. This is mainly due to technical difficulties. Three months is an interval of time which is more likely to make an article out of date than seven days, and an editor of a quarterly who postpones publication of an article which was written for a January issue until the April issue will be publishing it nearly six months after it was written. He has therefore to plan each issue more meticulously and spatially exact than the editor of the weekly. Looking through these numbers of the *Political Quarterly* over twenty years after I planned and produced them, I feel a certain parental pride in them, and I do not think it is merely parental infatuation which makes me think that journalistically the standard is remarkably high. I find them readable even today, though one must allow for the fact that almost every paper or journal is more interesting twenty years than it was twenty minutes after it was published. Most of the articles are written by intelligent experts—not a very common combination—and deal with events and problems, even contemporary events and problems, of political or sociological importance from the long-term, if not eternal, angles of incidence and reflection. The mere Contents of two issues, and the names of the writers, which I give below, are some evidence of this:

October–December, 1942

German Disarmament and European Reconstruction	by Mercator
The Meaning of the French Resistance	by Professor Paul Vaucher
Hitler's Psychology	by Leonard Woolf
Colonies in a Changing World	by Julian S. Huxley
Industry and the State	by Joan Robinson
'Grey Eminence' and Political Morality	by the Hon. Frank Pakenham
Christianity, Science, and the Religion of Humanity	by Anceps
Putting Britain Across	by Historicus
Parliament in Wartime	by H. R. G. Greaves

April–June, 1943

The Problem of the Public Schools	by R. H. Tawney
The Beveridge Report: an Evaluation	by William A. Robson
The Age of Transition	by Harold J. Laski
Parliament in Wartime	by H. R. G. Greaves
The Future of An Alliance	by Max Beloff

Another of my occupations was, every now and again, to sit on the Civil Service Arbitration Tribunal. As I recorded in *Downhill all the Way*,[1] in 1938 I was appointed a Member of the National Whitley Council for Administrative and Legal Departments of the Civil Service. What these many words meant was that Civil Servants were precluded from striking, and, if their Trade Unions and H.M. Treasury could not agree with regard to any claim about pay or other conditions of employment, the claim had to be remitted for trial and decision to a Civil Service Arbitration Tribunal. The Tribunal consisted of three arbitrators: a permanent chairman, appointed by the Government, an arbitrator from a panel appointed by the Treasury, and an arbitrator from a panel nominated by the staff or Trade Unions. I had been nominated by the staff and continued so to be for seventeen years. I used to enjoy my work as a District Judge or Police Magistrate when I was a Civil Servant in Ceylon, and I found my work as a Civil Service arbitrator in London hardly less interesting. To sit on the Bench and try almost any case as judge, magistrate, or arbitrator (provided that you think about the litigants and their case and characters, and not about yourself—a rule not always observed by judges) can give one an insight into the mind, motives, and methods of the human animal which it is not easy to obtain in any other way. To be above the battle, and to know that you must remain there and under no circumstances allow anything—even the shape of a litigant's nose or the colour of her eyes—to 'prejudice' one, purges the mind and purifies the vision so that one sees things and understands people in a way impossible in everyday life.

Even when the skies are falling about our ears—whatever may be happening to Justice—we eat our eggs and bacon for breakfast and go about our daily and nightly business. With German bombs falling about our ears in Regent's Park or with battles raging from Normandy to Rome to decide the fate of the world, the Arbitration Tribunal met from time to time throughout the war to decide such

[1] See above, pp. 342-8.

questions as whether a clerk in the Ministry of Labour should get an increment of 1s. or 2s. or whether a Prison Matron should work forty-four or forty-five hours a week. This is, I think, as things should be and indeed always have been: the ordinary person, except when he was being killed, starved, conscripted, or ruined by the great World Wars and the great World Conquerors and Pests of the World like Alexander the Great and Napoleon, has ignored them and got on with his eggs and bacon, or, like Jane Austen, ignored Napoleon's retreat from Moscow and got on with writing *Mansfield Park.*[1] So far as I was concerned, when the great battles which were to decide the great war were at their height in Poland, Hungary, Greece, Italy, and France, and the 'doodle-bugs' or V1s were falling on London, for instance, I spent a day in December 1944, in the house looking on to Regent's Park, with Sir David Ross and Mr Fairholme, deciding whether Chief Officers, Matrons, Superintendent of Weaving and the Superintendent of Printing and Binding in the Prison Service should be entitled to payment at time-rate-and-a-quarter for all hours worked in excess of eighty-eight a fortnight. And after listening for many hours to a recital of the hours and conditions of employment and of the scale of salaries, and to the arguments for and against by the Prison Officers' Association and the Prison Commissioners, we awarded the claimants what they asked for for a period of three years.

There is one thing I should like to say before finally leaving the Civil Service Arbitration Tribunal. For me personally and psychologically, as I have said, I always found the work interesting, though at the same time I always felt that from a public point of view the whole system was absurd and a waste of time. As I pointed out in *Downhill all the Way*,[2] the whole industrial structure of the

[1] See Jane's letter to Cassandra written in Chawton, Sunday evening, 24 January 1813, in which she says that she learns from Sir J. Carr that 'there is no Government House in Gibraltar', as she had said in *Mansfield Park*, and that she must alter it to the Commissioner's. There is no mention of the Great War, or of Napoleon, or of the retreat from Moscow, but she does write: 'My mother sends her love to Mary, with thanks for her kind intentions and enquiries as to the pork and will prefer receiving her share from the two *last* Pigs: she has great pleasure in sending her a pair of garters, and is very glad that she had them ready knit'. How right that the great writer should confer immortality, not on the great conqueror and his great war, but on Mary, the Pork, the two *last* Pigs, and the pair of garters.

[2] See above, p. 346.

Civil Service seemed to me crazily irrational. Each of the hundreds of Government occupations has, on the face of it, a scale of pay and conditions of employment peculiar to itself, but in fact, of course, in any particular case there will be close similarity with a large number of other occupations. Hence, if any change is made in the scale of pay or conditions of work in one occupation, it sets off an unending chain of claims in similar occupations throughout Government service. I said that I thought that the whole structure of Government service should be rationalised by constituting a small, limited number of classes for scales of pay and conditions of employment, and this classification and pay structure should be applied to practically all persons in Government employ. I am glad to see that the Fulton Commission on the Civil Service, which has recently reported, makes the same proposal.

Sporadically, from time to time and for short periods of time—a few days or a week or two—I used to edit the *New Statesman*. This was because the editor, Kingsley Martin, when he wanted to go on holiday for a week or more or when he went on one of those peregrinations in Europe or Asia which are essential stimulants to the life-blood of good journalists, had got into the habit of asking me to act for him. Thus in 1943 I did eight weeks in all, though I stipulated that I would come for only two or three days in the week. It was a pretty strenuous business fitting it in with my other work, but I must admit that, knowing that I would never be a permanent prisoner in the editor's chair, I got a good deal of amusement out of it. The staff which I had to deal with consisted of Dick Crossman, G. D. H. Cole, Aylmer Vallance, Norman Mackenzie, and on the literary side Raymond Mortimer.[1] I found them easy to get on with, but they were a formidable team and required some watching. We met together on Monday or Tuesday for the final decision on what the menu should be for the paper to offer for the week. I always contemplated Dick Crossman with amazement and the greatest admiration. He was the best journalist I have ever known. His mind was extraordinarily fertile of ideas; it teemed with them, and if you dipped into it, you brought up a shoal of brilliant, glittering ideas, like the shoal of shining fish that one sometimes sees in a net pulled out of the sea by a fisherman. It is true that Dick's ideas were almost

[1] It was only after the war that I had Dick as Assistant Editor. He was in fact Assistant Editor of the *New Statesman* from 1938 to 1955, but during the war he was in the army a brilliant Director of Psychological Warfare.

as kaleidoscopic in colour and as slippery to keep a hold on as the mackerel for, having written a glittering and devastating article one week, he would turn up the following Monday with the most brilliant idea for the most brilliant article contradicting his most brilliant article of the previous Monday. And on each of the two Mondays Dick, I am sure, believed passionately in each of the two ideas.

The rest of the staff were journalistically an almost perfect team. Douglas Cole was a very old friend; for years I had worked closely with him and Margaret, his wife, in the Fabian Society and the Labour Party. He was an extraordinarily able man. Academically, as a teacher in Oxford, and politically, as an intellectual providing the British Labour Movement and Party with ideas, principles, and policy, he had a large and devoted following, particularly among the young. To an editor he was what every editor prays for, being as reliable as the sun and moon. For one could be absolutely certain of receiving by the first post on Wednesday morning an impeccable article, of exactly so many thousand words, on one of those topical, but grimly gritty subjects, which are the despair of editors—and often of readers—for they lie in the depressing region where economics, industry, trade unionism produce the most important, insoluble, and boring problems.

Norman Mackenzie, when I first met him in the *New Statesman* office, was a young man at the beginning of what one thought (wrongly) would be inevitably a journalistic career. He was as reliable as Douglas, never putting a foot—or a pen or typewriter—wrong. He covered much the same field as Douglas; it is a field in which articles have to be written by 'experts' and, by their nature, do not make light or amusing reading. Sitting in Kingsley's chair, there was only one editorial grumble which I had when I read the articles of Douglas or Norman. They were uncompromisingly sound and solid, but verbally they were written by plain cooks. It was only when, after the war, Dick reappeared that one realised that it was possible for an article, even about the League of Nations or Ernest Bevin, to be sound and solid and yet at the same time brilliantly readable.

The last member of the *New Statesman* team was Aylmer Vallance. He was very much a professional journalist, for he had been the editor of the *News Chronicle*. During the war he combined his work on the *New Statesman* with that of a Colonel on the General

Staff at the War Office. In the technique of planning, writing, and preparing for press a weekly paper he was first class; he could knock off in an hour a good (but not a very good) article on any subject from mind to matter or from God to girls. He was a good fellow well met. But he was also one of the most indiscreet good fellows that I have ever met. For instance, one day in a room full of people going and coming, as they do in a newspaper office, he told us that he had been interrogating captured German officers and that they were all convinced that Germany would win the war with a new weapon Hitler was about to use against us—and he described in some detail what a little later we came to know as the V2. Hearing this from an officer in a colonel's uniform with red tabs and all, in a room full of heterogeneous people, it never struck me that there could be anything wrong about it. But later in the day when I met Bunny Garnett, who was in the Air Ministry, and asked him about Hitler's new weapon, hair and hackles rose upon his head and he told me furiously that I had no right to be in possession of—far less talk of—what was a top top secret—only that morning—with metaphorically all doors shut and blinds pulled down—for the first time the facts about this topmost secret had been revealed to the topmost red tabs of his office. I felt that I had only just escaped arrest and imprisonment.

This was not the only time I got into trouble through Aylmer. He was distinctly a Fellow Traveller, and may, for all I knew, have been a member of the Communist Party. I had lived long enough in the Fabian Society and the Labour Party, among denizens of the political Left, to know that you could never completely trust a Fellow Traveller, that dear friend who might or might not be a crypto-communist. But it was some time before I realised that one had to keep more than one eye on Aylmer. It was in May 1945 that my two eyes opened. I edited the paper during the four historic weeks in which Hitler's death and the end of the war with Germany were announced. It was a hectic time. After my third week of editing, I received an enraged letter from Maynard Keynes about the front page article celebrating the end of the war. I cannot now remember what the article was all about, but I think it must have been full of the slants, snides, sneers, and smears which Communists and Fellow Travellers habitually employ as means for building a perfect society. Maynard was outraged, and so was Lady Violet Bonham-Carter and several other highly respectable and respected persons who had written indignant letters to him. For some strange reason Maynard blamed the absent and innocent Kingsley instead of me. I wrote him the following letter in order to divert his anger on to my guilty, but not too contrite, head:

Dear Maynard,

I entirely agree about the article, although the responsibility is of course mine. It is appalling. I was in a difficult situation last week and I daresay looking back I made a wrong decision. The two days' holiday in the middle of the week meant that all the proofs had to be passed on Thursday. I arranged that Vallance should write the front page and leave it with the printer on Thursday morning so that I could not see it before it was in proof . . . It was understood that the printers could only print on Friday if there were no serious alterations to be made. The front page was only ready for me to read at 5. When I read it, I felt as you do about it. . . . It was considerably worse than it is now. The difficulty was that the article ought to have been rewritten entirely, but that in the state the printers were it meant beginning all over again on Friday for them and quite probably not getting the paper out until Monday. I also had an engagement which made it necessary for me to catch the 6.45 latest to Lewes. In the end I told Vallance that he must put in certain alterations and additions which I thought would make the article tolerable. But I agree that they did not and that it would probably have been better to have re-written the article and have held up the printing.

As regards what action it is your duty to take, I think it would be wrong to confuse this case with anything against Kingsley. It should be raised at the Board meeting, but the responsibility is mine and it shouldn't be counted against Kingsley.

I don't understand Vallance. Up to this incident I had always thought him to be a first rate journalist and second rate in everything else, but also someone one could trust to be reasonable up to a point.

Yours
Leonard

I think this incident and my letter gives a good idea of the hurry and scurry of editing a paper like the *New Statesman*. The scene described by me to Maynard took place, not in the *New Statesman*, but at the printers in Southwark. There one had to go on Thursday morning—in this case on Friday owing to the holidays—and pass the proofs, or sometimes write or rewrite the article on the front page. One sat in a kind of glass case and the page proofs came up to one straight from the machine. Usually it was merely a question of correcting the proofs, but sometimes something might have happened overnight to make the article written the previous afternoon now out of date. In that case one might have to do a great deal of rewriting or even write an entirely new article. One worked under high pressure with all sorts of comings and goings, with the printer metaphorically behind one's back clamouring for the copy. It was much the same turmoil, or even more so, all the week from Monday to Wednesday in the office in Holborn. I do not mind working under pressure and am not disturbed by disturbance, having to do two or three things at the same time with doors perpetually opening and shutting and people perpetually coming and going. Ceylon had taught me to work in its kachcheries, unprotected by doors or windows, impassively and imperturbably in a kaleidoscope of noise and perpetual motion, people talking in two or even three languages at the same time about two or three distinct questions at the same time. There is, in fact, a certain exhilaration in this kind of expertise, the administrator, journalist, or tycoon able to juggle with half a dozen problems at the same time like a juggler who can keep half a dozen billiard balls in the air at the same time. But to do this kind of thing all the time for a long time has a curious effect upon the mind. You live on the surface of things, on the surface of life and its problems, on the surface of your own mind. You become so slick, so skilful and astute, so knowing, that you no longer need to, or eventually can, think; you know all the questions and fortunately—or unfortunately—all the answers. I learned in Ceylon that if you have to settle any question which really requires some thought, whether in a Government office, a publisher's office—or even a newspaper office—it is essential to take it home with you. In your office you have bright ideas which seem to you brilliant. It is only at home, that, if you ever think, you may think.

I have already in *Downhill all the Way*[1] described what seems to me to be the effect of journalism, if persisted in for long, upon the mind of the journalist, and I will not repeat it here. There is, however, one rather interesting psychological effect of journalism upon journalists which I did not mention there, but which I noticed when I was Literary Editor of the *Nation*, and again when I temporarily edited the *New Statesman* for Kingsley. All occupations or professions, like individuals, create around themselves a kind of magnetic field. To me myself everything within and without myself acquires a curious and strong quality or aura of me myself—my pains and pleasures, my typewriter and my big toe, my memories

[1] See above, pp. 289-90.

and the view which I am now looking at from my window, the people I love and the people I hate, all these, when they enter the magnetic field which my ego and egocentricity have developed about me, acquire a meaning and value peculiar to myself. And everyone else walks through life, materially and spiritually, enveloped in a similar magnetic field of his own personality which gives to everything and everyone entering the field a magnetised reflection of his ego, a meaning and value which he alone in the world feels and understands.

Occupations and professions, even institutions, acquire the same kind of magnetisation. Everything entering the magnetic field surrounding a school or college, the occupation of a barrister or doctor, of a miner or electrical engineer, a cook or a gardener, acquires the same kind of peculiar meaning and value to those within the field. The psychology of this occupational hallucination or self-deception is shown most obviously and commonly in the enormous, sacred importance which the vocation and everything connected with it acquire in the eyes of those who practise it. Kings and queens, their families and relations, and all those who earn their living by some sort of Court service, have always reached the most fantastic heights of ludicrous hallucination, and they have been encouraged by the almost universal acquiescence of ordinary people whose passion for self-deception is so great and so deep that they are delighted to be deceived even by the self-deception of someone else. Judges and priests—particularly the higher classes, the Popes, Cardinals, Archbishops, and Bishops—come second to kings and queens in the quality and quantity of their vocational inflation and self-deception. I think journalists come third. I am thinking, of course, primarily of the daily paper and the intellectual weekly. The chief factor in the hallucinatory overestimation of the importance of journals and journalism by journalists is the obvious importance of the events and subjects on which they are daily or weekly pronouncing judgment anonymously *ex cathedra*, the cathedra being in fact the editor's chair. By the curious logic of history and human institutions, the Pope, a celibate virgin who is forbidden to have any relations with women, is entrusted with the power to make detailed and intimate regulations for millions of ordinary people regarding marriage and the sexual intercourse of husband and wife. Not unnaturally a man who is given the power to make infallible decisions with regard to such important matters claims successfully from millions of people an enormously inflated importance, the outward and visible sign of which is the fantastic fancy dress in which, as with queens and kings, he is habitually photographed.[1] Something of the same sort happens to the editor, the paper which he edits, and all those engaged in producing the paper. I think that they all—even the lowliest office girl—feel that the paper is important because it is daily or weekly pronouncing judgment on the most momentous events, persons, and policies which history causes to pass like a pageant from Monday to Thursday morning, when the paper goes to press, before the editor's and the assistant editor's desks. The competence of the editor to pontificate on some of these subjects is probably no higher than that of a celibate old gentleman in Rome to lay down the law on the intimacies and intricacies of copulation and the mechanics of contraceptives. But it is quite impossible not to believe that one is important if one is perpetually laying down the law upon important questions. And with journalists, as with Popes, judges, and M.P.s, the power complex also comes in. Every editor—certainly every good editor—believes, not only that he is continually pronouncing judgment about the most important questions but that he and his paper have a powerful influence upon public opinion with regard to those questions. Thus a magnetic field of highly charged importance, influence, and power is created around every newspaper, and everyone connected with it is subjected to its effect and to any vocational delusions to which it gives rise. I know from experience that the moment I sat down in the editor's chair in the *New Statesman* office, though I am by nature sceptical, an unusual sense of importance, a tinge of *folie de grandeur*, enveloped me. It emanated from the magnetic field of the *New Statesman* into which I had suddenly and importantly entered. Instinctively I was feeling that everything I was going to do or say during the next week was of importance. I was the (temporary) wielder of influence and power. I used to feel the same thing in the *Nation* office when I was Literary Editor there, and even as editor of the *Political Quarterly*.

[1] The credulity of human beings is so gigantic and unquenchable that millions of them not only accept the dictates of an old gentleman in Rome about contraceptives, but also believe that he is in direct communication with the Deity who created the universe, with its suns and galaxies and comets flaming through infinite space, and that it is direct from this Deity that he, the Pope, has received the detailed instructions with regard to how married persons are permitted to use or not to use contraceptives.

And this effect of the newspaper's magnetic field extends, as I said, far beyond the editor's chair. I am sure that Maynard Keynes, for instance, would never have taken so serious a view of Aylmer Vallance's indiscretions if he had not attributed such immense importance and influence to what appeared in the *New Statesman*.

In the last sentence I very nearly wrote 'exaggerated' instead of the word 'immense'. The question of whether or to what extent one exaggerates one's own importance and that of one's work or productions is a painful one and not entirely easy to answer accurately. I feel pretty certain that the magnetic field surrounding journalism induces the editor and staff of every newspaper to believe that his paper is much more important and influential upon public opinion than it really is. I have no doubt at all that I was a victim of this occupational delusion as editor of the *International Review*, the *Nation*, the *New Statesman*, and the *Political Quarterly*. Most of this is, of course, conjecture, but the evidence of facts, so far as it goes, seems to show that newspapers have very little positive effect on the formation of opinion. This is certainly true of the millions of copies of the popular dailies churned out and sold under the hourly direction of the great Press Lords, Northcliffe and Beaverbrook, both of whom aimed at moulding public opinion on almost any subject from sweet peas to Empire Free Trade, and seemed to believe—quite wrongly—that they succeeded. Some of their modern successors suffer from the same illusions. The truth is that an enormous majority of newspaper readers read them for either one or both of two purposes. The first purpose is simply to learn what has happened, the facts, whether about racing and football, crime and sex, the doings of the Queen and her family, or politics. The second purpose is to obtain entertainment, pleasure, reassurance, or irritation. Clearly an enormous number of people read papers mainly to get entertainment or amusement from them. A smaller number want to find in them a confirmation of their own tastes, beliefs, loves, hatreds, and delusions—they want to be reassured. A still smaller number read them because they want to be annoyed. This applies particularly to the intellectual weeklies. I am sure that many people have always read the *New Statesman* because it supplied them with a weekly dose of justified irritation. Finally I repeat what I have said elsewhere that I think it highly probable that the influence of newspapers is in inverse proportion to the magnitude of their circulations. The millions of copies of the *Daily Mail* or *Mirror* and the millions who read them are so formless and fluid that the papers have practically no effect upon the minds of the readers. Journals with a very small circulation, written by experts for experts on more or less technical subjects—the *Political Quarterly* is one of them—more often than not are dealing directly with opinion and are more likely therefore to influence it.

These facts about the magnetic field surrounding occupations and the occupational delusions which are involved in it lead to a question which almost everyone, I think, as he grows old, particularly if he writes his autobiography, must occasionally ask himself—and the autobiographer in particular must try to answer it honestly. Here I sit at the age of sixty, seventy, eighty, or (in my own case today) eighty-eight; behind me lies 'work', anything from forty to seventy years of 'work'. I am talking of males of the middle class; we began to 'work', to go into a profession or a business some time between the ages of eighteen and twenty-four. We had gone to prep schools (for seven years) and public schools (for five years) working to prepare ourselves for the work which we were going to do in our profession or business. What was the object of this 'work', of these hours and years of labour? What did we think was its object? What did it achieve and what did we think that it achieved? Of course, owing to the economic determination of history, classes, and individuals, we worked in order to make a living, and, since we are alive to ask these questions, we presumably achieved it. But, while there is a profound truth in Marx's analysis of society, psychology, and economics, it is only a half or possibly even a third of the truth. The vast majority of human beings regard their work, not only as economically determined, i.e. a source of income, but also as having a non-economic object and value producing effects of social, psychological, or artistic value.

It is sixty-four years since the November day when I set sail from Tilbury through fog and drizzle down the Thames in the P & O ship *Syria* for Ceylon. It was the beginning of my work in the technical sense, work in a profession, work to earn a living. In the sixty-four years which have passed since that November day I reckon that at a minimum I have worked 158,720 hours or the equivalent of 6,613 days. I feel sure that this is an underestimate, that I have, in fact, during the last sixty-four years spent on what everyone would agree was 'work' considerably more than 170,000 hours. The kind of work which I did in the seven years which I spent as a civil servant in

Ceylon I have described in *Growing*; the kind of work which I have done since I resigned from the Ceylon Civil Service I have described in *Beginning Again* and *Downhill all the Way*. In order to get some idea of its object and effect I propose to examine what exactly this work consisted of during the six years of the war, 1939 to 1945, at the end of which I was sixty-five years old.

The routine of my life changed considerably from time to time during those six years; the changes affected the amount of time which I could give to my various occupations, but not, I think, the total amount of time which I gave to work. What chiefly determined the kind of work which I could and did do was the proportion of my time which I spent in London and in Rodmell. Virginia's death which disrupted the whole of my life disrupted the rhythm and routine of my work; but what I could do and how I could do it was enormously influenced by the bombing of London. I have already described how in 1940, before Virginia's death, the early bombing wrecked our house in Mecklenburgh Square and made it uninhabitable. We now had nowhere to stay in London and became for the first time in our lives country folk, living permanently in Monks House, Rodmell. The first effect of this and of the evacuation of the Hogarth Press in September 1940 to Letchworth was that I could no longer take any part in the day-to-day control of the Press; my work as a publisher was reduced to remote control by correspondence with John Lehmann and by our meeting from time to time in London or Rodmell. I went up for the day to London whenever I had work to do in the Labour Party, Fabian Society, Arbitration Tribunal, or *New Statesman*; otherwise I sat in Rodmell writing or editing the *Political Quarterly*.

But after Virginia's death I felt that I must have somewhere where I could stay in London in order to be able to do my work there more intensively. So I took a flat in Cliffords Inn. I discovered that by nature I am not a flat-dweller; I have little or no sense of gregariousness; I find no comfort or security in the sound and smell and warmth of the herd, the coziness of the human rabbit-warren. I like my fellow-human beings, but I require considerable periods of absence from them, periods of silence and loneliness. I could not stand Cliffords Inn for long, and in April 1942 I got three rooms in my house in Mecklenburgh Square patched up and moved in there. 'Patched up' is the right description of the rooms and the house. There were no windows and no ceilings, and nothing in the house, from roof to the water pipes, was quite sound. I got my loneliness and my silence (except when the bombs were falling) all right, but I have experienced few things more depressing in my life than to live in a badly bombed flat, with the windows boarded up, during the great war. I stuck it out in Mecklenburgh Square for exactly a year, but by October 1943 I could bear it no longer and I took a lease of 24 Victoria Square. When that lease came to an end I bought a further ninety-nine-year lease of the house from the Grosvenor Estate, so that, if I live to the age of one hundred and fifty, I may still have a house in London.

Cliffords Inn, Mecklenburgh Square, and Victoria Square, in succession, made a new routine and rhythm of life for me from the winter of 1941 to the end of the war in 1945. I began again to do a good deal of political work in London. The routine which gradually established itself was two to four nights in London and the rest of the week in Rodmell. Looking through the list of my engagements I find that in the last years of the war my 'work' in London, most of it political, consisted of the following:

Labour Party: Secretary of the Advisory Committee on International Relations; Secretary of the Advisory Committee on Imperial Questions.
Fabian Society: Executive Committee; Chairman, International Bureau; Imperial Bureau.
Anglo-Soviet Society.
New Statesman: Board of Directors.
Civil Service Arbitration Tribunal.
Political Quarterly: Board and Editor

This 'work' took up many hours of my time, for, when in London, I often had two committees in a day and, quite apart from the committees, I often wrote reports for the Labour Party and for the Fabian Bureaux. All this work was unpaid, except the *Political Quarterly* and the Arbitration Tribunal. (My salary for editing the *Political Quarterly* was £80 and I was paid four guineas for each case which I heard on the Tribunal.)

Why did I do all this work year after year? I was sixty-five in 1945 when the war ended and sixty-five is the usual year for retirement. But I continued to grind away at much of this political or social work for many years after the end of the war. And even in Rodmell I did a lot of work of the same kind, of a political, social, or communal nature; for I was Clerk to the Parish Council for seventeen years, was for years and still am a Manager of the Rodmell Primary

School, and have been for over twenty years President of the Rodmell Horticultural Society. It is extremely difficult to answer honestly the question why I have spent so many thousands of hours in these drab occupations. I do not really like sitting on committees and am not a good rank-and-file committee man, though I can be a very good secretary and even, when I take the trouble, a good chairman. There is, of course, a kind of childish or ignoble pleasure in the feeling of male importance which everyone feels when he takes his seat at a committee meeting. If you are chairman or secretary, you can feel at least a faint additional pleasure in the exercise of power, however feeble. Then too, as I have said, I find it extremely interesting to watch the psychological antics of five, ten, or fifteen men sitting round a table, each with his own selfish or unselfish axe to grind. I have always found the battle of brains and wills, boxing, wrestling, or ju-jitsu, with no blows or holds barred, which goes on round the table fascinating. Indeed, one of the reasons why I am ordinarily not a good rank-and-file committee man is that I tend to forget everything in the silent amusement of observing highly intelligent men fighting for Will-o'-the-wisps or even windmills as if for their own dear lives, converting their own pet molehills into God's Mount Sinais. Looking back over the aeons of slowly passing minutes that I have spent in the House of Commons and other less distinguished committee rooms, I must admit that I have enjoyed the spectacle of many great men or little men of great political expertise performing as if for my personal benefit; the wily, treacherous Ramsay MacDonald in the old I.L.P.; the mouselike Clem Attlee, who, when you least expected it, would suddenly show himself to be a masterful or even savage mouse, in the New Fabian Research Bureau; Bernard Shaw's gala performances of irrelevant wit and dialectic in the Fabian Society; the ruthless virtuosity of Sidney Webb in the Fabian Society; the new school of hard-headed, no nonsense, common sense of Harold Laski, G. D. H. Cole, Hugh Gaitskell, Hugh Dalton, Harold Wilson in the Fabian Society and Labour Party; the strange succession of Maynard Keynes, Kingsley Martin, John Freeman, and Jock Campbell on the *New Statesman* Board.

But these are, of course, not the main reason why I have continued for so many years to do all this dreary work. It had an object, a political or social object. My seven years in the Ceylon Civil Service turned me from an aesthetic into a political animal. The social and economic squalor in which thousands of Sinhalese and Tamil villagers lived horrified me; I saw close at hand the evils of imperialism and foresaw some of the difficulties and dangers which is inevitable liquidation would involve. When I returned to England after this seven-year interval, I was intensely interested in the political and social system; I could observe it with the fresh eye of a stranger, and also to some extent with the eye of an expert, for as Assistant Government Agent of a District, as a judge, and as a magistrate, I had learned a good deal about the art of government and administration.

My first contact with the economic system of capitalism in the England of 1912 was, as I described in *Beginning Again*, through a Care Committee of the Charity Organisation Society in Hoxton. The immediate effect upon me I described in that book as follows:

> One only had to spend a quarter of an hour sitting with Marny Vaughan on a Care Committee and another quarter of an hour with the victim, Mr and Mrs Smith in the Hoxton slum, to see that in Hoxton one was confronted by some vast, dangerous fault in the social structure, some destructive disease in the social organism, which could not be touched by paternalism or charity or good works. Nothing but a social revolution, a major operation, could deal with it. I resigned from the Care Committee of the C.O.S. Hoxton turned me from a liberal into a socialist.[1]

A study of the co-operative societies of England and Scotland and seeing something of the lives of working class co-operators in the north confirmed my socialism. I became a member of the Fabian Society, the Labour Party, and the I.L.P.

The senseless war of 1914 deepened my conversion to a political animal. I was horrified by this spectacle of millions of human beings apparently driven by inexorable fate into communal madness, slaughtering one another by the million, scattering over the whole earth the most ghastly misery and pain and ruin, blindly destroying civilisation in the name of civilisation—and all this for objects which had no relevance, import, or even meaning for anyone outside a tiny ring of kings, rulers, aristocrats, statesmen, generals and admirals, and historians. I became obsessed by two questions: first, why human beings, and particularly Europeans, at intervals committed political and social suicide, like Gadarene swine, by rushing down a steep place into war. I could not accept the acquiescent resignation

[1] See above, p. 70.

of the old Kaspars, little Peterkins, and little Wilhelmines contemplating the skulls, the memorials of the Duke of Marlborough's victory at Blenheim or Lord Haig's 'victory' at Passchendaele Ridge near Ypres:

> 'But what they fought each other for
> I could not well make out.
> But everybody said,' quoth he,
> 'That 'twas a famous victory.
>
> They say it was a shocking sight
> After the field was won;
> For many thousand bodies here
> Lay rotting in the sun:
> But things like that, you know, must be
> After a famous victory.
>
> And everybody praised the Duke
> Who this great fight did win.'
> 'But what good came of it at last!'
> Quoth little Peterkin:
> 'Why that I cannot tell,' said he,
> 'But 'twas a famous victory.'

During the war itself I became absorbed in the problem of the fundamental causes of war and whether anything could be done to prevent it. During the last years of the war practically all my work was concentrated on this problem. The result was my book *International Government*, which originated from a report which I wrote for the Fabian Society. The deeper I went into the question, the more convinced I became that part of the solution depended upon the possibility of establishing some rudimentary form of international government. I did not believe that war could be abolished by international government, but came to the conclusion that war would almost certainly sooner or later be inevitable unless some sort of system of settling international disputes without war by methods of law or conciliation could be established. This led logically and practically to the idea of a League of Nations. In the Fabian Society, the Labour Party, and the League of Nations Society,[1] which I helped to establish, I worked with others to ensure that the creation of a League of Nations should be part of the peace settlement.

[1] See above, pp. 138-9.

The League was created at Versailles. For the next twenty-seven years I worked as Secretary of the Labour Party Advisory Committee on International Affairs to try to get the Executive Committee of the Labour Party and secondarily the Parliamentary Party to make the League and the League system and its development the essence, the motive power, of their international policy. The Advisory Committee consisted of 'experts' on foreign affairs, like Brailsford, C. R. Buxton, W. Arnold-Forster, Norman Angell, and Labour M.P.s who specialised in the same subject. As time went on, the scope of our work increased considerably; we 'advised' the Executive Committee and through it the Parliamentary Party by a stream of reports and memoranda, explaining, often intellectually in words of one syllable, complicated situations and problems, warning about approaching crises, continually suggesting ways in which the Party's proclaimed general policy should be applied practically to these situations and problems. In the Fabian Society International Bureau I was doing the same kind of political work, but, whereas in the Labour Party Advisory Committee we were trying to educate the Labour leaders, the political elite, in the Fabian Society we were addressing the rank and file as well as the elite.

As Secretary of the Labour Party Advisory Committee for Imperial Questions for twenty-seven years and in the Fabian Society Colonial Bureau I was trying to do the same kind of thing for imperialism, the Empire, the colonies which in the other committees I was trying to do for the League and international affairs. My aim, and I think the aim of the Advisory Committee and of the Fabian Society, was to put before the Labour Party and its rank-and-file supporters the facts and problems of the Empire and imperialism, to warn them of the dangers imminent in the inevitable demand for self-government and independence, to suggest a detailed, practical policy, varying from territory to territory, by which each should attain self-government or independence, and also by which economically and politically peoples could be prepared and educated for independence where that was not immediately possible.

I give these rather dreary political and institutional details because they are essential to finding a true answer to this question of the importance and effect of long years of 'work', and of my 'work' in particular. And I do not think that the particular aspect of the question, *my* work and *my* aims and *my* failure, is the only one involved; the unimportant particular case was related to and determined by the catastrophic historical events which led to the destruction of the League of Nations, Hitler's war, and the break-up of the British Empire. It is therefore in the light of this history that I ask myself the rather ludicrous question: What was the use of all this work? Was it of the slightest importance? Did it achieve anything substantial of what it was intended to achieve?

Looking back at the age of eighty-eight over the fifty-seven years of my political work in England, knowing what I aimed at and the results, meditating on the history of Britain and the world since 1914, I see clearly that I achieved practically nothing. The world today and the history of the human anthill during the last fifty-seven years would be exactly the same as it is if I had played pingpong instead of sitting on committees and writing books and memoranda. I have therefore to make the rather ignominious confession to myself and to anyone who may read this book that I must have in a long life ground through between 150,000 and 200,000 hours of perfectly useless work. Objectively—I will deal with the fact subjectively later—this is I think interesting, for it throws some light upon the political determination of history. There are thousands of people doing the kind of political work which I did. The work has a clear, direct object, to influence men's minds and so to alter the course of historical events in one direction or another.

I was no fool at this particular game. It is not conceited for me to say that in mind, temperament, and experience I was peculiarly fitted for the kind of political work which I tried to do. I have a clear mind, capable of quickly understanding both theoretical and practical problems; I proved in my seven years in Ceylon, by my rapid promotion, that I was above the average in practising the art of politics and government; I enjoy making difficult, dangerous, and 'important' decisions and acting on them; until age mellowed or emasculated me I suffered, as a politician, from the disadvantage of regarding fools not with gladness but with exasperation and despair—and in politics the number of fools whom one has to suffer is terribly high—yet the many years in which I successfully managed the Labour Party Committees—difficult teams of intellectuals and trade unionists—proves, I think, that I did learn the art of managing and persuading all sorts and kinds of politicians; finally—and this is peculiarly important—by luck and the run of the game I very soon became known to and in many cases intimate with those people in the Labour movement who sat in the seats of power and who when the time came were Prime Ministers and Cabinet Ministers, Ramsay MacDonald, Clem Attlee, Sidney Webb, Hugh Gaitskell, Hugh Dalton, and many other worthy men. The relevance of what in the last sentence I believe, quite modestly, to be facts is that my failure to achieve anything was not due to personal political inadequacy and incompetence, and that, if I achieved nothing, it is almost certain that the enormous amount of similar work done by other people is and has been equally futile.

In order to explain and justify what I have just said, I will put down bleakly and objectively what seem to me to have been the positive and negative results of my 200,000 hours of labour. First the positive. I can, I think, chalk up one or two items of worldly success. I was interviewed for three days, eight hours a day, by Malcolm Muggeridge for a B.B.C. television programme. A sixty-minute T.V. interview by Malcolm on one's life and opinions is in some ways a popular apotheosis for someone like myself. Malcolm's power to confer the crown of notoriety upon the obscure is remarkable and I can give a significant proof for it. For many years once a year I have opened my garden to the public in aid of the Queen's Institute of District Nursing. Up to and including April 1966 I never had more than one hundred visitors to the garden on the day it was opened. Malcolm's T.V. interview was in September 1966. The number of entrance-paying visitors to my garden was 384 in 1967 and 457 in 1968. It is clear that Malcolm, by interviewing one, increases one's notoriety (or the notoriety of one's garden) by 284 per cent the first year and 357 per cent in the second.

My second worldly success was winning the W. H. Smith £1,000 award. But I am, of course, here concerned not so much with 'success' in the wider worldly sense, as with the positive achievements, the positive effects of one's work and life. Well, I had some slight peripheral influence upon the establishment of the League of Nations and upon the constitution given to it. In *Beginning Again*[1] I gave the facts which show that my book *International Government* 'was used extensively by the government committee which produced the British proposals for a League of Nations laid before the Peace Conference, and also by the British delegation to the Versailles Conference'. From 1920 to 1935 I worked incessantly through the Labour Party Advisory Committee and the Fabian Society, and also

[1] See above, p. 136.

outside these organisations, to get British Governments, and of course Labour Governments pre-eminently, to strengthen the League, to use it as the main instrument of their international policy and of pacification and peace in Europe. This did have some effect. The Labour Party Executive and the Parliamentary Party did in fact adopt the policy which the Advisory Committee persistently recommended to them. With Will Arnold-Forster I prepared briefs for Arthur Henderson to use—and he did use them—on the League; and through Philip Noel-Baker I occasionally did something of the same sort for Lord Cecil when he represented a Conservative Government on the League Council.

I think the hundreds of hours which I spent working as secretary of the two Labour Party Advisory Committees—on international and imperial questions—had some slight effects of a different kind. When after the 1914 war the Labour Party began to recover from Lloyd George's coupon election and became the alternative to a Conservative Government, when in fact the tide turned and at the 1924 election so many Labour M.P.s were elected that Ramsay MacDonald formed the first Labour Government, the class structure of the Party in the House gave it a peculiar intellectual complexion. The great majority of Labour M.P.s were working class and trade unionist, but there was a small, influential minority—they held a disproportionate number of Cabinet posts—of middle-class intellectuals, many of whom had begun their political life as Liberals. The trade unionists knew or thought they knew everything that there was to know about the industrial and the economic system, but they were completely ignorant of and took little or no interest in foreign affairs, the League, and the problems of empire. It is significant that in 1924, when the future of the Empire, colonies, and 'colonialism' was one of the most important of all political questions, MacDonald sent to the Colonial Office as Secretary of State J. H. Thomas, an ignorant, frivolous political buffoon. The Advisory Committees did something to dispel this ignorance and apathy. Men of knowledge and experience like Charles Buxton and Will Arnold-Forster on the International Committee, and Buxton and Sir John Maynard on the Imperial Committee, did an enormous amount of work between 1920 and 1930 to educate the Party. A certain number of Labour M.P.s joined the Committees and regularly came to the meetings. We continually briefed them for debates in the House, and gradually we helped to create a nucleus of M.P.s with a real knowledge and understanding of the problems. M.P.s like Sir Drummond Shields, who became Parliamentary Under-Secretary of State, India Office, and later the Colonial Office, and Arthur Creech Jones, who became Secretary of State for the Colonies, always acknowledged that their education in imperial politics came very largely from the Committee. We also provided the Party with an 'advanced' policy with regard to the League of Nations, India, and the Empire or, as it became, the Commonwealth. When Charles Buxton and I in the early 1920s produced a detailed programme for developing and educating the African colonies for self-government and the Labour Party adopted and published it as their official policy, it seemed as if we had really accomplished something important.

It was a delusion. The work which we were doing was, of course, closely connected with the most historically important events between 1919 and 1939 and it created for us the kind of magnetic field which I have described above. It had the usual effect of such magnetic fields on all of us. However often one has been disillusioned one almost inevitably feels some (uneasy or even perhaps guilty) sense of importance when one goes down to the room of the Prime Minister, even if it is only Ramsay MacDonald, in the House of Commons to discuss with him a difficult and dangerous international crisis or the next tottering steps of India to self-government. The whole thing was as phoney as the Prime Minister. Take for instance the case of the League of Nations. I still believe that after the 1914 war the only hope of preventing a second war was in the establishment of an effective League, the beginnings of a new international order, based upon law, collective security, and the pacific settlement of disputes. I believe too that if British Governments had gone all out for establishing the League and had used it as the instrument of their policy in the turmoil of peace which followed inevitably on the turmoil of war, they might have succeeded, they might have obtained sufficient support from the other states of the world to persuade or even compel first victorious France and later a renascent Germany to work for peace instead of pursuing policies which could only end in war.

There was in fact never any real hope that this would happen. Conservative Governments and statesmen, from Baldwin and Samuel Hoare to Neville Chamberlain, never believed in the League or attempted to use it; though they occasionally paid lip-service to it, they thought that they themselves were 'practical men' and that the League was a gimmick of 'idealists'. It is the practical men, not the idealists, who ever since the dawn of history have, by their practical policies, produced the unending series of disasters, the catalogue of miseries, which we call human history. They produced Hitler and the second great war. The only Conservative statesman who saw that the collective security system could be used to prevent that war was Churchill—and it was too late when he was at last converted. As for the Labour statesmen and the Labour Governments, to work with them in the 1920s was a lesson in frustration. The Governments were shortlived and without a majority in the House. Ramsay MacDonald shilly-shallied in foreign policy as he did in other things. Only Henderson at the top had a real grasp of what a League policy meant and he was not supported by Ramsay. When, as I recorded in *Downhill all the Way*,[1] we urged the Labour leaders to offer to join Winston Churchill in a coalition Government as the last chance of deterring Hitler from starting a world war—the very step they took when it was too late and Hitler had started his war—not one of them would even consider it seriously. Statesmen, those who are supposed and pretend to control events, are almost always content complacently to be controlled by them. That is why, while scientists produce bombs so efficient that they could destroy the whole human race in the space of half an hour and can send men to the moon and back, statesmen and governments allow international relations and the peoples of Europe to be controlled for years by a psychopathic lunatic and tolerate political and economic chaos from Vietnam to Nigeria and from Moscow to Washington.

My work with regard to the Empire and imperialism was just as futile. In a way it was even more exasperating. During the 1920s there were two problems of primary importance: first, to work out with the inhabitants of territories like India, Burma, and Ceylon the methods by which they could pass immediately from subordinate status to independence; secondly, to prepare those territories, mainly African, not ripe for immediate independence, by education and economic development so that they could pass, as rapidly as possible, through stages of self-government to political independence. When we put this before the Labour leaders and bigwigs and worked out in some detail the process by which the

[1] See above, pp. 370-1.

policy could be implemented, our proposals, as I have said, were accepted and put out as the official policy of the Party. When the time came for Labour Ministers and Governments to put their policy into practice, they almost always failed to do so. In my memory two incidents (which I have previously described in *Downhill all the Way*[1]) stand out as characteristic of Labour Ministers. In the first Charles Buxton and I, as Chairman and Secretary of the Advisory Committee, sat fantastically in the empty House of Lords one on each side of Sidney Webb, then Lord Passfield and Secretary of State for the Colonies, and vainly urged him to carry out the Party's promises and insist that some nugatory sum should be included in the Kenya budget for the education of African children and the provision of roads in the African Reserves. In the second, once more with Charles Buxton, I sit in No. 11 Downing Street on one side of a long table and on the other side sits Clem Attlee, not yet a peer, but Deputy Prime Minister and Lord President of the Council in Churchill's war Cabinet; we met a stony refusal from him when we urged him in a recurrent crisis in Indian affairs to do everything possible on the lines of the Labour Party's declared policy.

Of course I may be completely deluded in thinking that the policies of the League in international affairs and that rapid progress towards independence and self-government in imperial affairs might have saved the world from Hitler and the war and might have ensured a less bloody and chaotic break-up of empires. There are however some facts which make it more than possible that I am right. No one can deny that the policies actually pursued have produced in the last thirty years more horrors, misery, and barbarism than occurred in any other thirty years of recorded history. It is surely significant that over and over again the measures which we were urging in the 1920s and were rejected by 'practical' statesmen as utopian were adopted by them some twenty or forty years later—adopted when it was too late for them to be effective. After all, practical statesmen, who had refused to use the League of Nations before the war as idealist and utopian, resuscitated it under the name of the United Nations after the war and are misusing it in exactly the same way as they did its predecessor. I have given in *Downhill all the Way*[2] reasons for believing that 'the perpetual

[1] See above, pp. 363-4 and 356.

[2] See above, p. 354.

tragedy of history is that things are perpetually being done ten or twenty years too late', and I will not repeat them here.

As to the subjective effect of looking back over a life of eighty-eight years and 200,000 hours of work and of coming to the sobering conclusion that they have been, if not completely futile, at least mainly ineffective, there are two aspects of this picture. First there is the direct effect upon me of the state of the world, the climate of civilisation or barbarism. I feel passionately for what I call civilised life; I hate passionately what I call barbarism. When as a small child I heard my father say one day at lunch that, as regards rules of life, a man need only follow that advice of the prophet Micah: 'What doth the Lord require of thee, but to do justly, and to love mercy, and to walk humbly with thy God', I am sure that I did not really understand what he was talking about, yet in some curious way, I think, the words entered into and had a profound effect upon my mind and upon my soul, if I can be said to have a soul—for though it must have been more than eighty years ago, I can still see the scene, all of us children sitting round the Sunday lunch-table, the great sirloin appearing from under the enormous silver cover, my father with his serious, sensitive face with the carving knife poised over the sirloin as he quoted the prophet Micah, and the rather surprised and sheepish face of my cousin Benny who was not prone to walk or talk humbly with his God or anyone else.

Like Benny, I have never been much concerned with God or with walking humbly with him, but I believe profoundly in the other two rules. Justice and mercy—they seem to me the foundation of all civilised life and society, if you include under mercy toleration. This is, of course, the Semitic vision, but, when later I found that the Greeks had added to it the vision of liberty and beauty—τὸ καλὸν καὶ ἀγαθόν—I saw, when I added the words of Micah to the speech of Pericles in Thucydides, what has remained until today my vision of civilisation. And my feelings with regard to communal justice and mercy and toleration and liberty are both ethical and aesthetic, and it is this combination which gives to my feeling about what I call civilisation both its intensity and also a kind of austerity. The visions of civilisation and the partial, hesitating, fluctuating activation of these visions in the barbarous history of man, and the classical instances in which individuals have risked everything in a fight for justice, mercy, toleration, and liberty against the entrenched forces of kings and emperors, states and establishments, principalities and powers, all these have always given me not only an intense feeling about what is good and bad, what is right and wrong, but also the kind of emotion which I get still more powerfully from a play of Sophocles or Shakespeare, the Parthenon or the Acropolis, a picture of Piero della Francesca, a cello suite of Bach or the last movement of the last piano sonata of Beethoven. Actual examples are the description of Athenian civilisation by Pericles; the process of abolishing the slave-trade and Pitt's speech as the sun rose upon the debate in parliament which had lasted all night; Voltaire in the Calas case and Zola in the Dreyfus case; the passionate campaigns of Gladstone for liberty in Ireland and for justice and mercy in Armenia.

All this is the positive aspect of my political philosophy, if that is not too pretentious a name for my political beliefs, feelings, desires. The negative aspect is more relevant to the feelings with which autobiographically I look back on the effect of my 200,000 hours of work. Injustice, cruelty, intolerance, tyranny fill me with a passion of anger and disgust, and again my feelings are both aesthetic and ethical. To watch the Governments of Britain, France, and the United States destroy the League as a potential instrument of peace and civilisation against Hitler and the Nazis; to see the savage insanity of Hitler ecstatically infecting millions of Germans and carrying Europe and the world inexorably downhill into war; to observe the crude cruelty and stupidity of Soviet communism and the Iron Curtain from Stalin's massacres to the invasion of Czechoslovakia; to watch millions of ignorant Chinese and many western Europeans, who should know better, hail the imbecilities and savagery of Mao and Chinese communism as divine political and economic revelations; to see Americans at one and the same time showing superhuman skill and intelligence by sending three astronauts round the moon and year after year fighting in Vietnam a stupid, unjustified, bloody, and useless war; to see, what one had hoped for, the break-up of imperialism and colonialism, and then to find in the place of empires the chaotic crudities and hydrogen bombs of Mao in China, the senseless hostility of Pakistan and India, the unending war of Arabs and Israelis, the primitive brutality of apartheid in South Africa and Rhodesia; the ebb and flow of chaos and bloodshed and bleak authoritarianism in the new independent African states—when I look round at these facts in the world of today, I feel acute pain, compounded, I think, of disappointment and horror and discomfort and disgust.

Such are my reactions to the facts; except in the word 'disappointment' they throw no light upon my reactions to my own failure and futility. I do not think that ultimately I am much concerned by failure or success as a subjective experience. When I was secretary of the Labour Party Advisory Committees irate members used from time to time to come to me and say that we should give it up; we did, they said, an enormous amount of work for the Executive and the Parliamentary Party, and nothing came of it; the Party accepted our memoranda and reports and even adopted our policies—and yet nothing really came of it. I tried and usually succeeded in soothing them. I pointed out that we did occasionally get some important policy officially adopted and even at rare intervals acted upon; we did help the Executive and M.P.s to understand the crucial international and imperial problems; we occasionally prevented some unimportant or even important politician from going hopelessly astray. It was a question of casting bread on the waters—Heaven rejoicing in the conversion of a single sinner—being contented with small mercies or achievements—etc., etc.

These crumbs of comfort with the slightly Pecksniffian or Micawberish clichés to sweeten them seemed, as I said, to soothe and even convince the M.P.s and other frustrated members of the Committees. I do not think that they ever convinced me or were the real arguments or motives which kept me doing for so long so much work for such invisible and probably imaginary results. My attitude to these things was and, I suppose, still is rather different. For the vast majority of men, who are not great men or great criminals or both, there are three alternative ways of resigning oneself to one's own impotence to control one's own fate or to affect in any way the march of events: the first, which the enormous majority of human beings adopt from birth to death, is to ignore it all, make the best of it, earn one's living, marry a wife or a husband, join a club, play a game of golf, do the pools, watch the telly, eat and drink for tomorrow we die, and in fact finally die. The second method of ordering one's life in what for them is a hostile world and a hostile universe is adopted by a small number of extremely intelligent and sensitive people. Most of them are artists—writers, painters, or composers—if they are great, they create a new world both for themselves and for other people. But I have known a very few people in this case who are not artists or creative who have found a slightly different way of defying fate. They are defeatists; they give up the struggle; they spin for themselves, and live in a cocoon of unreality and eccentricity. The most curious example of this kind of cocoon existence was that of Saxon Sydney-Turner whose character and way of life I tried to describe in the first volume of my autobiography *Sowing*.[1]

The third method is one which, with many other people, not by conscious intent so much as through innate character, I have myself pursued. I cannot disengage myself from the real world; I cannot completely resign myself to fate; somewhere in the pit of my stomach there is a spark of fire or heat which at any moment may burst into flame and compel me violently to follow some path or pursue some object—no doubt too often some shadow of a dream or political *ignis fatuus*—contrary to the calculations of reason or possibility. It is in the pit of my stomach as well as in the cooler regions of my brain that I feel and think about what I see happening in the human ant-heap around me, the historical and political events which seem to me to make the difference between a good life and a bad, between civilisation and barbarism. I have no doubt that, if at any moment I had become convinced that my political work produced absolutely no effect at all in any direction, I would have stopped it altogether and have retired to cultivate my garden—the last refuge of disillusion. But the shadow of the shadow of a dream is a good enough carrot to keep the human donkey going through three score years and ten (and in my case even four score years and eight), and that is why I never could and still cannot yield even to the logic of events. On these things apparently I will 'not cease from mortal fight' and my sword will not 'sleep in my hand', although I know quite well that not Jerusalem, but only hideous red brick villas will be built in what was once 'England's green and pleasant land'.

All these excuses and explanations of why I have performed 200,000 hours of useless work are no doubt merely another way of confessing that the magnetic field of my own occupations produced the usual self-deception, the belief that they were important. That brings me to the final excuse or explanation. As I have said before, all through my life I have always believed and, I think, acted on the belief that there are two levels or grades of importance. *Sub specie aeternitatis*, in the eye of God or rather of the universe, nothing

[1] Volume 1, pp. 65-8 and 72-5.

human is of the slightest importance; but in one's own personal life, in terms of humanity and human history and human society, certain things are of immense importance: human relations, happiness, truth, beauty or art, justice and mercy. That is why in his private and personal life a wise man would never take arms against a sea of troubles; he would suffer the slings and arrows of outrageous fortune, saying to himself: 'These things are momentarily of terrible importance and yet tomorrow and eternally of no importance.' And in a wider context, though all that I tried to do politically was completely futile and ineffective and unimportant, for me personally it was right and important that I should do it, even though at the back of my mind I was well aware that it was ineffective and unimportant. To say this is to say that I agree with what Montaigne, the first civilised modern man, says somewhere: 'It is not the arrival, it is the journey which matters.'

4
All Our Yesterdays

Looking back over one's life, one of the curious things one notices is how two or three small events happened years and years ago, then for years the consequences disappear beneath the surface of one's life like underground springs or streams, and then, like streams breaking out of the ground as tributaries to form a great river, years later the events reappeared with important consequences in one's life. This kind of thing happened to me in 1943. It began with a letter from Phil Noel-Baker nearly twenty years before in the early days of the Hogarth Press. Phil was for a time in the Secretariat of the League of Nations in Geneva. I got a letter from him asking me whether I could find a job for a young woman, Alice Ritchie, who had just been sacked, he thought rather unfairly, from a responsible post in the Secretariat. Alice was a remarkable young woman with a character entirely her own. I cannot now remember what brought about her downfall, but I think it was some inexcusable criticism of a superior which the superior ought to have excused.

I saw Alice and offered her the post of traveller for the Hogarth Press. She was the first woman to become what is called a publisher's representative in Britain. She proved to be a good, if unconventional, commercial traveller, and on the whole she enjoyed taking the Hogarth Press books round the booksellers and getting orders from them. But she was much more than a traveller in books. She also wrote them. She was born in South Africa and had been educated at Newnham, but her roots were in the north of Great Britain for her father, an architect, had been born in Scotland and her mother in Durham. She had a brother, Pat, and a younger sister, Trekkie. The whole family returned to England for good during the 1914 war, because her father, who had already fought in the Boer war, decided that he must fight for Britain in the first great war. Pat, who was still in his teens and had a passion for flying, joined the R.F.C. He remained in the R.A.F. after the war and reached the rank of Air Vice-Marshal. I look back with some amusement to his attempts in the early 1920s to prove to me that flying was already a reliable form of transport. I had rather tactlessly said to Alice that, in my opinion, it was not yet reliable. Pat was at that time stationed in the West Country but once a week had to come to London to attend the Air Ministry. When Alice reported to him what I had said, he offered to take me up in a plane from Hendon and prove I was wrong. For many weeks after this I was rung up by him every Friday, and every Friday the weather was not good enough for a flight. However, at last one day he rang me up to say that it was all right and Virginia and I set off to Hendon. Pat met us and took us to the airfield. There was a long wait and then the disconsolate Pat came and told us that owing to some hitch the plane could not be used. Next week he was moved to another station and to my regret I never left the earth in a plane piloted by Pat Ritchie.

Alice was, as I said, a remarkable young woman and too good to spend much of her life travelling books. She wrote two novels, *The Peacemakers* and *Occupied Territory*, which we published in the Hogarth Press. The first was based on her experience in the League of Nations, the second on her experiences in occupied Germany after the war, when her father, who had reached the rank of colonel, was in command of his regiment there. Both these books showed real talent and considerable promise. She had the mind of a novelist and the temperament of an artist, but there was a psychological twist in her which made it almost impossible for her to face the final word or stroke or note in artistic production. She belonged to that strange race of Penelope writers who unpick every evening all the stitches which they sewed in the morning. Day after day Alice would write all the morning and tear it all up in the afternoon. This disease of artificial sterility is not uncommon among writers, particularly novelists, and some who suffer from it are potentially very good writers. The cause of the disease is not always the same. In most cases, I think, it come from a horror of cutting the umbilical cord which binds the work of art to the artist, a refusal, usually unconscious, to throw the child to the wolves, the book to the reviewers or critics. Virginia, as I have said before, had this horror of the cutting of the umbilical cord, but, like several others of her family, she combined nervous instability and skinless hypersensibility with remarkable mental toughness, and the moment always came with every book she wrote when she said: 'Publish and be damned'.

Alice, I think, was not without this umbilical horror, but the principal cause of her artistic sterility, of her inability to finish a book, was different. It was the same psychology as Desmond Mac-

Carthy's. 'The best is the enemy of the good,' said the Greeks. Desmond's standards as an artist were so high that, knowing that he could never in practice attain them, he never really even attempted to write the novel which he so often talked of writing. There was in this shrinking and shirking a mixture of mental laziness and artistic cowardice. Alice suffered from the same kind of inhibitions. She was not as mentally lazy as Desmond, but she had the same fear of committing herself artistically. She did not, as he did, invent good and bad reasons for not writing at all; she wrote her novel daily before midday and tore it up before midnight. In the hope of curing her of this disease, at one time I got her to post off to me every morning what she had written as soon as she had written it, but this did no good. After a week or more she got bogged down and I had to send her back what she had sent me. Penelope started all over again, and her third novel was never written.

There was a streak of melancholy in Alice which may have been part cause or part effect of her sterility as a writer. After some years she gave up her job with the Hogarth Press, but Virginia and I liked her very much and continued to see her from time to time. But in the 1930s she disappeared into Palestine, for she went to keep house in Jerusalem for her brother Pat who had been seconded and lent by the R.A.F. to the Army in those troubled years. I heard little or nothing from her and she seemed, as sometimes people do, to have passed out of my life. But in the middle of 1941 I received a letter from her asking me whether I would come and see her in London as she was ill.

Pat, who was now a Group Captain, had been brought back from Palestine for war duties in England, and Alice had returned with him. I found her in Victoria Square, already very ill, dying of cancer. For the next few months—until, in fact, the cancer killed her—whenever I was in London I used to go and see her. She seemed to be facing death bravely with her eyes open, and we talked on the surface as we had always talked. Yet we talked under the shadow of death. When I see someone, particularly someone who like Alice is young, dying, when I sit talking to her knowing that she is dying, and in her case she knowing that I knew that she was dying—I get a terrible feeling that time has stopped, the earth is no longer revolving, the universe has slowed down—we are waiting in a void for the final catastrophe, the passing of life.

I do not think that there is sentimentality or self-deception in what

I have just written. However sophisticated and atheistic a man may be, there is in his bowels, in the pit of his stomach, at the bottom of his heart, in the convolutions of his brain, a primeval attitude towards death. I myself feel it and have always felt it strongly. I saw the puppy dying in the bucket of water; in Ceylon at the Pearl Fishery, with the dawn coming up like thunder, I looked down on the dead Arab lying on the sand at the sea edge[1]; I watched Alice dying of cancer in Victoria Square; years later, only a day before he died, I went to see Clive Bell, dying of cancer, no longer able to talk, but in the room in which time had stopped, his eyes watching for death, but still eager to hear from me the trivialities of living; I saw Virginia's body in the Newhaven mortuary. In all these cases, however acutely my own personal feelings were involved or not involved, I had the primeval sense of time stopping, the universe hesitating, waiting, in fear, regret, pity, for the annihilation or snuffing out of a life, of a living being.

If you are the Pope or the Archbishop of Canterbury or the rector of Rodmell or the Queen of England or the headmaster of Eton or the Lord Chancellor or the Director-General of the B.B.C. or a less distinguished person sufficiently terrified by the prospect of dying, you believe that absolute truth about life and death and immortality was revealed three, four, or five thousand years ago to Semitic savages in the sands of Sinai and in the craggy town of Jerusalem—or if you cannot quite swallow that, you believe that absolute truth about immortality can be found in the pit of one's stomach where by some strange psychological alchemy primeval fear and wishful thinking produce absolute truth. I wish I could believe this, but I have no faith in the pit of my or anyone else's stomach, and I see no more reason for accepting the dreams and nightmares of Semitic savages on death and immortality than on the nature of thunder or the origin of species.

Alice died. Some time later I had a letter from her sister Trekkie; she said that she had been ill, but was now practically recovered, and she asked me to come and see her. I had seen her once or twice in the far-off days when Alice was with us in the Press. She was then a very young woman, a painter at the Slade, extremely beautiful. She designed the jackets for Alice's novels and she did a few other jackets for us at that time. I do not think that we met at all between 1930 and 1942. She had married Ian Parsons, the publisher, a

[1] See Volume 1, pp. 191-2.

Director of Chatto & Windus, and they lived in a house in Victoria Square—Alice in the last months of her life was living with them.

I went to see Trekkie and I dined with her and Ian in Victoria Square, but I did not see much of them until towards the end of 1942. It was one of the gloomiest periods of a gloomy war. Ian was in the R.A.F., in the bowels of the earth in Westminster, poring over photographs of airfields in occupied Europe. Trekkie every day rode on a motor bicycle to a super-secret department of the War Office in Petersham. But towards the end of the year I began to see more of them and Trekkie came and stayed for a weekend at Rodmell. This altered both the rhythm of my life and the future of the Hogarth Press. As regards the Press, it was because I had got to know Ian so well that, as I have described in a previous chapter, when John Lehmann put the pistol of dissolving our partnership at my head, I went straight off to Ian and asked him whether he and his partners in Chatto & Windus would step into the shoes of John in the Hogarth Press. Hence the fortunes of the Press (which John, quite correctly, accused of practising amateur publishing and which was soon to be transformed into a more dignified Limited Company) and my amateurish career as a publisher were in the next twenty-two years indissolubly, happily, and profitably linked to those of Ian and Chatto.

As regards the rhythm of my life, as 1943 waxed and waned, I began to see more and more of Trekkie both in London in the dilapidations of Mecklenburgh Square and at weekends from time to time in Rodmell. In October I moved from Mecklenburgh to Victoria Square and so, when in London, I was living next door to the Parsons. In 1944, after the invasion, Ian went to France and Trekkie came and stayed at Monks House. They gave up their house in Victoria Square and decided that after the war they would have a house near me in Sussex. We searched the neighbourhood for many months and they eventually found and leased a house in Iford, which is the next village two miles away from Rodmell. We also arranged that they should share with me the first and second floors of my house in Victoria Square.

Thus when at last the war ended and Ian was demobilised, a new rhythm of life began for us. I stayed one or two nights a week in Victoria Square to do my work at the Hogarth Press and various political committees; Trekkie did the same, but stayed with me at Rodmell in the middle of the week. We cultivated our gardens passionately, the Parsons at Iford and I at Rodmell.

In 1946, when this rhythm of life began for me, I was sixty-six years old, a time of life when one has passed or is passing from middle age into old age, when in most spheres of life one is officially called upon to retire on a pension. I have slowly in the last twenty-two years shuffled off most of my political activities. In 1946, having done twenty-seven years of hard labour, I resigned from the Labour Party Committee and was slightly amused when I was informed by the Secretary of the Party that the National Executive has passed 'with acclamation' a resolution 'placing on record its deep appreciation of your great services to the Party by enthusiastic and persistent hard work, through many years and over periods of great discouragement'. I think that many of my fellow-members would have said that a good deal of the discouragement had come from the National Executive itself. However, the wise man gratefully accepts the fact that, if he is ever given a bouquet, it will only be when he resigns or dies.

In 1967 the Hogarth Press celebrated its fiftieth birthday. It is rather surprising that it should have existed for half a century and that it was still flourishing fifty years after Virginia and I began printing *Two Stories* by Leonard and Virginia Woolf in the dining-room of Hogarth House in Richmond.[1] I was thirty-seven when we printed and published our first book and I was therefore eighty-seven when the Press completed its half-century. It was and is, I suppose, equally surprising that I was and am still a Director taking an active, if modified, part in its activities. The advantage—perhaps, too, sometimes the disadvantage—of being what is called by the Inland Revenue self-employed is that there is no one who can authoritatively ask one to resign. Being in a modified degree still able to walk, see, hear, and think, I can still go up to London once a week to the office, read MSS, and deal with the larger problems of publishing.

On the surface the Hogarth Press, as a publishing business, has changed its nature considerably since John Lehmann left it in 1946. It is a limited company and I have several co-directors. In fact, though in the business and technique of printing, binding, selling, distributing, and accounting it is now part of a large and efficient organisation very different from the business machine which we

[1] See above, pp. 167-72.

relied on during the first thirty years of its existence, in its spiritual or intellectual nature it has not materially changed.

It is, of course, one of several subsidiary companies of Chatto & Windus Limited. When Ian in 1946 agreed that Chatto & Windus should step into John's shoes, the Directors of Chatto were, as I have said, Harold Raymond, Ian, Norah Smallwood and Piers Raymond. The attitude of all four towards books, literature, and publishing was the same as mine and consequently the list of books published by Chatto was fundamentally merely a very much larger version of the list of books published by the Hogarth Press. That is why we have never had the slightest disagreement as to what the Hogarth Press should be and do.

I think that our publications, therefore, during the last twenty-two years have not changed in number, nature, or standard. The Press remains a small publishing business with an annual list of at most ten or twelve books. We are and have always been unashamedly highbrow publishers, but in the last twenty-two years, as in the previous thirty, we have had a surprisingly large number of best-selling and long-selling books and authors.

In the previous paragraphs I have been dealing with the effect of the rhythm of my life since the war upon my political and publishing occupations as old age crept upon and over me. I have gradually disencumbered myself from many of my previous responsibilities and I now spend much less time on them than I did twenty years ago. The third great occupation of my life has been writing, and as I have ceased to be a politician and a publisher, I have become a much more prolific author. I published *Principia Politica* in 1953, *Sowing* in 1960, *Growing* in 1961, *Beginning Again* in 1964, and *Downhill all the Way* in 1967. I am, I think, a person who habitually throughout his life has got a great deal of pleasure from a great variety of things. Eating and drinking, reading, walking and riding, cultivating a garden, games of every kind, animals of every kind, conversation, pictures, music, friendship, love, people—all these things give almost unfailingly pleasure, varying, no doubt, in quality and intensity. The pleasure in all these things is not only very pleasant but also, I think, very good; indeed, the only pleasures which are bad are pleasures in other people's pain, aggressive and sadistic pleasures, pleasure in what is on the dark side of the moon. The most civilised civilisations have always counted pleasure to be a very good thing, and the most uncivilised civilisations have always puritanically frowned on happiness. I do not find that old age has decreased my capacity for pleasure, though it has, of course, destroyed one's ability to do some of the things which used to give one pleasure. It is regrettable that the impotence of the aged body results in my inability any longer to play cricket, football, squash rackets, hockey, or lawn tennis, and to function in still more important ways. But, if I can no longer have the satisfaction of hitting a six over long-on's head, I can still play a good game of bowls, and it is possible to find great happiness in love and affection long after one has to accept the fact that all passion is spent. And one of the pleasures which all my life I have found to be most reliable and to have remained unaffected by the vampirism of senility is the pleasure of writing. It is, oddly enough, a physical as well as a mental satisfaction. I like to feel the process of composition in my brain, to feel the mind working, the thoughts arranging themselves in words, the words appearing on the virgin white paper. When one is actually writing, one is not concerned at the moment with whether the result is good or bad—though that awkward question will have to be put and answered later. Sufficient for the morning is the pleasure thereof, and one of the most unfailing pleasures is to sit down in the morning and write.

Another pleasure of the last twenty years which has not been much dimmed by age is travel. Travellers' tales autobiographically are almost always boring, and I must avoid them, but there are one or two of my post-war journeys of which I must say something. One of the many deprivations of war that I have felt acutely is the fact that one is cut off from the rest of the world. A great deal of sedentary sediment seems to be rinsed out of the mind as soon as one has crossed the Channel and one sees again, if one is going to drive south, the straight white road of France which will take you to the Mediterranean. From 1939 to 1949 I never saw any sky but that which is bounded on the south by the very English Channel. It was a tremendous pleasure in 1949 once more to travel along French roads and I have done it a good many times since 1949.

I think that one of the great pleasures which I get from travel is the casual meeting and talking with some stranger in the foreign land with whom one is instantly in sympathy and understanding. It is not only their personal relationship which, for a moment, can make one forget the inveterate savagery, the ingrained nastiness of human beings; there is also the pleasure of suddenly getting a glimpse of a civilisation and barbarism widely different from one's own. I recall two instances of this. The first was in Greece on the Acropolis. I was sitting on the parapet overlooking the Agora when a man, the tout selling postcards, came up to me and said: 'Where did you get that walking stick, Sir?' I said that I had bought it the week before in Sparta. 'It is not a Greek stick,' he said; 'and it is painted; it is not a very good stick.' I said that I knew that, but I had a habit of buying a stick in any foreign country I visited. 'It is not a very good stick,' I said, 'but it is a rather curious stick, and, whenever I use it in England, I shall remember the market-place in Sparta and Greece and the Acropolis and you.' He laughed and sat down by my side and began to talk of Greece and England. An hour later we were still sitting on the parapet of the Acropolis talking. We began by talking about Greece and the economic conditions and Greek politics, and we ended by talking of life, his life and mine. At last he got up, took off his hat, and shook my hand, and said: 'Thank you, Sir; I have much enjoyed our talk.' I thanked him and said that I had much enjoyed our conversation. The Greeks, I think, are politically among the most uncivilised people of Europe, but in other respects they are the most civilised and intelligent. The intelligence, knowledge, humanity of this man were extraordinary. I do not think that there is any other country in the world, except perhaps Israel, in which it would be possible to have the kind of talk and relationship which I had with a tout selling photographs.

The other incident happened in Israel, to which I travelled with Trekkie in 1957. In the 1920s I was against Zionism and neither the great Namier nor the still greater Chaim Weizmann could convert me, though they tried to do so. I think that the whole of history shows that the savage xenophobia of human beings is so great that the introduction into any populated country of a large racial, economic, religious, or cultural minority always leads to hatred, violence, and political and social disaster. Whether it is the Negroes in America, white settlers in Kenya and Rhodesia, or West Indians in Wolverhampton the miserable story is always the same, and, therefore, until the human race becomes more civilised everything should be done to prevent the creation of new centres of conflict between minorities and majorities. That was why I thought originally that the Balfour Declaration and the introduction of a Jewish minority and a Jewish state in a country inhabited by a large Arab population was politically dangerous. But in politics and history once something has been done radically to change the past into a new present, you must act not upon a situation which no longer exists, but upon the facts that face one. When the Jewish National Home and hundreds of thousands of Jews has been established in Palestine, when Hitler was killing millions of Jews in Europe, when the independent sovereign state of Israel had been created, when the Arabs proclaimed their intention of destroying Israel and the Israelis, Zionism and anti-Zionism had become irrelevant. At any rate I went to Israel, with a comparatively open mind, to see for myself this return of the Jews to Jerusalem.

I have never felt so exhilarated—not even in Greece—by the physical climate of a country and the mental climate of its inhabitants. In Ceylon in the low country I lived for several years in a climate which has no autumn or winter and only an apology for spring; it is perpetual summer, a very hot, dry, and sometimes oppressive summer at that. I have not yet discovered any climate too hot for me, for I would always rather be too hot than too cold, and since most of my life I have lived in England, for most of my life I have been much too cold. I liked the heat of Jaffna and Hambantota in Ceylon, but sometimes it lay upon one like a physical weight; it was as if one was in bed with too many blankets on one. In Jerusalem and Haifa and Safed it was hot enough even for me, but there was an extraordinary sparkle and freshness, a keenness without a touch of cold in it. This was immensely exhilarating, but what was even more exciting was that the same qualities existed in the inhabitants. The physical and mental effervescence in the streets of Tel Aviv is something unlike anything I have ever felt in any other country. It reminded me of the busy buzz of productive ecstasy on the running-board of a hive on a perfect summer day and hundreds of happy bees stream in and out of the hive on the communal business of finding nectar and storing honey.

I had some introductions and therefore got to know a certain number of people, intellectuals all of them, journalists, writers, teachers in the university and in schools. But I also was able to see something of the kibbutzim and their inhabitants; moreover, Israel is a country in which the inhabitants everywhere talk to the stranger. What astonished me was the immense energy, friendliness, and intelligence of these people. It was the vision of a civilised community creating materially out of the rocky soil and spiritually out of the terrible history of all the peoples of the world, in all the millennia since Adam, a new civilised way of life. There was another curious thing in the mental atmosphere of Israel. It reminded me of the atmosphere of London during the worst days of the blitz. There was a feeling everywhere of comradeship, solidarity, good-will, and I suppose this was due, as in London, to the sense of a common menace and danger. It is impossible anywhere in Israel ever to forget that it is a small country surrounded by a ring of violently hostile Arab states, and people who consider themselves to be perpetually at war with, and pledged to destroy, Israel. It is, I suppose, only the threat of this kind of imminent death or of German bombs raining down upon one from the skies which can make the human herd feel its own unity and humanity.

The particular incident which gave me a glimpse into this civilisation of the Israelis occurred in Tiberias. We took a taxi to Nazareth. The taxi-driver began to talk to us as soon as we left Tiberias. Were we Roman Catholics? No. Were we Church of England? No, we were agnostics or atheists, though I myself had been born into the Jewish religion. He was, he said, glad to hear it, for now he could tell us the truth about the places through which he would be driving us. 'I do not like to upset people,' he said, 'and in many cases I find that it is impossible to tell the truth about what has happened in this part of the country without upsetting Roman Catholics and Protestants.' He was a remarkable man. He had an intimate knowledge of the country between Tiberias and Nazareth and a lively interest in and love for it. As we drove along he gave us a running commentary on the ancient and contemporary history of almost every small town, village, and hamlet through which we passed. His knowledge of world history was far greater than Trekkie's or mine. He spoke perfect English and I have never heard a talk or lecture in which knowledge, imagination, and humour were more happily blended. He was a man of quiet gentleness, humanity, and good-will. One felt the intensity of these qualities in him the moment one saw him talking with other people. The land between Tiberias and Nazareth is largely inhabited and cultivated by Arabs who did not leave Israel, as so many Arabs in other parts did, during the Arab–Israel war. Our driver several times stopped our car and took us to see some small mosque or other item of interest in an Arab village. It was obvious that he was well known and very well liked everywhere. Nazareth is a mainly Arab town and, as we drove into it, he said that he would hand us over to an Arab to show us the sights. 'I do not think it is fair', he said, 'for a Jew to show visitors over an Arab town.'

There is no other country in the world—except, perhaps, Greece—where you could pick up a taxi in the street and find that it was being driven by someone with the intelligence, knowledge, and humanity of this man. To find such a civilised taxi-driver in Israel, however, was not, I think, quite as remarkable as finding that very civilised seller of postcards in Athens. The driver came from a highly educated and sophisticated middle-class background, for his father had been a Professor in a Jugoslav university. What is remarkable is that the fantastic, muddled churning up of society by the barbarians in the last fifty years has condemned this cultivated East European to spend his life driving a taxi in the plains of Galilee.

I had another similar example of the fantastic kaleidoscope of contemporary history in the mountains of Galilee. Twenty years or more ago there lived in Rodmell a man whom I will call Mr X. He was in a shipping company, a member of the Rodmell Labour Party, and a Jew, though at the time I did not know that he was a Jew. He was a gentle, intelligent man, very much interested in and keen to discuss contemporary problems. One day he came to me and told me that he was going to Israel to become an Israeli and a member of a kibbutz. Mr X disappeared from the Rodmell Labour Party, the Sussex downs which he loved, and the London shipping office which I doubt whether he loved at all. He became Avraham ben Yosef, the shepherd of a kibbutz on the mountains of Galilee looking into Syria, and every Christmas for years he wrote me a long and very interesting letter describing his life and experiences. During our tour of Israel we went up into the Galilean mountains and spent two or three days in Safed. There I found that we were only sixteen miles from Avraham ben Yosef's kibbutz, so I hired a taxi to drive us out to see him. The kibbutz was perched on the top of a mountain with a magnificent, though stern and stark, view over the foothills to the Syrian plain. The kibbutz itself was rather stern and stark. There was no luxury, but, as everywhere in Israel, a hum and warmth of life and energy. My friend lived in a gaunt room, which was a kind of outhouse in which the only ornament and amenity was a cold-water tap. Every day he took his flock of sheep down to the plain on the Syrian border, and there, though officially there was a state of bitter enmity and perpetual war between Syria and Israel, the Syrian shepherds from across the border came and fraternised with the

Israeli, and the sheep grazed and the shepherds ate their lunch together.

I asked Avraham ben Yosef to come and have dinner with us at the hotel in Safed. He arrived at 7.30 carrying a large suitcase full of books and pamphlets which he wanted me to look at after dinner. At half-past ten he got up and said that he must go. I asked him how he was going to get back to the kibbutz sixteen miles away. He was going to walk, though, if a police patrol car happened to pass him, they would give him a lift. It was characteristic of the way of life in Israel today that a man who had been a sedentary worker in a London shipping office should think nothing of walking thirty-two miles, carrying a heavy suitcase on mountainous roads in order to meet someone at dinner.

Three things remain in my memory and I can still see them clearly when I think of Galilee. The first is Avraham ben Yosef setting off with his suitcase to walk sixteen miles over the mountain to his austere kibbutz. The second is the great silent wadi below Safed, so packed with wild flowers that we found twenty or thirty different species in the space of a few yards. The third is a regiment of crabs climbing up the staircase of the large hotel on the Sea of Galilee. When we got to the hotel, they told us that they could only take us in for two nights, as after that they closed down altogether during the hot season. But the day after we arrived the Syrians opened fire on an Israeli fishing-boat and killed or injured one of the fishermen. This was an international 'incident', and three officers of the United Nations Commission came up to investigate it. The hotel had to remain open for an extra day and we decided to stay on. No one else did and we and the three Commissioners were the only guests in this large silent hotel. We were sitting in the vast lounge hall after dinner when we saw suddenly a long procession of large and small crabs file past us and begin climbing up the staircase. When the hotel manager passed by us paying no attention to the long line of crabs, I asked him what it meant. He said that whenever the hotel closed down, it was immediately invaded by hundreds of crabs from the lake and they remained there, upstairs and downstairs, until the hotel re-opened with the cool season.

I must mention one other unexpected conversation which I remember to have had when travelling. It was in Ceylon; the plane in which I was to fly back to England was held up, I think in Burma, for some repairs and we hung about all day long awaiting its arrival.

At last we were told that it would arrive at midnight, and we drove out to the airport; but when we got there we found that there would still be a long delay. We sat outside the building in the gentle, drowsy, soft air of a tropical night. One of the Sinhalese employees of the airport came and sat down by me and began to talk, first about Ceylon and the years which I had spent in it as a civil servant and then, for some extraordinary reason, about philosophy. There are, I think, four sciences, departments of knowledge, or disciplines, as they are called in academic circles, which are almost completely phoney: the most bogus is theology; then comes economics; in third and fourth place I should put sociology and metaphysics, with little to choose between them. I was a little uneasy when I found that the airport official sitting by my side had a passion for the metaphysics of Kant and insisted upon my discussing with him what I think is called *Prolegomena to any Future Metaphysic*. For the next half-hour we forgot the non-existent plane and all other terrestrial things and lost ourselves, not in an O *altitudo*, but in the semantic fantasies and obscurities of the *Critique of Pure Reason*. I was soon metaphysically out of my depth, but the enthusiasm of my companion was such that it prevented him seeing my ignorance, and I had not the courage or the heart to reveal my misprision both of pure reason and any future metaphysic. At any rate, just as the Sea of Galilee will always remain inseparably connected in my memory with crabs, so Colombo is now inseparably linked in my mind with Kant.

My journey to Ceylon was in February 1960; I went there with Trekkie for three weeks. It was half a century since I had spent seven years there as a civil servant, a period of my life which I have described in the second volume of my autobiography, *Growing*. I wanted to revisit, before I was too old or too dead to do so, the strange places where I had, rather absent-mindedly, in my youth helped to govern the British Empire. I set out with some misgivings, for two reasons. First, there had just been throughout the island some very serious riots in which the Sinhalese attacked the Tamils with considerable loss of life and destruction of property. I thought that after that kind of bloody disturbance there might be restrictions on travel in some areas, and I did not want to go to Ceylon unless I was free to wander about anywhere and everywhere. However, when I went to the High Commissioner's Office in London, they assured me that there would be no difficulty of any sort, and, in fact, not only was this so, but it was surprising to find very few traces of this horrible inter-racial conflict.

My other misgiving arose from the fact that imperialism and colonialism are today very dirty words, particularly east of Suez. I hoped, if I revisited Ceylon, to be able to to go the places where I had worked as a Government servant and see something of how, now that Ceylon was a sovereign independent state, their administration compared with ours. But to do this I would need to have some help from the Sinhalese and Tamil administrators of today, and I feared that I might find them, not unnaturally, contemptuous if not hostile. Would they not say, or at any rate think: 'Fifty years ago you were here ruling us, an insolent, bloody-minded racialist and imperialist. Thank God we have now got rid of you and really we don't want to be reminded of how you lorded it over us and exploited us in the bad old days.'

My fears were entirely unnecessary; I have never had such an enjoyable or interesting journey as my three weeks travelling up and down Ceylon. It was mainly due to the welcome and the help which I got from every Government officer from the Governor down to the eighty-three-year-old Aron Singho, who had been my peon in the Hambantota kachcheri fifty years ago. Their attitude was the exact opposite of what I had feared it might be. I visited the four places in which I had worked as a civil servant: Jaffna, Mannar, Kandy, and Hambantota. In each of these places the Government Agents took me in hand and went out of the way to show me exactly how they were administering the districts and provinces. Every Government Agent whom I met, except one, went out of his way to impress upon me the fact that things were better in our time than they are today. This was the kind of thing which they said to me everywhere: 'In your time when you administered a district or a province things were really much better than they are for us today. You had no local axes to grind, nor had the central government in Colombo. When you were appointed Assistant Government Agent of the Hambantota District fifty years ago, all you were concerned with was the prosperity of the District—that is what you aimed at and worked for. And you were allowed to get on with the job—no one deliberately obstructed you; practically no one interfered with you; the central government in Colombo encouraged you. But for us today it is entirely different. For instance, here am I Government Agent administering the Province; I am trying to do what you British civil servants did: all I am after is the prosperity of my Province. But I am never left in peace to get on with my job, as you were; I am always being interfered with by the politicians. All I care for is the good of the Province, the good of the people here. All they care for is a vote. They will interfere and stop me doing something which will benefit the whole Province in order to win the votes of a few people who have some vested personal interest here. And if we oppose this kind of thing, the demagogues in Colombo try to put the people against us by saying that we civil servants are part of the old 'feudal system' of the wicked imperialist days. They have already abolished the old headman system as 'feudal', though if the truth be known they have abolished it in name rather than in fact: if you go into a village today, you will find someone doing exactly the same work as the village headman did fifty years ago, but he will be called by some newfangled title instead of vidane or village headman.'

The Sinhalese seem to be naturally courteous and honey-tongued, and in the East people are far more likely to say nice things to you, if you are a stranger, than they would be in, say, France or Germany. But I do not think this tribute to administration under the British Empire was simply flattery. There was much to be said against the imperialism of the British Empire in the years from 1904 to 1911, when I helped to run it light-heartedly in the Hambantota District of Ceylon, but there were also some very good things in it. All governments are evil in one way or another, and the worst thing about our rule in India and Ceylon was its democratic hypocrisy, its failure to fulfil its democratic professions and to associate the people of the country with the government of the country; this applied particularly to the upper regions of power, prestige, and government. Contrary to what we professed, we never did anything to prepare the way for self-government or responsible government. Our manners, officially and socially, were often deplorable and nearly always arrogant. But in 1900 the population of Ceylon was almost entirely agricultural, peasants and cultivators living in villages. In these villages the standards of living, education, and culture were low. Given these conditions, our provincial administration had some very good points; it was honest and, though patriarchal and paternal, i.e. no doubt 'feudal', the civil servant at the top, as ruler, was concerned solely with what he thought to be the good of the people and of the Province. There is evidence of this in the fact that in 1960 many years after we had left Ceylon to govern itself this local provincial administration was exactly the same as it had been fifty years before when I left the island in the heyday of imperialism.[1]

It was not only the Ceylon civil servants of today who handed these bouquets to the old imperialist civil service of my day. At the end of my three weeks' visit, on the day when I left for England, the *Ceylon Daily News* had an article which began as follows:

> Mr Leonard Woolf's presence here after a lapse of fifty years inevitably takes one's mind back to the public service of the colonial era. Immediately one remembers such names as Emerson Tennent, H. W. Codrington, Rhys Davies, Sir Paul Pieris, Senerat Paranavitane, and others who, like Woolf, not only worked conscientiously at their day-to-day tasks, but found time through their 'extra curricular' research to make an essential contribution in such fields as history, literature, and oriental studies.
>
> One quality characterised the public service in this period—the ideal of service to the community. The public servants of this era were not afraid to move among and with the people. In this they provided a striking contrast to the successors of today. The latter have deliberately built a wall between themselves and the people they are meant to serve.

I have a nostalgic and, I suppose, sentimental love of Ceylon and its people. Ceylon and youth! Youth and the sun and sand and palmyra palms of Jaffna; youth and the lovely friendly Kandyan villages and villagers up in the mountains; youth and the vast lone and level plain of the low country in Hambantota, the unending jungle which tempered in me the love of silence and loneliness. Youth and the jungle! Does not my invocation show that they hold in my heart and memory the place that youth and the sea held in the memory of Conrad and his sea captains and chief officers? Listen to the voice of Marlow and Conrad:

> Ah! The good old time—the good old time. Youth and the sea. Glamour and the sea! The good strong sea, the salt, bitter sea, that could whisper to you and roar at you and knock your breath out of you. By all that's wonderful it is the sea, I believe, the sea itself—or is it youth along? Who can tell? But you here—you all had something out of life: money, love—whatever one gets on shore—and tell me, wasn't that the best time, that time when we were

[1] I must add that I really agree with the Ceylon critics who object to the system as being 'feudal'. The rule of subject or colonial peoples by imperial powers through their own headmen used to be called the system of 'indirect rule'. In certain stages of economic and social development it was inevitable. But it was in many ways a very bad system and everything ought to have been done by us and by our successors by economic development and education to make it unnecessary.

young at sea; young and had nothing, on the sea that gives nothing, except hard knocks—and sometimes a chance to feel your strength—that only—what you all regret.

Substitute 'youth and Ceylon and the jungle' for 'youth and the sea' and, no doubt, it might be the nostalgic voice and purple patch, the slightly lachrymose memory of Leonard Woolf instead of Conrad and Marlow—though in the bottom of my heart I do not really feel quite so nostalgic and lachrymose for 'the good old time' as these sentimental seamen. But I did genuinely and profoundly feel something of all this for Ceylon and my youth, and to feel it again, not only in memory but in the sounds and scents of Kandyan villages and low country jungle and in the voices of Sinhalese and Tamils, was what made this three weeks' resurrection of time past so enjoyable.

It was also naturally extraordinarily pleasant to be received everywhere with a friendly and even affectionate welcome, and, though normally I much dislike official receptions and the pomp and circumstance of the upper crust in every society—from Kings and Dukes to the Dictators of the Proletariat—I must admit to the discreditable enjoyment of being treated as a V.I.P. all over Ceylon. This was partly due to the desire of so many people to know what a person like myself who had had an intimate knowledge of the country half a century ago thought of the country today now that the people were governing it for themselves. Over and over again I was asked: 'What do you think of Ceylon today? Has it changed much from your time?' But it is not just vanity if I say that my welcome was also due to other things; chief among them was *The Village in the Jungle*, the novel about Ceylon which I wrote in 1913. It has been translated into Sinhalese and a Sinhalese company is making a film of it. The book is still read in the island and has won me the reputation among many Sinhalese and Tamils of not only loving the country and sympathising with the people, but also of understanding them. That reputation was enhanced by what happened in 1916 when for a year or more I worked closely with the delegates of the Sinhalese who came to London to try to get justice with regard to the riots of 1915.[1]

Another thing which told in my favour, rather surprisingly, was

[1] The details of this story, discreditable to the British Government, are given above, pp. 166-7.

the official diary which I kept from 28 August 1908, to 15 May 1911, when I was Assistant Government Agent of the Hambantota District in Ceylon. All Government Agents and Assistant Government Agents of those bad old days had to keep a detailed day-to-day diary of what they did and send it each month to the Secretariat in Colombo, where it was read with some care. (Anything of particular interest—or discredit to the diarist—would be shown to the Colonial Secretary or even to the Governor, and I was once severely rapped over the knuckles by His Excellency for including in my diary, with the inexcusable arrogance and sublime courage of youth, some sarcastic—and not unjustified—criticism of my superior, the Government Agent of the Southern Province.) These official diaries go back in some provinces for over a century and a half; when I was stationed in the Northern Province I found that the first diary in the Jaffna kachcheri was written by the officer who at the end of the eighteenth century victoriously entered Jaffna after Britain had seized Ceylon from the Dutch in 1795. For the historian of imperialism these diaries give an extraordinary day-to-day history of British administration in a Crown Colony for more than one hundred years. In my case I took a great interest in writing my diary fully and frankly. That is why I find it rather surprising that I gained kudos from it from Sinhalese and Tamils in 1960; for it was not written for publication or for the eyes of the public; it was a highly confidential day-to-day report to the central government. It was the kind of document which should show up the iniquities of the ancient imperialists' regime.

I think that in fact it does, for it gives an accurate and vivid picture of British paternal colonial government half a century ago; to the unprejudiced eye both the dark and the light spots in the picture are visible. Luckily for me in 1960, at any rate during my visit, people generously ignored the dark and gave me credit for the light. As soon as I arrived in Colombo, Mr Shelton Fernando, who was then head of the Civil Service, came to see me and presented me with a copy of my diaries from the Government. Mr Fernando was, and still is in his retirement, a remarkable man. Many hard things are said about government servants—some of them no doubt justified—but all tip-top civil servants of the British species whom I have met have been admirable people, not only masters of their own strange and difficult art of administration and with the *robur et aes triplex circum pectus* without which in their position they could hardly maintain sanity or even life, but also men of exceptional humanity and civilisation. Shelton Fernando, who was Permanent Secretary of the Ministry of Home Affairs—the equivalent of Permanent Secretary of the Treasury in Whitehall—was as good as any of them when I first met him in Colombo. It was the beginning of a very pleasant and instructive friendship, for he is a man of wide interests and has a passionate interest in everything connected with Ceylon and its history; for the last eight years I have received from him almost monthly a long letter about what is happening or has happened in the island.

Mr Fernando took us to see Sir Oliver Goonetilleke, the Governor, and Mr Dahanayake, the Prime Minister. The Governor said that, when we went to Kandy, we were to stay as his guests in his official residence, The Pavilion. We did so, and it was a curious experience. In 1907 I had been sent to Kandy as Office Assistant to the Government Agent, Central Province, and I remained there for a year.[1] I lived there in the O.A.'s humble bungalow almost at the gates of The Pavilion. Now we were in the rich man's palace, looking down on the poor man's cottage which I had previously lived in. The palaces which our imperialist Proconsuls inhabited in Asia were often remarkable buildings, and the Kandy Pavilion was in its way, apart from its imperial pomp and circumstance, rather beautiful. It is embedded in a lovely semi-tropical garden, whose loveliness, in my eyes, is enhanced by a large troop of gubernatorial monkeys who swing from bough to bough of the great trees, and, like Luriana Lurilee, 'laugh and chatter in the flowers'.

When I went to see the Prime Minister in Colombo he talked to me about my Hámbantota diaries and later instructed Mr Fernando to have them printed and published by the Ceylon Government. They were published in Ceylon in 1961 through the *Ceylon Historical Journal*, and the Hogarth Press published them in England. When I read them in the Galle Face Hotel in Colombo fifty years after I had written them, they called up before my mind and almost my eyes the picture of what Ceylon had been (and what I had been) in those far-off days. I was very glad to have the opportunity of recalling that picture before setting off on my sentimental journey to Hambantota, Kandy, and Jaffna. It was strange to see how changed and in some respects how changeless the people, the gov-

[1] See Volume 1, pp. 217-21.

ernment, the land, and even the jungle had become since I had last seen it. I gave an account of what seemed to me the most important changes in the preface which I wrote for the edition of the diaries, and instead of trying to do the same thing all over again, I will quote what I wrote there.

To give an account here of what those changes have been would mean writing, not an introduction but a book; but I can summarily just mention three immense changes which I observed. The first is the revolution which comes to a people when they win 'independence', when they govern themselves. When I left the Civil Service in 1911, every Civil Servant administering in the provinces and districts was a European, indeed practically every member of the Civil Service was a European and so were nearly all the senior officers in all departments of government. Today the government, the administration, the public services are Sinhalese and Tamil from the highest to lowest. In other words the people of Ceylon today are governing themselves, instead of being ruled by young men (and old men) born in London or Edinburgh. The tempo of government and of life is quite different, it is more lively and vigorous in 1960 than it was in 1911, and that is mainly due to self-government.

The second change is also a change in tempo. When I was in the Civil Service, the motor car had hardly reached Ceylon. We travelled about our districts on a horse, on a bicycle, or on our feet. The pulse of ordinary life was determined by the pace of a bullock cart. There were no motor buses—even the 'coach' from Anuradhapura to the Northern Province was a bullock cart. Today the pulse of ordinary life beats to the rhythm of the motor car or motor bus, thirty, forty or fifty miles from village to village and from town to town. This has of course some great advantages, but also, I think, some disadvantages. One result has been that the kind of jungle village described by me in *The Village in the Jungle* is ceasing, or perhaps has already ceased, to exist. At any rate it would be quite impossible for a Government Agent to become intimately acquainted with it as I did fifty years ago. You could only get to know the villagers and their villages by continually walking among them, sitting under a tree or on the bund of a tank and listening to their complaints and problems. Today one drives through the village at thirty miles an hour.

The third change is economic. In a visit of three weeks one cannot of course really learn what the economic conditions of a country like Ceylon are. But my impression everywhere was that the standard of life is on the average higher today than it was in 1911 and that 'prosperity' is a good deal wider spread. At any rate the changes are great in a district like Hambantota. The poverty-stricken villages in the jungle, the Beddegamas of my time, have almost ceased to exist; where there were thousands of acres of irrigated paddy fields, good roads, and flourishing villages. These changes are very great and all to the good. And yet beneath the surface there is much, I feel, that has hardly changed at all. I revisited some of the out-of-the-way villages which I had known so well, both in the Kandyan hills and in the low country. Gradually the people, adults and children, gathered round, stared at me, and began to talk desultorily, sometimes about the old days. I may be wrong, but it seemed to me that something of the old village typically Sinhalese life still goes on beneath the modern surface. There were many bad things in those old days, but there were also some good things. At any rate it is to the Sinhalese way of life and the Sinhalese people who lived it that I look back with a kind of nostalgic, and no doubt sentimental, affection.

I have said that I had an almost universal flattering welcome in Ceylon. I did have one extremely hostile reception, which shows that some human beings, like the elephant, never forget—never forget and never forgive. The day before my departure, I was sitting in the Galle Face Hotel talking to Mr Fernando when I was told that someone wished to see me. My visitor turned out to be Mr E. R. Wijesinghe, aged eighty-six; he had been a Mudaliyar or Headman of East Giruwa Pattu in the Hambantota District when I was Assistant Government Agent there fifty years ago. I had only a vague, misty remembrance of him. He now stood in front of me and Mr Fernando and recalled to my memory an incident of which again I had a dim and misty recollection. It had happened during a terrible outbreak of rinderpest which ravished the district. The Government had instructed me to see that all cattle were kept in enclosures or tethered and all infected beasts immediately destroyed, and I had handed on these instructions to all my headmen, including the Mudaliyar. One day I received information that there was a buffalo, badly infected with rinderpest, wandering about in a village which was within the Mudaliyar's area. I sent a message to him to meet me there next day in the morning with the village headman. The village was some twenty miles from my bungalow and I rode out there in the early morning. The Mudaliyar and the village headman met me and took me to the bund of the village tank which was quite dry. Some distance away across the tank was a buffalo which, they admitted, was badly infected with rinderpest.

I had brought a rifle with me and I told the village headman to go across the tank and drive the buffalo down to me, so that I could shoot him. The headman went off but soon came running back, saying that the buffalo was savage, owing to the sores all over its head (the result of the disease) and would charge him. I gave my rifle to the Mudaliyar and told him that I would go and drive the buffalo down to him so that he could shoot it. This I did and the Mudaliyar shot the unfortunate beast, which was in a terrible state owing to the disease.

Under the bylaws made for dealing with the outbreak, it was an offence, punishable with a fine or imprisonment, to keep cattle untethered and also an offence not to destroy an infected beast, and the owner could be tried by the Police Magistrate. As Police Magistrate, I told the Mudaliyar that I proposed to charge and try the owner of this buffalo at once—'Who was he?' To my amazement I was told that the owner was the village headman standing hangdoggedly before me. I tried the owner of the buffalo for two offences—not tethering his cattle and not destroying an infected buffalo—and I fined him ten rupees. As Assistant Government Agent, I then tried the village headman for not carrying out his duties, i.e. reporting or prosecuting the offender (himself) for breaking the law, and I fined him ten rupees.

All this, which I had forgotten, the old Mudaliyar, standing in front of Mr Fernando and me in the Galle Face Hotel fifty years afterwards, recounted in great detail and considerable bitterness, and, as he spoke looking back over the long procession of years, I suddenly remembered and saw vividly again the scene of us three standing in the sweltering heat in the parched and waterless tank with the dead buffalo swarming with flies, near the village with the magnificent name of Angunakolapelessa. And when the Mudaliyar had finished his story, he fixed on me a beady and a baleful eye and said: 'Was it just, Sir? Was it just? The village headman paid the ten rupees which you had fined him as Police Magistrate, but he could not pay the ten rupees which you had fined him for not carrying out his duties as headman. I had to pay it for him—I had to pay it for him. Was it just, I say—was it just, I ask you, Sir?' 'Yes,' I replied, 'it was just. He had committed two entirely different offences, one as the owner of the buffalo and one as village headman, and I punished him for the one as Police Magistrate and for the other as Assistant Government Agent. Yes, Mudaliyar, it was just.' Of course, it was just. I was quite certain that it was just that day, 28 February 1960, in the Galle Face Hotel with the indignant Mudaliyar facing me, and yet I was not entirely comfortable about it, and I am quite certain that fifty years before in 1910 when I stood in the village tank, faced by the Mudaliyar and the unhappy vidane, I had the same ambivalent feeling. This ambivalence with regard to law and order and justice in an imperialist society was one of the principal reasons for my resigning from the Civil Service. Where the ethics of government and public service are concerned, I am a rigidly strict puritan both for myself and for other people. One of the bases of civilisation is honesty and justice in government and the officers of government; for a headman or any other government servant to commit an offence himself and conceal the fact that he had committed it, while prosecuting and punishing other people for the same offence, seems to me outrageous, and I thought and still think that it would have been unjust if I had not punished the headman for the two completely different offences committed by him, one as a private person and the other as a government servant. But there is a cliché—which normally irritates me because it is so often mouthed complacently by complacent judges—that a decision must not only be just, it must also be seen to be just. Even if the heavens had fallen upon our heads in the Angunakolapelessa tank or in the Galle Face Hotel, even if Jehovah or Gautama Buddha had appeared and proclaimed that it was just for me to fine the headman twenty rupees, neither the headman nor Mudaliyar E. R. Wijesinghe would have believed it. I find and found this profoundly depressing. Mr Wijesinghe had as good a right to his code of conduct as I had, and there was no real answer to his question: 'Was it just, Sir, was it just?' I thought it was, but I was not prepared to spend my life doing justice to people who thought that my justice was injustice. I felt a certain sympathy for the vidane of Angunakolapelessa and even for Mr Wijesinghe who had to fork out his ten rupees. At any rate I resigned from the Ceylon Civil Service as long ago as 1911.

I said that the Mudaliyar was the only person who, during my revisiting Ceylon, showed me hostility or reminded me that I had been an imperialist. After my visit, however, there were several articles in the Ceylon papers attacking me for arrogant imperialist behaviour fifty years before. The untrue story that, as a young man in Jaffna, I had deliberately struck a Tamil lawyer in the face with my riding-whip was resurrected. On the other hand Mr Fernando and other people wrote defending me.

I must return for a moment, before ending this volume, appropriately to the subject of old age. Ever since Cicero wrote his *De Senectute* old men have written pompous platitudes about it, truisms which nearly always contain ten per cent of truth to ninety per cent of untruth. Or they have suffered from the complacent hypocrisy of Seneca which allowed him to write: '*Ante senectutem curavi ut bene viverem; in senectute, ut bene moriar'* ('Before I grew old I took care to live a good life, in old age my care is to die a good death'). A few years ago I had to make an after-dinner speech and I chose the subject of old age, and most of my friends who heard it complained that I talked as much nonsense about it as Cicero and Seneca. I do not think that they were right. Their chief complaint was that my picture of old age was absurdly optimistic, leaving out all the miseries and aches and pains of the old body, the old mind, and the withered soul. I can, of course, only speak from my own experience. There are lamentable things in one's physical and mental decay as one goes downhill from middle age to death. But there are compensations. I admit that physically I am unusually tough and have so far escaped the major miseries of the moribund body. On the other hand a positive pleasure comes from the fact that, in Britain, one enjoys great prestige merely from not dying. If only you grow old enough, you get immense respect, affection, even love, from English people. Queen Victoria and the great W. G. Grace are well-known examples of this senolatry. Victoria, who had been unpopular in middle age, became more and more beloved of her subjects the longer she lived as a selfish, bad-tempered old woman. Grace, it is true, was the greatest of cricketers, but his enormous fame and popularity was due less to his genius than to the fact that he could make a hundred not out when he was sixty not out. Anyone who lives to the age of eighty, by acquiring the merit of not being dead, enjoys this irrational approval and even affection. It is a valuable asset, because it provides the basis for good relationships with other people. It is one reason why it is easier for a man of eighty to understand and get on with the young than a man of fifty or sixty.

There are other assets of old age. The storms and stresses of life, the ambitions and competitions, are over. The futile and unnecessary and false responsibilities have fallen from one's shoulders and one's conscience. Even the false proverbs tend to become true for old people, for instance, that it is no good crying over spilt milk—after the age of eighty. One has learnt the lesson that sufficient for the day is the good thereof. And one can almost say:

> Grow old along with me!
> The best is yet to be,
> The last of life, for which the first was made.

And one can say again: 'It is the journey, not the arrival, which matters.'

INDEX

Compiled by Patricia Utechin

More paperbacks from Oxford

LEONARD WOOLF

AN AUTOBIOGRAPHY
1: 1880-1911

Leonard Woolf (1880-1969), disciple of reason, colonial civil servant, author, editor, journalist, politician, publisher, husband of Virginia, was one of the central figures of the Bloomsbury group, and indeed of the English intellectual life of his time. His widely acclaimed autobiography, originally published in five volumes, is now in paperback for the first time, unabridged, in a two-volume Oxford Paperbacks edition. This first volume, incorporating *Sowing* and *Growing*, covers the author's childhood, his years at Cambridge, and his service as an increasingly reluctant 'imperialist administrator' in Ceylon, service which came to an end in 1911 with his decision to resign, partly in the hope of marrying Virginia Stephen.

For this new edition Quentin Bell, Virginia Woolf's nephew and biographer, has written an introduction which gives us a telling personal portrait of Leonard Woolf.

'Mr Woolf's memoirs are centrally important documents of our cultural history in his century.' *Guardian*

'The great quality in Woolf as an autobiographer is his utter truthfulness—rarer in this genre of literature than one might suppose.' Malcolm Muggeridge

'The narrative of the years which culminated in Cambridge is extraordinarily well done . . . Mr Woolf writes in an incisive, vigorous prose, admirably suited to his own uncompromising view of life.' Anthony Powell

THE SHORTER STRACHEY

Edited by Michael Holroyd and Peter Levy

Here is a provocative and entertaining selection of thirty of the best essays by Lytton Strachey, author of *Eminent Victorians, Queen Victoria,* and *Elizabeth and Essex.* His subjects range from Gibbon and Macaulay to Sarah Bernhardt; from Poe to Dostoevsky; from Boswell to Lady Hester Stanhope. There are wartime pieces, a childhood memoir, and a memorable description of a day spent with Vanessa Bell, Ottoline Morrell, and others from the Bloomsbury colony. All the essays are characteristically witty in tone, elegant in style, and eminently readable.

Also available in hardback

CARRINGTON
LETTERS AND EXTRACTS FROM HER DIARIES

Edited by David Garnett

Gifted painter, intimate companion of Lytton Strachey, friend of Virginia Woolf, Augustus John, Ottoline Morrell, and E. M. Forster, Dora Carrington led a fascinating life. At the age of 22 she met Lytton Strachey, a homosexual and an intellectual. Carrington detested her own femininity and had been haphazardly educated. Nevertheless, she and Strachey formed a deeply affectionate relationship which lasted until his death. Three months later Carrington shot herself. Despite her suicide, she was not made for tragedy. Her letters and diaries, punctuated by enchanting drawings, testify to a childlike exuberance of spirit which retains its power to captivate. This book constitutes one of the most candid, entertaining, and moving autobiographies ever written.

P. N. FURBANK

E. M. FORSTER
A LIFE

P. N. Furbank's biography of E. M. Forster has won such outstanding critical acclaim that there seems little doubt that it will stand as one of this century's finest biographies. John Bayley found it 'impossible to over-praise Furbank's style and sympathy as a biographer . . . He seems even more successfully and effortlessly *en rapport* with his subject than was Quentin Bell in his biography of Virginia Woolf. *The Listener*.

Edward Morgan Forster was born into a mixed family background of Bohemia and prim respectability. Indulged, cosseted, dressed up, and shown off by his adored mother, Lily, it was not surprising that he found public school life painfully harsh, nor that he should begin to tend towards homosexuality. Cambridge began the emancipation—intellectual, artistic, social, and sexual—which Forster's experiences abroad, his growing literacy reputation, his deep friendships, and his love affairs later extended. He died in 1970 at the age of 91, having achieved a world-wide reputation as an outstanding writer. Though best known for his novels, he was also a brilliant critic and essayist and the author of some remarkable short stories. In the 1930s he also emerged into the limelight as an active public figure: polemicist, broadcaster, and President of the National Council for Civil Liberties. In his closing years Forster invited Furbank, a close friend, to write his biography. Based on the full range of private diaries, correspondence, and personal reminiscences, this book is therefore the authorized and definitive life of Forster, as well as a remarkable literary *tour de force*.

LYNDALL GORDON

ELIOT'S EARLY YEARS

Described by Jonathan Raban in the *Sunday Times* as 'the most valuable single book yet published about Eliot', this unusual biographical study of T. S. Eliot's formative years opens a new perspective upon the career of one of our century's most influential poets and critics. Drawing on unpublished manuscripts (his Notebooks and early poems, his mother's poems, his wife's diaries), Lyndall Gordon traces Eliot's journey across the 'waste land' to his conversion to Anglo-Catholicism at the age of 38. Eliot's poetry has a strong autobiographical basis, and the author here shows us its essential coherence within the context of his life. First published in hard covers in 1977 (£4.95) and described by the *T.L.S.* as 'essential for all serious students of Eliot', *Eliot's Early Years* is now also made available in paperback.

JOSEPH FRANKEL

INTERNATIONAL RELATIONS IN A CHANGING WORLD

This analytical description of international relations today is such a fundamental revision of Professor Frankel's earlier work, *International Relations*, that it has been given a new title. The author takes into account recent events and basic changes in the international system in the last few years; he examines the rise in the numbers and importance of new states, of multi-national corporations, and of terrorist groups, and the shift of the main danger spots geographically from Europe to the Middle East and Africa. Particular attention is paid to the USA, the Soviet Union, and China—their foreign policies, interaction, and balance of power—and to the purpose and relevance of such international bodies as the UN and the League of Nations. 'A comprehensive and compendious piece of work.' *Times Literary Supplement*